MANAGEMENT:
A life cycle approach

David A. Tansik
Associate Professor of Management

Richard B. Chase
Professor of Management and Head of Department

Nicholas J. Aquilano
Associate Professor of Management

all of the
College of Business and Public Administration
The University of Arizona

MANAGEMENT:

A life cycle approach

 1980

RICHARD D. IRWIN, INC. Homewood, Illinois 60430
Irwin-Dorsey Limited Georgetown, Ontario L7G 4B3

ISBN 0-256-02278-X
Library of Congress Catalog Card No. 79–90540
Printed in the United States of America

1 2 3 4 5 6 7 8 9 0 H 7 6 5 4 3 2 1 0

Preface

This book was written to meet the common body of knowledge requirement of the American Assembly of Collegiate Schools of Business in management. It is designed to convey the concepts of management in an interesting way and, most importantly, to help prepare the reader for entry into the managerial world. The distinctive feature of this book is its structure—the life cycle approach—which quite simply presents the field of management in the context of the evolution of the organization itself. This structure was selected because it is logical and understandable, and effectively bridges the gap between management as an academic subject and management as an activity performed in organizations. It is also a flexible teaching device which permits the instructor to emphasize particular topics while maintaining a sense of continuity in a survey course.

Using this approach, the reader should obtain both the big picture of the organization and be able to recognize the types of problems (and their solutions) encountered when he or she enters the organizational world.

The book is organized around the following major phases in the organization's evolution:

1. Selecting the product or service.
2. Designing the organization.
3. Staffing the organization.
4. Starting up the organization.
5. Operating the organization in the steady state.
6. Improving the organization.
7. Revising or terminating the organization.

In each chapter we discuss where and how the subject matter fits into the life cycle. We also provide the basic terminology and theory that are essential in applying this subject matter. We draw upon insights from experts and anecdotes that illustrate the material. Some insights and anecdotes are humorous, some are profound, but all of them, we believe, are valuable to the practicing manager. Finally, we offer selected "guides to action" based upon our own knowledge and experience.

We have avoided segmenting material into behavioral and quantitative chapters for the simple reason that the life cycle approach makes such separations unnecessary. Quantitative and behavioral concepts are introduced at that point in the organizational life cycle where the manager would want to use them. Any other way of presenting them, to our way of thinking, is artificial and more importantly would not reflect reality.

If you are a student, we hope that you will judge this book by the ease with which you learn about management and by how much it helps you on the firing line of your job. If you are an instructor, we hope you judge the book by how well it assists you in conveying what you believe to be important to managers about management and organizations. For both students and instructor, we hope you judge the book by how well it enhances the classroom experience over the life cycle of your management course.

A book such as this one is the product of many persons' contributions. Today's idea is often the product of years of thought and many observations and inputs from others. For this, we must thank the many teachers, friends, and colleagues whom we have had over the years.

Then, there are those who had a more direct influence on this book. Larry Cummings (University of Wisconsin–Madison) and Kirby Warren (Columbia), our series editors, gave sound advice and encouragement. Dan Brenenstuhl (Arizona State University), Larry Foster (Michigan State University), and Rex Galloway (Murray State University) provided critical reviews at appropriate stages. Linda Tansik did the initial editing and typing, a chore that many times called on those skills that helped her turn in a perfect paper for a first place finish in the 1959 Texas Interscholastic League Spelling Contest.

January 1980   *David A. Tansik*
                                                           Richard B. Chase
                                                           Nicholas J. Aquilano

Contents

MANAGEMENT:
A life cycle approach

Level of Organizational Outputs

SELECTION OF THE PRODUCT OR SERVICE	DESIGN OF THE SYSTEM	STAFFING THE ORGANIZATION	STARTUP OF THE ORGANIZATION	OPERATING THE ORGANIZATION IN THE STEADY STATE	IMPROVING THE ORGANIZATION	REVISION OF THE ORGANIZATION	TERMINATION OF THE ORGANIZATION
Decision-making processes; social value; goals; forecasts; policies; plans	Authority and responsibility; power; organizational structure; communications systems; job design	Work force planning; personnel management functions	Startup planning and scheduling; monitoring; alternative startup approaches	Motivation; leadership; production and operations management; control	Individual improvement programs and techniques; group conflict management; MBO	Evaluation of organizational policies; strategic choices; organizational change; organizational development	Partial terminations; cutback management; complete terminations; mergers; born-again strategies

t_0

Time

Chapter 1
What is management all about?

Organizations, and managers, have existed on Earth for many thousands of years. The history of the human race is inevitably the history of people banding together in families, villages, nations, armies, and businesses for various purposes. The hunting parties (which we see pictured on cave walls) used by prehistoric Man and the giant multinational organizations of today exhibit a common element—people forming an organization when a task becomes too large or difficult for someone to do alone. Working together, a number of people can accomplish what the same number could never do individually—from hunting mammoths to building automobiles, exploring space, or to running a university. Organizations, then, are entities composed of two or more people, interdependent, and cooperating toward the accomplishment of a goal.

Management is a necessity in all organizations. Resources (land, labor, and capital) do not automatically come together as a finely run, well-organized system. Someone has to set goals, determine what is to be done, assemble resources, attract workers and assign them jobs, monitor performance, dispose of outputs, alter goals and work activities if desirable, and finally close down the organization if necessary. A number of people milling about in a parking lot outside of a well-equipped factory and a band of cave dwellers standing around looking at their spears exhibit a similar missing element. Someone—a manager or managers—must cause the resources (human and material) to be utilized properly (coordinated) to accomplish a goal.

WHAT DOES A MANAGER DO?

Throughout this book we will endeavor to show the reader key decisions that face a manager at various stages of an organization's life cycle. As the manager makes these decisions, he or she will act out a number of roles—roles that really describe what a manager "is" or "does."

Henry Mintzberg has attempted to describe how managers act and spend their time on the job.[1] First, he presents several "facts":

1. Managers work at a rapid, unrelenting pace, they are action oriented, dislike reflective activities, and their actions are brief, varied, and discontinuous.
2. Managerial work involves a number of regular duties including ritual and ceremony acts, negotiations, and analyzing information.
3. Managers strongly favor verbal interactions (face to face and telephone).
4. The "programs" managers use to make decisions, set up schedules, and so on are sophisticated but remain deep in the brain. It is not simply intuition and judgment, but rather complex analytical procedures that are used.

Given these facts of managerial life, Mintzberg goes on to present a number of roles acted out by managers.

4

Interpersonal roles

1. Figurehead—ceremonial; e.g., taking the customer to lunch, greeting the special visitor, attending the wedding of the plant manager's daughter.
2. Leader—responsible for the work unit; e.g., hiring and firing, motivating workers.
3. Liaison—contacts outside of the vertical chain of command; e.g., meeting with a peer in another department, checking up on a supplier, speaking with a government official.

Informational roles

1. Monitor—obtains information for the work group; e.g., gossip, hearsay, official reports, and so on.
2. Disseminator—passes on information; e.g., gives workers important data, acts as a "go-between" for data.
3. Spokesperson—sends information outside the work group; e.g., speech at a public meeting, report to the division manager.

Decisional roles

1. Entrepreneur—improver of the work unit; e.g., looks out for new ideas, develops new programs.
2. Disturbance handler—responds to pressure; e.g., what to do if a supplier goes bankrupt, how to get a union to call off a wildcat strike.
3. Resource allocator—who gets what; e.g., sets budget priorities, selects the "best" of several "good" proposals.
4. Negotiator—stepping into the middle; e.g., bargaining for a new union contract, listening to a grievance.

These ten roles form a "gestalt" or "overall whole" of a manager's job. We hope to use these roles in showing the reader how to make better management decisions in organizations. As Shakespeare has said:

All the world's a stage. And all the men and women merely players. They have their exits and their entrances. And one man in his time plays many parts. . . .[2]

We hope to help you learn your cues and your lines.

HISTORY OF MANAGEMENT

The history of management can be viewed in two distinct phases; not surprisingly, the ancient and the recent. What we know about the ancient phase we obtain from diverse sources such as cave drawings, archaeological sites, and biblical passages.

The ancient era of management

Early Man, the hunter, undoubtedly went out in small bands where one person perhaps chased an animal toward other people who were equipped with spears, rocks, or other specialized paraphernalia. Who told Arg to chase the beast? Trigh to stand on the cliff and drop rocks? And Burgh to throw the spear when he saw the whites of the beast's eyes?

Bones of large and dangerous animals have been found in human-occupied sites of the Upper Paleolithic period (40,000–10,000 B.C.) that indicate a high degree of cooperation and organization by human hunters.* Shortly (in geologic time) thereafter, evidence points to the use of nonhuman assistants (dogs) in hunting. (But for his ability to organize, could not Man have become "something" else's assistant?)

Religious leaders also probably were early managers. Stonehenge, built between 1900 B.C. and 1600 B.C., is widely thought to be a computer used in telling the seasons, predicting eclipses, and the like.[3] Imagine the work force and coordination needed to build that edifice so that the priests could use their knowledge to control and give direction to their people.

Also the pyramids of Giza built around 2500 B.C. stand as monuments to Man's ability to set a goal, assemble great amounts of resources, work to the accomplishment of a task over time, and then terminate the system. Undoubtedly, the laborers worked under a supervisor, had specialized jobs, and encountered many of the other aspects of organizational life so familiar to people today.† The largest of the pyramids covers an area of 13 acres and contains about 2,300,000 blocks of granite and limestone, each weighing up to 5,000 pounds. The logistical problems alone, housing and feeding the many thousands of workers, required an administrative skill that would be admired even today. The work itself was divided into many specialized tasks. A master builder had a number of subordinates, who in turn each had several superintendents, who managed a number of foremen who in turn supervised specialized teams of workers. Each "manager" had a scribe and a recorder to take down orders and pass these on to the proper person.

The Greeks and Romans also built monuments that required advanced organizational techniques. The Roman aqueducts, road network, public buildings, harbors, and lighthouses are testaments to exceptional skills in organizing vast amounts of labor and materials and in using a highly rationalized division of craftsmen.

In Arizona, the elaborate buildings and canal systems of the Anasazi Indians are examples of engineering and construction genius. Yet these were constructed around 700–1000 A.D.

More "recently" we have evidence of what may be the first large-scale assembly line. Shipbuilders around 1430 A.D. apparently used assembly line

---

* Or little cooperation and organization among large and dangerous animals.
† With the exception, of course, of labor unions.

techniques in the outfitting of ships at the Arsenal of Venice. The planning committee of the Arsenal issued regulations that required that bows be made to accommodate all types of arrows, that all stern portions of ships be of identical design so that rudders would not have to be custom fitted, and that all rigging and deck furnishings be uniform.

Despite these pieces of evidence we can only guess as to the actual process of how the organizations were created and managed. Unfortunately, written records do not exist that would allow us to gain insight into the many management techniques that were used. In Exodus 18, however, we do find a written record of a management practice still used today. Moses, in leading the Israelites from Egypt to Canaan, found himself being increasingly bogged down from dawn to dusk solving routine problems that arose with his people (a not uncommon plight facing many of today's executives). Discussing the problem with Jethro, his father-in-law, Moses received some advice that caused him to delegate authority differently than had been done in the past. This involved the management concepts that we know as span of control and decentralization. In Jethro's words:

It is not right to take this on yourself. You will tire yourself out. . . . The work is too heavy for you. You cannot do it alone. . . . Choose from the people at large some capable and God-fearing men, trustworthy and incorruptible, and appoint them as leaders of the people: leaders of thousands, hundreds, fifties, tens. Let these be at the service of the people to administer justice at all times. They can refer all difficult questions to you, but all smaller questions they will decide for themselves, in making things easier for you and sharing the burden with you.

Scientific management

The recent period of management thought begins with the Industrial Revolution. As people moved from relatively self-sufficient agrarian communities into urban societies, and as specialized "factories" emerged, the role of management became crucial. A hallmark of this recent period is that management theories became systematized and written down. This permits learning from others, rather than by trial and error.

Adam Smith. Adam Smith's 1776 observation of pin manufacturing points out the value of specialization (division of labor).

One man draws out the wire, another straights it, a third cuts it, a fourth points it, a fifth grinds it at the top for receiving the head. . . . Those . . . persons therefore could make among them upwards of forty-eight thousand in a day. . . . But if they all had worked separately and independently and without any one of them having been educated to this peculiar business they certainly could not each of them have made twenty, perhaps not one pin in a day. . . .[4]

Smith noted that a division of labor increased output for three reasons: (1) increased dexterity on the part of each worker, (2) avoidance of lost time due to handling, and (3) "the invention of a great number of machines which facilitate and abridge labor, and enable one man to do the work of many."

Charles Babbage.   In 1832 Charles Babbage (who was later to design the first modern digital computer, Stonehenge perhaps being *the* first) published *On the Economy of Machines and Manufacturers* in which he proposed using the scientific method in analyzing business problems, the use of time study, the performance of research and development, locating factories on the basis of economic analysis; and the use of skill differentials in wage payment plans.

Frederick Taylor.   Beginning in the late 1800s Frederick Taylor began to work on productivity improvements via time studies and devising a "best way" to do certain jobs. Augmented by proper hiring and training of personnel and by incentive wage plans, Taylor's "best way" yielded significant productivity and efficiency improvements. Taylor's philosophy was not greeted with unanimous approval, especially by many unions that feared or resented the mechanistic treatment of people. Also there were many instances of managers quickly embracing the "mechanisms" of Taylor's ideas—time study, incentive wages, and so on—but failing to perform their responsibility to organize and standardize the work. These abuses contributed to a bill in Congress in 1913 to prohibit the use of time study and incentive plans in federal operations. The unions advocating the legislation claimed that Taylor's subject in several of his time study experiments—a steelworker named "Schmidt"—had died from overwork brought on by Taylor's experiments. They even distributed pictures of Schmidt's "grave." Later it was discovered that Schmidt (whose real name was Henry Nolle) was alive and well and working as a teamster.[5] The bill was ultimately defeated, although amendments were later made to other bills that prohibited the use of certain time study techniques in post offices.

The Gilbreths.   Frank and Lillian Gilbreth in 1912 published in *Industrial Engineering Magazine* their work on motion studies and fatigue which involved breaking work down to the most basic human motions (e.g., left-to-right eye movement) called therbligs (Gilbreth spelled approximately backwards). Therbligs could then be combined in a sequence that would be most efficient and not overly fatigue certain parts of the body.

Henry Ford.   By 1913 Henry Ford had created the moving assembly line with its specialized jobs *and* in 1914 added the notion of high wages (then $5 a day, about twice the prevailing rate) to attract and keep good workers.

Before Ford introduced his assembly line in August of 1913, each auto chassis was assembled by one man in about 12½ hours. Eight months later, when the line was in final form, with each worker doing a simple task and the line being moved mechanically, the average labor time per chassis was 93 minutes. Ford controlled his workers closely by making them subservient to the mechanical line—a subservience many workers resented as reflected in Ford's high turnover rates.

In fairness, the whole story of Ford's $5 a day plan ought to be told. In the summer of 1913, Ford's wage was fixed at $2.34 per day maximum; the standard wage for the Detroit area. The assembly line technology was not popular with the workers and since other jobs were plentiful in the community, the turnover rate was very high—380 percent in 1913.[6] At the end of 1913, Ford is reported to have had to hire 963 men to increase plant employment by a net of 100.[7] Since it cost $50–$100 to hire and train a new worker, Ford was very concerned. The wage was to be very effective in cutting turnover. In 1914, the plant had 14,000 workers and it was necessary to hire 53,000 workers to keep it at the 14,000 level. In 1915, only 6,508 people were hired and the majority were hired for new positions.[8]

Labor unrest caused by the I.W.W. (Wobblies) was also concerning Ford in late 1913, with a strike rumored for the summer of 1914. James Couzens, Ford's business manager, proposed the solution. On January 5, 1914 with a showmanship any public relations agent would envy, the "Five-Dollar Day" was born. Beginning one week later, Couzens told the press, the Five-Dollar Day wage would be paid to all "qualified" workers, "even the lowliest laborer and the man who merely sweeps the floor." Over and above this "profit sharing" (which is what the Five-Dollar Day was) came a reduction in work hours from nine to eight.

The response was tremendous. Thousands of applicants stormed the plant. Of course, hiring was slow as Ford only wanted the best workers. Two weeks after the crowd appeared, it was still there; hiring was indeed at a snail's pace. Finally, patience wore thin and a riot ensued in the early morning hours of Monday, January 12, 1914. The Detroit *Journal* reported under the headline, "Icy Fire-Hose Deluge Stops Twelve Thousand in Riotous Rush for Ford's Jobs." The *Journal* wrote that "three thousand men were soaked, it is estimated. With the temperature hovering close to the zero mark . . . their clothes froze a moment after they encountered the business end of the hose."[9]

Though Ford got his workers, not all of them got the $5 "profit sharing" wage. To qualify as a "profit sharer," several qualifications had to be met. "Women workers, unmarried men under twenty-two, family men who were living by themselves or not supporting their dependents, married men involved in divorce actions, new employees with less than six months' seniority or any worker who in Ford's opinion was 'living unworthily as a profit-sharer'—all these were excluded from the beginning."[10] Approximately 30 percent of the plant workers never got the Five-Dollar Day.

About 5–10 percent of the workers failed to achieve Five-Dollar status because they failed to live up to Ford's code of conduct. Ford established a "Social Department" which at various times had between 30 and 150 investigators. The department sought to paternalistically aid the employees. Investigators visited homes, encouraged budgeting and savings accounts, and taught hygiene and good shopping techniques. A card catalog was kept on all workers with information gleaned from home visits, rumors, or almost any source. Taking in male boarders, frittering away an evening, sending money home to the "old country," simply spending money unwisely, using liquor, or having marital discord quickly relieved one of "profit sharer" status and his salary was cut in half. There was a six-point scale for measuring one's rehabilitation. If a worker failed to be rehabilitated within six months, he was simply fired.

Thus, Mr. Ford controlled his workers tightly at work and at home. Mr. Ford was, however, very skeptical of the large number of heretofore unknown "brothers" who were found living with workers (male boarders?) and of a sudden increase in the number of "orphaned nieces" his young male workers had to take into their homes.

Henry Gantt. In 1914 Henry Gantt proposed the idea of a bonus for the worker (and his foreman) for achieving the daily standard. To monitor progress Gantt devised a simple charting system (the "Gantt chart") that is still widely used today. A very simple concept, the Gantt chart was believed by Mr. Gantt to have had a significant influence on America's winning World War I. Gantt devised a system of monitoring the number of rivets used in Liberty Ships as a substitute measure for the amount of shipbuilding completed. Hence management was better able to plan and schedule completions in excess of the number of ships being sunk.

Limitations of the scientific management school.   The increased productivity associated with specialized workers in well-designed jobs is by now known to most all of us. The contributions of these early "scientific managers" to the economic system of the 20th century cannot be underestimated. Time and motion techniques, scientific selection of personnel, work design to select a "best way," and incentive pay systems contributed greatly to the professionalization of management.

Unfortunately, some aspects were overlooked. The emphasis on economic and physical needs of workers overlooked the social and other psychological needs of people and the tensions created when these were not met. Sometimes workers simply would not act "rationally" and scientific managers were at a loss to explain why.

Classical organization theory school

While the scientific management approach concerned itself with production efficiency at the "blue-collar" level of an organization, another body of thought developed around the management of complex organizations consisting of managers as well as "workers."

Henri Fayol.   Henri Fayol, a Frenchman, is acknowledged as the founder of this approach.[11] Fayol's main contribution was in describing the functions of a manager. These functions were: planning, organizing, commanding, coordinating and controlling. Fayol also observed that the abilities required of a manager depended on the manager's position in the organization. Lower level jobs required technical skills, but little conceptual managerial ability. As one moves up the hierarchy, less technical skills and more managerial abilities are required.

Based upon his five functions of management, Fayol proposed 14 "principles of management":

1. *Division of work (labor).*   Specialization allows people to produce more and better work with the same effort. Although epitomized by the assembly line, it is applicable to virtually all kinds of work.
2. *Authority.*   Authority involves the right to give orders and the power to exact obedience. Responsibility is a corollary of authority; where authority is exercised, responsibility arises. A distinction should be made between formal authority deriving from an office or position and informal authority deriving from intelligence, experience, and the like.
3. *Discipline.*   People in organizations must respect the rules, regulations, and customs of the organization. Fayol felt that discipline is the result of good leadership which is the product of good superiors at all levels of the organization, clear and fair agreements between organization members, and judiciously applied penalties where required.
4. *Unity of command.*   An employee should receive orders from only one superior. Authority is undermined and discipline threatened where this principle is violated.
5. *Unity of direction.*   Activities having a common objective should be supervised by one superior with one plan of action. For example, the bookkeeping department in an organization should not have two (or more) supervisors each with different policies and procedures.
6. *Subordination of individual interest to the general interest.*   The interest of any employee or of any employee group should not take precedence over that of the organization.
7. *Remuneration of personnel.*   Compensation for work done by organization members should be fair and satisfactory to both the employees and the organization.
8. *Centralization.*   Centralization refers to decreasing the role of subordinates in decision making (and increasing the role of higher level managers). Decentralization refers to increasing subordinates' roles. There is no universal optimum balance. The objective should be to make optimum utilization of the talents of personnel while retaining final responsibility for management.
9. *Scalar chain.*   The scalar chain is that line of superiors/subordinates rang-

ing from the highest to the lowest level of the organization. We usually conceptualize this via the boxes and lines of an organization chart. Fayol felt that all communications in an organization should follow these lines/ boxes much as we follow a road map.

10. *Order.*   There is a place for everyone, and everyone should be in his or her place. Physical materials should be where required and personnel should be in positions best suited for their talents.

11. *Equity.*   Managers should be fair and friendly so as to evoke devotion and loyalty from subordinates.

12. *Stability of tenure of personnel.*   High turnover is disruptive and costly. Also, it takes time for workers to learn their jobs well. Thus, a lack of stability of personnel should be avoided. Fayol even felt that an average or mediocre manager who stays is preferable to outstanding managers who come and go.

13. *Initiative.*   The willingness to act on their own to conceive and carry out plans should be instilled in employees. Mistakes will undoubtedly be made at times and the vanity of some managers may suffer. However, this is preferable to having unstimulated employees.

14. *Esprit de corps.*   Managers should promote a team spirit. Avoid splitting up personnel and use verbal (versus written) communications where possible in dealing with employees.

Max Weber.   Closely related to Fayol's ideas was the notion of bureaucracy advocated by the German writer, Max Weber.[12] Weber advocated a "rational" organization structure with a number of characteristics. First, tasks should be divided into specialized jobs. Second, a rigorous set of rules must be followed to ensure predictability and eliminate uncertainty in task performance. Third, a clear authority structure must be maintained. Fourth, an impersonal attitude must be used by superiors in dealing with subordinates. And fifth, employment and promotions must be based on merit; lifelong employment being an accepted fact.

While we often criticize unmoving bureaucracies, we can still find some value in Weber's ideas. In certain circumstances, bureaucratic structures may be very effective. Still, it is hard to practice many of Weber's prescriptions. Highly specialized tasks become monotonous, rules often unnecessarily restrict behavior, we can't always be impersonal, and we have difficulty clearly identifying the more capable worker. These are serious issues that we must address when analyzing the bureaucratic model. Other important classical organization theorists were James Mooney and Alan Reiley, two General Motors executives, who wrote *Onward Industry* in 1931 and Lyndall F. Urwick who wrote *The Elements of Administration* in 1943 based upon his military experiences.

Mary Parker Follett.   While the classical organization theorists primarily emphasized structural phenomena, two other people began considering the human variable more closely. Mary Parker Follett argued that managers and workers should be considered as a group; that a manager's authority should be based on *knowledge* and *expertise* not simply position power. In this way, the manager and his or her directives would be more acceptable to the work group. Follett's *The New State* was published in 1918.

Chester Barnard. In 1938 Chester Barnard published *The Functions of the Executive* which put forth the thesis that an organization can operate efficiently and will survive only when there is a balance between an organization's goals *and* the aims and needs of the individuals working in it. The ability to meet personal goals was the only thing that kept people working in organizations. Barnard thus anticipated a major point to be later proposed by human relations advocates.

Human relations school

Elton Mayo. From 1927–32 Elton Mayo and several associates conducted the now famous study of human behavior in a work setting at the Hawthorne plant of Western Electric in Cicero, Illinois. Mayo initially came into the Hawthorne study when other researchers began getting peculiar results in their work. Employees had been divided into a test group and a control group to study the effects of lighting on work; the hypothesis being that better lighting would lead to better work. Sure enough, as the lighting was increased, the production increased. To more completely test the theory, the lighting was worsened. But productivity kept increasing! To compound the situation, the control group's production kept rising every time a change was made with the test group.

Mayo then tried a new experiment with a test and control group. In the test group's room, a number of things were tried such as increased pay, coffee breaks, and a shortened workweek. Again *both* the control and test group had significant production increases. Mayo concluded that the productivity increases were not caused by the physical changes that were introduced but rather by complex emotional and behavioral factors within the workers. Because they had been singled out for the study, they felt important and their group pride led them to improve their performance. Mayo concluded that when special attention is given workers by management, production will likely increase regardless of changes in working conditions. This phenomena has been labeled the *Hawthorne effect.*

In another experiment in the "bank wiring room," Mayo found another example of a behavioral influence. Here workers were paid on a piece rate basis; however, it was observed that many workers never produced up to their known potential and thus earned less than they otherwise could have (this during the "depression years"). There was, Mayo found, a production norm to which the workers adhered. Those who didn't would get a "bing"—

a punch on the arm. The production norm was set at a "safe" level which all the workers could meet and which was tacitly accepted by management. This finding seriously compromised Taylor's notions of maximizing production via piece rate payment plans that would appeal to workers' desires to earn the maximum amount possible.

Mayo's findings dramatically pointed out the role of human behavior in organizations.[13] The concept of a "social" worker was thus balanced against the concept of a "rational-economic" worker. Later, especially in the 1950s, many managers assumed from Mayo's work that happy workers were productive workers. However, attempts to improve productivity in this manner did not produce the expected results. Apparently, economic aspects of work do play an important role as do social aspects. Further, emphases on social factors that neglect aspects of the task itself, worker skills, and organization structures will likely have detrimental effects for obvious reasons. Thus, the matter of productivity and worker satisfaction is a complex issue.

Behavioral science school

It is a short but significant step from the human relations to the behavioral science school of thought. Exemplified by such people as Chris Argyris, Abraham Maslow, and Douglas McGregor, this school of management thought emphasizes the many needs, especially growth, ego, and self-actualization of workers.[14] Being aware of these many needs, the manager should offer rewards tailored to the needs of the workers. Recently, the "contingency approach" which states cause-effect relationships among variables has been widely discussed by behavioral writers. We will more fully explain aspects of the behavioral science school of thought in later chapters.

The quantitative school

During World War II, Great Britain, faced with the need to counteract German attacks with limited resources, formed multidisciplinary teams of psychologists, mathematicians, physicists, and others to develop more effective ways of deploying forces. These *operational research* teams were very successful and, after the war, the concept was brought to the United States where it eventually evolved into the application of mathematical approaches to management decision making.

While many quantitative techniques have relevance to management, the behavioral aspects of organizations often diminish the impact of operations research methods. Still, where relevant, these tools need to be understood by managers. We will, in this book, attempt to show the reader where these tools are relevant and give advice as to applications. The remoteness of many of these tools from the practical problems facing many managers and the peculiar constraints in many situations pose limitations on the quantitative approach of which we must stay aware.

APPROACHES TO TEACHING MANAGEMENT

The various schools of thought discussed above all find their way into contemporary management books and courses. The functions of management approach set out by Fayol is widely used today in many texts and has perhaps been the most popular method of teaching this subject. The abstractness of this approach, however, often leaves the student aware of sets of concepts but without the awareness of when and where they should be applied.

The other schools likewise have particular faults—primarily their inability to deal with both behavioral and structural concepts *together* in a simple and useful way. Perhaps, then, an integrated approach is called for; one that begins with a focus on the *process* of organizing and the *role* of the manager at various stages of the process. This approach also should glean the valid concepts from all the schools of thought rather than be attached to only one. And, of greatest importance, it should be helpful to the student in understanding both the theory and practice of management. In our view, the life-cycle approach meets these requirements quite well.

THE LIFE CYCLE APPROACH

Life cycles in general

The notion of a life cycle has been widely applied in philosophy, religion, and the sciences to relate some variable or variables to the age of the system or concept under study. Not only do living organisms have life cycles but inanimate objects (planets and mountains) and intangible "objects" (philosophies and languages) do as well. Writers have often dealt with the human condition in life cycle terms (see Gail Sheehy, *Passages*) and even the RAND Corporation, the famous "think tank," has produced at least one paper with the label in its title ("The Household Life Cycle and Housing Choices").

Organization and management theorists too have long recognized that the age of an organization constitutes one of the major "contingencies" faced by the manager. Greiner, for example, suggests that "growing organizations move through five distinguishable phases of development, each of which contains a relatively calm period of growth that ends with a management crisis."[15] He also contends "that since each phase is strongly influenced by the previous one, a management with a sense of its own organization's history can anticipate and prepare for the next development crisis."[16]

Filley and his associates have identified three distinct stages of organizational evolution—craft, promotion, and administrative—which present unique demands on the organization's structure and leadership.[17] For example, during its craft stage, an organization requires the leader to have the technical skills of a craftsman, while during the promotion stage the leader needs entrepreneurial abilities, and during the administrative stage, professional manager skills.[18] Finally, Lippitt and Schmidt label developmental stages of an organization simply as "birth, growth, and maturity."[19] This structure roughly approximates the one described below.

The life cycle used in this book

Exhibit 1–1 shows the major phases in the life cycle of an organizational system along with some of the managerial questions that must be answered in each phase. All organizations pass through life cycle phases; obviously, not all organizations go through all phases (e.g., the termination phase), though most do in some fashion.

Exhibit 1–1
The major phases and issues in the life cycle of an organizational system

BIRTH OF THE SYSTEM	Is there a need for a new organization to provide a product or service? How is the product or service selected?
	What are the objectives of the system? Profit? Environmental? Social? Humanitarian?
	How do you set realistic goals for the organization?
DESIGN OF THE SYSTEM	How is the system to be segmented? By geography? By customer? By division? By product?
	Are there any peculiar cultural or behavioral characteristics in the environment in which the system will operate?
	Should the system operate with centralized or decentralized authority?
	What are the line/staff relationships?
	What types of communication and information flows should be established?
	What are the measures of system effectiveness? Cost centers? Budgets? Growth? Return on investment?
	Specifically, what are the duties of the managers, staff, and operatives?
	How do you measure individual performance?
	How do you determine equitable wage scales?
	What are the characteristics of the individuals who will occupy and influence the roles of management?

Exhibit 1-1 *(continued)*

STAFFING THE ORGANIZATION	What are the forecasted work force needs?
	What are the job descriptions for each position?
	How do you recruit, select, train, evaluate, reward, and develop personnel?
STARTUP OF THE ORGANIZATION	How do you get the system into operation?
	How long will it take to reach the level of planned output?
	What personnel will you use for startup?
	How can you develop a realistic schedule of operations?
THE ORGANIZATION IN STEADY STATE	What type of operating system should be used to manage day-to-day production?
	How do you control the system to reach desired objectives? By management audits? By budget reviews? By technology audits?
	How do you evaluate, control, and promote effective personnel?
	How can you motivate personnel toward achieving organizational goals?
	What styles of leadership are most effective?
IMPROVING THE ORGANIZATION	What techniques are available to improve management performance? Time management? MBO?
	What techniques are available to improve worker performance? Job enrichment? Participative decision making?
REVISION OF THE ORGANIZATION	How do you change objectives in light of new developments?
	How do you evaluate organization policies?
	What methods of change are available for externally and internally caused change?
TERMINATION OF THE ORGANIZATION	How does an organization die? By consolidation? By merger? By bankruptcy?
	How does one phase out personnel and capital assets?
	Should the organization start anew and embark with a different product or service or new objectives?
	Should the organization consolidate and/or phase out a particular office, product, division, and so on?

Let us briefly look at the life cycle phases that are the basis around which this text is organized.

Selection of the product or service (birth of the system). Organizations exist to provide socially desirable goods and/or services. Goals and objectives are thus created which require the efforts of more than one person. Also, the resources necessary to create the organization must be acquired. Thus, an organization is born.

Design of the system.   A scheme must be developed by which the human and material resources will combine to efficiently and effectively produce the good or service. An organization "structure" must be created and jobs designed so that the work that will be done will "add up" to the production of the desired output.

Staffing the organization.   All organizations require people. Once designed, the organization must attract and assign the human resources to the previously designed jobs.

Startup of the organization.   New organizations (including new components of large organizations) having been "born," designed, and staffed must now be put into operation. Rehearsals may have been held, training sessions run, and the Grand Opening announced. At some point, the action is "for real." Since the first real action is rarely (or never) of the type and intensity that will later be experienced, special skills and techniques must be used.

The organization in steady state.   Having progressed through the startup the organization settles down into a "normalcy" state. Routines are known and well practiced. Management must now be concerned with sustaining the organization. Of particular interest here are general questions of motivation, leadership, and control and the specific subfield of operations management (which is directly concerned with making the product of the organization).

Improving the organization.   Over time, improvement opportunities and problem areas will become apparent. Management will attempt to discover these opportunities and problem areas and then attempt to deal with them. The management literature contains proven techniques to help in both dimensions.

Revision of the organization.   As the world changes, perhaps so should the organization if the original output, system design, or operating strategy no longer seems appropriate. Changes can be structural (e.g., new technology, new outputs, new organization structure) or people oriented (e.g., new "type" of employee, new skills, attitudinal changes toward minorities). The March of Dimes going from an organization focused on polio to one focused on birth defects exemplifies this phase.

Termination of the organization.   The entire organization may be terminated (e.g., Penn Central Railroad, Office of Economic Opportunity) or portions of it may be closed down (e.g., the Edsel at Ford, the SST at Boeing). The key that differentiates termination from revision lies in the fact that termina-

Exhibit 1–2
Life cycle phases

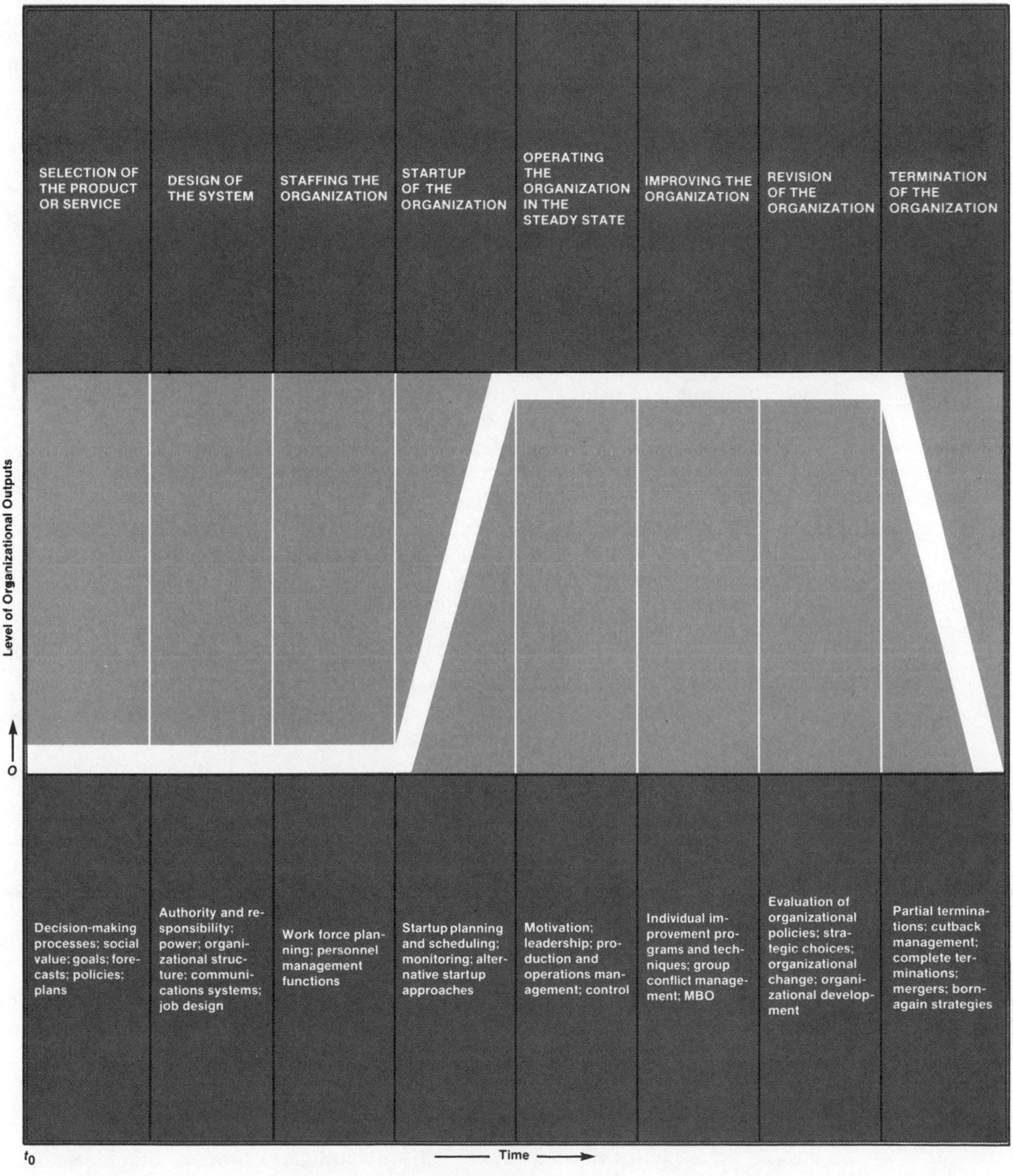

SELECTION OF THE PRODUCT OR SERVICE	DESIGN OF THE SYSTEM	STAFFING THE ORGANIZATION	STARTUP OF THE ORGANIZATION	OPERATING THE ORGANIZATION IN THE STEADY STATE	IMPROVING THE ORGANIZATION	REVISION OF THE ORGANIZATION	TERMINATION OF THE ORGANIZATION

Level of Organizational Outputs (vertical axis, 0)

Decision-making processes; social value; goals; forecasts; policies; plans	Authority and responsibility; power; organizational structure; communications systems; job design	Work force planning; personnel management functions	Startup planning and scheduling; monitoring; alternative startup approaches	Motivation; leadership; production and operations management; control	Individual improvement programs and techniques; group conflict management; MBO	Evaluation of organizational policies; strategic choices; organizational change; organizational development	Partial terminations: cutback management; complete terminations; mergers; born-again strategies

t_0 ⟶ Time ⟶

tion involves shutting down (personnel and assets are phased out). Revision involves a reassignment of these personnel and assets.

Exhibit 1–2 in graphical form portrays the outline of this book. It shows that an organization exists over time and that during this time span different phases are encountered. The management concepts and topics that we feel are important in each phase are shown and these topics will appear in that section of the book.

A major benefit to students of the life cycle approach is its logical sequence and the resulting structure it gives to a course in management. Managers face different types of problems in the various life cycle phases. Thus, being aware of this phenomenon, the student can be prepared to recognize these problems and develop problem solutions. Simply learning abstract concepts is not enough; one must be able to *apply* these at the right time and place. Recognition of the life cycle phases helps managers to determine the proper concept, time, and place.

As chapters are read, the student should always remember which life cycle phase is being considered and thus an overall perspective of the course can be maintained.

Another benefit is the "tool" approach of the life cycle outline. The step-by-step progression of the text through the phases can serve as a mental "dry run" in establishing a real organization. The *reality* of the life cycle approach is paramount; organizations do go through these phases; e.g., an organization must be designed and staffed before it can be started up. An operating organization has de facto been designed and staffed. Recognizing this and making conscious decisions probably separates the more successful from the more unsuccessful managers of organizations.

Finally, even if a new organization is not being considered and the student will enter an ongoing organization, the approach is still valid. Recognition of the phase the organization is in will serve to illuminate potential problem areas and solutions.

The life cycle and organization size

When we think of those entities we know as organizations, we usually first consider large ones such as K mart, U.S. Department of Defense, U.S. Steel, or the city of New York. The very size of these organizations and their impact on our lives due to the goods and services they do (or do not!) provide causes our awareness of them. Yet organizations such as these very rarely become "big" overnight. Such size is usually acquired as a result of an evolution through the life cycle phases discussed here. This evolutionary process, humble and straightforward as it perhaps seems, has profound implications from a management perspective. To borrow from an old saying: before one runs, he must learn to walk; before one walks, he must learn to crawl; and before one crawls, he indeed must be born. The same goes for organizations. Thus, we must consider small organizations (ones learning to crawl and walk) as well as running big ones. Consider the following information:

1. Of the 12 million businesses in this country, only 13.9 percent are corporations; the rest are organized as proprietorships or partnerships and tend to be small.
2. Of the active corporations, 57.7 percent have less than $100,000 in assets and 93.7 percent have less than $1 million in assets.
3. Approximately 95 percent of all businesses have fewer than 20 employees. These account for approximately 23 percent of all employment by industry.[20]

It is clear from the above that while smaller business organizations are dominant, Big Business is overwhelming in terms of employment. The 1979 *Fortune* 500 (a listing of the 500 largest, by sales, industrial organizations in the United States) has a total employment of 15.8 million. The 50 largest banks had 515,248 employees, the 50 largest retail firms 2,875,873, and the 50 largest utilities had 1,682,388.

Our point is that all sizes of organizations are important because to become large, an organization typically began small and progressed through what we feel are definable stages. Knowing this, we are in a better position to influence and adapt to that growth process.

Types of smaller firms.   Hosmer et al. discuss three major types of small organizations: (1) "Mom and Pop" companies, (2) stable, high-payoff companies, and (3) rapid growth companies.[21]

We are probably all familiar with the small retail or service organization that hires few (if any) employees and relies on the proprietor or members of the family. They are usually small because they serve a limited set of customers. Rarely are profits such that more than one store can be supported; hence, few chains emerge. These organizations typically start small, serve a limited market, and remain small.

Stable, high-payoff companies usually emerge from organizations that have a proprietary output. Often the market is such that it cannot support more than one firm; hence, the first one "in" has a "lock" on it and thus it is not attractive to others to enter. Again, though, size and outputs (volume and type) are restricted.

Rapid growth companies are the ones that start small and "grow up." These organizations are usually ones that operate in growing markets that can support competition and provide opportunities to innovate with newer, sometimes different goods and services. A different "kind" of management is required; one that can take risks (financially and psychologically), control diverse resources (human and material), and innovate.

The type of organization most often referred to in this book will be of the rapid growth type; one that will move through all or most of the life cycle stages.

THE ROLE OF AN ORGANIZATION IN SOCIETY

We have already made several important statements about organizations and managers:

1. Organizations are created when a job or goal is too large or difficult for one person to effectively accomplish alone.
2. Management is the process of coordinating human and material resources toward the accomplishment of that goal.

Let us for a moment consider the organizations in our lives. It is doubtful that anyone in this modern society could remember anything he or she has done recently that did not involve an organization. Star watching? Where did the telescope come from? Or the star charts? Whose land were you on while doing it? (To say nothing of your clothing on a cool night or where you initially learned about the stars.) How about hiking alone in the wilderness? Well, the boots and other equipment were probably an organization's output. Chances are the trail was built by a government agency or perhaps a local hiking club. We could go on and on.

We, a society, are *dependent* on our organizations. It is an irreversible fact of modern life. The die was cast as far back, perhaps, as the days of the cave dwellers.

Our questioning is not, then, *if* we will have organizations but rather *how* and of *what kind.*

First, think of our economic system. Organizations provide us with a multitude of goods and services. In the United States these are provided primarily by business organizations. In other societies (e.g., China, Russia, Italy, Great Britain) other "types" of organizations provide many of these goods and services. If an organization fails to provide a socially desirable good or service, society will attempt to eliminate it. The elimination may be as simple as failing to purchase the good or service; i.e., we eliminate economically via low profits, excess losses, and perhaps eventually bankruptcy. Also we eliminate via "social actions"; i.e., laws. The output of the Mafia is viewed by society as socially undesirable. Hence, through laws we attempt to eliminate it.[22]

Society, by its actions, can change the "rules of the game" and the definition of acceptable outputs at will via new legislation, regulations, or collective actions by citizens. Thus, we sense the role of an organization in society: to assemble and utilize resources in such a way as to provide a socially desirable good or service. Hence, profits may become a secondary objective of the business organization. Henry Ford has said: "There is nothing inherently wrong about making a profit. Well-conducted business enterprise cannot fail to return a profit, but profit must and inevitably will come as a reward for good service. It cannot be the basis—it must be the result of service."[23] If a desirable output (or "service" in Ford's words) is not forthcoming, society will attempt to close down the organization. Profits are "allowed" only *if* the output is acceptable. Step one is to determine the acceptable output. Step two is to produce/disseminate the output in a profitable manner. If profits alone were all that mattered, we could all simply act as gangsters or robber barons cleaning up as best we could. But society does not allow that. If you sell dope, make harmful toys, manufacture cars that pollute above certain levels, etc., society will *attempt* (but not always succeed, admittedly) to stop you.

Businesses are not all that needs to be considered here. Government organizations, charities, religious institutions, and so on likewise have to meet socially desirable standards. The recent spate of "sunset laws" which require a government agency to effectively "go out of business" and have to re-justify its existence every so many years exemplifies this process.

This, then, will lead us to the first step in our life cycle of organizations, determination of the product (i.e., the socially desirable good or service). Before we discuss this, we will, in the next chapter, analyze the decision-making process managers use in making this determination.

SUMMARY

The history of management is a fascinating field in its own right. It abounds with characters and scalawags, as well as with truly brilliant individuals. However, as we start on our trip though the life cycle it will quickly become apparent that this history is still being written—by dynamic managers, insightful philosophers, and ever-curious researchers. All aboard!

NOTES

[1] Henry Mintzberg, "The Manager's Job: Folklore and Fact," *Harvard Business Review,* vol. 53, no. 4 (1975), pp. 49–61.

[2] William Shakespeare, *As You Like It,* II, vii, 139.

[3] Gerald S. Hawkins, *Stonehenge Decoded* (New York: Dell Publishing Company, 1965).

[4] Adam Smith, *An Inquiry into the Nature and Causes of the Wealth of Nations* (London: A. Strahan & T. Cadell, 1776), vol. 1, pp. 6–9.

[5] Milton J. Nadworny, "Schmidt and Stakhanov: Work Heroes in Two Systems," *California Management Review,* vol. 6, no. 4 (Summer 1964), pp. 69–76.

[6] Keith Sward, *The Legend of Henry Ford* (New York: Rinehart & Company, Inc., 1948), p. 49.

[7] *Automotive Industries,* March 14, 1918, pp. 539–41.

[8] Henry Ford, *My Life and Work* (Garden City, N.Y.: Doubleday, Page & Company, 1924), p. 129.

[9] The Detroit *Journal,* January 12, 1914.

[10] Sward, *The Legend of Henry Ford,* p. 56.

[11] See Henri Fayol, *General and Industrial Management,* trans. by Constance Storrs (London: Pittman & Sons, 1949).

[12] Max Weber, *The Theory of Social and Economic Organization,* trans. by A. Henderson and T. Parsons (New York: Free Press, 1947).

[13] For a complete description of Mayo's work, see Elton Mayo, *The Human Problems of an Industrial Civilization* (New York: Macmillan, 1953), and F. J. Roethlisberger and W. J. Dickson, *Management and the Worker* (Cambridge, Mass.: Harvard University Press, 1939).

[14] See C. Argyris, *Integrating the Individual and the Organization* (New York: John Wiley & Sons, Inc., 1964), Abraham Maslow, *Motivation and Personality* (New York: Harper & Row, Publishers, 1964), and Douglas McGregor, *The Human Side of Enterprise* (New York: McGraw Hill Book Company, 1960).

[15] Larry E. Greiner, "Evolution and Revolution as Organizations Grow," *Harvard Business Review,* vol. 50, no. 4 (July–August 1972), pp. 37–46.

[16] Ibid., p. 37.

[17] Alan C. Filley, Robert J. House, and Steven Kerr, *Managerial Process and Organizational Behavior,* 2d ed. (Glenview, Ill.: Scott, Foresman and Company, 1976), chap. 22.

[18] Ibid., pp. 519–20.

[19] G. L. Lippitt and W. H. Schmidt, "Crisis in a Developing Organization," *Harvard Business Review,* vol. 45, no. 6 (November–December 1967), pp. 102–12.

[20] LaRue T. Hosmer, Arnold C. Cooper, and Karl H. Vesper, *The Entrepreneurial Function: Text and Cases on Smaller Firms* (Englewood Cliffs, N.J.: Prentice-Hall, Inc., 1977).

[21] Ibid. For an interesting article on the entrepreneurial personality and the type of small business most likely to succeed or fail, see Marlys Harris, "Do You Have What It Takes," *Money,* March 1978, pp. 49–54.

[22] For an enlightening comparison of the Mafia with legitimate business, see Radic C. Bunn and Anthony J. Tasca, "Mafia: Parallels with Legitimate Business," *Michigan Business Review,* vol. xxvi, no. 4 (November 1974) pp. 14–20.

[23] Ford, *My Life and Work,* p. 70.

DISCUSSION QUESTIONS

1. "The typical manager is really just someone who tells other people what to do." Comment.

2. Respond to the following statements:
   a. I'm going to be a high school P.E. teacher. Why should I study management?
   b. "Henry Ford was clearly a tyrant and would never .be effective in a modern organization."

   c. "Most U.S. businesses are corporations, so we should really limit our study of management to techniques that work best in big companies."

3. What are the major limitations of the Scientific Management school of thought?

4. Describe the Hawthorne effect.

5. Describe the various life cycle stages.

6. Why do we have organizations?

7. Why are profits a "secondary objective" of a business organization?

Section one
Selection of the
product or service

Organizations are allowed to exist in a society only if they produce a socially desirable good or service output. In this section we first discuss the decision-making process used in selecting this output. We then analyze the processes of goal setting, forecasting, and planning which will hopefully facilitate the efficient and effective provisioning of organizational outputs.

Level of Organizational Outputs

O

t_0

Time

SELECTION OF THE PRODUCT OR SERVICE	DESIGN OF THE SYSTEM	STAFFING THE ORGANIZATION	STARTUP OF THE ORGANIZATION	OPERATING THE ORGANIZATION IN THE STEADY STATE	IMPROVING THE ORGANIZATION	REVISION OF THE ORGANIZATION	TERMINATION OF THE ORGANIZATION
Decision-making processes; social value; goals; forecasts; policies; plans	Authority and responsibility; power; organizational structure; communications systems; job design	Work force planning; personnel management functions	Startup planning and scheduling; monitoring; alternative startup approaches	Motivation; leadership; production and operations management; control	Individual improvement programs and techniques; group conflict management; MBO	Evaluation of organizational policies; strategic choices; organizational change; organizational development	Partial terminations; cutback management; complete terminations; mergers; born-again strategies

Chapter 2
Managerial decision making

You can't solve a problem? Well, get down and investigate the present facts and its past history! When you have investigated the problem thoroughly, you will know how to solve it. Conclusions invariably come after investigation, and not before. Only a blockhead cudgels his brains on his own, or together with a group, "to find a solution" or "evolve an idea" without making any investigation. It must be stressed that this cannot possibly lead to any effective solution or any good idea.

Quotations from Chairman Mao Tse-tung
(Foreign Languages Press, Peking, 1972), p. 233.

The decision-making role of managers as discussed by Mintzberg was noted in the previous chapter. The centrality of decision making in management is becoming increasingly apparent. Herbert Simon, who won the Nobel Prize in 1978 for his work on administrative decision making, argues that decision making and management are indeed synonymous terms.[1] If one considers all of the aspects of decision making including problem recognition, data gathering, and decision implementation, as well as actual decision *making,* we could well argue that decision-making elements are present in the interpersonal and informational roles as well as in the decisional role per se.

We consider managerial decisions to be choices from among alternative courses of action that are intended to accomplish objectives. The three key elements of this definition require some elaboration. First is the notion of a "choice." If the manager does not have the ability to make a choice, there is no decision. Following a rule, obeying an order, or being physically required to act in a certain way does not constitute a decision.*

Second is the aspect of alternative courses of action. Note the plurality of the phrase. There must be more than one possible course of action for the manager to *have* a choice. Creativity on the part of managers in developing good alternatives is very important. The more successful managers tend to be the ones who creatively discover new, better ways of dealing with old problems. A well-known homily is: If you can only see one way of doing something, it is probably wrong. The point is that you are in all likelihood overlooking some key element in the problem if you are "blindered" onto one solution. Also, never overlook the status quo as a *potential* alternative. Perhaps the best thing is to live with the problem; anything you do might make things

---

* Except, one could argue, that there was a decision to obey or not obey the rule or order. However, assuming that the person wishes to stay on good terms in the organization, compliance is just that. It is not decision making.

worse. Thus, with the status quo as one alternative, the manager needs only to create one other alternative to have a situation where a choice is possible.

The third key element in the definition is the objective. If you don't have a goal or know what you are trying to do, why worry and fret over a decision? Flipping a coin or some other method of randomly selecting an alternative is as good as any other approach *if* you have no defined objective.

"Decisiveness" is a highly valued trait in our society. Knowing when as well as how to make decisions thus becomes a key aspect in the training and development of managers. Harry Truman's popular saying, "If you can't stand the heat, get out of the kitchen" and the plaque on his desk that read "The buck stops here" epitomize the notion that for a manager or administrator to keep his or her job, decisions have to be made and the blame (or credit) taken.

William James's famous observation that "There is no more miserable human being than one in whom nothing is habitual but indecision" illustrates the typical view of the decision avoider.[2] And, if being miserable isn't enough, remember that in *The Divine Comedy*, Canto III of the *Inferno*, Dante warns that the worst place in Hell is reserved for those who were incapable of making a decision. But, lest we be accused of advocating the creation of a generation of decision-making gunslingers, we point out still another famous observation, this one by Lord Falkland: "When it is not necessary to make a decision, it is necessary to not make a decision."[3]

The discussion that follows assumes that choices, alternatives, and objectives are present when we speak of decision making. The pervasiveness of decision making in the many tasks managers do will be apparent. In this chapter, we will first present a model of the decision-making process. We will then show how limitations of the human being impact on the decision process and result in what is probably "less than optimal" decisions as the norm. The impact of groups on decision making will then be considered. And finally, we will show how managers face different kinds of decision situations at different stages of an organization's life cycle.

A MODEL OF DECISION MAKING

As illustrated in Exhibit 2–1, there are ten key elements in the decision-making process: (1) the situational factors making up the original state of nature, (2) problem recognition, (3) development of alternatives, (4) assessment of the potential effects of each alternative including (5) their probability of occurring and (6) their importance, (7) a final weighting of each alternative, (8) selection of an alternative, (9) implementation, and (10) via feedback, an assessment of the implemented decision's impact.

Exhibit 2-1
A model of the decision-making process

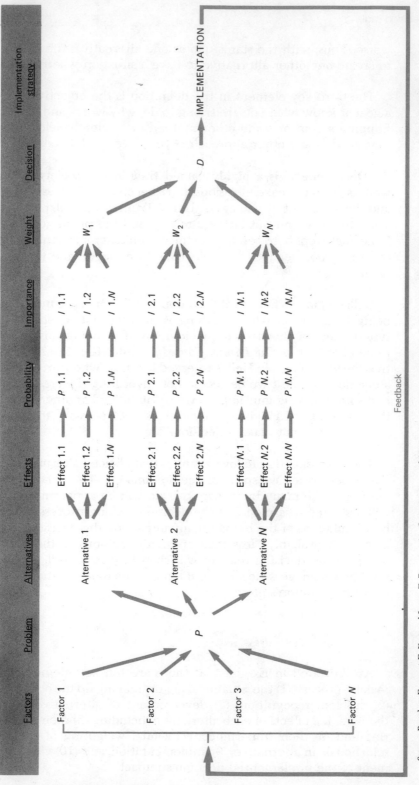

Source: Based on Fremont E. Kast and James E. Rosenzweig, *Organization and Management: A Systems Approach*, 2d ed. (New York: McGraw-Hill Book Company, 1974), p. 366.

Situational factors

The environment surrounding decision makers tends to be complex. Therefore, the adept manager must be capable of determining what factors are of importance to the organization and then must develop a means of monitoring these. A constant flow of relevant, up-to-date information is a necessity. As Chairman Mao has said, "Get the facts!" Obviously, there are limits upon the amount of information that any person can deal with effectively. Determining the key factors for which data will be collected and the presentation of this data in a concise, easily understood format is the basis for a sound management information system.

Problem recognition

Problems are situations where objectives are not, or will not be, met. Recognizing problems based upon the factors being monitored is crucial. Good managers will tend to recognize problems earlier than their less successful counterparts; they will be at work solving problems before the others even know they have a problem.

Kepner and Tregoe have developed a management training program, based on decision making, that is used in a large number of organizations.[4] The heart of the Kepner-Tregoe approach involves problem recognition and definition. "A problem is a deviation between what *should* be happening and what *actually* is happening that is important enough to make someone think the deviation ought to be corrected."[5] Once problems are "found," causes must be ascertained. "The cause of a problem is always a change that has taken place through some distinctive feature, mechanism, or condition to produce a new unwanted effect."[6]

Kepner and Tregoe were working for the RAND Corporation in the late 1950s. They believed that a key to improved decision making was to improve the use of logic in defining problems and ways of solving them.

They began constructing a step-by-step method for the human mind to follow in discovering the root cause of problems. After defining a "problem" as a deviation from the norm, they focused intensively on three things: problem solving, decision making, and potential-problem analysis. Although the approach has been called "unsexy," most people familiar with it concede that it works.[7]

Development of alternatives

Once a problem is recognized and its cause(s) determined, the process of finding several alternative solutions begins. The better decision makers tend to be creative in developing alternatives. They do not feel constrained to repeat past performances; new ways of solving old problems are always sought.

We mentioned earlier the relevance of the status quo as a potential alternative, and the need to avoid the "blinderedness" of developing only one (possible) solution to a problem. Creativity does not, however, require "offbeat" alternatives. One should always be cognizant of the factors at play in the situation and develop realistic alternatives in light of these.

Determination of possible effects

For each alternative, the decision maker should attempt to develop a scenario of what would be likely to happen *if* that alternative were implemented. Imagine yourself as a Hollywood scriptwriter and develop the story line for each alternative. As realistically as possible, try to determine what will happen, who will do various things, and so forth. You need not be *certain* that each effect will occur. At this stage, we simply want to determine what will *possibly* occur, good or bad.

Assignment of probabilities

Benjamin Franklin once said that ". . . Nothing is certain but death and taxes."* This philosophy should apply to the possible effects of the various alternatives. Each effect will only *probably* occur though some may well have higher probabilities of occurrence than others. The decision-maker must examine each effect and make an honest estimate of these probabilities.

Importance of effects

Each effect, with its probability of occurrence, will now have an importance level placed upon it. Importances are, obviously, influenced by the philosophy of the decision maker. We all have our own values and biases and these will be expressed as we assess the importance of various effects.

Weighting

After considering all of the probably occurring, variously important effects of the alternatives, we subjectively "weight" each alternative against the others. Trade-offs will be made. For example, is a low probability, high importance effect (e.g., being attacked by an alligator in San Diego) weighted more than a high probability, lower importance one (e.g., seeing an alligator during a routine visit to the San Diego Zoo with your children)?

---

* This quotation is often abridged to include regional insights, e.g., in Chicago, "Nothing is certain but death, taxes, and the fact that the Cubs will fold in August."

The decision

At the conclusion of the weighting process, a decision is made to either select one of the alternatives *or* to go back and develop other alternatives if none are presently good enough. Certainly, we should not be stifled by total inaction as is illustrated by the following parable: A 14th-century philosopher, Jean Buridan, invented an imaginary ass—known ever since as Burdian's ass. This ass was supposed to be placed exactly between two identical bales of hay. Buridan maintained that the ass must starve to death because it would have no reason to choose one bale over the other.

Implementation

Deciding what to do is only part of the process. Doing it is a major task yet remaining. Given that an alternative has been selected, the decision maker must now determine who will do what, when, where, and how to carry out the decision. Assume that your decision is to fire Bill. Who will tell Bill? Where? When? How? Who will do Bill's job until a replacement is found? And so on. For every decision, an implementation strategy must be developed. The best decision in the world, left unimplemented, will have no more effect than if the problem was never recognized, and a decision never made.

Feedback

Learning from experience requires determining the results of one's actions. The difference between someone with ten years' experience and someone with one year's experience ten times over is that the former typically has watched what happened after decisions were made and used this information to better assess the factors, the problems, alternatives, and so on in subsequent decision situations.

IMPLICATIONS OF THE MODEL

The general process outlined in Exhibit 2–1 is actually used whenever we make decisions. For example, finding oneself on one side of a street and wanting to be on the other side creates a problem. We have several alternatives: jaywalk, go forward to the next intersection to cross, go back to the previous intersection, and so forth. There are *effects:* getting across safely, being hit by a vehicle, receiving a ticket for jaywalking, going out of the way to get to an intersection and being late to an appointment, presenting a good impression and example for your young brother/sister who is with you, and so on. Within each alternative, each effect has a *probability* and an *importance*. These are *weighed* and you decide what to do. You then *do it* and *assess* the outcome. The next time you are in a similar situation, the information stored away about this event can be used to better assess factors (e.g., perhaps to be able to discover your problem at an earlier intersection versus at mid-block), develop new alternatives, assign more realistic probabilities and importances, better weigh alternatives, and develop better implementation and feedback strategies.

For most routine problems, we mentally go through this process very quickly. Imagine, for example, your decision-making behavior while driving on a crowded expressway. You constantly face problems and make decisions to avoid running into another car that pulls in front of you, to stop (or not stop) when an object blows across the road, or to change lanes (or not) in response to something you see up ahead.

For unique, major decisions in organizations, it is probably wise to go reasonably slowly through the steps in a deliberate fashion. Few administrative decisions require split-second action. Indeed, it is a rare managerial decision that does not have at least several minutes' cushion before a decision is mandated. Indeed, most significant decisions will have a cushion measured in hours, if not days.

Programmed decisions

When certain problem situations occur with regularity, it may be advantageous to develop programmed responses. Thus, when a given set of factors occurs, a given decision response is forthcoming without a step-by-step progression through the model. Much time can be saved and perhaps errors avoided. In a real sense, this is the process of establishing rules and hence the implementing of courses of action (technically speaking) may not be decision making. Obviously, though, the original programmed action was a decision and is noted here to point out the practical usefulness of finding repetitive problem situations and developing programmed responses.

In addition to repetitive situations, time-constrained situations also may benefit from a programmed response. Imagine a physician in an emergency room. An ambulance attendant bursts in and exclaims, "His heart just stopped!" The physician does not have the luxury of a few minutes' time to unhurriedly go through the decision-making model. Action, now, is imperative. Thus, physicians are trained *in advance* for situations like this one which have a good likelihood of occurring in the future. The problem was defined when the physician was a student in the calm of a classroom. Using the model, given responses (i.e., behaviors to be implemented) were then determined for given sets of factors (i.e., problems). Thus, the model *is* followed, but in a prearranged manner. Whenever time-constrained situations are likely to occur, advance decision making is the prescribed approach. Thus, we train physicians, pilots, quality control inspectors, etc. to relate various sets of factors directly to predetermined responses.

Programmed decisions, when used in repetitive or time-constrained situations, yield several benefits. Obviously, they save time and permit more rapid action. Having been made in a calm environment, there is less likelihood of overlooking new, unique alternatives due to the pressures of the "firing line." Further, a greater uniformity of decisions is usually forthcoming. This can be of benefit in such situations as approving loans in a bank or settling insurance claims. Finally, programmed decisions permit the utilization of personnel with lower skill levels than could otherwise be used in certain job situations. Needed are not the analytical decision-making skills, but rather skills of observation and reaction.

RATIONALITY IN DECISION MAKING

Administrative decisions, as well as the many other decisions we face in life, tend to be rather complex. Most often, there tends to be much information that is relevant to the decision. Unfortunately, some, if not most, of that information is not always readily available. For example, in starting a new business, how can we *accurately* predict areas of future sales, whether a source of raw materials (e.g., a mine) or energy will last another 10 or 50 years, whether the population will increase by 8 percent per year, and so on? Most of this data will be rough estimates or at best good guesses.

Because of the information problem, most administrative decisions are *not* made according to the "Economic Man" theory. The Economic Man is thought to possess all relevant data, and to use this data to pick that one course of action that optimizes the utilities (or objectives) for which the decision is being made.

Beginning in the late 1940s, Herbert Simon challenged the Economic Man assumptions as being undescriptive of actual decision-making behavior. Simon argued first of all that obtaining perfect information (i.e., all relevant facts) is virtually impossible. And even if all that data were obtained, few humans, even with computers, could make sense of it within any meaningful time frames. Thus, Simon contended that, by necessity, we are selective in our information gathering. We knowingly limit our data to a small percentage of all relevant facts; a percentage that includes what we feel are some of the more important factors and that is small enough for us to process it. We are obviously influenced in this *search*, or data gathering, by our own values, aspirations, and previous experiences.

Figuratively, we draw a fence around this limited set of information and then, based on that data, find the best solution. If this solution is satisfactory, i.e., appears to yield acceptable results, we stop there, implement that decision, and go on to another problem. If it is not satisfactory, we undergo additional search and slightly expand the fenced-in boundaries. We then look at the best solution with the new data. Is it satisfactory? If so, we stop. If not, we search and again expand our boundaries.

There are two important concepts here. First is *bounded rationality*. The most rational, optimal decision of the Economic Man was foregone when we accepted less than perfect information. By placing a fence (boundary) around our information and then making the "best" decision based on this limited set of information, we in essence bounded our rationality. Note that we do not behave *ir*rationally. We simply make the most rational decision we can with a bounded information set.

The second key concept is the notion of *satisficing* behavior. The bounded rationality decision was not examined on the Economic Man grounds of optimality. It was examined on the basis of whether or not it would yield satisfactory (not necessarily optimal) results. If, based on a bounded set of information, the best decision is not satisfactory, then search behavior is begun to expand the information boundaries by a small increment. A new "best" solution is then examined. If it will yield satisfactory results, the process stops. If not, search is again begun. And so on. The process continues until the first satisfactory decision is found.

Students may find satisficing behavior in their own actions. In studying for exams, rarely does one study until an optimal 100 percent exam score can be positively achieved. Perhaps, if one had nothing else in life to do but study for that one exam, optimality could be sought. However, most students will study hard enough to get a score that will yield an "acceptable" grade and then move on to other studies, a movie, or some other endeavor. In this way, more ground is covered (in an "acceptable" fashion) even though no perfect 100 percent exams are recorded. At graduation day, you could probably see the person who never settled for less than perfection still in the library cramming for that freshman accounting exam, while your 90 percent exam score four years ago did just fine! And you had time to study economics, marketing, management, finance, go to some movies, and so on. Perhaps, in administrative decision making, seeking perfect rationality can itself be a bit irrational.

GROUP DECISION-MAKING TECHNIQUES

Groups are important in organizational decision making for a variety of reasons. At times a group (e.g., committee) is the decision-making agent. At other times, groups are used to provide information and support for an individual decision maker. In addition, there is the potential impact a group may have on acceptance and implementation of decisions.

Groups as decision makers

Committees, as a form of a group, are often criticized for their lack of decision-making prowess (e.g., "a camel is a horse designed by a committee"). Whether we consider groups to be good or bad decision makers seems to depend upon the criteria we are using. Creativity, accuracy, implementability, and speed tend to be common measures on which groups are evaluated relative to individual decision makers.

Groups typically take more time and spend more worker hours to make decisions than do individuals. Yet a group typically brings to a situation far more information than one individual usually possesses. If this added information is important, the cost of added time spent may well be justified.

A group is usually more creative than an individual because of the diverse viewpoints possessed by members. This can, of course, be offset by composing a group of people who share similar backgrounds and work together. When difficulties exist in defining a problem and/or of finding new solutions when old ones begin to fail, groups made up of diverse individuals generate a creative spirit that is often beneficial.

There is evidence that for complex problem situations, where there is one clear-cut correct answer, groups using a consensus agreement approach tend to be more effective than individuals.[8] On problems of lesser complexity, but where special skills are needed (e.g., solving mathematical equations), individuals with the proper training tend to excell.

There is some disagreement on the relationship between groups and individuals regarding risk taking. On the one hand are arguments that groups are moderately conservative in that their decisions usually are based on "the lowest common denominator." Thus, they take neither very risky nor very conservative approaches. The contrary argument holds that since no one individual in a group tends to receive the blame (or credit) for decisions, there is a tendency to be more risky; if an individual were forced to act alone, there would be less of an incentive to take a chance.

Implementability usually improves with a group decision since group members often take it upon themselves to "sell" the decision to colleagues and co-workers once it has been made. Thus, the decision starts out with a cadre of advocates. This compares to the often-felt reluctance to go along with decisions made by one person and autocratically imposed.

Group decision-making approaches

Groups can use a variety of approaches in making decisions. Several of the more common ones are: (1) *lack of response*, i.e., don't argue with what is proposed by some individual; (2) *authority rule*, i.e., the "leader" announces the decision; (3) *majority rule*, i.e., take a vote; (4) *minority rule*, i.e., a few people dominate and take over; (5) *consensus*, i.e., find a common ground upon which everyone can agree at least somewhat; and (6) *unanimity*, i.e., do nothing unless everyone agrees completely.[9]

Charles Wolf of the RAND Corporation has posed as his Law of Decision Making:

Major actions are rarely decided by more than four people. If you think a larger meeting you're attending is really "hammering out" a decision, you're probably wrong. Either the decision was agreed to by a smaller group before the meeting began, or the outcome of the larger meeting will be modified later when three or four people get together.[10]

Wolf's law can be easily observed as politics are played out in group meetings. Quite often, a small coalition can be dominant, and influence votes, discussion, and so on. Obviously, this can thwart the creativity of a committee and make the committee perform more in line with the beliefs of the individual who dominates the coalition. Several techniques exist which may overcome this phenomenon.

Delphi.   The Delphi process, originally developed at the RAND Corporation, seeks to minimize the influence of any one person on a group. In using a Delphi approach, the group members are isolated from one another. An "administrator" who is not an actual member of the group then presents each group member with a statement of the problem. Each group member then writes down his or her decision. The administrator collects and tabulates the decisions and reports these back to each individual. At no time does any group member know which other person "owns" a given decision in the tabulations. After receiving the first round tabulations, each person makes a second round of decisions. You can change to another decision, keep the one you had, or make up an entirely new one. These are then given to the administrator who tabulates and reports them back. A number of rounds are usually held until some one decision tends to emerge as a clear favorite. Often, after three or four rounds, a short (one- or two-sentence) justification for one's decision is allowed and included (anonymously) with the tabulations report.

The Delphi approach tends to eliminate the undue influence of high power or aggressive people in a group. Further, it avoids the often subconscious downplaying of a suggestion made by someone we don't like or respect. We don't ever know *who* owns what decision; thus we objectively evaluate the decision per se and do not subjectively evaluate its source. The Delphi approach is usable with geographically separated group members when the administrator uses a telephone or teletype communications device. Obviously, the integrity of the administrator must be assured lest the data tabulations be manipulated.

Consensus group.   Consensus groups involve face-to-face discussions. However, the "rules" are that voting, trading, and averaging are *not* allowed. A discussion must be held until all members can agree at least somewhat with a decision. This requires even the low-power, nondominant individual to be included and thus typically precludes the "railroading" through of any given decision. The aggressive, dominant person can, however, often control the discussion. This approach usually takes substantial time. Yet, Jay Hall contends that the Consensus Approach is quite beneficial for complex problems in that it more often than not results in decisions that are more accurate than could be made by any one group member acting alone.[11]

Vroom and Yetton decision tree.   A recent framework has been proposed by Vroom and Yetton to help a manager determine when to share decision-making powers with subordinates.[12] They identify five decision-making styles, each of which can be feasible given certain conditions. The two key factors which dictate the best decision style are: (1) the assurance that a high-quality decision be made where required, and (2) ensuring the acceptance and implementability of the decision where necessary.

The Vroom and Yetton model is shown in Exhibit 2–2A. The model is used by asking question A (at point A). Depending on the yes/no response, the proper branch is followed to another node; e.g., say the answer is "no," then go to the node below E. Then that node's question is asked. Assume the answer here is "yes" and thus go to the F node, and so on. The prescribed decision-style approaches are described in Exhibit 2–2B. When multiple decision approaches are described, the manager may operate to either "save time" and opt for an autocratic approach or "invest time" and rely on a participative approach.

The utility of the model in real organizational settings is still being evaluated. Vroom found in one study that for 46 successful decisions, 65 percent were made in a manner as proposed by the model. For 42 unsuccessful decisions, 71 percent went against the model.[13]

"Groupthink."   Groupthink is a term coined by Irving Janis to describe a dangerous situation where a group makes a decision that no individual member acting alone would, in all probability, have made.[14] This occurs when the group strives for unanimity that overrides members' willingness to speak out and realistically analyze alternatives and point out flaws. Groupthink results from an overriding desire for cohesiveness to the point that valid criticism is withheld lest one be viewed as a troublemaker or outsider.

Exhibit 2-2: The Vroom-Yetton decision tree and decision-style approaches

A. Vroom and Yetton model

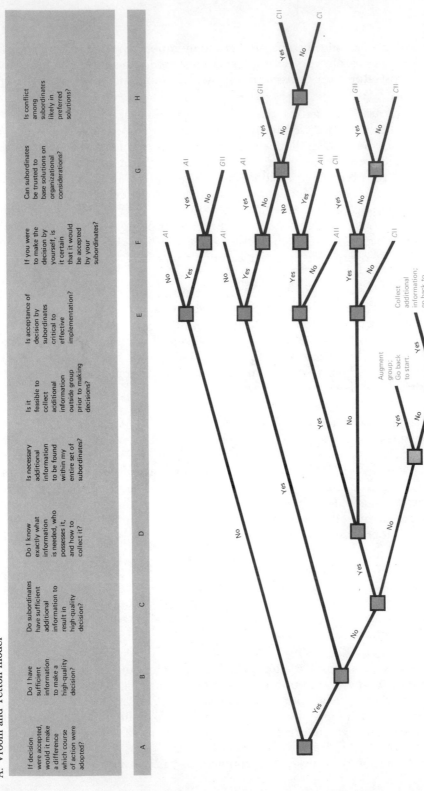

A	B	C	D	E	F	G	H
If decision were accepted, would it make a difference which course of action were adopted?	Do I have sufficient information to make a high-quality decision?	Do subordinates have sufficient additional information to result in high-quality decision?	Do I know exactly what information is needed, who possesses it, and how to collect it?	Is necessary additional information to be found within my entire set of subordinates?	Is it feasible to collect additional information outside group prior to making decisions?	Is acceptance of decision by subordinates critical to effective implementation?	If you were to make the decision by yourself, is it certain that it would be accepted by your subordinates?	Can subordinates be trusted to base solutions on organizational considerations?	Is conflict among subordinates likely in preferred solutions?

Source: Lyman W. Porter, Edward E. Lawler III, and J. Richard Hackman, *Behavior in Organizations* (New York: McGraw-Hill Book Company, 1975), p. 427.

B. Decision-style approaches

AI. The leader uses personally possessed information to make the decision.

AII. The leader makes the decision after obtaining the needed information from subordinates. The subordinates may or may not be told the nature of the problem.

CI. The leader meets with relevant subordinates individually, shares the problem and asks for suggestions. He or she then makes the decision.

CII. The leader serves as a chairperson in sharing the problem with the group and generating and evaluating alternatives while trying to reach a group consensus. The leader must ultimately make the decision which may or may not reflect subordinates' influence.

GII. The leader shares the problem with the group, and together they generate and evaluate alternatives and attempt to reach a solution.

In the book *Victims of Groupthink*, Janis reviews some well-known historical events in light of the probability that groupthink was involved.[15] Such events as the Bay of Pigs, the crossing of the 38th Parallel during the Korean War, and the escalation of the war in Vietnam are indicative of groupthink legacies.

Jerry Harvey has described the "Abilene Paradox" which seems to be a close relative of groupthink.[16] The Abilene Paradox was discovered by Harvey while visiting his in-laws in Coleman, Texas (population 5,608 in 1970), which is about 50 miles southeast of Abilene. One hot, summer day while playing dominoes and swatting flies, someone said, "Let's go to Abilene." Someone else said, "Sure," and before you knew it, there was a carload of sweaty people driving down a dusty road (called U.S. 84) to Abilene. There, they got a bite to eat in a fourth-class cafeteria, turned around and sweated their way back to Coleman. Upon their return home, someone said, "That was a lousy trip. It would have been better to stay home and eat leftovers." Someone else agreed, and before you knew it, nobody wanted to go to Abilene in the first place. "I went 'cause I thought you wanted to go" was the common complaint. Thus, an Abilene Paradox exists when everyone does the opposite of what they really want to do because they decide to do what they think everyone else wants to do. Sound absurd? It is, but a lot of people have made their own trips to Abilene.

The "solution" to both groupthink and the Abilene Paradox is to provide a nonthreatening atmosphere where people don't feel compelled to seek consensus just to promote harmony and cohesiveness. We must encourage and tolerate diverse points of view. We need not always accept these, but at least they will be heard by various group members who *could* voice their agreement with that other point of view.

DECISIONS OVER A LIFE CYCLE

While managers constantly make decisions, the nature and context of these decisions will vary depending upon the stage of development of the organization. (See Chapter 1.) As the organization proceeds through its life cycle, different topics become dominant issues. For example, selecting the organizational output must come before improving the system that produces the output; it is hard to improve something you don't have. Still, once an organization has progressed through several life cycle stages, this does not mean that decisions based on previous states will not occur. Certainly, any forward-looking organization in, for example, the steady state will be contemplating future changes in outputs to keep up with the changing world. The benefit to be gained from the life cycle perspective is to ensure that attention is paid to relevant decision areas at specific points in the life of the organization.

In reality, any large organization will have components that may variously be in any given life cycle stage. For example, a large firm could be starting up a new plant on the East Coast, terminating an outdated refinery in Oklahoma, and improving the steady state operations of a third plant on the West Coast. Adept managers will recognize the concurrent nature of the life cycle phases. They will thus be cognizant of the important decision-making issues in various components of the organization at any given point in time.

QUANTITATIVE TOOLS IN DECISION MAKING

A variety of quantitative tools are available to managers to aid in their decision making. (See, for example, Chapters 9, 12, and 13.) Likewise, the use of computers to process data has vastly improved many decision-making areas, allowing managers to quickly make accurate decisions that were heretofore impossible simply due to computational inabilities.

While modern managers are usually aware of quantitative tools and computers and have some familiarity with them, most large organizations typically have highly skilled employees whose job it is to aid managers in using these techniques. While a familiarity with these tools is beneficial, an even more important managerial skill involves knowing how to use the "management scientist" who is typically highly skilled at quantitative analysis but perhaps less skilled in understanding the rudiments of the given organization—how it works, with whom, its interrelationships with other organizations, and so on. We will develop this issue in later chapters.

SUMMARY

Decision making—making choices from among alternative courses of action to accomplish a given objective(s)—is something all managers do. Hence, we recognize why many people view management and decision making as synonymous terms.

Our model of decision making consists of ten steps: (1) *factors* that lead to (2) a *problem* for which (3) *alternative* solutions are developed, each of which has (4) *effects* that have (5) *probabilities* of occurring and (6) various *importance* levels which (7) result in a *weighting* of each alternative leading to the (8) *choice* of the "best" as the decision which will (9) be *implemented* and (10) its results monitored via *feedback*. For regularly recurring problems or for those which can be anticipated, we urge that the model be used to produce programmed decisions which can then be implemented immediately upon confronting a particular set of factors.

To deal with the complexity of most administrative decisions, Herbert Simon has developed a theory that describes decision making on the basis of bounded rationality and satisficing. Simon's concepts certainly appear to be descriptive of managerial decision making as well as logical in the sense that managers must keep their search for optimality within reason.

Organizations, being made up of people, naturally have situations where groups of people rather than individuals acting alone are involved in making decisions. Knowing the advantages and disadvantages of group decision making should lead to their utilization (or lack thereof) at appropriate times. The Delphi approach and consensus group techniques have found acceptance among many managers who wish to avoid various group-related difficulties in achieving a sound decision. The Vroom and Yetton model, though still being studied, has exhibited a potential for prescriptively advising managers as to when to use participative versus individual approaches for decision making.

Virtually all mature organizations will have components (subunits, products, and so on) that are in various life cycle phases. Within any phase, there are certain decision areas or topics that will have a dominant relevance. The adept manager will constantly be aware of the life cycle stage being occupied by the organization and/or its smaller unit and take these stages into account in making decisions.

Finally, the abundance of quantitative tools for decision making must be recognized. As well as developing some familiarity with basic techniques, managers must develop the ability to work with specially trained management scientists in applying these quantitative tools. We will review a number of these quantitative aids in the chapters on startup, operations management, and control.

GUIDES TO ACTION

1. Avoid groupthink and Abilene Paradox errors. Likewise, remember that the majority is often wrong.

2. Few decisions of importance are clearly right or wrong at the time they are made. Thus, after you have made the choice, don't stew about it later. Go on to the next one. Remember, ball players make the Hall of Fame if they can make a hit four out of ten times at bat.

3. Avoid making decisions under pressure; sleeping on a decision problem is sound advice.

4. Since it is unlikely that you will have this book handy for all decision situations to help you remember the decision-making model, at least remember to lay out the alternatives in writing before making an important decision.

5. Where possible, hold off committing resources till the last possible minute. It is very hard to get an egg back into the shell.

6. Seek out independent opinions if you believe that your biases are affecting your decision making. Be careful though. A truly objective opinion is not easily found, because many advisers have a vested interest in the outcome.[17] For example, don't ask your barber if you need a haircut.

NOTES

[1] Herbert Simon, *The New Science of Management Decision* (New York: Harper & Bros., 1960), p. 1.

[2] William James, *The Principles of Psychology* (New York: H. Holt and Company, 1890).

[3] Paul Dickson, *The Official Rules* (New York: Delacorte Press, 1978), p. 51.

[4] Charles H. Kepner, and Benjamin B. Tregoe, *The Rational Manager: A Systematic Approach to Problem Solving and Decision Making* (New York: McGraw-Hill Book Company, 1965).

[5] Ibid., p. 20.

[6] Ibid., p. 45.

[7] Stephen Singular, "Peering into the Corporate Id," *MBA*, vol. 9, no. 3 (March 1975), p. 27.

[8] Jay Hall, "Decisions, Decisions, Decisions," *Psychology Today*, November 1971, pp. 51–54.

[9] Fremont E. Kast and James E. Rosenzweig, *Organization and Management: A Systems Approach*, 2d ed. (New York: McGraw-Hill Book Company, 1974), pp. 424.

[10] Charles Wolf, in Dickson, *The Official Rules*, p. 137.

[11] Jay Hall, "Decisions, Decisions, Decisions."

[12] Victor H. Vroom and Phillip W. Yetton, *Leadership and Decision-Making* (Pittsburgh: University of Pittsburgh Press, 1973).

[13] Victor Vroom, "Can Leaders Learn to Lead?" *Organizational Dynamics*, vol. 4, no. 3 (Winter 1976), p. 21.

[14] Irving Janis, *Victims of Groupthink* (Boston: Houghton Mifflin, 1977).

[15] Ibid.

[16] Jerry Harvey, "The Abilene Paradox: The Management of Agreement," *Organizational Dynamics*, vol. 3, no. 1 (Summer 1974), pp. 63–80.

[17] George Odiorne, *Management and the Activity Trap* (New York: Harper & Row, Publishers, 1974), p. 143.

DISCUSSION QUESTIONS

1. What is a decision?

2. Pick one of the problems below and work the decision-making model:
   a. You've locked your keys in your car.
   b. You're trying to sleep but a neighbor's dog is barking.
   c. You got a parking ticket you don't feel is justified.

3. Why are programmed decisions beneficial? Under what circumstances are they useful?

4. Define satisficing and bounded rationality.

5. Why might "groupthink" and Abilene Paradox processes be "normal"? I.e., what human traits may predispose us to act that way?

6. Find three examples of problems that could well be solved via a Delphi process. Find three that could be solved via a consensus group approach.

7. What relevance is there between organizational life cycles and decision making?

8. Based upon your college curriculum, find three examples of quantitative decision-making techniques that you have learned (or will learn). Why might a "seat of the pants" manager not be inclined to accept your advice if you use these tools?

CASE: WRIGHT CLEANERS AND DYERS, LTD.*

Wright Cleaners and Dyers operated a number of retail branches throughout a large metropolitan area. Many of the older branches were located in neighborhoods which had become economically depressed. A few, such as the store established in Whitesdale six months earlier, were in upper–middle-class communities.

Richard Clark, 35, an executive in a rapidly expanding firm, lived in Whitesdale with his wife and two young sons. As Clark left for a short business trip on Monday, he asked his wife to take several of his shirts to Wright's. Mrs. Jackson, sole clerk at the Whitesdale branch, promised Mrs. Clark that the shirts would be ready by Wednesday.

Mrs. Jackson, 61, a widow, had been forced by the death of her husband to obtain employment. She had been working for Wright's for six months—

---

* From: Garrett L. Bergen, and William V. Haney, *Organizational Relations and Management Action* (New York: McGraw-Hill Book Company, 1966), pp. 754–56.

her first job since her marriage in her early 20s. Except for a brief indoctrination period at Wright headquarters, she had spent all of this time at the Whitesdale store.

Clark arrived home late Wednesday night and wasn't expected in the office until Thursday noon. The next morning he drove with his sons to Wright's. He walked into the store with his boys at 8:30 A.M.

Clark: Are my shirts ready yet?

Mrs. Jackson: Do you have your ticket?

Clark: Ticket? No, I didn't know you had to have one.

Mrs. Jackson: Oh, yes—I can't find your laundry without a ticket number.

Clark: Well, OK—I guess my wife has it at home.

Clark loaded his boys into the car, drove the mile back to his home, picked up the ticket, and returned with his children to Wright's.

Mrs. Jackson: (After glancing at the ticket number) Oh, that's not in yet.

Clark: But my wife said they were promised for yesterday.

Mrs. Jackson: Well, they may have come in this morning, but they would be in large boxes in the back, and it would take an hour to unpack them. You come back in an hour, and I'm sure I'll have them ready for you.

Clark: Why don't you let me help you go through the boxes? This running back and forth is getting ridiculous.

Mrs. Jackson: I can't do that—no one is allowed back of the partition.

At this, Mrs. Jackson walked behind the partition, leaving an exasperated Clark, who decided he could do no more with the situation at this point.

In an hour, Clark returned.

Mrs. Jackson: Here are the shirts—I got them out for you. I'm sorry about the delay.

Clark: If you're sorry, may I assume that you wouldn't like to have this sort of thing happen again?

Mrs. Jackson: Why, yes, of course.

Clark: Well, whose rule is it that no one is allowed to help you sort out the laundry in an emergency?

Mrs. Jackson: The supervisor's—that's a store rule.

Clark: Then I would suggest that you advise your supervisor that this store is in Whitesdale—not some blighted neighborhood. I think you can assume that people are honest here.

Mrs. Jackson: Oh, it isn't a question of honesty. I had a woman in here a couple of weeks ago who went through the cleaning bags hanging on the racks, tearing them open to find her clothing.

Clark: I don't see the similarity. I had my ticket number. Nothing would have had to be torn apart.

Mrs. Jackson: Well, no one is allowed behind the partition. That's a store rule.

Clark: I know, and most of the time it's probably a good rule. But don't you suppose there might be an exception—an instance when a rule might be broken?

Mrs. Jackson: No, that's what rules are for. (Mrs. Jackson quickly walked behind the partition.)

Later in the day, Clark telephoned Wright's main office and spoke to Anthony Conti, supervisor of stores.

Clark: Mr. Conti, I didn't feel like doing you people a favor this morning, but I'm a little more mellow now. I'd like to tell you about a practice which may lose you customers. (Clark recounted the incident with Mrs. Jackson.)

Conti: Well, I'll tell you, Mr. Clark—I'll tell you why that happened. You see, we train our workers all alike because we may have to transfer them from one store to another, and so on. Now, we tell them *never* and under *no* conditions to let anyone go back of the partition. And there are two reasons why we tell them this. Now, we find that nine times out of ten whenever we let a customer back there fooling around with the cleaning, there's going to be confusion. And the second reason is the safety of the workers. You know what I mean—we can't let a man back there with our female employees.

Clark: I know what you mean, but I don't think Mrs. Jackson should have been concerned. She's seen me several times in the store. And I don't exactly dress or look like an escaped convict—besides I had my two little boys with me.

Conti: Well, you have to have a rule, though—you never know, and those things can happen.

Clark: Yes, but the probability of their happening in Whitesdale is pretty remote, don't you think?

Conti: Well, maybe—but rules are rules, and we make the workers live up to them.

Question

What should Mr. Conti do, after concluding his discussion with Clark, about this incident?

SELECTION OF THE PRODUCT OR SERVICE

DESIGN OF THE SYSTEM

STAFFING THE ORGANIZATION

STARTUP OF THE ORGANIZATION

OPERATING THE ORGANIZATION IN THE STEADY STATE

IMPROVING THE ORGANIZATION

REVISION OF THE ORGANIZATION

TERMINATION OF THE ORGANIZATION

Level of Organizational Outputs

0

Decision-making processes; social value; goals; fore-casts; policies; plans

Authority and re-sponsibility; power; organi-zational struc-ture; communi-cations systems; job design

Work force plan-ning; personnel management functions

Startup planning and scheduling; monitoring; alter-native startup approaches

Motivation; leadership; pro-duction and operations man-agement; control

Individual im-provement pro-grams and tech-niques; group conflict manage-ment; MBO

Evaluation of organizational policies; stra-tegic choices; organizational change; organi-zational develop-ment

Partial termina-tions; cutback management; complete ter-minations; mergers; born-again strategies

t_0

Time →

Chapter 3
The product/service decision:
Organizational goals and plans

*The fundamental problem of business is to
think of something that would cost a dime, sell
for a dollar—and be habit-forming.*

John L. McCaffrey, former president
of International Harvester

Organizations exist to provide a socially desirable good or service. Organizations are not ends in themselves, nor does management exist except for purposes of assembling and guiding resources toward the attainment of organizational goals. The raison d'être of an organization is to accomplish a task(s) that a single person acting alone could not accomplish. In this chapter, we will develop this point and consider the major elements which initiate and direct organizational growth. Specifically, we will examine how the product or service is selected, the nature of organizational objectives, the entrepreneur who starts the organization, and the plans, policies, and procedures upon which the projected operation of the organization is based.

There is a "chicken and egg" paradox when considering the precise relationship between outputs and goals in the new organization. In general, the product or service idea is the spark that ignites a new company, but certainly the desire to make a profit is but a hair's breadth away. No doubt for every inventor who first stumbled across a new product and then wondered if it could be made into a profitable business, there is an entrepreneur who first set sights on a desired income level and then sought some business he or she could get into to achieve that goal.

THE PRODUCT/SERVICE DECISION

Product ideas originate from any number of sources; we have excited inventors and entrepreneurs with "better mousetraps" all the way to aspiring politicians with yet another new service for the public. Established organizations develop most ideas internally, though there are many that obtain their ideas from the successful outputs of other organizations. Notable is the appliance field where one can find many kinds of toasters, slow cookers, crepe machines, and so on. When one company promotes a product, many others join in the production of this same—often almost identical—product. Thus we see waves of similar appliances almost simultaneously.

Services, as exemplified by government organizations, go through an analogous process. The television show "Emergency" is thought to have led to many cities establishing sophisticated emergency paramedical units. Many states followed the lead of Pennsylvania's insurance commissioner in developing "no-fault" auto insurance, and Colorado's lead in the development of "sunset laws" which require that government organizations periodically justify the reasons for their existence. Sunset laws are particularly important in terminating organizations which no longer justify their cost but which have no market mechanisms to force them into a loss-bankruptcy position.

As implied above, some sources of new ideas are not obvious—a meat-packing company developed an onion soup based upon the suggestion of a wife of one of its executives, and a producer of plastic products designed a film slide viewer after reading a list of needed inventions published by a bank. In an established firm, however, new product ideas generally arise from internal sources (see Exhibit 3–1).

Many companies have overlooked the "golden idea" even when given the opportunity to examine it. Eastman Kodak and IBM passed over the opportunity and promise of Chester Carlson's copying machine. As we know, the then Haloid-Xerox Company which had been producing photographic paper did get into the copy machine business in a rather large way, to the envy of many.

We could cite numerous examples of companies that have developed a product for a market which does not exist. One company spent a great deal

Exhibit 3–1
Mortality of new product ideas by stage of evolution (51 companies)

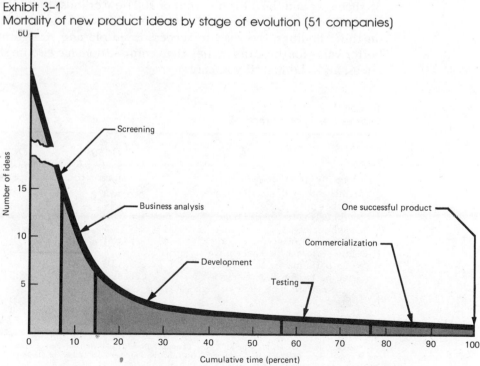

of time and money to develop and produce catsup with that "old-fashioned natural" flavor. The only problem was that the major part of the market for catsup was primarily those who have never tasted or do not remember "grandma's homemade" catsup. To their regret, the company found that the natural and delicate tomato flavor of this product was entirely foreign and unappealing to most catsup consumers.

What makes for a successful new product?

Though this question requires a marketing course to answer satisfactorily, a study by Davidson of new grocery brands suggests that three factors are of particular importance:[1]

1. A significant price or performance advantage to the purchaser over existing brands.
2. Some significant differences from existing brands. A brand that was radically different from existing brands had a much higher chance of success than a close copy.
3. New untried area.

Exhibit 3–2, drawn from the Davidson study, shows the distribution of the 50 successes and the 50 failures out of 100 new brands studied when comparing the differences in performances and the differences in distinctiveness. Based on these findings, the road to success is simple and straightforward: Offer a better value for the same money than competition, have some significant differences, and—be first, if you can!

Exhibit 3–2
Differences in performance

Difference from competitor	Of 50 successes (percent)	Of 50 failures (percent)
Significantly better performance, higher price	44	8
Marginally better performance, higher price	6	12
Better performance, same price	24	0
Same performance, lower price	8	0
Same performance, same price	16	30
Same performance, higher price	2	30
Worse performance, same or higher price	0	20
Total	100	100

Source: J. Hugh Davidson, "Why Most New Consumer Brands Fail," *Harvard Business Review*, vol. 54, no. 2 (March–April 1976), p. 119. Copyright © 1976 by the President and Fellows of Harvard College; all rights reserved. Reprinted by permission.

THE ENTREPRENEUR

The entrepreneur—the person with an idea and the fortitude to gamble in the marketplace—is a legendary figure in American business. Indeed, the names of entrepreneurs Ford, Hughes, and Rockefeller are household words.

There are two types of entrepreneurs: one type creates a firm, sells it, and creates another firm. The second type creates a firm and continues to run it. From an organizational standpoint, the most interesting entrepreneur is the one who turns manager and stays with the firm as its chief executive.

There have been a number of studies dealing with entrepreneurs, trying to determine what their characteristics are, and how they differ from the usual organizational managers. Though sketchy, following are some of the findings which characterize entrepreneurs:

Entrepreneurs are first-born, married, usually began a company by the age of 30, may have any education from high school to a master's degree, are psychologically unable to work for someone else, are doers and not planners, and are poor employees. Entrepreneurs are good at sports but poor as spectators. They are also secretive, not easily sharing their thoughts or feelings.[2]

Managers and entrepreneurs are completely different breeds. Additional traits of entrepreneurs show that they:

Spend considerably more time by themselves than do managers.
Like their job and don't need the escapes of vacations or hobbies.
Work on their own time schedules.
Are independent.
Work very hard (harder than managers).
Are lacking in interpersonal relationships.
Are skillful in communication.
Take greater risks than managers.

The most important requirement for success as an entrepreneur is managerial ability. Entrepreneurs want to be in control. One of the most difficult phases of an entrepreneur's life is when he or she is so successful that work must be delegated to others. Henry Ford came close to destroying Ford Motor Company in his later years because he insisted on centralized authority with himself as head, when the company was too large to allow him to make all the decisions.

Exhibit 3–3 shows a brief sketch of three well-known entrepreneurs: Curtis, the first manufacturer of airplanes; Land, of Polaroid fame; and Thomas Edison. All started off very young and exhibited the characteristics cited.

Exhibit 3–3
Profiles of several famous entrepreneurs

Glenn Curtis. Aviator, airplane designer. The first airplane manufacturing company in the United States was the Herring-Curtis Company which was created to produce Mr. Curtis' designs. Later, after its initial success the company expanded to produce pontoons to make its products into seaplanes and later to the development of catapults for launching these aircraft from ships.

Edwin H. Land. He developed a technique to make the use of polarized light practical. In 1932, at the age of 23, he started a laboratory in Boston. By 1936 he was using his polarized materials in sunglasses. In 1937 Land had developed a 3–D movie process, and in 1947, the now-famous Polaroid camera was first produced.

Thomas Edison. His first major endeavor was to improve the stock ticker for Western Union on Wall Street. The result was the development of the Edison Universal Stock Ticker, which he then manufactured. As we all know, Edison then went on to develop numerous inventions in electricity and sound reproduction. He also developed many other items we now take for granted—e.g., the double-drain sink and one of the forms of synthetic rubber.

One of the interesting questions is: "Can Entrepreneurship Be Learned?" Are there special aspects of the entrepreneur which can be taught? In 1973 the National Science Foundation funded three universities (MIT, Oregon, and Carnegie-Mellon) to encourage innovation and develop students' entrepreneurial skills. At MIT, training for students was emphasized; the University of Oregon evaluated ideas and inventions and directed the promising ones toward commercial development; and Carnegie-Mellon University concentrated on starting new ventures. Students at all three centers were trained in aspects of engineering, planning, management, and economics. Students followed the life-cycle process from idea creation through to product development.

Results of the experiment were mixed—there were some successful products and resulting profitable companies and there were some failures with companies going bankrupt. The science of entrepreneurship remains an inexact one.

Other studies have shown that while many characteristics of an entrepreneur must be inborn, many aspects can be learned.[3] Among these are methods of communication, management techniques, and behavioral skills which will help to increase the odds that the potential entrepreneur will be successful, or that the successful entrepreneur will be more effective. One of the more important entrepreneurial skills is effective goal setting and planning techniques.

ORGANIZATIONAL GOALS

We agree with the sociological contention that an organization is a social system with a specific purpose.[4] It is toward this purpose that an organization directs its resources, and the work of organizational members must "add up" to result in the accomplishment of this purpose.

At first glance, identifying the purpose of an organization would not seem to be a too difficult task. However, as is true of much of management theory, what at first seems obvious to the uninitiated does in fact have complex under-tones.

Classical management theory would hold that organizational goals are set by higher management and that successively lower level managers interpret these goals and engage in actions to accomplish them. The result is a coordi-nated set of behaviors by organizational members quite analogous to the di-verse efforts of members of a symphony that, under the conductor's direction, results in beautiful music. Different sections of the organization do their own task but the "parts" add up to the "whole."

In analyzing organizational goals, we take a pragmatic position. While we recognize the common stated goals of profit, return on investment, and growth, our interest is in how goals come to be. We are more concerned in identifying what an organization *actually* does rather than what organizational members *say* it does. A divergence often exists between real and stated goals for a variety of reasons; e.g., deliberate attempts to deceive, or pressures and power plays brought about by unions, stockholders, management, creditors. The logi-cal "symphonic" ordering of goals and actions as postulated by the classical scholars may well break down under close scrutiny.

To determine the *real* goals we must look at actual decisions and behavior in the organization. What would be "the goal" of the Saturday Evening Bridge Club whose "charter" states that it exists to provide skill building experiences and the accumulation of Master's points, but whose members actually spend more time socializing than playing bridge? Also, for example, consider a state prison. The governor and legislature might contend publicly that the goals are to rehabilitate convicts, to take dangerous people off the streets, and to punish and thus serve as a deterrent to committing crimes. Yet these goals may conflict. To achieve the custodial goal (keep them in jail and off the streets), the institution might best simply isolate convicts and keep them locked up (e.g., as Alcatraz did in its heyday). But this doesn't provide much chance for job training and other rehabilitation. How do we determine what the organization actually does? The answer is straightforward: "It is the decision to commit resources for certain activities and to withhold them from certain others that operationally defines the organizational goal—the [organization] must put [its] resources where [its] mouth is if something is to be considered a goal."[5]

Let us now look at organizational goals from a perspective that allows us to differentiate between what we refer to as goal levels.

Level I goals (production of goods or services)

We have already inferred an important aspect of an organization's purpose in Chapter One's discussion of the role of an organization in society. Thus, we start from the premise that the purpose of an organization is the production of the desirable good or service. Without that production the organization will ultimately fail due to economic distress (e.g., bankruptcy) or social action (e.g., direct government action to regulate or close, or to arrest organizational members). We will refer to the production of the desirable good or service as the organization's Level I goal. All organizational activities in some manner should contribute to accomplishing this goal.

In many cases Level I goals are reasonably well defined and even measurable. For example, Ford Motor Company produces a line of cars and trucks as its socially desirable output and hence its Level I goal. But, how would we define and measure the Level I goal of a hospital? Presumably, the hospital's output could be "quality health care." How do we measure this goal? Would we even agree on what "quality" is?

The stated "mission" (goal?) of the U.S. Department of Commerce ". . . is to foster, serve, and promote the Nation's economic development and technological advancement."[6] The Department of Agriculture ". . . is directed by law to acquire and diffuse useful information on agricultural subjects in the most general and comprehensive sense."[7] Where, for example, does the Rural Electrification Service (created in 1935 and still in existence within the USDA) fit into the above mission statement?

The point to be made is that reasonably intelligent people could easily disagree as to what the product is and hence on what the Level I goal is. For example, what is good health care for the hospital? Or, where does "information" stop and services begin in the Agriculture example? Sometimes the organization's product (Level I goal) is not very easily measurable. But there are ways of determining its accomplishment, and this leads us to the next goal level.

Level II goals (facilitating achievement of production)

In the Ford example above we saw that the Level I goal was the production of cars and trucks. But an analysis of Ford's actions will reveal other areas where the organization has "put its money where its mouth is." For example, after the 1967 riots in Detroit, Ford Motor Company engaged in a concerted effort to hire and train the hard-core unemployed. This would seem to have been a real (versus stated) goal also.

In addition, Ford spends a great deal of money on its safety programs. Thus, safety seems to be a real goal. Also, Ford sends many of its managers to schools and workshops to improve their administrative skills, another real goal.

The list could go on and on. Ford does many diverse things which could be termed real goals. However, their common element is that they facilitate advancement of production either directly by enhancing methods of output, or indirectly by avoiding problems which could interfere with providing the company's product.

The objectives we choose as Level II goals should, when possible, provide observable contributions to the Level I product or service output. Obviously, this linkage will be more observable when the Level I output is directly measurable (e.g., cars and trucks in the Ford example). When the linkage is not directly observable we rely on "secondary criteria."[8] A secondary criterion is an objective that is chosen because it is considered, for good reasons, to be positively related to the Level I goal. Thus, we "believe" that the objective of a reduction in the incidence of childhood diseases and influenza will improve the quality of health care. To the extent that we lack evidence as to the link between Level I and Level II goals, we have the potential for having inappropriate objectives. For example, did the 1976–77 swine flu inoculation program improve the quality of health care?

To add to our difficulties, Level II goals may often directly conflict. An objective of hiring the hard-core unemployed may well result in additional training costs which could decrease the amount of funds available for safety education.

George England in a survey of 1,072 American business managers attempted to determine the priorities placed on different classes of what we label Level II goals.[9] Exhibit 3–4 shows England's results. It is interesting to note in England's data that objectives closely tied to the production of the Level I good or service come first in the eyes of managers. Welfare of employees or society in general comes in a distance back.

Robert Townsend in *Up the Organization* gives an excellent example of the use of Level II-type goals:

One of the important functions of a leader is to make the organization concentrate on its objectives. In the case of Avis, it took us six months to define one objective—which turned out to be: "We want to become the fastest-growing company with the highest profit margins in the business of renting and leasing vehicles without drivers."

Exhibit 3–4
Organizational goal preferences of U.S. business managers (total group,
$N = 1,072$)

Type of goal	Percent rating goal as highly important	Percent indicating goal is significant for corporate success
Organizational efficiency	81	71
High productivity	80	70
Profit maximization	72	70
Organizational growth	60	72
Industrial leadership	58	64
Organizational stability	58	54
Employee welfare	65	20
Social welfare	16	8

Source: George W. England, "Organizational Goals and Expected Behavior of American Managers," *Academy of Management Journal,* vol. 10, no. 2 (June 1967), p. 108.

That objective was simple enough in that we didn't have to write it down. We could put it in every speech and talk about it wherever we went. And it had some social significance, because up to that time Hertz had a crushingly large share of the market and was thinking and acting like General Motors.

It also included a definition of our business: "renting and leasing vehicles without drivers." This let us put the blinders on ourselves and stop considering the acquisition of related businesses like motels, hotels, airlines and travel agencies. It also showed us we had to get rid of some limousine and sightseeing companies that we already owned.[10]

Level III goals (specific goals)

Given an organization's Level II goals in the form of direct or secondary criteria links to the Level I output, we still must further define what actions are to take place. Level III goals are specific goals tied to definite actions that can be observed. For example, given that safety is a Level II goal, what will we do in an organization to accomplish it? We must at this point describe specific goals or courses of action such as: Minimize lost-time accidents. Use safety equipment. Encourage workers to "talk safety," and so on.

For our hospital example of reducing childhood diseases, specific goals may be: Create a well-baby clinic. Provide immunizations to local residents. Promote good hygiene in the home.

Obviously, instances may occur where observers disagree as to whether a specific goal contributes to an objective—does "talking safety" really work to reduce accidents? Nonetheless, such specific goals are established and these tend to channel the work of organization members into specific areas or tasks.

Level IV goals (goal quantification)

The final level of goal we will describe is Level IV, measures or indicators. These measures define precisely what action is being encouraged and undertaken in the organization. For example:

Level II goal (objectives):
    An objective of the organization is to promote safety on and off the job.
Level III goals (specific goals):
    a. Minimize lost-time accidents
    b. Encourage workers to "talk safety."
Level IV goals (measures):
    a. Ratio of total hours worked and hours lost due to injuries.
    b. Ability of spouse, parent, or roommate to recite the weekly safety slogan.*

Another example is as follows:

Level II goal (objectives):
    An objective will be to reduce the incidence of childhood diseases.
Level III goals (specific goals):
    a. Provide a well-baby clinic.
    b. Provide immunizations for childhood diseases.
    c. Promote good hygiene in homes of newborns.
Level IV goals (measures):
    a. Number of patients served in the well-baby clinic.
    b. Number of immunizations given; percentage of school children immunized.
    c. Column inches of "good hygiene tips" ads in local newspaper; number of new mothers receiving good hygiene instructions.

It should be obvious that the Level IV goals which are actual performance measures must ultimately "add up" to the production of the Level I goal—the socially desirable good or service. It is incumbent upon management to select valid measures because other organization members usually have no other reference as to the actions desired/required by the organization. Management, not the workers, is to blame if these measured actions fail to achieve the Level I goal. Exhibit 3–5 shows the goal relationships described here.

---

* A number of organizations randomly (and secretly) select a worker's name each month/week and then call the spouse, parent, roommate (or "next of kin" if there are none of the above) to see if they can recite the slogan. If they can, a valuable prize is awarded. This encourages workers to "talk safety" at home.

Exhibit 3–5
A hierarchy of goals

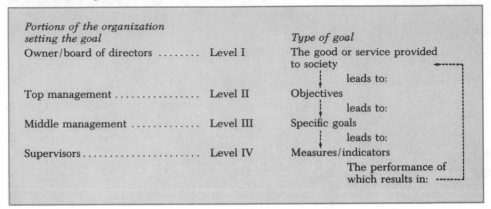

Portions of the organization setting the goal		Type of goal
Owner/board of directors	Level I	The good or service provided to society
		leads to:
Top management	Level II	Objectives
		leads to:
Middle management	Level III	Specific goals
		leads to:
Supervisors	Level IV	Measures/indicators
		The performance of which results in:

THE DYNAMICS OF GOALS

Goal succession

Occasionally, as an organization proceeds through its life cycle, a situation may occur where the Level I good or service is no longer appropriate. Buggy whip manufacturers in the early 1900s, or cyclamate producers in 1972 fall in this category. Organizations must constantly appraise the Level I goal and alter it if necessary. The acquisition of coal mines by many "oil companies" in the late 1970s and thus a shift to become "energy companies" is a good example of goal succession. Another example is provided by Sills's analysis of the National Foundation for Infantile Paralysis.[11] The initial Level I goal was to eliminate infantile paralysis. Through the "March of Dimes" and many other efforts, this disease was indeed conquered when a vaccine for polio was discovered. At that point a crisis occurred in the organization; its goal had been accomplished and the organization was thus no longer needed. Soon thereafter, the Foundation revised its Level I goal and became a funding source for a range of childhood diseases.

Similar examples exist in other areas. For example, the shift from the Department of War to the Department of Defense after World War II. The Boy Scouts of America in the late 1970s considered a name change to Scouting International as both girls and boys from numerous countries became members.

Goal displacement

Our categorization of Levels I to IV of organizational goals implies a definite sequencing. Level IV is a *means* to Level III, which is a *means* to Level II, which in turn is a *means* to the *end* which is Level I. We must constantly be aware of this means-end chain. Often organizational members lose sight of the ultimate goal (Level I) and focus only on their Level IV measures. This is understandable when organizational members are evaluated on the basis of certain measured phenomena. If a worker feels he or she is evaluated and rewarded on task X, that worker will probably maximize performance on task X even to the detriment of other (unmeasured) tasks that contribute to the Level I goal. Management must always observe these Level IV measures and note their contribution as a means; they are not ends in themselves.

For example, a department store owner must keep in mind the connection between bad credit losses, sales, and profits. Given wide enough authority, a credit manager could cut bad credit losses to zero. Some people would say, "Great!" But wait, to do that the credit manager will call in all the old credit cards, only give out new cards to the absolute best of credit risks, and even require that a bond be posted in the amount of a person's credit line. What will happen to sales? Customers probably will abandon the store for its competitors. Thus, to *maximize* the accomplishment of the credit department we have improperly displaced the Level I goal (the end) with a means (a Level IV measure). Management must set limits on these Level IV measures. Perhaps a 2 percent loss on sales is "correct." It just balances between credit losses and sales; a smaller loss and sales fall off rapidly, a larger loss isn't offset by more sales. We term this limiting process by management "suboptimization."

Goal displacement is often the result of the tendency to gravitate toward quantifiable performance measures. The saying, "What counts in business is what counts" is no laughing matter. Too often, what gets counted becomes the end in and of itself. How do we evaluate high school and university athletic teams? By how much character is built, or what amount of recreation was provided? Or, by how many tickets were sold, and on the won/loss record the coach has accumulated?

There are very important objectives such as public responsibility, employee welfare, and the like. However, these objectives often are displaced by the more quantifiable ones such as sales and profits. To the extent that measures are subjective and more difficult to justify, they tend to be ignored in favor of those that are quantifiable.[12]

Planning

The essence of planning is knowing what your goal is. In the previous section we have discussed a hierarchy of goals, and now, using this hierarchy approach, we will look at the planning process in organizations.

Lewis Carroll impressed us with the need to know one's goal in *Alice in Wonderland.* Shortly after falling down the rabbit hole, a very confused Alice was walking along when she came to a fork in the road. In a tree at the fork sat the Cheshire cat.

Alice: Would you tell me, please, which way I ought to go from here?

Cat: That depends a good deal on where you want to go.

Alice: I don't much care where.

Cat: Then it doesn't matter which way you go.

Either path would get Alice nowhere or anywhere just as quickly, it seems. We sympathize with Alice, but, like the cat, we caution you to not waste time planning if you don't have a goal. Plans without a goal as a basis are as valuable as the outcome of a coin flip. And the coin flip will probably be cheaper and faster.

Some basic definitions

Planning is the process of setting a course of action designed to accomplish a given goal(s) in a predicted environment. Plans are often viewed in a time dimension: long-range, intermediate-range, and short-range. *Long-range* plans involve determining the basic mission and structure of the organization, typically are thought to project five or more years into the future, and are usually made at the highest levels of the organization by the owner, board of directors, president, or similar person(s). *Intermediate-range* plans take the basic mission/ structure as a given and involve actions that manipulate the quantity and quality and the disposition of organizational inputs and outputs. These plans are generally made by the middle levels of management and involve time periods of one to five years. *Short-range* plans are those that have as givens the mission and the input/output considerations and involve scheduling of activities. The time dimension here is weeks or months, typically up to a year, and is a function most often performed at the supervisor level in organizations.

In addition to the time dimension of planning, certain types of plans are designed to set limits on actions and to specify how those actions are to be performed. Such plans fall under the headings of policies, procedures, and rules.

Policies are broad statements or guidelines that influence decision making in the organization. Though most often made at the higher management levels, policies can be created at almost all organization levels so long as those at lower levels do not conflict with higher level policies. "To provide realistic and practical incentives as a means of encouraging the highest standard of individual performance and to assure increased quantity and quality of performance" is an Armco Steel Corporation policy. This policy should give guidance to a personnel department attempting to set up an incentive pay plan. "Satisfaction guaranteed or your money back" is a policy that you will find over the entrance to every Sears, Roebuck store. What does this do to guide store managers' decisions about returned merchandise? Marshall Field, another retailer, built an entire organization around a single dominant policy: "Give the lady what she wants." This policy guided decisions involving everything from merchandise to be stocked to refunds or replacements for returned merchandise. "Spend the Company's money as if it were your own" was a policy set out by a firm attempting to cut down on expense account costs. If it *were* your money (e.g., you're on vacation) would you take the airport limousine or a taxi downtown from the airport?

Note that policies do not have to be written. The notion of "guidelines" implies that precedents or a number of consistent decisions also creates policies. If parking assignments have repeatedly been made on the basis of seniority, that may then become an organizational policy.

Procedures are detailed steps or functions to be performed in certain situations. A procedure for processing an automobile loan application at a bank might involve a series of steps such as: (1) complete loan application form A if for up to $5,000 and form B if over $5,000; (2) have applicant sign form; (3) obtain credit information from Credit Bureau, and so on. Procedures are obviously useful when certain situations occur with high regularity and management wishes to have a high level of consistency in how the activity is carried out. Thus, if an auto loan would be turned down (or approved) at one of the bank's branches, it should be turned down (or approved) at all others if the procedure was correctly carried out.

Rules are statements that require an explicit action in certain situations. "No smoking in Room A134." "The store will not be open on Sundays." The only discretion in a rule is in whether or not it will be obeyed.

Policies, procedures, and rules are termed *standing plans*. Standing plans are used to set a course of action designed to accomplish a goal in a predicted environment when there are organizational activities that occur with such regularity that management should (could) not have to spend time making decisions each time the given situation occurs.

When situations are not repetitive we rely on *individual plans* created for specific circumstances. Thus, a *budget* serves a given time period and must be redone periodically. Budgeting is a key planning process around which other organizational activities are in turn planned. *Projects* are also individual plans. For example, the construction of a large office building by a general contractor is usually a well-planned, almost choreographed set of activities taking into account predicted weather, labor unrest, and so on. *Programs* resemble projects but are larger. The Apollo Moon Program of NASA involved a multitude of projects to enable the United States to meet President Kennedy's goal of "land[ing] a man on the Moon by the end of the decade" (i.e., before 1970). One project in this program, for example, was the design and construction of the "Moon buggy" driven on the Moon's surface. Another was the design and construction of the launch rocket, and so on. These projects in some cases had to be completed in sequence or at least closely coordinated. For example the "Moon buggy" had to fit into a certain space in the LEM (Lunar Excursion Module) that landed the astronauts on the Moon.

THE NECESSITY FOR PLANNING

Once I was asked to head up a new long-range planning effort. My wife listened to my glowing description of my new job. Next evening she blew the whole schmeer out of the water by asking: "What did you plan today, dear?" Bless her.[13]

We point out Townsend's rather cynical view of planning not because we agree with it; to the contrary. Unfortunately, all too many people tend to agree with him. Mostly these are people who place a high value on action. Their reference point is always right now. They judge their success by how busy they keep themselves; by how much dust always seems to be stirred up around them. Frankly, we are led to recall a well-known definition of a fanatic when we see these people: $fa \cdot nat \cdot ic$\fe-'nat-ik\n—one who, having forgotten what he is trying to do, speeds up his efforts so as to finish it faster. Of course, there are other reasons why managers don't plan:

1. Fear of failure. "If I don't plan, then I won't fail if I don't meet it."
2. Low tolerance for ambiguity. "The future is so complex that I can't make sense out of it, so why should I plan?"
3. Fire fighting. "Things are too busy right now. I'll do it next month."
4. Takes time. "I'd rather spend the half day it takes to plan doing something else."
5. Uncertain payoff. "Why should I spend good money developing a plan when there is no guarantee of results?"
6. Takes money. "We ought to spend our money on workers, not planners."

Karger has shown that in the decade of the 1960s the relative pretax profits of firms with formal planning systems were far in excess of those with only informal planning systems.[14] In times of rapid changes in markets, product innovations, laws, social values and the like, management must be capable of equally rapid responses. If nothing else, planning for several possible contingencies and then implementing the plan that best fits the state of the world that does occur, allows management to indeed make a decision faster. Plus, a forward-looking management may be able to spot undesirable trends and to engage in activities to actually alter the future (e.g., lobby for new laws, build roads in certain areas to encourage housing development there versus elsewhere, and so on).

THE PLANNING HIERARCHY

Exhibit 3–6 enlarges upon the earlier presented Hierarchy of Goals to indicate the relationship between types of plans, the organizational goals being affected, and the position in the management hierarchy that is involved. Obviously, Exhibit 3–6 is a generalized view of the goal setting and planning process. The central point is that the upper levels of management are heavily involved in long-range issues that involve the basic goals of the organization. As one moves down into the organization, constraints on goals are incurred due to higher level decisions already made, and the time span of decisions decreases.

Exhibit 3–6

Type of plans		Level of management	Type of goal
Time dimension	*Specific plans*		
Long-range plans	Policies, budgets, programs, projects	Owner/board of directors	Level I— The good or service provided to society
Long- and intermediate- range plans..........	Policies, programs,	Top management	Level II— Objectives
Intermediate- range plans..........	Procedures, policies	Middle management	Level III—Specific goals
Short-range plans	Rules	Supervisors	Level IV—Measures/indicators

At the extremes, the board of directors establishes the basic mission of the organization but does not decide if Joe or Frank should work the drill press overtime tonight. The supervisor does make the overtime decision and has little say about whether or not to expand sales into Kansas.

THE PLANNING PROCESS

The process of constructing a plan as discussed earlier in this chapter involves answering four essential questions:

1. What is our goal? As noted above, this is the essence of the planning process.
2. Where are we now relative to the goal? This question involves an introspective look to determine what the current state of affairs is.
3. What does the future hold? We need to look into the future and make a good guess as to what will occur. What is there that could help or hinder? What can we influence?
4. How do we get there from here? This is the plan—the set of actions to be taken in a predicted environment to accomplish our goal.

We have discussed goals and the types of plans we can develop (i.e., aids to answer Questions 1 and 4). From the life cycle perspective we are initially assuming a ground zero condition; that is, no organization currently exists (Question 2). Thus, we now turn to a discussion of forecasting in order to develop answers to Question 3.

FORECASTING

Forecasting may be simply defined as "making predictions about the future." Before any organization can proceed to develop any product or service, it must have some idea about the future. It must estimate or forecast such factors as the demand for the product or service, the availability of resources, the probable number of units to be produced, and the expected profit or service level output.

To search for opportunities for new products or services, we can forecast from two approaches: (1) technological forecasting, which looks at the supply side, and (2) need forecasting, which looks at the demand side.[15]

Technology forecasting

As individuals, we would like to know what kind of a world we will be living in in the coming years. We would like to know what new developments might be coming along since it will influence our present lifestyle, our plans for the future, and our current purchases. Consider the quandary one faces today when trying to buy a watch, calculator, or other electronic device. Technology has been advancing so rapidly in electronics that obsolescence on a new purchase is often only months away. If you hold off buying that calculator today and wait a few months, you may find one available at a cheaper price with more features. It becomes a trade-off of current usage versus guaranteed obsolescence. Businesses have the same problems in areas such as computer software and hardware, and in plant and equipment investment.

How do we forecast changes in technology? Organizations need technological forecasts to make plans and set objectives. Technological forecasting can be divided into three phases.[16] Phase 1 involves the preliminary study of the technology and predicts potential levels of achievement. Phase 2 tries to compare the technology we're interested in with existing technologies to predict the probable output of the technology as well as its rate of development. Phase 3 examines the side effects which are the influences this technology has on other technologies and on various organizations.

To expand each of these phases, Phase 1 performs an in-depth analysis of the field through literature search, investigation of the firms in that business, and discussions with research and scientific experts. The objective is to find out who is doing what in the technology. What advances and applications have been made? Who is promoting research in this area and why?

Phase 2 compares this technology under investigation with existing technologies. If this new technology can be developed, is it worth it after all? For example, if one were developing some new technology in cable transmissions, he would have to look at what the current methods are now, and also what they will be in the future through improvements. Transmission techniques such as microwave networks, satellites, fiber optics, and laser propagation exist today, and others might also be developed.

Current developments challenging the incandescent lamp are the modified smaller fluourescent bulb which uses a conventional socket, and a bulb which has a paint on its surface which is translucent to light waves but reflects much of the infrared heat waves back to the filament, thereby preserving a significant portion of a bulb's greatest energy loss—through heat loss and not light generation. If one could develop a gas which would conduct electricity, giving off light at ambient temperature without requiring a transformer and starter, it is easy to visualize the possibility of taking over the lighting market. However, one would certainly still like to know what future improvements are possible in existing fluorescent and incandescent lighting.

Phase 3 involves the side effects or the influences on other technologies. The development of the transistor at Bell Laboratories was originally for communication application interests. At that time, probably no one ever visualized that we would be telling time by checking our electronic quartz watch with its liquid crystal display backlighted for night viewing with an atomic power tritium source.

The recent ban on fluorocarbons as propellants in aerosol cans is a case where the technology originally led firms up a less desirable path. Scientists using recently developed methods made studies which led them to comment that the ozone layer around the earth was being lost due in most part to the heavy use of fluorocarbons. The primary source was stated to be the billions of cans of aerosol sprays that are used annually in the United States alone, where the propellant is a fluorocarbon. Many firms predicted that any federal laws preventing the use of fluorocarbons in aerosol cans would drive them out of business. In response, some firms came out with manual pump sprays to appeal to ecology-minded consumers. As it happens, it was a blessing to all who were now able to stop using fluorocarbons. Through competition, firms were originally drawn into the use of this expensive propellant and could not independently abandon the propellant for fear of losing to competition. But, since all firms together were being forced into a less expensive but just about as effective propellant, all are living happily ever after.

For ongoing organizations, technological forecasting is a must in order to

Exhibit 3–7
Examples of basic forecasting techniques

Technique	A. Qualitative methods, Delphi method	B. Time series analysis and projection, Exponential smoothing	C. Causal methods	
			Regression model	Econometric model
Description	A panel of experts is interrogated by a sequence of questionnaires in which the responses to one questionnaire are used to produce the next questionnaire. Any set of information available to some experts and not others is thus passed on to the others, enabling all the experts to have access to all the information for forecasting. This technique eliminates the bandwagon effect of majority opinion.	This technique is similar to the moving average, except that more recent data points are given more weight. Descriptively, the new forecast is equal to the old one plus some portion of the past forecasting error. There are many variations of exponential smoothing.	This functionally estimates an equation using the least-squares technique. Relationships are primarily analyzed statistically, although any relationship should be selected for testing on a rational ground.	An econometric model is a system of interdependent regression equations that describes some sector of economic sales or profit activity. The parameters of the regression equations are usually estimated simultaneously. As a rule, these models are relatively expensive to develop and can easily cost between $5,000 and $10,000, depending on detail. However, due to the system of equations inherent in such models, they will better express the causalities involved than an ordinary regression equation and hence will predict turning

Short term (0–3 months)	Fair to very good	Fair to very good	Good to very good	Good to very good
Medium term (3 mo–2 years)	Fair to very good	Poor to good	Good to very good	Very good to excellent
Long term (2 years and up)	Fair to very good	Very poor	Good	Good
Identification of turning points	Fair to good	Poor	Very good	Excellent
Typical applications	Forecasts of long-range and new product sales, forecasts of margins.	Production and inventory control, forecasts of margins and other financial data.	Forecasts of sales by product classes, forecasts of margins.	Forecasts of sales by product classes, forecasts of margins.
Data required	A coordinator issues the sequence of questionnaires, editing, and consolidating the responses.	The same as for a moving average.	Several years' quarterly history to obtain meaningful relationships. Mathematically necessary to have two more observations than there are independent variables.	The same as for regression.
Cost of forecasting with computer*	$2,000+	$0.005	$100	$5,000+
Is calculation possible without a computer?	Yes	Yes	Yes	Yes
Time to develop an application and make a forecast	2 months+	1 day–	Depends on ability to identify relationships.	2 months+

*These estimates are based on using configuration: an IBM 360–40, 256 K and a Univac 1108 time-sharing system, together with such smaller equipment as G.E. Time-sharing and IBM 360–30s and 1130s.

Source: Adapted from John C. Chambers, Stinder K. Mullick, and Donald D. Smith, "How to Choose the Right Forecasting Technique," *Harvard Business Review*, vol. 49, no. 4 (July–August 1971), pp. 55–64.

keep informed for product improvements as well as the effects that other technology will have on the existing product lines.

Demand, or need, forecasting

The entrepreneur embarking on a first venture had better forecast the demand for his or her product or service reasonably accurately. The entrepreneur goes into operation to produce generally one product or service and this will determine the survival of the organization. The entrepreneur must forecast the demand for the product or service in terms of quantity required, price levels, the timing of the demand, and the particular styles, colors, or whatever variations exist in the product or service which he or she is planning on producing and marketing. If successful, then as previously mentioned, the entrepreneur will go on to forecast, develop, and market other products.

Forecasting product or service demand is a difficult problem because it is based in large part on the psychology of consumers—how they will react, their intelligence, and their ability to compare products and judge values.

Forecasting demand is done by one or more of the three major methods: qualitative, time series analysis, and causal methods. The qualitative methods are based on judgment, utilizing customer surveys, salespeople's surveys, jury of executive opinion, and Delphi-type techniques. This analysis, being subjective, is often based on intuition or the gut feeling of the individual who must make the forecast.

Time series analysis and projections include statistical techniques which utilize the past product or service data and average or extend this history into the future. The basic assumption of this analysis is that the past is, in fact, indicative of the future. This may not always be a good method; for example, fad items or fashion goods change demand patterns very rapidly and with little predictability.

Causal methods assume that the demand for the product or service of interest is in some way related to another factor which we may have data on. For example, the demand for gasoline or tires is related to the number of cars sold. In this case, models such as the econometric type, or leading indicators, may be useful to predict demand. Exhibit 3–7 shows three selected types of forecasting methods, one from each of the three major areas. For more detail, the reader is directed to the original publication which lists 18 forecasting methods. Although the article was published in 1971, the methods are still currently in use; the stated costs, however, should be at least doubled to account for increased prices (primarily due to inflation).

CONTINGENCIES

It is well to keep in mind that "fortune teller" abilities are nonexistent or at least very rare. Forecasts rarely will be found to have been completely correct. Thus, we often must develop several plans, each contingent upon different potential futures. A bank may have a plan to put in effect if and when the price of gold reaches a certain point. Another plan to use if the price holds constant for three consecutive days. And still another to implement if the price of silver increases relative to the price of gold. All of these plans are worked out well in advance and permit rapid response to changes in the environment. Chase and Clark have presented an example of this process used by a large school district.[17]

We compare the contingency planning process to that of several explorers rafting down an unknown river. They don't know what is around the next bend; a waterfall, wild natives, or a peaceful river. But they do know what to do at the point they see what the scene is. They have worked out the contingency plans well in advance and hence won't have to make plans about what to do as they quickly approach the rapids. Compare this to a "well-planned" European adventure by a travel agent. (If it's Tuesday, it must be Belgium.) If you don't know "for sure," it's best to have contingency plans.

SUMMARY

The purpose of this chapter has been to relate the concepts of organizational goals and plans toward the attainment of these goals. We have introduced the notion of goal levels and by looking at these levels we see a means-end chain that hopefully results in the production of a socially desirable good or service by the organization (viz the Level I goal).

The planning process is premised upon the determination of the Level I goal. Thus beginning any organization involves first selecting the product or service to be produced. We have discussed sources of new ideas and the role of the entrepreneur in the development of innovative ideas.

Given a basic product or service idea, one must begin the planning process with a forecast of the future environment. Actions are then designed to move the organization through this anticipated future. We emphasize that few forecasts are ever perfect and hence the planning process involves building in correcting mechanisms so as to keep organizational actions consistent with the reality of the environment.

Based upon its plans the organization proceeds to the next life cycle phase; that of designing the system that will put these plans into action.

GUIDES TO ACTION

1. Come up with a concise statement of what "business" you are in (and this de facto also tells you what to stay out of).

2. Remember that people in organizations will try hard to perform well in the areas that management can measure. Therefore, make sure that what you measure is what you want.

3. One can be an entrepreneur within an existing organization if it is recognized that innovation involves not only new products or services, but also new ideas for enhancing organizational performance.

4. You will rarely, if ever, forecast perfectly. Therefore, develop contingency plans to handle forecasting inaccuracies.

NOTES

[1] J. Hugh Davidson, "Why Most New Consumer Brands Fail," *Harvard Business Review*, vol. 54, no. 2 (March–April 1976), p. 119.

[2] J. R. Mancuso, "What It Takes to Be an Entrepreneur," *Journal of Small Business Management*, vol. 2, no. 4 (October 1974), pp. 16–22.

[3] See James P. Roscow, "Can Entrepreneurship Be Taught?" *The MBA*, June–July, 1973; Herbert Kierulff, "Can Entrepreneurs Be Developed?" *MSU Business Topics*, Winter 1974, pp. 39–44; and Douglas Durand, "Training and Development of Entrepreneurs," *Journal of Small Business Management*, vol. 12, no. 4 (October 1974), pp. 23–26.

[4] Talcott Parkson, *Structure and Process in Modern Societies* (Glencoe, Ill.: Free Press, 1960), p. 17.

[5] Vernon E. Buck, "A Model for Viewing an Organization as a System of Constraints," in James Thompson, ed., *Approaches to Organizational Design* (Pittsburgh: University of Pittsburgh Press, 1966), p. 109.

[6] *United States Government Manual, 1973/74* (Washington, D.C.: U.S. Government Printing Office), p. 125.

[7] Ibid., p. 94.

[8] Yehezkel Dror, *Public Policymaking Reexamined* (San Francisco: Chandler Publishing Co., 1968), p. 26.

[9] George W. England, "Organizational Goals and Expected Behavior of American Managers," *Academy of Management Journal*, vol. 10, no. 2 (June 1967), pp. 107–17.

[10] Robert Townsend, *Up the Organization* (New York: Alfred A. Knopf, 1970), p. 129.

[11] D. Sills, *The Volunteers: Means and Ends in a National Organization* (New York: Free Press, 1967).

[12] W. K. Warner and A. E. Havens, "Goal Displacement and the Intangibility of Organizational Goals," *Administrative Science Quarterly*, vol. 12, no. 4 (December 1961), pp. 539–55.

[13] Townsend, *Up the Organization*, p. 146.

[14] D. W. Karger, "Integrated Formal Long-Range Planning and How to Do It," *Long-Range Planning*, vol. 6, no. 4 (1973), pp. 31–34.

[15] Edward M. Tauber, "Forecasting New Opportunities for Products," *Journal of Marketing*, vol. 39, no. 1 (June 1975), p. 67.

[16] P. J. Lovell and R. D. Bruce, "How We Predict Technological Change," *New Scientist*, February 15, 1962, pp. 370–73.

[17] Richard B. Chase and Donald Clark, "Long Range Planning in School Districts," *Educational Technology*, October 1974, pp. 32–36.

DISCUSSION QUESTIONS

1. What determines whether or not an organization's output is "desirable"?

2. From your own experiences, try to think of several products or services that have gone "off the market." What made these different from some that have stayed on the market?

3. What makes entrepreneurs different from so-called normal managers?

4. Distinguish between real and stated goals.

5. Using an organization with which you are familiar, define several Level I, Level II, Level III, and Level IV goals.

6. Why does goal displacement hinder the attainment of organizational objectives?

7. What is planning? What is the distinction between long-range, intermediate-range, and short-range plans?

8. Distinguish between policies, procedures, and rules. Using an organization familiar to you, give an example of each.

9. Why do you feel that Robert Townsend has such a cynical view of planning?

10. List the steps in the planning process. Using these, develop a plan for you to graduate.

11. Using one or more of the forecasting techniques discussed in this chapter, forecast the job market for college graduates with skills like yours (or that you hope to have) in five years.

12. Develop several contingency plans for the possibility that your skills (per question 11) won't be in great demand. For the possibility that they will be.

EXERCISE: TESTING THE ENTREPRENEURIAL YOU

Your psychological makeup can play a strong role in making your business a success or a failure. Here are some questions based on ideas supplied by Richard Boyatzis and David Winter, two psychologists who have studied the entrepreneurial character. The questions are designed to reveal whether you have entrepreneurial attitudes. Even if no answer fits your feelings precisely, choose the one that comes closest. The answers are at the end of the exercise.

1. If you have a free evening, would you most likely:
   a. Watch TV?
   b. Visit a friend?
   c. Work on a hobby?

2. In your daydreams, would you most likely appear as:
   a. A millionaire floating on a yacht?
   b. A detective who has solved a difficult case?
   c. A politician giving an election night victory speech?

3. To exercise, would you rather:
   a. Join an athletic club?
   b. Join a neighborhood team?
   c. Do some jogging at your own pace?

4. When asked to work with others on a team, which would you anticipate with most pleasure:
   a. Other people coming up with good ideas?
   b. Cooperating with others?
   c. Getting other people to do what you want?

5. Which game would you rather play:
   a. Monopoly?
   b. Roulette?
   c. Bingo?

6. Your employer asks you to take over a company project that is failing. Would you tell him or her that you will:
   a. Take it?
   b. Won't take it because you're up to your gills in work?
   c. Give your employer an answer in a couple of days when you have more information?

7. In school, were you more likely to choose courses emphasizing:
   a. Field work?
   b. Papers?
   c. Exams?

8. In buying a refrigerator, would you:
   a. Stay with an established, well-known brand?
   b. Ask your friends what they bought?
   c. Compare thoroughly the advantages of different brands?

9. While on a business trip in Europe you are late for an appointment with a client in a neighboring town. Your train has been indefinitely delayed. Would you:
   a. Rent a car to get there?
   b. Wait for the next scheduled train?
   c. Reschedule the appointment?

10. Do you believe that people you know who have succeeded in business:
    a. Have connections?
    b. Are cleverer than you?
    c. Are about the same as you but maybe work a little harder?

11. An employee who is your friend is not doing his job. Would you:
    a. Take him out for a drink, hint broadly that things aren't going right, and hope he gets the message?
    b. Leave him alone and hope he straightens out?
    c. Give him a strong warning and fire him if he doesn't shape up?

12. You come home to spend a relaxing evening and find that your toilet has just overflowed. Would you:

    a. Study your home repair book to see if you can fix it yourself?

    b. Persuade a handy friend to fix it for you?

    c. Call for a plumber?

13. Do you enjoy playing cards most when you:

    a. Play with good friends?

    b. Play with people who challenge you?

    c. Play for high stakes?

14. You operate a small office cleaning business. A close friend and competitor suddenly dies of a heart attack. Would you:

    a. Reassure his wife that you will never try to take away any customers?

    b. Propose a merger?

    c. Go to your former competitor's customers and offer them a better deal?

Answers

1. c.	5. a.	8. c.	12. a.
2. b.	6. c.	9. a.	13. b.
3. c.	7. a.	10. c.	14. c.
4. a.		11. c.	

Score one point for each correct answer. Questions 1, 2, 3, 7, 9, and 12 suggest whether you are a realistic problem solver who can run a business without constant help from others. Questions 5, 6, and 8 probe whether you take calculated risks and seek information before you act. Questions 4, 10, 13, and 14 show you whether you, like the classic entrepreneur, find other people most satisfying when they help fulfill your need to win. Question 11 reveals whether you take responsibility for your destiny—and your business. If you score between 11 and 14 points, you could have a good chance to succeed. If you score from seven to ten points, you'd better have a superb business idea or a lot of money to help you out. If you score seven or less, stay where you are.

Source: Marlys Harris, "Do You Have What It Takes?" *Money*, March 1978, pp. 49–54.

CASE: THE ALCHEMISTS*

"I am Mr. Weslyn, of the Treasury Department," the rather prim man said.

"Yes, sir, what can we do for you?" John Ball asked. John was president of Allied, a small, research-oriented firm which was growing very rapidly. "I hope that our tax returns are in order?"

"It's not about taxes, Mr. Ball, although we checked carefully—very carefully," Mr. Weslyn said. "You see, your net income seems to be growing very fast, and we wondered about that. But extensive audits have shown no major discrepancies."

_____

* From: Richard N. Farmer, Barry M. Richman, and William G. Ryan, *Incidents for Studying Management and Organization*. © 1970 by Wadsworth Publishing Company, Inc., Belmont, California 94002. Reprinted by permission of the publisher.

John wondered what "major" meant. Had that tax accountant goofed? After all the money they paid him. . . .

"The question, Mr. Ball, is where all that gold is coming from." Mr. Weslyn leaned forward in his chair. "Our records indicate that you have sold some, ah, $9 million worth of gold to the mint in the past year." Mr. Weslyn consulted his notes. "It appears that you rather regularly send several hundred ounces of fine gold to the mint for sale."

John relaxed. He felt that he was on strong ground now. "Oh, that," he said. "We make it."

"You *what?*" Mr. Weslyn stared at him.

"I said we make it. You know, we take mercury and convert it to gold. I won't say how, since it's a proprietary secret. Quite simple, really, when you know how. Our attorney says that he doubts that the process is patentable, however, since something like it was done as early as 1948. But we prefer to keep the whole thing secret anyhow, since you are probably aware that patent law is in a terrible mess now. You can't depend on anything anymore," John sighed. "The world is really going to the dogs, I'll tell you. You can't trust anyone."

Mr. Weslyn looked pained. "You are probably aware, Mr. Ball, that the Gold Accord of 1988 set the price of gold at $500.00 per ounce on an international level. You may also be aware that gold was reinstated as the foundation of our monetary system. Congress passed legislation making gold the underlying base for our money supply. The reason for both actions was to make each country and each bank subject to fundamental monetary discipline. Without more gold, the money supply could not be expanded indefinitely, and price inflation thus was brought under control for the first time in 70 years."

"Look, I'm an engineer, not an economist," John said. "I know that the price of gold is $500.00, and a good thing too, since it cost us about $40 per ounce to make the stuff. With the old $35 price, we never could have gotten into business."

"Do you realize that you will destroy the entire world's monetary system if this absurd project continues?" Mr. Weslyn stood up and began to pace the floor. "For 15 years, since the Accord, the world has been in economic equilibrium. Now you are beginning to destroy it."

"You haven't seen anything yet, Mr. Weslyn. We are expanding fast, and within a few years we expect to get up to $1 billion a year in this market. Where else can you find a market that will take any amount you can make at a fixed price? It sure beats packaging isotopes. This company is going to be the biggest in the world in a few years. Incidentally, we have no trouble getting financing—the bankers sure think that this is a good thing."

"But what you're doing is illegal!"

"I beg your pardon," John said, "but it's not. Our lawyers checked that. It is illegal to hoard or hold gold, but we sell it to the mint as fast as we make it. Our product is excellent—purer than mined gold. I would think that your people would be pleased to get such a fine product."

"There will be legislation," Mr. Weslyn said. "This can't continue."

"Of course it can continue," John said. "And incidentally, you had better check Central Atomics, too. Our boys picked up a hot rumor that their gold-making process is even better than ours. A lot cheaper, they think. But we're working on it, and we should get our costs down soon." John smiled. "Besides, we really don't care about Central. In this market, any number can play. It won't be long before a dozen firms are making gold, but the market just keeps expanding indefinitely. I would suggest that you take a good look around, Mr. Weslyn—the gold market is due for some big changes."

Questions

1. Do you think that Allied should be allowed to make gold? Why or why not?
2. What could or should be done by the government?
3. What would you do if you were Mr. Ball?

Section two
Design of the system

A hallmark of organizations is that the product or service output is typically too big or too difficult for one person alone to produce it. Therefore, a system must be created which will enable the coordination of diverse human and material resources so that desired organization products will in fact be produced. An organizational structure must be created to effect a division of labor and a hierarchy of authority. A communications system must be developed to facilitate coordination, and specific jobs must be designed to ensure that all work necessary to produce the organizational output will be done.

SELECTION OF THE PRODUCT OR SERVICE	DESIGN OF THE SYSTEM	STAFFING THE ORGANIZATION	STARTUP OF THE ORGANIZATION	OPERATING THE ORGANIZATION IN THE STEADY STATE	IMPROVING THE ORGANIZATION	REVISION OF THE ORGANIZATION	TERMINATION OF THE ORGANIZATION
Decision-making processes; social value; goals; forecasts; policies; plans	Authority and responsibility; power; organizational structure; communications systems; job design	Work force planning; personnel management functions	Startup planning and scheduling; monitoring; alternative startup approaches	Motivation; leadership; production and operations management; control	Individual improvement programs and techniques; group conflict management; MBO	Evaluation of organizational policies; strategic choices; organizational change; organizational development	Partial terminations; cutback management; complete terminations; mergers; born-again strategies

Level of Organizational Outputs

t_0

Time

Chapter 4
Authority/responsibility concepts

As noted earlier, organizations are necessary because one person can't do all the work alone and hence needs help. Organizational design is concerned with specifying how the work is allocated among the helpers. Though there are many general objectives in organizational design, the basic one is to develop a structure and a set of authority relationships that enable the organization to function in a coordinated fashion to achieve its goals. In this first of two chapters on organization design, we focus on the authority relationships required to achieve the coordination. In the next chapter, we discuss the formal structure within which these relationships operate.

THE CONCEPT OF AUTHORITY

Authority may be defined as the right to command. In organizations, it is formally vested in a position, and is most often thought of as a boss telling a subordinate what to do. To understand the limitations of the concept, it is useful to contrast it with two related terms—*influence* and *power*. If one has *influence* with another individual, this means that he or she can sway that individual's general thoughts or actions. If one has *power,* he or she can influence another's actions in a particular direction. In a university setting, the instructor has the authority to require attendance, the power to require that students take exams, and (hopefully) the ability to influence students on subject matter by lecturing.

It should be emphasized that influence and power are behavioral phenomena which can exist quite outside an organizational framework. Formal authority, however, is ultimately derived from some organization of which the individual is a member, be it the state (through laws) or the organization (through policies and rules).

In practice, existence of authority is not sufficient to obtain action unless one or both of the following elements (depending upon the situation) is present.* These are the *power to levy sanctions or rewards* and *perceived legitimacy.* As we will discuss in more detail later in the book, a manager will have a difficult time getting subordinates to follow orders unless he or she has the ability to reward for good performance and punish for poor performance. Authority without such capability is meaningless. Perceived legitimacy refers to the acceptability of an order, policy, or rule in the mind of the individual within the organization. For authority to be executed, it must be perceived as legitimate for the situation at hand. But what is legitimate? In the past, more people would agree that certain rules in the work situation should be followed—arrive on time, perform the tasks usually associated with the job, follow safety regulations, and so forth. But now, however, there is an increasing

---

* People *may be inclined* to obey authority for other reasons (e.g., charismatic leadership, formal or informal status of the authority figure, cultural values, or reduction of anxiety by simply accepting authority).

questioning of what is legitimate authority in virtually every facet of a job. Among the more publicized issues in contemporary organizations are the following:

Does the military have the right to require that sideburns be no longer than three inches?

Should a secretary be obligated to make coffee for the boss?

Should an employee be required to dress a certain way?

Should an employee be required to sing the company songs at meetings?[1]

Should a female administrator be expected to type when her male counterparts are not required to?*

Should an employee be required to engage in a company physical conditioning program as a prerequisite for employment?[2]

Questions of legitimacy arise in most all organizations and from the excerpts above we can see that they arise not only in the expected areas of personal activities but in the content of the work itself. As far as the limitations as to what an employer will consider legitimate, much depends on the cultural setting—both national and local. In Japan, under the *Nenko* system, employees are sometimes hired for life and virtually any order from a superior is accepted without question; in Italy, where workers pride themselves on individualism, virtually every order or rule is subject to scrutiny.

Other factors which have been found to affect legitimacy are perceived relevance to the job, personal biases, perceptions of legality,† and credibility of the source.

A classic example of source credibility in getting people to behave in a way that is totally counter to their nature is found in the series of studies by Milgram.[3] In one study, subjects were asked to participate in an "experiment" to determine the effect of negative rewards on learning. What this entailed was for the subjects to apply electrical shocks to someone who gives an incorrect answer to a complicated math problem. The real subjects (those *giving* the shocks) were in a different room from the "subjects" receiving the shocks (who were really paid actors) and were told to administer shocks by turning a dial graduated from "light" to "heavy" electrical current amounts. (Of course, the actors never received the slightest real shock.) As a wrong answer was given, they were told by a researcher that they should administer the shocks, and that for every incorrect answer, the current should be increased, up to its maximum. The cover story in this case was that the "shock-giving" subjects were helping science and that the task they were performing—administering shocks—was imperative for the success of the study. At all times a person

---

* Many female managers now make it a point not to have typewriters in their offices lest they be asked to type.

† Many young military officers are thought to have altered their perceptions of legality on the basis of the *Calley* decision during the Vietnam War.

stood nearby and "demanded" that shocks be given if ever the subject hesi-tated. The actors gave ever louder cries and pleas for mercy as the "amount" of current was "increased."

The effect of source credibility was observed by the conditions under which the study was carried out. In one condition, the experiment was performed in a run-down building in an old part of town with monitoring done by a young researcher wearing street clothes. A second condition was administering the experiment at a university research center on campus with a distinguished-looking professorial type acting as the researcher. The results, measured in terms of how much pain the true subject was willing to apply to another person in the name of science, showed dramatic differences between the two conditions. In the run-down building environment, subjects stopped far short of high pain threshholds in applying shocks. In the university research center, on the other hand, subjects turned the current dial up to high despite anguished pleas for mercy from the next room. These results illustrate dramatically that legitimacy of authority can be greatly extended if the wielder of that authority and the setting where it is invoked are credible.

The zone of indifference

In the final analysis, the actual authority a manager can apply in achieving the organization's (or his) goals depends upon the attitudes of the subordinates. The subordinate's willingness to accept authority can be described in terms of his or her zone of indifference—that is, the limits within which employees will willingly do what is asked of them. It seems safe to say that this zone of indifference is narrowing. Workers no longer blindly follow orders even in military or religious organizations, much less business organizations. This, of course, makes the job of manager more difficult, and, arguably, more enlight-ened.

The concept of responsibility

Responsibility, in an organizational setting, refers to an individual being held accountable for certain decisions and actions on his or her part or on the part of other subordinates. In a well-designed organization, responsibility for all major activities will be clearly spelled out and the appropriate amount of authority will be provided to enable the individual to meet responsibilities.

With respect to the latter point, management writers historically have un-derscored the need for a parity between authority and responsibility, although obtaining exact equivalency is not always easy.

Problems of imbalance increase as the size and complexity of the organiza-tion increase. In small organizations, it is relatively easy to specify who should have responsibility for particular decisions and to provide that individual position with the requisite authority. In large organizations, especially those in civil service, the lines of responsibility and authority often become unclear.

When applying the concept to organization design, it is important to keep the following notions in mind:

1. Responsibility for the results of actions taken by a manager's subordinates cannot be delegated to those subordinates. Quite simply, the manager can't "pass the buck" for actions taken in the name of his or her general area of responsibility to those below.
2. Making "everyone" responsible for a particular job means that no one is responsible. Hence, sharing of responsibility is a bad practice in general.
3. An individual should not be held responsible for a particular action unless he or she has the authority to carry out that action.
4. A subordinate should be responsible to just one supervisor. This is often called "the principle of unity of command." Where this is violated, it often leads to confusion as to which boss's conflicting orders should be followed and, in many instances, severe organizational conflict results.

Linear responsibility charts

A linear responsibility chart is a simple method of describing "who is in charge of what" in an organization. Such charts are widely used in the management of temporary projects and are particularly valuable in making sure that all important decision areas are accounted for. Exhibit 4–1 illustrates a linear responsibility chart applied to a school district administration. Across the top are listed various positions in the school district and along the side are the various duties to be performed. The symbols Z, C, and I refer to levels of action responsibility.

Exhibit 4–1
Linear responsibility chart

Duties (from job description)	Job titles (from organization chart)			
	District superin- tendent	Assistant superin- tendent for finance	Assistant superin- tendent for personnel	Assistant superin- tendent for curriculum
Curriculum development	I	C	I	Z
Financial planning	C	Z	C	I
Facilities planning	C	Z	I	C

Key: Z = Makes decision.
      C = Consulted on decision.
      I = Informed on decision.

CENTRALIZATION AND DECENTRALIZATION OF AUTHORITY

Centralization and decentralization are labels applied to indicate the degree to which authority is dispersed throughout an organization. The greater the centralization, the greater the amount of decision-making authority at the top of the organization structure; the greater the decentralization, the greater the authority at lower levels of the organization structure. Quite often, it is possible to determine the degree of centralization by looking at the number of levels in the organization chart—centralized organizations usually having many levels, and decentralized organizations few. This is not an infallible measure, however, since two managers may differ in the amount of authority they are willing to give their subordinates—even though they are working under identical organization structures.

Taking a life cycle view of centralization and decentralization, we typically see changing attitudes of management and changing structural relationships as factors affecting the degree of centralization. In the young organization, authority is usually centralized in its founder. As the organization becomes more mature with a greater number of employees, authority is parceled out, often informally, to individuals so that they may execute specific functions. Sometime before the organization reaches its long-run operating size, authority becomes formally vested in specific functions—production, marketing, finance, personnel—with managers of these functions deciding on the degree to which they want to centralize authority within their departments. When the organization is mature, the degree of formal centralization is usually pretty well established, although it is rare for there not to be jockeying for authority even in stable organizations.

DELEGATION OF AUTHORITY

Though pleasing in concept, delegation of authority (the true meaning of decentralization) is often quite difficult in practice. Certainly the advantages of delegation are apparent—it relieves the superior of some duties so that time may be spent on others; it permits subordinates to grow in their jobs; and it permits balancing of work across all individuals in the organization. Indeed, if authority were not delegated, all decisions would be made by top management and the organization would operate in a ponderous fashion if at all. What makes effective delegation difficult is human nature—managers are often reluctant to give away much of their authority and subordinates are often reluctant to accept it (and the responsibility that goes along with it). Some of the reasons for this dual reluctance and suggestions for overcoming it have been offered by W. H. Newman and are summarized in Exhibit 4-2.[4]

Exhibit 4–2
Delegation: Problems and solutions

Reasons for reluctance to delegate:	*Recommended solutions:*
1. "I can do it better myself" fallacy.	Recognize the fact that the manager must get things done through others.
2. Lack of ability to direct.	The manager must cultivate the ability to communicate what must be done, often far in advance. This means that the manager must *(a)* think ahead and visualize the work situation; *(b)* formulate objectives and general plans of action, and then *(c)* communicate these to the subordinate.
3. Lack of confidence in subordinates	The choice is clear—either train the subordinate immediately, or, if this is impractical, find a new subordinate.
4. Absence of selective controls which give warning of impending difficulties.	Feedback mechanisms must be developed to allow reasonable monitoring of performance.
5. A temperamental aversion to taking a chance.	The manager may have to be trained to accept the fact that delegation, even under the best of circumstances, entails some risk.
Why subordinates avoid responsibility	*Recommended solutions:*
1. It's easier to ask the boss.	This is a habit that is best broken by agreement that the subordinate will make his or her own decisions. If this doesn't work, the less desirable option is for the boss not to give any advice and let the subordinate "sink or swim" on his or her own.
2. Fear of criticism for mistakes.	The boss must provide constructive review rather than negative criticism. Focus on the act rather than the actor.
3. Lack of necessary information and resources to do the job.	The boss's job includes developing the "enabling conditions" for the subordinate to get the job done.
4. Subordinate already has more work than he or she can do.	This may be the subordinate's own fault. Nevertheless, if one perceives her- or himself as being overworked, one will be unwilling to do more. The options in this case are obvious.
5. Lack of self-confidence.	In many cases, self-confidence may be developed by carefully providing experience with increasingly difficult problems to help the individual sense his own potentialities.
6. Positive incentives may be inadequate.	The manager must find the positive incentive that is important to the subordinate.

How much authority should be delegated?

Contrasting views on this question are offered by Robert Townsend who favors a good deal of delegation for motivational reasons, and Theodore Caplow who recommends caution in delegation for political reasons.

Many give lip service, but few delegate authority *in important matters*. And that means all they delegate is dog-work. A real leader does as much dog-work for his people as he can: he can do it, or see a way to do without it, ten times as fast. And he delegates as many important matters as he can because that creates a climate in which people grow.

Example. An important contract with a supplier comes up for renewal. There is your present supplier and a major competitor. How many managers would delegate that decision? You're right: none. But you should. Here's one way:

1. Find the man in your organization to whom a good contract will mean the most.
2. Take the pains to write out on one sheet of paper the optimum and the minimum that you expect from each area of the contract.
3. Give your organization (including John—the man you've picked to negotiate) a couple of days to discuss your outline, edit, subtract, delete, add, and modify. Then rewrite it, call John into the office (with his boss if there is one between him and you—I assume he's in favor of this or forget it).
4. With John on an extension, you phone the top man involved at each supplier, and after the amenities, you say: "This is John. I've asked him to negotiate this contract. Whatever he recommends, we'll do. There is no appeal over his head. I want a signed contract within 30 days."

Now, I know that 99 out of a hundred managers won't take this risk. But is it a risk? John is closer to the point of use. He will be most affected by a bad contract. He knows how much the company gains or loses by a concession in each area (and they know he does). And he'll spend full time on it for the next 30 days. Would you? I maintain the company will get a more favorable contract every time.

Note that you've given maximum authority and accountability to John. And you've been fair to (and put great pressure on) your suppliers by telling them the rules in advance.[5]

*   *   *   *   *

The principle that authority can be enhanced by giving it away is central to modern management, but it does have certain limitations that prevent it from being universally applied. In many operations, the need for precise coordination among the parts of an organization is so compelling that it takes precedence over the improvement of morale or even productivity. Most large organizations include operating units not fully committed to the organizational program and more likely to use an increase of autonomy to sabotage or abandon their tasks than to perform them with heightened zeal.

An even more fundamental limitation . . . is that subordinates as well as managers are capable of learning that the delegation of authority may be used to enhance a manager's power, and they may resist the manipulations of a manager oriented to human relations as stubbornly as the arm-twisting of an old-fashioned authoritarian.[6]

The process of delegation

The process of delegation involves the giving and receiving of orders. The following discussion, excerpted from an article by Paul Pigors, explains how this process can be done effectively using the following seven steps:[7]

1. Planning
   a. *What action* is required to answer the need of the situation?
   b. *Who* should act?
   c. *What kind of order* shall be used?
2. Preparation (of the order-receiver).
3. Presentation: actual communication of the order.
4. Verification: confirmation that the order has been received and that the order-receiver is ready to act.
5. Action.
6. Follow-up: the use of one or more control mechanisms to test the success of action and its results.
7. Appraisal or review: generalizing judgments as to the functioning of both the order-giver and the order-receiver throughout the process.

1. Planning. This is the process of determining "who, what, when, where, and how." There are basic considerations here. For instance, do certain people have the ability to carry out a course of action? Will they do it voluntarily, or will I have to watch them closely? And so on.

2. Preparation of the order-receiver. Subordinates should be developed or trained over time to take on work and responsibilities. By preparation is meant "continuous teaching." Also one should not just "give" an order. It should be explained, the objective pointed out, and the process to be used discussed. Thus, the order-receiver will be better able to deal with unforeseen problems because he or she knows what the intent of the order concerns.

3. Presentation of the order. At some point the order is given; e.g., "Gentlemen, start your engines!", the green flag is waved. The tone of the message and the manner in which it is delivered are very important considerations.

4. Verification. Was the order understood? Was it *really* understood? So often we "hear" what we want to hear, or expect to hear and not what was actually said. A two-way process is necessary. Get the order-receiver, in his or her own words, to repeat the order. Then you can be more sure that what you "meant" is what the order-receiver "understood."

5. Action. The starting gun was fired. Did the runners take off? Or did they stand there looking at you? If the preceding steps were done properly the correct action will likely begin. If floundering occurs some earlier step has likely gone awry.

6. Follow-up. Rarely do things go so smoothly that some corrective action is unnecessary. Even if the order-receiver is doing exactly what you intended, some unforeseen contingency—a strike, an accident, a broken machine—may occur. Another order may well be required to alleviate the problem.

7. *Appraisal or review.* How did it go? What went well? Badly? The order-receiver needs to know this for true learning to occur. The appraisal is too often neglected because the manager doesn't want to criticize or hurt someone's feelings. Remember, more damage is done by avoiding such problems than by hurt feelings from constructive criticism.

LINE AND STAFF

Line and staff are common terms in describing organizational relationships. Unfortunately, they can be interpreted in different ways depending upon whether they are applied to *authority relationships* or *organizational functions*. As an authority relationship, line refers to the formal right of a superior to give orders to a subordinate (and would be shown on an organization chart as a solid line between the two); staff refers to the formal right to give advice. (We will discuss organization charts in detail in the next chapter.) As a functional relationship, line refers to those functions which are directly responsible for the production and distribution of the organization's product or service; and staff refers to those positions which assist and support those directly responsible. These distinctions are noted in Exhibit 4–3.

The fact that a department may be staff in nature does not mean that it is less important to meeting organizational goals than a line department. Indeed, staff services should be major contributors to organization success or they should not be part of the organization.

The two authority/function concepts become intertwined in practice when we have, for example, a line relationship between manager and subordinate within a staff department. Thus, while the staff department is advisory to other departments, the hierarchical arrangement within the department would operate in the same general fashion as its line counterpart.

Where problems usually arise in applying the line and staff concept is in determining how much real "power" a staff department has in getting line

Exhibit 4–3
Contrasts in line/staff concepts

	Authority	Function	Typical departments
Line	Gives orders	Central to operations.	Production, marketing, finance, top management.
Staff	Gives advice	Support to operations.	Accounting, legal, personnel, R&D, industrial engineering, production control.

departments to follow its advice. As might be expected, a line manager would be likely to accept without question the advice of a legal department representative on, say, patent laws, an accounting department on bookkeeping procedures, and so on. Indeed, in these instances, acceptance is usually required by organizational policies and formalized under the heading of *functional authority* (i.e., authority to require compliance over certain prescribed functions within the expertise of a staff department).

The extent of authority found in staff departments ranges from *staff advice* where the advisee is free to listen or not to listen to staff; *compulsory staff advice* where the advisee must at least listen to staff; *concurrent line-staff authority* where the line manager and the staff manager must jointly agree on the decision to be made; and *functional authority* which as noted earlier, requires the line advisee to follow staff advice. Along a different dimension is the concept of *informal staff authority.* In this case, the staff manager may exert far more influence than granted by the formal organization by providing sound advice, by sharing information otherwise unavailable to the line manager, or by being a member of a powerful staff department.*

PLURAL AUTHORITY

While we often think of authority as vested in an individual, virtually every large organization has authority vested in groups as well. Usually going under the heading of committees, such groups may operate in a direct line capacity as in a board of directors, in a purely advisory capacity as a president's cabinet, or somewhere in between as is found in an industrial safety committee. We will have more to say about such group operations in Chapter 14, "Improving the Organization."

THE MANAGER'S USE OF POWER

Authority in practice—Power tactics

The success or failure of a manager often rides on his or her understanding of power tactics in day-to-day activities. Based upon an extensive study of successful leaders, Martin and Sims identify a number of areas and ways power tactics are employed:[8]

1. *Taking counsel.* The able manager takes counsel only when he or she alone desires it. "A vague sort of policy which states, 'I am always ready

---

* While a junior member of a methods department for a finance company, one of the authors of this book observed that senior members of the department were able to get every efficiency improvement suggestion, no matter how far-fetched, accepted immediately by line managers. The reason for this was that senior staff department members advised top management as to which line managers were expendable.

to hear your ideas and advice about anything,' will waste time, confuse issues, dilute leadership, and erode power."

2. *Alliances.* The hierarchical system in an organization is composed to a large degree of sponsor-protégé relationships. The wise manager recognizes this and will make a point to develop a devoted following of subordinates and close alliances with other executives.

3. *Maneuverability.* Wise executives maintain flexibility and never completely commit themselves to any one position or program. If forces beyond their control compel a major change in company policy, they can gracefully bend with the wind and cooperate with the inevitable, thus maintaining their statuses.

4. *Communication.* It is a poor strategy to communicate everything one knows. This is particularly true with respect to uncertain future plans or when such information would lead to organizational conflict.*

5. *Compromising.* Compromise is likewise a poor strategy for maintaining power. While managers must often appear to alter their views, their success often requires them to continue to press forward toward a clear-cut set of goals. Giving ground is frequently necessary, but concessions should be more apparent than real.

6. *Negative timing.* When an activity or decision is urged or when a decision which would have negative consequences for the managers is urged upon them, they may initiate action but retard the process of expedition. (In politics, this is approximated by the "pocket veto" in which the inadvisable program "dies on the vine.")

7. *Confidence.* The successful executive, like the successful baseball umpire, after making a decision looks and acts decisive even though inner conviction may be lacking.

8. *Always the boss.* Warm, personal relationships tend to interfere with organizational effectiveness and act to limit the power of the manager. No matter how cordial he or she may be, the executive must sustain a line of privacy which cannot be transgressed. In the final analysis, he or she must always be the boss.

Power plays

No discussion of power is complete without touching upon some of the insights about the subject from current writers focusing on symbols and situations where power is exhibited.

OFFICES†

Some top executives have gone through great lengths to establish an Olympian aura. Offices have been designed with raised platforms that perch a short boss

---

* We like the homily, "Never pass up the opportunity to keep your mouth shut."

† Size and location of an office have often been considered power symbols but before you evaluate your professor, note that a recent *Human Behavior* article (March 1978, p. 59) shows this to be a good indicator in business organizations but not in universities. (The three authors of this book have relatively small, corner offices.)

high above his visitors or with special lighting to place the "host" in a dramatic setting. One executive's floor was actually installed in reverse: it sloped downward from the door to the table desk so that the visitor seemed to grow smaller as he approached.[9]

Low, soft chairs making visitors sit lower than the executive, forcing them to peer "between their knees at him." It is particularly helpful to make sure that all ashtrays are just slightly out of reach so that visitors sitting in low chairs and unable to rise have to stretch awkwardly to dispose of their cigarette ash.[10]

WATCHES

More powerful executives wear watches that hardly show the time, so thin are the hands and so obscure the numbers on the face. People who are really secure in their power sometimes show it by not wearing any watches at all, relying on the fact that nothing important can happen in their absence.[11]

SHOES

One thing is basic: power people have their shoes polished, or do it themselves. In all shoe wearing cultures, and in every age, a dirty shoe is a sign of weakness.[12]

The ultimate in power shoes are authentic Gucci loafers. Korda cautions, however, that "you can't put Gucci's on Florsheim feet."[13]

SUMMARY

In this chapter we have introduced the concept of authority—how it is delegated, accepted, and built into a formal organization via line and staff relationships. We have also introduced its companion concept—responsibility—which goes hand-in-hand with authority via the process of delegation. Further, we have considered the role of power as it exists via formal authority and as it is often enhanced by "power tactics" and symbols. We have noted, too, that authority and power in the birth stage of the organization are centralized in the founder but as the organization grows, the necessity for coordinated action makes the disbursement of both inevitable. We should emphasize, however, that such disbursement is not irreversible—mature organizations (as we shall see) often experiment with re-centralization of authority as a primary means of responding to pressures of their internal and external environments. In the next chapter, we will discuss the structural forms which operationalize authority and responsibility concepts as an organization comes into being.

GUIDES TO ACTION

1. In entering an organization, make sure you know who has direct line authority over you and who is directly subordinate to you. This may seem obvious but it is surprising how often people in large organizations are unsure as to who is their boss.

2. Before accepting responsibility for a job, make certain that you know precisely what is required. If necessary, write down what is to be done, who is to help or interact with you, due dates, and expected results.

3. If your objective is to rise to the top position in an organization, you are generally well advised to get into a line department rather than a staff department. The line is where the action is even though entry level skill requirements and hence pay are usually lower in line positions.

4. Despite the publicity on power plays and office politics, the best way to assure success in an organization is to be technically competent and diligent in your work.

NOTES

[1] A fascinating book (if you can get a copy) is the *IBM Club Song Book* which contains such titles as "March on with I.B.M." with the verse:

"The fame of I.B.M.
    Spreads across the seven seas
Our standards fly aloft
    Proudly waving in the breeze,
With T. J. Watson guiding us we lead throughout the world,
    For peace and trade our banners are unfurled—unfurled." (p. 4)

Or try the little ditty titled, "To J. L. Barton: Resident Manager, Endicott Plant" which goes (to the tune of "Oh! Susanna"):

"In Endicott we have a man,
Whose thoughts will ever be,
To fill each need with greater speed,
Throughout our factory;
J. L. Barton, to I.B.M. you're true,
You'll ever go ahead we know
And we are back of you." (p. 7)

[2] See "The Brewmasters: Colorado Coors Family Has Built an Empire on One Brand of Beer," *The Wall Street Journal,* October 26, 1973, p. 1. Under certain circumstances Coors employees are required to participate in a competitive sport. "If you can't fight competition, you don't need to survive," says William K. Coors.

[3] Stanley Milgram, *Obedience to Authority* (New York: Harper & Row, Publishers, 1974).

[4] W. H. Newman, "Overcoming Obstacles to Effective Delegation," *Management Review,* January 1956, pp. 36–41.

[5] Robert Townsend, *Up the Organization* (New York: Alfred E. Knopf, 1970), pp. 46–47.

[6] From *How to Run Any Organization* by Theodore Caplow, pp. 27–28. Copyright © 1976 by Theodore Caplow. Reprinted by permission of Holt, Rinehart and Winston and Theodore Caplow.

[7] Paul Pigors, "How Can a Boss Obtain Favorable Responses to His Orders?" *Management of Personnel Quarterly*, Autumn 1961, pp. 40–44.

[8] Norman H. Martin and John Howard Sims, "Power Tactics," *Harvard Business Review,* November–December 1956, pp. 25–29. Copyright © 1956 by the President and Fellows of Harvard College; all rights reserved. Reprinted by permission.

[9] P. Preston and A. Quesada, "What Does Your Office 'Say' about You?" in Peter J. Frost et al., *Organizational Reality—Reports from the Firing Line* (Santa Monica, Cal.: Goodyear Publishing Company, 1978), p. 114.

[10] Michael Korda, *Power! How to Get It and Use It* (New York: Ballantine Books, 1975), p. 23.

[11] Ibid., p. 243.

[12] Ibid., p. 209.

[13] Ibid., p. 210.

DISCUSSION QUESTIONS

1. Based upon authority concepts, why has President Carter been unsuccessful in getting people to reduce their gasoline consumption?

2. Would you have behaved differently than the subjects in Milgram's experiments?

3. To which concept in the chapter does the following quote from the movie, *Network* pertain: "I'm mad as hell and I'm not going to take it any more!"

4. Give an example from your own life where the principle of unity of command was violated. What was the effect of this in your case?

5. You are the CEO (chief executive officer) of a fraternity or sorority which is planning a fund drive. The choices are narrowed to *(a)* an all-night country swing party featuring Chuck Wagon and the Wheels or *(b)* a 1950's "sock-hop" featuring records by The Five Satins, The Del-Vikings, and Danny and the Juniors. Assuming that you have a complete staff of chapter officers, set up a linear responsibility chart for making the decision and carrying it through.

6. Compare the amount of authority held by the store manager of a national supermarket chain with that of "Ma" or "Pa" in a "Ma and Pa" corner grocery.

7. In your present role of student, can you identify three decisions/actions you always delegate, and three decisions/actions which you *never* delegate. From these two extremes, can you formulate a personal "principle of delegation?"

8. Think of a boss you have had. Did he or she seem to use the eight power tactics recommended by Martin and Sims? Be specific on how each one was or was not used.

9. One of the authors of this book carried out a manufacturing management audit of three factories owned by a lighter company in Europe. His findings were that production capacity was poorly utilized, schedules had not been met, and costs in general were above those of the competition. The divisional manager over these operations was fired, even though he drove a classic Mercedes, wore a paper-thin watch, and Gucci shoes. What does this suggest to you about the relative importance of power symbols?

EXERCISE

As we pointed out in the chapter, people differ in what they perceive as legitimate authority. The questionnaire provided below was drawn from a study by Schein and Ott who examined the question of "what is legitimate?" We suggest that you take this list and compare your answers with those of your classmates. For purposes of rough comparison of attitudes, you may score your test by simply adding up the number of entries in each column. Some questions you then might consider are:

a. Do your attitudes suggest that you would make a "good" organization person?

b. How would you as a manager cope with a subordinate who had, say, 40 out of 55 "no" answers?

c. Does a "no opinion" for you mean that an item falls within your "zone of indifference" as defined in the chapter?

d. Would you be willing to work for a company that implicitly insisted that 40 out of the 55 answers be "yes"?

It is legitimate for a manager to attempt to influence subordinates in terms of:

Yes	No	No opin- ion	
____	____	____	1. How much importance s/he attaches to getting along with other people.
____	____	____	2. The amount of money s/he gives to charity (assuming contributions are made at work).
____	____	____	3. How much leisure time s/he spends with superiors.
____	____	____	4. Whether s/he wears long hair.
____	____	____	5. His/her attitudes toward unions.
____	____	____	6. Whether s/he uses profane language at work.
____	____	____	7. How much alcohol, if any, s/he consumes during the working day.
____	____	____	8. Whether s/he owns a house.
____	____	____	9. The kind of car s/he drives.
____	____	____	10. The amount of time s/he spends talking to spouse and children on the telephone while at work.
____	____	____	11. His/her willingness to play politics to get ahead.
____	____	____	12. Where s/he lives.
____	____	____	13. How active s/he is in recruiting others to join the company.
____	____	____	14. How much s/he competes with peers for promotion.
____	____	____	15. What political party s/he belongs to.
____	____	____	16. The type of clothing s/he wears at work.
____	____	____	17. The kind of person s/he marries.
____	____	____	18. Who his/her friends are.
____	____	____	19. The amount of time s/he spends doing job-related reading while at work.
____	____	____	20. How much s/he buys on credit.
____	____	____	21. How many children s/he has.
____	____	____	22. Where s/he spends vacations.
____	____	____	23. The kind of house or apartment s/he lives in.

Yes	No	No opin-ion	
___	___	___	24. How much leisure time s/he spends with subordinates.
___	___	___	25. The amount of additional education s/he obtains in job-related areas.
___	___	___	26. The location of his/her next job (assuming the company rotates its people to different geographical areas of the country).
___	___	___	27. His/her working hours.
___	___	___	28. How much leisure time s/he spends with peers.
___	___	___	29. The church s/he attends.
___	___	___	30. What clubs or organizations s/he belongs to.
___	___	___	31. Where his/her children attend school.
___	___	___	32. His/her attitudes toward money.
___	___	___	33. His/her attitudes toward smoking.
___	___	___	34. The kind of temperament s/he exhibits on the job (i.e., how excitable or phlegmatic or aggressive or passive).
___	___	___	35. His/her attitudes toward sexual morality.
___	___	___	36. How critical s/he is of the company in public.
___	___	___	37. How s/he supervises his/her own secretary.
___	___	___	38. The form of address s/he uses in talking to colleagues.
___	___	___	39. The degree of formality of his/her clothing.
___	___	___	40. Whether s/he uses the company product personally (i.e., drives the kind of car the company makes, or whatever the product is).
___	___	___	41. The amount of life insurance s/he carries.
___	___	___	42. The amount of company work s/he takes home.
___	___	___	43. His/her attitudes toward saving money.
___	___	___	44. The tidiness of his/her office.
___	___	___	45. How s/he divides up the working day among various duties.
___	___	___	46. How faithful s/he is to spouse.
___	___	___	47. How much s/he drinks at home.
___	___	___	48. The amount of leisure time s/he spends at company social functions.
___	___	___	49. How much s/he entertains.
___	___	___	50. Where s/he maintains charge accounts for personal shopping.
___	___	___	51. Whether s/he has close friends in a rival company.
___	___	___	52. How many drinks, if any, s/he has at lunchtime.
___	___	___	53. His/her degree of participation in noncompany public activities (i.e., working for local political parties, organizations, etc.).
___	___	___	54. Whether his/her spouse works.
___	___	___	55. Whether s/he participates on a company athletic team (assuming s/he has the talent and is needed).

Source: Adapted from Edgar H. Schein and J. Steven Ott, "The Legitimacy of Organizational Influence," *The American Journal of Sociology*, May 1962.

CASE: WHO IS RESPONSIBLE?*

Mr. Smithers, president of Electronics, Inc., needed a special cost-study report by 9:30 A.M. Friday for presentation at an urgent board of directors' meeting later that day. Shortly after lunch on that Friday, Tom Edison—the chief design engineer who is directly subordinate to Alex Bell, vice president of research and development—received a call from Mr. Smithers.

"Tom," he snapped, "where in the world is the BIM report? As I told you last week, it was to have been on my desk by 9:30 this morning, at the latest."

Tom Edison winced. "I'm very sorry Mr. Smithers," he said, "but I gave the project to Werner, our design engineer, who is the most qualified person to compile this report. He said that he would take care of it."

Mr. Smithers then called Werner, who said that he had completed the project and that three days ago he had given the report to Mr. Edison's secretary, Liz, to be typed. Mr. Smithers investigated further and found that Liz had been away for the past two days with the flu. The untyped report was later found in the "In Process" basket on her desk.

Questions

1. In your opinion, who is responsible?
2. Can such occurrences be prevented?

---

* From Richard N. Farmer, Barry M. Richman, and William G. Ryan, *Incidents in Applying Management Theory.* © 1966 by Wadsworth Publishing Company, Inc., Belmont, California 94002. Reprinted by permission of the publisher.

Level of Organizational Outputs

SELECTION OF THE PRODUCT OR SERVICE	DESIGN OF THE SYSTEM	STAFFING THE ORGANIZATION	STARTUP OF THE ORGANIZATION	OPERATING THE ORGANIZATION IN THE STEADY STATE	IMPROVING THE ORGANIZATION	REVISION OF THE ORGANIZATION	TERMINATION OF THE ORGANIZATION
Decision-making processes; social value; goals; forecasts; policies; plans	Authority and responsibility; power; organizational structure; communications systems; job design	Work force planning; personnel management functions	Startup planning and scheduling; monitoring; alternative startup approaches	Motivation; leadership; production and operations management; control	Individual improvement programs and techniques; group conflict management; MBO	Evaluation of organizational policies; strategic choices; organizational change; organizational development	Partial terminations; cutback management; complete terminations; mergers; born-again strategies

t_0

O

Time

Chapter 5
Structural concepts
of organizing

. . . each local and regional group would have considerable autonomy within its own jurisdiction; at the top there would be a national commission, like the board of directors of a . . . corporation, to establish major policy for the organization, and the leaders of all the larger outfits would sit on that panel, with each man an equal. Though [one person] would be the chairman—the unanimous decision of his peers—his vote and voice would be no stronger or more powerful than anyone else's.

Martin A. Gosch and Richard Hammer,
The Last Testament of Lucky Luciano[1]

One thing that successful armies, churches, and legitimate (and illegitimate) businesses have in common is a well-defined organization structure. Indeed, no large organization, whatever its mission, can compete effectively without grouping the work to be done into carefully defined organizational units and specifying the precise nature of the authority hierarchy which ties these units together. The objective in this chapter is to discuss the common approaches to this problem and to provide some conditions for evaluating alternative organizations. The focal point in this discussion is the organization chart—modern management's "road map" to the way in which authority and responsibility flow vertically and horizontally through the organization. It is also of great help to the outsider to understand how to best interact with the organization as a supplier of materials, funds, services, and so on, or as a user of the organization's services.

BASIC CONCEPTS

Consider the organization chart shown in Exhibit 5–1.
This simple chart displays several things:

— The manager is ultimately responsible for the performance of all individuals reporting to him or her.
— A chain of command extends from the manager through the two supervisors down to the six workers.
— The span of management (or span of control) for the manager is two and for each supervisor is three. The span of management refers to the number of subordinates who report *directly* to a supervisor.
— There are three organizational levels and two supervisory levels.
— There is only one supervisor for each subordinate.
— The adviser occupies a *staff* relationship relative to the manager as indicated

Exhibit 5–1

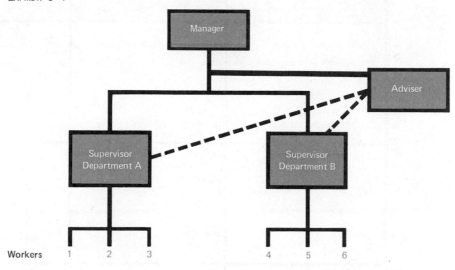

by the way in which the adviser's line relates to the main chain of command line.
— The adviser has functional authority over the two supervisors (usually indicated by a dashed line).

These characteristics give rise to several important questions about organizational design, the answering of which provides the "organizational structure" for this chapter:

1. What bases for *divisionalization* and *departmentation*—the grouping of work activities into subunits of the organization—are commonly used?
2. What *organizational forms* are commonly used to tie together those subunits?
3. What is an appropriate *span of management* for any given organization?
4. What is the nature of the trade-off between a *tall* organization (one with many levels) and a *flat* organization (one with few levels)?
5. What are the characteristics of good and bad organization structures?
6. What are the characteristics of flexible and inflexible organization structures?

Designing an organization involves two basic processes: differentiation and integration. Differentiation is concerned with taking the work to be done in the organization and assigning portions of it to different organizational units; i.e., effecting a division of labor. Integration refers to the mechanism(s) used to ensure that the differentiated tasks come together to produce the desired good or service output. The organizational designer thus asks two major questions: How do I divide up the work? How do I get the work to come together to produce what I want?

Exhibit 5-2

Basis for divisionalization or departmentation	Definition: Group activities according to:	Organization examples: Chart segment
1. Function	"Thing" to be done	Top Management — Marketing / Production
2. Product	Product or service provided	Top Management — Large Appliance / Small Appliance
3. Geographic	Location of production or sales	Top Management — Domestic Operation / Foreign Operation
4. Customer	Needs of customer	Top Management — Industrial Products / Consumer Products
5. Equipment	Operation of equipment	Top Management — Fabrication / Assembly
6. Time	Time of work activities	Top Management — Day Shift / Night Shift

Bases for divisionalization and departmentation

Divisionalization and departmentation are similar terms used to indicate the process of breaking an organization into its constituent parts. Divisionalization as used in industry refers to the first major "cut" or separation of organizational activities, the result being two or more large groupings or divisions of the firm. (From a historical standpoint, divisionalization refers to the division of labor which in fact occurs when organizational subunits are formed.) Departmentation usually implies grouping activities into specific, smaller units within divisions. As a rough generalization, large organizations, or organizations which have geographically separated operations, usually have divisions; small organizations, on the other hand, rarely do.

There are six common bases upon which divisionalization and departmentation are predicated in modern organizations:

1. Function.
2. Product.
3. Geographic locale.
4. Customer.
5. Equipment.
6. Time.

Exhibit 5–2 provides a definition and example of each.

Exhibit 5–3 illustrates a simple example of how all six bases of departmentation mentioned in Exhibit 5–2 might be combined for a large organization. Note that different levels of the organization can use different bases, but within a given level only one base is used.

Organizational forms

There are three commonly used organizational forms by which divisions or departments are tied together to yield an organizational structure. These are: (1) line, (2) line/staff, and (3) project or product. Examples of each type are illustrated in Exhibit 5–4.

Line. Because organizations commonly "grow a hierarchy" by adding functional departments first, the simple line structure is often referred to as a functional structure. This can lead to confusion if one is attempting to distinguish structural forms from departmentation as we are here. Thus, for our purposes, a line structure simply denotes an organization without staff units, which under some circumstances may contain departments based on persons, places, and so on [see Exhibit 5–4A]. The effect of the absence of staff units is that the manager of each department must have the skills normally provided by staff units available among his or her subordinates.

Exhibit 5–3
Four bases of divisionalization and departmentation applied to a hypothetical appliance manufacturer

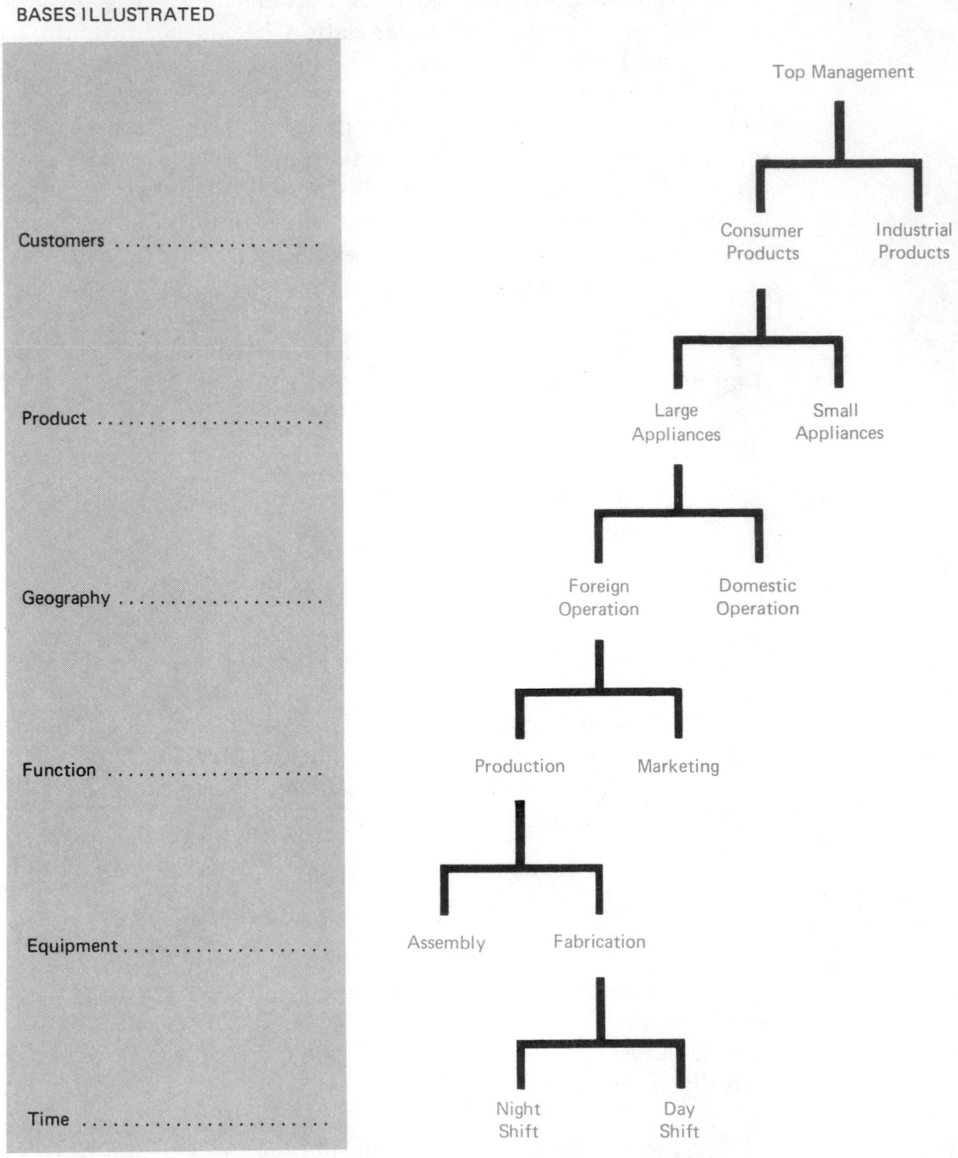

BASES ILLUSTRATED

Customers . . . .

Product . . . .

Geography . . . .

Function . . . .

Equipment . . . .

Time . . . .

Exhibit 5–4
Three common organizational forms

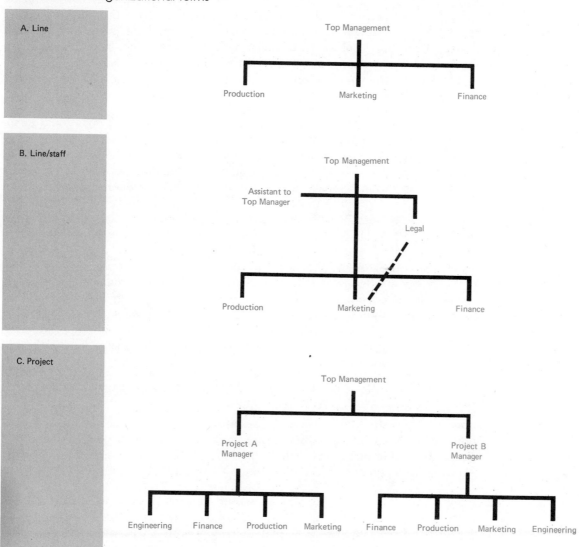

A. Line

Top Management

Production   Marketing   Finance

B. Line/staff

Top Management

Assistant to
Top Manager

Legal

Production   Marketing   Finance

C. Project

Top Management

Project A
Manager

Project B
Manager

Engineering   Finance   Production   Marketing   Finance   Production   Marketing   Engineering

Line structures are simple to understand and provide a good way to structure small organizations. Their major drawback is that they do not provide a structure for the infusion of specialized knowledge or help into the organization.

Line/staff. In Exhibit 5–4B, we see the addition of a staff function—a legal department. As mentioned in the previous chapter, staff functions act in an advisory capacity. The dashed line from legal to marketing tells us that the legal department has functional authority within marketing.

There are two types of staff units; personal and general. Personal staff acts as a "helper" or "adviser" to a specific line manager. An example would be the job of "assistant to the president." General staff units provide services to the broader organization. Examples here would include personnel, maintenance, legal, or purchasing. In charting an organization, personal staff are usually represented by horizontal lines linked to a vertical. Note the difference in connecting lines in Exhibit 5–4B for the legal staff unit and the assistant to top manager.

The line/staff structure is no doubt the most common organizational form. Rapidly changing laws and technologies require the addition of specialists to deal with them, and the staff department is a relatively easy way to build them into organizational structures. Research on the effect of staff departments in the organization typically focuses on the conflict between line and staff in decision making. Part of the problem is usually cast as one of differences in orientation between members of line and staff departments—staff personnel often are professionals (engineers, accountants, and so on) with an allegiance to their field; line personnel on the other hand are rarely "certified" professionals and have a stronger allegiance to their organization. Another part of the problem was alluded to in the previous chapter—the line manager is responsible for the consequences of the action he or she takes from staff advice. This point can be brought home by noting the role of the chicken and the pig in making ham and eggs: While chickens may be *concerned* about production of eggs, the pig is *committed* in the production of bacon. So it is with staff and line personnel.

A related problem in the operation of the line/staff structure is that top managers often do not use their staff effectively because they don't know how to motivate highly trained specialist groups. As George Odiorne has pointed out, "During the sixties, the effectiveness of such people [personnel managers, traffic managers, public relations people, and so on] was practically exterminated. They added cost without a corresponding output."[2]

Project/product.   In Exhibit 5–4C we see an organization which is designed around individual projects, in this case by having separate line functions under the direction of each project's manager. A common variant of this approach is one whereby the project manager is given authority over certain personnel or facilities from common production, marketing, finance, and other departments. This latter form is called a *matrix* structure since the project manager would be shown to the side of the other departments with authority lines flowing in a horizontal direction between the project department and other departments, thus forming a "matrix." Another common variation is the *product* or *brand management* form in which a product manager assumes control over almost all aspects of producing and marketing a particular product line.

While all three forms have the advantage over line and line/staff forms of being able to focus group efforts on particular projects or products, they often give rise to jurisdictional problems. For example, which project manager has priority over resources of the firm? Project workers are often assigned to several projects during the year; which manager evaluates their work? Is it a functional department manager (if they are following a matrix structure), or is it a particular project manager? In short, such structures tend toward dual chains of command and hence may violate the principle of unity of command.

Organizational forms—Growth dynamics

No organization starts with, say, 15 line and a dozen staff departments. Rather, they tend to add people to existing operating units until the size of the unit becomes unmanageable, or until new workers with particular skills must be added to the organization in sufficient numbers that they compel the creation of a new department. In essence, growth of an organization occurs by expanding the organizational structure either vertically or horizontally, usually one step at a time. For example, the organizations shown in Exhibit 5–5 grow vertically by adding a new supervisory position and grow horizontally by adding, say, an accountant. Subsequent horizontal growth might arise by adding a second supervisor, and subsequent vertical growth by adding a bookkeeper.

SPAN OF MANAGEMENT

One of the most intriguing questions in management is how many subordinates should report to a given manager? The basic trade-off considered in the span of management decision is the ability of the manager to supervise the number of individuals which report to him or her versus the ability of the subordinates (be they managers or workers) to work independently. As one might expect, the type of work performed by the manager and subordinates affects the size of the span. Writing in the *Harvard Business Review*, Fisch suggests that different spans be chosen for different levels of managers in the organizational hierarchy.[3] Specifically, he identifies four types of managers—supermanagers, general managers, middle managers, supervisors—and proposes some major differences between them which should be reflected in their span of management.

Supermanagers are the chief executives of large (super) organizations whose major role is dealing with corporatewide or policy level issues. Such individuals are by definition removed from close supervision of other managers.

General managers according to Fisch's classification are the top-level managers of small- to medium-sized organizations or divisional managers in large organizations. While they also engage in policy making, a large part of their job involves frequent interaction with subordinate managers. One of their jobs is teaching of subordinate managers, and as Fisch points out, it is in this

Exhibit 5–5
Growth dynamics in a simple organization

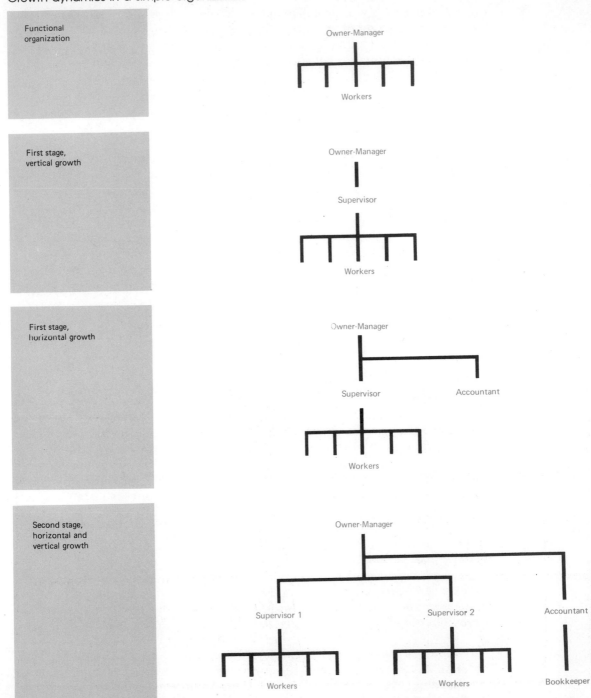

Functional organization

First stage, vertical growth

First stage, horizontal growth

Second stage, horizontal and vertical growth

group that the need for close contact with people is the major determinant to the span of management.

Middle managers, as the name implies, are positioned between the top and bottom levels of the management hierarchy. Much of their work consists of interaction not only with their subordinates but with other line, staff, or service departments (maintenance, data processing, and so on). Hence, selecting the right span of management must take into consideration the time required to lead and train subordinates and time required to deal with other units in the organization.

Supervisors are at the bottom of the management hierarchy. Their freedom of action with respect to many aspects of management is usually highly circumscribed—their subordinates are often hired by a personnel department and their use of personnel is constrained by union agreements covering job classification, compensation, and duties. The supervisor's typical responsibilities include setting work schedules, providing certain types of technical training, and maintaining morale.

Based upon his studies of the characteristics of the four types of managers, Fisch proposes a span of management *range* for each category and general methods by which more precise values can be obtained (see Exhibit 5–6).

Exhibit 5–6
The span of management and methods of determination

Group	Classification	Personnel involved		Analytical method recommended
I	Top management Large corporations	Supermanagers	50	*Overall conceptual analysis* of total enterprise and its needs now and in future
II	General management Medium to small organizational units	General managers	12	*Specific situational analysis* of overall needs of unit and personal leadership requirements
III	Middle management All sizes of organizations	Middle managers	50	*Economic analysis and cost optimization* of total middle management system, balancing savings of some increases against rising support-group costs
IV	First-line supervision All sizes of organizations	Supervisors	100	A. *Specific factor analysis* of each situation or group of situations for separate analysis and simplification; this method is similar in approach to common industrial engineering sequence of time study, work simplification, restudy, and standard rate setting B. *Situational evaluation* using analytical techniques similar in kind to those used in job evaluations

Source: Gerald Fisch, "Stretching the Span of Management," *Harvard Business Review,* September–October 1963, p. 84. Copyright © 1963 by the President and Fellows of Harvard College; all rights reserved. Reprinted by permission.

The Lockheed approach

The Lockheed Missile and Space Company has developed a direct method for determining the span of management which has been widely applied since its publication in 1963. This method is particularly useful since it presents both a listing of considerations affecting the span and a way in which they may be directly applied. This method first quantifies a given management job according to its degree of difficulty in each of six areas of "span factors." The resultant value is then multiplied by a weighting factor for the amount of direct organizational assistance available to the manager (e.g., direct line assistant) or in the case of a first-line supervisor, by the number of lead persons reporting to him or her. The appropriate span is then obtained from reading off the value corresponding to this weighted figure from a supervisory index table.

To illustrate the method, we will apply it to the job of a manager (actually a first-line supervisor) of a McDonald's type restaurant (all tables and calculations are shown in Exhibit 5–7; circled values within tables represent our

Exhibit 5–7
Application of Lockheed span of management determination

Span factor	Degree of supervisory burden				
Similarity of functions (performed by subordinates)	Identical 1	Essentially alike 2	Similar ③	Inherently different 4	Fundamentally distinct 5
Geographic contiguity of department members)	All together 1	All in one building ②	Separate buildings, one plant location 3	Separate locations, one geographic area 4	Dispersed geographic areas 5
Complexity of functions (performed by department)	Simple repetitive 2	Routine ④	Some complexity 6	Complex, varied 8	Highly complex, varied 10
Direction and control (required by subordinates)	Minimum supervision and training 3	Limited supervision 6	Moderate periodic supervision ⑨	Frequent continuing supervision 12	Constant close supervision 15
Coordination (with company-wide activities)	Minimum relationships with others 2	Relationships limited to defined courses ④	Moderate relationships, easily controlled 6	Considerable close relationship 8	Extensive mutual nonrecurring relationships 10
Planning (effort required by manager and subordinates)	Minimum scope and complexity ②	Limited scope and complexity 4	Moderate scope and complexity 6	Considerable effort required, guided only by broad policies 8	Extensive effort required, areas and policies not charted 10

Total for hamburger restaurant example = ㉔.

Exhibit 5–7 *(continued)*
Organizational assistance multiplier factors *(M)*

First-line supervisors (number of lead people)	(M)	Middle and general managers	(M)
1	.85	Direct line assistant and staff activities	.60
2	.70	Direct line assistant (only)	.70
3	.55	Staff activities (administrative, planning, *and* control functions)	.75
4	.40	Staff activities (administrative, planning, *or* control functions)	.85
5	.20	Assistant to (limited duties)	.95

Note: M = multiplier value.
Supervisory factor = $24 \times .70 = 16.8$.

Conversion of supervisory index into span of management

First-line supervisors		Middle and general managers	
Supervisory index	Span of management	Supervisory index	Span of management
40–42	9–10	40–42	4– 5
37–39	8–12	37–39	4– 6
34–36	8–14	34–36	4– 7
31–33	10–16	31–33	5– 8
28–30	12–18	28–30	6– 9
25–27	14–20	25–27	7–10
22–24	16–22	22–24	8–11
19–21	17–23	19–21	10–11
16–18	19–24	16–18	11–12

Span = 19 to 24.

judgments about this particular example). Assuming that the manager has two lead people, then the span factor of 24 totaled from the first table is multiplied by .70 (the multiplier value associated with two lead people for first-line supervisors). This yields 16.8 shown below the second table. The 16.8 figure lies between 16–18 in the "Supervisory index" column, which in turn is associated with a span of management of 19–24.

TALL VERSUS FLAT ORGANIZATION STRUCTURES

By this point in the chapter you should have some feel about organization structure. Test your understanding with respect to the effectiveness of the tall (many levels) and flat (few levels) organization structures pictured in Exhibit 5–8 by using the table that follows. (Answers are on page 118.)

Exhibit 5–8
Hypothetical tall and flat structures

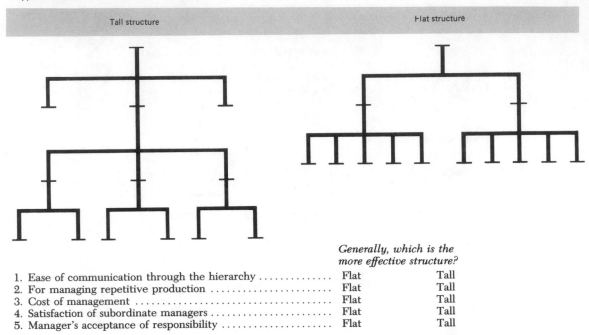

	Generally, which is the more effective structure?	
1. Ease of communication through the hierarchy	Flat	Tall
2. For managing repetitive production	Flat	Tall
3. Cost of management	Flat	Tall
4. Satisfaction of subordinate managers	Flat	Tall
5. Manager's acceptance of responsibility	Flat	Tall

The classic study of tall and flat structures was carried out by James C. Worthy on the flat structure of Sears. It was Worthy's contention that small organizations had better employee morale and productivity than large organizations. He stated that the advantages of small organizations could be incorporated into large organizations by using fewer levels of administration; that is, a flat organization structure with a wide span of management rather than a multileveled organization with a very narrow span. (The merchandising vice president at Sears has 44 senior executives reporting to him; the typical retail store has about the same number of department managers reporting to a single store manager.) Obviously, these wide spans force delegation to lower level managers and in theory at least, enhance their professional growth and development. However, Cummings and Berger's research suggests that where one is in a tall or flat organization makes a difference: "High-level executives in tall organizations and lower level executives in flat organizations experience more satisfaction than their opposites."[4] Further, the assertion that productivity is greater in flat organizations is questionable in view of the fact that each manager has to deal with substantial coordination problems which inherently limit the ongoing efficiency of his or her department. In summary, the tall-flat debate leads to an important conclusion about organization design in general—there is no one right structure for all organizations. The situation calls the tune.

CAPLOW'S SUGGESTIONS ABOUT STAFF IN THE ORGANIZATION STRUCTURE

Theodore Caplow suggests that a good organization chart includes the following provisions about the staff:

First, the major staff officials ought to be clearly unequal in rank, pay, influence, and other status attributes, since if two or more of them are nearly equal, their struggles for predominance will keep the organization in a constant state of turmoil.

Second, they ought to meet frequently with the manager as a council or cabinet so that most of their disputes can be resolved by direct interaction or by the persuasion of a majority opinion. If they meet frequently without the manager, they will probably come to perceive him as their common enemy. If they do not meet at all, they will use him as the rope in their tugs-of-war. In council, the manager's role as chairman enables him to develop a coalition against any malcontent without losing the benefit of the malcontent's advice, as in the famous case of President Lincoln and Secretary Stanton.

. . . Staff officials should be approximately equal in rank and perquisites to the subordinate managers with whom they deal, or perhaps a little lower to make up for the informal perquisites they acquire by proximity to the central authority. The people who carry out staff functions for a subordinate manager should report information to, and receive directives from the headquarters staff but remain dependent on the subordinate manager for pay and promotion. A subordinate manager should never be required to go through the staff to obtain access to the manager, nor should the manager allow his direct channels of communicaton to the line to be blocked by staff officials.[5]

COMMON ERRORS IN ORGANIZATION STRUCTURING

The trained eye can detect potential trouble spots in the organization by carefully examining the organization chart. In "The Organization Chart Returneth," Paul L. Harmon identifies a number of common structure errors he found in a survey of 78 firms.[6] Some of these (further described below) are:

1. Not enough authority to match responsibility.
2. Two doing the same job or "overlapping titles."
3. Overloading.
4. Nondescriptive titles.
5. The crabgrass problem—or no scalar chain.
6. The "palsy-walsy."

Exhibit 5–9 shows a mismatch of authority and responsibility. The company policy manual states that the assistant vice president of sales training is responsible for the performance of the sales force. This responsibility is shared with

Exhibit 5–9
Not enough authority to match responsibility

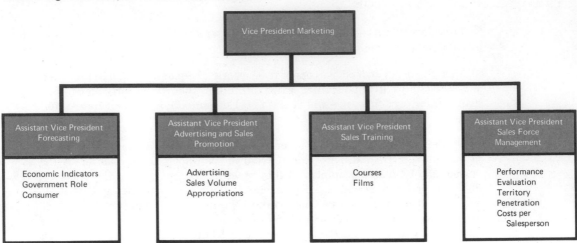

the assistant vice president of sales force management. However, the assistant vice president of sales training is paid and appraised according to the productivity of the salespeople. Thus, the manager must get confidential ratings and records on each of the salespeople to know which ones need training and in what areas the training should be given. As we can see, the manager does not receive this information—*he or she has been given responsibility without matching authority.* This is a violation of the parity of authority and responsibility principle, which often leads to frustration, low morale, and expensive turnover.

Exhibit 5–10 illustrates some problems arising from overlapping titles. For example, what is the "merchandise buying specialist" supposed to do? Are the specialist's duties the same as those of the "buyer"?

One justification for *overloading* the assistant vice president of wages in Exhibit 5–11 may be the high-level competency of the person holding this

ANSWERS TO THE TALL-FLAT TEST

1. *Flat.* Communication must pass through several levels and hence is slower and often distorted.

2. *Tall.* Repetitive production often requires close control to keep the work flowing.

3. *Flat.* Fewer managers means saved money in supervisory salaries, offices, secretaries, and fringes.

4. *Flat.* Fewer levels give supervisors more control and flexibility and hence greater job satisfaction.

5. *Flat.* Since each manager has many subordinate managers reporting to him or her, there is a reduction in the amount of time available for each one; hence the subordinates must make more decisions.

Exhibit 5-10
Two doing the same job or "overlapping titles"

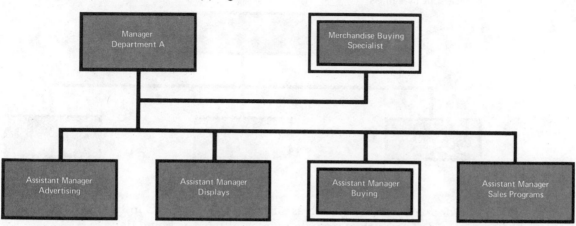

position. It may be better to place this position on a higher level than the other two assistant vice presidents. If left on the same level, whether paid more or not, personal friction may result. Another justification for this is the close interrelationship of the departments involved. Even though numerous, they require only one director. The excessive work load, if any, may be distributed to others or a new department could be created.

Exhibit 5-11
Overloading

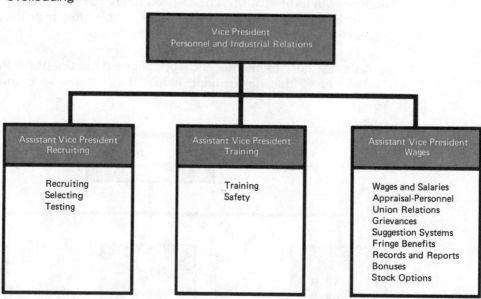

Exhibit 5–12
Nondescriptive titles

Research Department Manager

Subsection A   Subsection B   Subsection C

Nondescriptive titles such as Subsection A, B, and C in Exhibit 5–12 should be avoided since they provide no idea of what is being done.

Descriptive titles should be substituted for Subsections A, B, and C as in Exhibit 5–13. If you squeeze a clear description into the box, memos are sent to the right people, outsiders know who to contact, and a better picture of the organization's functions is conveyed to all.

Once upon a time three sons were left with an equal share in the top-level management of the family firm by their father. One was called the general manager, one was called the president, and one was called the administrative chief. The result of their sibling rivalry is the confusing *"crabgrass"* structure illustrated in Exhibit 5–14. (The dashed lines here represent the right to advise, rather than functional authority.) Clearly, a substantial restructuring is in order to move it toward a more useful pyramidal shape.

An assignment to monitor the work of one department should not be given to someone in that department. Exhibit 5–15 shows an example where the

Exhibit 5–13

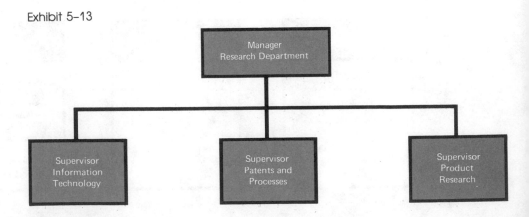

Manager
Research Department

Supervisor
Information
Technology

Supervisor
Patents and
Processes

Supervisor
Product
Research

Exhibit 5–14
The "Crabgrass" problem—Or no scalar chain

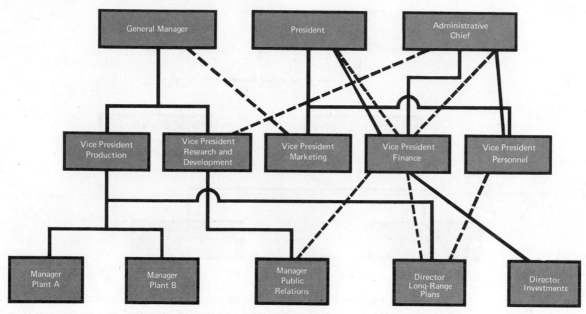

Exhibit 5–15
The palsy-walsy

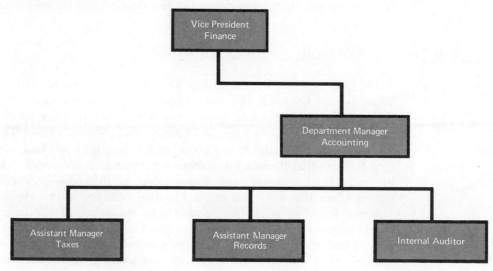

Exhibit 5–16
"Palsy-walsy" eliminated

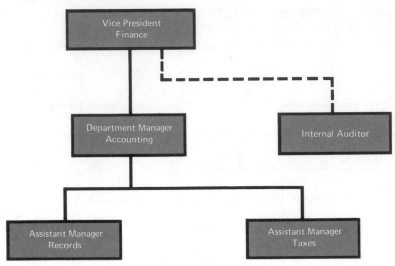

internal auditor reports to the department manager of accounting (who writes performance ratings, promotes him or her, and so on), and hence the auditor will be inclined to assume a *palsy-walsy* relationship with the manager and protect him. This violates what is known as the "separation principle"—one shouldn't be responsible to the individual or function which he or she is to monitor. This palsy-walsy problem can be solved by changing the organization to that in Exhibit 5–16 and having the internal auditor report to the financial vice president, thereby maintaining the desired checks and balances.

FLEXIBLE AND INFLEXIBLE ORGANIZATION*

Certain types of organizations are inherently more flexible than others. The need for flexibility derives primarily from the environment within which the organization operates, which commonly includes market forces, governmental restraints, work force availability, and cultural values. Though we usually conceive of flexibility as "good" and inflexibility as "bad," it is important to recognize that there are instances where an inflexible organization is desirable and a flexible organization undesirable. An inflexible organization is appropriate when the environment is relatively stable, where the nature of production activities is routine, and where the work of the organization as a whole is amenable to the efficiencies provided by specialization of labor. Examples of industries where inflexible organizations are generally applicable are agriculture, furniture, and most types of mining. A flexible organization, by

_____
* Our use of flexible and inflexible organizations is roughly equivalent to what many management researchers refer to as "organic" and "mechanistic" organizations, respectively.

Exhibit 5–17
Characteristics of flexible organizations and inflexible organizations

Flexible	*Inflexible*
Flat span of management	Narrow span of management
Loose job definitions	Rigid job definitions
Much lateral communication	Mainly vertical communication
Emphasis on individual judgment	Emphasis on rules and procedures
Decentralized decision making	Centralized decision making
Emphasis on short-run objectives	Emphasis on long-run objectives
Emphasis on product innovation	Emphasis on quality and service

contrast, is appropriate where there are frequent and dramatic changes in the environment such as rapid technological innovation, new laws, and shifting market patterns. Examples of industries where flexibility is important are airlines, plastics, electronics, and petroleum. Most other industries fall somewhere in between in terms of environmental uncertainty, and hence their need for flexibility varies.

Government organizations likewise face diverse environments. Some are relatively stable (e.g., U.S. Patent Office, Bureau of Customs), but most are rather dynamic (e.g., the military faces an ever-changing social profile of new recruits, the Department of Labor deals with dynamic shifts in the U.S. labor movement, the Internal Revenue Service deals with changing tax laws and citizens' ways of finding loopholes). Perhaps the inflexible nature of most government structures is not consistent with the dynamic environments being faced.

Contrasting characteristics of flexible and inflexible organizations are presented in Exhibit 5–17.

Building in flexibility

In addition to the characteristics listed in Exhibit 5–17, organizational flexibility may be built in at the design stage by establishing departments whose main purpose is to gather information about the environment, or to develop new products or processes which can be employed to competitive advantage. The most common type of information-gathering department in industry is the market research department. These departments are often subject to "attack" by outsiders seeking a competitive advantage. Consider the following example from the automobile industry:

On occasion, national security and nuclear secrets had been guarded less carefully than design details of future model cars.

Even staff designers were not allowed unhampered movement. Those least senior were restricted to one or two studios, their freedom increasing only after years of service. The precaution made sense. Designers were sometimes wooed by other auto companies and, since each studio held secrets of its own, the fewer an individual entered, the less knowledge he could take with him if he left. Generally, what a designer was told about activity on new model cars was based on the military principle of "need to know." However, as designers grew older in the company's service, and also more "locked in" financially through stock options and pension plans, security was relaxed and a distinctive badge—worn like a combat medal—allowed an individual past a majority of doors and guards. Even then, the system didn't always work because occasionally a top-flight, senior designer would move to a competitive company with a financial arrangement so magnanimous as to outweigh everything else. Then, when he went, years of advance knowledge went with him. Some designers in the auto industry had worked, in their time, for all major auto companies, though Ford and General Motors had an unwritten agreement that neither approached each other's designers—at least directly—with job offers. Chrysler was less inhibited.[7]

Some organizations go a step further than just finding out about the environment—they attempt to actively influence it in their favor through nonmarket-related activities (the classic case here being industry lobbyists in Washington). Dissemination of the "right kind" of information is another environment control strategy. Effective advertising, for example, can sustain a market for the inflexible organization and create a new market for the flexible organization. Looking at the issue from a broader perspective, a firm that can obtain control over its environment doesn't need flexibility!

Buffering the technological core

This high-sounding phrase is quite popular in the management literature and its meaning becomes the admonition of the garage mechanic: "Get away from the car and don't borrow my tools—the service manager will let you know when your car is ready." When placed in a theoretical context, this statement reflects the fact that production activities (the technical core of the organization) operate best when not interfered with. Any potential outside disturbances should be taken care of by nonproduction departments. In the words of the noted sociologist, James D. Thompson, "the technical core must be able to operate as if the market will absorb the single kind of product at a continous rate, and as if inputs flowed continuously at a steady rate with a specified quality."[8] Examples of departments which buffer the production organization are customer complaints, purchasing, distribution, public relations, and general management.

TECHNOLOGY AND ORGANIZATION STRUCTURE

No question in management has consumed so much recent attention by experts as the relationship between technology (the equipment, processes, and procedures of production) and organization structure. Some studies conclude that technology is the main determinant of the organization structure (particularly the number of levels, ratio of managers to workers, and span of management). Others conclude just as strongly that technology has no real or consistent effect on structure, and still others say that it doesn't make any difference because equally successful firms in the same industry have been found to use totally different structures.

One generalization which seemed to hold true in two major studies of technology and structure (by Woodward[9] and Hickson et al[10]) is that the span of management of first-line supervisors is sensitive to the kind of production processes used. Larger spans of management are found in mass production enterprises (e.g., automobile manufacturers) and smaller spans in job lot (e.g., shoes) and custom manufacture (e.g., large machine tools). The logic is that in job lot and custom manufacturing, the control by the supervisor is direct, and thereby calls for a narrow span of management. In mass production, mechanical control exists and the speed of the production process guides the work activities, enabling a broader span of management. Perhaps the safest way to view the structure technology relationships is as Porter, Lawler, and Hackman do: "If organizations are small, technology will be critical to structure and design; and if organizations are large, the impact of technology will tend to be confined to the structure of operations at the level of the rank and file employee."[11]

REAL-LIFE ORGANIZATION CHARTS

The Mafia

Exhibit 5–18 depicts an organization chart compiled from the testimony of a Mafia member. It is primarily a line form departmentalized on a geographical basis. The "production" work is carried out by the "crew" who are recruited by each Mafia family. All policy making is done by the Commissione consisting of representatives of each family, with decisions made by majority vote. The Commissione was formed to avoid problems encountered in having individual bosses who in the past had used their powers to extort excessive contributions from subordinate members of the organization. The mob wars of the 1930s and 1940s provided the impetus for this structural change. Some important operating features of the organization include absolute adherence to the chain of command, the use of the underboss to act as a buffer for each boss, and the consiglieri filling the role of personal staff adviser to each lieutenant.

Main rules of operation

1. Resort cities—always open.
2. One member may never lay a hand on another member except for "lawful" orders to kill him.

Exhibit 5–18
The Mafia

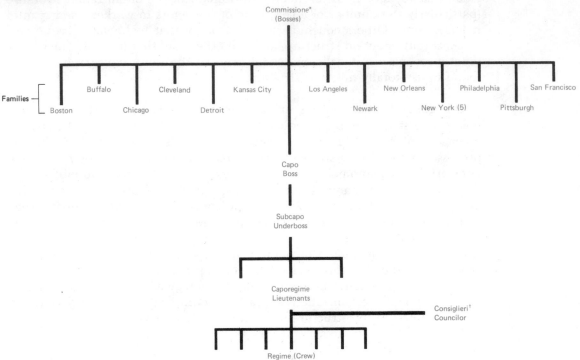

* Mob wars in the '30s and '40s, precipitated by one man autocratically ruling and extracting payment from other families, ultimately led to creation of the Commissione.

† Position only in New York City and Newark.

Source: Peter Maas, *The Valachi Papers* (New York: G. P. Putnam's Sons, 1968).

3. Must follow chain of command.
4. All major policy made by Commissione and majority vote.

Department of Labor

Exhibit 5–19 shows this structure. Note that it is a line/staff form, departmentalized on a geographic basis. It is apparent that the regional directors are on the receiving end of the substantial functional authority given to the staff units. Also, note the policy-making supermanager role of the secretary of labor and the operating or general manager role of the under secretary. Finally, the executive assistants and the counselor to the secretary are drawn in as advisory staff.

Department of Health, Education, and Welfare

The HEW chart (Exhibit 5–20) at first glance appears straightforward, but look again. All the work done in the field is carried out by ten regional offices,

Exhibit 5-19
Department of Labor

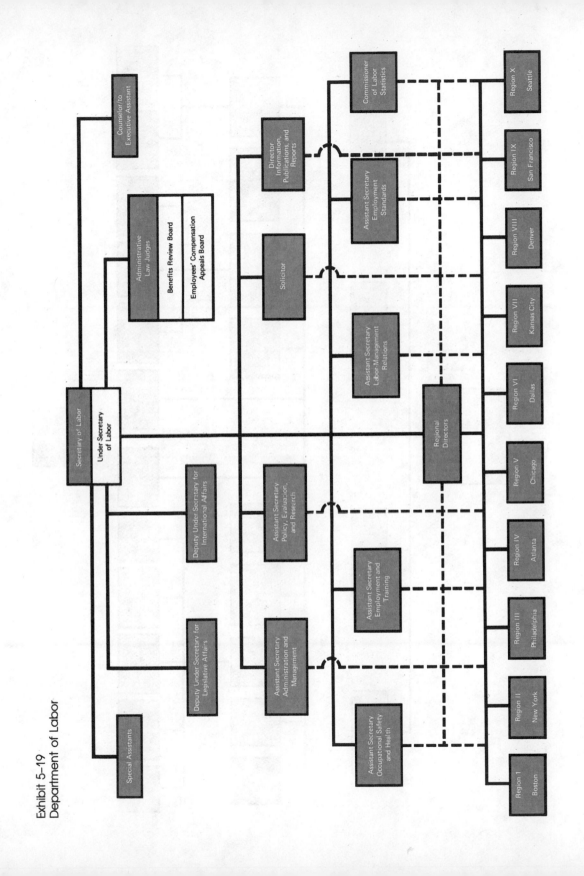

Exhibit 5–20
HEW organization chart

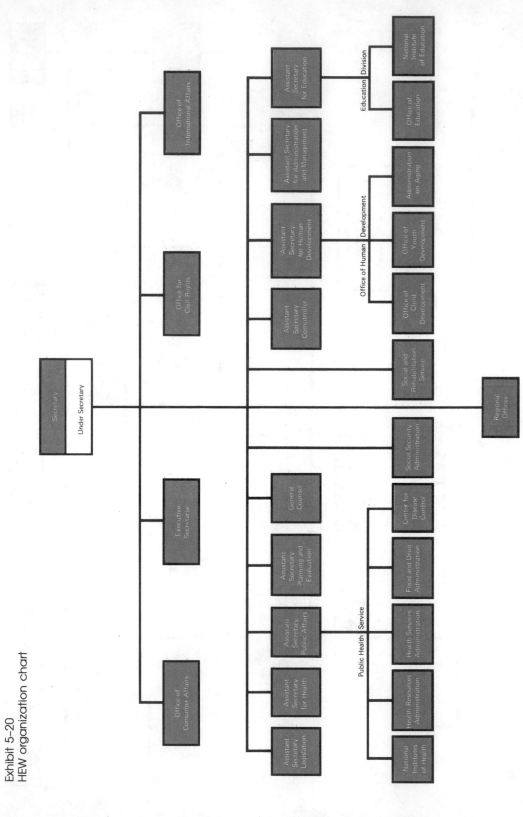

Exhibit 5–21

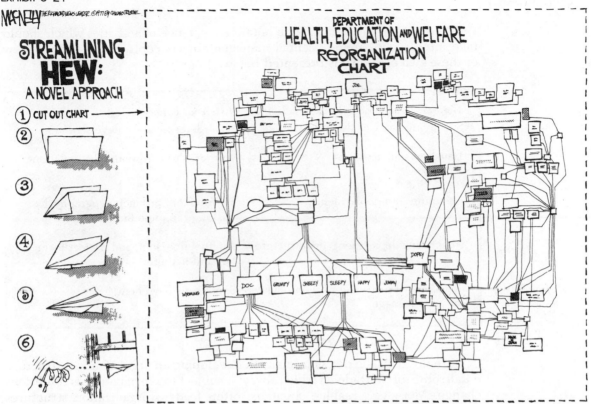

Reprinted by permission of the Chicago Tribune-New York News Syndicate, Inc.

who report directly to the under secretary. How does the under secretary control these offices? How do the other departments relate to these functions? Which offices are staff and which are line? Who would handle the problem of rehabilitating an over-65 alcoholic? —The Health Services Administration, Social and Rehabilitation Service, Administration on Aging, or the Regional Offices? Such questions as these have led to proposals to reorganize HEW in some more rational way. However, because of its size and mix of activities, the current secretary, Patricia Roberts Harris, has a difficult chore ahead of her. The recently created Department of Education may be a partial solution. The streamlining procedure (Exhibit 5–21) proposed by cartoonist Jeff Mac-Nally is at best a stopgap measure.

The message to be learned from this HEW example is that simplicity in organization charting does not lead to simplicity and effectiveness in actually running the organization. The organization chart provides a lot, but not all information that we need. Too often, it doesn't accurately describe functional responsibility and decision-making authority.

SUMMARY

The design of the organization entails a sequence of activities which should take into account some essential management concepts. A bare-bones view of these two elements is presented below.

General sequence of decision activities	Essential concepts
Specifying work of the organization. ↓	Goal determination (levels I–IV).
Line and staff activities. ↓	Authority and responsibility relationships.
Grouping into departments. ↓	By function, product, geography, customer, equipment, and time.
Integrating departments in a structure. ↓	By line, line/staff, and project form; tall and flat alternatives.
Specifying the number of subordinates for each manager.	Span of management.

Virtually all of the decisions made in developing an organizational structure entail some sort of trade-off which always is subject to reevaluation as conditions change. Moreover, real-life situations often lead to organization structures which are modified from some ideal form to take into account the particular strengths and weaknesses of individuals within the organization. A brilliant manager (or an incompetent one) can lead to substantial adjustments in the informal structure which never appear on the organization chart.

Despite the inherent shortcomings of organization charts, we find that they are of substantial value in examining any organization. In fact, in performing an organizational analysis, our first step is to construct several organization charts. One chart we elicit from the president, one we elicit from an operating manager, and one we elicit from a staff person who interacts with many departments. Inconsistencies in the charts are noted and we then try to determine those characteristics of the current organization structure that help or hinder performance. Quite often we find that a basically sound structure is being subverted by poor communication practices or poor leadership. These problems we then attempt to resolve using the relevant concepts from the next two chapters.

GUIDES TO ACTION

1. If you start a business yourself, hire a good bookkeeper first. Companies, both large and small, commonly fail due to lack of attention to funds flow. This occurs even though the product seems to be selling well.

2. If in need of a quick answer about the correct span of management for any situation, answer "six" since this seems to be the number which appears most often when experts give general answers. (Besides, any seasoned party giver knows this is the correct number for a dinner party.)

3. Despite the fact that experts constantly criticize organization charts as being out of date, not reflecting true power and communication relationships, and so on, when you are planning to go to work for an organization, request a copy of its chart, study it carefully, and find out where you will be on it. It is the single best piece of information you are likely to get before you get involved.

4. As a corollary to (3), if you are told that the organization chart is too complicated, being redone, or always ignored, think twice about your affiliation with that organization.

NOTES

[1] Taken from Martin A. Gosch and Richard Hammer, *The Last Testament of Lucky Luciano* (Boston: Little, Brown and Company, 1975), p. 146.

[2] George Odiorne, *The Activity Trap* (New York: Harper & Row, Publishers, Inc., 1976), p. 156.

[3] Gerald G. Fisch, "Stretching the Span of Management," *Harvard Business Review*, vol. 41, no. 5 (September–October 1963), pp. 74–85.

[4] Larry L. Cummings and Chris J. Berger, "Organization Structure: How Does It Influence Attitudes and Performance," *Organization Dynamics*, Autumn 1976, pp. 34–49.

[5] From *How to Run Any Organization* by Theodore Caplow, pp. 25–26. Copyright © 1976 by Theodore Caplow. Reprinted by permission of Holt, Rinehart and Winston and Theodore Caplow.

[6] Paul L. Harmon, "The Organization Chart Returneth," *Manage,* February 1971, pp. 22–36.

[7] Arthur Haley, *Wheels* (New York: Bantam Books, 1971), pp. 71–72.

[8] James D. Thompson, *Organizations in Action* (New York: McGraw-Hill Book Company, 1967), p. 20.

[9] Joan Woodward, *Industrial Organization: Theory and Practice* (London: Oxford University Press), 1965.

[10] D. J. Hickson, D. S. Pugh, and P. Pheysey, "Operations Technology and Organizational Structure: An Empirical Reappraisal," *Administrative Science Quarterly*, vol. 14 (September 1969), pp. 378–97.

[11] Lyman W. Porter, Edward E. Lawler III, and J. Richard Hackman, *Behavior in Organizations* (New York: McGraw Hill Book Company, 1975), p. 241.

DISCUSSION QUESTIONS

1. Is your university characterized by a tall or flat organization structure?

2. What is your professor's span of management? Is the concept appropriate for a teacher? Explain.

3. Draw a chart showing the organizational structure of your family. Is it hierarchical?

4. Which type of organization form is appropriate for:
   a. Producing a newsletter on jobs available for students.
   b. Preparing a "team" term paper.
   c. Running an off-campus beer parlor.

5. Use the Lockheed method to evaluate the span of management for the coach of your university's football team.

6. Paul L. Harmon has identified several other organization chart errors. These include:
   a. "Too many Indians report to one chief."
   b. "One Indian reporting to two chiefs."
   c. "The careless use of 'assistant'."
   d. "Improper [geographic] location of a service activity."
   Construct organization charts which might illustrate these points.

7. How would you determine if an organization structure is a good one?

8. Frederick W. Taylor proposed that since no one foreman had all the knowledge and expertise to do all of his duties perfectly, the foreman's duties should be divided among eight separate "functional" foremen. Each foreman in turn would give direction to a subordinate just in his area of specialization. These areas as defined by Taylor are: (1) order of work and route clerk, (2) instruction card clerk, (3) time and cost clerk, (4) shop disciplinarian, (5) gang boss, (6) speed boss, (7) inspector, and (8) repair boss. (The first four would be members of a planning department; the second four members of the shop.)
   a. This seems like a logical idea, so why hasn't it been applied?
   b. How are these functions formally allocated out in most modern organizations?

9. Camp Kiowa is beginning its first year of operation in San Diego. It will offer the usual range of services and activities including swimming, boating, tennis, hiking, and games. It will be using the facilities originally constructed for a marine boot camp. Uncle Ed, the owner, is hoping to attract 500 8- to 15-year olds his first year and very much wants a well-run operation.
   a. What type of organization structure is appropriate for the camp?
   b. Should the organization be flexible or inflexible?

CASE 1:   AJAX MANUFACTURING CORPORATION*

Ajax Manufacturing Corporation had a complex line-and-staff organization. Recently, Ned Forrester, who had spent his entire career in the production department, was elected president of the company. Shortly after assuming the presidency, Mr. Forrester wrote the following memorandum.

November 12

From: N. J. Forrester, President
To: All Vice presidents
Re: Line and Staff Relationships

Since I have been in this company there has always been friction between line and staff. I want this to stop.

The purpose of our staff people is to advise and assist our line managers. If that advice is worth anything, our line managers ought to be willing to pay for it.

I propose that our staff departments be set up on a consulting basis. They are to bill the line departments for any work done at a mutually agreed-upon price. The entire budget of the staff departments will consist of money earned in this fashion. No line manager will be charged for any staff services he does not desire. As usual, line departments will be evaluated upon their profitability, after deduction of funds paid to staff departments.

I shall appreciate your prompt cooperation in implementing this policy.

N.J.F.

The memo from President Forrester represented a radical change because the budgets of staff departments had previously been determined each year by the president. Visibly upset by the president's memo, Jack Worthy, administrative vice president, replied as follows:

November 19

From: J. P. Worthy, Administrative
            Vice President
To: N. J. Forrester, President
Re: Line and Staff Relationships

Your proposal of November 12 would effectively wreck the accounting, production control, industrial relations, public relations, and other staff departments for which I am responsible.

We do give advice to line functions, but we are also responsible for checking on, and in some ways supervising, the line. Most line managers would be glad to have us out of their hair; they certainly would not "hire" us, as suggested in your memo. I urge that you immediately withdraw your recommendation to put us on consulting basis.

J.P.W.

---

* From: J. Belasco, D. Hampton and K. Price, *Management Today* (New York: John Wiley & Sons, Inc., 1974), pp. 280–81.

Questions

1. What assumptions did Mr. Forrester make about the nature of line-staff relations?
2. What assumptions about the division of labor between line and staff did Mr. Worthy make in his memo of November 19?
3. If you were Mr. Worthy, what would you do? Why?

CASE 2: THE SPIDER WEB*

T. R. Ronson, the president and majority stockholder of a large construction company bearing his name, was explaining his organizational structure to William Prince in the process of exploring the possibility of Prince's employment in Ronson's company as the director of managerial development. Ronson had been considering creating such a position for many years, but for a variety of reasons, he had never actually hired someone to fill it.

Ronson had numerous outside interests; he owned an office building, an insurance company, and was extremely active in church and public affairs. These interests did not seem to interfere with his presidency of the Ronson Construction Company.

"I think that you will find the organizational chart of my company different from any that you have ever seen. Here we have no pyramid, no layers. I visualize myself as the center of a network, surrounded by all my chief assistants. They tell me what to do, not the other way around. Here is a chart which I don't show to many people." With those remarks he reached into a desk drawer and took out the chart shown in Exhibit 1. He did not ask for any opinion, and Prince did not volunteer any.

After some more general conversation, in which Prince's experience, education, and salary needs were briefly touched on, Ronson called in Arnold Duffer, his special assistant and a classmate of Prince at a graduate school of business. Prince and Duffer went to Duffer's office. While they were discussing problems and opportunities at the company, one of the vice presidents, Mr. Miles, dropped in, "I'm sorry to interrupt you, Arnold, but I badly need a preliminary PERT network and an estimate for the Bravos contract. The estimators either can't or won't do it for me. Can you put some pressure on them, so they will know that my request is important?"

"Miles, I'll look into the matter this afternoon and let you know as soon as I have an answer."

* From: Richard N. Farmer, Barry M. Richman, and William G. Ryan, *Incidents for Studying Management and Organization.* © 1970 by Wadsworth Publishing Company, Belmont, California 94002. Reprinted by permission of the publisher.

Exhibit 1

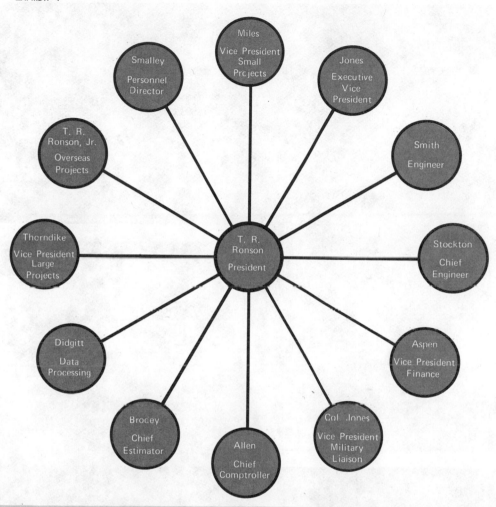

Prince left the office shortly thereafter to catch a plane back to his home. Two days later he received a letter from Ronson, containing a very substantial offer of employment. The letter proposed a fine salary, wonderful fringe benefits, a company car, a large insurance policy, and so forth. Prince declined this offer, although he had received no other.

Questions

1. In your opinion, why did Prince decline the offer?
2. What do you think of the organizational structure depicted in Exhibit 1?

Level of Organizational Outputs

| SELECTION OF THE PRODUCT OR SERVICE | DESIGN OF THE SYSTEM | STAFFING THE ORGANIZATION | STARTUP OF THE ORGANIZATION | OPERATING THE ORGANIZATION IN THE STEADY STATE | IMPROVING THE ORGANIZATION | REVISION OF THE ORGANIZATION | TERMINATION OF THE ORGANIZATION |

0

t_0

Time →

| Decision-making processes; social value; goals; forecasts; policies; plans | Authority and responsibility; power; organizational structure; communications systems; job design | Work force planning; personnel management functions | Startup planning and scheduling; monitoring; alternative startup approaches | Motivation; leadership; production and operations management; control | Individual improvement programs and techniques; group conflict management; MBO | Evaluation of organizational policies; strategic choices; organizational change; organizational development | Partial terminations; cutback management; complete terminations; mergers; born-again strategies |

Chapter 6
Organizational communication and information

While we perhaps once believed that Mankind's ability to communicate differentiated us from other creatures on Earth, it is now apparent that Man is not the only animal that communicates. The "Song of the Humpback Whale" provides substantial evidence of communicative ability.[1] Further, "danger signals" are given out by prairie dogs, monkeys, and other animals to call attention to invaders or other threats.

Exhibit 6–1
Far-out communications

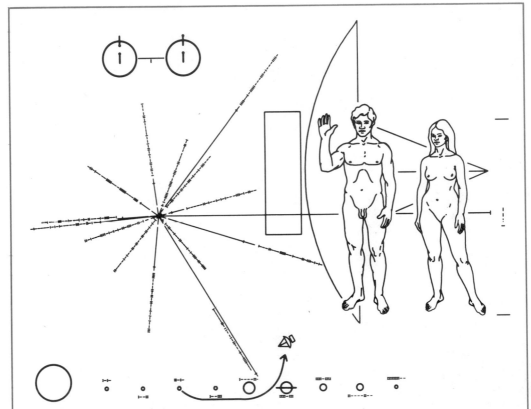

Carl Sagan, a Cornell University astronomer, is a seeker of extraterrestrial life. He and his wife, Linda, designed the plaque above which was attached to the *Pioneer 10* and *11* space vehicles. The plaque communicates many things in scientific fashion that other intelligent life should be able to understand. It shows, among other things, a map of our solar system along with hints as to its location, the dominant forms of life, and hydrogen atoms. Using the hydrogen atom as a reference, the size of the humans pictured is calculated. The *Voyager* vehicle launched in August 1978 carried on it a porcelain cartridge, diamond stylus, and a copper phonograph record sprayed with gold. Playing instructions in "scientific" language were included. Among many other things, the record contains greetings in 60 languages and sounds of a volcano, avalanche, surf, and animals. Songs range from Bach's Brandenburg Concerto No. 2, first movement, to "Johnny B. Goode" by Chuck Berry.

In perhaps the most noteworthy effort, Francine Patterson, a Stanford University graduate student, has taught Koko, a young female gorilla, to actually hold conversations using sign language as used by deaf humans.[2] Koko has a vocabulary of almost 400 words and has even learned how to lie! Recently, Koko was presented an infant gorilla to raise in an effort to see if she would pass on her language ability. Indeed, Rex Harrison may soon *really* be talking to the animals! Our *ability* to communicate [via a language (spoken and written), our actions, body language, music, paintings, sculpture, our dress, laughter, cries, and so on] is probably exceeded only by our *desire* to communicate. In 1978 the United States sent into space a small package that is our attempt to "speak" with inhabitants of other worlds (see Exhibit 6–1). Indeed, it is a rare person who does not feel compelled to, in some way, send messages of some sort to others.

As managers we must be aware of the many mechanisms by which people communicate as well as understand the benefits and pitfalls associated with these mechanisms. The person who controls the flow of information in a system controls that system.

In this chapter we will first discuss communications as a social process. What is it? How does it occur? What needs to be done or avoided to ensure "good" communications? Next, we will consider the role of the manager as an information center, and then move to the formal and informal tools at the manager's disposal in any organization. We will follow this with a discussion of management information systems and conclude with a comparison of how effective and ineffective organizations deal with a number of communication variables.

THE COMMUNICATION PROCESS

Communication is, quite simply, a transfer of information between two (or more) individuals.* Exhibit 6–2 shows a model of the communications process. Imagine that the sender and receiver are two men working in an office. It is warm in the office and the sender wants the other person to turn on the air conditioner switch. This "want" is the sender's *idea*. He then *encodes* this idea. What takes place here is a remarkably sophisticated process. The sender must decide how to approach the other person, whether to use language (i.e., words) or actions (e.g., panting and wiping brow with handkerchief while pointing at the switch). If language is chosen, he must decide what words to use, in what tone of voice, the rate and loudness of speaking, and so on. This is the *encoding* process. The idea to be communicated becomes a series of symbols in the mind of the sender to be used in expressing that idea.

---

* This definition allows for human-animal communications as with Francine Patterson using sign language with Koko or even giving commands to a pet dog (who, by the way, communicates back to you via barks, tail-wagging, or other such behavior).

Exhibit 6–2
A model of the communication process

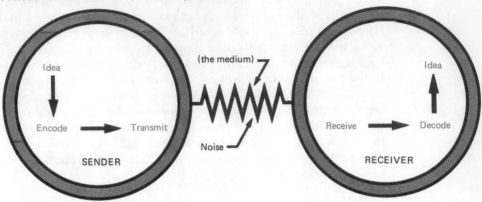

Next the message is *transmitted*. A memo might be written, the actions (panting, pointing) taken, or words spoken. Let's say the choice here is encoding with English language words to be spoken. The proper "sounds" are then made. For example, several approaches could be used:

a. Bill, please turn on the air conditioner switch.
b. Turn on the switch.
c. It sure is hot. Would you mind turning on the air conditioner?
d. It would sure be nice to have the air conditioner on.

The transmission passes through a medium, here air in which certain vibrations occur. (These vibrations are the sound waves.) "Noise" can occur, and other sound waves may mask ours. For example, a radio, telephone, airplane passing overhead, and so on all make "noise." Any interfering sound waves are noise, even a beautiful (but "interfering") symphony.

The sound waves reach the receiver's ear along with any other ambient sound waves. The message is thus *received*. Somehow, using mental processes that we do not yet fully comprehend, these sound waves are themselves converted into coded symbols within the receiver's mind. This is the *decoding* step. Finally, these decoded symbols are converted into an *idea* in the mind of the receiver.

The prime basis upon which we judge this communication process is whether the idea sent is the same as the idea received. The receiver may well receive the idea correctly (i.e., "he wants me to turn on the air conditioner switch"), but not take the action desired by the sender (e.g., refuse to turn on the switch). The communication per se was a success. It simply did not lead to the sender's desired result, and that is a problem of another kind.

Intricacies of encoding and decoding

As we noted, symbols are used in the communication process. Words, actions, and so on are, indeed, simply symbols. As noted by Lewis Carroll,

"When I use a word," Humpty Dumpty said, in rather a scornful tone, "it means just what I choose it to mean—neither more nor less."

"The question is," said Alice, "whether you *can* make words mean so many different things."

"The question is," said Humpty Dumpty, "which is to be master—that's all."[3]

Could not you and someone else agree that henceforth the letter *X* will stand for "table" and the letter *Y* will stand for "book?" The phrase "put the *Y* on the *X*" could, then, be "understood." There is nothing sacred about words. They are only symbols and can be altered at any time. As long as the "correct" symbols are encoded so as to result in the receiver decoding them to make the idea sent and the idea received the same, we, like Humpty Dumpty, can use any symbols to represent any meaning that we desire. Remember, words are *not* the thing that they represent. They are symbols that have meaning only in the mind.

How do words acquire meaning? The process of learning a language is a start. There is, à la a dictionary, a body of words with somewhat "standardized" meanings. Words also take on meaning by our experiences. Take the phrase "in a few minutes." Ask several people to write down *exactly* how much time (in minutes) that phrase means to them. Your answers will probably vary anywhere from 2 on up to, say, 10 or 12; maybe even higher. Why can't people agree on such a common, widely used phrase? Because, we all impart meaning based on experiences. Imagine that your mother once said, "You better be home in a few minutes." You then stayed away for ten minutes, came home and received a verbal (maybe even physical) lashing for staying away longer than "a few minutes." You learned something—Mom's conception of a few minutes is certainly less than ten. By age six or seven, you probably knew exactly how long "a few minutes" were to your mother. You maybe knew that to Sally's mother, it meant "less than three" but Bill's mother meant "five to six." By observing, asking questions, and so on you may eventually know what your father, your boss, your teacher, "mean" by the phrase "in a few minutes." Thus, when you receive a transmission containing the symbolic phrase "in a few minutes" you decode in light of the source. The true meaning is thus not inherent in the symbol alone.

What does this imply? It implies that *if,* for example, you honestly believe that Sue interprets "in a few minutes" as between six and seven and you want her to deliver something to you in less than four minutes, you should *not* tell her to deliver it "in a few minutes." If you do go ahead anyway, she will come two to three minutes later than you wanted. *And it is your fault.*

You knew how she would decode the symbols and you deliberately chose to send a set of symbols that would result in the idea sent *not* being the idea received.

False perceptions

We go through life acquiring information which we use in the decoding process. For example, look at the three triangles below and read the phrases:

Most people read these as "Snake in the grass," "Busy as a beaver," and "Paris in the spring." They are wrong, of course; take a closer look at the phrases in the triangles. What happens is that the phrases are so "common" to us that when someone says, "Snake in the" the word "grass" immediately comes to mind. We often gloss over typographical errors, and fail to accurately perceive many other things in life because of this perceptual problem.

Unfortunately, even when we are aware of the importance of perceptions and of the fact that words are *just* symbols, we still may fall victim to inappropriately linking "things" and "word labels." Consider the following true story reported by William Haney:

An incident occurred several years ago while the late Professor Irving J. Lee was giving his exceedingly popular course, "Language and Thought," at Northwestern University. Dr. Lee had several graduate assistants who were occasionally given the opportunity to lecture before a class of 200 to 300 undergraduates. On one such occasion, an assistant set out to "dramatize" the tendency to react to labels rather than to the objects the labels represented. He distributed bits of food that resembled dried biscuits and assured the class that the food was sanitary and nutritional and added that most of them had probably never eaten this type of food before. Each student was to taste the food and decide how much he liked or disliked it. Most students found it relatively tasteless and reported an indifferent reaction. A few said they liked it slightly and even fewer expressed a mild dislike. Not *one* said he liked or disliked it extremely.

The assistant tabulated the results on the blackboard and suggested that perhaps the food would be more tasty with cream and sugar. He added that it was quite inexpensive and readily available. At this point he reached behind his desk and held up a large, distinctly labeled box and said, "Just go to your grocer's and ask for _____ Dog Biscuits." The reaction was precisely what he had hoped for—a great deal of groaning, shrieking, laughing, feigned nausea (and some not so feigned). Whereupon he triumphantly cried out: "Now, just what are you reacting to—those innocuous bits of food—or to the words on this box!"

Elated by his success, the assistant repeated his "dramatization" in the next term. But the word had spread and students came to expect such things from the course "where they served dog biscuits." Undiscouraged, he changed his tactic. He baked some "special" cookies, passed them out to the class, and tabulated the results. The cookies were sweet and the reactions were unanimously favorable.

"Glad you liked them, I'll give you the recipe," he volunteered, "so you can bake some at home if you wish." The recipe: So much flour, sugar, shortening, . . . and two cups of carefully cleaned grasshoppers!

He admitted later that, even had he been able to restore order, he would not have dared to ask: "Now, what are you throwing up about?!"[4]

COMMUNICATION PITFALLS[5]

There are a number of important communication pitfalls which can trap the unwary manager. The following are some of the more common, yet avoidable, ones.

Bypassing

The same word can mean different things to different people. Our "in a few minutes" example mentioned earlier is a classic bypassing problem. The multiple-meaning characteristic of many words in the English language contributes to this problem. How many different usages can you think of for the word "fast"?

To run *fast.*
To be *fast* asleep.
To be in *fast* company.
To *fast,* as to refrain from eating.
Fast photographic film.
To be tied down and made *fast.*
To dye a cloth with *fast* colors.
A *fast* racetrack.
A *fast* wristwatch.
Fast (i.e., insensitive) bacteria, and so on.

How about "stock"?

A gun's *stock.*
Soup *stock.*
Stock in a company, and so on.

Exhibit 6-3
A police department's radio code signals

Code	Meaning		Phonetic alphabet	
10– 1	Receiving poorly	10–42	Malicious mischief at _____	A Adam
10– 2	Receiving well	10–43	Armed robbery	B Boy
10– 3	Stop transmitting	10–45	Meet party at _____	C Charles
10– 4	Message received OK	10–46	Gas your unit	D David
10– 5	Relay message	10–47	Winter uniform with coat	E Edward
10– 6	Busy, stand by	10–48	Winter uniform without coat	F Frank
10– 7	Out of service	10–50	Auto accident, property damage	G George
10– 8	In service	10–51	Auto accident, wrecker on way	H Henry
10– 9	Repeat message	10–52	Auto accident, persons injured, ambulance	I Ida
10–10	Out of service (subject to call)		dispatched	J John
10–12	Call in reports	10–53	Auto accident, fatal	K King
10–13	Any unit having report to make come in for	10–55	Drunk driver	L Lincoln
	traffic	10–58	Is wrecker on way?	M Mary
10–14	Convoy or escort	10–59	Is ambulance on way?	N Nora
10–15	Have prisoner in custody	10–61	What are the storm conditions in your area?	O Ocean
10–16	Pick up prisoner at _____	10–62	Check your arroyos, subways, dips, for rising	P Paul
10–18	Complete assignment as soon as possible		water	Q Queen
10–19	Return to station	10–63	Need barricades at _____	R Robert
10–20	What is your location?	10–64	Need flare pots at _____	S Sam
10–21	Call _____ by Telephone	10–70	Fire follow up at _____	

10-25 Come in for traffic
10-26 Holding subject—Rush reply
10-27 Request driver's license information
10-28 Check for full registration
10-29 Check for wanted or stolen
10-30 Vacation home check at _____
10-31 Family fight at _____
10-32 Drunk disturbance at _____
10-33 Disturbance at _____
10-34 Bogus check at _____
10-35 Larceny at _____
10-36 Burglary at _____
10-37 Burglary in progress at _____
10-38 Fingerprint kit—Take to _____
10-39 Major crime, quad set up—All units remain
         10-8 and 10-3
10-40 Prowler at _____
10-41 Drunk at _____

10-76 Fire equipment needed at _____
10-77 Grass/brush fire at _____
10-78 Set up command post
10-79 Report progress of fire
10-81 Stop for interrogation _____
10-82 Stop for interrogation, arrest or cite if possible
10-83 Units stop transmitting. You are covering
         other unit
10-84 Follow up _____
10-91–A Reporting to F-1
         or
10-91–B Change to F-1
10-92–A Reporting to F-2
         or
10-92–B Change to F-2
10-98 At Pima County Juvenile Court Center
10-99 Emergency traffic

V   Victor
W   William
X   Xray
Y   Young
Z   Zebra

Note: This replaces and supersedes the Radio 10 Series Code attached to 6-'0.506 dated 26 March 1967.

Source: Tucson, Arizona, Police Department.

There are ways to avoid many bypassing problems. First, be aware of the sender or receiver and look for words' meanings to the other *person*, not in the words themselves. You know what a word means to you, *but* what does it mean to the other person? Ask questions when in doubt. "Oh, you need this back in a few minutes. May I keep it until 3:15?" Finally, look for the context. A plaintive cry of "help" means one thing if it is a person standing in ankle-deep water with a burst pipe and still something else if the water is shoulder high and rising quickly.

Jargon or coded communications are useful in avoiding bypassing problems. Radio communications between control towers and pilots or dispatchers and

Exhibit 6–4
Illustrative CB radio transmission

> **Person 1:** Breaker 1–9 for that westbound 18-wheel thermos bottle at the 399 heading for Shaky City.
>
> **Person 2:** Hey, you got the Catalina Cowboy. Come back.
>
> **Person 1:** This is the Crazy Fox in that Cowboy Cadillac on the eastbound side. You got a Smokey takin' pictures at the 405. Better comb your hair and smile with a double nickel. How's it over your shoulder?
>
> **Person 2:** 10–4 on that bear. You're clean and green. Last thing I saw was way back at the 301. Had a County Mountie in a green wrapper flip-floppin'.
>
> **Person 1:** 10–4. Have a good one. We'll catch you on the flip side.
>
> Translation of this Citizen Band (CB) radio conversation between two motorists on Channel 19, the channel used by most highway travelers:
>
> **Person 1:** Attention all of you on Channel 19. I would like to talk with the tractor trailer tanker going west (toward Los Angeles) who is currently at the 399-mile marker.
>
> **Person 2:** This is the driver of that truck. My radio name is the Catalina Cowboy. What do you want?
>
> **Person 1:** My radio name is Crazy Fox and I'm driving a pickup truck on the other side of the road (going east). There is a police officer using radar to catch speeders at the 405-mile marker. You should make sure you're driving carefully at 55 miles per hour. How are driving conditions behind you (the direction I'm heading); especially, are there any police?
>
> **Person 2:** Thanks for telling me about that police officer. The road conditions are fine. I haven't heard of or seen any police in the area immediately behind me. There was a county sheriff in a green car at the 301-mile marker (98 miles back) who was driving a mile or so in the eastbound lane and then crossing the median to drive back a mile or so in the westbound lane, and so on.
>
> **Person 1:** Thanks. I received your message. Drive safely. If we pass on the return trip and I recognize your truck or your name on the radio, I'll say hello.

police officers made good use of this. Exhibit 6–3 shows some police radio code signals. There is no mistake between what a "10–43 in progress" is and what a "10–37" is. An officer responding to either of these will/should use different behaviors. It is far easier, faster, and more accurate for the dispatcher to simply use a 10-code rather than explain over the radio, in conversational English, what the call is all about.

Another example of radio jargon is shown in Exhibit 6–4. While more colloquial than police transmissions, it is nonetheless standardized.

Allness

Allness occurs when you think you've said all there is on a subject when, in fact, all you have done is to say what you can think of at a particular moment. "Listen" in on what takes place at a barber shop, beauty salon, or in a "Letters to the Editor" column of a newspaper. Many people fall into the "know-it-*allness*" trap. Try to *completely* describe something simple such as a piece of chalk or a pencil. Be careful!

One aspect of allness is stereotyping. Too often, we judge a whole on the basis of a part. He's a redheaded Irishman. She's a dumb blonde. Or, he's a typical used car salesman. In a humorous little poem, John G. Saxe tells of six blind men who confront an elephant.[6] The first man runs into the elephant's side and contends that an elephant is like a wall. The second grasps a tusk and says an elephant is like a spear. The third feels the trunk and exclaims that an elephant resembles a large snake. Feeling about the elephant's knee, the fourth compares it to a tree. The fifth encounters an ear and believes an elephant is like a fan. And, upon seizing the tail, the sixth swears that an elephant is like a rope. Who is right? All of them, partly! And wrong? Again, all of them!

How does one overcome allness? First, be humble. Admit that you don't know it all and don't communicate with people in a manner that leads them to believe otherwise. Realize that virtually everything you say is an abstraction of an ever broader reality. And, finally, realize that the sender, like the blind men, might not be as aware of the allness problem as you.

The "frozen evaluation"

Times change. People change. Too many people forget that. When you read or hear something, ask yourself "when?" A friend once said that he always dreamed of living in a $100,000 house. Little did he realize that it would be the one he bought for $25,000 that is now (due to inflation) worth over $100,000!

Either/or thinking

For the following words, think of the opposites:

Black   . . . .   _____
Honest   . . . .   _____
Correct   . . . .   _____
Cold   . . . .   _____
Polite   . . . .   _____

Did you, like most people, say white, dishonest, wrong (or incorrect), hot, and impolite? Fine. Now fill in the "in-betweens" on each of the scales. That is, what is a word that fits half way between, say, polite and impolite? What goes between this "center" word and the two end words?

It's not easy, is it?

In a fascinating article, Albert Rothenberg talks about many of the human race's most creative achievements coming about because of an awareness of a tension between opposites.[7] "Janusian thinking," as Rothenberg calls it (after the Roman god Janus who was able to look in two directions at once), is predicated on the ability to conceive of opposites existing simultaneously, equally operative, and valid. Creative people score quite well on their abilities to take word tests such as the one above.

It is easy to speak about the ends, or contrary positions. When you find yourself (or someone else) doing that, stop for a moment and examine the middle ground. It covers a lot more area and is usually more descriptive of reality.

Undelayed (thalamic) reactions

As we noted in Chapter 2, "Managerial Decision Making," society values people who act decisively. Too often, however, we equate decisiveness and "quick" reactions. Such quickness is fine for reflex actions. A knee's jerk when tapped just below the patella or the contraction of the eye's pupil when a light shines into it are examples of (desirable) fast reactions controlled by the brain's thalamus. Other actions are more voluntary. For example, spell your name backwards. Multiply your age by three. These involve "thinking" and are delayed reactions.

Most administrative issues do not require instantaneous reflex actions. Practice an old adage that your parents probably gave you: think before you speak. In addition, always be aware that the other person might not have had such intelligent parents. Therefore, be careful of saying things that could well *evoke* an undelayed, reflex-like response. For example, never start conversations like these:

> To a harried, behind schedule foreman: "Bill, I have to shut your line down for two hours today. . . ."
> To a CPA: "It doesn't balance. . . ."
> To a guard at a prison: "They're not all here. . . ."
> To a surgeon in an operating room: "Oops. . . ."

You will probably never be able to finish:

> To the foreman, ". . . but I'll be able to install a new gizmo that will more than make up the lost production by morning and give you double output forever and ever!"
> To the CPA, ". . . but it's not your fault and I've already corrected it."
> To the guard, ". . . because two prisoners are in court today."
> To the surgeon, ". . . I forgot to feed my cat this morning."

. . . . before they "fly off the handle" or faint.

Misuse of small talk

Beware of mistaking casual conversations that are merely attempts to be pleasant with real attempts to convey information. The big boss saying to a young management trainee, "Stop by my office anytime," will probably mean one thing after several drinks at an office party and something else toward the end of a difficult, but well-presented position paper during a staff meeting.

This is not to say that good contacts can't be made in social gatherings or that casual comments/rumors made after several cocktails aren't ever true. Just remember and evaluate the source and the situation.

NONVERBAL COMMUNICATION

> Fie, fie upon her!
> There's language in her eye, her cheek,
>   her lip,
> Nay, her foot speaks; her wanton spirits look out
> At every joint and motive of her body.[8]

As most successful poker players know, nonverbal cues such as a quivering lip, enlarged pupils, a smile, and so on mean something. Julius Fast, in his book, *Body Language,* analyzed what he called kinesics; i.e., body language.[9] Most body cues, he feels, are culturally induced and unconsciously (but "truthfully") exhibited.

Michael Argyris has identified a number of important nonverbal areas.[10]

First are static features. (1) *Distance*. How close one stands to another often has sexual or hostile meanings. This distance, as will be noted later, is culturally derived.* (2) *Orientation*. Side by side, back to back, turning one's back on someone, and so on all have connotations. Queen Elizabeth's chair in public places is always one inch higher than her husband's; after all she is the Queen and he is just a Prince. (3) *Posture*. Being seated or standing at various times *means* something. Further, for example, whether one sits or "slumps" says something. (4) *Physical contact*. Touching, holding, kissing, and so on are outward signals. Note how, even on a busy sidewalk, you can often "tell" if two people are "with" each other or if they are strangers who are simply walking closely together.

There are also dynamic features:

1. *Facial expressions.* Smiles, frowns, yawns, and the like all convey a message.
2. *Gestures.* While many gestures are "universal" (e.g., clenched fist, surrender via holding hands up), others aren't.†
3. *Looking.* Eye contact is the secret of the panhandler. Staring at people means something. The lowering of one's gaze is thought to have a sexual connotation.

In a book written some years ago, but still valid nevertheless, Edward T. Hall *(The Silent Language)* discusses the use of time and space as communicative devices; especially in cultures other than our own. Americans tend to view time as a line stretching into the future along which things can be planned. To be late to appointments or to keep someone who has an appointment with you waiting "says" something to an American. In Latin America, time is viewed differently. "¿Hora Americana, hora mexicana?" (American or Mexican time?) is a not too unheard of phrase when Americans do business south of the border. It is not uncommon for a visitor to an office to have to wait 45 minutes or an hour before being allowed to see the person with whom an appointment was made. It would be an insult to have to "cool one's heels" that long in New York, Washington, D.C., or most other U.S. cities.

Americans attempting to do business in China or Japan experience similar problems. It would not be unreasonable (to the Chinese) to expect an American to fly to China and then wait one, two, three, or more *weeks* before being allowed to see the merchant or other important person who is the object of the trip. To do business too fast in that culture is as serious an affront as to force people to cool their heels in ours. When in Rome, at least understand what the Romans are up to.

---

* An interesting experiment is, upon entering an elevator occupied by only one other person, to stand right behind that person or at least as close as possible! What does (would) this connote? Would the sex of the two people matter?

† One author remembers a fellow University of Texas student who reported that the first time his New Yorker mother watched a Texas football game, she thought that the "Hook 'em Horns" sign was an obscene gesture.

Space, too, communicates. How close can a business acquaintance get to you before you feel "crowded" or intimidated? In America somewhere between three and eight feet is a "normal" distance.

In Latin America the interaction distance is much less than it is in the United States. Indeed people cannot talk comfortably with one another unless they are very close to a distance that evokes either sexual or hostile feelings in the North American. The result is that when they move close, we withdraw and back away. As a consequence they think we are distant or cold, withdrawn and unfriendly. We, on the other hand, are constantly accusing them of breathing down our necks, crowding us, and spraying our faces.[11]

THE MANAGER AS AN INFORMATION CENTER

In Chapter 1, we listed the roles of the manager according to Mintzberg. Included in this list were the three informational roles of *monitor, disseminator,* and *spokesperson*. In the role of monitor, the manager is concerned with data gathering in order to understand what is going on inside and outside the organization. "He seeks information in order to detect changes, to identify problems and opportunities, to build up knowledge about his milieu, to be informed when information must be disseminated and decisions made."[12] As a disseminator, the manager sends "external information into his organization and internal information from one subordinate to another"; and as a spokesperson, "the manager transmits information out to his organization environment."[13]

To accomplish these roles effectively requires not only that the manager be an effective communicator (know how to listen, give orders, and instructions) but know how to use as well the tools of information flow which are commonly found in organizations.

THE TOOLS OF INFORMATION FLOW

The various tools of information flow* can be grouped into formal and informal categories as follows:

Formal tools	*Informal tools*
Memos and letters	Unscheduled meetings
In-house publications	Grapevines
Reports (routine & nonroutine)	Telephoning
Scheduled meetings (committees, conferences, speeches)	Observation and Inference
Bulletin boards	

---

* The focus in this chapter is on *intra*organizational communication. However, many of these devices are used in interorganizational and extraorganizational communication as well.

Formal tools

Memos and letters.   Memos are generally for intraorganizational use and have a standardized heading format—i.e., To:, Re:, From:, Date. Letters, on the other hand, are generally for interorganizational use and contain both introductory and concluding statements. Together, these documents account for the major formal information vehicles for managers in large organizations. This is not to say that managers treat either of these mediums as particularly important in their jobs. Regarding *incoming* mail (containing both memos and letters) Mintzberg observed that managers considered only 13 percent of it to be of "specific and immediate use." This "important" mail consisted of requests for authorization, advice on current situations, and problems related directly to the manager's job. Regarding outgoing mail, Mintzberg notes that the executives he studied averaged only one piece of correspondence per day, about half of which were replies to or acknowledgements of incoming mail.[14] From Mintzberg's studies and others, the following observations can be made about memos and letters:

1. Managers don't like them, most preferring face-to-face communication.
2. They can, if not screened by a secretary, waste the manager's time.
3. Subordinates are likely to have to deal with a large percentage of those requiring action since the manager will forward a sizable percentage to them.
4. Memos and letters are subject to criticism because *(a)* they are hard to write, *(b)* they take time to reach their recipient, *(c)* they are prone to misinterpretation, *(d)* feedback is delayed, *(e)* copies must often be reread and hence retrieved from a filing system, taking time and effort, *(f)* they can cause organizational problems if they are routed to the wrong people; or if some individuals *don't* get a copy, *(g)* they provide hard evidence of management decisions.*

Admiral Hyman Rickover (the father of the nuclear submarine) is one manager, however, who paid a great deal of attention to written documents. Recalling his days as a staff officer to Rickover, one of our colleagues at the University of Arizona reports that pink onionskin copies of *all* written documents originating in Rickover's division had to be routed to him each day by 4:30 P.M. (Any document that was not received by the division or completed internally by 4:30 was to be so noted and sent to him the following day.) He would then go through each item the same evening and require face-to-face answers to any questions the following morning. The Admiral insisted that the author of each document, and his supervisor, understand and be able to explain each item to his satisfaction; and woe to him who was not prepared to do so. As used by Rickover, the "pinks" were a valuable general communications tool. They were required reading for all Rickover's top navy and civilian personnel.

---

* This is, of course, a two-edged sword. If the manager was right, he or she has proof; if wrong, "they can be presented at the trial."

(As an aside, Rickover's demand for immediate feedback was so strong that when he summoned one of his officers to his office by phone, that officer's secretary had to stay on the line until the officer had left so she could report, "He's on his way over now.")

Joe Mancuso argues that memos can be used as a weapon in organizational politics and oneupsmanship battles.[15] The battle plan works on a point basis. If you receive a hostile or malicious memo from someone, rank it as follows:

	Points
If it is from someone who outranks you	4
If it is from someone equal or quite close in rank to you	2
If it is from someone who ranks below you	1

Next look at who received carbon copies. Each carbon recipient counts 4, 2, or 1 point(s) as above. Next, place a point value on the memo's contents. The mechanics are explained in Exhibit 6–5. Add up the total point value for the memo.

To retaliate you must write an equally hostile memo back to the original sender and "carbon in" people such that your memo's points add up to more points than the one you received.

Note that the typical method of listing carbon copy recipients is by name at the bottom of the memo in order of people's organizational rank. A mean trick is to deliberately take a person out of that order and place him or her at the end of the list. To twist the knife you could even misspell the name. All of this is intended to make a person feel less important and a little threatened and hence vulnerable.

Why do we tell you this? Because we strongly advocate these tactics? Not really, but you will encounter people who play the game this way, so you may as well be prepared to, as the boxing referee says, "protect yourself at all times."

In-house publications (such as newsletters) rarely, if ever, contain important and/or fresh information. They are used primarily as a means of recognizing good works of employees and announcements of general interest. The publisher of the "house organ" is usually of low organizational rank and is expected *never* to publish any controversial items. If a manager has to rely on this as a primary information source, he or she is in serious trouble.

Routine reports are those which come out at a specific time period on a regular basis. The critical routine reports for the typical manager are the

Exhibit 6–5
Memo points (for each person in the three categories below receiving a copy
of the memo, add the appropriate number of points)

	Vulnerable*	Not vulnerable†
Section 1		
1. People higher than you in the organization	7	4
2. Your organization peers	3	2
3. People below you in the organization	1	1
Add the following points to the score for each person in the prescribed category receiving a copy of the memo regardless of organizational rank:		
Section 2		
a. Blind carbon copies	2	1
b. Presidents	6	3
c. Members of the board of directors	7	4
Add the following points to the score for memo contents:		
Section 3		
d. If numbers are utilized to emphasize a point (dollars, time, etc.)	10	5
e. Quotations used	6	4
f. Harsh or foul language used	4	2

Note: Total score obtained by adding sections 1, 2, and 3.

* Vulnerable—only use the vulnerable scoring system when the memo is of impact in your climb up the corporate ladder.

† Not vulnerable—use the not vulnerable system when the memo will not affect your climb up the corporate ladder.

Source: Joe Mancuso, *No Guts—No Glory* (Port Washington, N.Y.: Ashley Books, Inc., 1976), p. 85.

departmental budget and the department's goals in the annual revision of the company's long-range plan. These documents tell the manager what is expected of the department and what resources are available to meet these expectations. It is undeniable that certain other routine reports are indispensible to management—profit and loss statements, hospital occupancy rate, steel tonnage shipped, factory inventory turnover, insurance claims filed, and so on. However, routine reports have a major shortcoming—they are usually too late for corrective action. To discover that for the past month an airline operated at a 50 percent seat occupancy rate does nothing to get the lost revenue back. It can only be used (perhaps) to spot trends and argue for a different route or pricing structure in the future. A second problem with routine reports is that they are rarely used selectively—often everybody gets a copy which means that everybody must sift through the material, file the report, or decide simply not to read it. A final problem, which stems from their mass circulation, is that they are not in the form usable to many if not most of the recipients. This is especially true of reports created by accounting departments, which are designed around accounting needs and conventions—not for the use of operating managers. Finally, some people find them impossible to throw out.*

Recognition of such problems with routine reports can, however, be a boon to the new manager. As Caplow states, "The easiest way to make one's mark as a manager is to improve the quality of routine reports the organization produces. . . ."[17] This is so because few people understand the importance of routine reporting or how to set up a reporting system. Furthermore, even good systems deteriorate over time and therefore would benefit from an analysis of their strengths and weaknesses.

For the individual manager, revising the routine reports which he or she receives requires first that they be prioritized as A, B, or C (or "1, 2, 3"), according to the manager's particular needs: "A" priority reports are those that the manager looks at the minute they come out, with no expense spared to assure their accuracy, completeness, and clarity. "B" priority reports are those which are examined and filed, and "C" reports are those which have little or no interest and if possible are eliminated at the source. Once the reports have been prioritized, the next step is to make sure that the report form is correctly designed. Some of the characteristics of a well-designed report are:

1. Indicates space for preparer, receiver(s), date, time period covered.
2. Should deal with specific rather than general information. Numbers, graphs, outlines attract attention better than general discussions.
3. Provides comparative data—relative to a standard or goal in + or − terms.
4. Indicates variation from past reporting periods—i.e., percentage change, statistical deviation.
5. Indicates trends in major variables in graphical or numerical form.
6. Most importantly, highlights exceptional information; e.g., dominance in a new market, impact of a new regulation, probability of a strike.

Nonroutine reports, if they deal with a significant organizational problem, are termed *special* reports. These reports are typically prepared by staff departments and deal with such questions as how do we get more business, how to cut costs, where do we locate the new franchise, or what should be in our new investment portfolio? Here again, the reports are most often too late for corrective action, but given that they are often developed for planning purposes (or in response to indicators on a routine report), this criticism is not too meaningful. A more valid criticism, however, lies in the common misuse of the special report, or more appropriately, the poor selection and execution

---

* The bookkeeper for Goldwyn Studios dropped in on his boss and said, "Mr. Goldwyn, our files are bulging with paperwork we no longer need. May I have your permission to destroy all our records before 1945?" "Certainly," replied Goldwyn. "Just be sure to keep a copy of everything."[16]

of it. In some organizations, the special report is make-work for individuals who, because of previous poor performance, have been given nothing of importance to do. Equally common is the report that though valid when initiated, becomes useless in the light of changed conditions, yet work on it continues nonetheless.*

Scheduled meetings

"Never just attend a meeting—Always 'win' it!"[18]

Committees.   Effective managers are generally highly skilled at committee-manship in the sense that they know when to set up a committee, when to disband one, how to chair one, and, most importantly, how to achieve their own goals from the meeting itself.

Committee meetings operate on two levels—the formal or content level and the informal or process level. The content level refers to the stated purpose of the committee as given in the agenda for the meeting; the process level refers to the unstated purpose which is on the "hidden agenda" members bring to the meeting. These content and process issues are self-explanatory and are given in Exhibit 6–6.

Exhibit 6–6
Content and process issues in committee meetings

Content issues or agenda items	Process issues or hidden agenda items
Inform	Obscure
Issue orders	Stonewall
Receive orders	Pass the buck
Develop alternatives	Rubber stamp
Make decisions	Display power
Consult	Obtain commitments
	Validate perceptions

The decisional power of a committee rests with the chairperson and to a lesser extent the formal agenda. Both of these features in turn reflect the relative importance of the committee within the organization. As a rule of thumb, the importance of a committee is directly proportional to the amount of money involved as a result of its recommendations. (Well-known, powerful committees in Congress include the House Ways and Means Committee and the Defense Appropriations Committee.)

---

* The ultimate result, if such individuals are "good" at this, is converting a special report to a routine report, thereby generating the need to retain the preparer.

Committees come in three varieties—standing committees, ad hoc committees, and special committees. *Standing committees* deal with repetitive issues calling for collective judgment; e.g., university curriculum committees, bank loan committees, and physician peer review committees. Standing committees work best with five to nine members. These sizes permit a diversity of views and at the low end (five) enable a majority vote of three which is likely to represent a range of constituent's views. Since the purposes of a standing committee are to obtain diversity of opinion and relieve the manager of administrative duties, the committee should not be chaired by the manager who sets it up. The chair of the committee should, however, be senior to other members of the committee since he or she will have to allocate work on occasion to the membership. (The manager may be an ex-officio member of the committee so that he or she may sit in when particular issues are considered.)

Ad hoc committees are normally appointed for some noncontroversial tasks such as selecting a new vendor, planning recreational activities, or preparing a notice for a newspaper. The manager's role in such a committee is usually nominal, such as supplying information to the membership.

Special committees may be established to deal with a difficult problem that can't be handled under the normal routine, to evidence concern (real or feigned) about some issue (Mayor Daley of Chicago was a master of this tactic) or to fulfill a ritual (e.g., a governmental "blue ribbon" committee to investigate UFO sightings). The membership of special committees should be broad enough to reflect a wide variety of interests in the organization as well as honoring individuals by inviting them to serve as members. "The best chairman for such a committee is a subordinate manager of considerable seniority, preferably with white hair and a good command of parliamentary procedure."[19]

Committee management. The formal agenda is of critical importance in most committees, yet we never cease to be amazed at how little effort is devoted to it in planning the meeting, and how little attention it is given during the conduct of the meeting. The result is that committee meetings inevitably go on too long and at best only partly accomplish their mission.* The blame for this mismanagement usually lies with the chairperson who does not appreciate the importance of the agenda and the need to stick with it. In preparing the agenda, the chair should balance the need to reach conclusions on specific issues with the desire for participation by all members of the committee. Since most committees are set up to render a recommendation to management, a good strategy is to develop at least two or three alternatives to be placed on the agenda itself. This gives the membership something to "chew on" before the meeting takes place.

---

* Several years ago a West German firm introduced a clocklike device into which each committee member's salary was programmed. In digital stopwatch fashion the device kept track of the amount of salary "used up" as a meeting progressed.

During the meeting, the chair should be both permissive and autocratic—permissive in the sense that diverse views are brought to light, autocratic in the sense of moving expeditiously from item to item, summarizing and initiating voting or consensus. There is a good reason to push committees toward fairly rapid decisions—committees are simply not too creative. The fact that members are representatives of other groups and bring with them one or two hidden agenda items virtually guarantees that no true innovation will arise from its deliberations.

Some rules of thumb for getting more from meetings are:

1. Start on time and quit on time.
2. Assign timekeeping and minutes responsibilities.
3. Hold a stand-up meeting (i.e., no chairs), if appropriate.
4. Start with and stick to the agenda.
5. Control interruptions (phone calls and beepers not permitted).
6. Chair should state his or her expectations about the meeting at the start.
7. Restate conclusions and assignments at completion.
8. Expedite the preparation of the minutes (48 hours maximum).
9. Use progress reports as inputs to the next meeting. Provide for "unfinished business" on the agenda.
10. Ask yourself if the meeting is necessary; then ask if the committee is. In this evaluation, don't forget the cost of the meeting in terms of members' salaries, overhead, travel, and lost time.

Conferences.   Performance reviews, providing instruction, presenting work schedules, and handling grievances are typical examples of formal conferences between the manager and the subordinates. Because these subjects fall under other headings in this book (e.g., leadership and motivation) we shall not dwell on them here, other than to point out that skillful managers don't treat these interactions lightly. They plan the conduct of these meetings and, above all, they appear organized and businesslike in carrying them out.

Bulletin boards.   Many organizations must use bulletin boards, since the law requires that safety regulations, fair employment practices, and so on be publicly posted. Who is "in charge" of bulletin boards usually doesn't matter much, however, great concern with bulletin boards indicates to us that the manager is out of touch, or can't cope with the real problems of the organization. In our study of school administrators, we found that those who had the greatest number of problems with teachers and parents were those who had the strictest rules for bulletin board control in the classrooms. Similarly, we have observed that administrators in business and universities begin to spend inordinate amounts of time studying and writing memos about bulletin boards when the organization is in turmoil. Thus, while there are obvious uses of bulletin boards in organizations, we tend to view excessive managerial concern with them as an indicator of other organizational problems.

Presentations.   Managers are occasionally called upon to make presentations before special committees. Staff personnel commonly make their recommendations both in writing and through formal presentations to line members. For those confronted with a presentation for the first time, our advice is careful organization and practice runs in front of friends. Many organizations are aware of the importance of good presentations as evidenced by the substantial market in audiovisual equipment and heavy enrollment in public speaking courses.

Informal tools

Unscheduled meetings.   Unscheduled meetings are, of course, a common way of exchanging information. However, the wary manager recognizes that what one says during these meetings even under the heading of "small talk" can be used for or against him or her. As Stephen Potter, author of satirical books on "gamesmanship" has said, certain individuals are always "in play." That is, they are always ready to take personal advantage from any interaction, no matter how casual.

The effectiveness of unscheduled meetings as information devices varies from manager to manager. Some managers as well as subordinates store questions in their minds on the off chance that they will be in contact with certain individuals during the day; thus while the exact time and place of the meeting is not planned, the information exchange process is. Hence, seemingly casual meetings are in fact carefully thought out intelligence forays.

Grapevines.   The following excerpt from "Banana Time" by Donald Roy conveys the spirit of a typical grapevine interaction.

The arrival of the pickup man [a material handler] was always a noisy one, like the arrival of a daily passenger train in an isolated small town. Interaction attained a quick peak of intensity to crowd into a few minutes all communications, necessary and otherwise. . . . During the course of the exchanges news items would be dropped, some of serious import, such as reports of accomplished or impending layoffs in the various plants of the company, or of gains or losses in orders for company products. Many of the news items, however, involved bits of information on plant employees told in a light vein.[20]

Such informal networks exist in every organization and fulfill the need which employees have for receiving information to which they would not have access through formal channels. The grapevine is notoriously fast, though its accuracy of information is always a question. Most experts agree that the grapevine is valuable for the manager if he or she has contacts in it (e.g., trusted staff members or secretaries) and can exercise some control over the information available to it. Though the grapevine is the epitome of informal communica-

Exhibit 6–7
Four grapevine forms

Type	Structure	Characteristics
"Single strand." Person A passes information to B, B to C, C to D, etc.	A → B → C → D	Generally inaccurate because of distortion as information is conveyed away from the source
"Gossip." One person seeks out others to share information.	A→ B, C, D (branching)	"Juicy morsels" often of little importance.
"Probability." Individuals share information at random with whomever is around.	A → B → E → F, C → D	Interesting but usually unimportant to formal or informal activities.
"Cluster." Selective sharing of information.	A → C → E → F, B, D	Most likely to convey information of importance.

tions, Keith Davis has identified four common structures of it and the nature of information each tends to convey (see Exhibit 6–7).[21]

Telephoning.* Telephones are the typical alternative to the unscheduled face-to-face meeting. In Mintzberg's study, presidents of small companies were on the phone 17 percent of the workday with the average duration of the calls being two minutes, and presidents of large companies were on the phone 6 percent of the time, averaging six minutes per call. Beyond this use as a communications medium, telephones are best known for their ability to break into a manager's prearranged schedule (a ringing telephone can disrupt a significant conversation and substitute an insignificant one); and as a means of jockeying for power between caller and receiver.† (Rules of the game: Secretary summons boss who does not answer until other manager, *not* his or her secretary, says "hello." The manager who speaks first "loses.")

Observation and Inference. The skilled manager can learn a great deal about his or her organization by taking "tours" of operating areas and drawing infer-

---

* Telephones are also used for formal communication, but probably less than for informal discussions.

† Another contribution by Michael Korda in his book, *Power:* "As a general rule, the power game in telephoning is to place more calls than you receive. The more calls you make, the less time is available for people to reach you. By carrying this procedure to its extreme, it is possible to delay any matter until it has ceased to be of importance to either party without your ever being accused of negligence or indifference" (Korda, p. 219).

ences from what is "observed." Top managers may often pose as customers or clients and observe how the organization treats them. Idle workers, waiting customers, cluttered aisles, absence of other managers from the premises all tell a manager something. On an interpersonal basis, patterns of speech and body language of superiors and subordinates often tell a story if the manager can "read" it.

CHOOSING BETWEEN ORAL AND WRITTEN TOOLS

What is the best way to convey information to a subordinate? A study by Level tested this question with respect to four methods: (1) written only, (2) oral only, (3) written methods followed by oral methods, and (4) oral methods followed by written methods. His results, with respect to ten varied communication situations, are summarized in Exhibit 6–8. (L refers to least effective; M refers to most effective.)

Analyzing this comparison, we can make two generalizations: oral communication alone is undesirable a large percentage of the time, and written followed by oral will tend to lead to in-between results—neither particularly effective or ineffective.

Exhibit 6–8

Situation	Written	Oral	Written/oral	Oral/written
1. To communicate information requiring immediate action	L	M		
2. To communicate information requiring future action	M	L		
3. To communicate information of a general nature	M	L		
4. To communicate a company directive or order.................		L		M
5. To communicate information on an important company policy change		L		M
6. To communicate with your immediate supervisor about work progress		L		M
7. To promote a safety campaign		L		M
8. To commend an employee for noteworthy work	L	M		
9. To reprimand an employee for work deficiency..................	L	M		
10. To settle a dispute among employees about a work problem	L	M		

Source: Modified from Dale E. Level, Jr., "Communication Effectiveness: Method and Situation," *Journal of Business Communication,* Fall 1972, pp. 19–25.

MANAGEMENT INFORMATION SYSTEMS

A management information system (MIS) may be defined as a formalized system for collecting and disseminating information for purposes of managerial decision making. While all organizations have some form of MIS, interest in the subject in recent years has centered on those organizations which must handle a large volume of information and hence require electronic data processing technologies. Therefore, when managers talk about MIS, they are usually referring to a computer-based system.

In addition to a computer, a management information system consists of three major elements: data inputs, computer programs, and output reports. In planning and developing an information system, the flow of activity among these elements is as follows:

$$\text{Reports} \rightarrow \text{Computer program} \rightarrow \text{Data}$$

That is, we start from the desired reports, developing the system around desired information. (In the operation of the system, the sequence is reversed; i.e., data gathering, computer processing, and then report generation.) As a general design objective a complete MIS should answer the questions which management needs to run the business:[22]

1. What are we selling? Products and dollars.
2. Where are we selling it? Geography and product mix.
3. What will we be selling and where? Forecast—units and dollars.
4. What do we own? Company inventories—product and dollars and age.
5. Where is it? Location of inventory.
6. What are we producing for sale? Production schedules.
7. When will it be ready for sale? Future product availability.
8. What will it cost us? Product cost.
9. What should we be producing and selling tomorrow? Product, dollars, and place.

Reports

Certain organizational functions need reports answering the nine questions stated above on a daily basis in a detailed form, while others need answers less frequently and in a summarized form. Indeed, while MIS is often thought of as an all-encompassing system, it more typically consists of a number of separate systems which are designed to meet the operating needs of each functional area and top management. Exhibit 6–9 provides a listing of the areas of reporting which are of particular importance to various organizational functions (or subsystems).

Exhibit 6–9
Major information systems and subsystems

Financial	**Personnel**
Cash budgeting	Personnel records
Capital budgeting	Payroll
Cost accounting	Employment
Profit planning	Placement
Responsibility accounting	Training
Profitability accounting	Material and maintenance
Production/operations	**Project control**
Production planning	PERT/CPM, cost, time, etc.
Inventory	**Other**
Distribution	R&D
Marketing	Strategic planning
Sales planning	Simulation
Sales and invoicing	
Sales analysis	
Credit control	
Market research	

Source: Robert G. Murdick and Joel E. Ross, *Information Systems for Modern Management* (Englewood Cliffs, N.J.: Prentice-Hall, Inc., 1977), p. 176. Reprinted by permission from *Information Systems for Modern Management.* © 1977 by International Business Machines Corporation.

The process of developing reports for each of these functions is, of course, simplified if management can use a "canned" program supplied by a computer company. Often as not, however, such programs aren't suitable and reports must be custom-made, giving rise to certain problems. In large measure the particular difficulties encountered in developing programs stem from two very different types of communication linkages—between the programmer and the manager, and between the programmer and the computer.

Problems in manager/programmer communication tend to arise from their diverse backgrounds and orientations. The manager is trained to deal with human and technical problems within a speciality area (marketing, finance, production, and so on), which often have a sizable subjective component; the programmer thinks in terms of computer languages, flowcharts, and computer capabilities which require adherence to precise rules. Thus when a manager asks in general terms for a report which provides a rough X, the programmer may well end up developing a program that provides a precise Y. There is rarely a simple way around this problem although organizations have improved the situation by training both participants to understand the other fellow's problem. They do this by having managers learn some computer basics, and programmers become exposed to management information needs. In most cases, however, successful communication takes a good deal of time, which means that top management must lend its full support to system development efforts.

The communication "link" problems between the programmer and the computer are, of course, technical in nature—does the computer have the capacity to store all of the data needed for the desired report? Has the programmer accurately translated the symbolic logic to the computer program language? Can the program be written in such a way as to reduce computer processing time? Is there a possibility of using a minicomputer? And so forth. For both communications problems, the manager is indeed fortunate if the programmer combines insight into management needs with solid technical abilities.

As a final comment on reports, computers are notorious for producing printed output that defies easy interpretation. Thus, many organizations have resorted to retyping or rewriting this output to make it more intelligible for the user. This is a particularly useful practice when the system is first installed since the users are most often skeptical about its value at this time and there is some learning and time needed to adjust to the new standard form reports.

Computer programs

The manager is well advised to gain some familiarity with what computers can and cannot do. Ideally, one should take a college level course on computer concepts and data processing. Other alternatives are special seminars such as those offered by the American Management Association or simply reading a recent book on management information systems. The value of such knowledge is threefold: (1) it is useful in determining whether a computer is needed at all in the organization, (2) it will help one converse with specialists in the precise language of "computerese" (bytes, files, cores, and so on), and (3) it will help the manager fend off computer company representatives who will not take "no" for an answer.*

The kind of programs employed depends upon what type of computer is available, the kind of software already on the shelf, and the technical ability of the programmer to create customized programs. The ultimate decision is, of course, a cost trade-off balancing program development time and computer operating cost (rent or purchase) with the particular information needs of the organization. In other words, if you really wanted to spend the money, you could develop a system which would tell you the amount of paper clips

---

* At least one computer company encourages its salespeople to approach every management level of a large company until they make a sale of their software or hardware. As one manager relates, "I told them on Tuesday that we were developing our own computer programs and on Wednesday they had set up an appointment with my boss 'to make sure'!"

used in the organization each day. Clearly, some judgment must be exercised on the value of each unit of information. Our discussion of satisficing and bounded rationality in Chapter 2 is of relevance here.

Data

The third element of a management information system is the data base which provides the input to the computer program. Of particular concern here is the amount of data which must be collected and then stored in the computer and the accuracy of that data. Gathering the data itself requires a formal system—forms to record the variables of interest, a standard procedure to collect the data, and an organization to convert raw data into computer input (e.g., clerks to keypunch data cards).

The importance of accurate data for an information system cannot be overemphasized, yet many organizations waste substantial amounts of money because they don't invest the time and effort to keep precise records. By way of example, numerous manufacturing concerns follow the practice of keeping an "open" stockroom so that workers can get the materials they need at any time. The managers of these companies justify this practice by saying that "they trust the workers" and that they would have to hire personnel to run a "closed" stockroom, thereby increasing their overhead. This reasoning is fallacious, however. Even if workers are perfectly trustworthy,* removing even inexpensive items from a parts supply room without a record of the transaction means that the production planners will overestimate what is on hand, and therefore may not place a reorder for it. Then, when it comes time to fill a new order for the product, one of its components will be unavailable. This, in turn, leads to costly rush orders, aggravated customers, idle workers, and, inevitably, a loss of faith in the information system.

The way to resolve data accuracy problems, particularly in manufacturing companies, involves changing attitudes and changing procedures. The attitude change comes from pointing out the substantial managerial cost of poor record keeping and pointing out to all employees that inaccuracies are absolutely unacceptable to numerous other types of organizations. Banks for example require that all tellers stay at the end of the day if the books don't balance; dentists may get sued if they pull the wrong tooth even if it is the result of an "honest error" in mixing up X rays. The common procedural change for an organization which maintains a physical inventory of parts as supplies is to put a high fence around the stockroom, put a lock on the gate, and give

---

* Consider the Johnny Cash song about the Cadillac built from parts smuggled out of the car factory: "I got it one piece at a time, and it didn't cost me a dime. . . ."

the key to *one* person who is totally responsible for disbursing materials and keeping records of each item.*

A working MIS for production control

The area of production control presents substantial problems in information systems development and operation. It must utilize information inputs from outside the production organization (orders, forecasts), provide cost and performance output data for general management, and assume coordination of the production process itself. It must also make provisions for keeping accurate records of finished goods, work-in-process (WIP), and planned work. The trade magazine article which follows describes one such system which was developed by William Sandman. Exhibit 6–10 shows excerpts of printouts illustrating the actual reports generated by the Sandman system.

The Sandman System of Production Planning and Control in a nutshell, is designed to provide the daily information needed by manufacturing management to schedule, control and measure productivity in job shop operations to maximize profits. It is based on the logical theory that the human mind is incapable of effectively scheduling large numbers of jobs on a daily basis through several manufacturing work centers or processes; hence, a computer is required.

Regulating work-in-process is key. An optimum flow of jobs through the shop must be planned by considering all possible jobs and their delivery dates, and then continually meshing them with the available men and machines at various work stations.

This complex trade-off between capacity and work-in-process utilization of hundreds of jobs, is determined by a computer which can plot the course of jobs through the shop. The logic and program which allow these trade-offs to be made to produce an orderly production schedule make up the core of the Sandman System.

This approach to production control was developed by Bill Sandman while running his own shop several years ago. Once he discovered that his firm could gain a dominant market position using realistic production control, he sold his holdings and went into the consulting business to sell the concept to other job shops.

---

* Workers at a manufacturing plant habitually maintained that while their counts of inventory were not accurate, they were "close enough." However, increasing inventory costs and stockouts led management to believe that these "minor" inaccuracies were in fact the source of these problems, and they undertook a little experiment to make the point. Without telling the workers, they withheld seven or eight cents from many of the workers' weekly paychecks (which, incidentally, were computed according to a very elaborate incentive plan). Immediately after the checks were received, the workers stormed their supervisors' offices complaining about the sloppy record keeping by the company. Management's rejoinder, of course, was "It's close enough." Needless to say, once the experiment was announced, inventory record accuracy took a dramatic and sustained improvement. (The source of this anecdote is Hal Mather, a noted production control consultant.)

Exhibit 6–10
Examples of output from the Sandman system of production control

```
                         DAILY WORK SCHEDULE
06/05/75  WES MFG                                            PAGE  1
          OPER   1  OPER   2  OPER   3  OPER   4  OPER   5  OPER   6
          BURN-CUT  OUTVEND   FITUP     MACHINE   DRILL     SPECIAL
          683540099           680780050 6884106   748610215 694711642
          690900099           6646012   684800878 6910003
    DAY   680726799           6848008   695306799 500800299
          680766799           212250099           691000799
     1                        683540099
```

```
   THE FOLLOWING OPERATIONS NEED MORE TIME
      ORDER   SUB   OPER   OLD ESTIMATE
      68480   06    13         31
      66460   12    3          5
      68841   06    4          8
```

```
ESTIMATE ERRORS FOR WES MFG                                 06/05/75
    THE FOLLOWING ESTIMATES ARE SUSPECT--PLEASE REVIEW
    ORDER    SUB    OPER   CAPACITY   ESTIMATE
    68072    01     2      1          8
    69471    16     6      9          120
    69530    67     10     36         280
    69770    00     13     9          175
    81446    01     10     36         300
              ↑
          Subassembly
```

```
   COST REPORT FOR WES MFG CO                               06/05/75
          STA      CITY      NAME     ORDER        SUB
          BKT      RADAR     BENDX    41412        21
          OP     ESTIMATE   ACTUAL          PCT DEVIATION
          4         8         2                25
          8         6         10               167
          10        8         11               138
          15        13        15               115
TOTAL               35        38               109
```

```
DAILY STATUS REPORT FOR WES MFG
     **BY SANDMAN ASSOCIATES**     06/05/75 IN ORDER-SUB SEQUENCE
STA CITY      NAME  CC   ORDER SUB   RLSE FAM  *  SHIP   SPCL
MIC GRAPD     ANCHR 23   08071 06    5116         606
MIC GRAPD     ANCHR 23   08071 24    5116         605    OP 9
FLA PLANT     PCSTL 23   21225 00    5101         605
CAL S ANA     GARSN 24   31616 00    5153         611
```

```
BACKLOG ANALYSIS FOR WES MFG
          ** SANDMAN ASSOCIATES **     06/05/75
   WORK              STANDARD   ** BACKLOG **      HRS TO
   CENTER  OPERATION MANHOURS   HOURS   DAYS   LEVEL B/L
      1    BURN-CUT     18       138     8        12
      2    OUTVEND      1        25      25
      3    FITUP        18       155     9        12
      4    MACHINE      15       98      7        8
      5    DRILL        11       104     9        8
```

Source: William E. Sandman and Associates Company, 715 Twining Road, Dresher, Pennsylvania.

"Too many times," says Sandman, "we hear that the job shop problem is the work force: either people in the shop don't work hard enough or production managers cause scheduling bottlenecks which create too much idle time. This erroneous thinking leads to production control methods which seek apparent utilization of machinery and equipment, resulting in employees and machines appearing busy, when in reality the production control method backs up work-in-process on the shop floor. This costs management money."

Sandman further states that this kind of production control is a common approach and leads many managers to believe that when the shop floor is crowded with work-in-process, business is great. "What these managers don't seem to understand is that work-in-process is an investment in working capital and the more work-in-process that is idly waiting to be worked, the more cash is tied up, and the lower profits are."

THE SYSTEM

After an order is taken, the detailed information of the steps necessary to complete it is fed into a computer. An optimum path is then plotted through the necessary work centers, comparing each job to all the other jobs in the plant. The result is the optimum feasible production schedule for a maximum amount of work-in-process.

The working tools for production management are a series of daily reports which show the timing of jobs from work center to work center. This report is the one managers work toward each day to maintain the production control schedule. Obviously, situations occur, such as unscheduled employee absences, machine outages and human error, which mean the plan is never perfectly achieved. Data is [sic] then fed into the computer at the end of each day to show what has been done, and the work flow for the next day is completely replanned.

The System also includes "management exception" reports to flag trouble spots for attention. Such reports include work exceptions (such as those noted above) showing which orders have used all their computer-estimated time for completion and require management attention.

A "bottleneck report" is also provided, showing production management which work centers will have the heaviest work load that day. A priority status report shows the delivery date promised the customer against the date when the optimized schedule says it will be finished.

For top management, the Sandman philosophy provides a labor analysis which shows utilization by hours worked by work centers, as well as an order flow analysis showing where flow was impeded daily, every month, and averaged over the previous 52 weeks.

"Management trend" reports reflect a monthly summary of what happened during the month and year to date. The reports graphically show additions to backlog, completions and the size of the backlog in both hours and in orders. In addition, there are charts showing how the firm's product mix is changing over time, as well as capacity utilization summaries, so management can find bottlenecks and correct them.

Sound too good to be true?

Zoom Fleisher admits he was a skeptic as well, until he began utilizing the system at Pilot with results as outlined above. He has utilized it with so much success in fact, he avidly espouses that "if many of the fabricators around the country used this type of system, productivity would accelerate tremendously."

THE SYSTEM AT WORK

At Pilot, preliminary steps which must be taken prior to implementing the Sandman System are as follows:

After an order is received, it is assigned a shop order number. The order is manually entered in a production file for scheduling to Methods Engineering for layout, programming, routing, and material requirements. Every procedure is laid out in detail so that production and purchasing know exactly what must be done and where everything is supposed to go.

From Methods Engineering, the item goes into production at which time the Sandman System enters the picture.

Much of the information generated manually to this point—sequence of operation listed on the routing cards, estimates to complete each operation—are fed into the computer. The computer analyzes both jobs running and jobs entered, on a daily basis.

Out on the shop floor, the production superintendent is in charge of the foreman and production control man. The foreman has a lead man in each department. A computer printout revised daily, guides each man in the performance of his job. This printout is studied first thing each morning by the foreman, who can then coordinate the work to be done in the shop.

"Basically, the readout indicates standard man hours per department, per operation," explains Fleisher. "We have the number of hours that are in the system and the number of days it will take to clear out a given area."

The "critical operation" of the day is indicated on the readout, and the system also warns of impending bottlenecks. Steps taken to eliminate those bottlenecks are management's responsibility. It may mean jobbing work out, or pulling idle workers into the critical areas. The plant superintendent and production control man ultimately determine what must be done to alleviate problems.

On some jobs in the shop, time runs out before the entire job is completed; in other work areas the work is ahead of schedule.

Either way, each evening the computer is fed information compiled by Production Control from progress reports in the shop. The information is entered onto a form which in turn is entered into the computer.

The processed information comes back several hours later in the form of a printout and a night foreman makes copies for each of the morning foremen. This report will then guide the shop through the next day's production.

After nearly five years, Fleisher is still enthusiastic about what the system has done for his operations. He is perhaps one of Sandman's strongest proponents.

Says Sandman: "Zoom has achieved hundreds of percents of improvement in productivity in due date delivery performance and in profit from using our system. But clearly the accomplishments were Zoom's, resulting from both a skill in metal working and a skill in managing. The advances came about when he found that our system was the perfect tool for his use; he has used it as a craftsman. Despite all the credit he bestows on us, our system truthfully is inanimate and will do nothing on its own. It takes people using the system with good business sense to enjoy the super gains experienced by Pilot Metal Fabricators."[23]

Dealing with computer companies

Computers can do great things for an organization but it's up to the manager to make certain that the right system is chosen for his or her operations. Some suggestions along these lines are as follows:

1. Do your own "systems analysis" to find out what information you actually have and what information you need. Even the most ethical computer companies can make a persuasive case for additional "Whistles and Bells" on the computer and in the software packages they have to sell.
2. Write up your own bid proposal and contracts, rather than relying on the computer company to provide such a free service. While a few computer companies won't bid for small jobs, most will.
3. Consider using a computer service bureau as your first step into automated data processing. (Service bureaus provide a complete range of data processing services—keypunching, program rental, computer operation, and report preparation, for a monthly fee.) This gives your company the opportunity to move more gradually into automatic data processing, which in turn allows for learning more about your firm's long-term data processing needs before committing a large amount of company resources.

SUMMARY

Few organizations are perfect in their communication practices, but there is a wealth of research which suggests that effective organizations are that way in part because of their handling of information. In Exhibit 6–11 we have contrasted how the major communication variables behave in effective and ineffective organizations. This material, drawn from Rensis Likert's *The Human Organization*,[24] provides both a useful checklist and a synthesis of the major topics covered in this chapter.

Exhibit 6–11
The nature of communication variables in effective and ineffective organizations

Communication variable	In effective organizations	In ineffective organizations
Communication on company goals	Much communication with both individuals and groups	Very little
Direction of information flow	Down, up, and lateral	Downward
Initiation of downward communication	Initiated at all levels	Top only
Extent to which superiors willingly share information with subordinates	All relevant information and all they want	Provide minimum of information
Extent to which communications are accepted by subordinates	Generally accepted, but if not, openly and candidly questioned	Viewed with great suspicion
Adequacy and accuracy of upward communications via chain of command	A great deal	Very little
Subordinate's felt responsibility to initiate upward communication	Considerable	None at all
Forces leading to distortion of upward information	Virtually none	Powerful forces to distort information and deceive superiors
Need for supplementary upward communication system	None	Great, by spy system, suggestion system, and similar devices
Adequacy and accuracy of lateral communication	Good to excellent	Poor because of competition between peers
Superior's knowledge and understanding of subordinates' problems	Knows and understands very well	No knowledge or understanding
Accuracy of perceptions by superiors and subordinates of each other	Usually quite accurate	Often in error
Adequacy and accuracy of information available at the place where decisions are made	Relatively complete and accurate due to efficient information system.	Generally inadequate and inaccurate

Source: Modified from Rensis Likert, *The Human Organization: Its Management and Value* (New York: McGraw-Hill Book Company, 1967), chap. 3.

GUIDES TO ACTION

1. Whenever possible avoid communicating through intermediaries. Go straight to the person involved. When you must leave a message, request that the message-taker read it back to you.

2. Always consider that the other person might fall into a communications pitfall. Construct and transmit your messages accordingly. (Remember Murphy's law: If anything can go wrong, it will.)

3. Be redundant. Send out important messages via several different media.

4. Be alert for your own nonverbal cues. Many people benefit from seeing themselves on film or videotape.

5. In deciding what should be communicated to a subordinate, ask yourself these questions: *(a)* What information is necessary for the subordinate not just to do his or her job, but what is necessary for that person to cope with the unexpected? *(b)* What information would *I* want to know about the work situation? You should use this as a guide for deciding the type and quantity of information you will provide.

6. Keep careful records of communications you initiate and receive. The human memory is not to be trusted, especially when agreements about jobs to be done and compensation are involved.

7. Listen (discreetly) to rumors, cross-check them if they have potential significance, but don't start them.

8. Assume that there is no such thing as a confidential letter, phone call, memo, or report. (Only physicians, lawyers, or clergy can guarantee that your words will be kept in confidence.) Therefore, before engaging in any form of communication in the organization, think through the ramifications of the wrong person finding out; then act accordingly.

9. Before adopting a new computerized information system, find out why the last one failed and the vast improvements which will be available in next year's model. Once you have these facts clearly in mind, write a contract with the vendor of the system that guarantees that you will get exactly what you want. In other words, make sure that you are receiving a finished product, not developmental work.

NOTES

[1] S. A. Earle, "Gentle Whales," *National Geographic,* vol. 155 (January 1979), pp. 2–17; and R. Payne, "Their Mysterious Songs," *National Geographic,* vol. 155 (January 1979), pp. 18–25.

[2] Francine Patterson, "Conversations with

a Gorilla," *National Geographic,* vol. 154, no. 4 (October 1978), pp. 438–66.

[3] Lewis Carroll, *Through the Looking Glass,* chap. 6.

[4] William V. Haney, *Communication and Organizational Behavior: Text and Cases,* rev.

ed. (Homewood, Ill.: Richard D. Irwin, Inc., 1967), pp. 164–65.

[5] Based on William V. Haney, *Communication and Organizational Behavior.*

[6] John G. Saxe, "The Blind Men and the Elephant," in Sarah Lowrey and Gertrude E. Johnson, *Interpretative Reading: Techniques and Selections* (New York: D. Appleton-Century Company, 1942), pp. 44–45.

[7] Albert Rothenberg, "Creative Contradictions," *Psychology Today,* vol. 13, no. 1 (June 1979), pp. 55–62.

[8] William Shakespeare, *Troilus and Cressida,* IV, v, 54.

[9] Julius Fast, *Body Language* (New York: Pocket Books, 1971).

[10] Michael Argyris, "Non-Verbal Communications in Human Social Interaction," in R. A. Hinde, ed., *Non-Verbal Communication,* Cambridge, England: Cambridge University Press, 1972, pp. 243–69.

[11] Edward T. Hall, *The Silent Language* (New York: Fawcett World Library, 1966), p. 164.

[12] Henry Mintzberg, *The Nature of Managerial Work* (New York: Harper & Row Publishers, 1974), p. 67.

[13] Ibid., p. 75.

[14] Ibid.

[15] Joe Mancuso, *No Guts—No Glory* (Port Washington, N. Y.: Ashley Books, Inc., 1976).

[16] Arthur Marx, *Goldwyn: A Biography of the Man behind the Myth* (New York: Ballantine Books, 1976), p. 3.

[17] Theodore Caplow, *How to Run Any Organization* (Hinsdale, Ill.: Dryden Press, 1976), p. 50.

[18] Richard S. Sloma, *No-Nonsense Management* (New York: Macmillan Publishing Co., Inc., 1977), p. 125.

[19] Caplow, *How to Run Any Organization,* p. 60.

[20] Donald Roy, "Banana Time: Job Satisfaction and Informal Interaction," in D. Hampton, C. Sumner, and R. Webber, eds., *Organizational Behavior and the Practice of Management* (Glenview, Ill.: Scott, Foresman & Co., 1978), p. 209.

[21] Keith Davis, *Human Behavior at Work,* 4th ed. (New York: McGraw-Hill Book Company, 1972), pp. 261–73.

[22] Ward Fredericks, "A Manager's Perspective on Management Information Systems," *MSU Business Topics,* Spring 1971, pp. 7–13.

[23] *Journal of the Fabricator,* 1978.

[24] Rensis Likert, *The Human Organization: Its Management and Value* (New York: McGraw Hill Book Company, 1967), chap. 3.

DISCUSSION QUESTIONS

1. Identify at least three examples of nonhuman communications (other than those described in this chapter).

2. What is the basis upon which a communication's effectiveness should be judged?

3. Using a personal example describe each of the communications pitfalls.

4. Former President Lyndon Johnson expressed a desire to meet in person with people when discussing important issues rather than to communicate via letters or telephone. Why do you think he felt this way?

5. Graph a grapevine of which you are a member. How does it compare with the four grapevine forms depicted in Exhibit 6–7?

6. According to Exhibit 6–8, which communication medium is most appropriate for each of the following situations:

   a. A grade protest.

   b. Introduction of a new registration procedure in college.

      c. An automobile recall.

      d. Collecting an overdue bill.

  7. What are the major errors in conducting a committee meeting?

  8. What are some major communication problems that exist between MIS specialists and managers?.

  9. What are the odds of finding a president of a small company talking on the phone?

 10. What's wrong with open stockrooms?

CASE 1:   DASHMAN COMPANY*

The Dashman Company was a large concern making many types of equipment for the Armed Forces of the United States. It had over 20 plants, located in the central part of the country, whose purchasing procedures had never been completely coordinated. In fact, the head office of the company had encouraged each of the plant managers to operate with their staffs as separate independent units in most matters. Late in 1940, when it began to appear that the company would face increasing difficulty in securing certain essential raw materials, Mr. Manson, the company's president, appointed an experienced purchasing executive, Mr. Post, as vice president in charge of purchasing, a position especially created for him. Mr. Manson gave Mr. Post wide latitude in organizing his job, and he assigned Mr. Larson as Mr. Post's assistant. Mr. Larson had served the company in a variety of capacities for many years, and knew most of the plant executives personally. Mr. Post's appointment was announced through the formal channels usual in the company, including a notice in the house organ published by the company.

One of Mr. Post's first decisions was to begin immediately to centralize the company's purchasing procedure. As a first step he decided that he would require each of the executives who handled purchasing in the individual plants to clear with the head office all purchase contracts which they made in excess of $10,000. He felt that if the head office was to do any coordinating in a way that would be helpful to each plant and to the company as a whole, he must be notified that the contracts were being prepared at least a week before they were to be signed. He talked his proposal over with Mr. Manson, who presented it to his board of directors. They approved the plan.

Although the company made purchases throughout the year, the beginning of its peak buying season was only three weeks away at the time this new

* Copyright © 1942 by the President and Fellows of Harvard College. This case was prepared by George F. F. Lombard.
Note: All names have been disguised.

plan was adopted. Mr. Post prepared a letter to be sent to the 20 purchasing executives of the company. The letter follows:

Dear_____:
The board of directors of our company has recently authorized a change in our purchasing procedures. Hereafter, each of the purchasing executives in the several plants of the company will notify the vice president in charge of purchasing of all contracts in excess of $10,000 which they are negotiating at least a week in advance of the date on which they are to be signed.

I am sure that you will understand and that this step is necessary to coordinate the purchasing requirements of the company in these times when we are facing increasing difficulty in securing essential supplies. This procedure should give us in the central office the information we need to see that each plant secures the optimum supply of materials. In this way the interests of each plant and of the company as a whole will best be served.

Yours very truly,

Mr. Post showed the letter to Mr. Larson and invited his comments. Mr. Larson thought the letter an excellent one, but suggested that, since Mr. Post had not met more than a few of the purchasing executives, he might like to visit all of them and take the matter up with each of them personally. Mr. Post dismissed the idea at once because, as he said, he had so many things to do at the head office that he could not get away for a trip. Consequently, he had the letters sent out over his signature.

During the two following weeks replies came in from all except a few plants. Although a few executives wrote at greater length, the following reply was typical:

Dear Mr. Post:
Your recent communication in regard to notifying the head office a week in advance of our intention to sign contracts has been received. This suggestion seems a most practical one. We want to assure you that you can count on our cooperation.

Yours very truly,

During the next six weeks the head office received no notices from any plant that contracts were being negotiated. Executives in other departments who made frequent trips to the plants reported that the plants were busy, and the usual routines for that time of year were being followed.

CASE 2: FINDING OUT IF THE MESSAGE IS COMING OVER LOUD AND CLEAR*

When Stone-Platt, the engineering group, wanted to find out just how good its internal communications were, the Board decided that the last people it

---

* From: Jason Crisp, *Financial Times of London*, May 17, 1979.

should ask were the senior managers. As Edward Smalley, the chief executive, puts it: "If you ask them they will tell you everything is wonderful and that we and they are good at communications."

The Board also realised that if the company management were to go around asking the shop floor the same question it was not only very likely to get biased answers, but the questions would raise suspicions about management's motives.

Unlike sales, profits or market share, an efficiency-minded company cannot objectively assess "communication" from the inside, which is why Stone-Platt called in Metra Oxford, the management consultants, to conduct an impartial audit and to make recommendations.

According to Smalley, Stone-Platt wanted to know: "whether we were telling people the right things, whether we were telling people the things they wanted and needed to know; whether there was a free flow of information in both directions: and whether our arrangements were consistent with good industrial practice and making the practice match the theory."

Metra's verdict on its performance was "six out of ten," says Smalley. One of the problems in assessing something as nebulous and intangible as communications in a group like Stone-Platt is its divergence of size, products and locations.

Stone-Platt has 20 plants in the U.K., from Glasgow to Bognor Regis, in units employing between 50 and 1,500 people, making anything from ships' propellors to air conditioning for trains. Although almost all the manual workers are unionised there is no central bargaining, and among white-collar staff there are varying degrees of unionisation.

The head office only employs 40 people and the group is divided into five divisions. The head office provides personnel services as well as the setting and monitoring of objectives and performance. But otherwise each division is responsible for the running of its own business.

Scepticism

With such a varied and decentralised organisation there was likely to be a great divergence in the nature of communication throughout the group. And as Smalley admits: "There was a good deal of scepticism as to whether anything would emerge."

Metra considered that communications in three of the five divisions were broadly satisfactory. In the fourth, the pumps division, Metra found a good deal of room for improvement. In the fifth, a fairly recent acquisition of a family firm, communications were described as being "virtually non-existant."

Perhaps the most significant finding was that the biggest gap in communications affected junior management and supervisors. They were, as often as not having to ask the shop floor what was happening in internal negotiation meetings. Another area where Metra found concern was from people who learned about new orders from the Press rather than from inside the company.

It also found, from talking to staff, that Stone-Platt was better at communications in manufacturing and finance than in the technical and R&D field, as well as in marketing. There was also a feeling that communications between marketing, engineering and manufacturing needed improving—a point which Smalley admits caused some surprise.

The management consultants made two other major points on communications within Stone-Platt: one that it tended to communicate the bad news rather than any good news, and second that although communication between the centre and the divisions was good, decisions often did not percolate downwards within these divisions.

William Keyser, a director of Metra, who was involved in the study, comments that in two of the divisions structure was the biggest inhibition to communication.

This was clearly true for the pump division, Haywood Tyler. The arrival last year of a new divisional chairman, Derrick Willingham, has resulted in both a re-organisation of the company as well as the implementation of a number of ideas to improve communications.

Willingham took over the division just after Metra had given it the label of being one of the problem areas in communication at Stone-Platt. Fortunately Willingham himself is a communicative man and he says the report "confirmed my previous views."

Reorganisation

He inherited a group making three different types of pumps in three separate locations in the U.K. and a number of others in North America, Europe and South Africa. He describes the old structure as a "three-headed monster," with such problems as having one sales force for three different products and markets based at Luton, the site of its biggest factory. The result was that some people were wearing two hats or that others were answerable to two or more people.

The reorganisation has put the lines of command and responsibility into a readily recognisable form. The pump division has been divided into three businesses in the U.K., each headed by a general manager running "profit responsible" management teams. The three businesses, producing different products are based at different locations, although certain functions such as engineering—responsibility for overall technical quality, design and new products—remain on a divisional level.

Willingham has also introduced a number of direct methods to try to improve communications. One of the first was to take advantage of an independent semi-social club organised by senior and middle management which had been going for about five years. Somewhat self-consciously called the "Maniacs' Club," it often discusses serious subjects and Willingham has begun to address them on what he likes to call "the state of the nation" at Haywood Tyler. This is very much a personal gesture, as his predecessor could well have taken the same opportunity.

On a more formal basis, he has set up "communications meetings" which are held throughout the division. At Luton, where the company has around 700 employees, the meetings are for about 70 people at a time and, Willingham says, are comprised of representatives from all over the works, "both union and non-union and from senior to junior levels." But at Keighley, which employs about 150 people making Sumo water pumps. "We call everybody together and I just stand on a soap box."

Regular meetings are held with foremen—"Rather a neglected breed"—and if there are any negotiations going on with the unions or there is an announcement being made to the shop stewards the foremen are briefed at the same time.

And the division now has its own house magazine, published every two months and mailed directly to each employee's home.

Willingham says there is still plenty of room for improvement: "I would like to get more instantaneous feedback at lower levels of the sort of things they are worrying about." For instance, he says, "We need to know much more quickly when wrong rumours are flying about."

As John Raimes, Stone-Platt's group personnel director, explains, the company is seeking a constant improvement, rather than a dramatic jump.

One of the most beneficial effects of Metra's study, says Edward Smalley, was that "It focused attention on the subject and made senior management more aware of communications."

For those who have doubts about the value of such an exercise the last word must go to John Raimes: "The more the employees are told the more they are involved with the company."

Questions

1. What types of communication devices are used at Stone-Platt? Does the company have a communications philosophy? Do you agree with it?

2. What kinds of information might be candidates for MIS?

SELECTION OF THE PRODUCT OR SERVICE

DESIGN OF THE SYSTEM

STAFFING THE ORGANIZATION

STARTUP OF THE ORGANIZATION

OPERATING THE ORGANIZATION IN THE STEADY STATE

IMPROVING THE ORGANIZATION

REVISION OF THE ORGANIZATION

TERMINATION OF THE ORGANIZATION

Level of Organizational Outputs

O

Decision-making processes; social value; goals; forecasts; policies; plans

Authority and responsibility; power; organizational structure; communications systems; job design

Work force planning; personnel management functions

Startup planning and scheduling; monitoring; alternative startup approaches

Motivation; leadership; production and operations management; control

Individual improvement programs and techniques; group conflict management; MBO

Evaluation of organizational policies; strategic choices; organizational change; organizational development

Partial terminations; cutback management; complete terminations; mergers; born-again strategies

t_0

Time

Chapter 7
Designing the work
of organizational members

*I have a darn good job with the Cardinals, but
please don't ask me what I do.*

Stan Musial on his front office job with the St. Louis
Cardinals after his playing days were over.

Work in organizations is divided into manageable sets of tasks that can be performed by employees. We term such sets of tasks *jobs*. Thus, we speak of jobs such as telephone switchboard operator, receptionist, mine safety inspector, keypunch operator, computer programmer, or police officer. Each job entails certain tasks and responsibilities which distinguish it from others. The sum total of *all* work done in the organization should result in the accomplishment of the organizational objective(s). In this chapter, we will consider the three major classes of jobs: operative, professional, and managerial. For each of these job classes, we will discuss major issues that affect job design.

CONCERNS ABOUT JOB DESIGN

Work in America, prepared in 1973 by the U.S. Department of Health, Education, and Welfare, described many problems facing workers in today's society. The thesis of this HEW report was that there is an urgent need to make jobs more "meaningful" and to improve the "quality of work-life." Increasing specialization and mechanization as well as the lack of workers' control over on-the-job behavior (e.g., lack of opportunity to be one's own boss or even decide when one could go to the toilet) were seen as major contributors toward worker dissatisfaction. Popular writers such as Studs Terkel *(Working)* and Paul Dickson *(The Future of the Workplace)* have expounded on this theme with vivid examples of workers performing in jobs they have come to despise. Periodically, Roy Walters, a management consultant, issues a list of the "Ten Worst Jobs."[1] The list is continually subject to change, probably because many people feel their job deserves inclusion. Walters' mid-1970s list included the following jobs: assembly line worker, highway toll collector, car-watcher in a tunnel, pool typist, bank guard, copy-machine operator, bogus typesetter (those who set type that won't be used), computer tape librarian, housewife (not to be confused with mother), and automated elevator operator.

Perhaps in response to these human complaints about "lousy" jobs, two psychologists, D. A. Bernstein and T. M. Alloway, have gone so far as to suggest the use of animals to perform those jobs that are supposedly beneath the dignity of humans.[2] Actually, using animals isn't a new idea. Dogs have long herded cattle, aided hunters, led the blind, and guarded buildings. Pigeons for centuries have carried messages. In addition, Verhave reports the use of trained pigeons by a pharmaceutical firm to inspect gelatin capsules for defects.[3] The birds "accepted" or "rejected" the capsules by pecking one of two keys. After a week on the job, they were 99 percent accurate. However, fearing adverse publicity, the company terminated the project. Bernstein and Alloway nicely conclude their article by contending that humans' quality of life may well be improved when we begin "sending a bird to do a bird's job."[4]

JOB DESIGN

Job design is defined as the process of specifying the work activities of an individual or group in an organizational setting. Its objective is to develop work assignments that meet the requirements of the organization and its technology and that also satisfy the personal and individual requirements of the workers. Because of the many factors included in arriving at the ultimate organizational job structure, job design is a highly complex function. Decisions must be made as to what tasks the job entails, who (what "kind" of worker) is to perform it, where (geographically) and when (in the sequence of work in the organization) it is to be performed, and finally how it is to be performed. This is illustrated in Exhibit 7–1.

Exhibit 7–1
Factors in job design

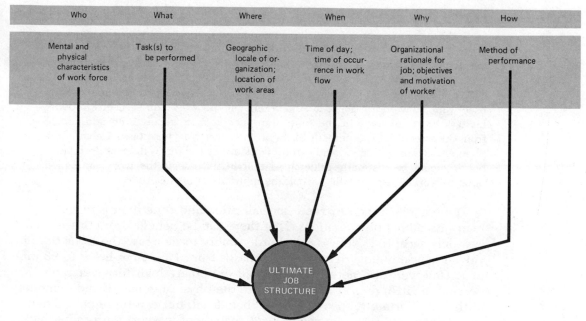

Who	What	Where	When	Why	How
Mental and physical characteristics of work force	Task(s) to be performed	Geographic locale of organization; location of work areas	Time of day; time of occurrence in work flow	Organizational rationale for job; objectives and motivation of worker	Method of performance

ULTIMATE JOB STRUCTURE

Source: Richard B. Chase and Nicholas J. Aquilano, *Production and Operations Management*, rev. ed. (Homewood, Ill. Richard D. Irwin, 1977), p. 457. © 1977 by Richard D. Irwin, Inc.

OPERATIVE JOBS

An operative worker is one who is directly responsible for some output. Operatives do not (normally) supervise any other workers. Assembly line worker, typist, police officer, bookkeeper, maintenance worker, and janitor are several examples of operative jobs. Depending upon the specific job(s) being considered, an operative job and the activities within it are composed of the following:

1. *Micromotion.* The smallest work activities, involving such elementary movements as reaching, grasping, positioning, or releasing an object.
2. *Element.* An aggregation of two or more micromotions, usually thought of as a more or less complete entity, such as picking up, transporting, and positioning an item.
3. *Task.* An aggregation of two or more elements into a complete activity, such as wiring a circuit board, sweeping a floor, or cutting a tree.
4. *Job.* The set of all tasks that must be performed by a given worker. A job may consist of several tasks, such as typing, filing, and taking dictation, as in secretarial work, or it may consist of a single task, such as attaching a wheel to a car, as in automobile assembly.

The scientific management school of thought carefully considered operative job design. Taylor's notions of the "best way" of performing jobs and the time and motion work done by the Gilbreths were mentioned in Chapter 1. The design of jobs from a scientific management perspective is illustrated by the following quote from Taylor's *Principles of Scientific Management:*

Perhaps the most prominent single element in modern scientific management is the task idea. The work of every workman is fully planned out by the management at least one day in advance, and each man receives in most cases complete written instructions, describing in detail the task which he is to accomplish. . . . This task specifies not only what is to be done but how it is to be done and the exact time allowed for doing it. And whenever the workman succeeds in doing his task right, and within the time limit specified, he receives an addition of from 30 percent to 100 percent to his ordinary wages. These tasks are carefully planned, so that both good and careful work are called for in their performance, but it should be distinctly understood that in no case is the workman called upon to work at a pace which would be injurious to his health.[5]

The emphasis upon extreme specialization and repetition is manifested in many assembly line operations. That there can be benefits from this approach is widely accepted. Note Henry Ford's ability to decrease the labor time involved in assembling an automobile chassis from 12½ labor-hours to 93 minutes. However, also note that Ford had extremely high turnover rates (380 percent in 1913) due, at least in part, to the physical demands and monotony of the job. Certainly, specialization is beneficial, but can there be too much? (See Exhibit 7–2.) As long ago as 1924, a study of workers performing highly simplified jobs showed that they were bored and took unauthorized breaks whenever possible.[6]

Exhibit 7–2
Advantages and disadvantages of specialization of labor

Advantages of specialization

To management:

1. Rapid training of the work force
2. Ease in recruiting new workers
3. High output due to simple and repetitive work
4. Low wages due to ease of substitutability of labor
5. Close control over work flow and work loads

To labor:

1. Little responsibility for output
2. Little mental effort required
3. Little or no education required to obtain work

Disadvantages of specialization

To management:

1. Difficulty in controlling quality since no one person has responsibility for entire product
2. "Hidden" costs of worker dissatisfaction, arising from
   a. Turnover
   b. Absenteeism
   c. Tardiness
   d. Grievances
   e. Intentional disruption of production process

To labor:

1. Boredom stemming from repetitive nature of work
2. Little gratification from the work itself because of small contribution to each item.
3. Little or no control over the work pace, leading to frustration and fatigue (in assembly line type situations)
4. Little opportunity to progress to a better job since significant learning is rarely possible on fractionated work
5. Little opportunity to show initiative through developing better methods or tools
6. Local muscular fatigue due to use of the same muscles in performing the task
7. Little opportunity for communication with fellow workers due to layout of the work area

Source: Richard B. Chase and Nicholas J. Aquilano, *Production and Operations Management*, rev. ed. (Homewood, Ill.: Richard D. Irwin, 1977), p. 458. © 1977 by Richard D. Irwin, Inc.

Physiological factors in operative job design

The human body can be viewed as an efficient machine that consumes fuel (e.g., food, oxygen) and produces energy (e.g., lifting objects, pushing buttons, thinking, and so on). A major aspect of operative job design concerns the efficient and effective use of the human machine to get work done. The machine, while an excellent one, still has its limits of performance.

Exhibit 7–3
Work task continuum

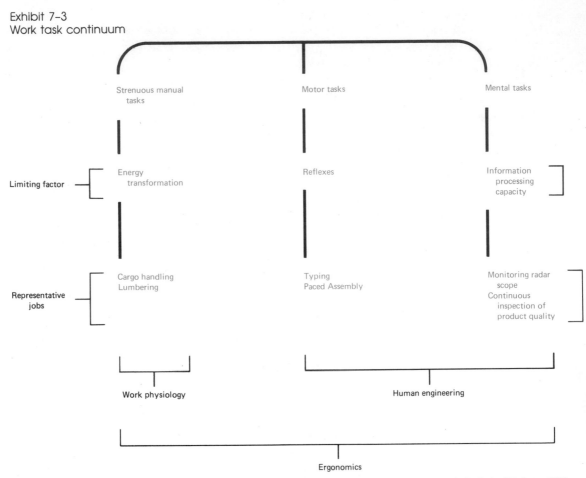

Source: Richard B. Chase and Nicholas J. Aquilano, *Production and Operations Management,* rev. ed. (Homewood, Ill.: Richard D. Irwin, 1977), p. 468. © 1977 by Richard D. Irwin, Inc.

Exhibit 7–3 shows three classes of human work, which together comprise the field of "ergonomics" (from the Greek noun for "work" and the Greek verb "to manage"). Strenuous manual labor is defined as work that places stress on large muscle groups in the body and leads to overall fatigue. Intermittent rest from strenuous work is required to allow the body to recover from increased heart, respiration, and sweat rates, as well as the other bodily functions affected by stress.

Motor tasks are controlled by the body's central nervous system and, from a job design standpoint, we are interested in the speed, precision, and degree of localized fatigue. Motor tasks refer to the use of small muscle groups, such as the fingers, hands, and arms in typing. Such muscle use does not cause overall fatigue, but rather fatigue is confined to those specific muscles used.

Mental tasks refer to a combined mental and physical response. This entails rapid mental decision making followed by a response. In this kind of work, we are interested in response time and in the kinds of decision-making errors that may result.

Arguments are often put forth contending that, due to mechanization, strenuous work is of diminished importance in modern organizations. While we cannot overwhelmingly dispute this contention, we still feel that there are sound reasons that the nature of such work be understood by job designers.

1. Due to simple economics, it is unlikely that we will ever eliminate all strenuous work. Humans are quite simply often less costly and more versatile than machinery.
2. Though many tasks are mechanized, those that remain are often of crucial importance. Poor performance by the worker may so hamper the machinery efficiency that the cost becomes about the same as before when many people did the task.
3. Time and space limitations often preclude mechanization. This is certainly true in many mines, cargo handling in aircraft, and some construction work.
4. There are many (if not most) parts of the world where large numbers of people are employed in manual work activities. Inefficiency here results in a true waste of resources.

Heart rate and oxygen consumption are the two most common methods used for work-stress evaluations. The "average" worker has a maximum sustainable heart rate of about 115 beats a minute. Of course, this level can be exceeded at times; however, the worker will then have to rest to permit the body to recover. The muscles must get a fresh supply of oxygen and rid themselves of carbon dioxide.

Oxygen consumption, converted to calories per unit of time, is the primary measure of energy expended by the body at work. By expressing this measure in calories, we have a basis for relating nutritional intake to work performed. The approximate number of calories per minute for a variety of activities is shown in Exhibit 7–4. The ability to relate necessary caloric intake to measurable work can be of great benefit to managers of isolated work sites (e.g., the trans-Alaska pipeline and off-shore drilling rigs), military leaders conducting a long march, and in a multitude of similar situations.

Exhibit 7–5 is a rough grading of work difficulty in terms of heart rate and caloric expenditure. Obviously, work physiology analysis is intended for moderate to heavy intensity jobs. Clerical and various other sedentary tasks do not lend themselves to heart rate of oxygen consumption analysis.

Exhibit 7–4
Calorie requirements for various activities

Type of activity	Typical energy cost in calories per minute
Sitting at rest	1.7
Writing	2.0
Typing	2.3
Medium assembly work	2.9
Shoe repair	3.0
Machining	3.3
Ironing	4.4
Heavy assembly work	5.1
Chopping wood	7.5
Digging	8.9
Tending furnace	12.0
Walking upstairs	12.0

Source: Paul Webb, ed., *Bioastronautics Data Book* (Washington, D.C.: Scientific and Technical Information Division, National Aeronautics and Space Administration, 1964).

Exhibit 7–5
Grading of work by physiological measurements

Work load	Energy expenditure (calories/minute)	Heart rate (beats/minute)
Very light	less than 2.5	less than 75
Light	2.5– 5.0	75–100
Moderate	5.0– 7.5	100–125
Very hard	7.5–10.0	125–150
Extremely hard	10.0–12.5	150–175

Source: E. H. Christensen, "Heart Rate and Body Temperature as Indices of Metabolic Rate during Work," *Arbeitsphysiologie* (March 1950).

Work methods

To determine how a job will be done, a methods analyst in an office (or industrial engineer in a factory) usually starts with charts describing the process and time study values for each of the operations to be performed.* For a worker who remains at the same work place continuously, job design is intended to simplify the way in which the work is being done and reduce the number of motions required by the worker. Here, the analyst can use some basic principles of motion economy, or "simo" charts, which examine the simultaneous motions of the left and right hands.[7] All in all, the analyst attempts

---

* "Standard" types of work (e.g., lifting a five-pound hammer) have been so regularly observed that such tasks have been reduced to "fact books" in terms of the time it takes to do them and how much work is involved.

Exhibit 7–6
Activity chart for a 10-minute automobile oil change and lubrication

Time	Worker 1	Worker 2	Worker 3 (in well under car)
0	Drive car in service bay	Idle	Idle
1		Open hood	Loosen oil plug and filter
	Check tire pressure	Remove oil fill cap	Put drain pan in place
2		Check pc v valve	Remove oil plug and filter
3		Check power-steering fluid	Grease car
4	Vacuum car	Check hydraulic brake fluid	
5			Squirt oil on springs
6		Check battery water level	Safety check under car
7	Clean windows	Clean air filter	Install new oil filter
8	Start car	Add oil	Replace oil drain plug
		Check automatic transmission fluid	Continue safety check
9	Idle time		Check for oil leaks from plug or filter
		Close hood	
10	Drive off bay	Clean up area	Clean up area

Work order was completed by a "greeter" or order writer specifying particulars such as filter change and oil type.

to devise a way of doing the job that uses the least amount of effort, or which spreads the work across different muscles so as to avoid fatigue.

When workers interact with equipment, the objective is to find the number or combination of machines to balance the cost of the idle time when the person is waiting for the machine to complete an operation and the idle time of the machine waiting for the person to reload it. Such study methods use "activity charts" and "worker-machine" charts. See Exhibit 7–6 for an example involving an automotive service organization.

To design a job for a worker, the analyst also needs to know how long the job takes. *Time study* separates a job into its tasks or elements and each is timed separately. In order for the result to be useful on a broader scale, the time must be adjusted by the "performance rate" of the individual worker. When the observation was made, the worker (for any number of reasons) may have been working faster or slower than a "normal" worker in that category and such variations must be accounted for. The performance rate used is simply a matter of judgment for the time study analyst. Was the person loafing, really going fast, or working normally? An allowance for fatigue is added to the time and the result is the so-called standard time of performance. Thus, on an automobile assembly line we "know" it should take 12.93 seconds to install bolt number 601–A3.

Current views of specialization

Recent research suggests that in today's society disadvantages dominate the advantages of highly specialized, repetitive operative jobs. We are not willing, however, to state that for simple, humanitarian reasons specialization should be avoided. Different workers still desire different things from their jobs; some want more freedom; others prefer to be directed.

Activation theory is helpful in understanding why some people react adversely to highly specialized, repetitive jobs.[8] Generally speaking, as an individual becomes familiar with the surroundings and learns the behaviors required for a given task, a decline in mental activation takes place. When this occurs, the individual is believed to attempt to increase the level of activation; humans don't like situations requiring such low levels of mental activity. Stimulation (activation) of the cortex of the brain can be brought about by a number of devices: thinking about an upcoming date, a football game, an exam scheduled for next week or by physical actions such as stretching, going to the water fountain, or even by slightly varying the task being done. Much behavior (horseplay, conversation, and so on) on the job may well be attempts to increase (or sustain) activation levels. If activation decreases far enough (each person probably has their own critical level of "enough"), and if the worker is unable to engage in activation-increasing behavior, performance will deteriorate.*

If the activation increasing behavior is detrimental to the job being done, we have the possibility of poor performance, yet a (reasonably) high level of morale or job satisfaction for the worker. On the other hand, noninterfering behavior may result in successful adaptation to a repetitive, usually boring task. Thus, those workers who seem happy in what most people consider "lousy" jobs may well have simply discovered an activation producing behavior.†

Of course, there are situations where activation levels could be too great. Air traffic controllers and emergency crews of various types are examples of

---

* Or, without the jargon: "If you're bored stiff, you'll probably do a crummy job."

† It takes all kinds: Several years ago we ran across a fellow whose job was simply connecting huge hoses to different spigots for the purpose of blending gasoline in a refinery. His work was performed in a semidark square pit and required that he snake through connected hoses on his stomach. When he emerged from his work area (covered with grease and grime), we asked him if he enjoyed his job. His answer was surprising—"Enjoy it? Heck yes! Nobody bugs me, it's quiet . . . the best job in the refinery!"

where workers must constantly deal with large amounts of rapidly changing data in a stressful situation. The divorce rate and incidence of stress-related medical problems is quite high for these workers. (See "The Rest of the Story," Chapter 18, for a discussion of how to cope with such stress.)

Two schemes exist to redesign jobs in order to make them less boring and/or more satisfying. *Job enlargement* refers to taking a repetitive, boring job and giving it variety by introducing different, but similar (as to skill and decision-making) tasks. Thus, instead of doing one repetitive task for eight hours, the worker might do four different but somewhat repetitive tasks for a total of two hours each during a day.

Job enrichment is similar to enlargement, but where enlargement introduces task variety at the same horizontal skill/decision-making level, enrichment gives task variety at perhaps the same horizontal level as well as new tasks demanding higher level skills (vertical) and decision-making responsibilities.

For example, a factory assembling household steam irons might abolish the assembly line method where each worker puts on one or two parts and begin having a single worker assemble the whole iron. Assuming that all these assembly skills are equal, this would be an example of job enlargement.

But now assume that management goes one step further. In addition to assembling the iron, each worker also has to test his or her own work (i.e., quality control). Further, the workers are required to keep tabs on the parts inventory and order new supplies when necessary. They are expected to produce X units per day and in so doing can work fast in the morning and slow in the afternoon (or vice versa) if they want. So long as they produce the required number of units, management is not concerned. This is an example of job enrichment. Sometimes, as in the Scandinavian Saab and Volvo automobile plants, teams of workers, instead of a single worker, produce the item. Motors, for example, at Saab–Scania and Volvo are made by teams of three or four people. Saab–Scania team members organize the work however they want, so long as they assemble 470 engines in each ten-day period.

The teams organize themselves as they wish and work at the speed they choose. While a worker on a conventional assembly line might spend his entire shift mounting one license-plate lamp after another, every member of a Kalmar work team may work at one time or another on all parts of the electrical system—from taillights to turn signals, head lamps, horn, fuse box and part of the electronically controlled fuel-injection system. The only requirement is that every team meet its production goal for a shift. As long as cars roll out on schedule, workers are free to take coffee breaks when they please or to refresh themselves in comfortable lounges equipped with kitchens and saunas.[9]

There are numerous examples of other job enrichment programs. The General Foods Gaines dog food plant in Topeka, Kansas, where teams of workers perform in enrichment fashion; and an AT&T subsidiary where workers were assigned to do all (install, repair, fix broken wires, deliver phone books, and so on) phone company work in certain parts of cities are two of the more well-known examples.[10]

However, it is clear that not all workers desire enlarged or enriched jobs. Six American workers from General Motors, Ford, and Chrysler spent four weeks at a Saab engine plant in Sweden and came away with doubts, especially about the group work feature. In general, they felt the pace was too fast and tedious. Said one: "If I've got to bust my ___ to be meaningful, forget it; I'd rather be monotonous."[11] In 1973 another dog food plant was opened by General Foods near the "enriched job" plant which began operating in 1971. The new plant was operated on a more standard assembly line model, and a number of workers elected to transfer to it from the enriched job plant. Obviously, we all have different needs and expectations from our jobs.

Where employees exhibit a desire to be more "in control" of their work, and if they have the capacity to perform well, enrichment strategies may prove highly effective. It is necessary, though, to have a "whole task" around which to enrich the job. The complete household iron, a functioning motor, and full bags of dog food are examples of complete, whole tasks. Have you noticed the "inspection tags" found in pockets of new clothes or in the iron's box? Often they say, "Inspected by No. 49875" or something similar. Under enriched jobs, the worker's name is usually substituted for the number and sometimes a phone number is given to call that person if the article is defective. Such a system now exists even in Russia, where all too often consumer products are *brak* (meaning "trash" or "rubbish"). *Kachestva* ("quality") is now stressed, and good workers are allowed to put on a five-cornered seal of quality called a *znak kachestva* on their output which then bypasses all regular inspections. It doesn't always guarantee quality, though: "A letter in a Soviet newspaper told recently about a new piece of farm machinery whose rear wheels dropped off after 25 miles. 'What is most amazing . . . is the *znak kachestva* proudly printed on the machine's hood.' "[12]

Clearly, job enlargement and job enrichment strategies are not panaceas to be applied to all situations. One must view jobs in terms of their entire framework; that is, the worker's motivation, prevailing cultural norms, quality of supervision, and other similar factors. It is interesting to note that sometimes benefits from job enrichment may be partially offset by losses elsewhere. In the above-mentioned General Foods dog food plant, some staff and management personnel felt that their own positions were threatened because operative workers were performing too well.[13] "Personnel managers objected because team members made hiring decisions. Engineers resented workers doing engineering work."[14]

Exhibit 7–7 summarizes a number of job design experiments involving operative workers. While the "specifics" of each case differ, all were involved with the provisioning of greater degrees of freedom and independence to the worker.

In summary, operative jobs lend themselves to rigorous analysis. Their performance can be broken down into small "pieces" of work or motions and these motions even measured as to heart rate and oxygen consumption. Still, this "efficiency" is only part of the problem. Boredom and lack of psychological activation may well lead to an inefficient operation of the human machine. Thus, we must often temper our specialization abilities with such strategies as job enlargement or job enrichment. Overall, our goal is to ensure that certain work gets done in the organization (i.e., organizational requirements are met) while certain requirements of individual workers are also met.

PROFESSIONALS' JOBS

One of the most important decisions to be made when designing organizations and jobs concerns the placement and role of the professional or "knowledge worker." The ever-increasing complexity of our modern world requires the continual use of the services of trained professionals in organizations. Yet, numerous problems exist in this endeavor.

By far, the more highly trained members of most organizations are found not in the highest levels of the organization, but rather in the middle levels. Further, these persons are most often not in line or command positions, but rather are "around" or "tangent to" them. These knowledge workers are usually referred to as staff, professionals, experts, advisers, specialists or simply by the name or title or the pertinent profession.

As a consequence of the organizational placement of professionals, we tend to find situations where authority and knowledge are not "equal"; i.e., the person with the authority to make a decision (line manager) is often not the one most knowledgeable about the pertinent technical issues (staff adviser). The role of staff adviser for line managers was discussed in Chapter 5.

Conflict between professionals and others

Professionals (physicians, lawyers, scientists, etc.) are deemed to have several characteristics:

1. *Expertise.* This is usually the result of special training and tends to be limited to a specific area. Certification or licensing based upon tests and/or graduation from a recognized training institution or apprenticeship program is common.
2. *Ethics.* There is a perceived obligation to serve society. This obligation often results in a published (and publicized) code of behavior. Behaving

Exhibit 7–7
Experiments in job design

	Organization			
	Netherlands PTT	*Kaiser Aluminum Corporation Ravenswood, W. Va.*	*Bankers Trust Company New York*	*Operations Divisi… Bureau of Traffic– Ohio Department … Highways*
1. Establishment(s) or employee groups	Clerical workers—data collection.	Maintenance workers in reduction plant.	Production typists in stock transfer operations.	Six field constructi… crews.
2. Year initiated	Not specified.	1971	1969	Not specified.
3. Number Employees affected	100	60	200	Not specified.
4. Problem	Jobs were routine. Workers and supervisors were both "notably uninterested" in their work.	Productivity was low. There were walkouts and slowdowns.	Production was low and quality poor. Absenteeism and turnover were high and employee attitudes were poor . . . Jobs were routine, repetitive and devoid of intrinsic interest . . . Too much overseeing.	Low productivity … poor quality of per… formance.
5. Technique used	Jobs were enlarged to comprise a whole collaborative process (e.g., listing, punching, control punching, corrections, etc.) instead of a single stage of this process.	Time clocks were removed and supervision virtually eliminated. Workers now decide what maintenance jobs are to be done and in what priority and keep their own time cards.	Typists were given the opportunity (1) to change their own computer output tapes, (2) to handle typing for a specific group of customers, (3) to check their own work, and (4) to schedule their own work. Training was given in these areas.	Three experiment… groups were establ… lished, each with a … ferent degree of s… determination of w… schedules. Crews … unaware that they … were participating … an experiment.
6. Human results	88% of the workers in the experimental group said the work had become more interesting.	"Morale has improved along with pride in workmanship," says the maintenance chief.	A quantitative survey disclosed improved attitudes and greater satisfaction.	Data showed that … participation in… creased, so did mo…
7. Economic results	There was a 15% increase in output per labor hour.	Tardiness is now "nonexistent." Maintenance costs are down 5.5%. Maintenance work is done with more "quality."	Absenteeism and tardiness were reduced while production and quality increased. Job enrichment programs were extended.	There was no signi… cant change in pro… ductivity.
8. Reference(s)	N. A. B. Wilson, *On the Quality of Working Life*, A Personal Report to the NATO Committee on Challenges of Modern Society, p. 36	Donald B. Thompson, "Enrichment in Action Convinces Skeptics," *Industry Week*, Feb. 14, 1971	William W. Detteback, Assistant Vice Pres. Bankers Trust, and Philip Kraft, Partner; Roy W. Walters Associates, "Organization Change through Job Enrichment," *Training and Development Journal*, August 1971	Reed M. Powell, a… John L. Schlacter, "… ticipative Manage… ment: A Panacea?" *Academy of Mana… ment Journal*, June 1971, pp. 165–73

Source: *Work in America*, Appendix—Case Studies in the Humanization of Work (Boston: MIT Press, 1973).

...nsanto-Textiles Co. ...sacola, Fla.	Alcan Aluminum Corp. Oswego, N.Y.	Micro Wax Department —Shell Stanlow Refinery, Ellesmere Port; Cheshire, England	Philips Electrical Industries— Holland	Ferado Company United Kingdom
...duction workers of ...n tire yarn.	Rolling mill operators.	Chemical operators.	Assembly workers.	Production workers making brake linings.
...1	1965	1963	1960	Not specified.
...0	Not specified.	Not specified.	240–300	Not specified.
...specified.	High rates of absenteeism and tardiness.	Low productivity, low morale, and possibility of "shutdown."	Not specified.	Not specified.
...r-day classroom ses...s were held to in...ve production work...in problem-solving. ...o, employees set ...duction goals and ...ted jobs.	Time clocks were removed and production jobs designed to give workers unusual freedom and decision-making responsibilities. Salaries were guaranteed during absences or layoffs.	Operators formed group teams that provided both more flexibility within shift teams and rotation in jobs. Time clocks were also removed.	Independent work groups were formed and made responsible for job allocations, material and quality control, and providing delegates for management talks.	Groups of six men were trained to use all machines involved in the process and allowed to move from one machine to the other. Each group sees the batch of marketable products they have made.
...r the employee the ...gram means 'hu...nized' working con...ons," the plant man...r reported.	"Monotony is relieved," says the plant manager.	"It is well known that absence and sickness may be symptomatic of alienation . . . from the work situation. Thus . . . [these] statistics are partly an indication of morale," said that plant manager.	The members of semi-autonomous groups derived more satisfaction from their work compared with workers in the old situation.	Job satisfaction in the plant has been found to increase.
...e cost of the pro...m more than pays ...itself in higher pro...tivity through ...er idle machines ...lower repair ...s—a possible gain of ...,000 pounds of yarn ...ar," says the plant ...ager.	Absenteeism decreased to about 2.5% compared to an industry average of about 10%. Productivity increased.	"Output" in three sections increased by 35%, 40%, and 100% over 1965. Absence and sickness decreased from 4.3% in 1963 to 3.3% in 1969.	By 1967, waste and repairs decreased by 4% and there was an unspecified savings of lower managerial personnel.	There is less turnover and original delivery times have been cut by seven-eighths.
...News and World ...ort, July 17, 1972, ...2	"The Honor System," Wall Street Journal, May 22, 1970 "Alcan Hails in Dumping Time Clock," The Plain Dealer, Sept. 29, 1969	Derek Burden, A Participative Approach to Management, Shell U.K., April 15, 1970	Louis E. Davis & Eric Trist—Work in America, Approaches to Improving Quality of Working Life, June 1972, p. 18	N. A. B. Wilson, On the Quality of Working Life, p. 40

toward "clients" with neutrality, making decisions based on objective and accepted standards, not being swayed by self-interest, and the like are common ethical guidelines.

3. *Standards of performance.* The typical belief is that only another professional can evaluate a professional's performance. Consequently, "peer review" is the norm used to police the specialty area (e.g., in promotion and tenure decisions for professors).

4. *Autonomy.* Professionals tend to seek freedom to innovate, define their own goals, and communicate with others without being constrained by hierarchical controls. Such freedom, it is claimed, is necessary to provide "objectivity."

5. *Identification.* A stronger loyalty to the profession rather than to the organization that employs them is thought to exist among professionals. Professionals are "cosmopolitans" who can pursue their calling in any number of possible organizations rather than "locals" who are long-time employees that identify primarily with a given organization.[15]

Each of these characteristics of a profession leads to potential conflicts in an organization. The professional's *expertise* may well make the person "too" specialized or "too" abstract for some organizational members. Often, the professional is seen as an ivory tower esoteric person thoroughly unfamiliar with the dirty fingernail reality of life on the firing line. Conversely, the professional often sees well-founded advice unapplied or misapplied because the person with authority "foolishly" decides to do something else. Clearly, expertise and authority are often vested in different persons in organizations.

The internalized *ethics* of the professional often invokes some suspicion by the more "loyal" organization-bound person. With a reference group consisting of colleagues outside the organization (some of whom may be employed by competitors) the professional is certainly not a strong candidate for someone to share secrets with. After all, when might the professional's ethics be detrimental to the organization? If as a medical scientist you helped develop a new vaccine for a dreaded disease, could/would you agree with the company's desire to "keep it secret and off the market" for a year or so in order to better protect the firm's position while it tightened up its patent application? Or, if you were the firm's psychologist, would you keep the trust of an employee who has confided in you that he is addicted to drugs while being employed in a sensitive area?

An emphasis on peer *review* (versus hierarchical review) *of performance* by the professional often evokes sardonic views by other organizational members. Often professionals deny that hierarchical superiors have the ability to determine whether performance standards are being met. Also, the professional may even deny the relevance of a superior's criteria. Such behavior by professionals, while often proper, may well lead other organizational members to view them as being aloof and uncommitted to the organization.

By demanding *autonomy,* professionals further isolate themselves from the organizational mainstream. Yet, this autonomy insulates them from bureaucratic pressures and permits an unbiased, "correct" application of professional actions. This autonomy often results in professionals not being bound by the same sets of rules enforced upon everyone else. This results in further conflicts; e.g., being able to order supplies direct from a specific supplier while the rest of the organization must go through the purchasing department on a bid procedure.

Finally, *identification* with an "outside" body of colleagues and the desire to gain recognition from outsiders more than from organizational superiors further serves to isolate the professional. The ability of the professional to easily cross boundaries to another job and still be doing similar work for another organization also is viewed as threatening by many organizational members. After all, where do the professional's loyalties lie?

Job design considerations

As noted earlier, the fact that modern organizations require professionals' expertise is well-accepted. Lawyers, accountants, physicians, scientists, and so on are necessary for our organizations to function effectively. Still, we must recognize the built-in potential for conflict that does arise between professional and organizational forces.

Professionals' jobs should be designed to permit the functioning of ethics, peer review, autonomy, and identification. Quite frankly, in so doing the organization makes available to it talented men and women who possess the necessary skills. To preclude or prohibit these professional trappings will usually result in attracting lesser qualified employees as the "better" professionals gravitate to more receptive organizations.

Still, this does not mean that organizations must place themselves at the mercy of the professional employee. An organization isn't required to provide paychecks, supplies, helpers, an office, and so on and simply satisfy itself with whatever outputs the professional chooses to deliver.

As discussed in Chapter 5, various principles of line-staff relationships exist which delimit authority to advise or make decisions. This leads to requirements or prohibitions over certain work by professionals. For example, outside professional organization memberships may well be allowed or encouraged but still formal restrictions and approval procedures can be placed upon the publication of certain data or papers in professional journals.

Finally, the organization must require a certain "kind" of output from the professional employee. Do not allow the professional to evade organizational scrutiny over performance by saying, "You wouldn't understand what I do even if I told you. It's difficult to explain or comprehend. It takes years of training." When faced with such a situation, put on your best "wise, analytical" look, scratch your chin, tap your forehead (Columbo-like) and then say: "Yes, I think I see what you're saying. But, tell me this, then. What would I lose if I fired you?"*

Such a question rarely fails to evoke a long list of observable "job outputs" that the professional contributes to the organization. (All expressed in lay language, of course.) It is around these outputs that the professional's job is, or should be, designed. Design here is, however, less rigorous or specialized than in the case of operatives. For example, the hospital administrator does not tell a staff surgeon step by step how to do an appendectomy. Those "specifics" are left to the professional surgeon. But the administrator can make one surgeon responsible for chest surgery, another for abdominal surgery, and so on.

In short, the professional is accorded much more freedom than the operative. However, because of the professional's ethics, standards of performance, and the like, we do have some "controls" over the design and performance of jobs; e.g., CPAs are "expected" to do certain things, and emergency room physicians do certain other things. Thus, some elements of job design are done, de facto, when the professional is hired. While we could well devise a certain set of procedures for a bookkeeper, we would refrain from so narrowly designing a CPA's job. This does not mean that the professional is totally free of organizational scrutiny, however. A firm understanding of "job outputs" and of on-the-job freedoms/restrictions makes the professional's job a "designed one" in the same spirit as is the operative's.

MANAGERIAL JOBS

In Chapter 1 we discussed Mintzberg's views of the roles enacted by managers in doing their jobs.[16] These roles were:

Interpersonal roles: Figurehead, leader, liaison.

Informational roles: Monitor, disseminator, spokesperson.

Decisional roles: Entrepreneur, disturbance handler, resource allocator, negotiator.

Due to the diversity of roles and the variety of situations managers find themselves in, it is not surprising that we have no single, universal statement of what a manager's job entails. Instead, job design for managers normally

---

* We're indebted to Dr. George Odiorne for this most effective managerial ploy.

involves delineating an area of *functional responsibility* (e.g., men's clothing department, sales of pharmaceuticals in the Pacific coast states, and so on), a statement concerning *persons/positions to be supervised,* and a statement concerning materials or other *physical resources controlled.*

All managers can be viewed as performing a similar generic task: coordinating human and material resources to accomplish an objective(s). The objective(s) for which the manager is responsible delineates the area of functional responsibility. Once that is ascertained, the job design variables involve the human (employees) and material (plant, equipment, supplies) resources over which the manager is given discretion. In essence, then, managers (from first-line supervisor to president) all do the same "type" of job, yet each differs according to: (1) functional area and scope, (2) employees supervised, and (3) material resources controlled.

The key design variables for managerial jobs thus reduce down to the decision-making prerogatives involved in these three areas. The most important such decision-making variable (once the "magnitude" of the three areas has been established) concerns the "type" of decisions to be made. According to Simon these are programmable decisions—those decisions which are repetitive and can be readily executed or delegated, and nonprogrammable decisions—those which are particularly complex or unique and must always be carried out by the manager.[17] For example, a typical programmable decision for a hospital administrator would be reducing the number of nurses on the night shift by 10 percent in response to a projected 10 percent decrease in bed occupancy rate. A typical nonprogrammable decision by a hospital administrator would be settling a dispute between surgeons over which one has priority on a particular operating room. Of course, there are decisions which are only partially programmable, so in fact we should look upon programmable/nonprogrammable decisions as end points on a continuum rather than as a sharp dichotomy.

Programmable decision areas lend themselves to delegation. Thus, a task or tasks can be removed from the manager's job and given to a subordinate(s). At the same time, the manager obtains as a new task the need to supervise the person to whom the task was delegated.

All in all, important as they are, managers' jobs are not very susceptible to rigorous design. In coordinating human and material resources to accomplish an objective, managers play a number of roles. Due to day-to-day pressures and events, the manager must often "ad lib." The operative usually always knows what the job will entail (minute by minute) today, tomorrow—next year. The professional also knows within certain limits, what the job is and will be. The manager, however, is subject to ever-changing situations. Rarely will any two days of managerial work be identical.

SOCIOTECHNICAL SYSTEMS

While we have looked at major job design considerations for operative, professional, and managerial jobs, we must caution that jobs and their technical components exist in a social system. An organization is comprised of both technical (jobs, knowledge, plant and equipment, and so on) and social (interaction of people, politics, social norms, and so on) dimensions. It is impossible to speak of or influence one without also touching upon the other. A change in plant or office layout influences interactions and friendship patterns. Job redesigns also often alter existing interaction patterns. And on and on. An organization is not simply a social or a technical system. It is, synergistically, a sociotechnical system.

The implication of this concept is that the job designer must recognize that there are these two dimensions, and that attempting to alter one may lead to unexpected consequences in the other. Certainly job enlargement and job enrichment strategies that involve groups of workers are important sociotechnical illustrations. Additionally, line-staff interactions concerning professionals will involve technical as well as social phenomena as line managers exhibit varying degrees of trust, openness, and so on with staff personnel. Personnel groupings for reporting to given managers also involve technical (e.g., functional similarity) as well as social (e.g., *who* will now have to work with *whom*) implications.

Because of the sociotechnical nature of the system as a whole, it may well be advisable, at times, to compromise some technical efficiency in job design in order to gain the acceptance and conformance of the social system.

SUMMARY

As people combine to form organizations, different work is usually assigned to different people; i.e., a division of labor occurs. Job design is concerned with delineating the scope of the work performed by various organizational members.

Our intent in this chapter has not been to design all jobs for all organizations. Obviously, that would be an impossible task. Rather, we have attempted to point out some of the more important implications involved in the design of the operative, professional, and managerial jobs that exist in organizations.

Job design is rarely a specific, formally defined duty in an organization. That is, there tends to be no one person who is "head job designer." Rather, it is an activity that comes into being as a result of departmentation. The statement, "We need somebody to do something, and he or she should probably do it this way," fairly represents the manner in which a job is typically "designed" the first time through. Later, often as a result of pressure for more output or dissatisfaction with a job content, staff specialists may be brought in to *redesign* the work.

For managers and professionals, job design is usually determined, respectively, by authority provided in the position and an externally derived code of behavior. However, regardless of the status of the job, the effectiveness of its incumbent can and should be measured by some output criterion. A job design which has no clear-cut measure of effectiveness is a poor one indeed.

In designing jobs, we must remember that an organization is a sociotechnical system. Jobs do not exist in a technical or in a social vacuum. An influence in a technical aspect of a job normally leads to social system influences, and vice versa. This fact becomes evident when we see the need for massive retraining of a workforce as the result of automation, or increased absenteeism when "minor" changes in procedures alter workers' interactions with their colleagues. Recognizing the interrelationship between the individual, the group, and the methods of task performance is the real challenge of job design.

GUIDES TO ACTION

1. The individual who has been doing the job usually has developed short cuts. Therefore, always ask the operative for his or her input for any job redesign.

2. Preselect workers with extreme care where possible. Some people like jobs that you might hate, and vice versa. The trick is to find the right match.

3. There is a difference between men and women in their capabilities to perform certain kinds of jobs. In case you hadn't noticed, women are generally narrower in the shoulders and broader in the hips than men. Thus, from a strictly anatomical standpoint, women are better suited to sedentary work (e.g., typing and light assembly). Also, women are generally more dextrous in their hand movements, and thus are usually desirable for high-precision tasks.

4. Don't overlook the benefits of hiring both physically and mentally handicapped workers. There are many jobs that people with disabilities can do quite successfully because of their desire to be productive individuals. Mentally handicapped people are often well suited to simple repetitive jobs requiring a high degree of care.

NOTES

[1] Roy Walters, *Job Enrichment Newsletter,* Roy W. Walters and Associates, Inc., April 1972.

[2] D. A. Bernstein, and T. M. Alloway, "On the Use of Alternative Organisms," *Journal of Applied Psychology,* vol. 53, no. 6 (1969), pp. 506–9.

[3] T. Verhave, "The Pigeon as a Quality-Control Inspector," in R. Ulrich, T. Stachnik, and J. Mabry, eds., *The Control of Human Behavior* (Glenview, Ill.: Scott, Foresman, 1966).

[4] Bernstein and Alloway, "On the Use of Alternative Organisms," p. 509.

[5] F. W. Taylor, *Principles of Scientific Management* (New York: Harper, 1911), p. 59.

[6] H. M. Vernon, "On the Extent and Effects of Variety on Repetitive Work," Fatigue Research Report No. 26 (London: H. M. Stationery Office, 1924), as reported by L. W. Porter, E. E. Lawler III, and J. R. Hackman, *Behavior in Organizations,* New York: McGraw-Hill Book Company. 1975, p. 278.

[7] See Richard B. Chase and Nicholas J. Aquilano, *Production and Operations Management,* rev. ed. (Homewood, Ill.: Richard D. Irwin, 1977), p. 484. © 1977 by Richard D. Irwin, Inc.

[8] W. E. Scott, "Activation Theory and Task Design," *Organizational Behavior and Human Performance,* vol. 1 (1966), pp. 3–30.

[9] "Volvo's Valhalla," *Time* Magazine, September 16, 1974, p. 92.

[10] See *Work in America,* Report of a Special Task Force to the Secretary of Health, Education, and Welfare, Boston: MIT Press, 1973.

[11] Quote attributed to Joe Rodriguez, (then) a 26-year-old, 10-year veteran of Ford, in *Time* Magazine, March 10, 1975, p. 42.

[12] Lloyd Shearer, "Russia Tries Quality," *Parade* Magazine, March 12, 1978, p. 6.

[13] "Stonewalling Plant Democracy," *Business Week,* March 28, 1977, p. 78.

[14] Ibid.

[15] See Robert K. Merton, *Social Theory and Social Structure* (New York: The Free Press, 1956); and Alvin W. Gouldner, "Cosmos and Locals: Toward an Analysis of Latent Social Roles," *Administrative Science Quarterly,* vol. 2 (1958), pp. 444–80.

[16] Henry Mintzberg, "The Manager's Job: Folklore and Fact," *Harvard Business Review,* vol. 53, no. 4 (July–August 1975), pp. 49–61.

[17] Herbert Simon, *The New Science of Management Decision* (New York: Harper & Row, Publishers, Inc. 1960).

DISCUSSION QUESTIONS

1. What is a "job"?

2. From your own experiences and observations, find several jobs that could compete for a spot on Roy Walters' list. Why do they belong?

3. Visit a local cafeteria or restaurant (a fast-food place would be good for this) and develop an activity chart for several jobs which you can observe.

4. Why can specialization be dysfunctional?

5. What are several issues that contribute to conflict with professionals in organizations? Can these be "designed out" of professionals' jobs?

6. Why are managerial jobs not very susceptible to job design efforts?

7. How does the social system influence job design?

8. Differentiate between job enlargement and job enrichment. Why might some workers *not* prefer enlarged or enriched jobs?

CASE: BUREAU OF STATE SERVICES*

Since 1972, the Bureau of State Services in the U.S. government has struggled to maintain satisfactory performance in its building maintenance activities. The employees in building maintenance include 150 janitors and laborers engaged in a number of general cleaning, sanitary, and custodial maintenance duties. The work force is recruited primarily from among the residents in the poorest sections of the city since the organization has been required to employ only "worker trainees" for such duties since 1972. "Worker trainees" is a job designation for individuals who are high school dropouts and have a history of unemployment. From the beginning of this program, the maintenance personnel have had recurring disciplinary problems, high absenteeism, and low performance.

The bureau's first approach to the correction of these problems was a significant increase in the amount of direct supervision. The workers were watched closely and performance was frequently reviewed with each individual. This program was followed by an increase in productivity. However, there was also an increase in absenteeism and in the number of disciplinary problems. With respect to the latter problem, there was a very significant increase in the number of supervisor-employee confrontations resulting in suspensions and removals. The resulting turmoil created several serious work disruptions.

The next program for correcting the personnel problems was a loosening of supervision along with the creation of work teams which had specific areas

* From Stephen J. Carroll, Jr., Frank T. Paine, and John B. Miner, *The Management Process*, 2d ed. (New York: Macmillan Publishing Company, Inc., 1977), pp. 273–74.

of responsibility. For example, a particular work team would be given the responsibility of maintaining the cleanliness of a specific wing of a certain building. Supervision was on a spot-check basis, carried out only by roving supervisors. The results were not good. The roving supervisors often found workers sleeping. Sometimes they could not find certain team workers at all.

Recently, a new change in supervision was made. The work teams were given leaders selected from their own ranks. These work team leaders were given a 10 percent pay differential over the other workers in the team. However, in a few months the majority of the new team leaders quit, saying the extra pay was not worth the abuse they took.

Questions

1. What might be the reasons for the employees' behavior?
2. What other programs might be more effective?

Section three
Staffing the
organization

Given an organizational structure and well-defined jobs, the manager still must bring people into the organization to actually perform the necessary tasks. An organization without people is simply an unproductive empty shell. In this section we discuss the basic processes whereby people with the required skills are brought into an organization and become a valuable organizational resource.

SELECTION OF THE PRODUCT OR SERVICE	DESIGN OF THE SYSTEM	STAFFING THE ORGANIZATION	STARTUP OF THE ORGANIZATION	OPERATING THE ORGANIZATION IN THE STEADY STATE	IMPROVING THE ORGANIZATION	REVISION OF THE ORGANIZATION	TERMINATION OF THE ORGANIZATION
Decision-making processes; social value; goals; forecasts; policies; plans	Authority and responsibility; power; organizational structure; communications systems; job design	Work force planning; personnel management functions	Startup planning and scheduling; monitoring; alternative startup approaches	Motivation; leadership; production and operations management; control	Individual improvement programs and techniques; group conflict management; MBO	Evaluation of organizational policies; strategic choices; organizational change; organizational development	Partial terminations; cutback management; complete terminations; mergers; born-again strategies

Level of Organizational Outputs

O

t_0

Time

Chapter 8
Staffing the
organization

Help-Wanted Ad in the Miami, Oklahoma, News-Record: "Bartender-Waitress. We need honest, sober, reliable help. Would settle for any two of the three above-named requirements."

L. M. Boyd

A government office in the South, advertising a job opening for an administrative technician, said applicants "must have demonstrated capacity to answer phone when it rings without having to be told."

Mike Ullman
The National Observer

Ad in Editor & Publisher: *"Small, fast-growing daily looking for honest-to-goodness reporter; no flim-flam braggodocio claims, just good, solid writing with 'the' and 'cat' spelled correctly every time."*

Reader's Digest[1]

One of the more difficult and often traumatic things we have to do in life is to find a job. Not just *a* job, *the* job we really want. Equally difficult is the role of the employer who wants to find the right person for the job. Not just *a* person, but *the* person who can and will perform up to certain expectations. The job of doing this selection (and subsequent training) is the responsibility of the personnel department and is referred to as *staffing*.

To begin with, there is *work* in the form of *tasks* which needs to be done. Collections of tasks are brought together to form *jobs* for which people are hired to perform. Managers must define this work, group it into tasks, assemble these tasks meaningfully into jobs and then acquire (and keep) the talent necessary to perform the jobs. As simple as it sounds, doing it is complex, and is a most crucial part of a manager's job.

The staffing process is not limited to the business and government organization with which we are most familiar. The Dallas Cowboys professional football team is one of the best examples of good personnel management in action. The Cowboys won the 1978 Super Bowl with only one player on the roster who had ever played for another professional football team.* All of the other players had been recruited by the Cowboys organization, and had "risen through the ranks." Their coach, Tom Landry, is the only coach the team has ever had since its formation in 1960.

---

* Preston Pearson had previously played for the Pittsburgh Steelers and the Baltimore Colts.

The Dallas Cowboys were put together . . . with a loan officer's eye for the sure, steady return and an actuary's fetish for minutiae. . . . [The] Cowboys have been, over the past 18 seasons, the most successful team in football. Dallas devised a computerized scouting system that catalogued the requirements of the sport in fractions of inches and split seconds. The Cowboys have turned up blue-chip players with clockwork regularity, including prospects found in fields foreign to the gridiron. Track stars, basketball players—not to mention the occasional Heisman Trophy winner—have contributed to the impressive return on Dallas' investments. . . .[2]

It is said that the Dallas Cowboys owner, Clint Murchison, purchased a computer company with the intention of complementing and exploiting Tom Landry's own style and ability. At the Cowboy's headquarters "part of a basement and a full wall upstairs are lined with 1,500 big black ledgers that detail the size, speed, strength and character of every professional football prospect known . . . to a Cowboy's scout."[3] (One wonders if similar effort goes into the selection of the 36 Cowboy cheerleaders each year.)

The Cowboy organization, with obvious efficiency, is constantly assessing its talent at every position. Expectations of how long players will continue playing at given skill/efficiency levels are calculated. Then an analysis is made of those prospects noted by the scouts. Thus, when the draft and signing take place, the Cowboys typically have insured a continued flow of good talent at precisely the positions where this talent is expected to be needed. One could even build the probabilities of injuries or unexpected retirements into the model. That such attention to detail is a hallmark of this organization was seen at the 1978 Super Bowl.

For its part, the Cowboy organization had learned from past experience—a Super Bowl victory over Miami in 1972 and losses to Baltimore in '71 and Pittsburgh in '76—that too much time can be squandered unless someone is there to take care of every little detail. Things like getting a car for a player or a plane reservation for his wife, or a dinner reservation for a distant cousin at Moran's or Antoine's. Thus, Dallas had a special squad of people assigned to do nothing but conquer the French Quarter. The organization set up an elaborate office with seven secretaries who were there to do nothing more than handle player requests, and those of Cowboy owner Clint Murchison, General Manager Tex Schramm, Landry and their pals. If Harvey Martin wanted to go to the King Tut exhibition to see what a real mummy looked like, as opposed to those in Pat O'Brien's or Galatoire's, a special secretary handled it. The Cowboys also were prepared to get tickets, sometimes in huge quantity, for any friend of the Texans'. They even had a team acupuncturist in town.[4]

In any organization, employees are considered to be a valuable resource. In professional sports, this is acknowledged in the context of players' (actually their contracts) being traded or sold. "Labor" as one of the components of an economic system (land, labor, capital, entrepreneurship) is viewed in terms of being something of value. But, unlike professional sports where players' contracts are bought and sold, employees aren't marketable slaves nor are they subject to being sold or traded. How, then, do we value them in economic terms? One easy way might be to consider what would happen *if* tomorrow morning a given organization (say, a local department store) suddenly lost, for whatever reason, all of its employees. What would it cost the organization to recruit, hire, and train a new set of employees? This cost is, in a sense, a reasonable approximation of the current value of those employees. If you were to add to this cost the lost business while recruiting and hiring and the lowered productivity of new employees as they are learning their new jobs, the cost (or value of the current work force) is even greater.

Because employees are normally free to leave the organization, the value of human resources does not show up on a normal balance sheet.* Some critics of this standard accounting practice argue that the value of human resources should appear on a balance sheet and in fact some companies (e.g., R. W. Barry Corporation, an Ohio shoe manufacturer) have been including a second so-labeled balance sheet in their annual reports. Consider why this might be plausible. A company could have, say, $100,000 available to either buy some new additional machinery or to use to train existing employees how to better use the current machinery. Either approach will increase productivity by 5 percent and profits will rise accordingly. At the end of the year the balance sheet will either show an added $100,000 in plant and equipment (less depreciation) and a decrease of $100,000 cash, or it will show a simple decrease of $100,000 cash and no increase in assets in the case of the training program.

The staffing process is concerned with the acquisition, training, placement, evaluation, development, and compensation of workers. But, before these activities can be done, the management of the organization must take steps to plan for the size and composition of the work force.

WORK FORCE PLANNING

Work force planning involves three major steps. First, the actual work to be done must be specified. Second, the specified work must be assembled into jobs for which people can be hired. And, third, an assessment must be made of the number of workers needed in various job categories.

Job specifications

The first consideration concerns the actual work to be done. Given that the organization has a goal or objective, what, *precisely*, must be done to

---

* In professional sports, this is not the case. There the values are shown and are even depreciated for tax purposes!

Exhibit 8–1
Some tasks common to operating a gasoline station

Pump gas
Wash windshields
Check oil, tires, belts, and radiator
Sell oil and pour it into engine
Sell tires
Sell miscellaneous accessories (e.g., headlight bulbs, fuses, and so on)
Clean up (janitorial work)
Change price signs
Operate cash register
Collect money from customers
Fill out charge card tickets
Order merchandise
Shelve (display) merchandise
Lubrication of cars
Tune-ups
Change oil
Miscellaneous "small repairs" (e.g., brakes, wheel bearings, and so on)
Hire, fire, and supervise employees
Compute and distribute payroll
.

.

.

There are undoubtedly others.

achieve it? For example, assume that we have decided to purchase a gasoline station via a "turnkey" arrangement.* What work has to be done to operate it? Exhibit 8–1 lists some tasks that might be required in a "normal" full-service station. (Of course, if this is to be a "self-service only" station, the tasks differ, but here we will deal only with the full-service example.)

After cataloging all the tasks necessary to operate our gas station, we need to ascertain what kind(s) of skills are necessary to do each task. Physical, mental, and behavioral skills are all open for consideration here, but obviously all required skills *must* be truly relevant to the task(s) being considered.

Once the tasks and skills are determined we must combine these tasks (and attendant skills) into "jobs." Obviously task groupings should consider the similarity of required skills and of the actual tasks or functions being performed. Thus, we might combine the tasks of pumping gas, washing windshields, checking oil, radiator, battery, fan belts and tires, collecting money

---

* Turnkey means you contract with someone to build the station and get it into operational condition. The key is then turned over to you.

or writing up charge tickets, and performing clean-up functions into a station attendant job. We could create a mechanic I job by combining the tasks of oil change, lubrication, tire changing, and installing batteries. A mechanic II job might involve tune-ups, brake jobs, engine troubleshooting, and other such tasks. The station manager will ring up all cash and charge tickets on the cash register, determine and post prices, keep track of gasoline and other items sold, order and stock merchandise, open and close the station, hire, fire, and schedule all workers, maintain the payroll, and provide supervision over all other workers.

If we run a 24-hour station, we might want to assign clean-up and building maintenance to the graveyard shift since they will probably have fewer customers. Also, we may not want to keep a mechanic or station manager on duty 24 hours. Thus, the night shift personnel may have to perform a greater variety of tasks; i.e., their jobs may be "different" from the day shift.

Regardless of the details inherent in our gas station jobs, the point is that all of the specific tasks involved in the organization must be assembled into jobs that people will do. These tasks all have requisite skills. The statements of the tasks and skills needed to do a job are termed *job specifications*.

Job descriptions

A job description provides a rather complete statement of what a job involves.* It covers:

1. What the worker does in relation to data, people, and things (i.e., the tasks the worker does).
2. The methodologies and techniques employed in doing the job.
3. The machines, tools, equipment, and work aids used.
4. The materials, products, subject matter, or services which result.
5. The traits required of the worker.[5]

In most cases these job descriptions are written documents. Although putting it in writing is desirable whenever possible, job descriptions can also exist as "understandings." For example, it is likely that your professor does not have a written job description. Yet the tasks, skills, and other requirements, and conditions under which work is performed are likely very well understood by the professor, department head, dean, and university president.

Job descriptions are very useful in ensuring that the necessary tasks are indeed assigned. As the organization's employees all act out their job descriptions, the resultant efforts should add together to accomplish the organization goal.

---

* There is another document which some organizations use. This is called a Job Procedure, which tells specifically how the job should be done. For example, a job description may state . . . make coffee daily. The job procedure may state that coffee is to be made at 7:00 A.M. in a ten-cup machine filled to the eight-cup level, with six tablespoons of Folger's electric grind coffee.

Likewise, job descriptions are also very useful in recruiting workers since they spell out what is expected of the prospective employee. Job descriptions should, where feasible, contain statements about the behavioral qualities required of an employee. For example, a specialist surgeon reduces paperwork by the extensive use of dictating equipment and a "special kind" of employee. After examining a patient, the surgeon, generally in the presence of the patient, uses a telephone device to "write" a report for the patient's file, transcribe a letter to the patient's family doctor on the patient's status, and gives the patient any instructions. In virtually all cases, by the time the patient reaches the outer office after listening to this dictation, a typed copy of the doctor's instructions is waiting. In all likelihood, the typist is also nearly done with the medical records and the letter. How? The surgeon actively sought out an exceptional typist who doesn't like to interact with other people; i.e., an introvert. The typist is located in a separate room, dresses however she desires, and rarely sees either the surgeon or other office staff. To quote the surgeon:

The typist has to be ready at all times to type my patient's instructions *immediately*. Also, the records must be updated by the end of each day and the letters mailed daily. We never know if there will be a 1-minute, 5-minute, or 30-minute period between my dictation. That typist has to be there, though. The first few typists I hired never lasted long. The noisy equipment had to be in a back room and the typist was always there—alone. They couldn't take the isolation nor my demand for constant vigilance. Then I got smart. I looked for a fabulous typist who hated other people. I'm happy I found her.

How to describe the behavioral qualities desired is not always easy. The following illustrates a level of description that we *don't* condone.

All Foreign Service officers should embody a balanced blend of integrity, good judgment and decisiveness, initiative, loyalty, intellect, creativity, capacity for growth, courage, sense of priority, appropriate attention to significant detail, ability to work with others, persistence in pursuit of sound objectives, willingness to accept responsibility, industry and productivity, honesty, dependability, self-reliance, adaptability, fairness including fair treatment of colleagues, honor, dignity, core skill and functional competence, independence of thought, humane and considerate conduct, acceptance of Service discipline, and an ability to meet reasonable and clear goals. The foregoing list of positive qualities and attributes is not meant to be all-inclusive. (*Foreign Affairs Manual Circular*, Department of State.)[6]

The U.S. Department of Labor publishes a very useful book which will aid in the development of job descriptions, the *Dictionary of Occupational Titles* (DOT). Included in this volume are short descriptions for almost any "normal" job (and a few that aren't). For example:

666 BORING OCCUPATIONS
This group includes occupations concerned with piercing wood by means of rotary cutting tools advanced into the wood in the direction of the tool's axis to make, enlarge, or thread holes.

666.382–010 BORING MACHINE OPERATOR (woodworking)
Sets up and operates single- or multiple-spindle boring machine and bore

holes in wooden parts: Examines blueprints, drawings, samples or written specifications to ascertain size, type, and setting of boring tools, stops, jigs, and guides to be used. Inserts specified number and size bits in chucks of boring heads according to location specified for holes in stock. Adjusts spindle locations and stops to regulate spacing and depth of bore, using rule or template and wrenches. Turns hand-wheels to move table and guides to center stock under bits and regulate depth of bore. Starts machine, places wood on table against guides, and moves lever or depresses pedal to engage wood with rotating bits. Measures location and depth of holes and compares measurements with work order and pattern specifications to verify accuracy of machine setup. Stacks bored material on hand truck and attaches work ticket when specified. Cleans machine, using airhose and rags. May be designated according to machine operated as BORING-MACHINE OPERATOR, DOUBLE END (woodworking); BORING-MACHINE OPERATOR HORIZONTAL (woodworking); BORING-MACHINE OPERATOR VERTICAL (woodworking); CLUSTER-BORE OPERATOR (woodworking); GANG-BORE OPERATOR (woodworking). May operate boring machine to bore, ream, and countersink bungholes in barrels and be designated BUNGHOLE BORER (cooperage).

Your professor could be described as follows:

090.227–010 FACULTY MEMBER, COLLEGE OR UNIVERSITY (education) Conducts college or university courses for undergraduate or graduate students. Teaches one or more subjects, such as economics, chemistry, law, or medicine, within a prescribed curriculum. Prepares and delivers lectures to students. Compiles bibliographies of specialized materials for outside reading assignments. Stimulates class discussions. Compiles, administers, and grades examinations, or assigns this work to others. Directs research of other teachers or graduate students working for advanced academic degrees. Conducts research in particular field of knowledge and publishes findings in professional journals. Performs related duties, such as advising students on academic and vocational curricula, and acting as adviser to student organizations. Serves on faculty committee providing professional consulting services to government and industry. May be designated according to faculty rank in traditional hierarchy as determined by institution's estimate of scholarly maturity as ASSOCIATE PROFESSOR (education); PROFESSOR (education); or according to rank distinguished by duties assigned or amount of time devoted to academic work as RESEARCH ASSISTANT (education); VISITING PROFESSOR (education). May teach in two-year college and be designated TEACHER, JUNIOR COLLEGE (education); or in technical institute and be designated FACULTY MEMBER, TECHNICAL INSTITUTE (education). Additional titles: ACTING PROFESSOR (education); ASSISTANT PROFESSOR (education); CLINICAL INSTRUCTOR (education); INSTRUCTOR (education); LECTURER (education); TEACHING ASSISTANT (education).

Some other interesting jobs that are described are: crab butcher, dinkey operator, deep submergence vehicle operator, turkey-roll maker, dehairing machine tender, head trimmer, and hide puller. Any bets on what these *really* are all about?

Personnel needs assessment

The staffing process is closely intertwined with the goals and plans of the organization. As an organization grows or contracts, as it expands into new markets or consolidates, it will require a certain "mix" of employees.

This mix is the basis of a personnel needs assessment which is developed in the following way: First, an employment profile is developed that shows the expected types and numbers of employees that will be needed at future dates. Next, an analysis is made of current employees (if any) and these current employees are "projected" into the future. Taking into account such human events as expected retirements, projections of possible deaths, injuries, resignations and terminations as well as expected results of current training and on-the-job learning, we estimate what our current employee group will look like at selected future points. The gap (if any) between projected needs and the future status of our current employee group delineates when and where staffing must occur. For example, due to an announced intention to retire in five years, we project a vacancy in the vice president of sales position. Is there an existing employee who should be groomed for that position? If so, how do we plan to cover *that* vacancy? If no current employee is likely to fill the requirements, when and where do we recruit?

The need to base this personnel assessment on organizational plans should be obvious. For example, if the organization plans to close the eastern U.S. office in three years, perhaps we can use those employees who might be willing to move to cover expected needs in our expanding southern office. Or, if the organization plans to introduce its product into three new states in the next four years, we should plan well in advance to obtain those employees needed to staff the facilities we will be establishing. Staffing then should be *anticipatory* rather than *reactionary*. Stewart shows an interesting way of looking at personnel planning from a project management/life cycle framework.[7] In Exhibit 8–2 we show Stewart's notion of how to view the personnel resources necessary for two projects; one the introduction of a new product and the other a merger of two departments in an organization. In both cases it should be noted that the number of workers and the nature of the task is being considered at different stages of the project.

A needs assessment program that is done correctly can yield another benefit. By planning for a progression through various jobs by certain employees or groups of employees, "job ladders" or career patterns can be viewed by employees. The ability to see where a person might go in the organization may serve as a powerful motivator to stay with the organization and develop one's skills. Of course, dead-end jobs may become very visible. In either case we can use that information for original employee hiring and placement.

The Dallas Cowboys, mentioned earlier, owe much of their success to their sound needs assessment program. Given the "style" of their coach, a certain "style" of play is planned for into the future. "Job descriptions" are created

Exhibit 8–2
Personnel planning for a project: A life cycle view

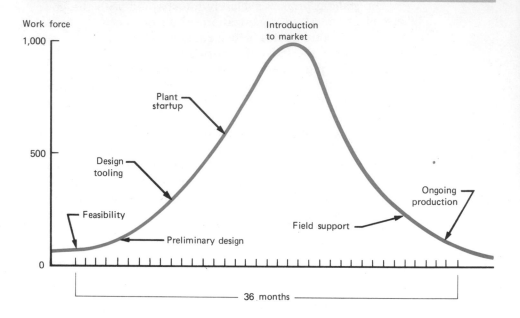

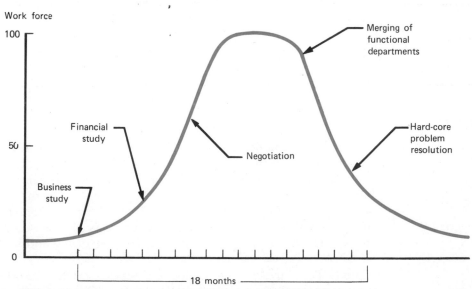

Source: Adapted from John M. Stewart, "Making Project Management Work," in David J. Cleland and William R. King, *Systems, Organizations, Analysis, Management* (New York: McGraw-Hill Book Company, 1969), p. 292.

to describe the various positions on the offense, defense, and special teams. The skills of current players are then analyzed and allowances made for predicted injuries, retirements, decreasing skills in older players, and improvement in younger ones. This is done position by position. Thus, the team knows with a reasonable amount of certainty what types of players it will need in various future years. Given this, the scouts' efforts can be channeled into the most productive areas. Thus, when it comes time for the NFL player draft, the team can make more rational selections. If the assessment shows a need for a top running back and if the Heisman Trophy winner looks like your man, then the strategy is to trade for a draft pick that will allow the team to get its man (i.e., obtain Tampa Bay's first round selection by trading away some players whose skills aren't badly needed and select Tony Dorsett). If the needs can likely be met by players expected to be still available when the team's own allocated picks come up, then no such dealing is necessary.

Exhibit 8–3 is a model that illustrates the staffing process we have been describing. Organizational goals lead to job specifications and job descriptions. We then assess our personnel needs. Employees are then obtained. Note that we should consider the use of temporary help (e.g., Kelly Services, Manpower,

Exhibit 8–3
The staffing process: Initial organization startup

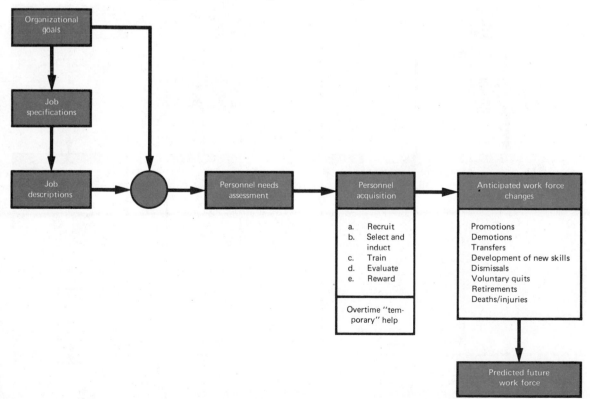

Inc.) and the use of overtime. We then predict our future work force based upon changes that we anticipate in our newly acquired work force.

In Exhibit 8–4 we elaborate on the model to show how a manager should take actions based upon the predictions made about the future work force. First, note the arrows from the predicted future work force to organizational goals and to personnel needs assessment. This indicates that we may wish to change some aspects of the organizational goals due to the predicted presence or absence of certain employee skills. In other words, we may wish to alter our good or service output in recognition of things that our employees are/ aren't capable of doing. Based upon this new personnel needs assessment we ascertain whether or not a gap exists between desired and expected personnel levels. If we find a negative gap (i.e., a lack of employees with desired skills), we should first call back any laid-off workers and if necessary then engage in the personnel acquisition process. If we have excess employees (a positive gap) we must engage in personnel cutbacks/layoffs. Cutbacks are appropriate where we do not expect to again need those employees for a reasonable period of time. Layoffs should be used if the positive gap is expected to be temporary.

Exhibit 8–4
The staffing process: A cyclical view

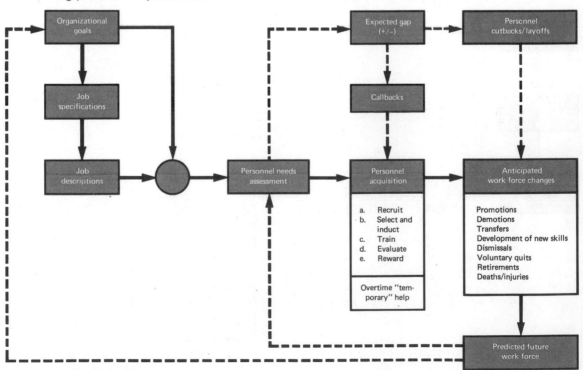

A major implication in Exhibit 8–4 is that staffing is a constantly occurring management task. Even in the absence of employee turnover (a very unlikely occurrence in any case) the constant reassessment of organizational goals leads to numerous personnel needs assessments. Thus, management is at least implicitly going through staffing decisions even if those decisions are to take no overt actions. An analysis was undertaken and a decision made in any case.

Now that we have discussed the general staffing process, we will turn to a discussion of some of the more visible staffing activities that we often see being done by personnel managers.

PERSONNEL ACQUISITION

Acquiring personnel is a process that involves several distinct phases. As was shown in Exhibits 8–3 and 8–4, acquisition comes only after a needs assessment and is thus based upon organizational goals, job specifications, and job descriptions.

Recruitment

Recruitment has as its major objective providing a large enough group of candidates so that the organization will be able to select those persons with the required skills. Thus, we usually do not recruit just the number of people we wish to hire; we recruit more so as to be sure we can obtain enough qualified candidates and to assure ourselves that of those people in the job market we have had the chance to acquire the best.

For lower level, operative jobs (both white and blue collar), we usually engage in what is known as *general recruiting*. For these types of jobs (e.g., janitor, drill press operator, typist, salesperson, bookkeeper) job descriptions are usually similar across many organizations. It follows that we can usually use rather straightforward and widely used means to assess a candidate's qualifications. For example, the typist can be given a typing test, the drill press operator can be placed in front of a machine and given a blueprint of a part and the bookkeeper can be given a test over the types of accounts the job covers. An organization may recruit a number of applicants for such jobs, note applicants' qualifications and then "stockpile" acceptable candidates. Then, when a vacancy occurs, candidates can be called in a predetermined order. General recruiting is appropriate where routine turnover tends to cause certain jobs to rather consistently have vacancies.

In many cases under general recruiting, the *exact* job is not known by the applicants until the first day on the job. The drill press operator is simply told that ". . . the job will be in Department 16 and H. O. Gauge will be your foreman."

For higher level, more "unique" jobs, we usually do not have a stockpile of talent primarily because the job description is "one-of-a-kind" in nature, or because we may have a person(s) in mind for the job who has not actually applied. When coaching vacancies occur in sports organizations, calls are often made to friends to see who might be interested/qualified. The organization may seek out and encourage applicants if they are perceived to be qualified. Other applicants hear of the vacancy and put their own names into contention. Management then chooses the "best." Such *specialized recruiting* occurs for higher level business organization jobs, executive level jobs in government, administrative and some teaching jobs in universities, and in other similar situations.

In comparison with general recruiting, note that the specific job is known to the applicant. Further, extensive interviewing with prospective co-workers and superiors is widely utilized. The applicant is often given travel funds for an on-site visit and much entertaining goes on.

Generally, there are "outside" and "inside" recruiting sources. Initially, an organization staffing for the first time will use outside sources. Newspaper advertisements, government and private employment agencies, schools, signs in front of the building (widely used for factories), and similar sources exist to inform the general public of personnel needs.

Inside sources are widely used for other than entry level jobs. Vacancies are often "posted" and promotions from within and transfers used to fill vacancies. Of course, this opens up another job, and this, too, must be filled. A series of promotions and transfers may be caused by an initial vacancy. Filling job vacancies from within can serve as a motivator in that employees see good work leading to advancement. Also, current employees need little or no indoctrination into the organization. And, such a procedure is often less expensive than an outside search even with the "chain reaction" promotions and transfers.

Selection

Two decisions take place in selection: (1) the organization decides to offer a job and (2) the individual decides whether or not to accept it. There is obviously a balancing of inducements made by the organization (pay, other benefits, and so on) and the performance contributions expected from the prospective employee (being at work or on call at certain times, amount of effort to be expended, and so on).

Often under a specialized recruiting situation the organization decides to offer the job even before the prospective applicant is made aware of the job. This could, for example, be the case where a baseball team seeks out a certain new manager or a university seeks out a particular professor. The organization must then talk the prospective employee into accepting the new job.

Under general recruiting there is usually a more explicit and ordered sequence in the selection process. The standard process is usually as follows:

1. An application is made and certain information collected.
2. A screening interview may then be held with each applicant. It usually is held with those applicants that appear to be potentially acceptable.
3. Testing of job-relevant skills.
4. Reference checks and background investigation. This includes past employment and any required licenses/credentials. Character investigations are also done if appropriate (e.g., FBI checks on prospective judges and cabinet officials, checks on criminal records of prospective bank tellers, and so on).
5. In-depth interviews.
6. Physical exam (if appropriate).
7. Job offer.

This process is shown in Exhibit 8–5. Note that the attention given each step may be perfunctory or significant depending on the specific circumstances surrounding the job.

The *application* is the starting point of the process. Where application forms are used the data can become a part of the employee's record (if hired). Deliberate misinformation may be a condition for later dismissal. Also, the application indicates at least an initial interest on behalf of the applicant, plus it serves as a basis for subsequent interviewing, testing, and background examination.

Based upon the Civil Rights Act of 1964, as amended, it is illegal to discriminate in employment on the basis of race, creed, nationality, color, or sex. The Age Discrimination Act of 1967 adds a further category. This requires the elimination from application blanks questions that would reveal information allowing the organization to so discriminate.

A review of federal legislation and the rights laws of most states indicates that the following are illegal questions: (1) asking applicants if they have ever worked under another name, or for the birthplaces of their parents, spouse, or other close relatives; (2) asking how abilities to read, write, or speak a foreign language were acquired; (3) asking for a list of all clubs, societies, and lodges in which membership is held; (4) asking for religious affiliation, name of church, or religious holidays observed; (5) asking whether and when the applicant was ever arrested. In general, these questions can be interpreted as seeking information which would reveal national origin, race, creed, or color of the applicant. Firms can ask what foreign languages are spoken as potentially usable for job

Exhibit 8-5
The selection process

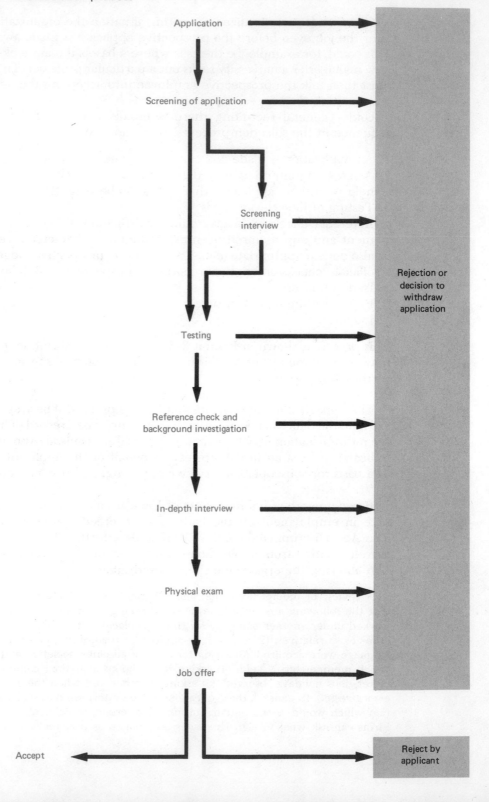

Application

Screening of application

Screening
interview

Rejection or
decision to
withdraw
application

Testing

Reference check and
background investigation

In-depth interview

Physical exam

Job offer

Accept

Reject by
applicant

assignment. They can also ask for prior conviction of crimes, but not for arrests, inasmuch as one does not always lead to the other.[8]

Also, it would be illegal to ask whether the applicant is male or female (unless the job is "sex specific," e.g., restroom attendant), whether a female (or male!) applicant had children or planned to have any, or even the age of the applicant (unless some age related law is involved; e.g., some states prohibit children under 16 to work full time). Note that the above do not pertain just to application blanks; you can't verbally request this information in an interview either.

Recent Civil Rights legislation puts a special burden on the recruiting process. Under Equal Employment Opportunity Commission (EEOC) guidelines, organizations must not restrict recruiting efforts in such a way that minorities become excluded. In fact, affirmative action programs often require an organization to take special efforts to recruit minority applicants.

The initial *screening of the application* serves to eliminate any clearly unqualified candidates. The person receiving the application can ask questions concerning experience, pay expectations and the like. Also note can be made of the applicant's behavior which is "job relevant." For example, was he/she able to communicate clearly, was the applicant dressed in soiled clothing, did the person appear to be under the influence of drugs? Where appropriate, the screening interview or the later in-depth interview should explore these observations.

Exhibit 8–6 illustrates (somewhat facetiously) why such screening is often necessary. Several examples are presented of how one can creatively write up experiences and qualifications tailored to the organization to which a job application is made. The applicant's "real" experience is as follows:

1. Worked in a grocery store while in high school. Primary responsibility was to remove rotten tomatoes and other vegetables from the display shelves.
2. Had a summer job helping a law student. Typed briefs and assembled papers for the law student who was at the time working in a lawyer's office.
3. Served as a swimming instructor at a pool used by foreign exchange students.
4. Served as a marshal in several protest demonstrations.

Testing is used to estimate the applicant's ability to do the job. Where possible the test should be under actual job conditions and should replicate the actual job insofar as is practical. For example, if the job will be done under noisy conditions with other people around, then test under those conditions.

Testing (especially psychological) has often been viewed as an invasion of privacy. William H. Whyte, Jr., in *The Organization Man,* has provided a set of guidelines entitled "How to Cheat on Personality Tests" designed to enable the reader to "pass" virtually any personality test and thus evade the invasion.[9]

Exhibit 8–6
A creative writing example of reporting prior job experiences

Prospective employer	Sorting rotten vegetables	Typing for student briefer	Teaching exchange students how to swim	Marshal in protest demonstrations
International Telephone and Telegraph	Decision making position with a vegetable marketing unit. Experienced in shredding rejects.	Assistant to chief briefer in a law firm. Coordinated security plan relating to internal documents.	In charge of a small, but important educational program with direct supervision of 15 trainees; emphasis on international programs.	Official position to moderate "shareholders" demands for change in management. Experienced in evading confrontation with domestic authorities.
Inter-American Development Bank	Variable grading of vegetables with emphasis on marketing factors.	Document preparation for use in policy determination.	Directed a technical assistance program with a focus on transference of skills.	Served as an adviser in fostering self-help efforts in the implementation of an international program with emphasis on local initiative.
Harpers Ferry High School (teaching position)	Worked on motivational consumer factors in a community-oriented enterprise.	Assisted in studies concerning the individual's relationship to community standards as reflected in local ordinances and state/national statutes.	In charge of a youth instructional activity with emphasis on individual needs and performance standards.	Motivational supervisor in a mass program designed to alter national goals and targets.
Department of the Army	Established parameters on product differentiation and implemented quality control program on specified food products.	Directly responsible for preparation of specialized documents that served as basis for strategic planning and action.	Planned and executed a program designed to meet student performance objectives of increased mobility in aquatic elements.	Key position in an organized effort to prevent unauthorized incursion and to foster self-discipline and prudence in a highly motivated and articulate group of citizens.

When in doubt . . . there are two general rules you can follow: (1) When asked for word associations or comments about the world, give the most conventional run-of-the-mill, pedestrian answer possible. (2) To settle on the most beneficial answer to any question, repeat to yourself:

a. I loved my father and my mother, but my father a little bit more.
b. I like things pretty well the way they are.
c. I never worry much about anything.
d. I don't care for books or music much.
e. I love my wife and children.
f. I don't let them get in the way of company work.[10]

Title VII of the 1964 Civil Rights Act has been used to fight tests that seemingly lead to discrimination. The Equal Employment Opportunity Commission has backed a number of complaints related to testing. In 1971, the U.S. Supreme Court in *Griggs* v. *Duke Power Company* declared that a high school diploma could not be used as a job qualification requirement since its relationship to job performance (in this case, shoveling coal) was unproved. At the same time, the Court also restricted the use of the Wonderlic Personnel Test and the Bennett Test of Mechanical Comprehension. Basically, the courts and the EEOC require that there be empirical statistical validity showing a significant relationship between a test score predictor and specific measures of job performance. The burden of proof is on the employer.[11]

EEOC actions have reduced the abuses of improper employment tests and requirements. However, organizations still have great difficulty in establishing tests and requirements that meet EEOC approval. AT&T, for example, has been hiring many females for the job of installing and repairing lines on telephone poles since 1973. These women were involved in on-the-job accidents at a rate three times that of men in the same jobs.[12] AT&T devised three tests that were believed to weed out the overweight, uncoordinated, and weak applicants (male and female) for these jobs: (1) balance on one leg on a beam three quarters of an inch wide that is laid on the ground, (2) stretch a steel cable across the chest, and (3) submit to a measurement of the proportion of body fat. AT&T claims that by using these tests it has substantially reduced accidents. However, since women fail the test in disproportionate numbers (especially the strength-related steel cable stretch test) the firm's tests may be struck down. According to EEOC guidelines, AT&T must *prove* that their test is the *least discriminatory* way to weed out the accident-prone.

Basically, EEOC rules state that if an organization can prove by its records that it hires minority group members at a rate of at least 80 percent of that at which it hires from the demographic group (usually, but not always, white males) that comprises most of the employees, then the organization is in compliance. For example, if out of every 100 white male applicants the firm hires 75, then if the firm hires 60 (i.e., 80 percent of 75) out of every 100 minority group applicants, it is "safe" in that "generally" the EEOC will leave it alone.

We wonder how the EEOC might react to the situation described by a British professor (Hans Eysenck, professor of psychology at the London University of Psychiatry):

In a U.S. company I studied we tried to find the real criteria by which staff were chosen. We were at a loss in the typing pool, because the women there differed widely by every measure of personality, work-quality, etc. . . . until we noticed they all had bust measurements of 38 inches or more.[13]

While we discuss relevant qualifications we should also point out the "over-qualified" phenomena which has arisen in recent years. When aeronautical engineers were laid off from California firms, they couldn't even get cabdriver jobs. The cab firms felt that the engineers would be on the lookout for better work and would probably quit very soon, thus forcing the organization into another round of hiring. Another aspect of overqualification was expressed by the founder of McDonald's:

Ray Kroc apparently knew from his own extensive commercial travels that an immaculate privy was a roadside phenomenon, sought after as much as gas and food. The brisk, happy rumble of good clean plumbing in a spotless white-tiled cubicle would rank high in the esteem of the suburban middle class that he targeted as McDonald's primary market. Like hamburgers and french fries, clean toilets were something basic and simple that everyone could understand. "You wouldn't hire a guy from Harvard?" someone asked Ray Kroc not long ago. And the founder answered, "I couldn't hire a guy from Harvard because the s.o.b. wouldn't get down and wash the toilets."[14]

The *reference check* and *background investigation* is made to ascertain the truth/validity of application form data. Studies have shown that a significant portion of all application forms contain data that is false.[15] Based upon recent legislation, applicants may often gain access to statements made about them by previous employers, friends, neighbors, and others. As a counter to this, many respondents will now give the investigator negative comments only via an unrecorded verbal response—one that will not become a part of a record that can be obtained by the applicant.

The *in-depth interview* is designed to do two things. First, the interviewer can probe for information on subjects raised in any of the previous steps. For example, why didn't the applicant state that he/she didn't quit the previous job but was fired? Why did the applicant type only 75 words per minute on the test rather than the 97 wpm capability stated on the application. Second, the interview should be used to seek data not thus far obtained. For example, why does the applicant want a job like this one? What is the applicant's career goal?

Recently a new voice-analyzer "truth machine" has been placed on the market to analyze verbal responses such as those in interviews.[16] Some organizations claim to use these devices to check on the applicants' responses. Also, there are organizations (e.g., CIA, and many businesses) that require an applicant to take a polygraph exam at this stage of the selection process. A survey by John Belt and Peter Holden of Wichita State University showed that 20 percent of the largest companies in the United States use lie detectors.[17] For example, Eckerd Drugs, a large chain, requires all employees (including the president) to undergo the test, and an Atlanta nursing home uses the tests to weed out potentially sadistic or otherwise disturbed nurse and orderly job applicants.[18] Only a few states forbid or restrict the use of polygraphs or voice-analyzers. Clearly, this is an area of extreme emotion as prospective employees worry about a loss of privacy and employers worry about entrusting their property (and sometimes lives) to potentially dishonest or disturbed people.

Recently, several researchers have cast doubts over the validity/utility of polygraph results.[19] A number of subjects first took a typical polygraph exam and tried to deceive the operator by lying about certain numerical data. The operator caught the deceit 88 percent of the time. Then the volunteers were randomly divided into three groups. One group received a month-long biofeedback training program where they learned to monitor and control galvanic skin response via relaxation techniques. A second group was taught to use autohypnotic suggestion to relax and control their arousal level. The third group was the control and received no training.

At the end of the month all volunteers again underwent the polygraph exam. For groups one and two, the polygraph operator caught the lie only 24 percent of the time. For group three (control) there was no significant change from the 88 percent rate. Apparently, biofeedback and autohypnotic methods allow people to influence what is measured during the polygraph exam.

This means that many industries which in the past have hired, threatened and fired employees through [lie detectors] have no longer a scientific basis for that action. It also suggests the possibility of a nationwide chain of biofeedback or hypnosis schools offering quick cram courses to those facing polygraph tests.[20]

The next to last step in the selection process is the *physical examination*. These exams are not required in all cases. However, where relevant they perform an important function. Customers and other members of the organization can be protected against contagious diseases (e.g., restaurants). The exam assures that the applicant (high-level manager as well as blue-collar employees) will be able to physically do the job. And the exam provides data to possibly protect the organization from improper worker's compensation claims.

Assuming that all the previous hurdles are successfully cleared, a *job offer* is made. The applicant must then weigh the benefits of the job against the demands of it and also compare the job with others that might be available.

Induction

The initial entry of a new employee into an organization is a crucial time. Often the experience is a new one; new sights, sounds, different types of people, perhaps a change in home life (e.g., getting up at 6:00 A.M. to drive 25 miles to work), and so on. Orientation programs are used to explain organization policies, rules, and benefits to the new employee as well as to introduce the new employee to the daily routine and to give the employee a review of the organization's history, its products, and where it fits in society at large.

The new employee must also be introduced to co-workers. This can be unsettling if the existing employee group for some reason decides to "test" the newcomer or indeed decides to "reject" the new employee (e.g., a rookie female police officer in a heretofore staunch all-male department).

A number of studies have shown that the work demands placed on the new employee will exert a strong influence on task performance in later years.[21] More demanding early work assignments are correlated with high performance in later years in that organization. This could be due to the new employee internalizing high-performance standards. Or it could be that the employees who did well on the early demanding task were noticed by management and were constantly given other challenging tasks. Other equally capable new employees not given the demanding tasks and thus not having the chance to show their capabilities could be doomed to a constant stream of mediocrity by not catching the attention of management.

Training

To paraphrase an old army saying, "There's a right way, a wrong way, and then there's *our* way." The new drill press operator has to learn the organization's method of maintaining the machine. The typist has to learn how this organization wants letters or reports set up. Training refers to the acquisition of skills necessary to do one's current job. Employee development, which we cover later, refers to teaching an employee skills that prepare one for another (usually higher level) job.

Training needs can be ascertained via several means. First, for example, the new employees may simply not know how to run a widget smasher. From the application and tests we can determine if the employee is capable of learning but does not now have the skill. Second, an analysis and appraisal of the employee's actual performance may point out a deficiency. Third, management can decide that a particular organization unit may need general training. For example, due to a high turnover rate of typists, all office supervisors will sit in on a class designed to teach human relations skills.

There is a wide variety of training techniques to choose from. Quite common is on-the-job training where the employee is simply placed on the "firing line" with perhaps some initial instructions and the watchful eye of the superior. Vestibule training is similar in that the employee is placed in the situation of actually doing the job; however, in this case it is not on the "firing line"; it takes place in a "vestibule" or simulation of the real situation. For example, before being allowed to run the widget smasher the new employee spends a week working on a simulator. The new typist spends three days typing a series of "training aid" letters and reports before being given the real thing. The objective in vestibule training is to reduce the pressures and fear inherent in actual on-the-job situations while the job is being learned. A variation of the vestibule approach involves sending new employees to a program run by machinery suppliers to learn how to operate equipment sold to the organization. (IBM often teaches new typists how to operate the word processing equipment owned or leased by the new employee's organization.)

Finally, a new worker can be placed under the tutelage of a skilled employee for some pointers.* Apprenticeship programs are formal versions of this approach that involve specified amounts of time doing various work under a "master." Internship programs usually combine job experiences with classroom training, with the job experience being closely watched by a "preceptor."

Hamburger University in Elk Grove Village outside of Chicago stands as one of 20th-century America's testaments to training. Established in 1968 by McDonald's, all new owner-operators and store managers attend Hamburger University, where they are taught how to do things the McDonald's way. Courses include "Buns," "Carbonization," "Big Mac," "Building Maintenance," and many others. Other firms have similar programs: Mr. Donut in Massachusetts, Kentucky Fried Chicken University (KFCU) in Louisville, and Holiday Inn's Learning Center, among others. (What would we call a football bowl game between Hamburger U. and KFCU?)

Evaluating performance

One of the most important yet most mishandled aspects of management is performance appraisal. Managers freely admit that evaluating and critiquing subordinates' performance is an often difficult and emotionally upsetting task.

Most organizations have formal performance appraisal systems where boss and employee meet to discuss performance and fill out certain forms that record the appraisal for inclusion in the employee's records. More informal appraisals take place whenever feedback (praise or criticism) is given on work

---

* Most hunting dogs get trained by being taken on hunts in the company of skilled dogs. Hopefully, the young pups learn by observing the older, skilled dogs. A danger here is that the new dog, while picking up the good techniques of the older dogs, will also pick up bad habits.

performed. This can take place at a casual meeting in the elevator, over coffee, or in the office.

Merit raises are often given out based on performance appraisal results. Also, training needs tend to be based on these appraisals. That abuses can take place unless the appraisals are done "properly" is shown by recent reports concerning performance appraisal and merit raises of Federal Civil Service employees. In 1977 only 226 out of 2.1 million federal workers were fired for incompetence. At least some of the problems of the Federal Civil Service can be blamed on a complacency and lack of forthright action in personnel performance evaluation by supervisors. Virtually all employees are given at least a "satisfactory" rating and for these people an "acceptable level of competence" certification normally follows. This makes them eligible for regular within-grade "merit pay" increases. Only about ½ of 1 percent of civil service employees receive "unsatisfactory" ratings. Is it really possible that 99.5 percent of all federal civil servants truly deserve "merit" increases? If not, why are supervisors unwilling to give even deserved unsatisfactory ratings? One reason is that such a rating is subject to appeal all the way up the line with higher authorities constantly questioning the supervisor's evidence and/or judgment. Also, an advance 90 days' notice must be given to an employee before an "unsatisfactory" can be given. Thus, the system itself encourages the cavalier attitude that everyone takes. All too often it is easier to transfer or promote(!) poor workers into numerous "turkey farms" conveniently buried in organizational hierarchies.

The 1978 amendment to the Age Discrimination in Employment Act of 1967 forbids mandatory retirement before the age of 70. While few organizations would openly admit it, in the past less effective workers were often eased out through mandatory retirement at an earlier age, though of course some productive workers were lost as well. Such behavior will probably now change as organizations will be quite concerned with the costs of keeping a "poor" employee until the age of 70.

When a guy is not doing so hot at 53 but only has two years to go before our pension plan kicks in at 55, we'll give him a token raise and let him stay. But now that we might have to keep him until 70, we will no longer have that compassionate alternative to let him stay till 55.[22]

This will necessitate an even greater reliance on productivity measures for old and young employees alike. This means that performance evaluations must be well done since employees can be discharged only "for cause."

We will discuss performance evaluations in detail in Chapters 13 and 14. However, note several problem areas that can occur. The halo effect refers to the evaluator viewing an employee's good (bad) performance on one task and then being subsequently biased in favor of (or against) that employee when other measures are taken. Also, evaluators tend to concentrate on recent behavior, especially the past six weeks. Thus, evaluations often fail to cover the entire review period. Finally, different evaluators have different standards. What is "excellent" to one evaluator may be only "very good" to another. Thus, the same actual performance can receive different evaluations (a circumstance many students have experienced when they got a "hard" or "easy" teacher and friends were in the other sections).

Rewarding employees

Several "types" of motivation are important when we discuss reward systems.* First, there is the motivation to *join* the organization. The jobs and the pay offered by the organization compete against other potential opportunities that exist for job applicants. Our rewards must be sufficient to induce applicants to accept our offers. Second is the motivation to *stay*. Once "in" an organization there are costs inherent in quitting for another job (e.g., financial and psychological costs of the move, possible loss of some retirement benefits, loss of seniority). Based on the attractiveness of these other opportunities as compared with what our organization offers, employees will stay or leave. The third area is the motivation to *perform* at more than the minimum acceptable level (i.e., to do more than just enough to keep from being fired). Perceptions of equity exist in the minds of employees and there is a tendency to put forth a level of effort consistent with the perceived equity of the rewards derived from the job.

These motivations are influenced by what we call *external* and *internal* equity. External equity is concerned with the comparison of our organization's pay and benefits for a given job with the pay and benefits for a reasonably similar job in other organizations with which we "compete" for employees.

These comparisons should be made job by job. For many "lower level" jobs (e.g., clerk-typist, janitor, bank teller, bookkeeper, and so on), especially those for which general recruiting is appropriate, there is great similarity of jobs among the "competing" organizations. For higher level jobs the similarity (task by task) may not be as great; however, a similarity by general functions is present (e.g., hospital administrator, vice president of personnel, comptroller—we "know" what these jobs entail).

Wage/salary surveys are the mechanisms used to acquire the data and make these pay comparisons. Several steps are involved:

1. Assemble up-to-date job descriptions of the jobs under consideration.
2. Determine which organizations are "competitors" with ours for employees.

---

* Rewards in organizations can be extrinsic or intrinsic. In this section we are referring to extrinsic rewards; more specifically, pay and benefits. This material is discussed in detail in Chapter 10.

3. Contact these organizations (usually through their personnel departments) to obtain their cooperation in the survey. This is usually not difficult in that wage data is most often at least "quasi-public" information. The promise of a summary of results is a very good bargaining chip. Five to ten representative competitor organizations are usually adequate.
4. In each cooperating organization, ask, one job description at a time:
    a. Does your organization have a job reasonably comparable to this one?*
    b. If yes to the above, What is the pay for that job at: (1) entry and (2) top of scale?†
5. After collecting this data from cooperating organizations, make comparisons, first at entry level and then at top of scale for each job to find where our organization fits (i.e., are we the highest payer, the lowest, the average?). This comparison is done first for actual pay since placing a monetary value on benefit packages is difficult. The analysis can then be subjectively annotated to include the benefit package data.

Exhibit 8–7 shows a comparison chart actually used by the authors for a wage/salary survey.

Based upon this wage/salary survey, we can ascertain whether or not our wages are "externally equitable." That is, are we paying the "going wage" or not? Since external equity is a major determinant in motivating employees to join and stay, this data is of obvious relevance.

Internal equity is concerned with the level of rewards (pay) being consistent with the actual contribution of jobs toward organizational goals. That is, if job A contributes more to organizational goals than job B, then job A should be paid more than job B. The technique used to make this determination is job evaluation. As with the wage/salary survey, up-to-date job descriptions are necessary for a sound job evaluation.

There are four commonly used job evaluation approaches. First is a simple *ranking* of jobs. This approach is most applicable to small organizations with only a small number of different jobs. A person or panel of people familiar with the jobs simply places them in rank order according to their perception(s) of the jobs' contribution to organizational goals. While ranking is a simple approach, it is crude. A major drawback is that it does not allow for the absolute level of differences between ranks. For example, jobs A, B, and C may be ranked in that order. However, A and B are very close with C a quite distant third. The simple ranking fails to point out this magnitude of differences.

---

* It is unusual to find organizations with perfectly identical jobs even for such jobs as janitor or typist. We usually use a 70 percent rule; i.e., if the other organization's job description is at least 70 percent the same as ours, we accept that job as a "comparable" one.

† Some surveys also ask for "average" pay or for the pay after so many years, and so on. The person(s) doing the survey should use their judgment as to what actual data are collected.

Exhibit 8-7
Sample wage/salary survey chart

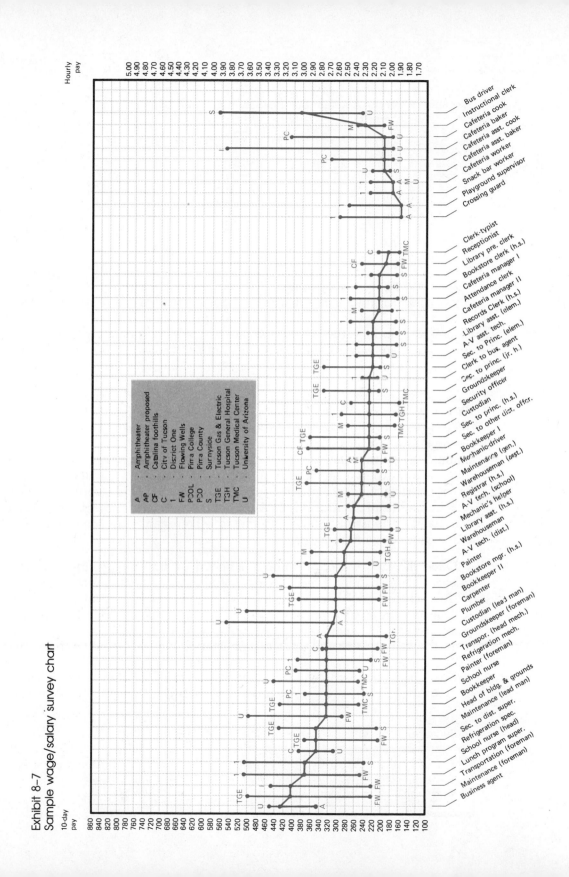

Exhibit 8–8
Example of the point system point allocation

Factor	Number of points	Percent
Skill	80	40.0
Education	25	12.5
Responsibility	30	15.0
Working conditions ...	35	17.5
Physical effort	30	15.0
Total	200	100.0

A second job evaluation approach is *job grading*. In this approach, a number of job classes or grades are established. For example, the Federal Civil Service has a scale of GS–1 to GS–18. Each class represents a pay grade. Based upon the job descriptions, the various jobs are assigned to various pay grades. This approach is an improvement over the simple ranking in that it establishes the magnitude of differences between jobs.

The third and most widely used job evaluation approach is the *point system*. With this approach management must first determine the *job factors;* i.e., those aspects of the jobs that are being compensated. For example, should the organizations be paying for skill, education, responsibility, effort, working conditions, or some other factors? Xerox has used a set of ten factors: education, training and experience, job complexity, accountability, internal contacts, external contacts, guidance of others' work, confidentiality of information, work surroundings, and physical effort.[23] Other organizations use others; those factors that are used must be relevant to the specific organization *and* understood and accepted by employees.

Once the factors are determined a specific number of points is assigned to each factor. Exhibit 8–8 shows a set of five factors with a total point value of 200. The person doing the analysis must decide how many total points will be used and then how to "weight" each factor by apportioning these points. Any "base" number of points can be used so long as each factor receives its number of points based upon its importance as determined by the analyst.

Next, scale values are constructed for each factor. Exhibit 8–9 shows a sample of this. After scale values are determined, each job is assigned a point value

Exhibit 8–9
Scale values for education factor

5	10	15	20	25
Ability to read & write	*Equivalent of 2 years high school*	*High school degree*	*Baccalaureate degree from university*	*Graduate degree*

Exhibit 8–10
Hypothetical allocation of pay for clerk typist

Skill	$2.35
Education	0.75
Responsibility	0.80
Working conditions	0.52
Physical effort	0.10
	$4.52

for each factor and a sum total of points computed. Jobs are then placed in order according to their point values.

The final job evaluation approach is the *factor-comparison* system. As with the previous discussion, job descriptions must be written and job factors must be determined. Next several *key jobs* are selected that management honestly believes are currently being paid a proper wage.

The person(s) doing the evaluation should then assign to each key job an amount of money for each job factor; the sum of these amounts, of course, equaling the actual wage. For example, assume a clerk typist job is one of the key jobs. It pays $4.52 an hour. Visualize a stack of 452 pennies and the job factors previously shown in Exhibit 8–8. Place various numbers of those pennies beside each job factor according to how you feel that job factor should be valued. The rule is that you have only 452 pennies and you have to assign them all. Exhibit 8–10 shows a possible allocation. Similar allocations of current pay are made for every other *key job*. The result is a set of scales as shown in Exhibit 8–11.

The next step is to take one job at a time and compare it to the key jobs factor by factor. For example, using Exhibit 8–11 and the job of secretary to the plant manager, first ascertain whether it requires more or less skill than the accountant. Let's say less. More or less than the clerk typist? Let's say more. OK. It is between those two jobs; i.e., between $2.35 and $3.00. Place it *exactly* where you think it should be. Let's say $2.75. Go on to education. More or less than the accountant?, and so on. Add up all the values and you get a dollar value for that job. Then, go on to the next job.

The factor-comparison method, while time consuming, is a very accurate method of job evaluation. A great benefit is that it always deals in money terms. There is no need to convert from ranks, grades, or points to actual pay rates.

Using the results of a wage/salary survey and a job evaluation, the organization can construct its pay program. The job evaluation process shows, on an

Exhibit 8–11
Factor comparison scales for a hypothetical organization

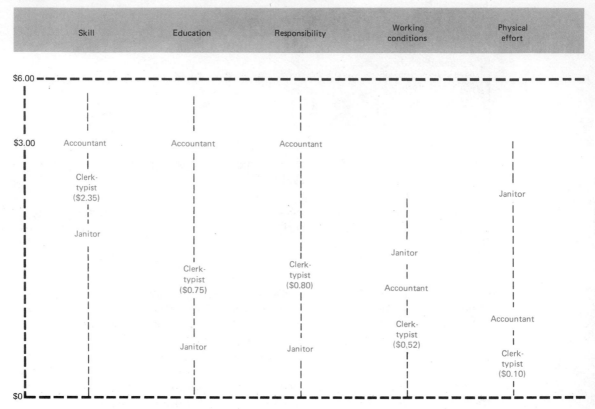

internal equity basis, the relative importance (and relative pay) of jobs, and the wage/salary survey shows on an external equity basis the competitive wage levels of the jobs in the community.

What happens if the results show that a given job (or person) is being paid more than is "appropriate?" We can cut the pay rate, of course. However, more often we "red flag" that job and give it no more raises until, via inflation and other jobs' raises, the pay becomes "appropriate" or until that person leaves the organization.

Developing employees

Promotion from within is a byword in many organizations. However, just because an employee can do the present job well does not mean that the employee can do a higher level job well, or even passably. For this reason, development plans are often created to both denote needed preparations as well as to monitor progress. Such plans are especially useful for managerial jobs but are by no means limited to them.

Development of talent prior to promotion (versus promotion and then training like mad to hopefully get up to speed) is an obvious way to avoid the infamous Peter Principle—"In a hierarchy every employee tends to rise to his level of incompetence."[24] The Peter Principle comes about from some all too common behavior: If a person does well in a job, a promotion is the likely result. Do a good job in the new position and another promotion should result. Keep doing good jobs and keep getting promoted. When do the promotions stop? When the person *stops* doing a good job. The result is that people rise up in a hierarchy to the point where they do poor work. However, if we do not promote simply because the person is doing a good job in their present position but because we also feel that the person has developed the skills necessary to do the new job well, we avoid the trap.

SUMMARY

To summarize, the staffing process includes two major functions: (1) work force planning and (2) personnel acquisition. Work force planning begins with an analysis of those tasks necessary to accomplish organizational goals. *Job specifications* are developed and jobs themselves created by *job descriptions*. Based further upon organizational goals and upon a flow of employees into and out of the organization, we *assess personnel requirements* for future points in time. Based upon this needs assessment, we acquire personnel. The personnel acquisition process involves seven stages: (1) *recruiting*, (2) *selection*, (3) *induction*, (4) *training*, (5) *performance evaluation*, (6) *rewarding*, and (7) *developing*.

In closing, staffing is one of the most highly refined processes in modern organizations. As we have indicated, there are clearly right and wrong ways of carrying out this function. Successful organizations are well aware of this fact and are willing to spend the money necessary to make it work. Their major initial investment in the staffing process is the recruitment and selection of a qualified personnel manager who typically operates in an advisory capacity to top management. The essential specifications of this position are: know the job, know the labor market, and know the labor laws.

GUIDES TO ACTION

1. Make sure your recruiting doesn't inadvertently exclude any minority groups. Go out of your way to reach them.

2. Have your application blank reviewed by a competent lawyer (call your local Bar Association to get names of those specializing in labor law). Also have the lawyer make a list of questions you *can't ask* in an interview. Have every interviewer memorize these. Keep the lawyer on retainer to advise of any law or guideline changes.

3. Work hard to develop appropriate "test" items that don't discriminate. Consider joining forces with other employers or industry groups to develop these.

4. Keep EXCELLENT records on recruiting efforts, applications received, tests given, and so on, so that any complaints won't automatically "win" simply because you couldn't defend yourself.

5. Above all, always keep in mind that your organization will never be any better than the people with whom it is staffed. Emphasize your staffing program accordingly.

And finally, here are several guidelines for hiring an "important" employee:*

1. Don't hire a reject. It is important to hire people who are currently employed. Good people don't leave one job before they have another. Those that do are "crapshooters" or "foolish." There are two exceptions: the recent graduate or someone who just moved into the area. But be sure to find out why the applicant moved!

2. Advertise. Some competitor may well have just the person you need without your having the expense of training them. It's worth a try.

3. Avoid employment agencies or "headhunters." People that go to headhunters usually lack the knowledge, experience, or confidence to "sell themselves" on their own. You don't need people like them.

4. Don't hire friends or friends of friends. You stand to hurt the organization or lose a friend if it doesn't work out. Didn't somebody once say something about mixing business and friendship?

5. Read the resume V-E-R-Y carefully. Be careful of people who emphasize that they "coordinated," "analyzed," "supervised," or "assisted." They probably never got their hands dirty. Also look for time gaps in the "previous experience" area. Find out where they were and what they were doing!

---

* Some of these hints are based on William Wayne, *How to Succeed in Business When the Chips Are Down* (New York: McGraw Hill Book Company, 1972). Others are our own. Check out Wayne's book to find out which is which. P.S.: Wayne's book has several suggestions (none listed here) that seem to us to be in violation of recent EEOC guidelines. (The book was written in 1972.) See if you can figure out which ones.

6. Check your "own" references. Would you list as a reference somebody you aren't reasonably sure will give you a good one? (The authors, while on a consulting assignment to recruit a school district superintendent, once put this one into practice. We called the Classroom Teachers' Association (union) president in the leading candidate's (then) current school district. If anybody would have the "dirt" on the applicant, this guy would! Next we called several members of the school board. We never did contact any reference given by the applicant. By the way, all their stories (union and school board) were consistent and the candidate was hired.)

7. Think about it. You might be able to get a real catch today, but will that person be moving on to even bigger and better things soon? Training is expensive. Maybe second best is best. Then again, maybe even a year or two from the superstar will be worth it. With our school superintendent, several board members thought our recommended applicant wouldn't stay two years, but they agreed he would be worth the expense if he only stayed one.

NOTES

[1] "Back to Basics," *Reader's Digest,* November 1977, p. 68.

[2] Reprinted by permission from *Time,* The Weekly Newsmagazine, January 16, 1978, p. 65. Copyright Time Inc. 1978.

[3] Ibid., p. 75.

[4] Jenkins, Dan, "Doomsday in the Dome," *Sports Illustrated,* January 23, 1978, p. 23.

[5] Benjamin Schneider, *Staffing the Organization* (Pacific Palisades, Calif.: Goodyear Publishing Co., 1976), p. 24.

[6] *New Yorker,* March 13, 1978, p. 110.

[7] John M. Stewart, "Making Project Management Work," *Business Horizons,* Vol. 8, no. 3 (Fall 1965), pp. 54–68.

[8] Edwin B. Flippo, *Principles of Personnel Management* (New York: McGraw-Hill Book Company, 1976), pp. 140–41.

[9] William H. Whyte, Jr., *The Organization Man* (Garden City, N.Y.: Doubleday & Company, Inc., 1956), pp. 449–56.

[10] Ibid., pp. 449–50.

[11] See Donald J. Peterson, "The Impact of Duke Power on Testing," *Personnel,* vol. 51, no. 2 (March–April 1974), pp. 30–37.

[12] Lee Smith, " 'Equal Opportunity' Rules Are Getting Tougher," *Fortune,* June 19, 1978, pp. 152–56.

[13] Michael Dixon, "Managers Fear Scientific Selection—Eysenck," *Financial Times (London),* May 23, 1978, p. 10.

[14] Max Boas, and Steve Chain, *Big Mac: The Unauthorized Story of McDonald's* (New York: New American Library, 1976), p. 19.

[15] See Robert Hershey, "The Application Form," *Personnel,* vol. 48, no. 1 (January–February 1971), pp. 36–43; and I. L. Goldstein, "The Application Blank: How Honest Are the Responses," *Journal of Applied Psychology,* vol. 55, no. 5 (1971), pp. 491–92.

[16] "Business Buys the Lie Detector," *Business Week,* February 6, 1978, pp. 100–4.

[17] Ibid., p. 100.

[18] Ibid.

[19] James Corcoran, M. David Lewis, and Richard Garver, "Biofeedback-Conditioned Galvanic Skin Response and Hypnotic Suppression of Arousal: A Pilot Study of Their Relation to Deception," *Journal of Forensic Sciences,* vol. 23, no. 1 (1978), pp. 155–62.

[20] "Beating the Polygraph at Its Own Game," *Psychology Today,* July 1978, p. 107.

[21] See David E. Berlew and Douglas T. Hall, "The Socialization of Managers," *Administrative Science Quarterly,* vol. 11 (1966), pp. 207–23.

[22] "When Retirement Doesn't Happen," *Business Week,* June 19, 1978, p. 82.

[23] Jay R. Schuster, "Job-Evaluations at Xerox: A Single Scale Replaces Four," *Personnel,* vol. 43, no. 3 (May–June 1966), pp. 15–19.

[24] Lawrence J. Peter and Raymond Hull, *The Peter Principle* (New York: Bantam Books, Inc., 1969), p. 7.

DISCUSSION QUESTIONS

1. How can the value of an organization's human resources be ascertained?

2. Develop a work force plan for an organization such as:
   a. Your college football or basketball team.
   b. A fraternity or sorority.
   c. A local restaurant.
   d. Or some other similar organization that you are familiar with.

3. Identify the steps in the personnel acquisition process.

4. Discuss the laws and regulations concerning job application forms or interviews.

5. What is the "job relevancy" requirement for tests and required skills?

6. Discuss the EEOC criteria by which an organization would be evaluated regarding minority hiring.

7. Why does the recent Age Discrimination in Employment Act place a burden upon the performance evaluation system?

8. Distinguish between internal and external equity. How is each ascertained?

CASE: NO ROOM AT THE TOP*

Lewis Latimer, supervisor of Special Test Operations, has a motivational problem created by organizational structure and work rules. The problem is a familiar one to many managers in business and industry even if the titles here are different. Let Lew Latimer explain:

"My problem is easy to explain but beyond me in terms of solution. I'm a supervisor at an electronics company which manufactures desk top electronic calculators. I head a group of about 20 special electrical test technicians. These men don't test parts on the assembly line but conduct special electrical tests on completed units as directed by management. We do such things as:

1. Conduct systems tests on field failure units.
2. Conduct ongoing reliability testing.
3. Conduct experimental testing for engineering.
4. Conduct special customer product testing (e.g., units for special applications).

_____

* From: Robert D. Joyce, *Encounters in Organizational Behavior: Problem Situations* (Elmsford, N.Y.: Pergamon Press, Inc., 1972), pp. 148–51.

"My men are electronics specialists typically, with military electronics background or are graduates of electronic trade schools. Some have certificates of completion from junior colleges which specialize in the sciences. We train the men we hire on the use of our test equipment and procedures but require practical electronic test experience as an employment prerequisite.

"The company currently has three technician classifications. They are:

Technician C *Trainee.* (Six months maximum.)

Technician B *Equipment Test Technician.* Familiar with all usual systems tests. Can perform all tests without assistance other than use of test manuals. (Up to four years.)

Technician A *Senior Equipment Test Technician.* Must perform all functions of Technician B plus be able to calibrate test equipment and write test specifications. (No limit.)

"Most men are hired as Technician C, which is considered an entry level position. If they learn their job well, they are promoted to Technician B at the end of six months. Technician B carries a higher pay scale and a limit of four years that the classification can be maintained. The purpose of this is to force a man to qualify for a broader range of responsibility. The same is true for Technician A. Most men qualify for Technician A in about three years.

"So, in my department, the majority of men are now in the top pay classification. It breaks out like this:

	Men
Technician C	1
Technician B	5
Technician A	14
Total	20

"We're a young company in a fast-moving industry. We make a good, reliable line of calculators, and most of our employees are proud of their products and the company. This has certainly been true of my technicians. You couldn't find a more highly motivated bunch of guys anywhere in the company.

"In recent months attitudes have begun to change. Several of the men have soured on the company and their jobs, after they reached the top of the pay scale for Technician A. For them, there's no place to go in the company and they know it.

"It's beginning to show up in their work too. A few of the men are taking a much more casual attitude toward their work than they used to . . . the old team spirit is really gone. When five o'clock comes the whole area is deserted. And these are guys that I used to have to chase home each evening.

"I talked to Frank Duncan about the problem. Frank is my boss and the director of operations at our facility. I suggested that the most promising persons in the Technician A category should be allowed to move to the Junior Engineer classification. But Frank didn't care much for this solution. He said that all engineering classifications should be used only for professionals (he means college graduates), and that if we opened this classification to nonprofessionals (he means my technicians), morale problems will develop in other areas.

"Duncan said he would consider a Super-Grade classification for outstanding men in the Technician A category, and asked me to write a new job description for this classification.

"For the moment I'm going along with that approach for lack of anything better, but I feel it is a short-range solution and the problem will be back with us in a year or so."

Questions

1. What is the fundamental issue(s) involved in this case?
2. What are the implications of the Super-Grade technician classification from the viewpoint of employee performance, job attitudes, and morale?
3. What are the implications of allowing technicians to move to a "professional" classification?
4. How else might this problem be effectively resolved?

Section four
Startup of the
organization

Setting an organizational system into motion requires special skills. Organizations must be started with care and brought up to a desired operating level. It is naïve to believe that a new organization will not contain unanticipated flaws, that personnel will not have to learn on the job, or that a "normal" output level can be immediately achieved. In this section we discuss a variety of techniques which can highlight and smooth many potential startup problems.

Level of Organizational Outputs

| SELECTION OF THE PRODUCT OR SERVICE | DESIGN OF THE SYSTEM | STAFFING THE ORGANIZATION | STARTUP OF THE ORGANIZATION | OPERATING THE ORGANIZATION IN THE STEADY STATE | IMPROVING THE ORGANIZATION | REVISION OF THE ORGANIZATION | TERMINATION OF THE ORGANIZATION |

| Decision-making processes; social value; goals; forecasts; policies; plans | Authority and responsibility; power; organizational structure; communications systems; job design | Work force planning; personnel management functions | Startup planning and scheduling; monitoring; alternative startup approaches | Motivation; leadership; production and operations management; control | Individual improvement programs and techniques; group conflict management; MBO | Evaluation of organizational policies; strategic choices; organizational change; organizational development | Partial terminations; cutback management; complete terminations; mergers; born-again strategies |

t_0

Time

Chapter 9
Startup of the organization

TWO STARTUP HORROR STORIES

How can I describe my emotions at this catastrophe. . . . I saw the dull yellow eye of the creature; it breathed hard, and a convulsive motion agitated its limbs.

Mary Shelly
Frankenstein

Automotive News *reported that in general the earliest Edsels suffered from poor paint, inferior sheet metal, and faulty accessories. . . . A former executive of the Edsel Division has estimated that only about half of the first Edsels really performed properly.*

John Brooks
The Fate of the Edsel

The startup phenomenon is an important issue in management for several reasons: Every organization undergoes some sort of startup at least once during its lifetime, so it is a common event across all organizations. Also, startup is different from other organizational activities and time periods and as such makes special demands on managers and workers. Finally, startup, depending upon how skillfully it is managed can set a positive or negative pattern for subsequent organizational processes. For the new business, startup is usually the make-or-break period for survival; for the existing firm, the startup of a new department or product line can drastically affect the contribution which these new endeavors can make in the long run.

STARTUP TYPES AND COMPLEXITY

Though our focus in this chapter is on the startup of a new organization, startup also occurs in a variety of other ways as indicated by the examples in Exhibit 9–1.

We can place startup of a new organization in sharper perspective by contrasting the general types of decisions which are made during this period with those of the prior and subsequent periods in the life cycle—design and operation (or steady state). Exhibit 9–2 illustrates that startup uses as known inputs decisions made about the product, objectives, structure, and jobs at the design state. Then, a startup plan is developed which has the objective of getting these diverse elements to operate as a system. Though variable from company to company, startup for purposes of our discussion may be thought of as completed when the organization is operating at its long run output level. From this point on, management turns its attention to the day-to-day problems of operation, and the broader questions of improvement, revision, and change.

The complexity of a startup is generally related to the number of employees in the organization and the sophistication of the productive processes (or technology) of the organization. In Exhibit 9–3 we have shown employee/technol-

Exhibit 9–1
Examples of different startup situations

The formation of a new organization from mergers, expansions, or reorganization.

The shakedown cruises of a newly built ship (initially with shipyard personnel to determine its seaworthiness and later with the new owner's crew aboard to acclimate them to the new "system").

A Broadway play opening (dress rehearsals, previews, road tours prior to Broadway).

The installation of a major piece of equipment (vendors usually have a major role in checking the operation).

The first operation of a pipeline (the Alaskan oil pipeline was filled with water at startup—a "wet" dry run).

A changeover to a new model year in automobile manufacture (an annual startup).

Opening a new department store (some have a "dry run" night complete with "customers" using Monopoly money).

Exhibit 9–2
Startup decisions contrasted with design and steady state

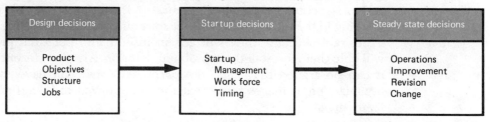

Design decisions	Startup decisions	Steady state decisions
Product Objectives Structure Jobs	Startup Management Work force Timing	Operations Improvement Revision Change

Exhibit 9–3
Hypothesized effect of number of employees and technology level on startup complexity

	Complexity of startup			
	Little	*Moderate*	*Moderate*	*Much*
Number of employees ...	Few	Many	Few	Many
Technology	Simple	Simple	Sophisticated	Sophisticated
Examples	Ma & Pa store	Copper mine	Electronics firm	Hospital

ogy combinations and some examples of organizations which display these characteristics. It should be obvious that small organizations which have simple production processes present less complicated startup situations than large ones having sophisticated production processes.

STARTUP PLANNING

Startup planning requires that decisions be made in two general areas:

1. Organization and staffing during startup.
2. Scheduling and execution of the startup.

We will spend the next few pages developing each of these areas.

Organization and staffing

Under this heading we are concerned with the organization structure of the startup and the personnel (both managerial and nonmanagerial) who carry it out. The broad strategies available to management for this purpose are:

1. Use the same organization structure and personnel as are to be used for the steady state operation (i.e., after startup).
2. Organize a special startup team under the direction of a project manager.
3. Use outside specialists who will either direct permanent personnel during the startup period or perform all startup activities with their own personnel.

Use of the same organization structure and personnel.   Using the same organization structure is appealing because it is one under which people will be working in the long run, so why not start out with it? Using the same personnel is desirable because they will get an insight into potential problems, which will help them forestall these problems later on. Also, in reference to personnel, it can be argued that since the permanent staff will have to live with the organization, it makes sense that they be allowed to "bend and shape" it in its infancy.

The general disadvantage of using the same organization structure and personnel is that one or both may be unsuited for the unique demands of the startup period. For example, functional organization structures while often suitable for long-run operations are far less effective in situations calling for the centralized (and rapid) coordination called for during startup. Similarly, certain managers are better suited for a stable work environment than for the variable, often "crisis" environment which typifies the startup period.

Likewise, operating personnel may be able to perform admirably when the system is debugged, but be inefficient or even frustrated when trying to work in the confusion which commonly attends a startup.

Startup teams. There are two common variants of this approach. One is to have "flying squads" of startup experts whose ongoing job is to startup new facilities. This approach is one often taken by large organizations which are expanding into new geographic areas by establishing new factories, branch offices, or stores (depending, of course, upon what their business is). The primary advantages of this structure is that teams can become highly proficient at coping with startup pressures by virtue of their experience with them at other installations. The disadvantage of this approach is that once the startup team's responsibility ends, unless great care is taken to train regular personnel in the system's operation, the latter may not be able to cope effectively with the inevitable problems which arise. A second problem centers on the job satisfaction of startup team members themselves. Such individuals must be away from home for extended periods, they are usually under severe time pressure to get the job done, and they are often not on a clear promotion pathway like other employees who have the opportunity to run the organization and show a profit.

A second common variant of the startup team approach is to select key members from the regular work force. In starting up a chemical plant, for example, it has been suggested that the startup team should consist of the following four groups, under the direction of the chief operating engineer:

1. A technical operating group, composed primarily of graduate engineers chosen especially for the startup.
2. A plant management group, which is expected to maintain supervisory and line control over the nontechnical operating personnel and which will assume technical control of the plant when the startup phase is over.
3. A maintenance group, which may be part of the normal plant staff but which may be supplemented with additional engineering members for the startup phase.
4. A laboratory group, which will be part of the normal plant staff but will be reinforced with additional technical advisers during the startup.[1]

This approach has much to recommend it—it takes advantage of the benefits of project structure* and it draws on individuals who have vested interest in the startup's success. However, whether or not it will work as well as the "flying squad" approach depends on the extent to which regular personnel are technically (and emotionally) qualified to handle the demands of startup.

Use of outside specialists. A number of construction firms specialize in what are termed *turnkey operations* in which they assume total responsibility for breaking in, as well as building, a new plant. Their services include hiring and training operating personnel and performing pilot runs in the completed

---

* Projects are designed around a particular goal which is to be accomplished in a specified period of time. Project structures as discussed in Chapter 5 are meant to do just this.

facility. When they turn over the "key" to permanent management, the system—theoretically at least—is ready for full-scale production.

Another approach, also using outside specialists, involves development of mixed startup teams, in which certain skills not possessed by in-house personnel are provided by consulting firms. For example, systems engineering capability is generally required to initiate a computerized control system in a steel plant, but it might be unnecessary or too costly for a steel company to retain systems engineering specialists on a permanent basis.

The advisability of employing outsiders depends upon the type of organization being set up, availability of internal startup skills, and the geographic location of the facility. Multinational organizations often use consulting engineers for turnkey operations. Such consultants usually are aware of the local culture and operating skills of the work force and naturally are in a better position to implement a new system than are foreigners who must get themselves started in a strange environment.

Startup scheduling

The way in which a typical organization sets about scheduling a startup is pretty much how any logical individual would go about scheduling any major project such as a move to a new house. That is, making a list of the things that have to be done and estimating the time to do them. Obviously, the major difference between the two projects is one of scale—a large organization has many more activities to perform and many more people to do them. Both projects, however, can be more easily carried out with the aid of graphical techniques which clearly display the necessary performance sequence of activities over time. The simplest type of such techniques is the Gantt chart (named for its developer); more complicated are critical path diagrams such as developed for the *Critical Path Method* (CPM). We will now demonstrate how these techniques are applied in the context of a small business startup situation—the opening of a fast-food restaurant called "Burgers Gourmet."

For both Gantt charts and CPM we need a list of the activities which must be performed by Burgers Gourmet, their required sequence, and our best estimate of the time it takes to complete them. In developing this list, we want to identify activities which are important aspects of the startup and which are consistent in detail relative to one another. We also want to make sure that we have activities which are unambiguous so that we may assign the responsibility for one or more to members of the startup team. A list which meets these criteria is shown in Exhibit 9–4.

Gantt chart.   A partial Gantt chart for the Burgers Gourmet startup is shown in Exhibit 9–5. Note that we have assumed that we are five weeks into the startup (and are a week behind schedule).

Exhibit 9–4
List of startup activities for Burgers Gourmet

Activity	Estimate of required time in weeks
Legal aspects	8
Facility design	12
Site selection	8
Financing	5
Determine work methods	6
Acquire equipment	8
Construct building	18
Hire and train help	4
Install equipment	6
Preopening readiness	3

Exhibit 9–5
Partial Gantt chart for Burgers Gourmet startup

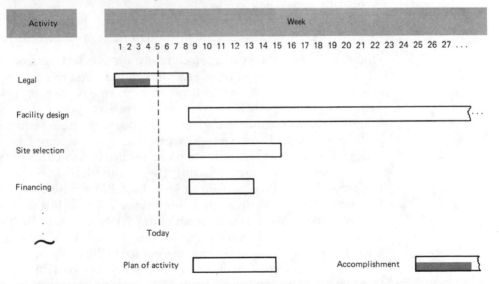

Critical path method.   In a book describing the history of the opening of a new plant making Jell-O products, the authors provide a nice summary of how and why CPM is used in startup:

The critical path method, which was employed in determining the plant production schedule was also used to set up a schedule for moving and starting up various administrative functions. It proves to be a very valuable tool because it demanded the following:

1. Planning in depth before scheduling.
2. Effective utilization of manpower with recognizable results.

3. Evaluation of major changes in plans to provide a minimum disruption in manpower and maximum assurance of fulfillment according to schedule.
4. Coordination among all areas involved in the move.
5. Continual checking of construction schedule changes to evaluate the effect on administrative functions.[2]

To use CPM requires the construction of a network and making some calculations to determine which *individual* activities within it must be completed within their scheduled time if the schedule for the entire startup is to be met.

In Exhibit 9–6 we have sketched the network listed in Exhibit 9–4 for the Burgers Gourmet startup. Note the following characteristics of the network:

1. All activities are well-defined jobs whose completion (in total) marks the end of the startup.
2. The activities are ordered in that they must follow a given sequence (as indicated by the direction of the connecting arrows).
3. Some activities can be carried out simultaneously, if adequate resources (usually personnel) are available.
4. Each activity is limited to one circle which implies that an activity once started must continue without interruption until completion.

Once the network is constructed (really the hardest part of CPM), the times when each activity must be started and completed are computed.* After these calculations are made, the "critical path" through the network can be identified. The critical path is the particular sequence of activities which takes the longest time to perform relative to any other possible sequence. The critical path indicates to the manager which activities must not be completed late if the startup is to be completed on schedule. It also indicates which activities can be delayed without affecting the completion date. Those activities on the critical path have no free time or (in CPM terminology) zero "slack." In Exhibit 9–6 we have indicated the critical path with a dashed line. We can also infer from this network the amount of slack associated with the noncritical activities. Site selection, for example, has two weeks of slack since the activity immediately following it cannot begin until facility design is completed. (Compare the times: Legal aspects (8) + Facility design (12) = 20, versus Legal aspects (8) + Site selection (10) = 18.)

Obviously, in controlling the startup, management would want to make sure that activities on the critical path are proceeding on schedule; in fact, one of the benefits of CPM is that it directs attention to these activities. However, management must also recognize that the time associated with each activity is only an estimate. This means that it is quite possible that some activity which was not on the critical path before the startup began could very well go over its estimated time and in turn become critical.

---

* For the sake of simplicity we have indicated earliest possible start times only on the diagram in Exhibit 9–6. A complete CPM network would give early start and late start times and early finish and late finish times.

Exhibit 9–6
Network diagram for Burgers Gourmet with start and completion times and critical path

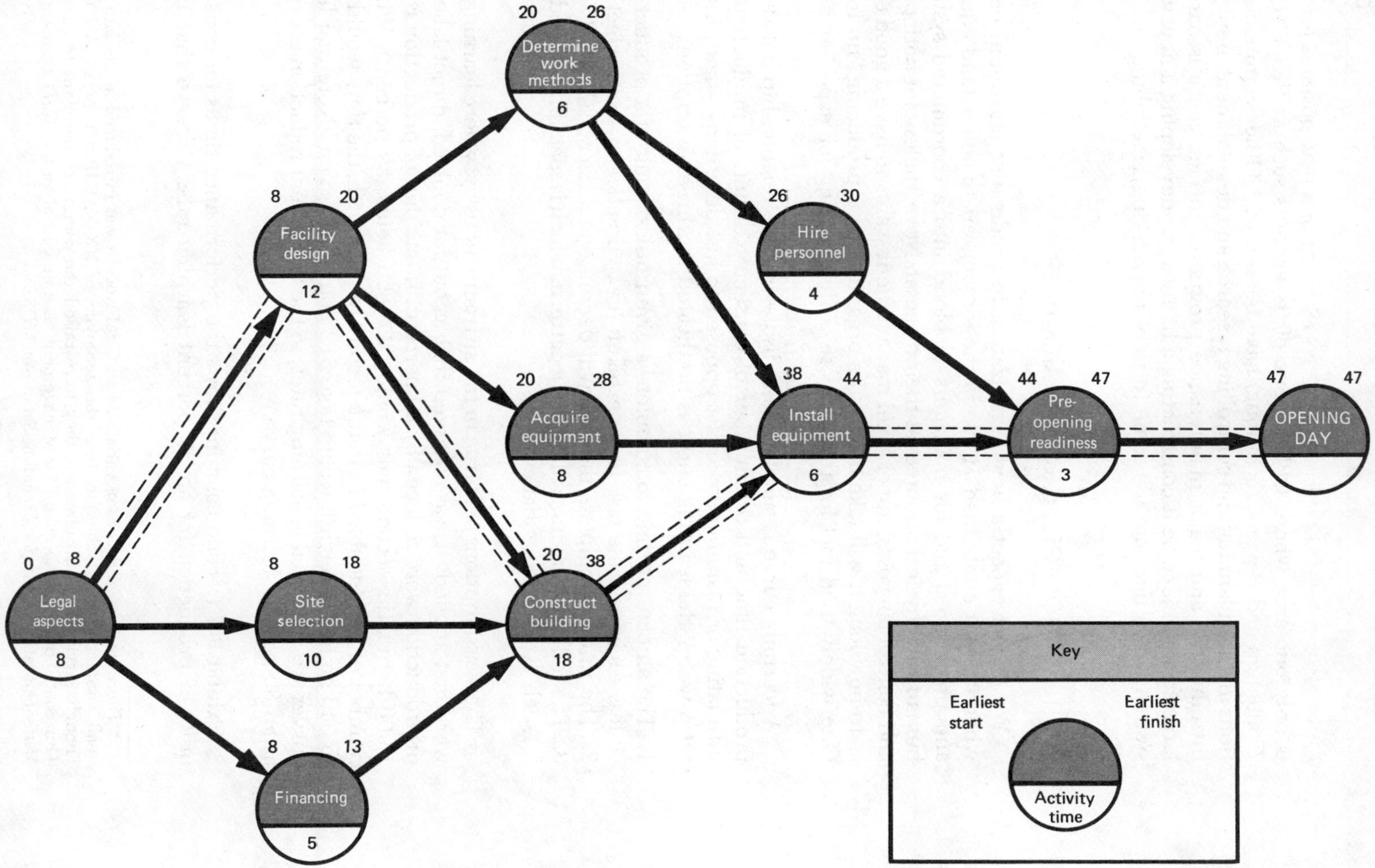

Key

Earliest
start

Earliest
finish

Activity
time

OPENING
DAY
47 | 47

Pre-
opening
readiness
44 | 47
3

Hire
personnel
26 | 30
4

Install
equipment
38 | 44
6

Determine
work
methods
20 | 26
6

Acquire
equipment
20 | 28
8

Construct
building
20 | 38
18

Facility
design
8 | 20
12

Site
selection
8 | 18
10

Financing
8 | 13
5

Legal
aspects
0 | 8
8

Other uses of critical path techniques.   Startup of a new business (or facility) is only one area where CPM or one of its variants such as PERT (*Program Evaluation and Review Technique*) have been used.* Other common applications include planning and controlling research and development, new product introduction, and major maintenance programs. In fact, there is hardly any large-scale project, be it constructing a highway or developing a new weapons system which does not use some form of networking scheduling.

Predicting startup progress: Learning curves

We do not expect a new organization to produce at maximum efficiency when it is just established. It takes time for workers to understand equipment and procedures, and for managers to blend into a coordinated system the human and physical resources at their disposal. Nevertheless, for both planning and control purposes, upper level management wants to have a good estimate as to how long it will take before the organization is producing "up to snuff." One widely used tool for this purpose is the learning (or experience) curve.

A learning curve is simply a line displaying the relationship between unit production time and the number of consecutive units of production. As an estimating or planning device (as opposed to just describing what production rates were), the learning curve is predicated on three assumptions:

1. The amount of time to complete a given task or unit of a product will be less each time the task is undertaken (i.e., "practice makes perfect").
2. The time to complete the task will decrease at a decreasing rate.
3. The reduction in time will follow a pattern, which is specific and predictable, such as an exponential curve.

These assumptions held true in the airframe industry, where learning curves were first applied. It was observed that as output doubled, direct labor-hours in production were reduced by 20 percent. If one unit of production required 1,000 hours, the second unit would take 800 hours (80 percent). When the number of units doubled from the second to the fourth, the time would reduce to 640 hours; the eighth would take 512 hours, and so on. (Note that learning curves are expressed in learning rates, so the 20 percent reduction is expressed as an 80 percent learning curve.)

Exhibit 9–7 (second column) shows the performance times for consecutive units of production for an 80 percent learning rate. Observe that the first

---

* There have been dozens of variations on CPM since it was introduced in the late 1950s. A small sample of such techniques bear the acronyms of ICON, IMPACT LOSS, AND SPERT. Though varying little in substance, they have raised the coining of acronyms to an art form. (Our contribution to "Acronyms for Management" is a new label for the Ten Commandments—*Man's Operating Strategies Excluding Satan*—or MOSES.)

Exhibit 9–7
Unit, cumulative, and average labor-hours required for an 80
percent learning curve

(1)	(2)	(3)	(4)
			Average
Unit		Cumulative	labor-hours
Number	Labor-hours	labor-hours	per unit
1	100	100	100
2	80	180	90
4	64	314	79
8	51	535	67
16	41	892	56
32	33	1,468	46
64	26	2,392	37
128	21	3,874	30
256	17	6,247	24

unit took 100 hours, the second 80 hours, the fourth 64 hours, and so on;
the same rate as in the previous discussion. This pattern of numbers results
in an exponential distribution (Exhibit 9–8) and is the most common relationship in learning experience.*

In presenting learning curve data, total time or average time values are
far more useful than unit times when used for product planning, pricing, or
budget preparation (see colums 3 and 4, Exhibit 9–7).

Learning curves have also have been applied to costs (see Exhibit 9–9).
Manufacturing cost, for example, falls as volume rises for standard products
such as calculators, computers, watches, copy machines, and small appliances.
Experience has shown that in these products as well as in distribution operations the cost declines will follow approximately a 70 percent learning curve
(in terms of constant dollars). Average total costs, including overhead and
administrative costs, also decrease as volume grows. Texas Instruments, Inc.,
for example, has found great success in using experience curves in their market
analysis, product planning, and product pricing. (See Chapter 15 for a discussion of how TI uses learning curves in strategic planning.)

During startup, costs are relatively high and therefore prices must also be
initially high to offset the production cost. Through the effects of learning,
improvements are made in product design, work methods, and material utilization. As volume increases, there are also opportunities to reduce costs through
volume purchases, taking advantage of quantity discounts, savings in transportation costs, and so on.

---

* Learning curves are often converted to straight lines (through the magic of log-log paper)
in order to more conveniently plot learning rates for an entire industry.

Exhibit 9–8
Graph of the 80 percent learning data in Exhibit 9–7 showing actual labor-hours

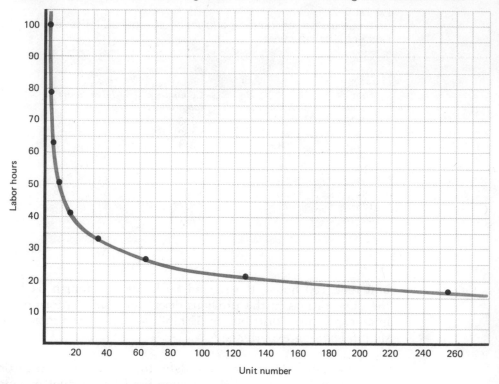

Exhibit 9–9

During World War II an executive of a home-appliance manufacturing company chanced to cross paths with an executive of a large West Coast aircraft firm. The appliance executive mentioned that it had taken his company two years to determine the exact cost of the electric refrigerator which it manufactured.

The aircraft executive pointed out that in many cases his company had been forced to determine costs on similar items in a matter of minutes, and said, "I'll bet you a steak dinner that I can predict the cost of your 100,000th refrigerator within 10 percent accuracy by using a learning curve based on aircraft production."

The manufacturing executive accepted the bet. The only information he furnished was the weight of the refrigerator and the cost of the first unit produced. During the next few minutes he watched while the aircraft executive worked with pencil, ruler, and log-log graph paper.

When he had completed plotting the curve, the aircraft executive stated: "Your 100,000th unit should cost you $162.50."

"Just drop the 50 cents," the appliance executive said. "It was actually $162.00."

Source: Frank J. Andress, "The Learning Curve as a Production Tool," *Harvard Business Review*, vol. 32, no. 1 (1963) p. 87.

Summary observations on learning curves. A common misunderstanding about learning curves is that the concept pertains only to individual operator learning. As the foregoing examples indicate, learning in industry is a far broader concept. While the individual worker can improve by practice, his or her output is greatly affected by how well management does its job. In other words, learning curves really depict both operator learning and management learning. The operator learning component has to do with the methods the worker uses, and is achieved by working smarter, not harder. The management component has to do with coordinating work flows, keeping the resource pipelines open, and assuring that equipment and facilities are adequate.

A related issue is that learning doesn't just happen. A job of management is to make sure that it does occur. Learning curves are both plans and standards. In this regard, some might argue that specifying a learning rate objective (e.g., a learning rate of 80 percent for the first 5,000 units) biases the learning phenomenon and creates a self-fulfilling prophecy. It is our belief that while bias of this type is undesirable if one wants to study the psychology of learning in organizations, it is quite in order if one is "simply" managing the organization.

Finally, there are some technical questions about learning curves which merit comment. The first is, how should management develop a curve for a brand new system? The answer is that the manager must do some research on learning rates in similar organizations in the same industry.[3] Sometimes this is available through trade associations, the Small Business Administration, or in the library. Other times, the manager will have to make enlightened guesses based upon discussions with other members of the organization and comparisons with learning rates in similar industries. (As a rule of thumb, the greater the labor component in production, the greater the opportunity for learning improvement. Thus, we would expect capital intensive chemical plants to have a small learning potential and labor-intensive assembly plants to have a large learning potential.) If the system is already in the startup phase, management can simply look at the brief production history now available and calculate the improvement rate from available data. If the rate is unsatisfactory, then corrective action is in order.

Another technical question has to do with the length of the learning period. Does an organization "run out of learning"; that is, does the learning curve become flat? The answer is yes. However, since learning is related to volume, many companies may never stop improving for every product they produce, since they will change products, or modify them before the curve reaches its limit.

Last, what about discontinuous production? If a company incurs a strike or has a month-long vacation period, can it climb back on the learning curve and continue making improvements at the previously set rate? The answer here, based upon research, is that discontinuous production almost invariably hurts learning progress and requires some relearning to get back to the previous production (and learning) rates. Compare your own experience in your first several days back to school after summer vacation or your search for "the old cannonball serve" after a winter without playing tennis.

FRANCHISES—AN ALTERNATIVE STARTUP

Since franchises are part of a chain of similar operators, there is normally a base of experience upon which to draw. A major benefit of a franchise is that one can draw upon home office skills which have been developed through earlier implementations. Questions such as where to buy equipment, how to hire help, and what job descriptions to have have already been answered by the parent company. Even site locations may have been previously selected by the parent franchise company.

In a franchised operation, the franchisee is buying management skill and is thus paying to avoid the mistakes the franchisors have made before and learned to correct. As a consequence, the speed of startup is greatly accelerated. (As they say in the game of bridge, "one peek is worth ten finesses"; and a franchise offers more than "peeks.")

Franchise cost is usually quite high compared to independent operation. In addition to the cost of the franchise license, there is normally a fee based on a percentage of the gross sales. On top of this, typical franchise agreements contain clauses requiring franchisees to buy equipment from the franchisor or "acceptable" sources, often at prices higher than they might pay if they were an independent.

Nevertheless, franchises offer considerable benefits. Wendy's International Hamburgers sells franchises for $10,000 per unit and 4 percent of sales. In return, the franchisee has available:

1. Building plans for a standard Wendy's outlet.
2. Site approval.
3. Training at Wendy's headquarters.
4. On-site inspection and evaluation.
5. Business counseling.
6. List of recommended suppliers.
7. Quality control standards.
8. Assistance in advertising and promotion.
9. Complete operations manual on how to run a Wendy's hamburger outlet.
10. Continued research in better methods of operation.
11. Continuous reports of interest from headquarters.
12. National and regional meetings.[4]

In summary, startup in a new franchise location is a repeat of previous similar startups. All the learning from past experience makes franchise startups frequently less costly, quicker, and with fewer problems. It must be pointed out, however, that franchise organizations often spring up which offer little in the way of managerial support. The business of these organizations seems to be in selling franchises. Without follow-up managerial support, when the sale of franchises goes down, revenue to the parent organization goes down, and the business goes out. Recall the short existence of franchises such as Minnie Pearl Chicken, Roy Rogers restaurants, and Vic Tanney athletic clubs.

TWO CONTRASTING CASE HISTORIES

Gates Learjet Corporation

In 1977, the Gates Learjet Corporation began construction of a second plant in Tucson, Arizona, to fabricate and assemble a new model of aircraft which could not be efficiently produced at their home plant in Wichita or their existing plant in Tucson. The hallmark of their startup was careful and detailed planning of how they were to recruit and train their work force. First of all, they specified all of the steps that were required in making the new model Learjet and, using a critical path schedule, set a target date (in 1980) when the first plane would be completed. This told them how many people would be required for each job (both supervisory and operative), which in turn indicated the size of the personnel staff needed for selecting and training. Early on, they developed in-house training programs, which among other things, involved practicing the new tasks on prototypes located in leased facilities in the Tucson area. This enabled the company to select workers who were suited to the work and enabled the development of time estimates for detailed scheduling and learning curve estimates. Because of this interest in obtaining only good workers, they also were building staff in advance of need—essentially building a work force inventory. In 1979, Gates Learjet was right on schedule, but as one might surmise, it has been an expensive startup. The expense can be more than recovered, however, by decreased personnel and operating costs during 1980 and subsequent production.

General Dynamics Trident Submarine Program*

In 1974, the Electric Boat Division of General Dynamics signed a contract with the U.S. Navy to deliver four Trident nuclear submarines, with the first one to be delivered by April 1979. In July 1978, the company said that the first sub wouldn't be delivered before November 1980, about a year after

---

* This material is drawn from Louis Kraar, "Electric Boat's Whale of a Mess: The Trident Sub," *Fortune,* July 1978, pp. 105–8.

the oldest Polaris sub is due to be retired. The delay stems from the fact that the company took on contracts for both attack submarines and the Trident. "As the work force was doubled to a peak of 30,000 in mid-1977, the [Groton, Connecticut] shipyard suffered the corporate equivalent of a nervous break-down." As one naval officer reported, "Electric Boat expanded its work force too rapidly, which lowered productivity. It lost control of its materials for Trident, and everything cascaded at once on the heads of its managers." Specific problems faced during this startup were lack of materials control, inadequate worker training, indiscriminate hiring, and unrealistic cost estimates. "The dominant cause of delays and cost increases that were avoidable boils down to shipyard management."

"General Dynamics is trying to clean up the mess with a tough new manager at Electric Boat, its third in four years . . . to get payroll costs under control."

"The new manager, P. T. Veliotis, took over at Electric Boat in October [1977], and began firing people his first day on the job. The initial batch of 2,000 salaried employees, including engineers and designers, were given a half hour to clean out their desks and leave." The total number of layoffs reached 5,000. "Gradually, Electric Boat is hiring back some of the journeymen who were made instant supervisors—this time as production workers."

In January, Veliotis ordered a nine-day curtailment of production in order to take the first inventory of parts in 25 years, cataloging 60 million items. At last costs are becoming controlled, but the effort has been wrenching; the startup is only now coming to an end.

When comparing the costs inherent in the Learjet and General Dynamics cases, we are inclined to remember a TV commercial urging the use of a company's automobile air filters as a preventive maintenance device. The key line went, ". . . you can pay me now [for the air filter] or pay me later [to rebuild the engine]."

SUMMARY

Despite the fact that all organizations go through a startup period, there is very little research on the subject in the general management literature. Rather, it has been the technology-oriented disciplines, notably chemical and petroleum engineering, that—by necessity—have considered management aspects of the problem in detail. However, this is not to say that certain standard concepts from management cannot be brought to bear on the problem. As we have suggested, certain management skills are required for startup and standard planning techniques are available to help in its conduct. Thus, the basic problem in startup management is recognizing its existence and applying what already exists for similar turbulent situations. As Bayloff points out:

Most startups are periods of intense and difficult adaptation on the part of direct and indirect labor, engineering, and supervisory personnel. Thus, adaptive efforts often have a fragile momentum that can be disrupted easily. . . .[5]

We believe that understanding this "fragility" is the critical first step in achieving a successful startup.

GUIDES TO ACTION

1. It is often helpful to treat startup as a project which has a definite sequence of activities that are different from design and steady state activities.

2. Startups of new organizations should not be rushed. Most customers expect that the service or product they buy is produced by an organization that knows what it is doing. Thus poor performance will hurt, even if the organization has the "excuse" of a hurried startup.

3. Keep in mind that startups are a learning period for an organization. Don't expect high productivity during startup. Overstaff at the outset and then gradually work on becoming efficient.

4. Trial runs in both service and manufacturing startups are highly recommended.

NOTES

[1] Manfred Gans and Frank A. Fitzgerald, "Plant Start-Up," in Ralph Landau and Alvin S. Cohan, eds., *The Chemical Plant from Process Selection to Commercial Operation* (New York: Reinhold Publishing Corporation, 1966), p. 280.

[2] S. S. Whitman and W. J. Schmidt, *Plant Relocation: A Case History of a Move* (New York: American Management Association, 1966), p. 78.

[3] For a discussion of learning curves in vari-ous industries, see Alan R. Fusfeld, "The Technological Progress Function," *Technology Review*, February 1973, pp. 29–38.

[4] Harvard University, *Wendy's Old-Fashioned Hamburgers* (Boston: Intercollegiate Case Clearing House), Case 9–677–122, revised July 1977.

[5] Nicholas Bayloff, "Start-Up Management," *IEEE Transactions on Engineering Management*, vol. EM17, no. 4 (November 1970), pp. 132–41.

DISCUSSION QUESTIONS

1. Have you ever been involved in a startup situation? If so, what problems unique to this phase of the life cycle did you encounter?

2. What are the three alternative organizational forms for startup described in this chapter? What are their advantages and disadvantages?

3. What information does a CPM network convey directly that a Gantt chart doesn't?

4. Under what conditions would there be more than one critical path in a CPM plan?

5. What are the managerial benefits of CPM relative to planning and controlling a startup?

6. Why does the learning curve in industry depend on more than just operator learning to gain its full benefit?

7. From the summary evidence provided, do you believe that the new manager of Electric Boat, P. T. Veliotis, acted appropriately? Would you have done the same thing?

8. Ask a franchise owner what help he or she received in startup. Also ask, "Would you go the franchise route again?"

9. What is the critical path and earliest possible completion time for the following network? (Letters refer to activity designation; numbers refer to activity times in days.)

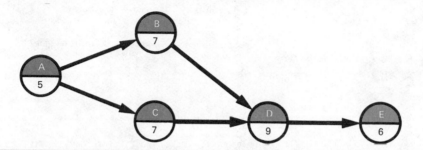

10. With reference to the preceding problem, which of the activities would you shorten by one day if you save $50 for saving one day and it costs you to cut a day from each activity at the rates given in the following schedule:

A $25, B $10, C $24, D $21, E $30?

11. Draw a Gantt chart for the network in Problem 9.

12. Suppose that it takes you one hour to read the first chapter of this book, and 50 minutes to read the second chapter. How long should it take you to read Chapter 16 at this learning rate? What reservations do you have about this figure?

CASE: THE LUCKY LUGGAGE COMPANY

The Lucky Luggage Company (LLC) fabricates and assembles "soft sided" suitcases at a plant in Chicago but is contemplating shifting to a "twin plants" operation. The twin plants concept is a simple one: a firm fabricates the parts of its product in the United States and then ships them to assembly plants just across the border in Mexico. Tariff laws in both countries make this a realistic and economic manufacturing strategy. The assembled product is then shipped back to the U.S. plant (usually located near the border), where it is packed for shipping to wholesale and retail outlets. The primary advantage of a twin plants operation is the savings in labor cost in assembling the item.

In Mexico the average hourly pay at a border plant is about 80 cents, as opposed to about $3.50 in the United States.

If LLC decides to embark on a twin plants strategy, it will close its facilities in Chicago and open a fabrication plant in Tucson, Arizona, and a "twin" assembly plant in Nogales, Sonora, Mexico. The general flow of operations between the two facilities is shown in the following diagram:

Stamp sides of luggage and load in plastic bins in Tucson

↓

Ship by truck across the border

↓

Assemble suitcases and box them in Nogales

↓

Ship by truck back across the border

↓

Crate boxed suitcases in Tucson

↓

Load on railcars and ship to retailers

Neal Herrick, the young staff assistant at LLC, was called in by his boss, John Dickson, to discuss the impending decision.

John: Neal, I'd like you to do some planning on this matter. It seems to me that we have a classic startup problem here and since you studied this issue in your management course, perhaps you might analyze some of the aspects of it.

Specifically, I would like to have a list of, say, the three major problems we should expect to encounter in this move. Then assuming that these can be surmounted, I would like to know what organizational alternatives are available for managing the startup and how long it will take before we can start production (I hope we can be ready to go in five months.) Lastly, I would like to know how many suitcases we will have to make before we reach our break-even suitcase assembly rate of five and a half minutes per suitcase on our five-person assembly lines.

Neal: Have you any background information to help me get started?

John: Not much, I'm afraid. About all we have is some production data and time estimates made by our manufacturing manager, Bob Sweek. According to Bob, it will take these times [see "Startup Activity Time Estimates" below] to get the project completed.

Bob has also told me that based upon his studies, we can expect a 95 percent learning curve for the assembly teams. In Chicago, it takes about 10 minutes for a new team to assemble its first suitcase. As you probably know, we expect to use only local workers and first-line supervisors in the Mexican plant. (We anticipate hiring 75 direct workers and two supervisors for the plant.)

Neal: That's it?

John: That's it. I would appreciate it if you would do an analysis of this material and get back to me tomorrow at 3:00. Many thanks.

Neal: I'll give it a try.

Neal (to himself): Oh, wow!

Startup activities

		Activities that must be done before
a. Locate and purchase factory building	2 months	—
b. Relocate and/or select new managers and supervisors	2 months	—
c. Hire local direct workers	1 month	a, b
d. Transfer equipment from Chicago plant	4 months	a
e. Train local direct workers to output level of 10 minutes per suitcase	1 month	a, b, c, d
f. Begin full-scale production	—	a, b, c, d, e

Case assignment

Give Neal a hand on his assignment. Be specific in your analysis and be sure to state your assumptions.

Section five
Operating the organization in the steady state

After being set into motion, an organization enters a period of "regular" or steady state operations. To operate effectively and efficiently, a number of important topics must be considered by management. First, there are behavioral issues involved in assuring that personnel carry out their job assignments. Second, there are techniques which should be used to ensure that the production of the organizational output proceeds in an economical and expeditious manner. Lastly, control systems must be used to compare actual versus desired (planned for) outputs and initiate corrective actions where necessary.

271

SELECTION OF THE PRODUCT OR SERVICE	DESIGN OF THE SYSTEM	STAFFING THE ORGANIZATION	STARTUP OF THE ORGANIZATION	OPERATING THE ORGANIZATION IN THE STEADY STATE	IMPROVING THE ORGANIZATION	REVISION OF THE ORGANIZATION	TERMINATION OF THE ORGANIZATION
Decision-making processes; social value; goals; forecasts; policies; plans	Authority and responsibility; power; organizational structure; communications systems; job design	Work force planning; personnel management functions	Startup planning and scheduling; monitoring; alternative startup approaches	Motivation; leadership; production and operations management; control	Individual improvement programs and techniques; group conflict management; MBO	Evaluation of organizational policies; strategic choices; organizational change; organizational development	Partial terminations; cutback management; complete terminations; mergers; born-again strategies

Level of Organizational Outputs

0

t_0 Time →

Chapter 10
Motivation and rewards

*Lawrence: You will not go to Aqaba for gold,
and you will not go to Aqaba to kill Turks;
but you* will *go to Aqaba because it
pleasures you!*
*Arab Chieftain: Your mother mated with a
scorpion!*

Scene from the film, *Lawrence of Arabia*

This chapter is intended to examine what "pleasures" people to do something—
to join an organization, to show up on time, and to on occasion make the
big push "to Aqaba." In short, what are the factors which *motivate* people's
behavior?

In dealing with this multifaceted question, we will pay particular attention
to the major theories of motivation put forth by behavioral scientists and the
actions which the manager can take in carrying out the motivation function.
A discussion of organizational and individual goals sets the stage for these
theories, and "tailoring rewards to employee wants" suggests how they may
be operationalized.

ORGANIZATIONAL AND INDIVIDUAL GOALS

A typical business has as one of its goals providing a high level of shareholder
return on investments. Is it reasonable to assume that the average employee
has this same goal as the reason for working in the organization? For example,
is it reasonable to assume that the typical telephone company operator is
working primarily to improve AT&T shareholders' return on investment? Not
likely. That telephone operator's goals probably revolve around a paycheck,
some companionship on the job, clean and safe conditions on the job, and so
on. Shareholder return is important to the operator mostly because the job
will probably cease if the company goes under. Bankrupt organizations have
a way of terminating jobs.

What we find in most cases is that employee and organization goals aren't
identical, but nor are they totally dissimilar. Exhibit 10–1 illustrates what we
usually find. While there is considerable dissimilarity, there is usually some
mutually agreeable areas. Managers should not fall into the trap of assuming
that employees have the best interests of the organization always foremost
in their minds. The organization, and its job, may well be only a means to
the employee achieving some desired goal(s) totally unrelated to the organization. A job is just a job. If this organization goes under, one can always find
another job.

Exhibit 10–1
Overlap of organization and employee goals

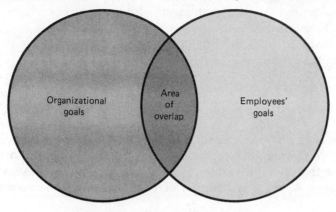

Organizational goals

Area of overlap

Employees' goals

Obviously, some people's goals have a greater overlap with organizational goals than others. An owner-manager, for example, would show considerable overlap. The greater the vested interest one has in the organization, the greater this overlap. Vested interests can come about from financial investment, seniority, inability to get another job, loyalty to the ideals of the organization, differential rewards based on organizational goal attainment, and so on.

This leads us to examine the crux of the matter—what we call *the* motivation problem: The problem is to create conditions on the job such that a worker acting to attain personal goals acts in such a way that the work desired by the organization gets done. What this means is that management must realize the potential divergence between employee and organizational goals and then take steps to design jobs and reward systems that cater to both. Is it really "wrong" for an organization to cause an employee to act in a certain manner (a manner ethically and legally acceptable to the employee) in return for desired rewards, with the net result that the organization gets the production or outputs desired from that employee? We think not. The employee gets what is desired. The organization gets what is desired. No laws were broken, and no one's ethical foundations were shaken. Some people call this manipulation, but frankly we're hard-pressed to see who is the real object of the manipulation since both parties (organization and employee) get what they want. We shall return to this thesis throughout the chapter as we attempt to uncover what the employee really wants and what rewards are available to the organization to enable it to induce the employee to act in some desired manner.

Before we proceed, however, several definitions should be provided.
1. Motive. A felt need or desire; internal to the organism. Hunger is an example. No one has ever seen a motive (behavior based on a motive, yes; but never a motive per se). Thus, you have never seen "a hunger;" hungry people's behavior, yes, but never "a hunger" itself.

2. *Incentive.* Something which if acquired satisfies the felt need or desire and that exists externally to the organism. A nice meal is an incentive based on the hunger motive. We learn about which incentives reduce which motives as we go through life.

3. *Motivation.* The driving force that causes an organism to acquire incentives to reduce motives.

PERFORMANCE IN THE ORGANIZATION

Ability is an obvious influence on performance, but we have all seen cases of very able people not performing up to their capabilities. Motivation is the key factor that influences the degree to which abilities will or won't be used. Performance is, then, a function of both ability and motivation. Expressed another way:

$$\text{Performance} = f(\text{ability, motivation})$$

The efforts of coaches and players to "psych up" a team are legend. "Win one for the Gipper" worked for Knute Rockne. "You Gotta Believe" statements by Tug McGraw spurred on the Mets some years ago. And Dick Motta's "The opera ain't over 'til the Fat Lady sings" (related to "The ball game isn't over until the last man is out") helped the Washington Bullets in 1978. There are others, but the point is clear. Abilities alone don't always lead to top performance. One must have the desire to use these latent abilities before they do any good.

The willingness to use one's abilities is in large part related to the options open to the worker. In recent years some Australian organizations have been experiencing problems with extreme amounts of absenteeism. Many workers are well-off enough financially so that they simply stay off the job in favor of more leisure time. The "sickies," as it is called, usually strike hardest when the weather is good, or right after holidays when a hangover might be the legacy of a party. Several years ago, absenteeism at an Australian Goodyear plant ran at just under 10 percent daily and 80 percent of the plant's workers took all eight paid sick days per year. The company was able to reduce absenteeism by 12 percent via offering prizes in raffles that could be won only by workers who showed up every day for a month.[1]

Thorn Lighting Company in Merthyr Tydfil, Wales (about 25 miles from Mynyddislwyn), experienced similar high absenteeism (14 percent daily) and offered the equivalent of an extra $8.80 pay per week to workers who were present each day.[2]

Closer to home, the authors were presented with a problem by the president of a firm manufacturing computer equipment. Ten percent absenteeism on Mondays and on Friday afternoons wasn't uncommon. (Paychecks were given out at Friday noon!) The "average" employee was an 18-year-old female, high school graduate, living either at home or sharing an apartment. The president's initial response was to raise the pay of all workers by 25 to 50 cents per hour, because, he said, he himself could be motivated by money; therefore, so could the workers. The result was a higher absence rate on Tuesdays! His workers were, by and large, already so well paid that they preferred more leisure time to more pay. It is quite possible that this company could have gotten better attendance (and better production) if it had *lower* pay scales.

Former Federal Reserve Chairman Arthur Burns termed this leisure-seeking behavior a "lessened sense of industriousness" that impedes the nation's ability to produce goods and services. Even on the job, "the extraordinary number of hours spent on coffee breaks, wash-up time, retirement parties and other social rites . . . have increasingly become part of our working lives."[3]

The U.S. economy has in recent years experienced far less of a productivity rise than most other industrialized nations; and this at a time when wages are sharply rising.[4] Indeed, the deficits in our balance of payments accounts, along with ever-increasing numbers of foreign automobiles, televisions, and so on are tied directly to our productivity problems.

MANAGERIAL APPROACHES TO MOTIVATION

Managers seek to "motivate" workers by performing certain actions of their own. Obviously, the manager will attempt to determine what "turns on" workers and then act accordingly. Thus, the viewpoint held by the manager is crucial. Several basic approaches have been observed.

Traditional approach

In Chapter 1 we noted the contributions of the scientific management school of thought as exemplified by Frederick Taylor. Taylor believed that jobs should be designed so that workers would do repetitive tasks at which they could become very skilled. Further, it was felt that people worked for only one basic reason—pay. Thus, if jobs could be designed in the best way, and then if pay was based on the amount produced, things should work out very well indeed. The employee would strive to maximize pay and in so doing would maximize production.

Human behavior being what it is, the system didn't work very well. All too often workers had high production and then management began to reduce the incentive pay or raise the minimum standard of production. As worker efficiency rose, layoffs often occurred. Eventually workers came to view job security as being more important than some pay increments which might

be earned via harder work. In other words, it soon became evident that pay
per se wasn't the only thing that motivated workers, especially if management
doesn't play fair.

Human relations approach

Based upon observations of the traditional approach to motivation and especially the Hawthorne studies in the 1930s, it became apparent that social
contacts and interactions were of great importance on the job. In fact, the
simple, repetitive tasks prescribed by the traditional approach were seen as
boring and as impeding motivation. Managers began to appeal to the social
and ego needs of employees by such devices as praising good work, keeping
workers informed, and all in all trying to promote a happy work force. Happy
workers were thought to be productive workers. Whereas compliance is obtained from workers by pay in the traditional approach, the human relations
approach attempts to gain compliance by causing employees to be more satisfied because they are treated humanistically.*

Human resources approach

The human resources approach departs from the human relations approach
in two significant areas. First, it views workers as being capable of providing
creative inputs to the job (versus simply doing as they are told). Second, it
views information sharing with employees not as simple attempts to promote
morale and satisfaction, but rather as attempts to gain valid employee inputs
into the decision-making process. The human relations approach views employee satisfaction as a cause of improved performance. The human resources
approach views improved performance as the result of increased participation,
with employee satisfaction as a by-product. Exhibit 10–2 illustrates these differences.

A summary of all three approaches (or models)—traditional, human relations,
and human resources—is given in Exhibit 10–3.

MOTIVATION THEORIES

There are two "kinds" of motivation theories: *content* and *process*. Content
theories express the *what* of motivation. That is, what is the basis of the motives
experienced by a person? These theories attempt to present a compendium
of the needs or desires that drive or motivate people.

---

* Eventually, we *may* try this with our doctoral students.

Process theories express the *how* of motivation. Taking as givens the fact that we have various motives or needs, process theories seek to develop frameworks that explain the behavioral choices that are made which lead to actions intended to acquire rewards.

Exhibit 10–2
Comparisons of human relations and human resources models

Human relations

Participation → Improved satisfaction and morale → Improved compliance with management demands and greater performance

Human resources

Participation → Improved decision making and performance → Improved satisfaction and morale

Source: Based on Raymond E. Miles, "Human Relations or Human Resources," *Harvard Business Review*, July–August 1965, pp. 148–63.

Exhibit 10–3
Comparison of the three approaches to motivation

Traditional model Assumptions:	*Human relations model*	*Human resources model*
1. Work is inherently distasteful to most people.	1. People want to feel useful and important.	1. Work is not inherently distasteful. People want to contribute to meaningful goals that they have helped establish.
2. What they do is less important than what they earn for doing it.	2. People desire to belong and to be recognized as individuals.	2. Most people can exercise far more creativity, responsible self-direction, and self-control than their present jobs demand.
3. Few want or can handle work that requires creativity, self-direction, or self-control.	3. These needs are more important than money in motivating people to work.	

Exhibit 10–3 *(continued)*

Traditional model	*Human resources model*	*Human relations model*
Policies:		
1. The manager's basic task is to closely supervise and control subordinates.	1. The manager's basic task is to make each worker feel useful and important.	1. The manager's basic task is to make use of untapped human resources.
2. The manager must break down tasks into simple, repetitive, easily learned operations.	2. The manager should keep subordinates informed and listen to their objections to his or her plans.	2. The manager must create an environment in which all members may contribute to the limits of their ability.
3. The manager must establish detailed work routines and procedures and enforce these firmly but fairly.	3. The manager should allow subordinates to exercise some self-control on routine matters.	3. The manager must encourage full participation on important matters, continually broadening subordinate self-direction and self-control.
Expectations:		
1. People can tolerate work if the pay is decent and the boss is fair.	1. Sharing information with subordinates and involving them in routine decisions will satisfy their basic needs to belong and to feel important.	1. Expanding subordinate influence, self-direction, and self-control will lead to direct improvement in operating efficiency.
2. If tasks are simple enough and people are closely controlled they will produce up to standard.	2. Satisfying these needs will improve morale and reduce resistance to formal authority—subordinates will willingly cooperate.	2. Work satisfaction may improve as a by-product of subordinates making full use of their resources.

Source: Richard M. Steers and Lyman W. Porter, eds., *Motivation and Work Behavior* (New York: McGraw-Hill Book Company, 1975), p. 17.

Content theories

As noted above, the content theories seek to explain what our motives (i.e., felt needs or desires) are. In general the theories are consistent, but, as we will note, important differences do exist.

The hierarchy of needs.   Abraham Maslow's need hierarchy is one of the best known content theories.[5] Exhibit 10–4 presents an outline of what is involved. Humans are thought to have five general needs as follows:

1. *Physiological.* Need for air, water, food, shelter, sex, and so on; i.e., the necessities to sustain life.
2. *Security.* Need to be free of fear, to be safe, and to have provided for a continued supply of life's necessities (e.g., water, food, shelter) into a foreseeable future. Illustrated by a secure job, some savings, a secure pension plan, and so on.
3. *Social.* Need for human companionship, love, a sense of belonging, affection. Illustrated by membership in a club, the desire to have friends and entertain them, the "need" to talk to others on the job. All in all, to *not* be a hermit.
4. *Ego–esteem.* Need for self-respect, to differentiate oneself from others, to have a sense of achievement, to be respected by others. Illustrated by keeping up with the Joneses, not allowing one's name to be dishonored, and so on. Also included here is the need to acquire power over others and autonomy for oneself, as illustrated by the desire to win arguments, avoid signs of weakness, and the like. This is probably what "drives" many politicians to seek election and to be "in" on decisions affecting people's lives.
5. *Self-actualization.* Need to accomplish that which one feels compelled to accomplish. This varies from person to person. Examples are to be president, to actually climb Mt. McKinley, to be the best garbage collector in Murraysville, to run the United Fund, or to be a respected professor at a good school. All in all, to do your own thing, whatever it is.

Exhibit 10–4 portrays these needs in a stair-step fashion. As with a set of stairs, one begins at the bottom and moves up. Thus, initially physiological needs are dominant. Once these are *reasonably* satisfied, we move up to security needs. Once these are *reasonably* satisfied, we move up to social needs . . . all the way up the hierarchy. What is "reasonable" depends on each person and is based upon that person's personality and past experiences. The hierarchy thus is "individual bound." People who were very affected by the

Exhibit 10–4
The Maslow hierarchy of needs

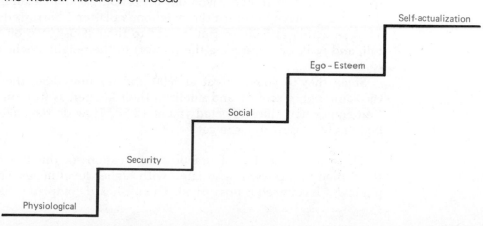

depression of the 1930s probably have a higher "level of reasonability" about security needs and material possessions than do people who have never been so deprived. In early 1978 Evel Knievel was reported to be quite concerned because he was down to his last two yachts. It's all relative, isn't it?

The key to using the hierarchy lies in the acceptance of this major contention: we are dominantly motivated by our lowest (on the stairstep) level unsatisfied (in "reasonable" terms) need. Thus, if all four lower level needs are reasonably satisfied, we will work on self-actualization. When that need becomes satisfied (or more likely even before) we tend to reevaluate our definitions of "reasonable" of lower level needs. What, for example, once seemed to be a reasonable level of financial security now is less than desired. Thus, we "cycle" back to a lower level stairstep whenever a need's reasonable level of satisfaction is redefined upward or where a need is actually jeopardized (e.g., the insurance company that holds your retirement program is threatened by bankruptcy).

An important aspect of this is another important contention: Satisfied needs are not dominant motivators. Once a need is reasonably satisfied and the person has moved up the stairstep, incentives associated with the satisfied need are not "motivating" forces. To grasp this thought, imagine the story of a Thanksgiving dinner.

It's Thanksgiving Day and you have slept later than normal. Say it's 10:00 A.M. That big turkey dinner will be served by your mother at 2:00 P.M. You don't eat breakfast because you don't want to ruin your appetite. The sights, sounds, and smells coming out of the kitchen are really something! That turkey dinner will be great! Come noon, when you normally eat lunch, you still hold out. Still the sights, sounds, and smells coming out of the kitchen continue. Boy, are you ever hungry! Watch the clock and hope two o'clock gets here fast.

Finally, it's time to eat. You do. In fact, you "pig-out!" Both drumsticks, a breast, dressing, and two helpings of pie. You're so stuffed you can hardly move. Then your mother, who has been doing some cleaning up, says, "It's 3:30 and we have to return the neighbor's platter I borrowed for the turkey. They're eating at 5:00, so run it over to their house." So off you go, stuffed full, and walk over (carrying the platter) to the neighbor's house.

Since they're going to eat at 5:00 and it's now 3:30, there are basically the same sights, sounds, and smells in their kitchen as were in yours at 12:30. Remember how these affected you at 12:30? How do they affect your stuffed body now? Positively or negatively?

There are a number of practical implications of this theory. Foremost is the notion that rewards associated with higher level needs won't "motivate" if a lower level need is unsatisfied. The oft-heard complaint that "Recognition won't buy bread" may well be a response to an ego–esteem-based reward (e.g., recognition, praise) where rewards based on physiological needs (e.g., increased pay to buy food for yourself and a hungry bunch of children) are really what are desired.

Additionally, when these lower level needs are reasonably satisfied, continuing to appeal to them will probably be nonproductive. If there is enough bread on the table already, the offer of an additional 25 cents an hour of pay may not be as "motivating" as would praise, recognition and maybe a promotion even if no more money were involved. Workers that refuse overtime work and tell us that they would rather spend more time with their families are probably saying: "Physiological and security are reasonably satisfied; social is now dominant."

Finally, management must be cognizant of the many ways there are of providing work-based incentives that appeal to all five need levels. Paychecks, retirement plans, insurance, and safety programs usually satisfy or come very close to satisfying most workers' physiological and safety needs. If so, management should allow for other needs to be satisfied as a motivation tool. Thus, allowing workers to form a social unit may be feasible. Being "one of the boys" or "one of the girls" may well promote a sense of teamwork and belonging that gets translated into better on-the-job performance.

The ego–esteem needs can be affected by offering the opportunity to gain a sense of accomplishment on the job. Also, status symbols can be powerful motivating devices. Often far better quality/quantity of production can result from selecting an "Employee of the Week/Month" than could be effected with a small pay increase.

We will take a closer look at reward systems later in this chapter.

ERG need structure.   Alderfer has provided a slight revision of the Maslow hierarchy.[6] Exhibit 10–5 illustrates Alderfer's revision. The physiological and security needs are combined into a single *existence* category. The ego–esteem category is split and the esteem-related desires to be creative, self-confident, and productive are combined with self-actualization to form *growth* needs. Social and the ego needs of status symbols, feelings of keeping up with the Joneses and the like combine into a *relatedness* category. Alderfer contends that his ERG revision does not require that lower level needs be satisfied before a higher level need becomes activated. Thus, a person can be "multiple motivated" at any one time. Also, Alderfer predicts that a lack of satisfaction of higher level needs will lead to an increased importance being placed on lower level needs. Thus we find employees in occupations where it is difficult to acquire rewards associated with higher level needs who therefore make increased demands for more lower level satisfaction, such as pay. Witness the salary demands behavior of some factory workers, plumbers, postal employees, police, fire fighters, pilots, and so on.

Exhibit 10–5
Alderfer's modification of the Maslow hierarchy

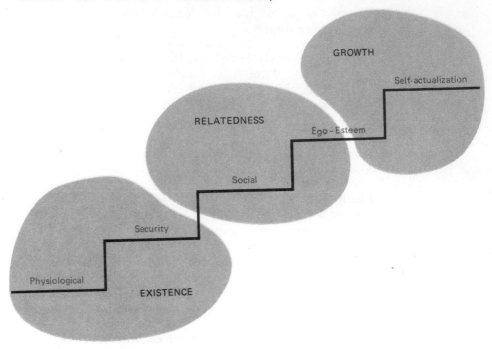

As was noted earlier, the need hierarchy is individual specific; that is, the emphasis placed on reasonable satisfaction of any level is based upon each person's own perceptions and biases. The hierarchy is also culture-bound to the extent that people's upbringings in various cultures differ in degrees of emphasis placed on different needs. For example, the Kwakiutl Indians of the Pacific Northwest exhibit a strong drive for status and power while the Zuni tribe of the Pueblos in the Southwest consider such behavior strange, if not evidence of insanity. Additionally, a number of studies exist indicating that the ordering (from physiological to self-actualization) of the needs varies for workers in different countries. One study, for example, compared Mexican and American workers employed by a parent U.S. company where the jobs and plants and equipment were identical; one plant was in Mexico, one in the United States.[7] The American workers placed a far higher importance on the need to self-actualize, to grow and develop, and to have a sense of accomplishment. The Mexican workers in turn placed a far greater emphasis on the lower level needs, especially security.

The adept manager will be aware of the importance of cultural biases in the need hierarchy. The tendency to infer that everyone shares one's own cultural outlook is clearly improper.

The need to achieve. David McClelland has for many years investigated the notion of an achievement drive in people.[8] McClelland found that the need to achieve (*n*Ach) was related to how people performed tasks. Also, the economic success of nations as measured by GNP seemed to be associated with *n*Ach in business and government leaders.*

*n*Ach is defined as the need to excel or succeed when in competitive situations. People exhibiting high levels of *n*Ach tend to:

1. Desire personal responsibility for task accomplishment.
2. Set moderately difficult goals and take calculated risks. (Easily accomplished or impossible goals are avoided.)
3. Desire constant feedback on performance.

High *n*Ach people tend to be very frustrated when jobs do not allow for the above three conditions. Conversely, low *n*Ach persons probably should not be placed in jobs where these conditions are present.

Theory X–Theory Y.   Douglas McGregor introduces a dual set of assumptions about people, Theory X and Theory Y.[9] Exhibit 10–6 presents descriptions of both theories. Theories X and Y are at opposite ends of a continuum along which other "theories" may also exist.

Notice how these theories relate to our earlier presented traditional and human resources motivation approaches. It seems quite likely that a Theory Y person will be highly motivated by needs high up on the hierarchy while Theory X people are probably more motivated by physical and security needs.

McGregor's message seems to be that management should tailor its actions to the profile (X or Y) exhibited by workers; i.e., different strokes for different folks. Further, he contends that the capability to be Theory Y is in everyone, although it is often latent.

Maturity–Infancy.   The needs and drives described by Maslow, Alderfer, McClelland, and McGregor may well be in all of us. How, though, do these become activated? Chris Argyris attempts to explain this in the context of our moving from a state of infancy to that of a mature adult.[10] Exhibit 10–7 presents Argyris's descriptions. There is a continuum between these two states and people can be in varying stages of maturation.

Argyris contends that the demands for conformance, adherence to rules, and so on made by modern organizations are in conflict with the profile of a mature person. When mature employees are faced with jobs over which they have little control, allow little use of abilities, are of short-time duration, and so on they will be psychologically distressed. These employees will *escape* via quitting or absenteeism, *fight* via a union or informal group for changes in the job, or *adapt* by becoming apathetic or indifferent and accepting one's fate.

---

* As well as oil reserves.

Exhibit 10–6
Theory X–Theory Y

Theory X Assumptions

1. The average human being has an inherent dislike of work and will avoid it if possible.
2. Because of this human characteristic of dislike of work, most people must be coerced, controlled, directed, and threatened with punishment to get them to put forth adequate effort toward the achievement of organizational objectives.
3. The average human prefers to be directed, wishes to avoid responsibility, has relatively little ambition, and wants security above all.

Theory Y Assumptions

1. The expenditure of physical and mental effort in work is as natural as play or rest.
2. External control and the threat of punishment are not the only means of bringing about effort toward organizational objectives. People will exercise self-direction and self-control in the service of objectives to which they are committed.
3. Commitment to objectives is a function of the rewards associated with their achievement.
4. The average human being learns under proper conditions not only to accept but also to seek responsibility.
5. The capacity to exercise a high degree of imagination, ingenuity, and creativity in the solution of organizational problems is widely, not narrowly, distributed in the population.
6. Under the conditions of modern industrial life the intellectual potentialities of the average human being are only partially utilized.

Source: Douglas McGregor, *The Human Side of Enterprise* (New York: McGraw-Hill Book Company, 1960), pp. 33–34.

Exhibit 10–7
Infancy–Maturity states

Infant	*Mature person*
Passive	Active
Depends on others	Independent
Limited set of behaviors	Capable of behaving in many ways
Casual, erratic, shallow, quickly dropped interests	Deeper, longer lasting interests
Short-time perspective	Long-time perspective
Desire to be subordinate	Desire to be equal or superordinate
Lacks self-awareness and control	Very self-aware and in control

Source: Chris Agryris, *Personality and Organization* (New York: Harper & Row Publishers, 1957).

Motivation–Hygiene. Frederick Herzberg has proposed that employee "wants" are best classified into two separate classes.[11] One set is the *hygiene* factors which if not present on the job lead to *dissatisfaction*. When present they simply lead to *no dissatisfaction, not* to satisfaction. In other words, the presence of hygiene factors leads to a "neutral" state. Examples of hygiene factors are pay, working conditions, status, supervision, and job security. They are called hygiene factors because they are like personal hygiene relative to physical illness: they may keep one from getting ill but they don't cure the illness.

Motivating factors lead to *satisfaction* if present and to *no satisfaction* if not present. Thus, their absence does not lead to dissatisfaction, just as the presence of hygiene factors does not lead to satisfaction. Some motivating factors are recognition, challenging work, sense of achievement, and the like.

Note the relationship between hygiene factors and lower levels of the need hierarchy while motivator factors seem associated with higher level needs.

No other motivation theory has caused as much controversy over its validity as this one. While most observers and managers seem to identify with Herzberg's message, other researchers have not always been able to replicate his work. There seems to be a general agreement though that the ". . . Herzberg motivators are related to productivity, and his hygiene factors are related to turnover."[12] Relate this statement to our remark earlier in this chapter that we are concerned with several aspects of people's behavior: Why they *join* and *stay* in our organizations, and why they *produce* while they are in the organization.

Similarity of the content theories. Maslow, Alderfer, McGregor, Argyris, McClelland, and Herzberg have all presented ideas that pertain to the "what" behind our motivations. Generally, they all allow for a highly motivated person who seeks recognition, responsibility, and the like. But they also allow for individuals who do not seek such on-the-job opportunities. The message behind these theories is that management should be aware of employees' needs and offer appropriate rewards. (Exhibit 10–8 shows these theories' relationship to one another.)

Process theories

As noted earlier, process theories seek to explain *how* behavior is motivated. Based upon the content theories just discussed, we take as given the fact that people have certain needs or motives. How, then, do these motives become translated into behavior?

Exhibit 10–8
Similarity of the content theories

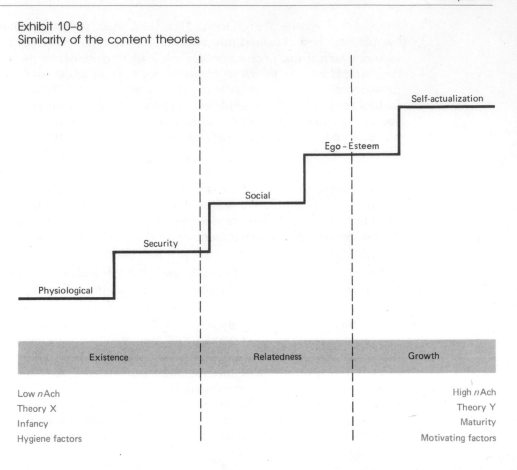

Expectancy theory.   In essence, expectancy theory seeks to explain a person's behavior with respect to: (1) the person's *perception* that a given behavior will lead to a given outcome, and (2) the *value* or attractiveness placed on that outcome by the person.

In discussing this theory we will use the illustration of a person employed by an organization to do a job. Several definitions are in order:

1. Primary outcome.   Those received directly from the job; e.g., pay, prestige, social interaction, and so on.

2. Secondary outcome.   Those which come about via a primary outcome; e.g., the new car (status symbol) purchased with pay, social acceptance in the community due to having a high prestige job, and so on.

A secondary outcome chain exists. For example, one's pay (a primary outcome) can be used to obtain an airplane ticket (secondary outcome) to Hawaii where one can stay at a certain hotel (secondary outcome). Guests at that hotel have the first chance to play golf at a certain country club (secondary outcome) if enough members choose not to play. Thus, pay leads to a chain of outcomes: a ticket which leads to Hawaii, which leads to a hotel, which leads to the special golf course.

3. Valence. The value placed on an outcome. This can be negative (i.e., not getting it is better than getting it, e.g., punishment), or positive. Valences range from −1 (worst possible thing) to +1 (best of all) with 0 being absolutely neutral.

4. Expectancy. The probability that an outcome will result from a given action(s). For example, what are the odds that if you skip class today, you will miss an important piece of information? Expectancies range from 0 (no chance) to +1 (certainty). Given these definitions, expectancy theory can be stated as follows:

Motivational force equals expectancy times valence, or $MF = \Sigma(E \times V)$.

Exhibit 10–9 illustrates an expectancy theory application. As a worker, you have been asked to work extra hard this week and produce an additional 1,000 units that the boss has said the organization needs. This would be 1,000 units "over quota" but you (and your boss) know you could probably do it. If you do make the extra 1,000 units, you stand to get bonus pay (a 90 percent chance) which you could use to take a better vacation (80 percent chance) and also paint the house (70 percent chance). For sure, you will get your regular pay (100 percent) which you are 90 percent sure will cover this month's expenses. There may (10 percent chance) also be enough money to paint the house. There's also a 30 percent chance you will get that promotion the boss has been talking about if you make the extra 1,000. If you do, you're sure (100 percent) to get more pay, enough in fact to make the vacation 90 percent certain and the house painting 100 percent sure.

On the other hand, there is an 80 percent chance your co-workers will get mad, since there's an unwritten agreement among all of you to not produce over a certain amount so as to not cause the company to raise the quota. Also, there's an 80 percent chance you'll really be tired if you work hard enough to do this extra production. Still in all, there's a 90 percent chance that if you do make the extra 1,000 the boss will be happy, and keeping him happy with you is important because he assigns the work (you don't like the dirty details he is capable of assigning).

Valences are subjectively assigned to each possible outcome and $E \times V$ computed. Add all the $E \times V$ products and you get the total motivational force, 1.568 in this case.

Part B of Exhibit 10–9 takes the other position: not producing the extra 1,000 units. For example, it is certain you will get your regular pay (100 percent)

Exhibit 10–9
Expectancy theory model of behavior

OUTCOMES	Combined expectancies	Outcome valence (-1 to +1)*	Motivation force
A. Produce 1,000 more units			
0.9 Bonus pay → 0.8 Vacation	(0.72)	0.8	0.5760
0.9 Bonus pay → 0.2 Paint house	(0.18)	0.2	0.0360
1.0 Regular pay → 0.9 Meet expenses	(0.9)	1.0	0.9000
1.0 Regular pay → 0.1 Paint house	(0.1)	0.2	0.0200
0.8 Rejection by co-workers	(0.8)	-0.5	-0.4000
0.9 Make boss happy with you	(0.9)	0.8	0.7200
0.8 Feeling tired	(0.8)	-0.7	-0.5600
0.3 Promotion → 1.0 More pay → 0.9 Vacation	(0.27)	0.8	0.216
0.3 Promotion → 1.0 More pay → 1.0 Paint house	(0.3)	0.2	0.060
			1.568
B. Don't produce 1,000 more units			
1.0 Regular pay → 0.9 Meet expenses	(0.9)	1.0	0.9
1.0 Regular pay → 0.1 Paint house	(0.1)	0.2	0.02
0.9 Remain a buddy to co-workers	(0.9)	0.5	0.450
0.6 Make boss mad at you	(0.6)	-0.8	-0.480
0.9 Don't feel tired	(0.9)	0.7	0.630
0.2 Promotion → 1.0 More pay → 0.9 Vacation	(0.18)	0.8	0.144
0.2 Promotion → 1.0 More pay → 1.0 Paint house	(0.2)	0.2	0.04
			1.704

* E.g., how much from −1 to +1 is the vacation worth? Here we gave it a +.8. Painting the house is only worth +.2. Being rejected by co-workers hurts, hence −.5.

with which you are 90 percent sure of meeting regular expenses and 10 percent sure of having enough to paint the house.

All things considered, you would have a greater *MF* to not produce the extra 1,000 units than to do so.*

The key point to be noted in the expectancy theory model is that the *ultimate* goal or outcome desired by the worker does not have to be presented as a reward by the organization. Through the use of secondary outcomes the worker acquires what is truly desired; the organization's primary outcomes may simply be a means to achieving this end. Early in this chapter, Exhibit 10–1 illustrated that the organization and employee may not share many goals. Thus, we noted a potential problem in getting an employee to engage in work which did not necessarily (directly) result in the employee achieving his or her goals. Expectancy theory resolves this problem. It doesn't matter whether the employee's and the organization's goals coincide so long as (on balance) primary outcomes can be used to acquire the desired secondary outcomes *and* there are not sufficient negatively weighted primary outcome valences to offset the positive $E \times V$ motivations. Expectancy theory thus "explains" why people stay in jobs that they dislike; the work itself is disliked but they like the (secondary outcome) rewards. On balance a better total set of outcomes couldn't be obtained with a job that had inherently "better" work associated with it. Thus, we could quit this job we hate (cleaning sewers) and take a new job we would like better (selling real estate). However, all things considered, the sewer job "pays" more.

The message to managers who wish to utilize the expectancy theory model is clear:

1. Make sure employees are capable of doing what is expected of them. (This ensures that the actions *can* indeed lead to an outcome. You wouldn't be motivated to work hard to produce the extra 1,000 units, as much as you want the rewards, if you "know" it is physically impossible to produce that many.)
2. Make the relationship(s) between performance and outcomes (rewards) clear.
3. Attempt to build into the system rewards that are associated with employees' needs or motives. (In other words, build in as many rewards as primary outcomes that are associated with employee motives [à la the content theories] as you can.)
4. Where you cannot build in the desired primary outcomes (as noted immediately above in 3), ensure that you provide primary rewards that can be used (are "negotiable" enough) to obtain the desired secondary outcomes.

---

* Although by the time you actually calculate the MF, you might be two hours into your overtime! (Of course, we do this mentally in a matter of seconds or, at most, a few minutes.)

5. Recognize that often you may inadvertently build in factors that are perceived as negative primary outcomes. Eliminate these if possible.

Positive reinforcement theory.   Operant conditioning and behavior modification (both positive reinforcement theories) are becoming popular yet controversial management tools. This theory is most closely associated with B. F. Skinner.[13] Generally these techniques are based on the belief that the consequences of a person's behavior in a given situation influences the person's behavior in future, similar situations. Those people who believe that people always "freely" choose how they behave are disturbed by the contention that we somehow become "programmed" based on past experiences and are therefore not so "free." The manipulative or Machiavellian aura of conditioning people's behavior has likewise met some resistance.

Notwithstanding its criticism, operant conditioning finds itself in many of our "normal" behaviors. Praising a child for picking up toys, giving a pay bonus for extra work, grading papers, and using "dog yummies" to train Spot to shake hands are all examples of operant conditioning in action. The theory holds that we learn to associate certain behaviors with desired outcomes and thus we are led to continue that behavior. Through punishments, we extinguish undesired behavior (e.g., spank the child, scold the dog, put foul-tasting substances into the cigarettes of people trying to quit).

The operant conditioning model is as follows:

Stimulus → Voluntary behavior response → Outcome → Future voluntary
response to the stimulus

Note how this differs from the classical conditioning of Pavlov's dogs. Dogs normally salivate when presented food. Pavlov rang a bell when presenting the food, and the bell became associated in the dogs' minds with food. Ultimately, they began to salivate (in anticipation of food) when they heard the bell. Classical conditioning is defined as the formation of a stimulus-response link (i.e., an "habitual" behavior) between a conditioned stimulus (Pavlov's bell) and an unconditioned (i.e., "normal") response (salivation when given food) via the repeated pairing of the conditioned stimulus with an unconditioned stimulus (presentation of food).

In the operant conditioning of your dog, you present a stimulus, e.g., the command, "Sit!", and when the dog sits (either "voluntarily" or with the help of your gentle push), you reward with praise or a yummy. Eventually, the dog learns that when it hears the stimulus (sit!), it can receive a desired outcome (reward) if it engages in certain behavior (sitting). Thus, to get the reward, it exhibits the behavior.*

---

* Interestingly enough, newer approaches to dog obedience focus on providing elements of love—petting, soothing words—rather than food. Do dogs have higher level needs?

A key difference to note between operant and classical conditioning is that with operant conditioning the initial stimulus-response link (e.g., salivation when given food) isn't there. You probably had to "help" the dog sit the first few times. With operant conditioning, one has to somehow "cause" that desired behavior to be exhibited so it can be rewarded and the learning link established. With the dog, you "helped" it sit. With humans, you could "tell" what the desired behavior is—"When I say, 'Jump!', you jump." Or you could (more deceptively) "train in" the behavior. An interesting example of this once occurred in a psychology class. After getting an operant conditioning lecture, members of the class decided to try it out. Henceforth, every time their professor moved to his left during a lecture, they would yawn, shuffle around in their seats, and appear generally disinterested. Every time he moved to his right, they became the best behaved, most interested, attentive class every seen at the university. Of course, the professor was totally unaware of the students' game. After only a few classes, he found himself walking into the classroom, going over to the right side wall, leaning against it, and delivering his lecture. Suddenly, it all occurred to him. He had been trained!

Associated with operant conditioning are a variety of reward systems or (in the vernacular) reinforcement schedules. To illustrate these, take the situation of the manager of a restaurant trying to train the hostess to greet customers more cordially. The manager could praise the hostess every time she correctly greeted a customer *(massed reinforcement)*. Alternatively, the hostess could be praised on the basis of time; e.g., every two hours so long as she behaves properly. This is called *fixed interval reinforcement.* The manager could do it on a *variable interval* by praising now, waiting 20 minutes before doing it again, then waiting two hours, then say 55 minutes, and so on. Note how fixed and variable interval reinforcement are based on *time.* Another way is to base on the action itself rather than on time. *Fixed ratio reinforcement* would have the manager praising the hostess after she properly greeted, say, every 5th or 16th customer. *Variable ratio reinforcement* would occur if the manager flipped a coin, drew a number or a card, or used some other random way of deciding when to reward the desired behavior. Exhibit 10–10 summarizes these approaches.

Interestingly, most people at first assume that massed reinforcement would work best. If we take what is called "resistance to extinction" as our criterion (i.e., how long does the newly learned behavior remain intact after being trained in), we find that massed reinforcement is the *least* effective. Variable ratio reinforcement approaches work best. This really should be obvious to anyone who has been to a casino in Las Vegas, Reno, or Atlantic City. There you will find individuals doggedly playing the slot machines according to a variable ratio reinforcement approach to payoffs.

In recent years there have been numerous innovative reward systems used in organizations that are based upon operant conditioning theory. We will analyze a number of these later in this chapter.

Exhibit 10–10
Operant conditioning reward schedules

Massed reinforcement .	Reward the desired response every time.
Based on time:	
Fixed interval	Reward on a fixed time basis (e.g., pay systems where one earns so much per hour, week, or month).
Variable interval	Reward on a variable time basis.
Based on responses themselves:	
Fixed ratio	Reward every given number of correct responses (e.g., piece rate pay plans, commissions on sales).
Variable ratio	Reward desired responses on a random basis (e.g., slot machines).

Equity theory.   The thesis behind equity theory is that if people perceive a discrepancy between the value/amount of rewards they receive and the value/amount of the effort expended to get the rewards, they will be motivated to reduce the effort.[14] The value/amount calculation may be real (in objective terms) or subjectively perceived.

We are interested here in a person's ratio between *job inputs* and *job outcomes* and a comparison of that ratio to the ratio of another person(s). Job inputs are such things as education, skills, effort, physical danger, and performance ability. Job outcomes are the rewards received such as pay, status symbols, sense of achievement, recognition, and the like.

Workers are thought to compare their ratio with the ratios of other workers of roughly the same level or status in (or outside of) the organization. If the ratios aren't in balance, the worker is motivated to reduce the perceived inequity. Most equity theory discussions center on money/pay as the crucial job outcome. Workers who feel they are receiving less than they equitably (i.e., ratio comparison) should are believed to resolve the imbalance by reducing their inputs. Thus, they won't work as hard, will make more "mistakes," and so on. Overpayment—feeling that one is receiving more pay than equitably warranted—is also possible and may lead to one's working harder or longer hours.

The precise method of resolving the equity will probably vary among people. Some may simply revise their perceptions of the inputs and outcomes (e.g., "I guess I'm really not as good as I thought," or "Maybe the fringe benefits around here aren't so bad after all"). Other people may quit. We have seen actual cases of janitors quitting a school district job for a lower paying new position because they felt they were underpaid *in comparison to* the school district's secretaries. In the new organization, they got a little less pay, but the secretaries got a *lot* less. This made the janitors happy, or at least not angry.

In Chapter 8, we discussed wage/salary surveys and job evaluation as tools management can use to uncover and correct pay inequities. Pay is a major, though not the only, job outcome that enters into the input/outcome ratio.

The ability to understand the "feelings" inherent in equity theory is important for managers; it's not only the actual magnitude of rewards that is important; their *perceived fairness* is crucial, too.

WHY DO PEOPLE WORK?

Why do people work? is an age-old question. Quite simply, there is no universal, agreed-upon answer. A slave would answer one way, a "workaholic" entrepreneur another. Some people enjoy their jobs. Other people hate theirs.

Most of us would contend that we work in order to acquire the resources we need to first of all survive and then to enjoy life; i.e., we get primary outcomes (pay, and so on) that are used to acquire secondary outcomes. The economic systems of the world being what they are, few of us would like to not have these primary outcomes. Still, there are those who will remain unemployed for extensive periods of time and yet survive. Public and private welfare systems, at least in the so-called developed countries, typically step in to ensure physiological needs.

Some people report that if a better paying and/or more interesting job came along, they would immediately take it. Others seem very content with their present jobs.

The "instant millionaires" created by the lotteries run in several states give us some insight into the behavior of those who, economically anyway, don't have to work. By and large, these people tend to exhibit frustrations with a life of total leisure and tend to take up "work" activities in the form of actual jobs or some self-employed endeavor. Perhaps there is a little Protestant ethic in people after all, or the old homily, "You are what you do" is generally valid.

Clearly, different people work for different reasons. Some can derive great satisfaction from jobs and others, for whatever reason, can't. All we can really say is that since we know all behavior is caused, we know something must be causing people to work. By intelligent observation, by listening, and by experimenting, we may well be able to infer these causes.

Employee wants

Flippo and Munsinger list eight common employee wants:[15]

1. Job security.
2. Pay.
3. Comfortable and attractive working conditions.
4. Congenial associates.
5. Credit for work done.
6. Opportunity to advance.
7. Competent, fair leadership.
8. Appropriate job requirements.

This list is consistent with a study done by Hinrichs where some 250 "wants-oriented" questions were asked.[16] Answers to these 250 questions grouped around several factors:

1. Challenging work.
2. Commitment to job and company.
3. Reasonable job demands.
4. Pay.
5. Good supervisor.
6. Congenial associates.
7. Job security.
8. Opportunity to advance.
9. Absence of "obstacles" like incompetent associates or too demanding a supervisor.

Based on a study of 57,000 job applicants over a 30-year period at the Minnesota Gas Company, Jurgensen lists in rank order the ten factors felt to make a job good or bad.[17] The order for men is security, advancement, type of work, company, pay, co-workers, supervisor, benefits, hours, working conditions. Women ranked type of work first, followed by company, security, co-workers, advancement, supervisor, pay, working conditions, hours, and benefits.

Given these studies, we feel that employee wants can be grouped into four categories. First is *remuneration*. Included here is the pay and benefits "package"; i.e., the tangible rewards received from the job. Second is *security*. We include here physical safety, opportunity for advancement as well as preservation of the job. The third area is *intrapersonal job satisfaction*. Included here are comfortable working conditions, appropriateness of job requirements, doing interesting work, and the like. The fourth, and last, category is *interpersonal satisfactions*. Satisfaction with one's supervisor, congenial work associates, and a feeling of identification with the organization are included here.

TAILORING REWARDS TO THE WANTS

While classifying rewards under the remuneration, security, intrapersonal, and interpersonal categories, we should still not lose sight of their relationship to the need hierarchy categories. Exhibit 10–11 illustrates a number of these reward-need relationships. In the following sections, we will review a number of these rewards and discuss some novel or unique reward applications.

Remuneration wants

One of the oldest, most reliable rewards for behavior is money. The scientific management school of thought used incentive pay plans as a basis of many

Exhibit 10–11
Needs and potential rewards

Needs	Associated factors	Things an organization can provide
Self actualization	Growth Achievement Advancement Sense of accomplishment	Challenging job Advancement in the job Allow creative behavior
Ego–esteem	Self-respect Recognition Status Power Autonomy	Job Title Merit pay Responsibility Status symbols Autonomy/freedom on job Public recognition
Social	Companionship Affection Sense of belonging	Interaction with co-workers Friendly/capable supervisor
Security	Safety Stability Competence to adapt Freedom from fear	Pensions Insurance General pay increases (cost of living) Safe working conditions
Physiological	Air Food Water Shelter Sex	Sound physical working conditions Direct provision, or resources to acquire food, shelter Cafeteria Heat and air conditioning Safety equipment

of its prescriptions. Interestingly, money can relate to all levels of the need hierarchy discussed in the last chapter. Money helps purchase social need gratification all the way from buying a round of drinks after work to belonging to a country club. Further, money is itself a status symbol; how much misery has been caused by someone making a little more money than someone else we'll never know. Plus, money buys status symbols (cars, clothes, houses, and so on) and other ego satisfactions. Finally, as a vehicle to self-actualization, money can play a significant role by *permitting* one to pursue the goal. It costs a lot to run for governor, take a year off to run the Heart Fund, or climb that mountain. Money rears its head, too, in expectancy theory as a means to the desired end and in equity theory. Clearly, then, money plays a role in both content and process theories.*

Again in reference to Chapter 8, we discussed how wage/salary surveys and job evaluation are applied to help specify proper wage payments. However, even given the "fair" pay rate, we must further choose the compensation plan or system.

Exhibit 10–12 illustrates several types of compensation plans: base pay or salary, variable pay for an individual or group, and supplementary pay that is not directly related to the job. Base pay is a rate paid to a worker or workers in a given job. This can be the minimum wage or the corporation president's salary. In effect, it is the "guarantee" that the worker has. Supplementary pay often takes the form of a bonus or incentive for some extra level of performance. Note that this could be delivered via a number of different reinforcement schedules (see Exhibit 10–10). In addition, seniority or other similar factors may lead to extra, variable payments. Finally, supplementary pay is that given to all workers regardless of job. For example, everyone might receive, as a fringe benefit, health insurance. In general, supplementary pay does little to stimulate an "extra" level of performance. At best, it serves to improve morale and lower turnover.

The bonus payments offered by Thorn Lighting Company and Goodyear that were discussed earlier in this chapter are variable pay examples and, in the "a rose by any other name . . ." department, some organizations use "well pay" in the manner of Goodyear and Thorn Lighting. To stay ahead of all those people trying to build better mousetraps, Parsons Pine Products in Ashland, Oregon (maker of almost 80 percent of the wooden mousetraps manufactured in the United States), gives an extra day's pay at the end of each month to workers with perfect attendance. Absenteeism dropped 30 percent and tardiness is virtually zero.[18] Piece rate production and commission pay schemes are likewise examples of this pay approach. Various studies have revealed

---

* In a recent survey reported in *The Wall Street Journal* (Febrauary 21, 1978) the Higher Education Research Institute of Los Angeles reported that money ranked lower than location for professors weighing job changes. Pay as a consideration ranked highest for economics professors and lowest among psychology professors. At least they practice what they teach.

Exhibit 10–12
Compensation and behavior

Pay plans			Projected behavior
Base pay (job)			Attraction to organization by meeting physiological needs and security needs. Satisfaction in terms of (1) relative pay of peers, superiors, and subordinates, and (2) inputs of skill, education, and effort.
Variable pay (people)	Seniority		Stability of employment. Long tenure.
	Merit		Higher quality of general performance.
	Incentive	Individual	Higher output. Acceptable quality.
		Group	Greater cooperation. Higher quantity and quality of output. Less waste. Less resistance to change. More suggestions.
Supplementary pay	Economic (pensions, insurance, etc.) . . .		Maintenance of work force. Maintenance of morale.
	Time off with pay (vacations, holidays, etc.)		Maintenance of work force. Maintenance of morale.

Source: Edwin B. Flippo and Gary M. Munsinger, *Management*, 4th ed. (Boston: Allyn and Bacon, Inc., 1978), p. 362.

that workers on incentive pay plans tend to be more highly motivated and produce more than hourly paid workers although the latter were more satisfied with the pay they actually received.[19]

A lottery game compensation system has also been used by some organizations as an attempt to reduce absenteeism. Here "tickets" are given to workers for each day (or each hour) of attendance and then a drawing for a valuable prize held. Those who have "attended" more often clearly have the advantage. A variation of this is to award the tickets on a random basis; e.g., everyone at work at 9:03 A.M. gets two tickets. (Note how this uses the *variable interval* reinforcement schedule.)

We are not really sure how to classify the pay scheme used by a firm in Florida selling commodity options by telephone to gullible people around the country.

Authorities and former salesmen say that prospects are referred to as "mooches," and that supervisors exhort salesmen with such rallying cries as, "The mooch has your money in his pocket!" Sales figures for each phone man often are posted on a wall, and managers openly say they won't tolerate a salesman who can't bring in at least $20,000 a month. One [brokerage] house is reliably reported to have brought in a prostitute each night at 11 to reward the evening's top salesman.[20]

Nor, are we able to classify per se as base, variable, or supplementary the pay scheme used by an unnamed eastern city's port authority for the toll takers on its bridges. There seemed to be a high relationship between turnover and the control of employee theft by management:

The personnel manager, together with the director of the toll-collecting operation, determined between themselves that the total cost of reducing theft to a minimum was excessive. Admittedly, they saved money in tolls, but personnel turnover (because toll collectors seemed to quit if they couldn't steal to supplement their pay) cost them more than the amount saved. By this time, the authority knew almost to the penny how much money should be collected per toll booth—as a function of traffic. They determined that they could tolerate toll-taker thefts of $10.00 a week a man.[21]

If thefts seemed to exceed $10, a police car was parked in front of the toll taker's booth. Thefts never failed to drop back to the tolerable level.

Security wants

Security is manifested in several ways. First, self-preservation is a predominant motive for most people.* Occupational Health and Safety Administration (OHSA) rules and regulations attempt to provide safe working environments. Yet black lung disease, asbestosis, and other poisonings, as well as accidents, will in all likelihood always occur. Workers will probably always make some sort of trade-off between the risk and the rewards of money, status, macho behavior, and the like. There will probably always be circus aerialists, Evel Knievel types, and iron workers putting up bridges and tall buildings.

Until recently the Japanese Nenko system was all that rivaled the job security of most government workers and tenured professors. Nenko is a system whereby a Japanese worker is hired by an organization for life. If necessary, the organization will even provide an education. Housing, recreation, and so on are provided at little or no cost to Nenko workers. Company loyalty under Nenko is understandably high. Wages are based on seniority and age rather than the job performed. In the late 1970s, however, economic conditions

---

* One author, on a mule ride in the Grand Canyon, was quite worried for a while; the drop-off is all the way to forever and the mule walks mighty close to the edge. He relaxed when told by the guide that only man has a greater sense of self-preservation than the mule.

have forced some Japanese firms to abolish the lifetime employment practice and introduce layoffs.

Security wants certainly can be influenced by economic conditions. After the massive mid-1970s layoffs in the U.S. auto industry and the subsequent recalls, attitudes among auto workers seemed to be different than before.[22] Security and making good cars people will buy to prevent future layoffs was the byword.

Opportunity to advance via promotions is another security-related area. Many organizations have promotion-from-within-when-possible schemes.

Recently, Information Terminals Corp., an electronics firm faced with decreased sales and the need to lay off skilled employees took a unique approach. The firm contacted other companies in the area that needed employees and then "leased out" the surplus workers, who continued to draw pay from the original employer (who was reimbursed by the other firm) and retained their seniority and fringe benefits.[23]

Similar strategies have been used by several European firms. AG Wester, an ailing West German shipbuilding firm, has "loaned" employees to Daimler-Benz, an automobile manufacturer; and Luxembourg's Arbed (short for Acieries Reunies de Burbach-Eich-Dudelange, S.A.), the world's 27th largest steel firm, has "rented out" employees to other business or government organizations when production slackened.[24]

A more precarious job security arrangement is practiced by some automobile dealers. In at least one dealership known to the authors, the lowest selling (by volume) salesperson each month is fired. No excuses or exceptions. Fired! Only baseball managers and football coaches seem to face more uncertainty.

Intrapersonal job satisfaction wants

An improved quality of work life has been a much sought after goal of social scientists in recent years. Studs Terkel's book *Working* (1974) in which a variety of workers talked about their jobs, *The Long Tunnel* (1976) by Dennis Smith about the rigors of coal mining, and *Blue-Collar Journal* (1974) by John Coleman, a college president on sabbatical digging ditches and washing dishes, are but several well-written pieces of the era.

The blue-collar trap has been widely blamed for much of the job dissatisfaction claimed to have occurred as jobs become more and more boring and meaningless to workers. The trap phenomena (applicable to white-collar as well) refers to a situation where workers are given relatively high pay to do "lousy" work (e.g., tighten bolts on an assembly line). After a short time, the worker's standard of living rises to match that income. But the job, boring as it is, becomes oppressive. The worker wants to quit, to do something more meaningful or interesting in a different job. But, those jobs don't pay enough. Hence, the worker is trapped. A lousy job; good pay; but no escape. Remember the sewer cleaning versus real estate job discussed earlier under "Expectancy Theory?" That is, perhaps, the *why* behind the trap.

Most often, jobs like this offer little in the way of good working conditions, credit for work done, opportunity to advance, and the like. Rarely are rewards other than pay emphasized. The worker is expected to satisfy needs through secondary outcomes. Indeed, "trapped" workers often exhibit high need gratification *off the job,* using pay from the job to purchase it. "We aren't implying that assembly-line work fills people with delight and satisfaction. . . . But they're getting about what they expect: a paycheck, vacations and retirement."[25]

However, what if workers want more than a paycheck, vacation, and retirement? Can we build in reward systems aimed at social, ego, even self-actualization needs? The answer seems to be, "Yes, sometimes."

Freedom.   Robert Schrank, a sociologist-worker of the Eric Hoffer mold, writes,

I dwell on the amenities of the job—the freedom to work at one's own pace, to break when you wish, to come in late, to go home early or late, shop in the middle of the day, take a long lunch hour, get paid by the week or month— because I believe this may be the stuff of which high levels of job satisfaction are made.[26]

In this view freedom is a major "want." To control one's own life a little more, to not be so tied to the system—that is what is desired. Schrank argues that jobs should be designed to give this freedom, or at least a dose of it. For example, at the Harmon automobile-mirror plant (Bolivar, Tennessee) workers may earn "idle time" by completing a certain agreed-upon amount of work. They can go home or attend training courses to upgrade their job status.[27] It is surprising how fast/hard someone can work in order to gain a measure of free time.

Even on assembly line jobs freedom is sought and gained. In auto plants workers very often "double up," that is they learn each other's job. One worker then will work feverishly on both jobs, allowing the other to be off. A half hour on and a half hour off tends to be the norm.[28]

The worker who is on is obliged to do both jobs by superhuman effort. But workers would rather race to keep up with the line than work steadily—in anticipation of a half-hour off to read, lie down, go to the toilet, or roam the plant to talk to a buddy.[29]

Another freedom-related scheme is flextime—allowing workers within limits to set their own hours. Many organizations allow workers to put in an eight-hour day anytime between 7:30 A.M. and 6:30 P.M., except for a fixed time in the middle of the day when everyone must be on the job. Where jobs are not so interdependent, such systems can work well (e.g., it would be hard to use flextime on an assembly line). Absenteeism often is reduced since workers can take several hours off to do something important whereas before they took the whole day. Many organizations now use flextime; e.g., numerous U.S. military bases, Blue Cross/Blue Shield of California, Pacific Gas and Electric, Exxon, Hewlett-Packard. SmithKline Corporation, John Hancock Insurance, and Continental Telephone.[30]

A "cousin" to flextime is the four-day workweek where a worker puts in 40 hours by working four 10-hour days. This gives an additional "leisure" day; i.e., three days per week off instead of the normal two. While once advocated as the wave of the future, there is currently disagreement as to whether "4–40" actually has a future. For sure, it has run up against some states' overtime laws (anything over eight hours in one day is often time and a half overtime), difficulties in employers' scheduling, and outright opposition by some unions. The U.S. Department of Labor estimates that in 1978 only 2 percent of the full-time workers in the United States worked less than five days a week.[31] *

Status. Status symbols have long been of concern to human beings. Pieces of bone, feathers, and other objects which were worn as body decorations by cave dwellers were very likely status symbols. Man's love affair with these symbols continues.

Exhibit 10–13 presents in somewhat random order a number of objects/ privileges often used as status symbols. While some symbols tend to be well-accepted as "high" status, others can be high in one organization and low in another. Status is simply a subjective ranking and thus depends upon the subjective assessments of those involved. What is "high" in one organization may be "nothing" or "low" in another. For example, large private offices, nicely decorated, are usually associated with high status. However, in one Wall Street bank, the high status vice presidents' desks (i.e., offices) were out in the open, arranged along the walls. Their secretaries shared the center of the room. To be in a private office would have taken them out of the flow of the business and thus make it appear that the bank no longer felt them valuable. Exhibit 10–14 depicts the arrangement.

Status systems in organizations are both formal and informal. Formal systems are those sanctioned by the organization. For example, all division managers receive wood desks, only certain people are allowed in the executive dining

---

* At the time of this writing, a movement has begun by several labor unions to introduce the 35-hour work week in order to boost employment. Workers would get the same amount of pay as for a 40-hour week. We are skeptical about this.

Exhibit 10–13
Miscellaneous status symbols

Rating factors/status symbols

1. Concrete or tile floor
2. Rug on floor
3. Wall-to-wall carpeting
4. Venetian blinds on windows
5. Curtains on windows
6. Drapes on windows
7. Filing cabinets in office
8. No filing cabinets in office
9. Black telephone
10. Call director
11. Small room
12. Large room
13. Office with windows
14. Office with windows, no view
15. Office with windows, with view
16. Small desk
17. Large desk
18. Single-occupant office
19. Double-occupant office
20. Multioccupant office
21. Two or more hard chairs
22. Upholstered chairs
23. No couch
24. With couch

25. No coffee table
26. With coffee table
27. With refrigerator
28. No refrigerator
29. Assigned secretary
30. Secretary from secretarial pool
31. Picture prints on wall
32. Original paintings on wall
33. No water pitcher
34. Plastic water pitcher
35. Silver water pitcher
36. Coffee served in paper cups
37. Coffee served in white glass cups
38. Coffee served in china cups with saucer
39. No pen set on desk
40. Plastic pen set on desk
41. Onyx or marble-base pen set on desk
42. Private toilet in office
43. Office located next to noisy toilets
44. Office with no copy machine
45. Office with copy machine

Nonoffice rating factors (when observable)

1. Access to executive dining room
2. Access to cafeteria
3. Regular passport
4. Official passport
5. Telephone answered with bureaucrat's name
6. Telephone answered with number or "hello."
7. Bust size of secretary, if any (secretary)

8. Assigned parking space
9. No assigned parking space
10. Parking space assigned, parking lot
11. Parking space assigned, within building, distant from door
12. Parking space assigned, within building, close to door
13. Parking space assigned, by name

Source: James H. Boren, *When in Doubt, Mumble: A Bureaucrat's Handbook*, pp. 153–54. © 1972 by Litton Educational Publishing, Inc. Reprinted by permission of Van Nostrand Reinhold Company.

room, and so on. Informal systems tend to evolve via the interaction of workers and may or may not be recognized by management. Desk location is often a phenomenon seen here. In a large open office area, desks may seem to be arranged in no particular order, but let someone quit and note what happens. Do others begin trading desks so that by the time a replacement is hired

Exhibit 10–14
Desk (office) arrangement of high-status vice presidents of a New York bank

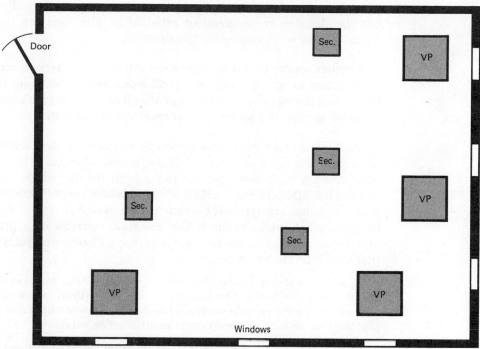

Desk positions were basically as noted. Sofas and chairs were scattered around for guests to sit in.

the now-vacant desk may be somewhere else in the room? If so, check to see whose desk is closest to the boss. That's probably the high status place. The other desk locations have their own rank order.

John Dean (of Watergate fame) tells of how office/desk location was important in the White House.

The White House, far more than any other government office, was in a state of perpetual internal flux. Offices were constantly exchanged and altered . . . Everyone jockeyed for a position close to the President's ear, and even an unseasoned observer could sense minute changes in status. Success and failure could be seen in the size, decor and location of offices. Anyone who moved to a smaller office was on the way down. If a carpenter, cabinetmaker, or wallpaper hanger was busy in someone's office, this was a sure sign he was on the rise. . . . We learned to read office changes as an index of the internal bureaucratic power struggles. The expense was irrelevant to Haldeman. "For Christ's sake," he once reported when we discussed whether we should reveal such expenses, "this place is a national monument, and I can't help it if the last three Presidents let it go to hell." Actually, the costs had less to do with the fitness of the White House than with the need of its occupants to see tangible evidence of their prestige.[32]

Management should try to assess the impact on informal status systems when making decisions affecting a work group. A rule of thumb is that if a manager makes what honestly looks like a sound, technically good decision, but the decision is criticized or rebelled at, the odds are that the informal status system was violated by the decision.

Another source of status is personal attributes. Whether one likes it or not, such factors as age, sex, physical good looks, race, education, religion, competence, and the like are qualities that are often viewed as desirable/undesirable by work groups and serve to help create status hierarchies.

One of the major problems caused by status symbols is *status incongruence*. There are usually a number of official/unofficial status symbols in operation. Most often a high-status person ranks high on the whole range of symbols and the low-status person ranks low on the whole range. Incongruence happens when high and low symbols become mixed in one person's "status collection." Imagine what might occur if the low-status person in a plant was (for no other reason) assigned the best parking place. Continuing John Dean's description of White House offices:

> By all White House standards my office was shabby. The walls needed painting and the furniture looked like military discards. . . . From my window I could gaze on an interior asphalt courtyard filled with delivery trucks and parked cars plus the rear ends of air conditioners in other office windows.

> I spoke with Larry Higby about this situation, which I felt did not befit a man with my title. "Larry, I don't want to sound like a complainer, but I'm embarrassed to invite anyone to my office for a meeting, it's such a dump. Also it's sometimes hard to concentrate, listening to the urinals flush all day, since you've got me right beside the men's room."

> "It's only temporary," he said. He agreed to have the walls painted and some decent furnishings delivered but added a teaser: "Bob hasn't decided where he wants to put you yet." Then he dangled "possibilities" before me—nice big offices of people Haldeman might move out in order to move me in. I did not have to be told what was happening. I was being tested and my performance would determine what I would get. I was at the bottom of the ladder, and instinctively, I began to climb.[33]

That people are quite cognizant of status symbols (often without necessarily understanding the theory behind them) is illustrated by the experience of a colleague's wife. Look for status symbols and their use in this anecdote: She quit her job as secretary to a lawyer to take a new secretarial job with a large corporation.* She quit after the first day. Why? Her office and the offices of all other people reporting to her boss were the only ones of all those she saw in the building that still had manual typewriters; everyone else had electric machines. She felt that if her boss had so little power that he couldn't get his staff high-status electric typewriters, then he probably had little power over a lot of other things. Why work for a weak boss? So she went back to

---

* American Cyanamid, if you must know.

the lawyer and asked for her old job back. He said, "OK, how much money do you want?" When she replied that her old salary would be fine, he told her no, that wouldn't do. "I just hired another new secretary to work in the area you're in at $50 more than that. You have to take that extra $50, too, since I couldn't stand it otherwise."

Motivation by the use of status symbols is something management ought to consider. People will often work hard to acquire a fancy job title, better office furniture, or to get any number of other desired symbols. Remember that people value these symbols; dispense them accordingly. However, also remember that the value of the symbol is subjective and thus depends upon the people concerned. Just because the boss thinks having a gold-plated pen and pencil set is high status doesn't mean anyone else does. Managers cannot simply create and introduce a new symbol without its subjective acceptance by the work force.

Job design.   How a job is performed is an often overlooked variable in management decision making. Too often, people simply assume that it has to be done that way because that's the only way they've seen it done.

Chapter 7, devoted to job design, illustrated a variety of "other ways." As was evident in that discussion, much motivation potential exists within the work itself.

Interpersonal relations wants

The social/relatedness categories of the need hierarchy point to the importance of opportunities to satisfy these needs. Though we all seem to need some time to be alone, few of us could go for long without companionship. Some of our most extreme punishments involve the withdrawal of social interaction (e.g., solitary confinement, shunning in the Mennonite religion, or the silence at West Point).

Jobs that restrict or prevent interaction tend to be viewed as boring or harsh. Several years ago a British labor union demanded a "lonely pay" bonus for a worker whose redesigned job caused him to be isolated. Sometimes interaction is difficult, not due to proximity problems, but rather to noise or the fact that the work pace is too fast to allow time to socialize (e.g., most assembly lines). In many organizations, especially factories, jobs that allow or require a worker to move about and interact with other people are valued highly. Workers in these jobs can partake of the communications grapevine and are able to have variety and change in their work routines.

Interpersonal relations center around co-workers, yet we must not exclude one's own supervisor or management in general from our analysis. The "climate" of an organization is determined in large part by the quality of management. Organizations with established policies and procedures, where the system seems to run well, and where there is a minimum of hassles, tend to be "good," friendly places to work. The "System" can create "mean streets" or "fun city," depending on its quality.

In recent years the National Institute for Occupational Safety and Health (NIOSH) has been investigating "mass illnesses" that strike organizations.[34] For example, on a hot summer day at an electronics assembly plant a woman becomes ill, claiming to feel dizzy and nauseous. Within several minutes several dozen other women report to the first aid room with the same symptoms. Management is concerned and shuts down operations. Teams of investigators find no toxins, bacteria, or anything else capable of causing the symptoms.

In another case in a seafood packing plant a worker mentions a "strange smell." Several minutes later, other workers also complain of a smell. Almost immediately, workers begin to fall ill. They have trouble breathing. Again, medical investigators find no causes.

NIOSH investigators are now calling this phenomena "assembly line hysteria" or "mass psychogenic illness." Several characteristics seem to be common to organizations experiencing the phenomenon:

1. Stressful jobs—due to noise, pressure for production, or some similar reason.
2. Boredom—primarily due to repetitive work at fixed work stations and an inability to communicate with co-workers.
3. Poor labor-management relations—evident in virtually all NIOSH investigated situations.

Assembly-line workers' inability to communicate easily with one another seems to contribute to mass psychogenic illness. . . . [T]he noise of keypunch machines made it impossible for the operators to talk with one another. Staggered lunch breaks further cut down social contacts. . . . [Studies] suggest that some workers who succumb to mass psychogenic illness are social isolates, people who aren't chosen as friends by others in the study samples.[35]

What can management do to facilitate social interaction without compromising production? Where possible, office/plant layout and job design should be done with an eye to permitting co-workers to maintain visual/verbal contact. Lunch and coffee breaks should, where possible, allow groups of workers to socialize. One of the most "lonely" scenes ever encountered by one of the authors was at a telephone exchange. The company representative giving the tour proudly opened the door to the "break room" where gaily painted walls, nice furniture, and vending machines were present. One woman was in the room sitting at a table staring at the wall, elbow on the table, chin in hand. "She's on her break," said the proud company representative. "With facilities like this, I can't understand why we have so much turnover among the operators."

Robert Schrank argues that one of the main things workers want from their jobs is a chance to "schmooz"—to talk about TV, sports, the movies, politics, lovers, gossip, the boss, and so on and to even fool around somewhat, maybe even use the telephone during the workday.[36] Clearly, workers can be allowed such freedoms in most organizations. In reality, managers already spend considerable schmoozing time each day and they get their jobs done, don't they?

STRUCTURE, MOTIVATION, AND JOB DESIGN

Exhibit 10–15 illustrates some predicted relationships among job design variables and individual motivation considered in this chapter and the topic

Exhibit 10–15
Predicted relationships between organization design, job design, and individual motivation factors

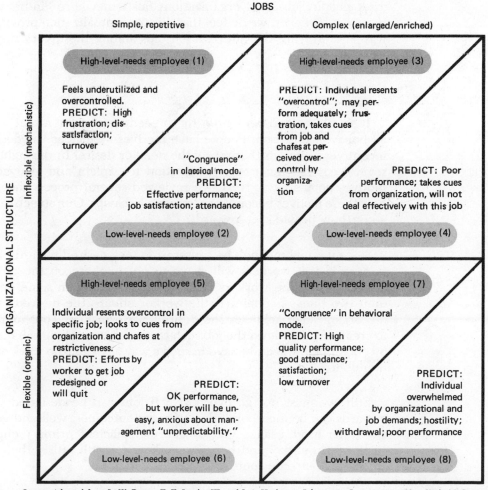

Source: Adapted from L. W. Porter, E. E. Lawler III, and J. A. Hackman, *Behavior in Organizations* (New York: McGraw-Hill Book Company, 1975), p. 309.

of organizational design (Chapter 5). The implication here is that job design must certainly be considered in the context of other factors and cannot exist in a vacuum. The figure is basically a $2 \times 2 \times 2$ table with the dichotomized variables of (1) organization design (flexible versus inflexible), (2) job design (simple, repetitive versus complex), and (3) individual motivation (high-level needs versus low-level needs—à la the need hierarchy). Note that two of the eight cells indicate a "congruence" situation; the other six predicting ineffective matching between people, jobs, and the organization. These cells are (2) low-level-needs employee, inflexible organization structure, and a simple job, and (7) high-level-needs employee, flexible organization structure, and a complex job.

We stress that Exhibit 10–15 represents predictions based on theory and some limited evidence. Also note that in expressing the variables in dichotomy form (i.e., endpoints only), we present mere caricatures of the real world; most people, jobs, and organizations fall somewhere "in-between" on each measure. However, we do feel that this conceptualization provides an effective way of conveying the interrelationships among these very important topics.

SUMMARY

It should be apparent from the preceding discussion that we believe that all behavior is caused. People have motives—felt needs or desires—and seek incentives—rewards that satisfy the need or desire. In this light, we reviewed several content theories of motivation to explain and analyze the kinds of motives people have. Next, we reviewed several process theories to explain how these motives become expressed in behavior. Our objective was to explain when/how people seek rewards.

Since it is in someone's best interest to seek desired rewards, it is reasonable to assume that workers will strive to obtain them on the job. If, to obtain these rewards, the workers are caused to perform in some desired manner, then two things happen: (1) the worker obtains the desired reward, and (2) the organization achieves the desired performance. Thus, our philosophy is to create conditions on the job such that workers seeking to satisfy their needs by obtaining rewards, behave in such a way as to get the work of the organization done.

Still, we must not go overboard. If jobs can be designed so that desired rewards can be incorporated as primary outcomes, well and good. Do it. On the other hand, realize that by offering sufficient primary outcome rewards in the form of pay and benefits workers can still satisfy their needs via the secondary outcome route.

Certainly, there are many people who do not view their jobs as something that is central to their life interests. A job is a job; a way of getting the resources to do what they really want to do. For the most part, these people will be difficult to motivate with anything but remuneration rewards. However, these persons should not blind the manager to the fact that other people do get great pleasure and satisfaction from their jobs.

GUIDES TO ACTION

1. Always try to determine what motives are dominant in those people with whom you work (your boss, your peers, your employees). Don't fall into the trap of believing that everyone else is like you in terms of what "turns you on."

2. Remember that for learning to take place under the operant conditioning model the manager must monitor behavior and dispense rewards or punishments as soon after performance as possible. This means that the manager has to observe behavior closely.

3. As needs become satisfied, the dominant motives of people will change. Watch for these changes as you maintain the awareness discussed in (1) above.

4. You have probably heard the saying, "Different strokes for different folks." Well, we agree. Within the limitations of equity, union agreements or other restrictions, be willing to provide different kinds of rewards to different workers. You often have to search for those "different strokes." Constantly look for and "collect" rewards that you can use to influence the behavior of employees.

5. "You get what you reward." It's a well-worn saying, but believe it. Be sure you understand the behavior-reward relationship that your employees *perceive.* Their *perceptions* are what channels their behavior. So, you have to figure it out.

6. Keep an open mind toward how jobs are done. Job redesign is often an effective way of improving employee-need satisfaction. Too often people fall into the, "But, we've always done it this way" trap.

7. Remember, all of your employees will strive to satisfy needs off the job if satisfaction isn't forthcoming as a primary outcome. Sometimes jobs can't be redesigned or novel reward systems developed. If such is the case, realize that the employee will probably emphasize financial rewards which will then be used to gain need gratification off the job. Manage that employee accordingly.

NOTES

[1] David Lamb, "In Australia They Bribe Men to Work," *Los Angeles Times,* August 13, 1974, p. 1.

[2] "At This Firm It'll Pay to Show Up," *Arizona Daily Star,* October 23, 1977, p. 10A.

[3] "Burns Ties Time off Job to a 'Productivity Slump'," *The Wall Street Journal,* May 16, 1977, p. 6.

[4] See Barbara Boner and Arthur Neef, "Productivity and Unit Labor Costs in 12 Industrialized Countries," *Monthly Labor Review,* vol. 100, no. 7 (July 1977), pp. 11–17.

[5] See Abraham Maslow, *Motivation and Personality,* 2d ed. (New York: Harper & Row, Publishers, 1970).

[6] Clayton P. Alderfer, "An Empirical Test of a New Theory of Human Needs," *Organizational Behavior and Human Per-*

formance, vol. 4, no. 2 (May 1969), pp. 142–75.

[7] John Slocum, Jr., "A Comparative Study of the Satisfaction of American and Mexican Operatives," *Academy of Management Journal*, vol. 14, no. 1 (March 1977), pp. 89–97.

[8] David C. McClelland, *The Achieving Society* (New York: Free Press, 1961).

[9] Douglas McGregor, *The Human Side of Enterprise* (New York: McGraw-Hill Book Company, 1960).

[10] Chris Argyris, *Personality and Organization* (New York: Harper & Row, Publishers, 1957).

[11] Frederick Herzberg, *Work and the Nature of Man* (Cleveland: Harcourt, Brace, and World, 1966).

[12] T. J. Atchison, and E. A. Lefferts, "The Prediction of Turnover Using Herzberg's Job Satisfaction Techniques," *Personnel Psychology*, vol. 25, no. 1 (Spring 1972), p. 61.

[13] See B. F. Skinner, *Beyond Freedom and Dignity* (New York: Alfred A. Knopf, 1971).

[14] See J. Stacey Adams, "Toward an Understanding of Inequity," *Journal of Abnormal and Social Psychology*, vol. 67, no. 5 (November 1963), pp. 422–36; also, Paul S. Goodman and A. Friedman, "An Examination of Adams' Theory of Inequity," *Administrative Science Quarterly*, vol. 16, no. 3 (September 1971), pp. 271–88.

[15] Edwin B. Flippo, and Gary M. Munsinger, *Management*, 4th ed. (Boston: Allyn and Bacon, Inc., 1978), pp. 351–52.

[16] John R. Hinrichs, "A Replicated Study of Job Satisfaction Dimensions," *Personnel Psychology*, vol. 21, no. 4 (Winter 1968), pp. 485–95.

[17] Clifford E. Jurgensen, "Job Preferences (What Makes a Job Good or Bad?)," *Journal of Applied Psychology*, vol. 63, no. 3 (June 1978), pp. 267–76.

[18] See "A Better Mousetrap," *The Wall Street Journal*, May 2, 1978, p. 1.

[19] Donald P. Schwab, and Marc J. Wallace, Jr., "Correlates of Employee Satisfaction with Pay," *Industrial Relations*, vol. 13, no. 2 (February 1974), pp. 78–89.

[20] Jonathan Kwitney, "Commodity Options Sold by Phone Often Fail to Ring True," *The Wall Street Journal*, November 18, 1977, pp. 1, 33.

[21] Lawrence R. Zeitlin, "A Little Larceny Can Do a Lot for Employee Morale," *Psychology Today*, June 1971, pp. 22–26, 64.

[22] John R. Emshwiller, "Recalled Auto Worker Finds His Outlook on Life Is Different," *The Wall Street Journal*, Febraury 3, 1977, pp. 1, 19.

[23] "Farming out Work," *The Wall Street Journal*, July 11, 1978, p. 1.

[24] Bill Paul, "Too Many Workers? Try Lending Them to Another Firm," *The Wall Street Journal*, May 3, 1979, p. 1; and Eric Morgenthaler, "Big Company Learns How to Lose Francs and Influence People,"*The Wall Street Journal*, May 21, 1979, p. 1.

[25] Quote attributed to Dr. H. R. Spiro. *Newsweek*, April 29, 1974, p. 40.

[26] See Robert Schrank, *Ten Thousand Working Days* (Cambridge, Mass.: MIT Press, 1978). Quote taken from *Business Week*, July 10, 1978, p. 10.

[27] Robert Schrank, "How to Relieve Worker Boredom," *Psychology Today*, July 1978, pp. 79–80.

[28] See Stanley Aronowitz, *False Promises* in Peter Frost, V. F. Mitchell, and W. R. Nord, eds., *Organizational Reality* (Pacific Palisades, Calif.: Goodyear Publishing Co., 1978), pp. 175–79.

[29] Ibid., p. 176.

[30] Barry Stein, Alan Cohen, and Herman Gadon, "Flextime: Work When You Want to," *Psychology Today*, June 1976, p. 40.

[31] *The Wall Street Journal*, July 25, 1978, p. 1.

[32] John Dean, *Blind Ambition* (New York: Pocket Books, 1977), p. 20.

[33] Ibid., p. 21.

[34] See Michael J. Colligan, and William Stockton, "The Mystery of Assembly-Line Hysteria," *Psychology Today*, June 1978, p. 93.

[35] Ibid., p. 94.

[36] See Schrank, *Ten Thousand Working Days*.

DISCUSSION QUESTIONS

1. What is *THE* motivation problem?

2. To what extent must there be an individual-organizational goal overlap for a person to be "motivated" to perform in an organization?

3. Differentiate between motives and incentives.

4. Why must both ability and motivation be considered in determining performance level?

5. Distinguish between the scientific management, human relations, and human resources approaches to motivation.

6. What are the content theories? The process theories?

7. Explain why (à la Maslow) satisfied needs are not dominant motivators.

8. Discuss the implications of Alderfer's modification of the Maslow hierarchy.

9. Describe the Theory X and Theory Y assumptions.

10. List several hygiene factors. Several motivation factors.

11. Differentiate between primary and secondary rewards.

12. Describe: $MF = (E \times V)$.

13. Using the Skinnerian operant conditioning theory, describe how one might train a cocktail waitress to be "more polite" to customers.

14. What are some major "wants" from a job?

15. Discuss the relationship between motivation, job design, and organization design.

CASE: SEABOARD RADIO AND APPLIANCE COMPANY*

The Seaboard Radio and Appliance Company, a large major appliance dealer in an eastern city, sold and serviced a wide range of home equipment, including radio, television, and high-fidelity installations; refrigerators, freezers, washers, and dryers; air-conditioning units and dehumidifiers. The sales manager of Seaboard often said, "Service is our biggest and most important asset. Competent servicing gives us an edge over our competition, including the fly-by-night discounters. That is why our advertising and promotion emphasize 'service with a smile' instead of price."

Philip Alger managed the Repair Service Division, which was organized into three departments, each under a department manager. The radio and television department was supervised by Sam Franklin.

It was not possible to schedule repair and service calls evenly throughout the workweek. A customer's call for service was, to the customer, "an emergency"—whether her dishwasher suddenly failed to work, a freezer full of steaks suddenly ceased operation, or the TV set blew a tube the night before

---

* From: Garret L. Bergen, and William V. Haney, *Organizational Relations and Management Action* (New York: McGraw-Hill Book Company, 1966), pp. 674–75.

the All-star game. Considerable overtime was therefore required of employees. Overtime was paid at the rate of time and a half. It was the policy of the Repair Service Division to distribute overtime evenly among all employees doing the same kind of work.

In the radio and television department, an exception to the overtime policy had been made with the knowledge and permission of Philip Alger. Sam Franklin usually called on Peter Cardoza, 1 of 11 technicians in the department, when overtime was required on particularly difficult service or repair assignments. This practice had been in effect for several years.

Pete had been with Seaboard ever since he got out of the service in 1951. He was a careful, highly skilled workman and, in addition, had won a reputation for handling himself well in the homes of customers, many of whom had written complimentary notes to the management of Seaboard about his attitude and satisfactory work. The other ten repairmen in the department voiced no objection to the practice of giving the lion's share of overtime work to Pete. Some were unable to handle the more difficult assignments. Others just didn't seem to care.

Relations between Seaboard and the union representing the servicemen had been excellent for years. Alger could not recall the last time a complaint had gone beyond the first step of the grievance procedure.

In June, the international representative of the union telephoned Philip Alger to call his attention to abuses of the overtime policy in the two other departments of his division. Alger verified the allegations of the union and decided that it was necessary to enforce the overtime policy in all departments.

The next day, during, his daily inspection tour, Alger told Sam Franklin of his decision. Franklin protested at the time, but Alger cut him short and said that he was not in a position to make any exceptions in the division. He knew he would be getting gripes from the other departments when he cracked down on their abuses, and he thought the other department managers would try to use Cardoza's case as an excuse for the way they distributed overtime in their own areas.

Sam Franklin wanted to avoid an argument with Cardoza. He walked out in the shop, where Pete was testing some hi-fi components to be installed that evening in the home of the president of the city's largest bank. "Pete, I've just had orders from Alger to spread all overtime equally among all the boys in the department. I'm sure you'll understand—it's the policy, you know." Cardoza looked bewildered. "Look, boss, I don't see how we can divide the tough jobs up evenly. Now, take this baby, for example. As soon as I'm through, I'll drop in your office to see what it's all about." Franklin turned away as he said, "Sorry, Pete, but that's the way the ball bounces."

Pete's performance steadily deteriorated. Late in July, he left to take a similar job with Seaboard's leading competitor.

Questions

1. Why did Pete quit?
2. What should be done now?

SELECTION OF THE PRODUCT OR SERVICE

DESIGN OF THE SYSTEM

STAFFING THE ORGANIZATION

STARTUP OF THE ORGANIZATION

OPERATING THE ORGANIZATION IN THE STEADY STATE

IMPROVING THE ORGANIZATION

REVISION OF THE ORGANIZATION

TERMINATION OF THE ORGANIZATION

Level of Organizational Outputs

O

Decision-making processes; social value; goals; forecasts; policies; plans

Authority and responsibility; power; organizational structure; communications systems; job design

Work force planning; personnel management functions

Startup planning and scheduling; monitoring; alternative startup approaches

Motivation; leadership; production and operations management; control

Individual improvement programs and techniques; group conflict management; MBO

Evaluation of organizational policies; strategic choices; organizational change; organizational development

Partial terminations; cutback management; complete terminations; mergers; born-again strategies

t_0

Time

Chapter 11
Leadership

Geez, I don't get no respect around here.

Rodney Dangerfield

The buck stops here.

Harry Truman

I shall return.

Douglas MacArthur

Dangerfield doesn't have it. Truman did. So did MacArthur—until Truman took it away.

"It" is that elusive, difficult to describe, quality called *leadership*. Leadership (especially how to get and use it) has been a topic that has perhaps forever fascinated the human race. Still, we have few answers to such questions as: What makes a leader? Who can be a leader? What does a leader do? Can leader skills be learned? Why do followers follow? What do followers want from a leader? And so forth.

Leadership tends to be discussed in terms of three main meanings. First, it is an attribute of a particular position (e.g., the president is our leader). Second, it is the characteristic of a particular person (e.g., Bill certainly showed real leadership when he took charge of all the survivors of the shipwreck). Finally, leadership is a category of behavior (e.g., the football team needs leadership to get it back on a winning track).

WHAT IS LEADERSHIP?

Our definition of leadership evolves from a chain, or series of definitions:

1. To *influence* is to cause some behavior in another person.* Approaching someone from behind and yelling loudly to make them jump is an act of influence. So is causing someone to catch a baseball thrown at them, or causing someone to move aside or to duck to avoid being hit by the baseball. To influence is simply to cause *some* behavior. We don't necessarily know what (exactly) the person will do when we yell or throw the ball. But we "know" the person will (probably) do something.

2. *Power* is the ability to influence in such a way as to cause a particular behavior. Assume that every time you sneak up behind Sharon and yell, she says, "Oh, my gosh" and stamps her right foot. You then have power over her to the extent that you can make her say, "Oh, my gosh" and stamp her right foot simply by sneaking up behind her and yelling. Anytime you want her to perform in that manner, you can cause the behavior by

---

* Or any organism. Our concern here, of course, is with people.

doing what you have to do. Thus, you have power, even though you may choose not to use it.

3. *Authority* is legitimate power; power vested in certain persons for certain purposes. For example, your boss can cause you to report to work at certain times by simply so setting your schedule. It probably would not be legitimate for your boss to order you to cheat customers. Unless, that is, you believed that cheating customers was appropriate for you to do. Legitimacy, then, is defined in the "mind of the beholder" and tends to be defined in socially acceptable terms. Thus, if a mugger says, "Give me your money" and you respond by giving up your money, that is simply a response to power. If the Internal Revenue Service says, "Give me your money," that's authority. The result is the same either way. However, one way tends to be more socially acceptable.

4. *Leadership* (as a class of behavior) is seen as the way, or style, by which authority is exercised. Thus, leadership is a social process by which followers are influenced to willingly engage in certain behaviors; behaviors the followers feel are legitimate for the leader to influence. Note that it is possible for some leaders to have more legitimate power (i.e., authority) than others (e.g., "I'll work overtime tonight if Smith asks me, but not for Jones!").

We tend to view leadership as something that involves more than simple compliance with legitimate demands placed upon employees by an organization's managers. With respect to those managers at a given organizational level, they may have all been "created equal" but they don't remain equal for long. Some managers will tend to gain more willing compliance with a broader range of requests than others. There tends to be an area within which an employee willingly complies with a manager's requests. This area, as noted in Chapter 4, is commonly termed the zone of indifference. The zone broadens or constricts depending upon the manager's leadership skills. Thus, we agree with a widely accepted definition of leadership: ". . . we consider the essence of organizational leadership to be the influential increment over and above mechanical compliance with the routine directives of the organization."[1]

WHY DO FOLLOWERS FOLLOW?

In the preceding chapter, we contended that people's behavior in organizations is based upon the attainment of rewards or other outcomes that satisfy various needs. It would seem, then, that subordinates will obey managers' orders to the extent that such obedience will lead to these desirable outcomes.

John French and Bertram Raven suggest that there are five bases or sources of power that managers can have in effecting the attainment of desired outcomes by subordinates.[2] These bases are:

1. Reward power. The power to give or withhold rewards (e.g., pay, promotions, and so on).

2. Coercive power.   The power to punish (e.g., to fire a poor worker).
3. Legitimate power.   Power which is based upon legal or other formalized authority (e.g., police officers have the right to perform certain acts, managers can require employees to report to work at a certain hour).
4. Referent power.   Power based on a person's liking or identification with another person (e.g., we like and respect someone, therefore we are inclined to allow ourselves to be influenced by that person so as to establish or maintain a good relationship with that person).
5. Expert power.   Power based on knowledge, skills, or ability (e.g., obeying a physician's orders).

It is relatively easy to understand how reward, coercive and legitimate powers influence people's behavior in organizations. The power to hire, fire, give raises, administer discipline, give demotions, and so on are (within various limits) areas deemed legitimate for management to influence. These powers, by and large, can simply be conferred by the organization on a manager. Hence, as noted earlier, all managers can be "created equal," but equal they do not long remain. The inequality stems from the "influential increment" expressed in our definition presented above.

The "influential increment" concept thus seems to be related to a manager's use of expert and referent powers. These two powers represent an addition to the organizationally allocated powers and create the inequality among managers. Further, these powers represent an ability to go beyond the control or influence of workers via the use of simple reward/punishment systems. People who participate in an organization only for monetary rewards will soon devise ways of attaining the rewards with a minimum of effort. Those who participate only to avoid punishment will do what is minimally acceptable and look for the opportunity to escape. And, legitimate power, unless supported by reward and/or punishment power, will tend to lead to only a grudging compliance with orders.

Clearly, then, there are several reasons why "followers follow." And there are likewise several reasons why some leaders have more of an "influential increment" than others. What separates the more effective leaders from their less effective colleagues would seem to be the former's ability to use more than a formal, organizationally allocated role in dealing with subordinates.

In the remainder of this chapter, we will examine several approaches to the study of leadership. First, we will examine an approach that attempts to view leadership in terms of the physical and personality *traits* possessed by effective leaders. The second approach is based on studies of the *behavior* engaged in by effective leaders.

The final approach looks at leadership in terms of *contingency* variables. That is, effective leadership traits and behaviors may vary according to particular factors inherent in particular situations.

THE TRAIT APPROACH

Many people have believed that leaders possess certain traits or characteristics that cause them to rise from the masses. Ralph M. Stogdill has carried out several studies of the nature of those traits thought to be possessed by leaders.[3] Lists of such traits could be virtually endless but typically include such things as size, energy, knowledge/intelligence, self-confidence, integrity, fluency of speech, good looks, imagination, endurance, emotional balance and control, task orientation, sociability/friendliness, drive for dominance, enthusiasm, courage, and the like. Exhibit 11–1 presents a list of traits for which Stogdill found the greatest evidence in his 1974 study.

There are obvious limitations with the "traitist approach" to leadership. For example, we "know" that people like General George Patton, Mahatma Ghandi, Vince Lombardi, John D. Rockefeller, Martin Luther King, Jr., Joan of Arc, Jesus, Adolph Hitler, Mao Tse-tung, Alexander the Great, Susan B.

Exhibit 11–1
Leader Traits

1. Social and interpersonal skills.
2. Technical skills.
3. Administrative skills.
4. Leadership effectiveness and achievement.
5. Social nearness, friendliness.
6. Intellectual skills.
7. Maintaining cohesive work group.
8. Maintaining coordination and teamwork.
9. Task motivation and application.
10. General impression (halo).
11. Group task supportiveness.
12. Maintaining standards of performance.
13. Willingness to assume responsibility.
14. Emotional balance and control.
15. Informal group control.
16. Nurturant behavior.
17. Ethical conduct, personal integrity.
18. Communication, verbality.
19. Ascendance, dominance, decisiveness.
20. Physical energy.
21. Experience and activity.
22. Mature, cultured.
23. Courage, daring.
24. Aloof, distant.
25. Creative, independent.
26. Conforming.

Source: Ralph M. Stogdill, *Handbook of Leadership: A Survey of Theory and Research* (New York: Free Press, 1974), p. 81.

Anthony, Fidel Castro, Geronimo, Al Capone, Winston Churchill, Abraham Lincoln, and Irving Fellerman* are somehow different. Also cases abound where a leader is successful in one situation (e.g., a military unit) but not in another (e.g., a hospital, university, or political party). Finally, Ben Solomon points out that while most (if not all) of the listed traits might be desirable in a leader, none seems to be absolutely essential.

The world has seen numerous great leaders who could hardly lay claim to any kind of formal education. History is replete with nontrained, nonacademic Fords, Edisons, and Carnegies who couldn't even claim a grammar school education yet managed to become leaders whose influence was felt around the globe.

As for appearance or robust health, need we mention more than the delicate Ghandi; or George Washington Carver, the frail, shriveled (physically) insignificant little Negro who was one of America's greatest scientists? And so many more like them? As for high ideals, fine character, etc., where would Hitler, Capone, or Attila the Hun rate here?[4]

As a final look at the trait approach, we note the work of Professor G. Edgar Folk (University of Iowa) in studying leadership characteristics of Arctic wolves. "Leadership: It's still a mystery. But we do know it is present at birth. Courage, boldness, adaptability. . . . There is a very definite rank order or hierarchy. The male is always more dominant."[5] (Sound familiar?) One interesting finding by Folk is that the leader always has a much higher heart rate than others in the pack—a case of executive stress, no doubt. Folk is interested in further studies comparing the behavior of wolf pack and human leaders. We fear that he will undoubtedly come up with a "lone wolf" leadership style.

THE BEHAVIORAL APPROACH

As it became obvious that the trait approach was yielding few clues as to what caused effective leadership, attention shifted to studying the actual behavior of leaders. There are important implications for this approach. First, by focusing on what leaders *do* (versus what they *are*) we tacitly assume that there is some "best" way to lead. Second, while traits are rather stable, behavior can be learned. Thus, leaders aren't only "born," they can be "created."

The behavioral approach stresses two important functions of leadership: task direction and psychological supportiveness.[6] This distinction involves viewing leadership as both a process of maintaining social relationships within an organized work unit and getting the unit to perform tasks at some acceptable level.

---

* One of the authors' former Boy Scout leaders, "a really neat guy."

Exhibit 11-2
Consideration and initiating structure

Consideration. Reflects the extent to which a person is likely to have relationships with subordinates characterized by such things as:

1. Mutual trust.
2. Respect for their ideas.
3. Consideration of their feelings.
4. Friendship.
5. Good rapport and two-way communication.

Initiating Structure. Reflects the extent to which a person is likely to define and structure both their own role and those of subordinates toward goal attainment. This is characterized by individuals who:

1. Actively direct a work group's activities.
2. Emphasize meeting deadlines.
3. Set definite standards of performance.
4. Criticize poor performance.
5. Encourage uniform procedures.

Source: Based on Edwin A Fleishman, *Manual for Leadership Opinion Questionnaire* (Chicago: Science Research Associates, 1969), p. 1.

The Ohio State Studies

The pioneering work in this area was done at Ohio State University and has become appropriately known as the Ohio State Studies.[7] The two leader functions were called "initiation of structure" which pertains to the task or performance dimension and "consideration" which relates to the social relationship between the leader and followers. Exhibit 11-2 describes these in greater detail.

Numerous research studies have been carried out to determine the effects of consideration and initiating structure on performance and morale of subordinates. Much work was predicated on the belief that the most effective leadership style would be high on both consideration and initiating structure measures. However, the results of many studies (which we will discuss shortly) indicated that no single style emerged as best. It was found that there were many *situational* factors which influenced what was "best." For example, in a study of research and development and engineering workers in several industries—petroleum, business machines, aircraft—it was found that there was a positive relationship between initiating structure and employees' job satisfaction. The relationship was, however, weakest in the aircraft industry (less formally structured). Thus, formality of organization structure seemed to be an important situational consideration.

The main point to be made about the Ohio State Studies is that they were an early attempt to rigorously determine the behaviors of leaders. The sound theoretical basis they provided served as a foundation for many later studies.

At about the same time as the Ohio State Studies, another group of researchers at the University of Michigan's Institute for Social Research distinguished between "employee-centered" and "production-centered" supervisors.[8] The close relationship with the Ohio State Studies should be obvious.* The Michigan researchers found that, in general, the higher productivity work groups had leaders who were more employee than production centered. For the most part, the Michigan findings were similar to those of the Ohio State group.†

The Managerial Grid®

Robert Blake and Jane Mouton, formerly at The University of Texas at Austin, also dealt with production-oriented and people-oriented dimensions.[9] Blake and Mouton propose a framework whereby leadership styles can be plotted on a two-dimensional Grid. Exhibit 11–3 presents this Grid. Since the Grid is a 9 by 9 matrix, there are 81 possible "styles." Only five are represented in Exhibit 11–3; however, these are sufficient to understand the ideas behind the Grid theory.

1,1 *Impoverished.*   The leader shows a low concern for both production and people. The leader exerts a minimum effort. This is sometimes also known as laissez-faire management.

9,1 *Task-oriented.*   The leader shows a very high concern for production and very little concern for employees' development or morale.

1,9 *Country club.*   The leader is concerned with promoting a friendly atmosphere and is interested in employees' morale. Very little concern is shown for production and efficiency.

5,5 *Middle-of-the-road.*   A moderate concern for both production and people. The leader is not highly concerned with either dimension.

9,9 *Team.*   This position shows a high concern for both the production and people dimensions.

Blake and Mouton argue that the 9,9 position is the ideal toward which all leaders should strive. They go so far as to propose a specific management training program which is designed to help move managers toward this position from any of the other 80 positions on the Grid.[10] We will mention this program again in Chapter 16.

---

* While we are aware of the long-standing football rivalry between these schools, we have no evidence that academic departments from these institutions were using this forum for some other kind of bowl game.

† A great defensive battle resulting in a 0–0 tie.

Exhibit 11-3
The Managerial Grid®

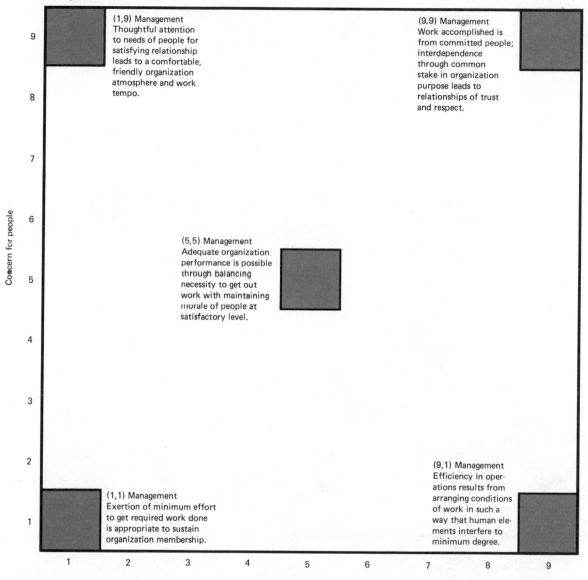

Concern for people

(1,9) Management Thoughtful attention to needs of people for satisfying relationship leads to a comfortable, friendly organization atmosphere and work tempo.

(9,9) Management Work accomplished is from committed people; interdependence through common stake in organization purpose leads to relationships of trust and respect.

(5,5) Management Adequate organization performance is possible through balancing necessity to get out work with maintaining morale of people at satisfactory level.

(1,1) Management Exertion of minimum effort to get required work done is appropriate to sustain organization membership.

(9,1) Management Efficiency in operations results from arranging conditions of work in such a way that human elements interfere to minimum degree.

Concern for production

Source: Robert R. Blake and Jane Srygley Mouton, *The New Managerial Grid*® (Houston: Gulf Publishing Company, 1978). Copyright © 1978, p. 11. Reproduced by permission.

Likert's continuum

Rensis Likert (associated with the previously mentioned Michigan studies) provides us with our final behavioral approach to leadership styles.[11] Likert's conception is of a continuum of styles ranging from autocracy to participation.

Exhibit 11–4
Likert's system approach

System I	*System II*	*System III*	*System IV*
Exploitative autocracy	Benevolent autocracy	Consultative leadership	Participative group leadership

These are illustrated in Exhibit 11–4. In System I, managers make all important decisions and pass on orders to subordinates. There is little, if any, concern for employee morale, and little trust or confidence in subordinates.

System II management still issues orders but subordinates are free to comment on them. Further, subordinates are permitted some freedom, albeit within narrowly defined limits. Managers tend to be somewhat critical of subordinates, and subordinates tend to avoid contact with supervisors whenever possible.

System III management is consultative in nature. Orders are issued only after subordinates have been consulted. Some authority is delegated to subordinates to carry out certain tasks. Positive rewards (versus punishment) are used to motivate workers. Subordinates tend to be trusted and feel free to discuss problems with their supervisor.

Exhibit 11–5
The linking pin

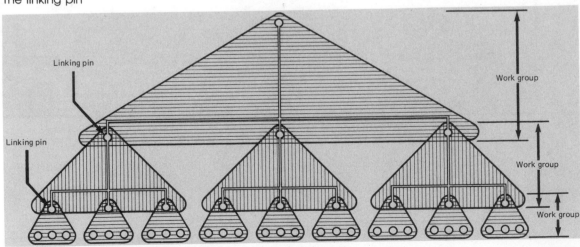

Note: The arrows indicate the linking pin function.

Source: Rensis Likert, *New Patterns of Management* (New York: McGraw-Hill Book Company, 1961), p. 113.

The final (and Likert's most favored) style is System IV or participative management. Where possible decisions are made and implemented by the work group rather than by the manager alone. Where managers must formally make a decision, it is done after incorporating ideas, suggestions, and opinions of group members. Workers are thought to be self-directed and motivated by higher level (Maslow and Alderfer) needs.

By emphasizing System IV throughout the organization, the manager is thought to provide a linking between groups in the organization. Exhibit 11–5 illustrates this concept. In System IV managers rely on much self-direction by subordinates and then "lead" or "manage" in a very low-key manner.

Synopsis of the behavioral approaches

All of the behavioral approaches utilize similar concepts though they are all couched in different labels. The notion of leaders having to influence both social and work output factors is thus accepted by all of the theories.

Exhibit 11–6 serves to illustrate the commonality of these theories.

Arguments against a "one best" leadership style

The Blake and Mouton Grid® seems to postulate that a participative, supportive, goal-oriented leader will be universally effective.

Yet, we pointed out that the Ohio State Studies found several instances where situational variables influenced whether high or low consideration and/ or initiating structure were associated with effective leadership.

In general, studies made by the Ohio State group using consideration and initiating structure leadership dimensions found that high consideration was related to low turnover and absenteeism, and high degrees of worker satisfaction. Supervisors who rated high in initiating structure and low in consideration tended to have higher rates of grievances and turnover. It was further found that *situational* factors sometimes tended to influence the perceived effectiveness of supervisors. For example, in situations where the boss was "expected" to make quick, important decisions (e.g., a hospital emergency room, military unit in combat), high initiating structure ratings were related to effectiveness. In situations not so time- or production-constrained, supervisors were rated more effective if they had higher consideration scores. In situations where the work flow or technology itself exerted a strong degree of structure (i.e., little discretion was allowed on how to do the job by virtue of the technology itself) supervisors who scored high in consideration tended to be seen as more effective.[12]

Exhibit 11–6
The behavioral approaches

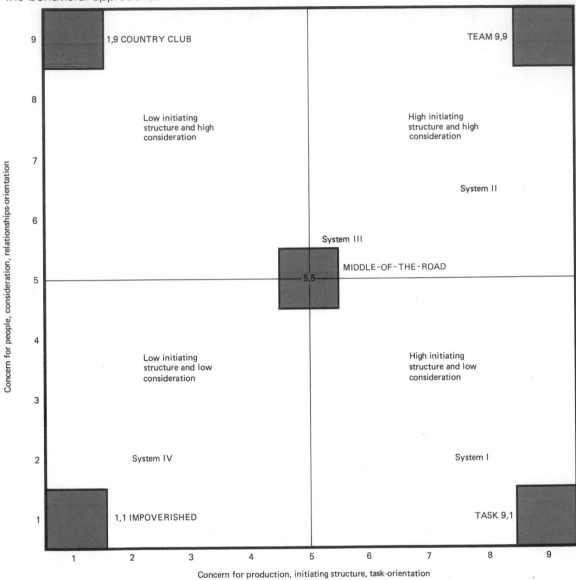

Note: Placement of Systems I–IV is based on the opinion of the authors.

For example, in a large food products organization, consideration was significantly related to sales supervisors' effectiveness evaluations by top managers.[13]
This relationship endured over the five-year period of the study. In a pharmaceutical company, warehouse supervisors showed significant relationships between their consideration scores and employees' reports of favorable attitudes

toward their supervisor, feelings of group achievement, and perceived recognition for good performance. Initiating structure was also related to favorable attitudes toward the supervisor and also to certain errors in employees' work (e.g., incorrectly marked prices).[14]

A recent inquiry by Kerr and Schriesheim has looked at some of the moderating variables in organizations that seem to influence whether consideration or initiating structure will affect supervisory effectiveness and subordinate behavior.[15] Their analysis seems to point to a circular relationship in many instances. Thus, a poorly performing employee may "cause" the supervisor to engage in more initiating structure-related behavior rather than the other way around (that is, leader style causing poor performance). We may well be faced with a classic "which comes first, chicken or egg" situation. This "reciprocality" between leader and subordinate behavior indeed hinders researchers' attempts to postulate conditions under which certain styles are most appropriate.

Larson, Hunt, and Osborn conducted a study which used as the criteria of effectiveness both subordinate satisfaction and the leader's performance ratings (done by the leader's boss).[16] Using the consideration and initiating structure measuring devices, they found that the high-high combination was not superior. In fact, no particular combinations could claim superiority.

Miles and Petty performed a study in several large and small "bureaucratic" (governmental) organizations to see how organizational size influenced the effectiveness of consideration and initiating structure.[17] Their effectiveness measures included the same subordinate satisfaction variable and leader's performance appraisal variable as was used by Larson, Hunt, and Osborn. In addition, Miles and Petty measured the tension/anxiety level and propensity to resign of subordinates. They found that high levels of initiating structure are "effective" in smaller (by size) organizations and that the effectiveness of consideration was unrelated to size. Thus initiating structure is most usable in small organizations and consideration can be effective in both large and small organizations. Miles and Petty did not find that being high on both consideration and initiating structure was related to effectiveness.

Paul Nystrom has likewise found little support for the high-high or 9,9 position.[18] In fact, he found that the low initiating structure and high consideration combination was "best" for business managers. "Best" was indicated by the manager's (1) need satisfaction (à la the Maslow hierarchy), (2) salary levels, and (3) upward career progression.

In yet another study, Gary Johns has looked at consideration and initiating structure and subordinate satisfaction in the context of various job or task moderators (e.g., task variety, autonomy, feedback, identity and significance).[19] Johns found that the relationship between high leader initiation of structure and subordinate satisfaction was positively influenced by task variety, autonomy, feedback, identity, and significance. High levels of consideration were positively associated with satisfaction regardless of the task moderator variables' measures. Thus, workers seem to be receptive to high initiating structure-oriented leaders only when their jobs are challenging and interesting. Boring jobs and high initiating structure leaders don't mix well.

Given the evidence of these studies, we conclude that while the two dimensions (task and social) of leadership seem appropriate, it does not appear that any particular combination of these task and social behaviors is "best" for all cases. The "best" leadership style (i.e., the one that gains the most influential increment) seems to depend upon a variety of factors. It is to a discussion of leadership approaches based upon contingency factors that we now turn.

CONTINGENCY APPROACHES

The objective of the contingency approaches is to describe those situational factors which influence leadership style effectiveness and to then recommend the leadership style that will be most effective under a particular combination of factors.

Situational factors

Robert Tannenbaum and Warren Schmidt were among the first to look at certain aspects of the leader's behavior in light of factors that might influence the behavior's effectiveness.[20] They identified three sets of forces that a manager should consider in deciding how to manage or lead:

1. Forces in the manager.
2. Forces in the subordinates.
3. Forces in the situation.

The manager's personal beliefs and biases will exert a strong influence on leadership behavior. Such things as the manager's value system, confidence in subordinates, personal leadership inclinations, and feelings of security or insecurity will all be powerful forces acting on the manager.

Subordinates, too, have personalities and abilities that they bring to a work setting. Such things as their need for independence, readiness to assume responsibility, tolerance for ambiguous situations, identification with the organization and their job, knowledge, and the like will be powerful forces that the manager must consider. According to Tannenbaum and Schmidt a manager can allow greater worker participation and freedom when the above factors are present.

Exhibit 11–7
Continuum of leadership behavior

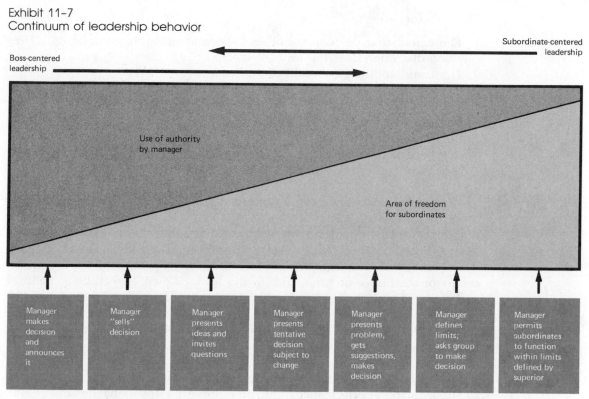

Source: Robert Tannenbaum and Warren Schmidt, "How to Choose a Leadership Pattern," in Michael T. Matteson and John M. Ivancevich, eds., *Management Classics* (Pacific Palisades, Cal.: Goodyear Publishing Co., Inc., 1977), p. 368.

Finally, there will be a set of situational-based forces that stem from the organization, the problem(s) at hand, and pressures of time. Some organizations have traditions and values that preclude/prescribe certain leader behaviors. The work group itself may be effective or ineffective producers. A particular problem situation may require specialized knowledge. And, time pressures in a given situation may preclude involving others in making a decision. Thus, depending on the particular combination of these forces the manager will be inclined toward different behaviors.

A continuum of leader behaviors developed by Tannenbaum and Schmidt is shown in Exhibit 11–7. What style a manager selects is not important so long as it is *appropriate* for the particular set of forces faced by the manager. Thus, adaptability and the ability to "read" the forces and select the appropriate strategy is what is desired.

Constraints and influences on leader behavior

Richard Steers presents a variety of factors that he finds act as constraints or limiting factors on a leader's choice of behaviors.[21]

These factors are:

1. The extent that decisions or other actions are preprogrammed (i.e., How much discretion does the leader have?).
2. The traits, abilities, and skills of the leader.
3. The leader's ability to vary his or her behavior (versus being rigid).
4. The leader's control over rewards for subordinates.
5. The openness of the organization itself to a particular style (e.g., Would the Marines like permissiveness?).
6. The particular situation (e.g., How much power does the leader have? How important is the decision? How quickly must it be made?).

Many other writers have also described sets of factors that they feel affect leadership behavior.[22] These authors tend to view leadership behavior as being influenced by: (1) organizational policy and climate, (2) one's own superiors' expectations and behavior, (3) peers' expectations and behavior, (4) subordinates' characteristics, expectations, and behavior, (5) the nature and requirements of the task(s) at hand, and (6) the leader's own expectations, abilities, and traits. These are illustrated in Exhibit 11–8. Clearly, Steers's "constraints" fall within the categories set forth in this exhibit. A key notion is the reciprocal relationships expressed by the arrows. Several recent studies point out the importance of this.

David Herold found that leaders' behaviors and attitudes varied in response to subordinates' performance.[23] Further, subordinates' behavior and perfor-

Exhibit 11–8
Sources of influence on leadership behavior

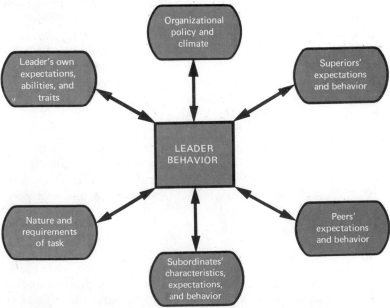

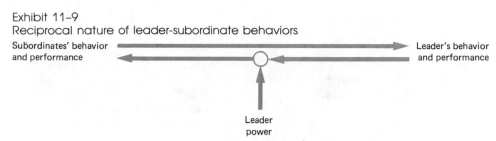

Exhibit 11–9
Reciprocal nature of leader-subordinate behaviors

Subordinates' behavior
and performance

Leader's behavior
and performance

Leader
power

Source: Based on David M. Herold, "Two-Way Influence Processes in Leader-Follower Dyads," *Academy of Management Journal*, vol. 20, no. 2 (June 1977), pp. 224–37.

mance varied as a function of the leader's behavior. This is, again, the reciprocality mentioned earlier. However, the effect of a leader's behavior on subordinates' performance was conditioned by the power held by the leader. Thus, depending upon subordinates' perception of the power held over them by their leader, they behave in various ways in response to the leader's own actions. The leader then views the subordinates' behavior and responds accordingly. Exhibit 11–9 illustrates this.

In another study, Durand and Nord found that subordinates' own personality characteristics influenced their perceptions of their leader's behavior.[24] Coupled with the study noted above, these results emphasize the reciprocal nature of situational factors in the leadership process.

Given the situational factors as important influences on leadership behavior, we now turn to a discussion of several leadership models that advise certain leadership styles in response to certain situational configurations.

The Fiedler contingency model

Fiedler proposes that certain elements in a leadership situation influence the effectiveness of various leadership styles.[25] The three elements described by Fiedler are: leader-member relations, task structure, and position power of the leader. Fiedler's general contention is that a leader's style is normally highly ingrained and not easy to change. Thus, an effective leader is one who is able to alter the elements of the situation to effect a proper fit between style and the situational or contingency elements. Further, we should, where possible, match and assign managers with a given style to situations that are favorable for that style.

Fiedler measures leadership via the Least Preferred Co-worker (LPC) scale shown in Exhibit 11–10. People who describe their least preferred co-worker in relatively favorable terms tend to be more permissive, human relations oriented, and emphasize the relationships (versus task) dimensions of leadership. On the other hand, people who describe their least preferred co-worker in harsh terms tend to be more autocratic and task-oriented.

Exhibit 11–10
The Least Preferred Co-worker (LPC) questionnaire

Think of the Person with Whom You Can Work Least Well.
He May Be Someone You Work with Now, or He May Be Some-
one You Knew in the Past. He Does Not Have to Be the Person
You Like Least Well, But Should Be the Person with Whom
You Had the Most Difficulty in Getting a Job Done. Describe
This Person as He Appears to You.

Pleasant	__ : __ : __ : __ : __ : __ : __ : __ 8 7 6 5 4 3 2 1	Unpleasant
Friendly	__ : __ : __ : __ : __ : __ : __ : __ 8 7 6 5 4 3 2 1	Unfriendly
Rejecting	__ : __ : __ : __ : __ : __ : __ : __ 1 2 3 4 5 6 7 8	Accepting
Helpful	__ : __ : __ : __ : __ : __ : __ : __ 8 7 6 5 4 3 2 1	Frustrating
Unenthusiastic	__ : __ : __ : __ : __ : __ : __ : __ 1 2 3 4 5 6 7 8	Enthusiastic
Tense	__ : __ : __ : __ : __ : __ : __ : __ 1 2 3 4 5 6 7 8	Relaxed
Distant	__ : __ : __ : __ : __ : __ : __ : __ 1 2 3 4 5 6 7 8	Close
Cold	__ : __ : __ : __ : __ : __ : __ : __ 1 2 3 4 5 6 7 8	Warm
Cooperative	__ : __ : __ : __ : __ : __ : __ : __ 8 7 6 5 4 3 2 1	Uncooperative
Supportive	__ : __ : __ : __ : __ : __ : __ : __ 8 7 6 5 4 3 2 1	Hostile
Boring	__ : __ : __ : __ : __ : __ : __ : __ 1 2 3 4 5 6 7 8	Interesting
Quarrelsome	__ : __ : __ : __ : __ : __ : __ : __ 1 2 3 4 5 6 7 8	Harmonious
Self-assured	__ : __ : __ : __ : __ : __ : __ : __ 8 7 6 5 4 3 2 1	Hesitant
Efficient	__ : __ : __ : __ : __ : __ : __ : __ 8 7 6 5 4 3 2 1	Inefficient
Gloomy	__ : __ : __ : __ : __ : __ : __ : __ 1 2 3 4 5 6 7 8	Cheerful
Open	__ : __ : __ : __ : __ : __ : __ : __ 8 7 6 5 4 3 2 1	Guarded

From *A Theory of Effective Leadership* by F. E. Fiedler. Copyright © 1967 McGraw-Hill Book
Company. Used with permission of the publisher.

The three situational elements are each measured in terms of a dichotomy:

1. Leader-member relations; good or poor? Are the leader and group members on friendly terms? Do they show respect for each other? If so, relations are good (i.e., "favorable").
2. Task structure; structured or unstructured? Is the job one that is routine and well-known? If so, it is structured (i.e., "favorable" for the manager).
3. Leader position power; strong or weak? Does the leader have power and authority over subordinates? Can the leader control rewards and assign tasks at will? If so, it is strong (i.e., "favorable").

Three elements with two possible "scores" for each result in eight possible combinations as is shown in Exhibit 11–11. To determine whether a task- or relationships-oriented leader was "best" for given combinations Fiedler measured actual productivity. (Note that subordinate satisfaction and measures other than actual performance were used in several earlier cited studies.) Thus, a baseball team would be measured in terms of games won, a bomber crew by hits on target, a retail outlet by net return on investment, and so on. The data shown in Exhibit 11–11 indicates that in situations I, II, III, and VIII a task-oriented style is best, and in situations IV, V, VI, and VII a relationships-oriented style is preferable.

Note that Fiedler says that the task-oriented style is best under two types of conditions: when the combination of situational elements is (1) very favorable or (2) very unfavorable for the leader. In contrast, situations of intermediate favorableness are best filled by relationships-oriented leaders.

Why might these results occur? First, remember that Fiedler's main criterion was productivity. Under very favorable conditions (I, II, III) the task-oriented leader will probably feel reasonably at ease and be able to use a task orientation to overcome unstructured task elements or weak power situations. In very unfavorable situations (VIII) only under highly directed, task-oriented leadership will anything get done.

In the intermediate to moderately unfavorable situations (IV, V, VI, VIII) relationships-oriented leaders are thought to use their abilities to interact well with subordinates to overcome those difficulties that present themselves. Further, research has indicated that relationships-(high LPC) oriented leaders are able to demonstrate greater flexibility in their behavior and thus may be better able to meet the conflicting demands of the intermediate situations.[26]

Numerous studies have been made on the Fiedler model. Generally, field studies in real organizations have tended to support the model, while laboratory experiments have been less supportive.[27] A recent study in U.S. military organizations by Csoka and Bons has given support to the prescribed matches between leader style and situation. However, it failed to demonstrate that leaders could manipulate situational variables to better conform to their style.[28]

Exhibit 11–11
Correlations between leaders' LPC scores and group effectiveness plotted for each situation

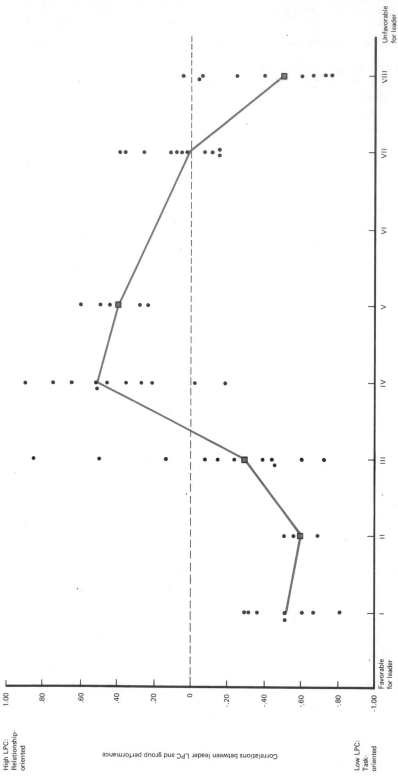

Source: F. E. Fiedler, "Validation and Extension of the Contingency Model of Leadership Effectiveness: A Review of Empirical Findings," *Psychological Bulletin*, vol. 76 (1971) p. 131. Copyright 1971 by the American Psychological Association. Reproduced by permission.

While we recognize the need for still more research we feel that the Fiedler model is a highly plausible one and has given us a useful framework by which to analyze leader behavior.

Path-goal leadership theory

The path-goal theory is highly related to the expectancy theory of motivation discussed in Chapter 10.[29] Expectancy theory provides us with an explanation of the thought processes of subordinates which managers must be able to influence. Managers must "lead" by influencing the availability of rewards (i.e., the "goals") and by clarifying the "paths" (i.e., things the subordinate must do) to be taken by subordinates to attain these "goals."

It is argued that a manager's style is an important determinant of the nature and scope of rewards which can or will be made available to subordinates. A relationships-oriented leader will use praise, emotional support, encouragement, and similar socioemotional "strokes" in addition to the standard rewards of pay, promotions, and so on. Further, such leaders can be expected to be cognizant of individuals' differences and will likely tailor "reward packages" for individual workers.

A task-oriented leader is expected to emphasize a narrower set of rewards— a set less tailored to individual workers. The task-oriented leader will stress pay (perhaps incentive plans) and job security, and may threaten to withhold pay (fire or lay off the worker) as a response to poor performance.

As we noted in Chapter 10, different workers want different things ("goals") from their jobs. Path-goal theory is suggesting that a leader's style, to be effective, must be aligned with the rewards being sought by workers.

Robert House postulates that (1) the *personality characteristics of subordinates* and (2) *environmental pressures and demands* are the two contingency factors that influence leadership style in path-goal theory.[30] Workers who feel that blind luck or predestined fate determine life's events tend to prefer task-oriented leadership. Those who feel they have more control over their lives desire relationships-oriented leaders. Further, skilled workers possessing a good self-image tend to desire a relationships-oriented leader. Less skilled, more self-effacing workers desire more task-oriented leadership.

The environment is a contingency parameter primarily because of what it *does* or *does not* provide; effective leader behavior will provide that which the environment doesn't. For example, if the workers' tasks are very structured and repetitive (an environmentally given factor) a leader who behaves in a rigid task-oriented manner will probably be resented since the *task* itself already determines what is to be done. Why add "insult to injury"? However, in an unstructured, complex situation the worker may well desire some guidance and task direction. Additionally, where the worker already receives a great deal of intrinsic satisfaction from the job, praise and recognition by the leader probably is of little, if any, benefit.

Another environmental element is the workers' own *work group*. A highly cohesive, supportive group probably needs little relationships-oriented behavior from the leader. Less cohesive and supportive interpersonal situations will require more relationships-oriented behavior from the leader.

Finally, the *organizational system* exerts a strong environmental influence. To the extent that formal rules, policies, and procedures already spell out the cause-effect relationships between rewards and punishments, a more informal, relationships-oriented style is likely to be more effective because the "structure" is already present. Under less well-defined conditions workers will probably prefer a leader who is relationships-oriented and always lets them know where they stand.

The effective manager must be aware of these many contingency factors and must constantly assess their impact on the relationship between leadership style, work productivity, and subordinate satisfaction.[31] Of special note are those job design variables over which a manager has some discretion. We noted earlier that Gary Johns has shown that the relationship between a task-oriented leadership style and worker satisfaction was positively influenced by task variety, task identity, perceived task significancy, autonomy, and feedback.[32] Thus, the "more" of these task variables present in a job, the more satisfied workers will be with a task-oriented manager.

In summary, it appears that there is some general set of both intrinsic and extrinsic "things" workers desire from jobs. The effective leaders will provide via their "style" some of these "things" that are not forthcoming from the job itself. Thus, managers should lead by providing the paths by which subordinates attain goals.

A life cycle theory of leadership

Throughout this chapter we have discussed the two general dimensions of leadership behavior—task and relationships. We have indicated that numerous situational or contingency factors seem to influence the effectiveness of different leadership styles; that is, the effectiveness of different "combinations" of task and relationships orientations. The leadership studies reviewed here point to a reciprocal relationship between leadership style and a number of other factors. Our discussions of the various contingency theories would indicate that different researchers have, in various studies, found that these factors seem relevant, although no one theory seems to include all of the factors.

Exhibit 11–12
A life cycle theory of leadership

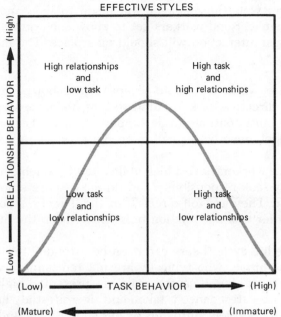

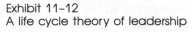

Source: Paul Hersey and Kenneth H. Blanchard, *Management of Organizational Behavior: Utilizing Human Resources*, 2d ed. © 1972 (Englewood Cliffs, N.J.: Prentice-Hall, Inc., 1972), p. 135. Reprinted by permission.

Hersey and Blanchard have proposed a life cycle theory of leadership (not to be confused with this book's life cycle) which relates task and relationships behavior, and the "maturity" of followers in terms of an effectiveness criterion.[33] The level of maturity of followers is defined in terms of their achievement motivation, Theory Y characteristics, and educational/experience background relevant to the task(s). While age *can* be a factor, it is not directly related to this life cycle-oriented definition. We are interested here in psychological, not chronological factors.

Exhibit 11–12 illustrates the life cycle leadership theory. The theory indicates that high task–low relationships leader behavior is effective with immature workers. As workers mature, the leader should move to a high task–high relationships position, then to a low task–high relationships position, and finally, with mature workers, to a low task–low relationship position.

The logic behind this theory is straightforward. "New" workers may well lack experience and understanding concerning their task(s). As they are learning their jobs, they are not likely to want to accept much responsibility. In general, management must instruct workers, see that rules and procedures are followed, and make sure work gets done.

As workers learn their jobs management still needs a reasonably high task orientation until workers are willing/able to accept responsibility. However, as workers perform well, the manager will begin to show more confidence in them. As the manager and workers get to know each other, it is expected that a more collegial interaction will/should take place. The manager should not remain aloof.

In the next phase, workers begin to accept responsibility. They know their jobs and a highly directive, task-oriented style is not necessary nor desired. Still, the manager must continue to be supportive of workers and encourage them to learn the job even better and to accept even more responsibility.

In the final phase workers have a high ability and high achievement motivation. They actively seek responsibility and do not require emotional support from the manager. They are self-directed in the Theory Y context. Hence, workers need neither task nor relationships "help" from the manager.

The logic of the life cycle theory can even be extended to student-teacher relationships.[34] Freshmen, who typically are not too familiar with a college setting and haven't yet chosen career goals, are presented highly structured, lower division courses, attendance is taken and rigorous study habits are often enforced. As the student gets "into" his or her chosen field and has the basic courses completed, the teacher often begins to interact more frequently with students to counsel them. At some point courses become less rigorous with some selection of topics for papers and reading lists left to the student. This is certainly true at the senior or masters degree level. By the time a student reaches the doctoral level, the teacher becomes available only on an "as needed" basis and responsibility for fulfilling requirements is largely left to the student.

While this life cycle theory is based upon a life cycle of workers' maturity, it relates to the life cycle of an organization as well. A new organization with new employees, new jobs, and so on will require a rigorous, task-oriented style as the organization begins to function and people begin to learn their jobs and roles. Eventually, as discussed above, the general culture of the organization work force may move to the maturity side of the scale. Thus, management must be adaptive and alert to changes on the maturity continuum. Hersey and Blanchard propose that the maturity continuum be divided into three levels as shown in Exhibit 11–13. Below average (maturity) workers will be most effectively led with a high task–low relationships style. Workers of average maturity respond best to a high task–high relationships or a low task–high relationships style. Finally, above average workers are best led with a low task–low relationships style.

Comparison with the contingency theories.   Exhibit 11–14 presents a synopsis of the variables inherent in the contingency theories discussed in this section.

Exhibit 11-13
Maturity levels

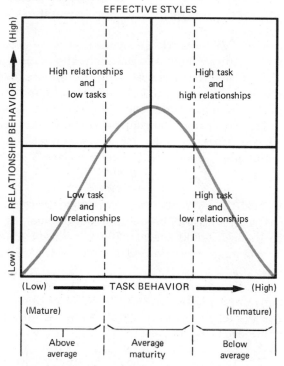

Source: Paul Hersey and Kenneth H. Blanchard, *Management of Organizational Behavior: Utilizing Human Resources*, 2d ed. © 1972 (Englewood Cliffs, N.J.: Prentice Hall, Inc., 1972), p. 142. Reprinted by permission.

Exhibit 11-14
Synopsis of contingency theories

Theory	Contingency variables
Tannenbaum and Schmidt	1. Forces in the leader
	2. Forces in followers
	3. Forces in the situation
Fiedler	1. Leader power
	2. Leader-member relations
	3. Task structure
Path-goal theory	1. Personality characteristics of subordinates
	2. Environmental pressures and demands
Life cycle theory	1. Follower's maturity level

While recognizing the diversity of variables' definitions and measures used by these various approaches, we are nonetheless led to (speculatively) point out a common theme which runs through at least several of the theories.

Taking the Hersey and Blanchard life cycle theory as a focal point, we see a high potential for maturity factors to influence the contingency variables associated with several of the other theories. For example, as followers mature would not "forces in followers" change? They would accept more responsibility, be more committed to their jobs, and so on. "Forces in the leader" may also change as the leader feels less pressure to supervise closely or rigorously define tasks. Situational forces may also be influenced by followers' maturity as problems become better defined, operating procedures are known and agreed upon, and so on.

Similarly, in path-goal theory maturity seems directly related to subordinates' personality characteristics and, based upon our discussions of the dynamics of the life cycle theory, would seem to have a direct effect on various environmental factors (e.g., group norms and pressures, agreement on work practices, and so on).

The eight situations proposed by Fiedler do not lend themselves to direct comparisons with the worker maturity concept. Thus, we refrain from matching Fiedler and the life cycle framework.

SUMMARY

Leadership is indeed a complex issue. It seems that a leadership style is something that managers must adapt to changing conditions. Or, in Fiedler's conception, where possible we can change the conditions to better fit the leader's given style.

Leaders are more than mere power holders. Leaders somehow are able to energize the "wants" or "needs" of their followers. In so doing, leaders must be aware of changes in their followers and react accordingly. "True" leaders perhaps do even more; arouse needs and then lead followers in their attainment. Leadership ultimately becomes a transactional process between a leader's behavior, subordinates' behavior, and organizational and environmental forces.

We have little confidence in using the trait method of describing leaders. The lack of a common set of traits among the various studies points out the dubious nature of this approach.

The behavioral approaches are valuable in that they give us the task-social dimensions of leader behavior. We agree that leadership behavior can be viewed in terms of these two dimensions, and we are aware of the difficulties in prescribing a particular "set" of task-social behaviors. The situational factors found in numerous studies indicate that while these behaviors exist, their relative magnitudes must vary under differing conditions.

This leads us to the contingency approaches which attempt to define those situational factors and propose relevant leadership behaviors. Our view is that the life cycle theory provides an important unifying basis for several of the contingency theories.

GUIDES TO ACTION

1. Recognize that the "best" style of leadership depends on some contingency factors and that a reciprocality exists with subordinate performance. Get the "lay of the land" before you implement any given style.

2. Attempt to ascertain your subordinates' zones of indifference. Beware of attempting to influence them beyond the limits of their zones.

3. There are very few perfect leaders. Remember this if you think you aren't leadership material or before you criticize someone else's leadership abilities.

4. In any group, a leader will eventually emerge. Be sensitive to the fact that people will be competing for this position in committees, bowling teams, and so on. Aggressive behaviors, controlling communications, and power plays are obvious indicators.

NOTES

[1] Daniel Katz and Robert L. Kahn, *The Social Psychology of Organizations*, 2d ed. (New York: John Wiley & Sons, Inc., 1978), p. 528.

[2] John R. P. French and Bertram H. Raven, "The Bases of Social Power," in Darwin Cartwright and Alvin Zander, *Group Dynamics: Research and Theory*, 3d ed. (New York: Harper & Row, Publishers, 1968), pp. 259–69.

[3] Ralph M. Stogdill, "Personnel Factors Associated with Leadership: A Survey of the Literature," *The Journal of Psychology*, vol. 25 (1948), pp. 35–71; and Ralph Stogdill, *Handbook of Leadership* (New York: The Free Press, 1974).

[4] Ben Solomon, *Leadership of Youth* (New York: Youth Services, 1950), p. 15.

[5] *Arizona Daily Star*, October 29, 1975.

[6] See Katz and Kahn, *Social Psychology of Organizations*, pp. 559–65.

[7] There are numerous books and articles concerning the Ohio State Studies. A good overview reference is: R. M. Stogdill, and A. E. Coons, eds. *Leader Behavior: Its Description and Measurement* (Columbus, Ohio: Bureau of Business Research, Ohio State University, 1957).

[8] Rensis Likert, *New Patterns of Management* (New York: McGraw-Hill Book Company, 1961).

[9] Robert R. Blake and Jane S. Mouton, *The New Managerial Grid®* (Houston: Gulf Publishing Company, 1978).

[10] Robert R. Blake and Jane S. Mouton, *Building a Dynamic Corporation through Grid Organization Development* (Reading, Mass.: Addison-Wesley Publishing Company, 1969).

[11] Rensis Likert, *The Human Organization* (New York: McGraw-Hill Book Company, 1967).

[12] For a review of studies using the consideration and initiating structure variables, see Victor H. Vroom, "Leadership" in Marvin D. Dunnette, ed., *Handbook of Industrial and Organizational Psychology* (Chicago: Rand McNally & Co., 1976), pp. 1527–51.

[13] B. M. Bass, "Leadership Opinions as Forecasts of Supervisory Success: A Replication," *Personnel Psychology*, vol. 11 (1958), pp. 515–18.

[14] T. C. Parker, "Relationships among Measures of Supervisory Behavior, Group Behavior, and Situational Characteristics," *Personnel Psychology*, vol. 16 (1963); pp. 319–34.

[15] S. Kerr, and C. Schriesheim, "Consideration, Initiating Structure, and Organizational Criteria—An Update of Korman's 1966 Review," *Personnel Psychology*, vol. 27 (1975), pp. 555–68.

[16] L. L. Larson, J. G. Hunt, and R. H. Osborn, "The Great Hi-Hi Leader Behavior Myth: A Lesson from Occam's Razor," *Academy of Management Journal*, vol. 19, no. 14 (December 1976), pp. 628–41.

[17] Robert H. Miles, and M. M. Petty, "Leader Effectiveness in Small Bureaucracies," *Academy of Management Journal,* vol. 20, no. 2 (June 1977), pp. 238–50.

[18] Paul C. Nystrom, "Managers and the Hi-Hi Leader Myth," *Academy of Management Journal,* vol. 21, no. 2 (June 1978), pp. 325–31.

[19] Gary Johns, "Task Moderators of the Relationship between Leadership Style and Subordinate Responses," *Academy of Management Journal,* vol. 21, no. 2 (June 1978), pp. 319–25.

[20] Robert Tannenbaum and Warren H. Schmidt, "How to Choose a Leadership Pattern," in Michael T. Matteson and John M. Ivancevich, eds., *Management Classics* (Pacific Palisades Cal.: Goodyear Publishing Company, Inc., 1977), pp. 265–80 (originally published in 1958 *Harvard Business Review*).

[21] Richard M. Steers, *Organizational Effectiveness: A Behavioral View* (Pacific Palisades, Cal.: Goodyear Publishing Company, Inc., 1977), p. 156.

[22] See, for example, Paul Hersey and Kenneth M. Blanchard, *Management of Organizational Behavior,* 2d ed. (Englewood Cliffs, N.J.: Prentice-Hall, Inc., 1972), p. 110; H. Joseph Reitz, *Behavior in Organizations* (Homewood, Ill.: Richard D. Irwin, Inc., 1977), pp. 516–24; and James Stoner, *Management* (Englewood Cliffs, N.J.: Prentice-Hall, Inc., 1978), p. 449.

[23] David M. Herold, "Two-Way Influence Processes in Leader-Follower Dyads," *Academy of Management Journal,* vol. 20, no. 2 (June 1977), pp. 224–37.

[24] Douglas E. Durand and Walter R. Nord, "Perceived Leader Behavior as a Function of Personality Characteristics of Supervisors and Subordinates," *Academy of Management Journal,* vol. 10, no. 3 (September 1976), pp. 427–38.

[25] See Fred E. Fiedler, "Engineer the Job to Fit the Manager," *Harvard Business Review,* Vol. 43, No. 5 (September–October 1965), pp. 115–22; Fred E. Fiedler, *A Theory of Leadership Effectiveness* (New York: McGraw-Hill Book Company, 1967); Fred E. Fiedler and M. M. Chemers, *Leadership and Effective Management* (Glenview, Ill.: Scott, Foresman and Company, 1974).

[26] Robert W. Rice and Martin M. Chemers, "Personality and Situational Determinants of Leader Behavior," *Journal of Applied Psychology,* vol. 60, no. 1 (February 1976), p. 27.

[27] F. E. Fiedler, "Validation and Extension of the Contingency Model on Leadership Effectiveness: A Review of Empirical Findings," *Psychological Bulletin,* vol. 76 (August 1971), pp. 128–48.

[28] Louis S. Csoka, and Paul M. Bons, "Manipulating the Situation to Fit the Leader's Style: Two Validation Studies of LEADER MATCH," *Journal of Applied Psychology,* vol. 63, no. 3 (June 1978), pp. 295–300.

[29] For a fuller description of path-goal theory, see Martin G. Evans, "Leadership and Motivation: A Core Concept," *Academy of Management Journal,* vol. 13, no. 1 (March 1970), pp. 91–102; and Robert J. House, "A Path-Goal Theory of Leader Effectiveness," *Administrative Science Quarterly,* vol. 16, no. 3 (September 1971), pp. 321–38.

[30] House, "Path-Goal Theory of Leader Effectiveness,"; also see Robert J. House and G. Dessler, "The Path-Goal Theory of Leadership: Some Post Hoc and Priori Tests," in J. Hunt and L. Larson (eds.), *Contingency Approach to Leadership,* (Carbondale, Ill.: Southern Illinois University Press, 1974), pp. 29–55.

[31] See H. Kirk Downey, John E. Sheridan, and John W. Slocum, Jr., "The Path-Goal Theory of Leadership: A Longitudinal Analysis," *Organizational Behavior and Human Performance,* vol. 16 (1976), pp. 156–76.

[32] Johns, "Task Moderators of the Relationship between Leadership Style and Subordinate Responses."

[33] Paul Hersey and Kenneth H. Blanchard, *Management of Organizational Behavior: Utilizing Human Resources,* 2d ed. (Englewood Cliffs, N.J.: Prentice-Hall, Inc., 1972).

[34] Ibid., p. 140.

DISCUSSION QUESTIONS

1. What are the three main meanings used in discussing leadership?

2. Differentiate between influence, power, authority, and leadership.

3. What is the zone of indifference? Discuss the zone typically found to exist between students and their teacher.

4. Define each of the five bases of power.

5. Why is the "influential increment" the essence of leadership?

6. Compare the following theories:
   a. Ohio State Studies.
   b. Blake and Mouton.
   c. Likert.

7. What are several of the arguments against a "one best" leadership style?

8. Discuss the "reciprocality" problem in studying leadership.

9. How does measuring the least preferred co-worker relate to leadership?

10. Discuss Fiedler's suggestions that changes in situational variables are more appropriate than changing leader behavior.

11. Can you show how the following studies' findings can be "explained" by the Life Cycle Theory?
    a. Miles and Petty.
    b. Nystrom.

CASE: "GENTLEMEN, THE COMMANDER"*

Each November, captains, majors, and a few foreign officers gather at Fort Mudge for a career course, a nine-month professional school that is a capstone of a man's early military career. The course is widely known as a "gentlemen's course," and no one—but no one—makes the next promotion without having been there. So the attendees have a sense of having made it. The satisfaction is mixed with only a little anxiety about doing well. The program is demanding, but having been assigned is by far the hardest part of it. They are all in the Fort Mudge Club now.

Attendance is also happily anticipated by the chosen officers, who look forward to nine months in an academic community removed from the demands and frustrations of their normal duties. For most of a year, the officers will

* From: Robert T. Golembiewski and Michael White, *Cases in Public Management*, 2d ed. (Chicago: Rand McNally College Publishing Company, 1976), pp. 83–86. Copyright © 1976, 1973 by Rand McNally College Publishing Company.

be released from the myriad burdens of the company-grade officer—responsibility for vast amounts of property as well as the day-to-day performance and problems of several hundred subordinates. For a while, at least, they will be removed from their normal uncomfortable position halfway between the irresistible force of the senior officers and the immovable object of the junior enlisted men. For a while, at least, the officers can leave behind the practical agonies of racial conflict and drug addiction; and they can indulge in the infinitely more pleasant exercise of talking about problems without having to do anything about them.

The course also will be, in many ways, like a college reunion. For those attending are career officers, men who have served in their specialty for five, six, or seven years. By now, the participants will know most of their classmates personally from shared experiences in far-off posts, or compounds, or jungles.

So it was that Class XXIV came together. They were officers gathered from many installations in many lands, weary of wars and domestic problems, welcoming the months of freedom. They settled into the processing at Fort Mudge amid handshakes and smiles and the casual banter of old friends well-met. The fragments of conversation buoyantly reflected how this was to be a time to be savored and enjoyed and remembered.

"They tell me you get through at 1400 every day."

"I'm going to see a real live pro football game, if I don't do anything else."

"They give you Sundays off."

"I thought you were still lost in Cambodia."

"They give you Saturday, too."

"All right!"

On the first Monday of the school year, the officers were a little weary from a weekend of drinks and war stories, but they were generally at peace with God and Man. They gathered leisurely for the school commander's welcoming address.

The commander was new, but the address—like all its kind—would surely follow a prescribed pattern. Everyone would rise, the commander would enter, saying genially: "Be seated, gentlemen, be seated." And, smiling, he would spend 15 minutes explaining how delighted he and the faculty were to have this splendid group of officers at the school. The commander would dwell on how much they would learn from each other—the army's finest faculty and this military specialty's finest officers. In short, all the right things would be said. All would leave the assembly with the unspoken but genuine feeling that "God's in his Heaven, and all's well with the world."

That was as it should be. They were all—students, faculty, and commander—brothers in their difficult fraternity, men whose maturity, competence, and hard work had raised them, from whatever level, to their present status of competent public servants. And they had all been brought together for a while to teach and to learn for the common good.

In such pleasant anticipation of meeting their new commander, the officers waited. The customary solemn voice finally intoned: "Gentlemen, the Commander." The chatter ended, the officers rose, and the Commander entered. The Commander walked to the podium and surveyed the officers before him. In a voice stripped of emotion, he said:

You may be seated. Let us understand each other from the start. While you are part of my command you will—note that I do not say "I hope"; I say "you will"—participate fully in the activities of this school. Whatever I do, I do 100 percent and so do those under my command.

Those of you who have not seen fit to join our professional association will do so this week, and the sooner the better.

Your wives will, without exception, participate in the ladies' social functions. And, I might add, any officer whose wife does not participate is only half an officer. This fact will be duly noted on his Academic Report, with foreseeable career consequences.

The [local charitable fund] campaign is now in progress and the school will participate 100 percent. I do not concern myself with the amount of money collected, but I will have 100 percent participation. The senior member of your class, Major Eager, whom I now designate as class leader, would do well to ensure such participation. Any failure to exercise appropriate leadership will be made a matter of record.

Welcome to the Fort Mudge school. Welcome to a 100 percent organization.

The Commander stepped from behind the podium, the officers rose, and, looking neither right nor left, the Commander walked down the aisle and out the rear door.

The silence in the room was absolute. Then the officer standing beside the newly appointed leader said:

Here's two dollars. A penny apiece for every son of a bitch in the class. I've always wanted to be part of a 100 percent organization.

Directions

You are the class leader, Major Eager, to whom is directed the sarcastic comment following the Commander's talk. What do you do? What do you say?

You are not certain how many of your colleagues heard the remark. But the voice sounded like thunder to you.

The two dollars are being waved gently in front of you.

SELECTION OF THE PRODUCT OR SERVICE	DESIGN OF THE SYSTEM	STAFFING THE ORGANIZATION	STARTUP OF THE ORGANIZATION	OPERATING THE ORGANIZATION IN THE STEADY STATE	IMPROVING THE ORGANIZATION	REVISION OF THE ORGANIZATION	TERMINATION OF THE ORGANIZATION

Level of Organizational Outputs

0

Decision-making processes; social value; goals; forecasts; policies; plans	Authority and responsibility; power; organizational structure; communications systems; job design	Work force planning; personnel management functions	Startup planning and scheduling; monitoring; alternative startup approaches	Motivation; leadership; production and operations management; control	Individual improvement programs and techniques; group conflict management; MBO	Evaluation of organizational policies; strategic choices; organizational change; organizational development	Partial terminations; cutback management; complete terminations; mergers; born-again strategies

t_0 Time →

Chapter 12
Operating the organization: Production and operations management

The mechanics of running a business are really not very complicated, when you get down to essentials. You have to make some stuff and sell it to somebody for more than it cost you. That's about all there is to it, except for a few million details.

John L. McCaffrey,
"What Corporation
Presidents Think about at Night"

The management subfield of production and operations management (POM) provides a variety of concepts and techniques for running any organization. Essentially, POM deals with the management of materials, equipment, and work force utilized in producing the products of the organization. In manufacturing, in a medium-sized plant, management responsibilities for this function typically fall to the production manager. For a manufacturing organization with several plants or a large, high-volume, single plant, responsibility generally lies with the vice president of manufacturing. Often included within the domain of production and operations management is production control and quality control, and closely allied with it are such engineering specialties as industrial engineering, process engineering, and maintenance. In our survey of POM in this chapter, we will first review the required activities of POM and discuss how the field pertains to service systems (in addition to manufacturing). Then we will look at the basic elements of production planning and quality control. Finally, we will discuss two quantitative techniques (linear programming and Monte Carlo simulation), and flowcharts, all of which are widely used in POM as well as other functional areas of the organization.

Required activities of POM

While this chapter focuses upon continual POM activities after the organization has reached its steady state operating level, POM is involved in *periodic* activities as well. These activities by definition are carried out less frequently and fall under three headings: selecting, designing, and updating. These are summarized in Exhibit 12–1.

Service systems

POM exists in service organizations as well as manufacturing. However, service organizations tend to use other labels for managers (and departments) which carry out their production function. Operations managers in banks, chief administrators in hospitals, and unit managers in restaurants, hotels, gov-

Exhibit 12–1
Organization of operations management activities

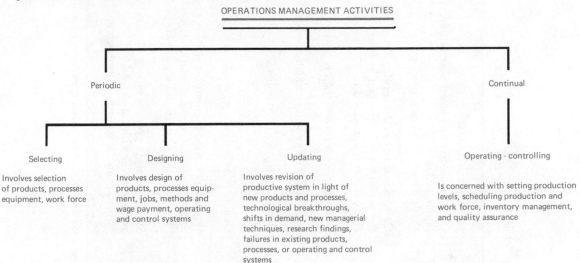

OPERATIONS MANAGEMENT ACTIVITIES

Periodic

Selecting

Involves selection
of products, processes
equipment, work force

Designing

Involves design of
products, processes equipment, jobs, methods and
wage payment, operating
and control systems

Updating

Involves revision of
productive system in light of
new products and processes,
technological breakthroughs,
shifts in demand, new managerial
techniques, research findings,
failures in existing products,
processes, or operating and control
systems

Continual

Operating - controlling

Is concerned with setting production
levels, scheduling production and
work force, inventory management,
and quality assurance

ernment offices, and so on are in fact charged with overseeing production in their respective concerns. It is important to note, however, that there are some rather distinct differences between how POM concepts are applied, not only between manufacturing and service industries, but within service industries themselves. In a recent article, Richard Chase suggests that production management concepts of efficiency are well-suited to service systems where customers are not physically in the service system during production of the service (e.g., a home office of a bank); and conversely, efficiency concepts are less easily applied where the customer is in the service system during production (e.g., a restaurant).[1] This is true generally because the customer can, by his or her very presence, influence the production process. To put it another way, each time you "have it your way" in a system designed for "our way," the operations manager groans. Consider the case of Gino, Inc.'s ill-fated hamburger which appeared on the market in 1976:

The ¼-lb. hamburger copied the approach used successfully by Wendy's and Burger King of offering customers a choice of dressing. But the Heroburger's truly unique feature was its unusual shape—a rectangle. So convinced was Gino's management that the new burger would be a hit that it pulled all its other hamburgers off the market. But the made-to-order feature turned into such a nightmare that the company had to reinstate its traditional products, and the four executives who had concocted the new burger departed. "We shot ourselves out of the water with that one," moans Louis C. Fischer, Gino's chairman.[2]

Exhibit 12–2 contrasts the effects of high and low customer contacts in some important production management decision areas.

Exhibit 12–2
Major design considerations in high- and low-contact systems

Decision	High-contact system	Low-contact system
Facility location	Operations must be near the customer.	Operations may be placed near supply, transportation, or labor.
Facility layout	Facility should accommodate the customer's physical and psychological needs and expectations.	Facility should enhance production.
Product design	Environment as well as the physical product define the nature of the service.	Customer is not in the service environment so the product can be defined by fewer attributes.
Process design	Stages of production process have a direct immediate effect on the customer.	Customer is not involved in the majority of processing steps.
Scheduling	Customer is in the production schedule and must be accommodated.	Customer is concerned mainly with completion dates.
Production planning	Orders cannot be stored, so smoothing production flow will result in loss of business.	Both backlogging and production smoothing are possible.
Worker skills	Direct work force comprises a major part of the service product and so must be able to interact well with the public.	Direct work force need only have technical skills.
Quality control	Quality standards are often in the eye of the beholder and hence variable.	Quality standards are generally measurable and hence fixed.
Time standards	Service time depends on customer needs, and therefore time standards are inherently loose.	Work is performed on customer surrogates (e.g., forms), and time standards can be tight.
Wage payment	Variable output requires time-based wage systems.	"Fixable" output permits output-based wage systems.
Capacity planning	To avoid lost sales, capacity must be set to match peak demand.	Storable output permits setting capacity at some average demand level.
Forecasting	Forecasts are short term, time-oriented.	Forecasts are long term, output-oriented.

Source: Richard B. Chase, "Where Does the Customer Fit in a Service Operation?" *Harvard Business Review*, November–December 1978, p. 189. Copyright © 1978 by the President and Fellows of Harvard College; all rights reserved. Reprinted by permission.

PRODUCTION PLANNING AND INVENTORY CONTROL

Production planning and inventory control is the essence of POM. In carrying out this function, the production manager must decide on:

1. The production capacity required to meet the firm's long run steady state demand (i.e., five years or more).
2. The required production rate to satisfy customer orders in the near term (i.e., the next month or year).
3. The schedule of specific orders (i.e., the next day or week).
4. The level of inventory required to support production and sales.

For *capacity planning*, the production manager is dependent upon information inputs from the marketing department relative to sales projections over the life of the product line and anticipated new products; and is dependent upon general corporate level management for guidance with respect to required flexibility in capacity needed in order to compete in the firm's market.[3] Here, for example, a production manager would have to know whether the strategy of the firm was to introduce new products frequently in order to skim the market, or if it is to have a narrow product line which must be produced at low cost. This decision in effect constrains the production manager in his or her choice of equipment, work force, use of subcontractors, and so forth.

In *setting production rates*, the production manager must respond to a short-term forecast of orders and in addition must decide upon how much inventory must be accumulated to meet unanticipated demand. Once it is decided how much to be produced, then the production manager must make certain that raw materials will be ordered in the proper amounts, that an adequate supply of workers (as measured in labor-hours) are on hand, and that sufficient machinery (as measured in machine hours) is available.

The next step in the production management process is the *scheduling* (typically using Gantt charts) *of specific jobs* on specific machines or work centers. The difficulty of this process depends upon the type of technology employed. This may be seen in the contrast between two extreme forms of manufacturing processes: assembly lines and job shops. With assembly lines, scheduling entails deciding on the amount of time available to each worker to do his or her portion of the work on a sequentially assembled product. The objective is to balance the work load across all workers on the line in such a way that output requirements are met and that the task times for each worker are the same. By way of example, a production plan may specify that 60 units per hour be produced by a line assembling toys. Assuming that 60 workers are assigned to the line, and of course are working simultaneously, each one should perform a task or combination of tasks which total to no more than one minute. If any worker takes longer than one minute to do his share, there will be a delay in passing that part downstream to the next worker, and parts will begin to pile up at this point. In dividing up the tasks into groups of one minute or less, those with less than one minute mean that some workers assigned these will have idle time. Some idle time is inescapable in line balancing, but amounts greater than, say, 10 percent are undesirable. Perhaps a better arrangement can be achieved by dividing some tasks into smaller units or having two or more workers performing the same tasks.

Scheduling a job shop presents a different set of problems.* In this situation characterized by companies that have different processing steps for different customer orders (e.g., machine shops, auto repair facilities, hospitals), the basic question is determining which jobs have priority (at each machine, work bay, or hospital department).† Suppose, for example, that your college computer center has 200 programs to be loaded and ready to run on the computer at the beginning of a certain day. Some of these jobs are very short, some are very long, and some are of intermediate length. Assuming that they can't all be run on the same day, which should be done first? Classical scheduling theory says that to complete the most jobs they should be scheduled according to the shortest processing time. That is, the shortest one first, the next shortest one second, and so forth. The rationale behind this is that the average time over all programs will be minimized by this rule. Unfortunately, if you happen to put in a long program, there is a good chance that it won't be run at all if the computer center manager sticks to the one measure of schedule effectiveness—minimum average processing time (i.e., there may always be someone inputing a job just a little "shorter" than yours). Other problems arise if other scheduling rules such as longest job first, first come–first served, "most important" job first, are employed.

The fourth major production control decision deals with *how much inventory* must be on hand to enable each production operation to be carried out without interruption, and how much finished goods inventory must be stored to fill sales orders. In both instances, the production manager must answer two basic questions: "How much do I need?" and "When do I need it?" Current production management practice is to set up one of two types of inventory systems depending upon whether or not the item under consideration is an end item or a component of an end item made by the company. If it is a component, its order quantity is a direct function of the demand for the product it goes into. That is, if a company plans on producing 500 watches, it will need 500 stems, 500 faces, 500 bezels, and so on. If each 100 watch faces require one gallon of plating compound, then five gallons are required for

---

* See the Sandman system of production control in Chapter 6 for a discussion of computer-aided job shop scheduling.

† "Forced labor?": Some hospitals have encouraged expectant mothers to elect induced childbirth during off-peak hours during the week. This smooths out the production schedules and increases facility utilization. (Some cynics maintain that this also permits obstetricians to maintain the same tee-off times for Wednesday golf matches throughout the year.)

the 500 watches. Thus, the product structure of the end item determines the inventory needs and timing of receipt of its components. The inventory method for controlling these amounts and their timing is called materials requirements planning (or MRP) and is the "hottest" topic in production control in the past decade. (The reasons behind this interest are discussed in Chase and Aquilano[4] and Miller and Sprague.[5])

In those situations where item demand is not a function of demand for another item—that is, the item in question is not a component item or is an end item itself, then mathematical inventory models are relevant. These models, referred to generally as *economic order quantity* (EOQ) models, focus on the unique demand history of the items themselves and attempt to minimize the total costs involved in carrying too much inventory on the one hand and placing too frequent reorders on the other.

A material requirements planning example

Consider a bicycle manufacturer who must decide upon the quantity and timing of parts needed to make 1,000 rear wheels. Under MRP, a product structure tree* such as that shown in Exhibit 12–3 would be set up. The numbers in parentheses indicate the number needed to make one unit of its parent. (E.g., a hub sprocket assembly is made of one hub unit and one sprocket unit. One complete wheel is made of one rim, 50 spokes, and one hub sprocket assembly.)

Assume that it takes five days lead time in order to complete the wheel rim given that the rim, spokes, and sprocket assembly are available. (The term "lead time" is an all-inclusive one; that is, it consists of waiting or idle times, delivery times, assembly or process times, and any other delays involved from the time the order is released for the item until the item is received.)

Exhibit 12–3
MRP product structure tree

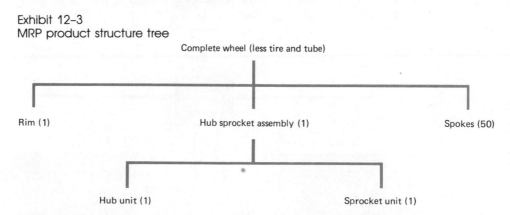

* This is also similar to a *gozinto chart*, named after the famous Italian mathematician, Zepartzat Gozinto.

Assume also that it takes 7 days lead time for the rim, 2 days for the spokes, 10 days for the sprocket assembly, 10 days for the hub unit, and 15 days for the sprocket unit. Referring back to Exhibit 12–3 we can see from the product structure tree that the total time to complete the wheel rim will be 5 days plus 10 days for the hub socket assembly and 15 for the sprocket unit, for a total of 30 days. The other three components do not delay the assembly process.

We can see that the product structure tree (called the *bill of materials*, or BOM, in MRP) tells us how much we need of each component to meet end item demand (for example, we need 50 × 1,000 spokes). And the "when" for each component and subassembly is specified by the lead time to purchase or manufacture.

MRP, though simple in concept, has many more aspects than described above. MRP virtually always implies the use of a computer since keeping track of current inventory usage and requirements would quickly overwhelm a manual system even for a relatively small producer. Further, MRP systems generate information for the scheduling function and can answer "what if"

Exhibit 12–4
Overall view of the inputs to a material requirements planning program and the reports generated by the program

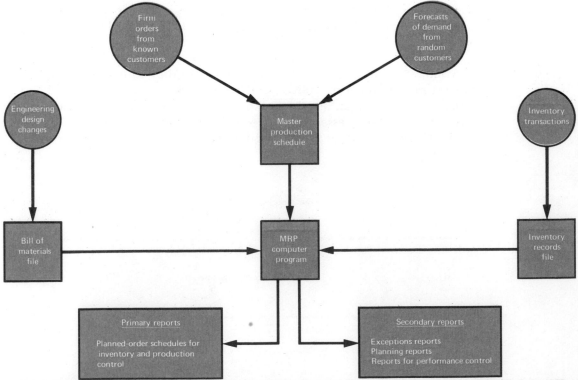

Source: Richard B. Chase and Nicholas J. Aquilano, *Production and Operations Management,* rev. ed. (Homewood, Ill.: Richard D. Irwin, 1977), p. 425. © 1977 by Richard D. Irwin, Inc.

questions about the effect of new orders, changes in the product structure, changes in lead time, and so forth by running the program with different input data. Exhibit 12–4 illustrates the major elements of a computerized MRP system.

Economic order quantity models

Economic order quantity models for inventory control require the use of demand and cost estimates which become the basis for the "how much" and "when" inventory decisions. Such models attempt to determine the specific point, R, at which an order will be placed and the size of that order, Q (quantity). The order point, R (often referred to as reorder point) is always a specified number of units actually in inventory. The solution to an economic order quantity (EOQ) model may stipulate something like this: When the number of units of inventory on hand drops to 56, place an order for 200 more units.*

Exhibit 12 5
Basic order quantity model

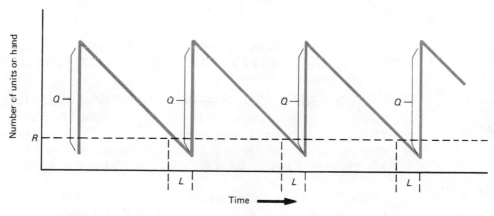

Exhibit 12–5 and the ensuing derivation of the optimal order quantity are based on the following characteristics of the basic model:

1. Demand for the product is constant and uniform.
2. Lead time (time from ordering to receipt) is constant.
3. Price per unit of product is constant.
4. Inventory holding cost is based on average inventory.

---

* It is interesting to note that some products contain a "built-in" reorder point to encourage the user to "stock up." Some cough medicine bottles, for example, have a line near the bottom with a reminder to purchase a new bottle when the quantity remaining falls below the line. (The more "mature" readers of this book will recall the jingle, "When the bottle gets down to four, that's the time to buy some more [product name].")

5. Ordering or setup costs are constant.
6. All demands for the product will be satisfied (no back orders are allowed).

The "sawtooth" graph relating Q and R in Exhibit 12–5 shows that when inventory drops to point R, a reorder is placed. This order is received at the end of time period L, which doesn't vary in this model.

In constructing any inventory model, the first step is to develop a functional relationship between the variables of interest and the measure of effectiveness. Let's assume that we would like to minimize the total annual cost for the number of items needed, the cost to order, and the cost to carry them in inventory.

The following equation would pertain:

$$TC = DC + \frac{D}{Q}S + \frac{Q}{2}H$$

Where

TC = Total annual cost.
D = Annual demand.
C = Purchase cost per unit.
S = Cost of placing an order or making a production setup.
H = Annual holding and storage cost per unit of average inventory.
Q = Quantity ordered.

On the right side of the equation, DC is the annual purchase cost for the units, $(D/Q)S$ is the annual ordering cost [the actual number of orders placed, D/Q, times the cost of each order, S], and $(Q/2)H$ is the annual holding cost [the average inventory, $Q/2$, times the cost per unit for holding and storage, H]. These cost relationships are shown graphically in Exhibit 12–6.

The second step in model development is to find that order quantity, Q, for which total cost is a minimum. (This Q is defined as the EOQ or simply $Q_{\text{opt(imum)}}$). In the basic model, a formula may be derived by simple algebra if we recognize that DC is not a decision variable and hence not a factor in the ordering decision. Then—with reference to Exhibit 12–6—total cost is minimum at the point where the cost of ordering is equal to the cost of carrying, or

$$\frac{DS}{Q} = \frac{Q}{2}H$$

which in turn is solved as follows:

$$Q_{\text{opt}} = \sqrt{\frac{2DS}{H}}$$

Exhibit 12–6
Annual product costs, based on size of the order

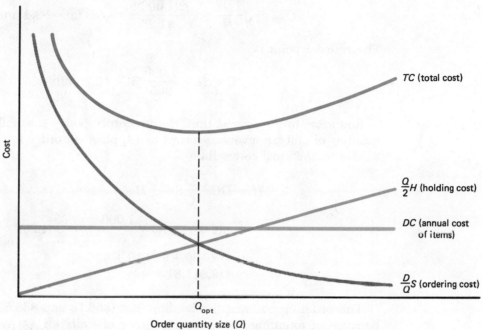

Those knowledgeable in calculus will recognize that this equation can also be derived by differentiating the total cost equation with respect to Q, setting it equal to zero, and solving for Q.

The final step in a simple inventory problem is finding R, the reorder point. The reorder point is the amount needed during the time between when the order is placed and when it arrives. *Assuming* that lead time to make or order the product doesn't change (this is a *big* assumption), then R is simply equal to $\bar{d}L$, where

$\bar{d}$ = Average demand per day.
L = Lead time in days.

Example. Find the economic order quantity and the reorder point, given the following data:

Annual demand (D) = 1,000 units.
Average daily demand $(\bar{d})$ = 1,000/365.
Ordering cost (S) = $5 per order.
Holding cost (H) = $1.25 per unit per year.
Lead time (L) = 5 days.
Cost per unit (C) = $12.50.

The optimum order quantity is

$$Q_{opt} = \sqrt{\frac{2\,DS}{H}} = \sqrt{\frac{2(1,000)5}{\$1.25}} = \sqrt{8,000} - 89.4 \text{ units}$$

The reorder point is

$$R = \bar{d}L = \frac{1,000}{365}(5) = 13.7 \text{ units}$$

Rounding to the nearest unit, the inventory policy is as follows: When the number of units in inventory drops to 14, place an order for 89 more.

The total annual cost will be

$$TC = DC + \frac{D}{Q}S + \frac{Q}{2}H$$

$$= 1,000(\$12.50) + \frac{1,000}{89}(5) + \frac{89}{2}(1.25)$$

$$= \$12,500 + \$56.18 + \$55.63$$

$$= \$12,611.81$$

The ordering cost and the holding cost ($56.18 and $55.63) are not equal because of rounding to an even number of units for Q. (Note that in this example the purchase cost of the units was not required to determine the order quantity and the reorder point. It is, of course, required to determine the total cost of the solution.)

There are a number of practical questions in inventory which we can only mention here. One is determination of safety stock: How much extra inventory should be carried to be assured of meeting unforeseen demand? Another is categorizing inventory items in such a way that management spends its time and effort on controlling important (i.e., high cost or high volume) items rather than spreading its efforts equally over all items. Also, there are questions of how frequently one should count inventory and whether or not it should be made or purchased.

EOQ on a different plane

The problem involved the training of stewardesses, of whom the company employed approximately 1,000. Most of these girls left the airline before they had given two years of service, primarily to get married. . . . Because of the high rate of attrition, the airline had a continuous need to recruit and train additional stewardesses.

The company had set up a stewardesses training school. It was capable of conducting three classes of 50 girls each. Actual training took five and a half weeks. An additional half-week was required for outfitting: a week was required to bring the girls from their homes to school and another was required to get them to their bases after training. This made for a total of eight weeks "lead time."

The company wanted to know how often it should run a class and how large the classes should be. On examination it became apparent that this was a familiar problem in production and inventory control. The conversion of a young lady (the raw material) into a stewardess (the finished product) by training (the production process) has associated with it an inventory carrying cost (the salary paid to excess girls whose available time for work is not completely used), shortage costs (those associated with emergency measures or cancellations of flights arising out of shortage of stewardesses), and setup costs associated with preparing the school for a class. The problem, then, was one of determining the size and frequency of "production runs" so as to minimize the sum of these costs, that is, to find the economic "lot sizes."

The appropriate mathematical analysis was applied to this familiar problem and it was solved, yielding a set of tables which the school administrator could use to conduct his operation in an optimal way. The savings indicated were impressive.[6]

QUALITY CONTROL

> Quality is our most important product.
> 99 and 44/100ths percent pure (soap).
> 100% pure beef patties.
> . . . the "lonely Maytag repairman."

The above advertising slogans indicate the importance of quality as a means of promoting a company's product and as an operating objective. The production or operations manager is concerned with quality because he or she has the direct responsibility for producing products which meet the organization's quality objectives.* In thinking about quality, it is important that one distinguish between quality of the product and quality of the quality control (QC) system. That is, while a high-quality product usually requires a substantial investment in QC procedures, it does not follow that a small investment in QC will suffice for an inexpensive product. For example, we know that a Rolls Royce undergoes a large number of quality checks during its production. However, we should also be aware that less expensive cars are also subjected to a variety of QC tests as well. In fact, it is generally conceded that all of the major Detroit auto companies have more sophisticated *systems* for controlling quality than does Rolls Royce, even though the intrinsic quality of a Rolls Royce is viewed as higher than its U.S. competition. The reason, of course, lies in the great difference in the number of cars produced (and in the differences in care and maintenance after purchase).

---

* Even though quality control is often a separate department, the actual monitoring of product quality during production may be carried out by inspectors who report to a production manager.

In operating, as well as in designing a QC system, management must have a good understanding of the following five factors.[7]

1. Degree of conformance to product design specifications.
2. Acceptance sampling procedures.
3. Process control procedures.
4. Location of inspection activities.
5. Personnel considerations.

Degree of conformance to specifications

Quality control implies the existence of a standard to provide a basis for comparison. That standard, in turn, must be stated in quantitative terms if it is to be easily enforced. In some situations, management can use *variables* (i.e., physical measurements—weight, length, breaking strength, circumference, and so on). In others, management is forced to use *attributes* (i.e., characteristics which are either present or absent in the product) and define quality according to how many of the items have the particular characteristic. For example, "2 out of 20" lenses have scratches, "95 percent of all transistors work," or "all flights took off within 5 minutes" of scheduled departure times.

Acceptance sampling procedures

This refers to the use of statistical methods to test whether products or components are satisfactory. Acceptance sampling entails either looking at all items and comparing them to a standard, or taking a statistically derived sample and letting tests on the sample determine whether to "accept" or "reject" all of the items. Sampling is relied upon heavily in quality control for a number of reasons: looking at every item (100 percent inspection) is time consuming, is often costly, and in some cases may damage the product (exploding all firecrackers, or biting into every "Big Mac"). In addition, the inspection process itself is often so tedious that inspectors may make more errors from lack of attention about overall item quality from examining all of the items than they would from a more careful scrutiny of just a small sample of items. In any event, statistical sampling procedures are so highly refined in most manufacturing industries that managers can readily weigh the costs of inspection to discover bad items versus costs of not inspecting and therefore accepting bad quality items which will result in another cost later on in the process. Statistical acceptance sampling is also used in service industries, but as one might expect, it is most easily applied to office operations such as checking the accuracy of invoices, rather than subjective measures such as patient diagnoses in a clinic.

Process control procedures

Process control procedures also imply the existence of a standard. But in this case, the objective is to make adjustments (where needed) in the production process itself while there is still time to avoid making poor quality items. It should be noted that acceptance sampling can be used between processes as well as at the beginning and end of production.

A classic example here is where the diameters of successive parts being trimmed on a lathe are gradually increasing in size, indicating that the cutting tool is wearing down and should be replaced before subsequent parts are made "off spec." The monitoring of the process might entail sampling of every tenth item and plotting this on a control chart to allow a trend to be observed. Naturally, the production of bad parts due to some other cause (tool breakage, malfunction of the lathe, and so on) would signal that the process should be stopped immediately and repaired. Exhibit 12–7 illustrates a control chart for a lathe cutting parts with acceptable diameters of 6.0 inches ± .05 inches. Note that this is termed a "dynamic" control chart since it shows that the

Exhibit 12–7
Control chart for monitoring production of parts made on a lathe

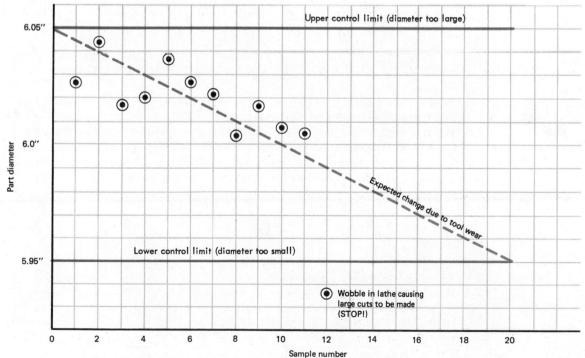

mean of the process is expected to change over time. Note also that samples 1 through 11 vary slightly from the expected average line, indicating that there is some inherent (and generally unavoidable) variation in the cutting process. Note that sample number 12 was outside of the acceptable limits, requiring that the machine be shut down.

Location of inspection activities

Most organizations are pretty consistent in requiring that inspection be carried out on raw materials and on the finished product. The tougher issue, however, is deciding where during the process inspection should be carried out. Should management place an inspector next to each machine in a machine shop? Next to each clerk in an insurance office? In each classroom in a high school? Obviously, in answering these questions, a trade-off must be made between sending along defective parts, wrongly completed forms, students with reading problems, and so on, with the cost of positioning inspectors at multiple points in the process. While this trade-off is rarely easy, the points brought out in Exhibit 12–8 provide some interesting rules of thumb for making it.

Exhibit 12–8
Rules of thumb for locating inspection stations

Locate inspection point:

1. Where raw material is received.   Defective materials can be sent back to supplier before value is added to them.
2. Prior to a costly operation.   Don't goldplate a defective watch or start assembly on an engine when the crankshaft is bent.
3. Prior to potential damage.   An off-standard part or material can cause damage in subsequent operations.
4. Prior to a series of operations.   In chemical processing, for example, a number of processing steps may be linked together in such a way that no inspection is possible during production.
5. Prior to the point of no return.   Some materials can't be economically reworked after they go through a particular process. Typographical errors in books, demolishing the wrong building, cutting a diamond, and so on.
6. Prior to stocking.   Work-in-process and finished goods should be inspected before they are stocked, especially if there is a high spoilage rate or a high cost if they are not available.
7. Where quality responsibility changes hands.   This allows tracing the source of defectives in a multidepartment organization. This also pertains to situations where incentives are paid to production workers.

Source: Drawn in part from J. William Gavett, *Production and Operations Management* (New York: Harcourt, Brace & World, Inc., 1968), pp. 406–7.

Personnel considerations

Besides the boredom that attends many quality control inspection jobs, personnel problems often arise due to two other factors: (1) Inspectors inspect work of others and hence are subject to the variety of pressures one might expect when passing judgment on someone else's efforts (and "bread and butter"). (2) Inspection work is itself difficult to measure and therefore to compensate. That is, unlike most production work where compensation is based essentially upon units produced, quality control work requires that compensation be keyed to the number of units inspected, the number of defects discovered, and the number of defective units missed. This requires that the inspector's work be inspected for quality. Furthermore, deciding between good and bad in some instances is highly subjective, and in fact may be an art. For example, how do you compensate such QC jobs as wine taster, proofreader, or egg candler?* This is not to say that sound pay schemes can't be designed for quality control work; only that finding the right payment formula is usually more difficult to develop and administer than for the typical production job.

GENERAL-PURPOSE PROBLEM-SOLVING TECHNIQUES

To this point, we have described quantitative techniques developed expressly to deal with POM problems. Now, we will examine two techniques (linear programming and Monte Carlo simulation) which have application to other management decision areas. (These, as well as other mathematical techniques, are often referred to as "management science" or "operations research" tools.)

Linear programming

Several years ago a recent M.B.A. graduate went to work for a midwestern meat-packing firm. One of the company's products was the common hot dog. Among the ingredients of the hot dog were beef and pork (plus a lot of other things that you would probably rather not know if you like hot dogs and want to keep eating them). The company's quality control kitchen had discovered that within certain limits the percentages of beef and pork could vary in the hot dogs without causing any noticeable change in quality or taste. Being an astute former farm boy, the M.B.A. knew that beef and pork prices varied quite a bit; even hourly, not just day to day or month to month. Soon, he had written a computer program which did marvelous things. In the hot dog plant a computer terminal was installed. From the home office, the *hourly* prices of beef and pork on the Kansas City market were plugged into the program. The program calculated and very quickly printed out for the factory supervisor a recipe for that hour's hot dog production which respected the

---

* Ask an agriculture student to explain the method.

quality control limits on beef/pork variation and also made sure that the absolutely lowest cost (based on that hour's market prices) hot dog was being made. After six months, the M.B.A.'s boss said that enough money had been saved to pay the M.B.A.'s salary for the next 15 years even if he never did another productive thing for the company.

Linear programming (LP) is basically a mathematical method to help decision makers allocate scarce resources in an optimal way. It is also a useful way of getting a handle on the problem. The methodology involves building a mathematical model of the situation, introducing actual cost or profit figures as constants of the problem, and solving via an algorithm (i.e., a "computational procedure") for that combination of variables which gives the best solution in terms of cost or profit.

Every LP problem consists of a mathematical statement called an *objective function* which is to be maximized or minimized depending upon the nature of the problem at hand (for example, maximize profit or minimize cost). In addition, an LP problem contains a set of *constraint equations* which specify the quantities of the various resources available and the proportion of each resource required to make a unit of the item of interest.

A mathematical statement and a verbal description for a hypothetical LP problem could be as follows:

Objective function

> *Maximize* $\$5x + \$8y$ Maximize the revenue from making xs and ys, where xs sell for $5 and ys sell for $8.

Subject to the following constraints

> Resource A: $4x + 5y \leq 10$ xs take 4 hours each and ys take 5 hours each on machine A. There is up to 10 hours available on machine A.
>
> Resource B: $6x + 3y \leq 15$ xs take 6 hours each and ys take 3 hours each on machine B. There is up to 15 hours available on machine B.

Once the problem is formulated in mathematical terms, the next step is simply to solve it using one of the several LP algorithms. We will now go through a complete LP problem demonstrating one such algorithm, the graphical method.

Graphical linear programming.   Though limited in application to problems involving two decision variables (or three variables for three-dimensional graphing), graphical linear programming provides a quick insight into the nature of linear programming and illustrates what takes place in the general (or "simplex") method briefly defined later in this chapter.

We will illustrate the steps involved in the graphical method in the context of a production planning problem faced by the Puck and Pawn Company, which manufactures hockey sticks and chess sets. Each hockey stick yields an incremental profit of $2 and each chess set an incremental profit of $4. A hockey stick requires four hours of processing at machine center A and two hours at machine center B. A chess set requires six hours at machine center A six hours at machine center B, and one hour at machine center C. Machine center A has a maximum of 120 hours of available capacity per day, machine center B has 72 hours, and machine center C has 10 hours.

If the company wishes to maximize profit, how many hockey sticks and chess sets should be produced per day?

1. Formulate the problem in mathematical terms. If H is the number of hockey sticks and C is the number of chess sets, the objective function may be stated as follows:

$$\text{Maximize } Z = \$2H + \$4C \text{ (profit)}$$

The maximization will be subject to the following constraints:

$$4H + 6C \leq 120 \text{ (machine center A)}$$
$$2H + 6C \leq 72 \text{ (machine center B)}$$
$$1C \leq 10 \text{ (machine center C)}$$
$$H, C \geq 0 \text{ (nonnegativity requirement)}$$

2. Plot constraint equations. The constraint equations are easily plotted by letting one variable equal zero and solving for the axis intercept of the other. (The inequality portions of the restrictions are disregarded for this step.) For the machine center A constraint equation, then, when $H = 0$, $C = 20$, and when $C = 0$, $H = 30$. For the machine center B constraint equation, when $H = 0$, $C = 12$, and when $C = 0$, $H = 36$. For the machine center C constraint equation, $C = 10$, for all values of H. These lines are graphed in Exhibit 12–9.

3. Determine the area of feasibility. The direction of inequality signs in each constraint determines the area wherein a feasible solution will be found. In this case all inequalities in the resource equations are of the less-than-or-equal-to variety, which means that it would be impossible to produce any combination of products that would lie to the right of any constraint line on the graph. The region of feasible solutions is shaded on the graph and forms a convex polygon. A convex polygon exists when a line drawn between any two points in the polygon stays within the boundaries of that polygon. If this condition of convexity does not exist, the problem is either incorrectly set up or not amenable to linear programming.

4. Plot the objective function. The objective function may be plotted by assuming some arbitrary total profit figure and then solving for the axis coordi-

Exhibit 12–9
Graph of hockey stick and chess set problem

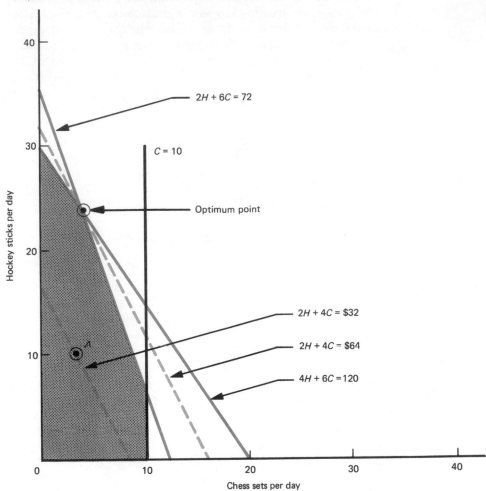

nates, as was done for the constraint equations. Another term for the objective function, when used in this context, is the *iso-profit* or *equal contribution line,* because it shows all possible production combinations for any given profit figure. For example, from the dashed line closest to the origin on the graph, we can determine all possible combinations of hockey sticks and chess sets that will yield $32 by picking a point on the line and reading the number of each product that can be made at that point. The combination yielding $32 at point *A* would be 10 hockey sticks and three chess sets. This can be verified by substituting $H = 10$ and $C = 3$ in the objective function:

$$\$2(10) + \$4(3) = \$32$$

5. *Find the optimum point.*   It can be shown mathematically that the optimum combination of decision variables will always be found at an extreme point (corner point) of the convex polygon. In Exhibit 12–9 there are four corner points (excluding the origin), and we can determine which one is the optimum by either of two approaches. The first approach is to find the values of the various corner solutions algebraically. This entails simultaneously solving the equations of various pairs of intersecting lines and substituting the quantities of the resultant variables in the objective function. For example, the calculations for the intersection of $2H + 6C = 72$ and $C = 10$ would be as follows.

Substituting $C = 10$ in $2H + 6C = 72$ gives $2H + 6(10) = 72$, $2H = 12$, or $H = 6$. Substituting $H = 6$ and $C = 10$ in the objective function, we get:

$$\text{Profit} = \$2\,H + \$4\,C$$
$$= \$2(6) + \$4(10)$$
$$= \$52$$

A variation of this approach is to read the H and C quantities directly from the graph and substitute these quantities into the objective function, as shown in the previous calculation. The drawback in this approach is that in problems with a large number of constraint equations, there will be many possible points to evaluate, and the procedure of testing each one mathematically is somewhat inefficient.

The second and generally preferred approach entails using the objective function or iso-profit line directly to find the optimum point. The procedure involves simply drawing a straight line *parallel* to any arbitrarily selected initial iso-profit line so that the iso-profit line is farthest from the origin of the graph. (In cost minimization problems, the objective would be to draw the line through the point closest to the origin.) In Exhibit 12–9 the dashed line labeled $\$2H + \$4C = \$64$ intersects the most extreme point. Note that the initial arbitrarily selected iso-profit line is necessary in order to display the slope of the objective function for the particular problem. This is important since a different objective function might indicate that some other point is farthest from the origin. Given that $\$2H + \$4C = \$64$ is optimum, the amount of each variable to produce can be read from the graph: 24 hockey sticks and four chess sets. No other combination of the products will yield a greater profit.

Simplex method.   The simplex method is an algebraic procedure that, through a series of repetitive operations, progressively approaches an optimum solution. Like the graphical method, it investigates solutions at each intersection of constraint equations. Through the use of matrix algebra calculations, an optimum combination of products can be found. The simplex method can solve a problem consisting of any number of variables and constraints, although its use for problems containing several variables and several constraint equations necessitates a computer.

Monte Carlo simulation

One of the problems in applying mathematical tools such as linear programming and EOQ formulas is that they become difficult or impossible to use when the variables under study become uncertain, too numerous, or require non-linear relationships. In both techniques we had to assume that demand for the products was known with certainty, that the time to produce the products was constant, that costs didn't change, and so on. Alas, the real world often is not quite so predictable and hence we must use different techniques which are less restrictive in their assumptions.

One such technique is Monte Carlo simulation. This technique, named after the famous gambling resort city, is expressly "designed" to study situations in which the variables can be described as a range of values with probabilities of each occurring rather than a single value. The method is extremely simple in concept although simulation models themselves can be very complex and require computerization for problems of any size. (For an excellent coverage of computer simulation, see the classic work of McMillan and Gonzalez.[8])

The essence of Monte Carlo simulation is the sampling from probability distributions to indicate how a system under study will respond to demands upon it. For example, we might simulate a baseball player's batting performance the next four times at bat by constructing a cardboard "pie" with the pieces sized according to the player's past history of walks, singles, doubles, triples, strikeouts, flyouts, and groundouts. Then, we could attach a "spinner" at the center of the pie with a pin, spin it with a finger and use where the

Exhibit 12–10
Data for baseball simulation

Outcome	Based on past history	Associated* random numbers	Partial random number table	
HR	5%	00–04	36	61
Single	10	05–14	76	82
Double	6	15–20	55	00
Triple	3	21–23	25	03
Walk	5	24–28	97	14
Groundout	20	29–48	01	44
Flyout	18	49–66		
Strikeout	33	67–99		
	100%			

* Actually any random numbers may be used, providing that their absolute number reflects the probability of drawing them from the random number table. That is, we could assign numbers 06, 21, 38, 89, and 99 to the HR outcome, providing that we don't use them for any other outcomes.

spinner stops to come up with the outcome of each turn at bat. (This in fact is how the children's game with the trade name of "All-Star Baseball" operates.) In formal simulations, the concept is the same, except that probabilities for events are given as a range of numbers in proportion to these probabilities of occurrence and the simulation is carried out by drawing random numbers from a table or computer program. For the baseball player, a formal simulation would be set up as shown in Exhibit 12–10.

The simulation would proceed by simply going in order down the random number table and tabulating the outcomes. Thus, 36 falls into the "groundout" category; 76, "strikeout"; 55, "flyout"; and 25, "walk." Hence, our batter is 0 for 3, plus a walk.*

A business simulation for, say, determining daily ending inventory for a retailer might be set up as follows:

Customer demand per day	Probability	Associated random numbers
10	.1	0
20	.5	1–5
30	.4	6–9

Stock deliveries per day	Probability	Associated random numbers
10	.5	0–4
20	.3	5–7
30	.2	8–9

And a simulation using, say, the first number of the two-digit number in column 1 of the random number table in Exhibit 12–10 for customer demand and the second number in column 1 for deliveries would be:

Day	Random numbers	Demand	Deliveries	Daily ending inventory
1	36	20	20	0
2	76	30	20	−10
3	55	20	20	0
4	25	20	20	0
5	97	30	20	−10

---

* Actually, simulation has been used rather widely in the sports world. Several football teams predicate their defense on simulations of probable plays used in specific situations by the opponent. Look for a computer terminal in the pressbox at your next home game. In Europe, wagers on snowed-out soccer matches have been won or lost depending upon the results of a government sanctioned simulation.

Exhibit 12–11
Partial flowchart of a chemical processing firm

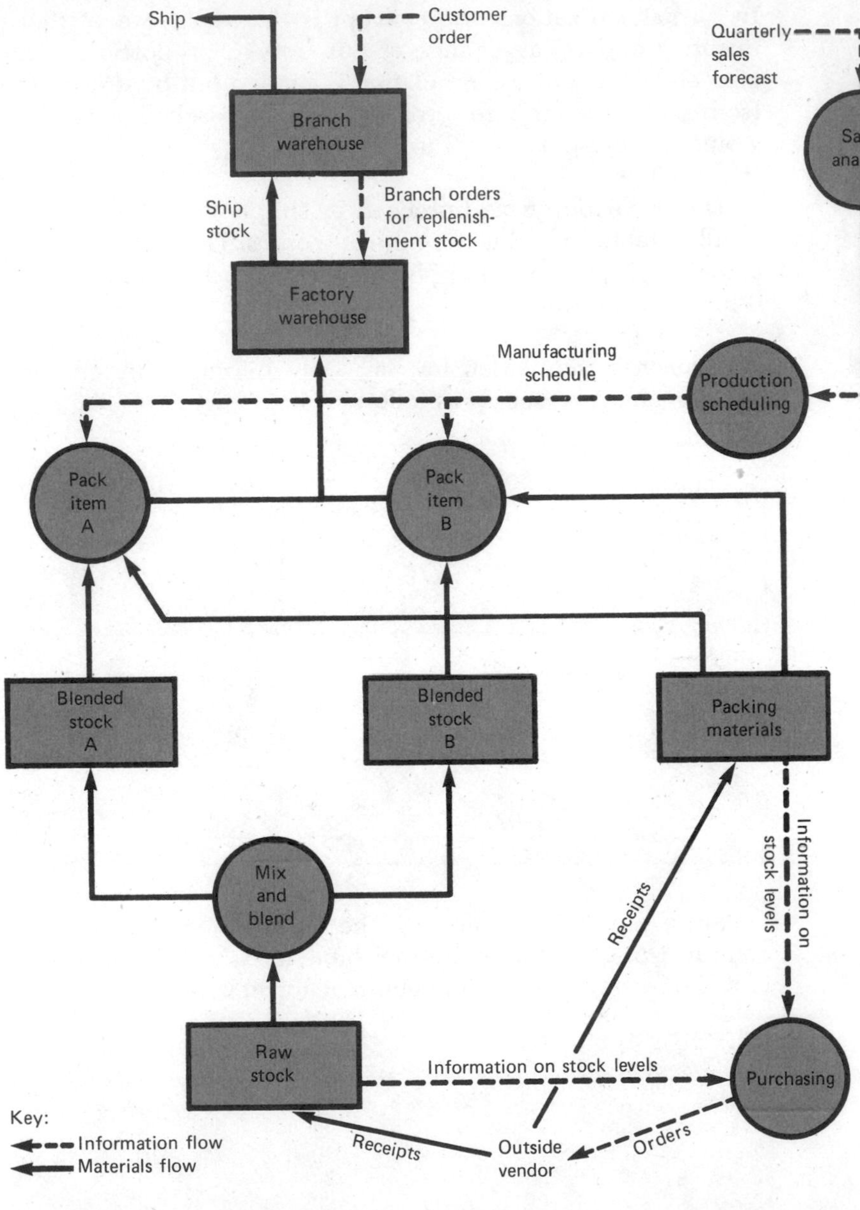

As we can see, the simulation indicates that a stockout will occur 40 percent of the time. Management may have to add stock, and consider if and how they will deal with back orders.*

---

* Actually, a five-day run is much too short to make decisions. The simulation normally would be run perhaps 5,000 times (taking about two seconds of computer time).

From the foregoing brief discussion, we can say the following about Monte Carlo simulation:

1. Each simulation model is special purpose in that it is designed for a unique set of conditions.
2. A large problem can be time-consuming. (Writing a simulation computer program can take a great deal of time.)
3. It does not guarantee an optimum solution. It is really just a sampling process.
4. It is often the only feasible way to study complex probabilistic systems. (Even so, the real thing is often too complex to model and simulate in every respect.)

Flowcharts

The best single tool for analyzing a production system is a flowchart which describes the steps in the production process. Such charts need not be complex but should illustrate the material and information flow from raw material input to finished goods output. Exhibit 12–11 shows a "macro" flowchart of major material and information flows. Within this there will be numerous "micro" flowcharts showing in detail the operations, transports, inspections, delays, and storages that occur along the way in the production process. It is surprising to many nonproduction specialists how much information can be gained about the pros and cons of a given system through the use of this simple mapping device. Indeed, the flowchart is to operations management as the organization chart is to general management. "Don't leave home without it!"

SUMMARY

It is becoming increasingly recognized in business schools* that POM is often the difference between success and failure of an organization. If the factory, office, or hospital doesn't run efficiently, sooner or later it will lose out in the marketplace. Indeed, no competitive organization can survive unless it tends to the technical problems of production planning, scheduling, and quality control. For the student planning a management career, these problems present a challenge and an opportunity. POM is a fairly difficult academic field and in the real world, it is a demanding one. Nevertheless, opportunities abound within it and rewards come to those who master it.

---

* It has always been recognized in the business world.

GUIDES TO ACTION

1. The best production systems are simple in design, operation, and control. Making a complex product doesn't mean that the system which produces it must also be complex.

2. How a production system works can best be understood by drawing a flowchart of material and information flows through the system.

3. One doesn't have to be an expert to sense whether or not a production organization is operating efficiently. Messy work areas, crowded aisles, idle workers, and idle machines are factors which signal the existence of production problems.

4. For any production problem to be studied, try to form a simplified symbolic or mathematical model. Even if you are unable to solve the problem mathematically, going through the experience of creating the model will help you understand the problem more clearly and will usually lead to a better solution.

5. To find out about opportunities in manufacturing POM, join the American Production and Inventory Control Society in your area.

NOTES

[1] Richard B. Chase, "Where Does the Customer Fit in a Service Operation?" *Harvard Business Review,* vol. 56, no. 6 (November–December 1978), pp. 137–42. See also Richard J. Matteis, "The New Back Office Focuses on Customer Service," *Harvard Business Review,* vol. 57, no. 2 (March–April 1979), pp. 146–59.

[2] "The Fast-Food Stars: Three Strategies for Fast Growth," *Business Week,* July 11, 1977, p. 58.

[3] For an excellent introduction to capacity planning, see George W. Plossl and Oliver W. Wight, "Capacity Planning and Control," *Production and Inventory Management,* vol. 14, no. 3 (Third quarter 1973), pp. 31–67.

[4] Richard B. Chase and Nicholas J. Aquilano, *Production and Operations Management* rev. ed. (Homewood, Ill.: Richard D. Irwin, 1977), chap. 9 © 1977 by Richard D. Irwin, Inc.

[5] Jeffrey G. Miller and Linda G. Sprague, "Behind the Growth in Materials Requirements Planning," *Harvard Business Review,* vol. 53, no. 5 (September–October 1975), pp. 83–91.

[6] Russell L. Ackoff and Patrick Rivett, *A Manager's Guide to Operations Research* (New York: John Wiley & Sons, Inc., 1963), p. 13.

[7] A thorough discussion of quality control from product development through usage is presented in J. M. Juran and Frank M. Gryna, Jr., *Quality Planning and Analysis* (New York: McGraw-Hill Book Company, 1970).

[8] Claude McMillan and Richard F. Gonzalez, *Systems Analysis: A Computer Approach to Decision Models,* 3d ed. (Homewood, Ill.: Richard D. Irwin, 1973). © by Richard D. Irwin, Inc.

DISCUSSION QUESTIONS

1. "We don't have any production manager in our company. After all, we're a new car dealership." Comment.

2. "We can make our fast-food restaurant just as efficient as a General Motors assembly plant." Comment.

3. How would you determine if an assembly line is properly balanced?

4. What factors would you have to consider in scheduling the following:
   a. Classrooms at your university next year.
   b. A new airline route.
   c. Payment of your school bills.

5. Under what conditions would you use mathematical inventory models in preference to MRP?

6. What is a "bill of materials?"

7. What factors limit the use of 100 percent inspection? When would you insist upon it?

8. A supplier of radio-controlled dog collars has an annual demand for a particular collar of 800 units. Each unit costs the supplier $200. Because the technology in electronics is changing so rapidly thereby decreasing selling price and because competition is fierce, the supplier places a 40 percent annual carrying cost on the collar.

   The cost for a clerk to keep track of the inventory level and place an order when the reorder point is reached is $10 per order. Lead time to obtain the order is 5 days.

   a. What is the economic order quantity?
   b. If demand is assumed uniform over the 365-day year, what is the reorder point?

9. Develop a simulation model of two people, A and B, who are matching coins where A is to match B. [Explanation: A and B each flip a coin. Simulate the flip of a coin. If both coins are heads or both are tails, A wins; otherwise, B wins.] Use the following random numbers or any part thereof to simulate the results of five repetitions or matchings by A and B.

   Random numbers 534, 786, 127, 538, 769, 254, 207, 982, 717, 219, 015, 444, 816, 271, 832, 910.

10. Solve the following problem using the graphical method of linear programming.

$$7x + 2y \leq 14$$
$$6x + 5y \leq 30$$

   Each unit of x produces $2 profit and each unit of y produces $10 profit. That is, maximize $2x + 10y$.

11. Shown below is the product structure tree for product X with the number of units required to make each parent item shown to the right.

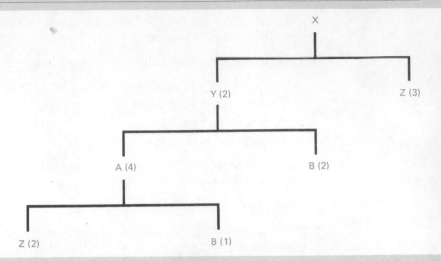

Lead times for Y and Z are 1 week and lead times for A and B are 2 weeks. The final assembly lead time for X is 1 week.

a. In order to make 100 units of X, how many units of A, B, Y, and Z are required?

b. Considering lead times, how many weeks would it take to complete the order for the 100 Xs?

CASE: THE BANKS COMPANY*

The Banks Company is the manufacturer of a highly specialized electronic product and, mainly due to the name and reputation of the founder, is virtually without competition in its field.

The company began its operation in 1957 in a stable at the home of the founder and initially employed the founder (a woman) and three part-time employees. Almost instant success in terms of customer acceptance was realized, and the operation grew out of its quarters in 1963. By that time it had been incorporated.

By then the firm employed five full-time employees, three part-time workers, and the founder, who was manager. All of the employees had two or more functions, which resulted in quite loose lines of authority and responsibility. Also, some of the employees were personal friends of the founder and went on record as stating that they would take orders from nobody but her.

At that time numerous problems plagued the company. Because of a magazine article which commented on the firm's tentative plans to market the

* From: William Voris, *Production Control: Text and Cases,* 3d ed., (Homewood, Ill.: Richard D. Irwin, 1966), pp. 329–30. © by Richard D. Irwin, Inc.

product through other supply houses, they were flooded with orders far beyond their capacity. They adopted a policy of returning orders and checks if an early delivery date was not foreseeable, or doing so upon receipt of the first complaint of slow delivery.

Recently a friend of the founder-manager assumed the role of unpaid adviser-organizer to the firm. He had some experience in electronics as well as plant experience with a New York firm. Among the major problems that he attacked was that of stock control. He found that at one time all new units were held up for three weeks for lack of one type of battery. He attempted to inventory the stock numbers for general classifications of items, but before he could complete a second page of inventory the first was obsolete because no account was kept of materials used. Although there was a general lack of documentation throughout, there was a notebook containing a list of parts and where each was used, but even this was out of date by about a year. The adviser attempted to establish an inventory by updating this record but was still frustrated due to stock being scattered in different unrelated areas and unrestricted access to any stock by any worker. A bench bin system reduced the travel time of the workers, but the bulk of the stock was still stored haphazardly on shelves, and shortages still occurred.

Another serious problem was the lack of drawings, schematics, and specifications. The firm's part-time engineer left the firm, with much of the technical data in his head. He had never quite gotten around to making drawings or writing specifications.

In the area of personnel the same problems persisted with clear lines of authority not defined. Due to a mutual interest in the field in which the product was used, the workers engaged in frequent "bull sessions" which interfered with the progress of the work. One of the full-time employees functioned as a general foreman but was not fully supported by the founder-manager.

The firm continues to grow, and as it expands and matures, more problems will develop and must be anticipated. The founder is eager to get the firm on an eight-hour day, five-day week, profitable basis, and has expressed a willingness to authorize constructive changes, while imposing the restriction that all changes and improvements be paid for from current income.

Questions

1. What is needed to set up an inventory control system for this plant?
2. Develop a plant reorganization which will include a production control department.

Level of Organizational Outputs

SELECTION OF THE PRODUCT OR SERVICE	DESIGN OF THE SYSTEM	STAFFING THE ORGANIZATION	STARTUP OF THE ORGANIZATION	OPERATING THE ORGANIZATION IN THE STEADY STATE	IMPROVING THE ORGANIZATION	REVISION OF THE ORGANIZATION	TERMINATION OF THE ORGANIZATION
Decision-making processes; social value; goals; forecasts; policies; plans	Authority and responsibility; power; organizational structure; communications systems; job design	Work force planning; personnel management functions	Startup planning and scheduling; monitoring; alternative startup approaches	Motivation; leadership; production and operations management; control	Individual improvement programs and techniques; group conflict management; MBO	Evaluation of organizational policies; strategic choices; organizational change; organizational development	Partial terminations; cutback management; complete terminations; mergers; born-again strategies

t_0 **Time ⟶**

Chapter 13
Organizational controls

There is always something to upset the most careful of human calculations.

> Ihara Saikaku (1642–93)
> From *The Japanese Family Storehouse* or *The Millionaire's Gospel*

The best laid schemes o' mice an' men Gang aft a-gley. *

> Robert Burns,
> From *To a Mouse*

If anything can go wrong, it will.

> Murphy's Law.†

Once plans are made, an organization structure created and staffed, and the system set into motion by management, "things" will happen. Some of the "things" will be as expected and others will be surprises; some will be desirable and others unwanted. As the above quotes indicate, we will rarely design and operate a "perfect" organization. It is probable that some employees will not be as motivated as we desire and their production may not be up to par. Other well-motivated people might simply make mistakes. Managers must build mechanisms into the organizational system that will help spot problems and facilitate correcting them. These mechanisms are what we call controls.

It should be apparent that control is closely tied to planning. When we plan, we set goals and objectives. The control process is involved with assessing the progress being made to meet these goals and objectives. Without planning, there is nothing to control!

In this chapter, we will discuss the basic elements and processes involved in management controls. We will identify a number of characteristics of effective control systems and will illustrate a number of specific control techniques. Lastly, we will discuss the impact of controls on people in organizations and consider what behaviors might be stimulated by control systems.

THE BASIC CONTROL MODEL

Control is the process of comparing actual performance against a desired standard (which is based on organizational plans) and taking action(s), if neces-

---

* Ayrshire dialect for "Go awry."

† There is no consensus on who the "real" Murphy is. The best possibility is Capt. Ed Murphy, an engineer at the Wright Field (Ohio) Aircraft Lab in the late 1940s who is known to have said, "If there is any way to do it wrong, he will" when referring to a young technician. This leads to a corollary to Murphy's law. If authorship can be lost, it will be. And, isn't it fitting that it happened to Murphy? After all, he seemed to "know" it would happen.

sary, to bring actual performance into conformity with the desired standard. This definition contains five key elements:

1. Organizational plans.
2. Desired standards.
3. Measures of actual performance.
4. A comparison of actual versus standard to note any discrepancy.
5. Corrective action(s) if deemed necessary.

Exhibit 13–1 illustrates the relationships inherent in these five elements of a control system.

Organizational plans.   The necessity of having plans upon which to base performance standards was noted above.

Standards.   Standards must be based upon plans and should be expressed in measurable terms. Sales quotas, turnover rates, absences, tolerance limits on machine parts, safety records, and production quotas are but a few areas for which standards can be created. Note the implicit assumption that *if* the standards are met, plans will be achieved. Thus we could plan to gain X percent of the market for a new product. We would then set production quotas, sales

Exhibit 13-1

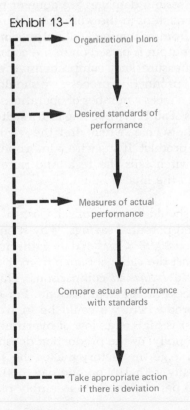

Organizational plans

Desired standards of
performance

Measures of actual
performance

Compare actual performance
with standards

Take appropriate action
if there is deviation

volume targets and other standards. If we meet the standards we "should" attain the planned for market share.

Typically, standards are based on four areas of measurement:

1. Quantity of outputs (e.g., produce 1,000 units per day).
2. Quality of output (e.g., all newly manufactured clocks keep the correct time within two minutes per month).
3. Timing or scheduling of output (e.g., all customer inquiries are answered within two business days).
4. Monetary (e.g., cost per unit of production will be less than $1.5327; or spend no more than $10 per month on paper towels).

Measures.   There are two major considerations in taking measures. First, *what* gets measured? And, second, *how often?* We could, perhaps, measure at every step in the process of producing our good or service. But, this may be very time-consuming and costly. Ideally, we would like to utilize measures at key points whereby we can minimize the costs of control, yet still catch errors before they become serious. We call these key points of measurement *strategic control points.*[1] A strategic control point has several characteristics. First, the measurement should be taken at a point where corrective actions can *remedy* any problems before serious damages are done or before the mistake gets covered up by subsequent steps in the work flow. Thus, good control will attempt to *prevent* mistakes from becoming final outputs in lieu of simply catching the mistakes before the output is passed on to the consumer. Second, strategic control points should measure key, comprehensive events. Rather than measure at every step of the production process, we should utilize points in the system where one measure checks a number of operations. For example, rather than check the connections of all 12 wires going into a switch mechanism as each is installed, simply test the whole switch after the wiring is done but before it gets installed in the final product. If any wire is improperly connected, it will be apparent when the switch fails the test. And note that the test comes *before* the switch goes into the final product.

Third, strategic control points should be economical. Costs of measurement and comparison should not exceed potential savings. Why spend $1 to check something that at best will save you $0.99? Costs of data gathering and analysis must constantly be balanced against the value obtained from the data. Finally, strategic control points must yield *balanced* comparisons. Thus, we usually measure several aspects of a process rather than just one. For example, if all we measured was quantity of production, we could be in trouble and not know it because our per unit cost is high (e.g., lots of overtime) or quality is low (e.g., they're making them sloppily) or the production doesn't "sequence" with the rest of the organization (e.g., the factory makes the 1,400 bumpers per week we need, but sporadically with 100 on one day, 500 the next, and so on, rather than the steady 200 per day the auto assembly plant needs).

How often we measure is the second major consideration. We could test every tube of toothpaste or audit the bank teller's cash box after each customer transaction. Such a volume of measurement would be expensive and time-consuming. Instead, we select appropriate intervals. Thus, we count the bank teller's cash box once a day (rather than once a week or once an hour) because this interval is economically feasible and because it is of long/short enough duration to spot most mistakes and take action to remedy them. Also, some measurements are destructive (e.g., as noted in the preceding chapter, testing firecrackers to see if they explode); thus we *have to* sample at intervals if we are to have any products for our customers.

Comparison. Standards and measures usually require ingenuity and creativity to establish. In contrast, the comparison step is relatively easy to conduct. One need only ask: Does the actual performance measure conform to the standard? Usually, this is a yes/no proposition. At times, however, even though the system is "up to standard," a trend may be observed that will eventually lead to a problem. Refer to Exhibit 12–7 in the preceding chapter for an illustration.

Corrective action. This is the essence of a control system. Without the corrective action step, all that has happened is that an evaluation was made; we compared an actual result against a desired standard. Unless we take needed actions, we have done nothing to prevent or correct undesired deviations. Imagine a baseball manager who simply keeps track of the game on his scorecard but who does nothing to alter the lineup or influence the play of his team when it is losing (or winning!).

As indicated by the feedback line (dotted) in Exhibit 13–1 sometimes the corrective action may be to change plans and standards. Perhaps goals are too high (or too low) and thus our standards are unattainable (or outlandishly easy). We can then revise the standards to conform more closely to actual performance. Thus, a bank trust department may change its desired return on investments in conjunction with movements in the prime lending rate of major city banks. Alternatively, the corrective action can be aimed at influencing the measures; i.e., by making changes in the work process so that (hopefully) actual performance, and hence the measures, is influenced in the desired direction.

It should be noted that control is not always concerned with bringing actual performance "up to standard." Just the reverse may sometimes be desired. For example, assume that the tolerance limit for ball bearings that go into a bicycle wheel is ± 0.005 inches. However, your ball bearing shop is always within ± 0.002 inches, and even brags about it. If ± 0.005 is "OK," are you willing to absorb the added costs (time, attention, "scrapping" ± 0.003 items, and so on) to get the "unneeded" accuracy? Perhaps in this case you need to take corrective action to cause performance to get worse rather than better!

TYPES OF CONTROLS

Controls can be classified into three categories: pre, current, and post. Each of these types of controls has important uses, and it is probable that an organization will utilize all three.

Precontrols

These types of controls, also called "steering" or "feed-forward" controls, are intended to spot deviations from a standard *before* some sequence of actions is undertaken. Thus, in a manufacturing plant, samples are often taken of raw materials to ascertain their quality *before* the materials are used in production. For example, assume that you operate a plant that makes catsup. One of your preproduction measures will be to determine sugar content in each truckload of raw tomatoes. Based upon this measure, you are able to vary the amount of sugar (and other ingredients) used to produce catsup from that batch of tomatoes. Thus, by using a precontrol, you seek to prevent problems from occurring (i.e., you shouldn't simply use the same recipe for all batches and then scrap or reprocess those finished and packed production lots that have abnormally high-/low-sugar concentrations).

A personnel manager may measure an applicant's or newly hired person's ability to run a certain machine or perform some set of actions. These measures, when compared to some standard(s), will lead to certain actions in determining who needs training or in deciding upon job assignments *before* the need for such actions becomes obvious due to faulty workmanship.

Current controls

These controls involve standards/measures/comparisons/actions during the production or work process. Not all aspects of a production process can be checked with precontrols. In the catsup plant, preproduction controls can be used to monitor raw materials and initially set up the production process. However, we will still need to check on things as our product is produced. For example, the temperature of the catsup going into bottles must be kept within certain limits (too low and bacteria can be present; too high and the bottles break). Also, we need to ensure that we put 12 ounces (or close to it) of catsup in a bottle if we are so labeling our products. These aspects of manufacturing our product can be checked only *as* the production process occurs. Thus, we may install thermostats to help regulate temperature, and we will have to be sure of the volume of catsup going into bottles. One way of measuring volume could be to sample every so many (e.g., every 100th bottle or every 22.5 minutes, and so on) bottles as they come off the line and accurately measure how many ounces are inside. A chart of the general type shown in

Exhibit 12–7 would then be kept to spot trends and deviations. The person tending the machine that injects the catsup into the bottle would then use this data to increase/decrease the flow. Again, note that the emphasis is to discover and correct "problems" *before* the finished product is completed. That is, mistakes or bad outputs are prevented.

Postcontrols

These controls are concerned with completed products or "units of work." The intent is to spot deviations from standards and then to take action to prevent more "faulty" units of production. Checking over the finished automobile, making sure the electric toaster "works" before packing it, or operating newly manufactured clocks for 24 hours to see that they run properly fit into this category of controls. In accounting, auditing is an example of postcontrols in that an audit analyzes what was done (actual performance) in line with what should have been done (standards).

An illustration

Most readers who have watched television in recent years have probably seen Maytag commercials featuring the actor Jesse White who plays the role of a bored Maytag repairman. "Not all Maytag repairmen are this lonely, but we're trying" goes the announcer's line. The point of the commercials is that Maytag's products (mostly washing machines and dryers) are so well made they rarely need service. Well, then, how does Maytag do it?

Long before the machines reach the final testing stage, inspectors from the 177-person quality-control department have watched them take shape at critical points on the assembly lines, and before that have sampled and tested the purchased materials and parts that went into them.[2]

Note the use of precontrols to screen inputs, the notion of strategic control points (i.e., the "critical points") for current controls, and, of course, the postcontrol "final testing."

Every Maytag appliance is operated just before it is packed for shipment. Clothes washers are hooked up on a slowly revolving "merry-go-round" and run through every function in a fifteen-minute test. Machines that don't work properly go to the "boneyard" for repair or dismantlement.[3]

A popular management homily is "The best control is self-control." This implies that workers can and should use pre-, current, and post controls wherever relevant on their jobs; this in contrast to having "doers" and "inspectors." "The main role of inspectors . . . [at Maytag] is to 'audit' a quality-control job that must be done by everybody."[4] Further, by using certain job design techniques discussed in Chapter 7, Maytag has a system whereby ". . . each worker puts the whole unit together and stamps his own number on it. The worker can set his own pace, and he also tends to make fewer mistakes. . . . Bench assembly [as this work design is called], Maytag officials say, has cut defects on clothes-washer transmissions by 62 percent. . . ."[5]

CHARACTERISTICS OF EFFECTIVE CONTROL SYSTEMS

Thus far, we have shown the elements of a control system and discussed types of controls (pre, current, post) that can be used. In this section, we will review some characteristics of better control systems.

Timing

Since the prevention of mistakes is a major aspect of control systems, measures must be taken and comparisons made in such a timely manner that action can be taken early enough to be preventive. Otherwise, managers will be forced to act or make decisions without relevant information. Data collection, transmission, and analysis *must* take into account where and when control decisions are to be made.

Economics and practicality

As noted earlier, it makes little sense to spend $1 to save $0.99; the benefits derived from a control system must offset its costs. Thus, an analysis must be made of costs and benefits and perhaps the control system modified to better reflect economic realities. Using the catsup factory example discussed earlier, in line with Federal Trade Commission regulations, the contents of each bottle of catsup should be within, say, ±.5 ounces with an average of 12 ounces. Thus, there is no consumer fraud from "short weighting" nor does the company "give anything away." Hence, the control system need not be so rigorous as to ensure a ±.001-ounce tolerance limit. But what if this were pharmaceuticals and not catsup? With medicine, we need a closer tolerance. Thus, we would need a more rigorous set of measures and a more fine-tuned set of corrective actions for a pharmaceutical firm. The moral is that we must use a control system that is compatible with the realities of our organization; not a system that is necessarily perfect or successful in another organization.

Integration

A control system should be compatible with the work flow of the organization. Thus, parts from suppliers are tested and approved *before* the time they are needed by the assembly division. Further, data collection should, where possible, tie in with other organizational processes rather than duplicate them. For example, if raw materials are checked for conformance to the purchase order before payment to the supplier is approved, that sample can be used as the basis for the precontrol measure as in the check for tomatoes' sugar content mentioned above. It makes little sense for the purchasing department to take one sample and for the quality control inspector to follow with another.

Credibility

The system must be objective in that it uses valid standards, measures what it is supposed to be measuring, makes accurate comparisons, and initiates valid corrective actions.

If quality is an objective, it would be wrong to emphasize quantity or cost standards to the exclusion of ones for quality. The standards must be consistent with plans as noted earlier. Few things make a mockery out of a control system faster than saying one thing (via plans) and doing another (via standards). A statement such as, "They talk quality around here, but all they ever do is look at quantity produced each week," is a sure sign of trouble.

If, for example, temperature accuracy is a crucial variable, then measure it with a thermometer rather than a subjective guess. Further, where possible, measure directly rather than by inference; e.g., use a thermometer to indicate air temperature rather than by counting sweaty brows of workers. It is all too common for well-designed, sophisticated control systems to fail due to a lack of rigorous attention to assure the integrity of basic data.

Flexibility

A control system must be subject to change and "human interpretation." For example a computerized inventory control system in a sporting goods store may initiate a notice that a certain number of units of Setshot basketball shoes should be ordered. However, if the store manager "feels" that basic customer tastes are changing and that the product will be displaced by something new coming on the market next month (e.g., black, high-topped basketball shoes versus new Addidas or Nike models), should not the control system be overruled? Or, perhaps due to abnormal weather, the manager "knows" that the store better keep a supply of heavy coats on the floor three weeks longer than "normal." Any control system that is so static and omnipotent that management cannot overrule it is sure to cause problems.*

---

* Remember the problems with HAL the computer in *2001: A Space Odyssey?*

Acceptability

Ultimately, organization members can probably sabotage most any control system if they desire. Falsification of data (i.e., subverting the measuring aspect of the system) is probably the most common attack, yet this is usually caught sooner or later. A potentially greater problem lies in more sophisticated subversions. A well-known study of employment agency interviewers makes this point.[6] A new agency manager noticed that the waiting room was always crowded with applicants and decided to improve productivity. He began measuring the number of interviews held by each interviewer. Not surprisingly, the number went up. However, job placements went down. Why? Because interviewers were more interested in padding their number of interviews than in doing rigorous interviews to find applicants' skills, strong points, and so on. Thus, their referrals were poor and few people got jobs. However, there was a noticeable drop in the number of applicants in the waiting room. Seeing what happened, the manager changed the system and began measuring job placements. The interviewers immediately changed their behavior and held long interviews to ascertain applicants' skills, and so on. Also, the interviewers began bribing the receptionists to try and get assigned the more "promising" applicants (e.g., applicants who were well dressed, spoke fluently, were well-mannered, and so on). Further, interviewers began to hoard notices of job openings so as to not have a colleague discover an applicant who might fit the job and thus get credit for the placement. Placements did increase, but the waiting room was always full again. At this point, the manager conceded and quit taking work measures.*

The moral is clear. Unless organization members accept both the rationale for the control and the measures themselves, efforts will be made to subvert the system.

CONTROL SYSTEM ILLUSTRATIONS

Virtually all areas of an organization's operations can be subject to management scrutiny via a control system. The design of a control system is often a creative undertaking, and there is no reason to believe that some given set of systems will be appropriate for all organizations. Each organization must weigh its own needs and then design and implement the system(s) it requires. The illustrations here are intended to show the diversity of control systems and to give an understanding of some of the more common systems. Also, note that controls can be unique separate entities designed especially for

---

* This situation illustrates one of the common problems inherent in high contact service systems (alluded to in the previous chapter). That is, that the input (the customer) is highly variable in its characteristics. Thus it is impossible, as the system is currently operated, for the interviewers to know beforehand how long the production process (the interview) will take for each applicant.

the purpose of control, or they can be naturally derived from other ongoing processes in the organization. We will discuss these illustrations in the context of three areas: personnel controls, operations controls, and financial controls.

Personnel

Personnel controls are often overlooked or underutilized as management tools. The basis for personnel controls begins with the development of sound job descriptions as discussed in Chapter 8. These job descriptions provide the basis for developing standards for use in the control system.

Hiring. Given the skills required of personnel as defined by job descriptions, an analysis can be made of the skills of job applicants. Based upon the comparison of actual versus desired skills, management may retain or revise the recruiting program. Sound personnel management requires continual checks on desired (à la job descriptions) skills as an organization's needs may change. Thus, "standards" are constantly being appraised.

Performance evaluation. This important management activity is essentially the "comparison" portion of a control system. Based upon the comparison of actual performance against the desired standard an evaluation is made, and deficiencies or above standard work noted. In the case of deficiencies, training, disciplinary action, or other appropriate actions are normally undertaken.

Training. In a sense, training is a "corrective action" phase of the control model. Training is the attempt to bring people's skills up to the desired standard. Thus, if the hiring program is unable to acquire personnel with the desired skills, training may be instituted to ensure that workers have these skills prior to placement on the job. Further, training can be used on an "inservice" basis to upgrade or introduce new skills in response to changes in job requirements for existing employees. Or, training may be instituted in response to deficiencies noted in the performance appraisal process.

Of course, training after hiring, but before being placed on a job, is a form of "precontrol" in that it attempts to assure certain future behaviors/outcomes.

Discipline. This is also a "corrective action" portion of a control system. The intent of discipline should be to correct inappropriate or undesirable behavior so that future behavior is as desired. Philosophically, we do not feel that discipline should be used as a form of retribution. The magnitude of disciplinary action ranges along a continuum and depends upon the frequency and severity of the inappropriate behavior. The following sequence of penalties is common:

1. Verbal warning/reprimand.
2. Written warning/reprimand.

3. Disciplinary layoff or suspension.
4. Demotion.
5. Discharge.

Due to the potential volatility in a situation where discipline is being administered, numerous guidelines have been advocated for managers:

1. The manager should exhibit the attitude of assuming that all employees desire to conform to reasonable organization requirements. One should not appear to invite trouble.
2. The act, rather than the person, should be condemned.
3. Although the act may be the basis for penalty, a model of future desired behavior should be communicated.
4. Reasonable promptness is important so that the employee can connect the penalty to the violation.
5. A managerial listening role is highly essential to (a) effect greater understanding of the reasons for the act and (b) prevent hasty decisions that may lead to unjustified penalties.
6. Negative disciplinary action should be administered in private so that the employee can save face among colleagues.
7. Definite, but tactful, follow-up should occur to determine the degree of success of the conditioning effort.
8. Consistency and flexibility, though apparently contradictory, are both desirable elements of a superior's style of disciplining.[7]

Consistency in administering discipline is a widely debated topic. Shull and Cummings have identified five "styles" on a traditional to behavioral continuum as shown in Exhibit 13–2.[8]

The *purely legalistic* manager enforces all the rules, all the time, equally. The *legalistic-judicial* manager tends toward consistent application, yet may be swayed by extenuating circumstances. A concern for "why" behind behavior is exhibited by a *judicial-clinical* manager. If a subordinate did not intend to violate a rule, discipline may be withheld. The *clinical-humanitarian* manager disciplines only those who consistently and deliberately violate rules. Most violations, it is felt, are inadvertent and punishment will have no effect on subsequent behavior. The *purely humanitarian* manager tends to overlook or ignore rule violations in the belief that workers are mature individuals who will exercise any necessary self-control.

Large employee groups, and especially unionized workers, tend to have discipline imposed from the legalistic end of the continuum. For situations

Exhibit 13–2
Discipline styles continuum

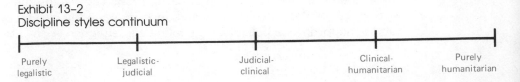

| Purely legalistic | Legalistic-judicial | Judicial-clinical | Clinical-humanitarian | Purely humanitarian |

Exhibit 13–3
A subordinate's rights where discipline is involved

1. The right to be disciplined in privacy.
2. Freedom from "entrapment" by a manager who creates a situation where the employee can't help but make a mistake and thus be disciplined.
3. The right not to be used as an example when other, perhaps more flagrant, offenders receive a lesser punishment or even go free.
4. The right not to have a rule, past violations of which were deliberately overlooked or condoned, suddenly enforced without due notice.
5. The right to have just the violation condemned and not one's total dignity as a human subject to castigation.
6. The right to treatment which is consistent with that received by others.
7. The right to be told how well one is doing; not just being told when one does badly.

Source: Based on George S. Odiorne, *How Managers Make Things Happen* (Englewood Cliffs, N.J.: Prentice-Hall, Inc., 1961), p. 136.

where consistency seems appropriate, the "hot-stove rule" may prove valuable.[9] This rule draws on an analogy between undergoing discipline and touching a hot stove. When the hot stove is touched, the "discipline" is immediate, consistent, and impersonal.*

1. The burn is immediate and the cause/effect is clear.
2. It is consistent. Everyone who touches a hot stove gets burned.
3. It is impersonal. People aren't burned because of who they are but because they touched the stove.

Further, there is a warning in that everyone knows what happens when one touches a hot stove.

Exhibit 13–3 illustrates a set of "rights" which we feel that any employee should have whenever discipline is involved. The manager who honestly respects these rights should never be viewed as "petty" or "small."

Operations

We have already discussed a variety of operations control devices in Chapter 12. As noted earlier, performance standards are usually expressed in terms of quantity, quality, time, and cost. In this section we will present control devices related to the first three of these categories. Cost-based standards will be discussed in the following section on financial controls.

---

* Or, as a former player said about the legendary Green Bay Packer coach Vince Lombardi's discipline style, "He treats us all equally—like dogs."

A key component of both operations and financial controls is an effective data gathering and processing activity. In Chapter 6 we discussed the role of a management information system (MIS). The role of MIS in the control process is to collect data (i.e., take measures) at selected points and to process this data to facilitate a manager's ability to make meaningful comparisons of actual versus desired performances.

Quantity-time.   The most widely used device to assist in controlling quantity of outputs in relation to time is the Gantt chart. As was shown in Exhibit 9–5, the Gantt chart portrays the actual quantity of output in relation to planned quantities over specified time periods.

A major benefit of the Gantt chart is its inherent simplicity and the magnitude of information that is revealed by but a quick glance.

Quality.   Control charts are also simple but popular control devices. Exhibit 12–7 previously referred to in this chapter is an example of a control chart. An important aspect of control charts is that trends can be observed and thus action(s) taken to prevent mistakes from occurring. Simple observation of the direction of the line connecting sample measures is usually sufficient to note these trends.

The indicator lights found on most automobile dashboards are, in essence, control devices of this type. When the engine temperature exceeds a certain temperature, or when the oil pressure drops below some point, or when the generator fails to provide adequate output, a light comes on indicating a problem. It is then up to the driver to take some action(s).

Many organizations have, in essence, "indicator lights." For example, the hospital administrator may receive a message whenever occupancy rates reach a predetermined level. Or, the personnel manager is informed whenever turnover in any branch exceeds 10 percent.

The "indicator" light approach reports only abnormal performances; those that are "out of standard" and require corrective action. This approach is termed reporting by exception and implicitly assumes that the manager need act upon only exceptionally bad (or good) performance; corrective actions not being required when things are "normal." Such an approach constitutes an important communications filter and may relieve a busy manager of many routine, but "unneccessary" reports.

Depending upon the particular circumstances and priorities in an organization, managers will need to receive certain regular data about operations in lieu of "indicator lights" information. Whenever such data is needed, the management information system should collect the data and assemble it into a readily usable format. For example, if downtime of a particular assembly

Exhibit 13–4
Example of a routine report

	Actual	Standard	Normal variation
Downtime on line 37B:			
Line downtime this week	43	38	36–38

	Average last month		Average last week
Line downtime	57		52

unit or machine is a critical variable, the manager may wish to receive reports such as shown in Exhibit 13–4. This report quickly shows recent performance, the norm, and recent measures so as to help spot trends.

In many factories, machines are equipped with devices that continually measure key operations, compare these with programmed norms, and even "self-adjust" when necessary. Known as numerical controlled (NC) operations, this type of equipment has become very popular as computer technology has advanced and computer costs have declined. Many steel mills are now showplaces for NC activities. In such a mill, a device might measure the thickness of sheet steel that is produced in a continuous strip but which is periodically cut and rolled according to customer orders. If the device senses that the thickness is getting too great, a signal goes to another NC device back up the line to increase temperature (to make the steel more malleable) and increase the pressure of the rollers that "squash" the strip. As the thickness decreases, the measuring device will signal for slightly decreased temperatures and pressures in an effort to stabilize the system around the desired standard of thickness.

The common thermostat found in most homes is also a member of the NC family of control devices. First, the desired temperature is set. Then, the thermostat measures the room's air temperature and when the room becomes cooler than the setting, the thermostat activates a relay that turns on the furnace. The furnace warms the air in the room and when the room temperature reaches that of the setting the thermostat's relay turns off the furnace.

Time. The critical path method (CPM) was illustrated in Chapter 9. As was noted there, CPM, in addition to its obvious role as a planning device, can also be an effective control device: By observing planned/actual completion times for various events, managers are able to spot actual (and potential) points where delays will have negative consequences. Actions can then be initiated to either overcome these delays or to take actions to minimize any adverse effects.

Financial

Probably the most widely known financial control device is a budget. Budgets are statements of planned expenditures, by category, of money, time, personnel, space, or equipment. Obviously, planning is an integral part of any budget. Once the budget is created, measures of expenditures are periodically made and compared with budgeted amounts. Management may then observe over, under, or "on target" expenditure levels and take action if warranted.

Responsibility centers.[10]   In many organizations managers have responsibility for certain activities or results. This responsibility can be established and results measured by using budgetary processes.

1. *Expense centers.*   In expense centers monetary inputs are measured but outputs are not. Most departments in a university have "operating budgets"—money for salaries, supplies, postage, telephones, and so on—and "capital budgets"—money for equipment such as desks, copy machines, and typewriters. Components of a business such as the personnel department or auditing are typically on expense center budgets.
2. *Revenue centers.*   These centers have outputs measured in monetary terms but not inputs. A sales division, for instance, may budget for a certain level of sales, and sales quotas can be given to individuals. Revenue centers are used where the organizational unit can influence the volume of outputs (i.e., sales) but not, for example, the costs of production. Thus, it isn't appropriate to control such a unit on the basis of profits.
3. *Profit centers.*   When an organizational unit is autonomous enough to have control over inputs and outputs, it is appropriate to use a profit center approach. Thus, expenses (inputs) are subtracted from revenues (outputs) and the resultant figure is profits (or losses). Divisions of General Motors (e.g., Chevrolet or Pontiac), individual J.C. Penney stores, or similarly autonomous units are amenable to profit center management. We can also find profit centers "within" an organization. This can occur when, say, a maintenance department "sells" (via some internal bookkeeping transfer) its services to the rest of the organization, or a manufacturing division "sells" its completed units to the assembly division.
4. *Investment centers.*   Return on investment is sometimes a more appropriate measure of performance than any of the above three measures. In none of the above three cases did we consider the assets of the unit. When an investment center approach is used, expenses are subtracted from revenues and the resultant profit viewed as a percentage of total assets. For example, we could, using this basis, compare a small with a large hospital. With the above three methods we could not since a large hospital will normally have higher revenues, expenses, and profits. However, if the small hospital had a 10 percent return on investment compared to the other's 6 percent, we have a more realistic appraisal of the functioning of both entities.

Variable and fixed budgets.   Budgets can, but need not, be static once they are established. Most government agency budgets, once approved, are fixed. Some businesses have similar budgets. However, assume that we have a toy factory. If there is high demand for our toys, we may want to hire more workers, buy more machines, and run 24 hours a day. Obviously, expenses will be higher. If we were on a fixed budget, we would be stuck with our fixed limit and may not be able to expand production. On the other hand, we could have a budget that provides for higher expenditures in various categories depending on the level of production. Such variable budgets are obviously practical where total demand for our outputs is not known in advance *and* where a significant portion of costs are variable (versus fixed).

Recent budgeting developments.   Two recent developments in the budgeting process have largely come from government.* The planning–programming–budgeting system (PPBS) was introduced into the Department of Defense in 1961 and later into the entire executive branch by President Johnson in 1965.[11] As governor, Jimmy Carter used zero-based budgeting (ZBB) in Georgia and later, as President, he ordered it used in the executive branch.[12]

The basic steps in PPBS are:[13]

1. Specify and analyze the basic *objectives* in each major area of activity.
2. Analyze the *output* of the program in terms of these objectives.
3. Measure *total costs* of the program for as many years into the future as is practical.
4. Apply the *alternatives* that may be used to reach objectives.
5. Make the analysis an integral part of the overall budgetary process.

PPBS did, for a time, compel government agencies to better plan and control specific output-oriented endeavors. While it "failed" in the sense that it is no longer used, per se, it "succeeded" in that this mode of thinking about outputs lingers on.

ZBB is a process that forces an organization to budget "from scratch." That is, each budgeting period the organization reviews its operations from the assumption that everything starts the budget with zero resources (dollars) and must justify receiving any funds. Such an approach obviously differs from the incremental approach to budgeting which began not with zero, but with last year's budget, and then added to or subtracted from it. ZBB has three basic steps:

1. Formulate "decision packages" that define an organizational activity, its costs, and benefits.
2. Rank those activities done by an organization (or an organizational unit) in order of priority. The "decision packages" obviously aid in the ranking.

---

* It is beyond the scope of this book to discuss these developments in detail. However, the references cited will provide substantial coverage of both of these budgeting methods.

Exhibit 13–5
Some commonly used ratios

Profitability:

$$\text{Return on investment} = \frac{\text{Net profit}}{\text{Net worth}}$$

$$\text{Profit margin on sales} = \frac{\text{Net profit}}{\text{Total sales}}$$

Liquidity:

$$\text{Current ratio} = \frac{\text{Current assets}}{\text{Current liabilities}}$$

$$\text{Acid test} = \frac{\text{Current assets} - \text{inventory}}{\text{Current liabilities}}$$

$$\text{Average collection period} = \frac{\text{Accounts receivable} \times 365}{\text{Net credit sales}}$$

General financial
condition:

$$\text{Debt ratio} = \frac{\text{Total debt}}{\text{Net worth}}$$

$$\text{Times interest earned} = \frac{\text{Earnings before interest and taxes}}{\text{Total interest charges}}$$

$$\text{Inventory turnover} = \frac{\text{Cost of goods sold}}{\text{Average inventory}}$$

$$\text{Turnover of stockholders' equity} = \frac{\text{Net sales}}{\text{Net worth}}$$

3. Allocate resources first to the top ranked activity, then to the next, and so on, until the funds are no longer justified by the benefits, or until funds run out, whichever comes first.

Ratio analysis. Ratio analysis is concerned with using financial statement data to express relationships in terms of ratios or percentages. By using ratios (rather than comparing absolute figures), we can better observe relative changes over time in an organization's performance and we facilitate comparisons between organizations. Ratios are commonly computed for several categories: profitability, liquidity, and general financial condition.[14] Ratios can be devised and computed between virtually any financial measures. Many financial analysts have favorite (sometimes even secret!) ratios which they believe in. Exhibit 13–5 illustrates some of the more commonly used ratios.*

Depending upon particular operating problems, the general economy, competition, and similar factors, management will use different ratios. The desired values of these ratios tend to be similar among firms within the same industry, but these values may be significantly different from industry to industry.

---

* Reference to a basic text in accounting or managerial finance will provide many more ratios than shown here.

Cost controls.   Managers often find it useful to compare various costs within and between organizations. For example, in a firm manufacturing airplanes the accounting system keeps track of the direct labor costs (of those actually working on the planes) expended on various segments (e.g., fuselage, avionics, interior) as well as the indirect costs (e.g., maintenance, heat and lights) allocable to each unit produced. By keeping track of these costs, the plant manager is able to rapidly spot problem areas where costs seem to be rising. Also, the manager will be able to determine if improvements (e.g., a new machine in the paint shop, or extra training for radio installers) seem to be paying off in terms of increased productivity and/or lower costs.

REACTIONS TO CONTROL SYSTEMS

It should be obvious that controls are a necessary and valuable part of an organization. Yet controls can cause undesired, and sometimes unexpected, consequences.

Unanticipated consequences

At times a management desire for "better control" results in the establishment and imposition of sets of rules that are intended to regulate behavior and to result in a desired level of performance. However, such management behavior often stimulates the social system of the organization to react. The "increased control" may be resented by workers and they may well respond in a manner not anticipated by management. Exhibit 13–6 shows a model of the response developed by Gouldner.[15]

In this model we see that the use of rules was intended to increase management's power and raise the "tension state" of workers so as to put management more "in control." At the same time these rules create a situation where workers focus on what their minimum required behavior is (e.g., how few can I make before the boss yells at me?). Thus, organizational performance decreases which causes even closer supervision and an even more visible power orientation by management. The result is an even greater tension level which upsets the equilibrium originally based on the initial implementation of the rules.

Impact on morale

The restriction on personal freedom or the "big brother is watching" feeling brought on by many controls may lead to decreased job satisfaction.

On each landing, opposite the lift shaft, the poster with the enormous face gazed from the wall. It was one of those pictures which are so contrived that

Exhibit 13–6
Gouldner's model of response to control

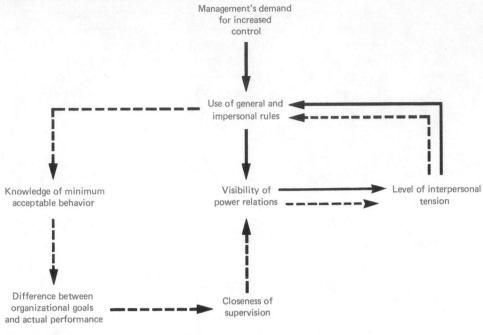

Source: Based on James G. March and Herbert A. Simon, *Organizations* (New York: John Wiley & Sons, Inc., 1958), p. 45.

the eyes follow you about when you move. "BIG BROTHER IS WATCHING YOU," the caption beneath it ran.[16]

Where increased control leads to changes that run in opposition to, say, job enrichment, the human response may well be negative. Management must weigh this possibility against the benefits brought about by the control system.

Narrow perspective

"You get what you measure" is a message that derives from the "you get what you reward" Skinnerian orientation discussed in Chapter 10. So long as workers *perceive* a connection between control system measures and their rewards (pay, promotions, and so on), they will be motivated to "look good"; i.e., to perform well on the measured items and perhaps ignore other relevant, but unmeasured factors.

Such behavior can obviously be detrimental to the organization. The phenomena of "bleeding the line" is a common response. Here a supervisor would force work-in-process through checkpoints toward the end of a period. Hence, the supervisor "looks good." But the disruption to the system and resultant increased costs are not measured. Police detectives measured on the number of completed cases may be "encouraged" to focus on easily solved burglary and car theft cases and thus leave the hard-to-solve murders and assaults on the "back burner."

Joseph Berliner relates an interesting case concerning Russian farmers which requires no elaboration:

For many years it had been the practice to take the livestock census on January 1. It would seem that January 1 is a rather harmless date; presumably it was selected by an innocent planner with the primary objective of facilitating schedules. However, the collective farms have targets of livestock holdings which they are required to meet as well as targets of meat deliveries to the State. Ordinarily the peasants would bring their stock for slaughter in the early fall, when they are fattest from the summer grazing. But in order to meet their livestock targets on January 1, they kept their stock through the cold early winter months so that they could be counted in the census. The consequence was a disastrous loss of weight. . . .[17]

Deliberate evasion and falsification

When measures aren't "audited" or if the audits are infrequent or poorly done, there may be ample opportunity for reporting false data. More than one person has "made out with a pencil" when in fact little was really done.[18]

Dalton provides an interesting glimpse at a well-organized falsification "system."[19] In a manufacturing plant "surprise inspections" were used to assure that foremen and shop managers did not have unauthorized equipment or spare parts. However, the inspectors, to maintain friendly relationships with their colleagues, the foremen, telephoned in advance of any inspection trips.

Notification that a count was under way provoked a flurry among executives to hide some of the parts. Motor and hand trucks with laborers and skilled workers who could be spared were assembled in a given department. Then, materials not to be counted were moved to: (1) little known and inaccessible spots in the plant; (2) basements and pits that were dirty and therefore unlikely to be examined; (3) departments that had already been inspected but could be approached circuitously while the counters were en route between the official storage areas; and (4) areas where other materials and supplies might be used as a camouflage for parts.[20]

A breakdown in management's authority system is the usual cause of a subversion/falsification system as far advanced as the one described by Dalton. When management is physically isolated from a plant or worksite, the propensity for this breakdown is increased. This is not to say that management must always behave in a traditional, autocratic, Theory X manner in order to preclude such behavior. Rather, it is to say that the control system itself should be subject to periodic controls or audits. Management should take steps to ensure that measures are valid, and do what can be done to prevent subversive behavior.

It is much easier to prevent the development of systematic cheating in an organization than to cure it once it has developed. Illegitimate practices that have become customary are likely to be defended like legitimate rights. The secretary feels entitled to take office supplies home for her children's schoolwork. The intern regards the free thermometers as a routine perquisite. The foreman cannot imagine operating his shop without a store of parts that do not have to be accounted for.[21]

Quantiphrenia[22]

"Hard data drives out the soft."* In other words, more measurable (i.e., "objective") phenomena tend to displace the qualitative (i.e., "subjective"). This problem would not exist if all objectives could be quantified; however, some admirable and desirable objectives are not so amenable. For example, "corporate good citizenship" or "social responsibility" are far less measurable than production rates or return on investment.

Quantifiable objectives are not necessarily more important just because they are measurable, but they often seem to receive greater attention *because of* the measurability. Perhaps in the future more enlightened and creative managers will be able to develop quantifiable measures for these current "unmeasurables."

SUMMARY

Controls are premised on plans and involve taking corrective action when actual performance deviates from a standard. We use controls on a pre-, current and postproduction basis with a major objective of preventing, rather than simply catching, mistakes.

A control system must strike a balance between its costs and the benefits it provides. Further, it must be timely and where possible, fit in with other organizational processes so as to minimize costs and system disruptions.

---

* Known as "Gresham's Law of Data." Compare this to the "real" Gresham's law ("bad money drives the good out of circulation") from economics.

The areas of personnel, general operations, and financial data are those in which controls are most commonly found. While some control devices are popular, every organization must develop and use controls that are pertinent to its particular needs.

While an obvious necessity, controls can have negative consequences. The reaction of the human element in organizations must be considered in designing and administering a control system.

GUIDES TO ACTION

1. Remember Caplow's admonition that it is easier to prevent systematic subversion of controls than to stop it once it has developed.

2. Always assess the costs inherent in control and assure yourself that the savings from mistakes prevented is worth more than the cost of the prevention.

3. Sometimes being "too accurate" is a problem. Being far above standard may be unnecessary and expensive.

4. All measures are subject to a margin of error. If something seems "out of sync" take another measure—quickly. The problem may be your measure and not the system being measured.

5. Use the control system not as a threat, but as a motivating tool. Standards that are known, appropriate, and adhered to give people a target at which to shoot. Achievement-oriented people welcome such a system.

6. "Never accept a 'numbers only' financial report; insist on prose: 'Good/bad' statements and prognosis."[23] Requiring subordinates to include judgmental statements presents a better picture of what is going on, saves you time, and develops their abilities.

NOTES

[1] Edwin B. Flippo and Gary M. Munsinger, *Management*, 4th ed. (Boston: Allyn and Bacon, Inc., 1978), p. 462.

[2] Edmund Faltermayer, "The Man Who Keeps Those Maytag Repairmen Lonely," *Fortune*, November 1977, p. 195.

[3] Ibid., p. 195.

[4] Ibid., p. 195.

[5] Ibid., p. 195.

[6] Peter M. Blau, *The Dynamics of Bureaucracy* (Chicago: University of Chicago Press, 1963).

[7] Flippo and Munsinger, *Management*, p. 467.

[8] Fremont A. Shull and Larry L. Cummings, "Enforcing the Rules: How Do Managers Differ?" *Personnel*, vol. 43, no. 1 (March–April 1966), pp. 38–39.

[9] See Leonard Sayles and George Strauss, *Human Behavior in Organizations* (Englewood Cliffs, N.J.: Prentice-Hall, Inc., 1966), pp. 329–38.

[10] See Robert N. Anthony and John Dearden, *Management Control Systems*, 3d ed. (Homewood, Ill.: Richard D. Irwin, 1976). © 1976 by Richard D. Irwin, Inc.,

[11] See Frederick C. Mosher, *Program Budgeting: Theory and Practice* (New York: Public Administration Service, 1954); Harley H. Hinrichs and Graeme M. Taylor, *Program Budgeting and Benefit-Cost Analysis* (Pacific Palisades, Calif.: Goodyear Publishing Company, Inc., 1969); George A. Steiner, "Program Budgeting," *Business Horizons*, vol. 8, no. 1 (Spring 1965), pp. 43–52; Samuel M. Greenhouse, "The Planning-Programming-Budgeting System," *Public Administration Review*, vol. 76, no. 4 (December 1966), pp. 271–77; and Allen Schick, "A Death in the Bureaucracy: The Demise of Federal PPBS," *Public Administration Review*, vol. 32, no. 2 (March–April 1973), pp. 146–56.

[12] See Peter A. Pyhrr, *Zero-Base Budgeting* (New York: John Wiley & Sons, Inc., 1973).

[13] Charles L. Schultze, "Why Benefit-Cost Analysis?" in Hinrichs and Taylor, *Program Budgeting and Benefit-Cost Analysis*, pp. 2–3.

[14] Earl P. Strong and Robert D. Smith, *Management Control Models* (New York: Holt, Rinehart & Winston, Inc., 1968), pp. 67–71.

[15] A. W. Gouldner, *Patterns of Industrial Bureaucracy* (New York: Free Press, 1954).

[16] George Orwell, *1984* (New York: The New American Library of World Literature, Inc., 1962), p. 5.

[17] Joseph S. Berliner, "A Problem in Soviet Business Administration," in George Grusky and George A. Miller, eds., *The Sociology of Organizations: Basic Studies* (New York: The Free Press, 1970), p. 561.

[18] F. J. Jasinski, "Use and Misuse of Efficiency Controls," *Harvard Business Review*, vol. 34, no. 4 (July–August 1956), pp. 105–12; and E. H. Caplan, *Management Accounting and Behavioral Science* (Reading, Mass.: Addison-Wesley Publishing Co., Inc., 1971).

[19] Melville Dalton, "Managing the Managers," *Human Organization*, vol. 14, no. 3 (Fall 1955), pp. 4–10.

[20] Ibid., p. 8.

[21] Theodore Caplow, *How to Run Any Organization* (Hinsdale, Ill.: Dryden Press, 1976), p. 113.

[22] Ross A. Webber, *Management* (Homewood, Ill.: Richard D. Irwin, 1975), p. 335. © 1975 by Richard D. Irwin, Inc.,

[23] Richard S. Sloma, *No-Nonsense Management: A General Manager's Primer* (New York: Macmillan Company, 1977), p. 41.

DISCUSSION QUESTIONS

1. Using the basic control model, develop a control process for use in producing a graduate from your college or university.

2. What are the characteristics of a strategic control point?

3. Using your college or university as in Question 1 above, list several pre-, current, and postcontrols for the academic (applicant becomes student becomes graduate) "manufacturing" process.

4. Why is discipline a control process?

5. How could you use a control or $\bar{X}$ chart, a Gantt chart, the critical path method, and a budget to monitor your progress as a student?

6. In exhibiting "unanticipated" responses to controls, what are employees *really* illustrating?

7. If your professor recommends a book, but then tells you that it won't be covered on a test, what is likely to occur? How does this relate to a control system?

CASE: OLD DOMINION RAILROAD

Old Dominion Railroad is a large north-central firm with headquarters in a large city. Each year, due to the large increase in summer railway passengers and vacations taken by regular employees, the company hires vacationing college students to help meet their personnel shortage. The large bulk of these workers are recruited by Old Dominion as waiters, cooks, and porters in conjunction with a federal program to help young black college students from the South meet their college expenses. The rest of these positions are filled by friends, neighbors, and relatives of Old Dominion employees. Old Dominion ex-

Exhibit 1
Rate of pay

Employee	Salary paid by company	Average hourly rate of tips	Gross hourly rate of pay
Waiter	$3.21	$0.75	$3.96
Cook	4.01	0	4.01
Steward	4.50	0	4.50

Total gross pay of summer employees (all waiters)

Average number of runs per summer	8
Average number of hours per run	×65
Total hours worked	520
Average hourly income	× 3.96
Total gross pay	$2,059.20

periences little difficulty in obtaining these temporary employees due to their attractive pay rates for summer workers (see Exhibit 1).

Mark West, a sophomore at a western university, was lucky enough to land one of these jobs through a friend's father who was employed by Old Dominion. Mark was one of the few non-blacks hired for this summer. Upon completing a physical examination and a two-hour orientation session, Mark was assigned to a dining car crew. Having never been a waiter and not having ridden a train since he was three years old, he was naturally apprehensive about his new job.

At 6:00 A.M. on June 15, Mark reported to the Old Dominion Commissary. He opened the door and was greeted by five middle-aged black workers who were changing into their uniforms. Each asked several questions and soon discovered that Mark was a "complete rookie." They humorously informed Mark that this wouldn't be an "easy job" but that they were happy to have him on their crew.

After several runs (see Exhibit 2), Mark was amazed to find himself still with the same crew. At the end of each run, the steward filled out a report evaluating the performance of each man. A summer employee job rested in the steward's hands because a bad report meant that he would either be fired or be placed on another crew. Placement on another crew often took a considerable amount of time and thus resulted in lost wages. After all of his blunders, Mark often wondered if they were just keeping him around for laughs.

Exhibit 2
A typical run

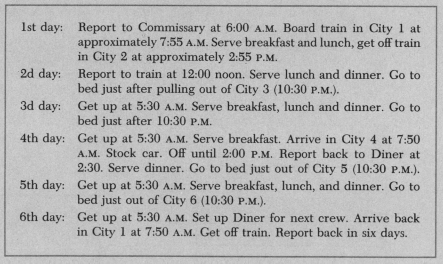

1st day:	Report to Commissary at 6:00 A.M. Board train in City 1 at approximately 7:55 A.M. Serve breakfast and lunch, get off train in City 2 at approximately 2:55 P.M.
2d day:	Report to train at 12:00 noon. Serve lunch and dinner. Go to bed just after pulling out of City 3 (10:30 P.M.).
3d day:	Get up at 5:30 A.M. Serve breakfast, lunch and dinner. Go to bed just after 10:30 P.M.
4th day:	Get up at 5:30 A.M. Serve breakfast. Arrive in City 4 at 7:50 A.M. Stock car. Off until 2:00 P.M. Report back to Diner at 2:30. Serve dinner. Go to bed just out of City 5 (10:30 P.M.).
5th day:	Get up at 5:30 A.M. Serve breakfast, lunch, and dinner. Go to bed just out of City 6 (10:30 P.M.).
6th day:	Get up at 5:30 A.M. Set up Diner for next crew. Arrive back in City 1 at 7:50 A.M. Get off train. Report back in six days.

Mark established many friendships, mainly with the black workers. During his early months on the job, he concluded that the best way to get along with the steward, cooks, and other waiters was to keep quiet. "Nobody likes a know-it-all 'rookie'." He also noticed that many of the rules that he had heard at orientation weren't enforced unless there was an inspector on the train. From the minute an inspector stepped on the train until he got off, all employees obeyed the rules to the letter. Cooks no longer drank on duty, waiters refrained from smoking and reading while on duty, and porters no longer ate in the dining car instead of the ranch car. Mark had often been told by these inspectors that if he saw anything out of the ordinary to let them know. Mark knew that this "reporting" was required by company policy and that summer employees who indeed reported infractions had always been rehired for the next summer. Mark was aware that he would need a job for next summer and that jobs at this rate of pay were hard to find.

Mark had also heard rumors to the effect that the railroads hired many undercover agents to check on the reliability of each worker. An agent could be the little old lady that you had just served or the young man with three children who just sat down in the dining car. Mark remembered what Bob Smith, a fellow waiter, had said about a young college student who had been caught by one of these people.

BOB: He just simply got up a tree and forgot to place an extra order on the check. Sure enough the lady he was waiting on was an undercover agent and railway officials were waiting for him when he got off the train. Ya know, Mark, he was a nice kid, something like you.

Mark's problem

It was late in the afternoon one day in July. The train was rolling along somewhere in Montana. The waiters and cooks were sitting around waiting for the evening customers to arrive when a young man with four children came into the car. Naturally, the youngest waiter would have to take care of these people while the others rested. The steward walked over and took their order and handed Mark, the youngest waiter, the top half of the check (see Exhibit 3). The steward said, "Five steak dinners, please." Mark proceeded

Exhibit 3
A check

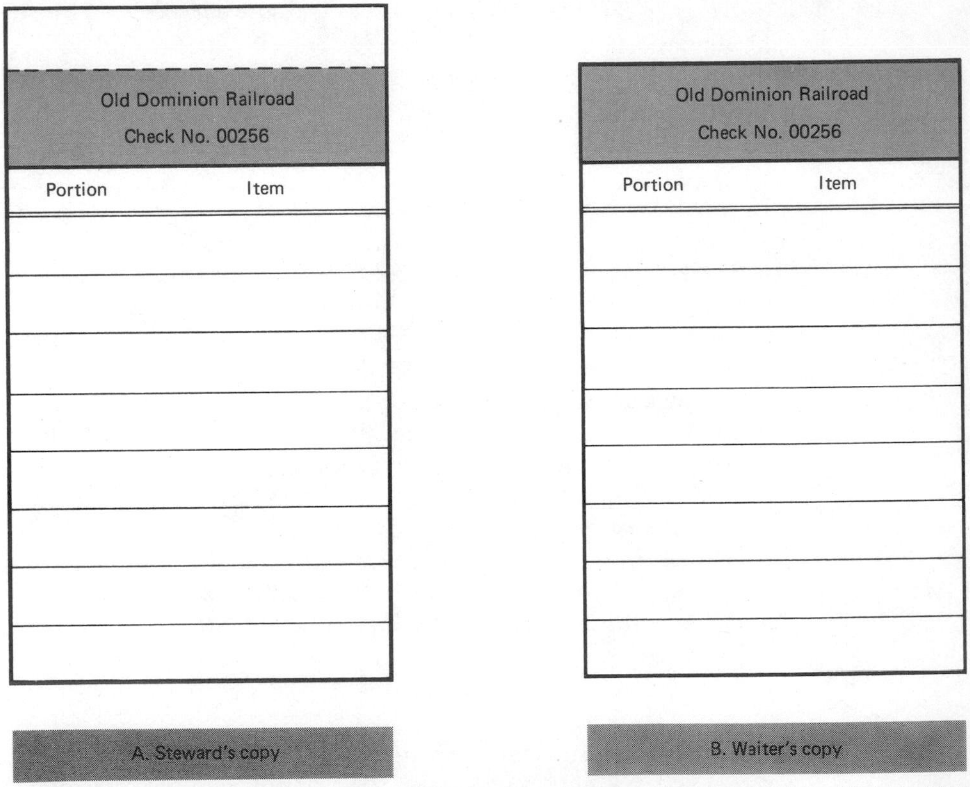

Old Dominion Railroad	
Check No. 00256	
Portion	Item
A. Steward's copy	

Old Dominion Railroad	
Check No. 00256	
Portion	Item
B. Waiter's copy	

back to the kitchen to place the order. Suddenly, he stopped. In the portion section of the check, there was nothing written. Thus, the steward could collect from the customer for five dinners and later fill in the check for one, while pocketing the cost of the additional four meals. Mark called Bob Smith over to ask what he should do.

BOB: Why don't you call him on it and tell him you want half? You could make about ten bucks on the deal.

MARK: I don't know.

BOB: Go ahead, I've seen Tow-Head* do it all the time.

MARK: Well, I just wouldn't feel right. What if that man's an undercover agent?

BOB: Oh, that's just one chance in a thousand.

MARK: Here, you can have the table and get half the money.

BOB: No thanks! Just do what you want, but you would be stupid not to collect half of that money.

Exhibit 4
Organizational chart—dining and sleeping car department

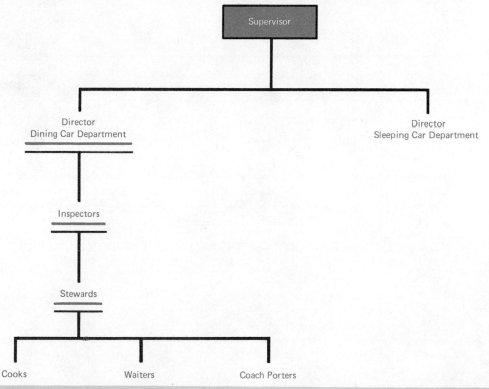

Question

Mark thought it over while he was preparing the appetizers. What should he do?

---

* Nickname of another waiter.

Section six
Improving the
organization

When the organization has reached its steady state, the focus of management is on searching for refinements in the ongoing system and applying improvement techniques.

Level of Organizational Outputs

SELECTION OF THE PRODUCT OR SERVICE	DESIGN OF THE SYSTEM	STAFFING THE ORGANIZATION	STARTUP OF THE ORGANIZATION	OPERATING THE ORGANIZATION IN THE STEADY STATE	IMPROVING THE ORGANIZATION	REVISION OF THE ORGANIZATION	TERMINATION OF THE ORGANIZATION
Decision-making processes; social value; goals; forecasts; policies; plans	Authority and responsibility; power; organizational structure; communications systems; job design	Work force planning; personnel management functions	Startup planning and scheduling; monitoring; alternative startup approaches	Motivation; leadership; production and operations management; control	Individual improvement programs and techniques; group conflict management: MBO	Evaluation of organizational policies; strategic choices; organizational change; organizational development	Partial terminations; cutback management; complete terminations; mergers; born-again strategies

t_0

Time

Chapter 14
Improving the organization

There's a better way to make everything, except babies.

Anonymous

A tantalizing question for any manager is "How do I make the organization run better?" In this chapter, we will propose some answers to this query by describing some widely used approaches for improving the management of human resources in the organization. In proceeding, we will cover concepts and methods developed to improve:

1. The individual manager.
2. The group with which the manager deals.
3. The system by which organizational goals are achieved.

THE INDIVIDUAL MANAGER

To our way of thinking, improving the performance of the individual manager entails two separate elements: (1) improving his or her use of time to facilitate getting the management job accomplished; and (2) developing the appropriate skills to permit that job to be done effectively. The two improvement approaches commonly applied to these elements are *time management* and *management development*, respectively, and we will consider them in order.

Time management

Peter Drucker has stated, "Those executives who really get something done, don't start with their work, but with their time." How true. And how true for doctors, lawyers, professors, and even students.*

___
* And scientists. A whimsical article by S. Evershamen entitled, "The Average Working Hours of a Scientist," shows the net working time out of a 60-year lifetime for scientists as follows:

	Years
Childhood, school, high school, college, university	24
Sleeping—8 hours a day*	20
Vacations, weekends, holidays (73 days per year)	12
Unspeakable necessities, ½ hour a day	1.25
Feeding, 1 hour per day	2.50
Total	59.75
Net working time	0.25 years = about 90 days

 * Sleeping hours during scientific discussions, lectures, and seminars are not taken into consideration.

Source: In Robert A. Baker, *Stress Analysis of a Strapless Evening Gown* (Englewood Cliffs, N.J.: Prentice Hall, Inc., 1963), p. 157.

Managers, because of the unstructured nature of their job, have the need for careful time control and, if they know some basic concepts of time management, have the opportunity to become highly effective in their use of time.

According to Oncken and Wass, there are three kinds of management time.[1] These are:

1. Boss-imposed time.   To accomplish those activities which the boss requires and which the manager cannot disregard without direct and swift penalty.
2. System-imposed time.   To accommodate those requests to the manager for active support from his peers. This must also be provided lest there be penalties, though not as direct or swift as from boss imposed time.
3. Self-imposed time.   To do those things which the manager originates or agrees to do himself. [Part of this kind of time is taken by subordinates and the remaining portion is discretionary. Self-imposed time, of course, is not subject to organizational penalty.][2]

Because the boss and system can impose penalties for not meeting time requirements of activities they initiate, the main area for time management improvement lies in careful use of self-imposed time. "The manager's strategy is therefore to increase the 'discretionary' component of his self-imposed time by minimizing or doing away with the subordinate component. He will then use the added increment to get better control over his boss-imposed and system-imposed activities."[3]

Reducing subordinate-imposed time basically entails avoiding entanglements in subordinates' decisions by requiring that they, not the manager, handle their own problems. Procedurally, this involves the manager setting the following ground rules with his or her subordinates:

1. Requiring that appointments be set for discussing a problem with the clear understanding that the subordinate's problem will at no time become the manager's problem.
2. Requiring "completed staff work"—the subordinate gathers data, summarizes, and has a recommended solution. (This step often will eliminate the problem being brought to the manager in the first place.)
3. Recognizing that "sharing" of a problem in a memo or in a casual conversation can transfer the decision-making "monkey" from the back of the subordinate to the back of the manager. (We refer to this as "upward delegation" and it is to be avoided at all costs.) This implies that subordinates will be rewarded for acting on their own and reporting routinely on what they have done. In the infrequent situations when this is not possible, the less desirable practices of recommending and then taking resulting action, or acting, and then advising at once, will be acceptable. A subordinate waiting to be told, or asking what to do will not be accepted, since this invariably transfers the monkey to the manager.

Exhibit 14–1
A $25,000 secret

Charles M. Schwab, one of the first presidents of Bethlehem Steel, asked an efficiency expert to suggest a way to improve the efficiency of his business. The efficiency expert, Ivy Lee, handed Schwab a blank sheet of paper and said, "Write down the six most important tasks you have to do tomorrow. Now number them in the order of their importance.

"The first thing in the morning start working on Number One until it is finished. Then tackle Number Two and so on. Don't be concerned if you have finished only one or two by quitting time. You'll be working on the most important ones. The others can wait. If you couldn't finish them all by this method, you couldn't have done so by any other method, and without some system, you'd probably have failed to finish the most important.

"Do this every working day and after you've convinced yourself of the value of this system, have your men try it. Try it as long as you wish, then send me a check for what you think it has been worth to you."

It is said that a few weeks later Schwab sent Lee a check for $25,000 with a letter saying this lesson was the most profitable he had ever learned. In five years, this plan was largely responsible for turning the unknown Bethlehem Steel Company into the largest independent steel producer in the world. And it helped to make Charles Schwab $100 million and the best known steel man in the world.

There are a number of handy hints for the manager dealing with his or her remaining discretionary time more effectively. Perhaps most valuable is the daily setting of priorities (see Exhibit 14–1, "A $25,000 Secret"). Longer range priorities are touched upon in Exhibit 14–2, "Getting Control of Your Time and Your Life."

Exhibit 14–2
Getting control of your time and your life

Probably the best known time-management expert is Alan Lakein, author of a popular paperback titled *How to Get Control of Your Time and Your Life.* Lakein glibly advises executives to "work smarter, not harder." He urges them to set lifetime goals, three-year goals, and six-month goals, which he says should then be subdivided into categories "A," "B," and "C" in order of precedence. Don't be afraid to include such "far-out wishes as losing forty pounds" or such uncensored fantasies as "climbing the Matterhorn or attending a group-sex party," he recommends. Businessmen, he feels, should identify both their "internal prime time" (when they do their clearest thinking) and their "external prime time" (the best period for dealing with others). These prime times should then be used for pursuing "A" goals.

Source: Ray Rowan, "Keeping the Clock from Running Out," *Fortune,* November 6, 1978, p. 77.

In setting priorities, the 80–20 rule* is a useful guide. That is, roughly 80 percent of a manager's time can be consumed by devoting attention to the many trivial duties which yield low results, while he or she should concentrate attention on the 20 percent of the duties—the vital few—which yield significant results.

To provide time to deal with the prioritized vital few, time management specialists have focused on eliminating time wasters. A sampling of time wasters and ways to eliminate them are given in Exhibit 14–3.

Exhibit 14–3
Eliminating time wasters

Telephone misuse
1. Use a callback system.
2. Have secretaries screen calls.
3. Group calls for specified times during the day.
4. Develop a commonly used list of phone numbers.
5. Learn how to terminate conversations, e.g.
   a. "I hope that information helped."
   b. "Joe, I have someone here in the office."
   c. "I'll see you Friday."
   d. Hang up on yourself in mid-sentence (last resort).

Excessive paperwork
1. Stop filing letters received (Instead, scribble your reply on each and send back).
2. Never handle a memo twice.
3. Set up an effective filing system.
4. Throw out everything possible every day.
5. Learn how to use a dictating machine.

Visitors
1. Let everyone know your available time.
2. Close your office door.
3. Go to subordinates' offices rather than your own. (This violates a power precept, but it allows you to leave quickly.)
4. Stick to appointment schedules.
5. Meet drop-ins at the door.
6. Remain standing if you wish a short conversation (or always have some object on office chairs).
7. Schedule your own small-talk time.

Miscellaneous
1. Learn to say "no."
2. Make that decision—give yourself a deadline.
3. Set realistic time estimates.
4. Take ten minutes every day to plan the day.

---

* This evolved from the "Pareto principle" named after economist Vilfredo Pareto, who discovered in the late 19th century that 20 percent of the people in Italy controlled 80 percent of the wealth.

Management development programs

One of the boom industries in the world today is management development programs. In addition to business school degree programs, formal management development programs are offered by consulting firms, moonlighting professors, and assorted experts in the social sciences, business, and government. From our experience, such programs are undertaken by organizations for any of several reasons:

1. A perceived need to bring the managers of the organization up to date in the latest management practices.
2. To eliminate some deficiency in the manager's prior training for his or her current job. (Promotion from a nonmanagerial position, or a broadened managerial responsibility typically initiate a need for management training.)
3. A company policy or philosophy which encourages its members to continue developing their skills. (This may be for recruiting purposes.)
4. Unspent money in a training budget near the end of the fiscal year which the responsible manager must disburse or face the risk of a reduced budget the next year.
5. To cope with the rapid expansion of the work force. General Motors and Motorola are examples of two firms which set up in-house training programs to deal with a pressing need for middle managers and first-line supervisors stemming from the opening of new facilities.

Whether designing or selecting a management development program, it is crucial that there be a close match between development needs and program content. In this regard, care should be taken to avoid the following pitfalls:

1. Incorrect match between program material and organizational position of participants. (E.g., superiors receiving broad policy level training, or middle managers receiving narrow, specialist training.)
2. Mixing of superiors and subordinates. While this *can* work successfully sometimes, the odds are against it because the boss brings his or her positional power to the meeting, thereby inhibiting the subordinate; or the subordinate outshines the boss with negative feelings carried back to the work setting.
3. Sending people to a course just because it looks good rather than following a carefully laid out development plan.

To get the most out of a development program, management should do the following:

1. Develop a list of the topics and goals of the program beforehand. Ideally, a committee consisting of the training specialist in the organization, the manager(s) who request the program, and representatives of the participant groups should be formed for this purpose.
2. Check out the credentials and experience of the training groups available and select that group which is willing and able to customize its program to fit the organization's objectives.
3. Require course evaluations at the conclusion of the program, and if possible

develop a means for determining the effectiveness of the course at a later point in time (at least six months later).

THE GROUP
Conflict

Managers manage people, and hence must confront the vagaries of human nature every day. In keeping score on these confrontations, a "victory" occurs when the subordinates work together effectively to achieve the goals of the organization, and a "defeat" occurs when conflicts between individuals inhibit movement in the right direction. One approach to dealing with such confrontations focuses on creating an organizational climate which fosters better working relationships. This falls under the heading of *organizational development* and is discussed in Chapter 16. The approach we will now describe looks at conflict as an ongoing characteristic of groups, and is concerned with ways to manage conflict directly.

The nature of conflict.   A scholarly definition of conflict might read as follows: "Opposition which arises due to scarcity of resources, unequal power and/or status, differing perceptions, or different value systems." While such a definition is quite accurate, it is often impractical in day-to-day interaction. Dues offers a more straightforward approach: "Conflict arises between two individuals when they disagree, and when one or both parties experiences sufficient discomfort with the situation. Such disagreements may concern disputes over scarce resources, value systems, jurisdictional issues, issues of fact, or other problems."[4]

How a manager will approach these situations is heavily influenced by the way in which he or she perceives conflict per se. If conflicts are seen as disruptions to be "dampened" or eliminated, it is viewed as a negative or undesirable occurrence. Indeed, some conflicts are unnecessary, and wasteful of the manager's time. However, many conflicts are capable of yielding new insights, or are likely to open up problems which the manager should address. Here conflicts are valuable feedback mechanisms and can serve a constructive purpose. These conflict types, which may be termed "constructive" and "destructive" are characterized by the outcomes presented in Exhibit 14–4.

Because conflict is a fact of human nature, it is also a recurring phenomena in modern organizations. If some conflicts are ultimately beneficial for the system, then the manager may actually wish, on occasion, to stimulate conflict. This strategy is especially useful when the problem is likely to arise in the future, and current procedures or plans are found wanting. Another reason for stimulating conflict is to increase sales. A healthy competition among salespersons can lead to greater profits. In essence, then, conflicts may have positive or negative consequences for the organization, and the way in which it is

Exhibit 14–4
Constructive and destructive conflict

Conflict is constructive when:	Conflict is destructive when:
1. It makes people sharpen their goals, methods, and procedures.	1. It syphons off energies which could otherwise be spent on productive activities.
2. It moves individuals or groups to higher accomplishments.	2. "Might" conquers "right."
3. Its resolution fosters mutual understanding.	3. It focuses on personalities rather than issues.
	4. It leads to such individual actions as frustration, aggression, withdrawal, obstruction and such group actions as strikes, slowdowns, and "jungle warfare."

framed or defined will in part determine the result. Of course, the method selected for the resolution/stimulation of conflict will contribute significantly.

Methods of managing conflict. A number of mechanisms have been identified to manage conflict. These include (1) expansion of resources, (2) avoidance, (3) smoothing, (4) compromise, (5) authoritative command, (6) changing human behavior, (7) changing organizational relationships, and (8) problem solving.

Expansion of resources. A classic cause of conflict is the fight over scarce resources—two dogs, one bone; two supervisors, one management position; two professors, one available office; and so on. Obviously, providing a second bone, managerial position, or office would be an easy way to resolve these conflicts. In practice, however, resources are usually scarce and hence other means must be found to deal with such situations.

Avoidance. One faculty acquaintance of ours used to make it a point to schedule all of his classes at locations where he would not encounter a particular administrator. He was thus able to state that for an entire year, no conflicts arose between them (alas, until he was thrust into a luncheon and three-hour meeting with him).

Smoothing. This can take the form of suppression—"sweeping the problem under the rug." The risk of this approach is that the conflict does not get resolved and in fact may become worse.

Compromise. The distinguishing feature of compromise is that it requires each party to give up something. Voting and arbitration—the formal methods of compromise—usually result in winners and losers and don't necessarily remove the cause of conflict. These methods also usually involve a third party who may increase tension and heighten differences simply by the process of negotiation. Still, compromise can be an effective mechanism for certain types of conflict. In disagreements between groups over "matters of principle," for example, Caplow suggests that the manager bring the factions together, make them work out a mutually acceptable compromise, and then throw all of his or her weight behind the compromise.[5] The zealots on each side will continue to argue but eventually will be forced to yield in light of the superior authority backing the compromise.

Forcing by authoritative command. The hierarchical structure in organizations is one of supervisor-subordinate relationships, with the supervisor the natural person responsible for resolving conflicts. When the supervisor resolves a conflict by using his or her authority, however, some important issues in the conflict may not be brought out. Also, the subordinate who is the loser in this conflict may not completely carry through the decisions of the supervisor. On the other hand, using authoritative power is often the only way of dealing with conflicts which are emotional or irrational, such as feuds. In such cases, Caplow suggests that the manager simply take one side or the other.[6] By giving full support to one of the feudists (preferably the strongest), the supervisor stands the best chance of keeping others out of the fray and may then prevent either the quitting or necessary firing of those involved in it. The logic of using authority to resolve this type of conflict is that others, seeing the supervisory backing of one of the participants, will realize that supporting the apparent loser wouldn't make sense. By quickly settling such conflicts, stronger feelings are avoided and both parties can get over the feud more easily.

Changing human behavior. Changing behavior traditionally means that people become educated to see the other fellow's problem, to look at the facts, or to come to grips with his or her own values and emotions in the conflict situation. Providing such education, of course, has implications far beyond just conflict resolution. Organizations would like to have their members embody these attributes but the process is time-consuming, uncertain, and costly. (See the section on "Organization Development" in Chapter 16.)

Changing organizational relationships. Conflict can be reduced by transferring people, developing new organizational relationships (setting up a new department, developing a coordinator position, or by decoupling conflicting units*), or expanding departments to include conflicting units. To illustrate

---

* Decoupling can take several forms: One is to set up buffer inventories so that interdependence between two groups can be loosened; e.g., Department X furnishes work-in-process and Department Y uses this to make the final product. A buffer inventory may be set up so that Department X places its components in a big bin ahead of Y's needs. If X falls behind, Y will have the inventory to draw upon. Another approach is to decouple by duplicating the facilities of one department upon which another is dependent. For example, many departments may maintain a backup Xerox machine in case central duplicating bogs down, a hospital operating room maintains a backup generator in case of power failure, or the sales division may maintain a reserve pool of gasoline in case the central motor pool runs dry.

the latter case, a social welfare function might be made part of a police task force to stop crime, rather than being a separate unit which is placed in an advisory position. Related to this approach is identifying a superordinate goal which requires conflicting sides to "bury the hatchet" in order to deal with a more important problem of mutual concern.

Problem solving. This method of resolving conflict attempts to confront the issue directly, focusing on identifying and clarifying the underlying causes of the conflict and moving systematically toward its resolution. Emphasis is on issues rather than people, with the end objective of identifying mutually acceptable ways of dealing with "the problem." The approach attempts to bring forth similarity of views rather than differences and to avoid deciding who is right or wrong. Unfortunately, while the method is inherently appealing, its use is generally limited to situations involving misunderstandings rather than basic differences in values. Thus, conflicts involving religion, politics, or pot smoking are unlikely to be resolved by problem solving.

A comparative study of conflict resolution methods. Robert R. Burke asked 53 managers to describe their experiences in particularly good and particularly bad conflict resolution attempts. The results of the study are given in Exhibit 14–5. An analysis indicates that where resolutions of conflict were perceived to be effective, problem solving was the most common method (58.5 percent), followed by forcing (24.5 percent), and compromise (11.3 percent). When resolution was perceived as ineffective, forcing was most common (79.2 percent). Interpreting the results, Burke notes that forcing was seen as effective by the "winners" and ineffective by the "losers" of a win-lose conflict. Whether the organization truly won or lost in terms of more effective performance by the managers involved was not known. As Burke points out, more research is needed, yet these findings indicate that problem solving is generally a good strategy.

Exhibit 14–5
Methods associated with effective and ineffective conflict resolution

	Effective resolution (percent)	Ineffective resolution (percent)
Withdrawal	0.0	9.4
Smoothing	0.0	1.9
Compromise	11.3	5.7
Forcing	24.5	79.2
Problem solving	58.5	0.0
Other (still unresolved; unable to determine how resolved, etc.)	5.7	3.8

Source: Adapted from Ronald J. Burke, "Methods of Resolving Superior-Subordinate Conflict: The Constructive Use of Subordinate Differences and Disagreements," *Organizational Behavior and Human Performance*, July 1970, p. 403.

Methods for stimulating productive conflict. At the outset, we wish to point out that there is a fine line between stimulating productive conflict and simply poor management. Thus, a big mental "caution" sign should be placed in front of this section to make the reader aware that the techniques for stimulating conflict should be invoked only after the manager is well attuned to his or her people (and secure in his or her job).

Communication overload and information repression. Providing "too much" information can be thought of as a strategy to force individuals to separate in a competitive fashion the important actions from the unimportant ones. Essentially, subordinates are forced to think.

Repression of information from certain individuals while providing it to others alters power relationships by giving those with more information greater (potential) power than those with less information. As was noted in Chapter 6, those who control the information in an organization control the organization. Also brought out in Chapter 6 was that simply replacing or adding people to the list of memo recipients can stimulate an individual to find out about why he or she is bypassed or why others have suddenly become equals.

Changing the organization structure and size. People can be perceptually demoted by raising the position of someone else. In manufacturing, for example, if the quality control manager is rejecting too many parts coming off the assembly line, the previously lower ranking production manager might be elevated to the same organizational level to equalize the desire for output with the desire for, say, perfect quality.

Management style. A manager may easily stimulate conflict by unequal rewards, task assignments, or status awarded to his or her subordinates. Even in situations where there are enough resources to go around, the manager may find it desirable to engage in "unfair" treatment to get people moving, to ask questions, or simply to make the have-nots try harder. Perhaps the most common way a manager may stimulate conflict is by forcing all subordinates to solve disagreements among themselves. In essence, this leads to survival of the fittest.

THE SYSTEM

Management by objectives (MBO)

The basketball coach of Duke University "has instituted something called Management by Objectives, a system borrowed from the head of the University of Utah business school wherein a player's weekly performance in everything from grades to free throw shooting . . . is monitored." (*Sports Illustrated,* November 23, 1978).

MBO is a formalized procedure for setting goals and appraising performance of individuals within an organization. What makes it different from the general process of management is its focus on measuring and rewarding output as opposed to the activities which lead to that output. That is, under an MBO system employees are not rewarded for being "good guys," for being "sharp dressers," or for being "fast talkers." They are rewarded for achieving objectives which measurably contribute to the overall objectives of the organization. At first glance, the reader may be surprised that MBO is worthy of extended discussion because it would seem that "good management" would naturally focus on results, both in planning and appraising performance. Unfortunately, however, as has been shown time and time again, this is not standard operating procedure in many organizations. The reasons for this vary: objective setting is hard work; things have been going OK, so why rock the boat; nobody ever thought of it; it's just one more thing for managers to worry about; and so

Exhibit 14–6
Linking of functions and objectives

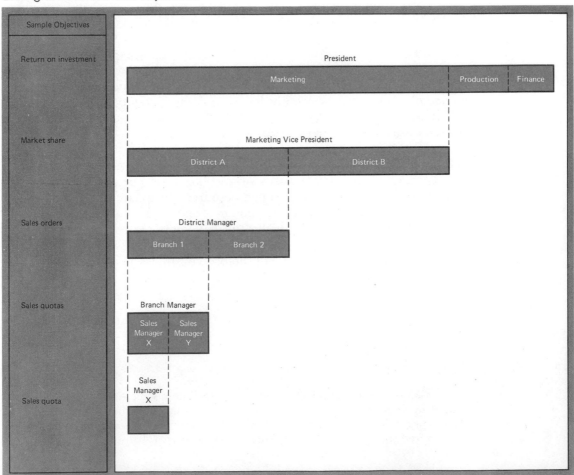

on. In short, there are many excuses for not having some type of MBO system, but unless management is content to operate at a lower level of effectiveness than it might, no excuse is compelling.

The MBO process. There are two essential components of an MBO system. One is the linking of objectives through the hierarchy in such a way as to assure achievement of the overall objectives of the organization as identified by top management. The other component is the interpersonal objective setting and performance appraisal process carried out between boss and subordinate. As we shall demonstrate, these two components are closely interrelated.

Linking of objectives. The way in which objectives are linked can be illustrated by reference to Exhibit 14–6. At the top of the exhibit, we see the objectives of the president of the organization which are met by the accomplishment of the objectives of various segments of the firm. If marketing, production, and finance achieve their objectives, the president of the firm will meet most, if not all, of the objectives for that position. The linking process is indicated by the breaking out of smaller and smaller boxes which reflect the relative narrowing of objectives (and responsibilities) from the top of the organization down to the first-line supervisor or to the sales manager. In practice, the linking process (or as it is often called, the cascading of objectives) follows the planning and budgeting cycle of the organization. Top management articulates its general objectives for the coming fiscal year; lower organizational levels use these for guidance in proposing their own more specific objectives, which are then discussed and modified (as we shall describe in a moment), and finally codified as premises for the plan and budget for the year.

Objective setting and performance appraisal. The heart of an MBO system is the joint development of objectives and periodic review sessions on accomplishment of objectives. An important prerequisite to these activities, however, is the clarification of the boundaries of the subordinate's job responsibilities. It is interesting (and somewhat surprising) to note that boss and subordinate often disagree on what the subordinate's job really is. The results of one widely cited study (Exhibit 14–7) show a high degree of misunderstanding between boss/subordinate pairs about various aspects of the job.

Exhibit 14–7
Perceptual differences of boss/subordinate pairs regarding subordinate's job

	Agreement on half or less of components (percent)	Agreement on more than half of components (percent)
Job duties	54	46
Job qualifications	67	33
Performance	92	8

Source: Norman Maier et al., *Supervisor-Subordinate Communication in Management* (New York: American Management Associates, 1961).

Joint objective setting entails categorizing the subordinate's job into (1) standard or routine objectives, (2) problem solving/innovation objectives, and (3) personal development objectives. These become the basis for agreeing upon specific output targets for the coming year for various objectives within each category. (Procedurally, the subordinate does this before meeting with the boss.) Standard or routine objectives relate to the basic elements of the job as stated in the job description. Problem solving/innovation objectives or opportunities refer to significant problems facing the subordinate. Personal devel-

Exhibit 14–8
Examples of objectives on MBO worksheet

STANDARD OR ROUTINE OBJECTIVES

(1)	*(2)*	*(3)*	
		Involvement I, M, L*	
Weight	*My major standard duties according to my job description*	*Supervisor*	*Other*
B*	1. Sales forecast accuracy within ± 10 percent	L	I
A	2. Achieve a market share of 30 percent	I	I

PROBLEM SOLVING/INNOVATION OBJECTIVES

(1)	*(2)*	*(3)*	*(4)*	*(5)*	
	Nature of innovation/ problem	*Means of achievement/ solution*		*Involvement I, M, L**	
Weight			*Output*	*Supervisor*	*Other*
B*	Evaluate radically new product	Market survey	Report by 10/30/80	L	M
A	High turnover of salespeople (25 percent)	Turnover analysis with recommendation	Reduce to 10 percent within 12 months	L	M

PERSONAL DEVELOPMENT

(1)	*(2)*	*(3)*	*(4)*
Weight	*Growth area*	*Means for achievement*	*Growth indicator*
C*	Understanding of psychology	American Marketing Association Training program	Certificate of completion

*Key: Weight: Involvement:
  A—Critical   I—Important role in accomplishment.
  B—Necessary   M—Moderate role in key situations.
  C—Moderate   L—Light role—mostly informational.

opment objectives refer to improving the subordinate's job-related skills. Exhibit 14–8 illustrates examples of each of these objectives as they might appear on an MBO work sheet for a marketing manager. After the objectives are agreed upon by both supervisor and subordinate, they are then typed and copies are retained by each party. This listing of perhaps 8 to 12 objectives becomes a performance contract providing a basis for an annual performance appraisal.

Note that the work sheets have a provision for setting priorities among objectives and for indicating the extent of support required by the job holder in meeting the objectives. Both of these elements are extremely important. Setting priorities permits the employee to really focus on what counts, and provides a natural basis for more effective time management. Identification of support required indicates to the boss what resources (time and financial) will have to be allocated to assist each subordinate in getting the job done. This, in turn, forces the boss to weigh the relative importance of all objectives within his or her department—a very healthy exercise indeed.

Performance appraisal under MBO is used as a means for supervisor and subordinate to look dispassionately at results achieved or not achieved over the year. Usually, raises and bonuses are not discussed directly at this meeting, since they tend to create an atmosphere of debate rather than objective evaluation. The financial aspect is brought into play in a separate review session. In addition to the end of the year reviews, many MBO systems call for periodic review sessions two or three times a year. The purpose of these meetings is for the boss to give feedback on progress to date and reallocate resources if need be, or in some cases to change objectives in light of changing circumstances. A simplified summary of the major steps in MBO are given in Exhibit 14–9.

Exhibit 14–9
Summary of major steps in MBO

Objectives for each department suggested by top management
as part of annual planning process

Specific objectives prepared by each manager

Meetings between each manager and subordinate managers to discuss
feasibility of objectives and assistance needed to achieve them

Periodic performance appraisal to see if objectives have been
met or need to be reviewed

Exhibit 14–10
Philosophy and rationale of the objectives approach

Rationale	Percent
1. Link evaluation to performance	35.4
2. Aid manager in planning	25.0
3. Motivate managers	22.9
4. Increase boss-subordinate interaction and feedback	22.9
5. Develop management potential	16.6
6. Link company objectives to department objectives	16.6
7. Managers know what their job is	12.5
8. Give management information about what's going on at lower levels	8.3
9. Management club to pressure performance	6.3
10. No mention	14.5

Source: Stephen J. Carroll, Jr., and Henry L. Tosi, Jr., *Management by Objectives, Applications and Research* (New York: The Macmillan Company, 1973), p. 23.

Evaluation of MBO.   A survey by Carroll and Tosi indicates the philosophy and rationale of MBO as perceived by 48 managers (Exhibit 14–10).

It is interesting to note that empirical research on MBO tends to confirm that reasons 1–8 as to why MBO is used do in fact mark a successful MBO implementation, while reason 9 is a major source of unsuccessful implementations.

Other factors which affect the success of MBO are: top-management support of the program both at the start and continually thereafter; setting of individual objectives which are both challenging and attainable; carefully documenting planned objectives and their extent of attainment; and fostering the philosophy that MBO is part of management, not just "something else to do." Recent research on MBO suggests also that MBO can be made more effective if teams of managers on the same organizational level get together and develop objectives which take into account their needs to collaborate in goal achievement. For example, many sales objectives and production objectives are interrelated and it only makes sense for some of them to be developed jointly. Extending this notion, French and Hollmann propose that a senior manager and his or her subordinates meet as a group to identify objectives which must be accomplished by integrated team effort.[7] This proposal corresponds directly with the original description of MBO by Peter Drucker: "Right from the start . . . emphasis should be on team efforts and team results."[8]

SUMMARY

The topics covered in this chapter are often interrelated in application. Time management, conflict management, and MBO are common topics in management development programs. Effective use of any one of the improvement techniques can show positive results in application of the others.

There are, of course, other techniques used in improving organizational performance. But, with the exception of organizational development approaches discussed in Chapter 16, most of these are oriented toward specific organizational functions or problem areas. Examples of those which have received broad application are:

1. *Zero defects programs.* Focusing on improving product quality.
2. *Human resource accounting.* Recognizing personnel as an investment and hence an accounting asset rather than an expense.
3. *Cost reduction programs.* Attempting to make employees cost conscious by setting up awards for identifying cost savings.
4. *Work simplification programs.* Improving productivity through better work methods.
5. *Value analysis/value engineering.* Setting up departments which are charged with reducing costs associated with product design or manufacture.

The reader will no doubt discover other improvement programs during the course of his or her career. Also, many organizations have taken such concepts as MBO and modified them, or even changed their name. Retitling often is done to give a technique the company's own distinctive stamp, or to avoid the negative connotations which arise from unsuccessful applications of the technique elsewhere.

GUIDES TO ACTION

1. Improvement programs of any kind work best when top management is committed to making them work.

2. The only true measure of top management commitment to an improvement program is the amount of money allocated to it in the budget. While proclamations are important in getting the attention of the rank and file manager, earmarked funds indicate the extent to which a program has management's attention.

3. Beware of "packaged programs." Consultants (including on occasion, the authors) think that they have *the* solution to your management problems. "Just use the XYZ system and your troubles will vanish." Alas, "a one-size improvement program" does not fit all. Improvements should be customized, and this takes work on the part of the user as well as the developer.

4. Any improvement program works best if it is simple. The more complex the mechanics to administer the program, the more the manager will have to rely on specialists to keep it going. Thus, beware of "whistles and bells" accessories to a program which sound good in theory but are difficult to use in practice.

NOTES

[1] William Oncken and Donald L. Wass, "Management Time: Who's Got the Monkey?" *Harvard Business Review,* vol. 52, no. 6 (November–December, 1974), pp. 75–80.

[2] Ibid., p. 75.

[3] Ibid., p. 76.

[4] Michael T. Dues, "A Manager's Guide to Conflict Resolution," California State University, Sacramento, Communication Studies Dept. Occasional Paper, 1978, p. 2.

[5] Theodore Caplow, *How to Run Any Organization* (Hinsdale, Ill.: Dryden Press, 1976), p. 173.

[6] Ibid., p. 170.

[7] Wendell L. French and Robert W. Hollmann, "Management by Objectives: The Team Approach," *California Management Review,* vol. 17, no. 3 (Spring 1975), pp. 13–22.

[8] Peter F. Drucker, *The Practice of Management* (New York: Harper & Bros., 1954), p. 126.

DISCUSSION QUESTIONS

1. What are your three greatest time wasters? How might you eliminate them? Do you *want* to eliminate them?

2. Has anybody put a "time monkey" on your back this week? Have you put one on anybody else?

3. Time management really means "organize your life to get more work done." Comment?

4. Why should a manager be wary of "packaged" training programs?

5. Your younger brother and sister, ages 8 and 9, respectively, are fighting over who gets to watch his or her "favorite TV show," since both shows are appearing at the same time on different stations. Which approach would you follow to resolve the conflict?

6. Why is the Middle East conflict so difficult to resolve?

7. Which of the methods listed in Exhibit 14–5 do you usually apply in resolving conflicts. Has it worked?

8. What are the two basic components of an MBO system? Have you ever worked under an MBO system?

9. Use the format given in Exhibit 14–8 to specify your personal development objectives for the next school term.

10. When do you think you would encounter significant conflict between boss and subordinate in MBO?

11. Is it possible, in your opinion, to manage effectively without some form of MBO?

CASE: THE CASE OF THE MISSING TIME*

It was approximately 7:30 Tuesday morning when Chet Craig, manager of the Norris Company's central plant, swung his car out of the driveway of his suburban home and headed toward the plant, located some six miles away just inside the Midvale city limits. It was a beautiful day. The sun was shining brightly, and a cool, fresh breeze was blowing. The trip to the plant took about 20 minutes and gave Chet an opportunity to think about plant problems without interruption.

The Norris Company owned and operated three printing plants with a nationwide business in quality color work. It was a closely held company with some 350 employees, nearly half of whom were employed at the central plant, the largest of the three. The company's main offices were also located in the central plant building.

Chet had started with the Norris Company as an expediter in its eastern plant ten years earlier, just after he graduated from Ohio State. After three years, he was promoted to production supervisor and two years later was made assistant to the manager of the eastern plant. A year and a half ago, he had been transferred to the central plant as assistant to the plant manager; one month later, when the former manager retired, he was promoted to plant manager.

---

* From Garret L. Bergen and William V. Haney, *Organizational Relations and Management Action* (New York: McGraw-Hill Book Company, 1966), pp. 169–73.

Chet was in good spirits as he relaxed behind the wheel. As his car picked up speed, the hum of the tires on the newly paved highway faded into the background. Various thoughts occurred to him, and he said to himself, "This is going to be the day to really get things done."

He began to run through the day's work, first one project, then another, trying to establish priorities. After a few minutes, he decided that the open-end unit scheduling was probably the most important—certainly the most urgent. He frowned for a moment as he recalled that on Friday the vice president and general manager had casually asked him if he had given the project any further thought. Chet realized that he had not been giving it much attention lately. He had been meaning to get to work on this idea for over three months, but something else always seemed to crop up. "I haven't had much time to sit down and really work it out," he said to himself. "I'd better get going and hit this one today for sure." With that, he began to break down the objectives, procedures, and installation steps of the project. He grinned as he reviewed the principles involved and calculated roughly the anticipated savings. "It's about time," he told himself. "This idea should have been followed up long ago." Chet remembered that he had first conceived of the open-end unit scheduling idea almost two years ago, just prior to leaving the eastern plant. He had talked it over with his boss, Jim Quince, manager of the plant, and both agreed that it was worth looking into. The idea was temporarily shelved when he was transferred to the central plant a month later.

A blast from a passing horn startled him, but his thoughts quickly returned to other plant projects he was determined to get under way. He started to think through a procedure for simpler transport of dies to and from the eastern plant. Visualizing the notes on his desk he thought about the inventory analysis he needed to identify and eliminate some of the slow-moving stock items, the packing controls which needed revision, and the need to design a new special-order form. He also decided that this was the day to settle on a job printer to do the simple outside printing of office forms. There were a few other projects he couldn't recall offhand, but he could tend to them after lunch, if not before. "Yes, sir," he said to himself, "this is the day to really get rolling."

Chet's thoughts were interrupted as he pulled into the company parking lot. When he entered the plant, Chet knew something was wrong as he met Al Noren, the stockroom foreman, who appeared troubled. "A great morning, Al," Chet greeted him cheerfully.

"Not so good, Chet; my new man isn't in this morning," Noren growled.

"Have you heard from him?" asked Chet.

"No, I haven't," replied Al.

Chet frowned as he commented, "These stock handlers assume you take it for granted that if they're not here, they're not here, and they don't have to call in and verify it. Better ask personnel to call him."

Al hesitated for a moment before replying. "O.K., Chet, but can you find me a man? I have two cars to unload today."

As Chet turned to leave, he said, "I'll call you in half an hour, Al, and let you know."

Making a mental note of the situation, Chet headed for his office. He greeted the group of workers huddled around Marilyn, the office manager, who was discussing the day's work schedule with them. As the meeting broke up, Marilyn picked up a few samples from the clasper, showed them to Chet, and asked if they should be shipped that way or if it would be necessary to inspect them. Before he could answer, Marilyn went on to ask if he could suggest another clerical operator for the sealing machine to replace the regular operator, who was home ill. She also told him that Gene, the industrial engineer, had called and was waiting to hear from Chet.

After telling Marilyn to go ahead and ship the samples, he made a note of the need for a sealer operator and then called Gene. He agreed to stop by Gene's office before lunch and started on his routine morning tour of the plant. He asked each foreman the types and volumes of orders they were running, the number of people present, how the schedules were coming along, and the orders to be run next; helped the folding room foreman find temporary storage space for consolidating a carload shipment; discussed quality control with a pressman who had been running poor work; arranged to transfer four people temporarily to different departments, including two for Al in the stockroom; talked to the shipping foreman about pickups and special orders to be delivered that day. As he continued through the plant, he saw to it that reserve stock was moved out of the forward stock area; talked to another pressman about his requested change of vacation schedule; had a "heart-to-heart" talk with a press helper who seemed to need frequent reassurance; approved two type orders and one color order for different pressmen.

Returning to his office, Chet reviewed the production reports on the larger orders against his initial projections and found that the plant was running behind schedule. He called in the folding room foreman, and together they went over the lineup of machines and made several necessary changes.

During this discussion, the composing room foreman stopped in to cover several type changes, and the routing foreman telephoned for approval of a revised printing schedule. The stockroom foreman called twice—first to inform him that two standard, fast-moving stock items were dangerously low; later to advise him that the paper stock for the urgent Dillon job had finally arrived. Chet made the necessary calls to inform those concerned.

He then began to put delivery dates on important and difficult inquiries received from customers and salesmen. (The routine inquiries were handled by Marilyn.) While he was doing this, he was interrupted twice: once by a sales correspondent calling from the West Coast to ask for a better delivery date than originally scheduled; once by the personnel vice president asking Chet to set a time when he could hold an initial training and induction interview with a new employee.

After dating the customer and salesmen inquiries, Chet headed for his morning conference in the executive office. At this meeting, he answered the sales vice president's questions in connection with "hot" orders, complaints, the status of large-volume orders, and potential new orders. He then met with the general manager to discuss a few ticklish policy matters and to answer "the old man's" questions on several production and personnel problems. Before leaving the executive office, he stopped at the office of the secretary-treasurer to inquire about delivery of cartons, paper, and boxes, and to place a new order for paper.

On the way back to his own office, Chet conferred with Gene about two current engineering projects. When he reached his desk, he lit a cigarette and looked at his watch. It was ten minutes before lunch—just time enough to make a few notes of the details he needed to check in order to answer knotty questions raised by the sales manager that morning.

After lunch, Chet started again. He began by checking the previous day's production reports, did some rescheduling to get out urgent orders, placed appropriate delivery dates on new orders and inquiries received that morning, consulted with a foreman on a personal problem. He spent some 20 minutes at the TWX,* going over mutual problems with the eastern plant.

By midafternoon Chet had made another tour of the plant, after which he met with the personnel director to review with him a touchy personal problem raised by one of the clerical employees, the vacation schedules submitted by his foremen, and the pending job evaluation program. Following this conference, Chet returned to his office to complete the special statistical report for Universal Waxing Corporation, one of Norris' best customers. As he finished the report, he discovered that it was ten after 6 and he was the only one left in the office. Chet was tired. He put on his coat and headed through the plant toward the parking lot. On the way out, he was stopped by both the night supervisor and the night layout foreman for approval of type and layout changes.

With both eyes on the traffic, Chet reviewed the day he had just completed. "Busy?" he asked himself. "Too much so—but did I accomplish anything?" His mind raced over the day's activities. "Yes and no" seemed to be the answer.

---

* Leased private telegram communication system using teletypewriter.

"There was the usual routine, the same as any other day. The plant kept going, and I think it must have been a good production day. Any creative or special project work done?" Chet grimaced, "No."

With a feeling of guilt, he probed further, "Am I an executive? I'm paid like one, respected like one, and have a responsible assignment, with the necessary authority to carry it out. Yet one of the greatest values a company derives from an executive is his innovative thinking and accomplishments. What have I done about it? An executive needs some time for thinking. Today was a typical day, just like most other days, and I did little, if any, creative work. The projects that I so enthusiastically planned to work on this morning are exactly as they were yesterday. What's more, I have no guarantee that tomorrow night or the next night will bring me any closer to their completion. This is a real problem, and there must be an answer."

Chet continued, "Night work? Yes, occasionally. This is understood. But I've been doing too much of this lately. I owe my wife and family some of my time. When you come down to it, they are the people for whom I'm really working. If I am forced to spend much more time away from them, I'm not meeting my own personal objectives. What about church work? Should I eliminate that? I spend a lot of time on this, but I feel I owe God some time, too. Besides, I believe I'm making a worthwhile contribution in this work. Perhaps I can squeeze a little time from my fraternal activities. But where does recreation fit?"

Chet groped for the solution. "Maybe I'm just rationalizing because I schedule my own work poorly. But I don't think so. I've studied my work habits carefully, and I think I plan intelligently and delegate authority. Do I need an assistant? Possibly, but that's a longtime project, and I don't believe I could justify the additional overhead expenditure. Anyway, I doubt whether it would solve the problem."

By this time, Chet had turned off the highway onto the side street leading to his home. "I guess I really don't know the answer," he told himself as he pulled into his driveway. "This morning everything seemed so simple, but now——"

Questions

1. How does Chet waste time? (List his "time wasters".)
2. Can you identify some monkeys placed on Chet's back?
3. Suggest ways in which Chet might improve his use of time.
4. Based upon Chet's situation, should the Norris Company introduce an MBO system for its employees?

Section seven
Revision of the
organization

Times change, and hence the organization must change. Goals and plans must be reassessed and perhaps new strategies adopted. Managers must be capable of analyzing strategic choices and of implementing change in organizations in such a way that technical as well as behavioral issues are effectively considered.

SELECTION OF THE PRODUCT OR SERVICE	DESIGN OF THE SYSTEM	STAFFING THE ORGANIZATION	STARTUP OF THE ORGANIZATION	OPERATING THE ORGANIZATION IN THE STEADY STATE	IMPROVING THE ORGANIZATION	REVISION OF THE ORGANIZATION	TERMINATION OF THE ORGANIZATION
Decision-making processes; social value; goals; forecasts; policies; plans	Authority and responsibility; power; organizational structure; communications systems; job design	Work force planning; personnel management functions	Startup planning and scheduling; monitoring; alternative startup approaches	Motivation; leadership; production and operations management; control	Individual improvement programs and techniques; group conflict management; MBO	Evaluation of organizational policies; strategic choices; organizational change; organizational development	Partial terminations; cutback management; complete terminations; mergers; born-again strategies

Level of Organizational Outputs

t_0

Time

Chapter 15
Evaluation of the organization and strategic planning

A business can tolerate a truly enormous number of errors in detail—if the strategic direction is relevant and correct.

Richard Sloma
No-Nonsense Management

I don't meet competition, I crush it.

Charles Revson,
president of Revlon

Every organization from time to time should "look in the mirror" to see where it is now, and "in the crystal ball" to see where it will be in the future. To conjure up these images requires (1) an evaluation of current activities, and (2) the development of a general plan of action, or corporate strategy, to help shape its destiny. These evaluation/planning undertakings are usually carried out by a planning staff in large organizations at periodic intervals (typically every three to five years). Because the outcome of their endeavors provides the general thrust of the organization in its competitive environment, they are naturally of great concern to top-level management. In addition, the resultant overall strategic plan provides the "marching orders" for middle management in leading their own specific functions or departments. The process of evaluation and strategic planning can be quite involved, but it can be readily placed in perspective if we recognize that it entails answering three basic questions: Where are we now? Where do we want to be? How do we get there?

"WHERE ARE WE NOW?"

Evaluating organizational performance to answer this question usually entails an audit of each operating department and top-level management. The audit process is generally initiated by the board of directors as a response to perceived problems on the horizon; a potential shift in organizational involvement in a new market; a personnel change in top management; or simply a periodic undertaking which is prescribed by organizational policy.

The activities involved in such an audit entail extensive data gathering on costs, markets, technology, and personnel and may take six months or more of staff or consultant involvement to complete. While a detailed treatment of the questions asked and procedures used is far beyond the scope of this book, the reader can get an appreciation for the issues considered in it by examining Exhibit 15–1.

In examining the evaluation outline, we can see that there are four vital areas about which questions should be asked: (1) product lines and competitive

Exhibit 15–1
Outline for evaluation of a firm

I. PRODUCT LINES AND BASIC COMPETITIVE POSITION

A. Past

What strengths and weakness in products (or services) have been dominant in this firm's history—design features, quality-reliability, prices, patents, proprietary position?

B. Present

What share of its market(s) does the firm now hold, and how firmly? Is this share diversified or concentrated as to number of customers? In what phases of their life cycles are the present chief products and what is happening to prices and margins? How do customers and potential customers regard this firm's products? Are the various product lines compatible marketing-wise, engineering-wise, manufacturing-wise? If not, is each product line substantial enough to stand on its own feet?

C. Future

Is the market(s) as a whole expanding or contracting, and at what rate? What is the trend in this firm's share of the market(s)? What competitive trends are developing in numbers of competitors, technology, marketing, pricing? What is its vulnerability to business cycle (or defense spending) changes? Is management capable of effectively integrating market research, R&D, and market development into a development program for a new product or products?

II. R&D AND OPERATING DEPARTMENTS

A. R&D and engineering

What is the nature and the depth of its R&D capability? Of engineering capability? What are engineering's main strengths and weaknesses re creativity, quality-reliability, simplicity? Is the R&D effort based on needs defined by market research, and is it an integral part of an effective new product development program? Are R&D efforts well planned, directed, and controlled? What return have R&D dollars paid in profitable new products? Have enough new products been produced? Have schedules been met?

B. Marketing

Nature of the marketing capability—what channels of distribution are used? How much of the total marketing job (research, sales, service, advertising and promotion) is covered? Is this capability correctly tailored to match the nature and diversity of the firm's product lines? Is there a capability for exploiting new products and developing new markets? Quality of the marketing capability—is market research capable of providing the factual basis that will keep the firm, especially its new product development and R&D programs, truly customer-oriented? Is there a capability for doing broad economic studies and studies of

Exhibit 15–1 *(continued)*

particular industries that will help management set sound growth and/or diversification strategies?

C. Manufacturing

What is the nature of the manufacturing processes, the facilities and the skills—are they appropriate to today's competition? How flexible are they—will they be, or can they be made, appropriate to tomorrow's competition? What is the quality of the manufacturing management in terms of planning and controlling work schedule-wise, cost-wise, and quality-wise? Is there evidence of an industrial engineering capability that steadily improves products and methods? Does manufacturing management effectively perform its part of the process of achieving new products?

D. Summary on R&D and operating departments

Is this a complete, integrated, balanced operation; or have certain strong personalities emphasized some functions and neglected others? What is the quality of performance of key R&D and operating executives; do they understand the fundamental processes of management, namely planning, controlling organizing, staffing and directing? Are plans and controls in each department inadequate, adequate or overdeveloped into a "paperwork mill?" Is there throughout the departments a habit of steady progress in reducing overhead, lowering break-even points and improv-

ing quality? Are all departments future-minded? Do they cooperate effectively in developing worthy new products geared to meet the customer's future needs?

III. FINANCIAL ANALYSIS AND FINANCIAL MANAGEMENT

A. Financial analysis

What main strengths and weaknesses of the firm emerge from analysis of the trends in the traditional financial data: earnings ratios (to sales, to tangible net worth, to working capital) and earnings-per-share; debt ratios (current and acid tests, to tangible net worth, to working capital, to inventory); inventory turnover; cash flow, and the capitalization structure? What do the trends in the basic financial facts indicate as to the firm's prospects for growth in sales volume and rate of earnings? Does "quality of earnings" warrant compounding of the earnings rate?

B. Financial management

What is the quality of financial management? Is there a sound program for steadily increasing return on investment? Do the long-range financial plans indicate that management understands the cost of capital and how to make money work hard? Have balance sheets and operating statements been realistically projected for a number of years into the future? Is there careful cash planning and strong controls that help the operating departments lower break-even points? Are capital

Exhibit 15–1 *(concluded)*

expenditures inadequate or excessive with respect to insuring future operating efficiently? Are capital investment decisions based on thorough calculations? Does management have the respect of the financial community? Is the firm knowledgeable and aggressive in tax administration?

IV. TOP MANAGEMENT

A. Identification of top management and its record
What person or group constitutes top management? Has present top management been responsible for profit and loss results of the past few years?

B. Top management and the future
What are top management's chief characteristics? How adequate or inadequate is this type of management for coping with the challenges of the future? Will the present type and quality of top management continue? Will it deteriorate, will it improve, or will it change its basic character?

C. Board of directors
What influence and/or control does the board of directors exercise? What are the capabilities of its members? What are their motivations?

Source: Robert B. Buchele, "How to Evaluate a Firm," in H. Koontz and C. O'Donnell, eds., *Management: A Book of Readings,* 3d ed. (New York: McGraw-Hill Book Company, 1972), pp. 806–7.

position; (2) R&D and operating departments; (3) financial data and the quality of the financial management; and (4) top management's past record and its ability to cope with the future.* We will now comment briefly on each of these.

Product lines and competitive position

"The firm that has sound, pertinent market data usually has achieved the first step to success" in evaluating its product line and competitive position.[1] One way of focusing on the basic facts of life about a product life is the building of life cycle curves. These curves plot sales and/or margins for a product against time. See Exhibit 15–2. Composite graphs showing several life cycle curves can illustrate whether the firm has achieved a balance among products relative to their market maturity. For example, Exhibit 15–3A illustrates product life cycles for three different lines. As we can see, the company is in a poor competitive position since these products are likely to enter the period of decline at about the same time. The company whose product life cycle

---

* Not included is long-range human resources planning. However, much of the material in Chapter 8 "Staffing the Organization" bears directly on this issue.

Exhibit 15–2
Product life cycle curve

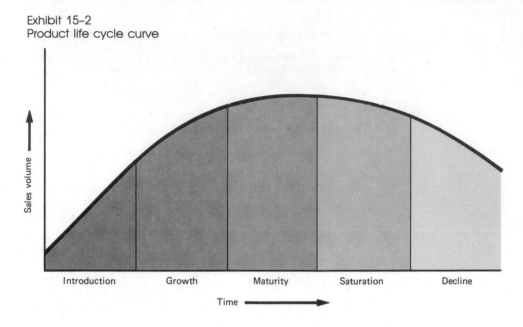

curves are depicted in Figure 15–3B is in a much safer position since a balance exists between growing products and declining products.

R&D and operating departments

R&D (research and development) is an area of critical concern to certain types of firms. Pharmaceutical companies, electronics firms, toy companies, and cosmetics firms typically devote a substantial amount of funding to developing new products. In the case of the first two, the ability of competitors to get around patent protection, coupled with less stringent patent regulations, means that high technology firms must always be on the prowl for new products to maintain their profit margins. In the case of the latter two, the fad type nature of their markets puts pressure on R&D (and advertising) to continually innovate. The burden on engineering is to be able to translate product ideas into producible products. Not emphasized in the evaluation outline but of crucial importance to companies producing goods for high-volume markets is the ability of R&D and engineering to develop process improvements. Usually, this boils down to whether or not automation can be introduced at a reasonable cost. Newspaper production, paper manufacture, and food processing are examples of diverse industries where "process R&D" plays a critical role in the firm's competitive position.

Because it deals in ideas, R&D presents unique problems in evaluation. In many respects, it is similar to universities, medical centers, and government

Exhibit 15–3
Contrasting product life cycle "portfolios"

A. Unbalanced life cycles portfolio—each product at or near maturity stage

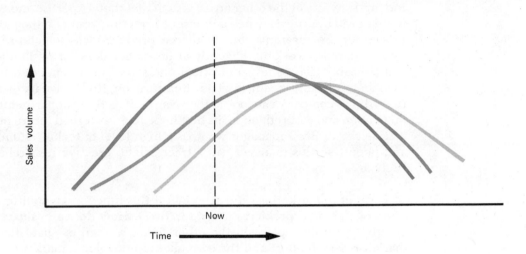

B. Balanced life cycle portfolio—each product at different stage

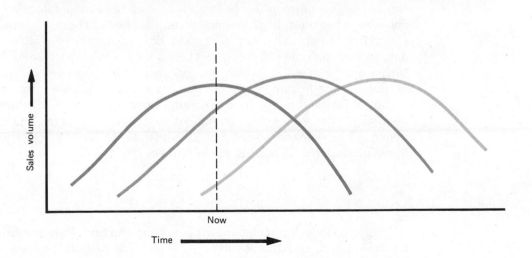

(e.g., legislators and judges). All have multiple (and often fuzzy) objectives, standards of performance are imprecise, and for better or worse, are dominated by professionals.

The nature of professionals (scientists and engineers in R&D, teachers, doctors, and lawyers in the other areas) is such that their expertise and contribution is measured by criteria which is different from time spent on the job or numerical output. For example, ten mediocre product ideas which are developed by a researcher working diligently at his or her desk for a full 40-hour week will probably lead to less profit than one sound idea generated by a seldom seen but brilliant eccentric. The literature on R&D management suggests that while a company can look at the records of its R&D department in product innovation and cost reduction, its best hope to ensure good future performance is to select an R&D manager who has a high level of technical understanding and hope that this manager can attract bright, creative researchers into the R&D area.

Turning to marketing, in evaluation of this function an auditor encounters some of the same problems noted for R&D. How do we evaluate marketing creativity, for example? On the other hand, we can evaluate the vigor of a market research effort and the care taken to develop a marketing diversification strategy. And, of course, we can measure directly the sales, market penetration, advertising, and promotional results of the marketing department.

The manufacturing area is the easiest of the major functional areas to audit. Here, we can look at cost per unit, meeting due dates, stockouts, product failure rates, inventory turnover, and capacity utilization. However, despite the availability of quantifiable variables, an audit of manufacturing should also consider what the task of manufacturing has been. That is, a company which consciously accepts all orders for production, no matter how big or how varied (i.e., customized), should not expect better cost performance out of its manufacturing arm than a firm which has less variety in its orders and product mix. Manufacturing flexibility is the most "expensive" flexibility for the firm. An organization can change its advertising, financial base, or distribution outlets generally far more quickly and easily than it can alter its manufacturing technology. Thus, demands to make major adjustments should be clearly recognized in evaluating manufacturing performance.

Financial data and financial management

"Figures alone don't tell the complete story of a firm. Its money management must be rated, and this involves an evaluation of both policies and men."[2] The policies of interest relate to the existence of sound programs for money management, care in keeping accurate cost records, and the existence of strong financial controls. The individuals involved are not only the financial manager but top management as well. The financial managers should be creative in the investment and acquisition of funds, know the money market well, and be able to operate effectively in providing financial resources to the rest of the organization. Top management ultimately determines the allocation of funds either through its planning or its spending policies. If a company decides to acquire another firm, for example, it is top management's decision, not the financial manager's. Thus, evaluation of a financial activity must consider both the quality of data preparation and the quality of the decisions made with that information.

Top management

Evaluation of (and prescription about) management is what much of this book is about. Evaluating top management in an audit sense refers to the chief operating officers (president and senior vice presidents) and the board of directors along several dimensions. For the president, in addition to corporate profitability, that individual's skill in setting goals, knowledge of the organization's strengths and weaknesses, leadership ability, and development of able successors are usually focal points in an audit. Much the same criteria are applied to senior vice presidents. For boards of directors, an audit should clarify the contribution made by each member, and its effectiveness as the major committee of the organization. More specifically, does it reach decisions? Does it use all of its resources? Is it an appropriate blend of philosophies and abilities for the company? And, most important, has it chosen an effective president?

"WHERE DO WE WANT TO BE?"

Large profit-seeking organizations

Rational management suggests that an organization would "want to be" in a strong competitive position in a growing market. For planning and analysis purposes, however, management must be more specific and define its goals in terms of market share, new product innovation, corporate image, and so on. And, most certainly, an organization is dependent upon its current skills and resources in identifying what really can be done in the way of future achievement. The evaluation process described in the previous section is most important in this respect because it will provide factual information about two basic issues: (1) the organization's *distinctive competence*, and (2) the organization's *primary task*.

An organization's distinctive competence is what it is good at; e.g., a unique product line, a strong marketing capability, low-cost production, or innovation skills. Put in another way, it is the special set of weapons with which the organization competes.

A company's primary task is what it must do well in order to compete and survive. In contrast to distinctive competence, which is determined by

Exhibit 15–4
BCG matrix

Market		Share	
		High	Low
Growth	High	II Stars	I ?
	Low	III Cash Cows	IV Dogs

the internal capabilities of the organization, the primary task is determined by forces in the organization's environment.

In deciding where we want to be, then, the job of management consists of looking jointly at these two factors to see if the organization is *able* to do what it *must* do. Does its distinctive competence match its primary task?

Turning now to the process of determining this match, several different approaches have been proposed under the general heading of "assessment guides." The Boston Consulting Group (BCG), for example, has developed a widely used method which uses a matrix to relate a company's current (or future) product line to its current (or potential) market share. Exhibit 15–4 illustrates such a matrix with the colorful terms used to describe the characteristics of products in each quadrant. Many products start out in the unknown quadrant (I). They have a low market share, but high growth potential. If things go well, then the product moves into the star category (II). If the company is successful at matching its distinctive competence to its primary task, the product will move into the cash cow category (III) where it becomes "old reliable," providing revenue to support the company's ongoing operations and new ventures. Naturally, management wishes to avoid selecting products (or services) which start out, or end up, as dogs (IV). The "where do we want to be" question, in terms of the BCG model, is answered by identifying through market research those products which have a high probability of becoming stars or cash cows.

If we focus on return on investment (ROI) as the measure of how well an organization matches its primary task and distinctive competence, we find from a famous research study (the PIMS project*) that market share, product quality, investment intensity, and company factors are the major determinants.

* Profit Impact of Market Strategies, initially develped by General Electric and later transferred to the Strategic Planning Institute.

Market share, the percentage of sales in a given market by a firm, is a major influence on profitability. In the PIMS study of actual experiences of 350 businesses, it was discovered that ROI goes up steadily as market share increases. Specifically, it was found that businesses with market shares above 36 percent earned more than three times as much as businesses with less than a 7 percent share of their respective markets.

Product quality (i.e., inferior, average, or superior) also has an effect on ROI. A firm with high-quality products will generally do better than one with low-quality products. This holds true when comparing companies with large market shares or small ones. However, good quality does not *guarantee* a large market share.

Investment intensity, the ratio of total investment to sales, has a negative correlation with ROI. The reason for this is that companies with heavy capital investments have to produce at very high volumes in order to achieve the same profit margin as those who can produce at a lower fixed cost base. Obviously, then, certain industries such as automobiles tend to be less profitable, than, say, electronics by virtue of the fixed investment needed to sustain auto production. This is not to say that electronics is a safer investment than cars; only that the ROI in electronics is likely to be higher.

Company factors are characteristics of the company that owns the business. The most significant characteristics in regard to ROI were found to be size and diversity. Large companies (in terms of annual sales) have the largest average ROI, while companies which are average in size have the lowest ROI. (See Exhibit 15–5.)

The authors of the PIMS study attribute the relatively poor performance of the average companies noted in Exhibit 15–5 to the fact that they are not large enough to achieve the benefit from economies of scale like the large companies and are not small enough to be flexible like the small companies.

Exhibit 15–5
Total company sales

	Annual sales (in millions)		
	Under $750 Low	$750–$1,500 Average	Over $1,500 High
Average ROI	15.8%	12.5%	21.7%
	Degree of diversity		
	Low	Average	High
Average ROI	16.1%	12.9%	22.1%

Source: S. Schoeffler, R. Buzzell, and D. Heany, "Impact of Strategic Planning on Profit Performance," *Harvard Business Review*, March–April 1976, p. 144. Copyright © 1976 by the President and Fellows of Harvard College; all rights reserved. Reprinted by permission.

In reference to diversity, "ROI was practically identical for businesses belonging to highly diversified corporations and for those operated by nondiversified companies. Presumably, the diversified corporations achieve good results through effectiveness as innovators."[3]

To summarize this research, the best situation is to be a large, diversified company with a large market share making a high-quality product.

Non-profit organizations and small businesses

Where a nonprofit organization "wants to be" must be related to performance measures other than ROI. In general, the focus of such organizations is on the service provided, either through offering more services, better services, or more cost-effective service. The following samples serve to illustrate this point.

Organization	*Service enhancements (where we want to be)*
Hospital	A leading center for heart transplants
Business school	Become one of the "top ten" in the United States
Postal service	Automated letter processing to speed deliveries
Law enforcement agency	Reduction in crime rates in certain categories (e.g., auto theft, robbery)

Small businesses usually want to become big businesses in terms of sales. In some instances, however, the owner-manager does not want the headaches associated with growth, preferring to make a reasonable profit from a reasonable amount of effort. Unfortunately, while this constitutes an answer to "where I want to be," it is not quite the same as taking a look at the business' product/market mix and making a reasoned judgment. In short, it is our belief that a small business owner should go through the exercise of examining the business' distinctive competence and primary task to see if a match exists, or if the situation will change in the near future. In particular, small businesses are highly vulnerable to competition from large ones (ma and pa stores versus supermarkets, small construction companies versus large ones, and so on). Thus, in rapidly growing communities especially, the little guy can't sit back and expect the good times to continue forever.

"HOW DO WE GET THERE?"

Achieving the goals identified in the previous section requires the development of what is called a *strategic plan*. A strategic plan differs from other types of planning (sometimes called tactical planning) in several respects.

Exhibit 15–6
Steps in the strategic planning process

1. Settle on the values, character, or personality of the company by open discussion among top executives.
2. Take a look *outside the company* to see what is going on, what the future will be like, and what opportunities exist for a firm of the general nature yours can be.
3. Take a look *inside the company* to determine what your resources and *capabilities for change* are.
4. Creatively match your internal capabilities to external opportunities to define the kind of company which you want to *be* in five or ten years. This definition of the "shape" of the company is in the form of a set of strategic goals:
   a. Scope—Products, markets, channels, price/quality categories, market position.
   b. Dynamics—Timing for goal achievements.
   c. Competitive edge [i.e., distinctive competence].
   d. Risk—Probability of gain as related to probability and size of loss for major substrategies.
   e. Specifications—quantitative goals such as market share, ROI, number of customers, assets, profits, and so on.
   f. Deployment of resources—Allocation of resources among human, capital, and liquid categories. Acquisitions and divestments.
5. Develop the long-range master plan for achieving the strategy (goals) in (4).
   a. Develop milestones (major subgoals).
   b. Develop the timing or schedule for these milestones.
   c. Specify the task, the personnel, and the other resources required to achieve each milestone.
   d. Estimate elements of costs for all tasks, milestones, and strategic goals.
   e. Prepare pro forma statements, work descriptions, and budgets.

Source: Robert G. Murdick, Richard H. Eckhouse, R. Carl Moor, and Thomas W. Zimmerer, *Business Policy: A Framework for Analysis*, 2d ed. (Columbus, Ohio: Grid Publishing, Inc., 1976), p. 101. Reprinted with permission.

1. It is a long-range plan, typically three to five years into the future.
2. It involves a large segment of the organization. As Ackoff has noted, "Planning becomes increasingly strategic as the portion of the organization encompassed by it approaches unity."[4]
3. It focuses on the establishment of major goals set by top management for the organization as a whole. Tactical planning focuses on the subgoals derived from these major goals.

The process of strategic planning varies from organization to organization and for some firms, the evaluation of current activities and the actual setting of goals are considered part of strategic planning. A nice summary of the steps involved has been developed by Murdick et al.[5] (See Exhibit 15–6.)

Types of strategies

The following strategies are illustrative of the kinds of corporate strategies used in industry. Obviously, there are others, and the ones described here could be combined to form hybrid strategies.

Innovator strategy.   In this strategy, the company competes by being first in the market with a new product or process. Examples of large companies which have followed this approach are RCA with color television and General Motors with "downsized" cars. A characteristic of this strategy is that it requires substantial amounts of cash reserves to sustain marketing and production while the product is gaining acceptance. Both RCA and GM spent millions in the early stages of their products' life cycles.*

A particularly successful exponent of the innovator strategy is Texas Instruments. The following excerpts from a 1978 *Business Week* article suggest how TI has used technological innovation and a practical understanding of the learning curve to become "the most feared competitor in the consumer electronics business."[7]

What TI really is . . . "is an innovator in applying technology and exploiting it." TI, in fact, is the only semiconductor producer that is building end-user products and developing new applications for all market areas—consumer, military, and computers.

The learning curve certainly is chapter one in the TI "bible." The concept is fundamental to the success of TI's strategy in driving for the leadership position in a high-volume market because, the gospel goes, the company with the largest share of the sales has the best opportunity for profit.

[Learning curve] theory says simply that manufacturing costs can be brought down by a fixed percentage, depending on the product, each time cumulative volume is doubled. . . . It involves constantly forcing manufacturing costs down through design improvement of the product and the production process. So the faster a producer can get into volume production, the faster he can drop the price.

Follower strategy.   Under this strategy, an organization never innovates, but rather introduces its product after its competitor's product has established the existence of a market. Sometimes, a company simply plans on remaining number two or three in an industry, thereby avoiding the high risks which go with innovation and capitalizing on the mistakes of "number one." Consider the following example from Murdick et al.:

---

* Another type of innovation is in mass distribution as is exemplified by McDonald's blanketing an area with outlets. But as the president of McDonald's says, "If there are 6,000 dealers selling Chevrolets, I don't see why we can't have at least twice as many outlets for selling hamburgers."[6] [Burp]

Early in 1965, the marketing intelligence system of Schick Safety Razor Co. warned that "number one" was about to launch an attack that would tear vast holes in Schick's share of the market. The secret "competitive edge" was truly a revolutionary competitive edge, namely, a ribbon razor blade. Schick also suspected that Gillette would launch its new product during the World Series so that a rapid response was needed.

Schick decided to go all out to thwart this threat by getting into production of such a band within the very short time of 14 months. In this time it had to find a plant, design production equipment, and develop effective manufacturing methods. But this would not be enough to give Schick a competitive edge. It achieved this edge by designing its band to fit the Gillette razor but making the reverse impossible! It turned a disadvantage of being second into a unique opportunity![8]

Flexibility strategy.   In some industries, aerospace, for example, it is impossible to forecast what products will be demanded since sales are based upon acquiring contracts via competitive bids. Under these circumstances, companies like Hughes Aircraft and General Dynamics Corporation concentrate on securing and maintaining organization structures and physical facilities which can be adapted to a range of potential products. This, of course, has the advantage of permitting relatively rapid startups and has the disadvantage of relatively high operating costs.

Vertical integration strategy.   Vertical integration refers to an organization adding value-added stages to its production sequence. An oil company which drills for oil and refines the oil is one example; another would be a hamburger chain which raises and slaughters its own cattle and uses the beef in its end product. This strategy is appropriate when all stages in the manufacturing are profitable or when a company wants to assure itself of an uninterrupted supply of raw material. One of the risks involved, however, is that central management may not be effective when they get out of their main business. Another is that full vertical integration leads to inflexibility, making it vulnerable to new techniques and products introduced by competitors.

Horizontal integration strategy.   Horizontal integration consists of an organization seeking ownership or increased control of some of its competitors. Obtaining one's competitors can be accomplished by purchasing their assets, buying their common stock, or by a merger. The major constraint in employing this strategy is Section 7 of the Clayton Act which prohibits acquisition of competitors where the effect "may be substantially to lessen competition, or tend to create a monopoly."

Some specific strategy options

Thompson and Strickland have described additional strategies, some of which are appropriate in particular situations, some of which are risky, and others which should be avoided entirely. (See Exhibit 15–7.)

Exhibit 15–7
A catalog of specific strategy options: Some winners and some losers

Strategies for underdog or trailing firms:
1. *Vacant niche strategy.* Search out and cultivate profitable *segments* of the market that larger firms are not catering to or are ignoring.
2. *"Ours-is-better-than-theirs" strategy.* Try to capitalize on opportunities to improve upon the products of the dominant firms and develop an appeal to the quality-conscious, performance-oriented buyer. (Example: Zenith's attempt to overtake RCA with its "the quality goes in, before the name goes on" theme.)
3. *Channel innovation strategy.* Find a new way to distribute goods that offers substantial savings or that reaches particular group of buyers more efficiently. (Examples include Avon's door-to-door selling of cosmetics and Timex's use of drugstores and discount stores as outlets for its watches.)
4. *Distinctive image strategy.* Seek to achieve a differential advantage via some distinctive and unique appeal—Dr. Pepper's taste, the VW beetle, Avis' "We're No. 2. We Try Harder" campaign.

Strategies for dominant firms:
1. *Seize-the-offensive strategy.* Refuse to be content with just being a leader. Seek to continue to outperform the industry by breaking records the firm itself has already set. Become firmly established as *the* source of new product ideas, cost-cutting discoveries, innovative customer services, and better means of distribution. In general, exercise initiative, set the pace, and exploit the weaknesses of rival firms.
2. *Fortification strategy.* Surround the chief products with patents; foreclose the attractiveness of entry by introducing more of the company's own brands to compete with those already successful company brands; introduce additional items under current brand names.
3. *Confrontation strategy.* Defend the company's market base by being quick to launch massive promotional wars which underdog firms cannot hope to match; promptly meet all competitive price cuts of lesser sized firms to neutralize any benefits to would-be price-cutters; make it hard for aggressive-minded smaller firms to grow by selling at prices so low that smaller firms are denied the profit margins and total earnings needed to make further expansion attractive.

Strategies to be leery of:
1. *"Me too" or "copycat" strategy.* Imitating the strategy of leading or successful enterprises; trying to play catch-up by beating the leaders at their own game. Weakness: Ignores development of firm's own personality, image, strategy, and policies.
2. *Take-away strategy.* Trying to achieve greater market share and market penetration by attacking other firms head-on and luring away their customers via a lower price, more advertising, and other attention-getting gimmicks. Weakness: Invites retaliation and risks precipitating a fierce and costly battle for market share in which no one wins—including the firm trying to play take-away.
3. *Glamor strategy.* When a firm gets seduced by the prospects of a new idea for a product or technology which it thinks will sweep the market. Weakness: The best laid plans. . . .

Exhibit 15–7 *(continued)*

4. *Test-the-water strategy.* Often arises when an enterprise is engaged in developing new opportunities or is reacting to market-technological-environmental changes which call for a fundamental reformulation or redesign of the basic corporate strategy. In such cases, firms may "test the water" in venturing out into new fields of endeavor. Weakness: A halfway effort or "sideline stepchild" seldom succeeds for lack of adequate corporate commitment; it's usually best to either get in or stay out entirely.

5. *Hit another home-run strategy.* This strategy is typified by a firm which has hit one "home run" (pioneering a very successful product and strategy) but which is now looking for ways to hit a second home run (by getting into a second line of business either related or unrelated to its first home run), so as to continue to grow and prosper at its former rate. Seeking out a second home-run strategy may be necessary because growth of the initial business is rapidly slowing down and becoming more competitive. Weakness: It may be questionable whether the distinctive competence gained from the first home run is transferable to other products, markets, and technologies and whether the firm has the know-how to make an effective transfer.

6. *Arm's race strategy.* May emerge when firms of relatively equal size enter into a spirited battle for increased market share. Commonly, such battles are waged with increased promotional and advertising expenditures and/or increased R&D and new product development budgets and/or aggressive price cuts and/or extra services to customers. As one firm pours more money into its efforts, other firms feel forced to do likewise for defensive reasons. The result is escalating costs, producing a situation much like an arm's race. Weakness: Seldom do such battles produce a substantial change in market shares, yet they almost certainly raise costs—costs which must either be absorbed in the form of lower profit margins or else passed on to customers via higher prices.

Strategies to avoid:

1. *Drift strategy.* When strategy is not consciously designed and coordinated but rather just evolves out of day-to-day decisions and actions at the operating level.

2. *Hope for a better day strategy.* Emerges from managerial inertia and tradition and is exemplified by firms which blame their subpar sales-profits-market share performance on bad luck, the economy, unexpected problems, and other circumstances "beyond their control." Such "entrepreneurial coasting" until good times arrive is a sure sign of a dim future and managerial ineptness.

3. *Downhill strategy.* Arises in companies where a once successful (and perhaps spectacularly so) strategy is fading and no longer viable. Nonetheless, management, blinded by the success-breeds-success syndrome, continues to be reluctant to begin to reformulate its strategy, preferring instead to try to rekindle the old spark with cosmetic changes—in hopes of reversing the downhill slide.

4. *Popgun strategy.* Seeking to go into head-to-head competition with proven leaders when the firm has neither a differential competitive advantage nor adequate financial strength with which to do battle.

Source: A. Thompson, Jr. and A. Strickland III, *Strategy and Policy, Concepts and Cases* (Dallas, Tex.: Business Publications, 1978), pp. 84–86. © 1978 by Business Publications, Inc.

Making the strategic choice

The aforementioned authors write that there are three pivotal elements in reaching a decision on strategy:

1. The risk/reward trade-off.
2. Timing the strategic move.
3. The vulnerability to strategic counterattack.[9]

Risk/reward trade-off.   This element "involves the willingness of an organization to assume risk."[10] Some organizations are inherently conservative and thus are inclined toward strategies which yield modest returns; others are gamblers, willing to assume a high-risk strategy which offers potentially high returns. Low investment and little innovation are characteristics of the conservative firm, while the opposite use of resources is characteristic of the risk-taking firm.

Timing considerations.   When a firm decides to employ a particular strategy can have as much profit impact as the strategy itself. Consider the difference in returns one might expect in producing a full-size line of cars in 1973 compared with the same product in 1980. Or buying the same house in Los Angeles in 1973 or in 1980. We like to think that proper timing is a result of careful planning, but we know from experience that luck often plays a big role. Who at MGM could anticipate that the Three Mile Island nuclear plant problem would coincide with their film on a nuclear disaster, raising their stock by 25 points; or who in Arizona could anticipate that a partially completed nuclear power plant would encounter severe public opposition because of a chance event in Pennsylvania?

Strategic counterattack.   It is a naive manager indeed who does not consider the likely strategic responses of a competitor when selecting a strategy. Similarly, the alert manager should also be contemplating potential reactive strategies to those aggressive strategies of competing firms. Though more tactical reaction than business strategy, the programming actions on the part of the three major TV networks present an ongoing "show" for aficionados of counter-punching strategies. Using weekly ratings as a means of quick scorekeeping, we see such counterprogramming maneuvers as strong lead-in programs to buttress weaker programs, and of course the hiring away from one network by another of programming experts (e.g., Fred Silverman from ABC to NBC).

If one wishes to avoid head-to-head strategy confrontations such as found in network programming, the obvious approach is to keep a low profile either by remaining small or by being positioned in an industry where successful strategic counterattacks are likely to put the victor in possible violation of antitrust laws.

Policy analysis

Strategic planning in the public sector is carried out under this broad heading. While there are many things which distinguish the planning in schools, welfare organizations, prisons, and so on from private business, perhaps the main distinction is the relationship between investment and payoff. First of all, the policy analyst must look at the impact of strategies not over a three- to five-year period, but over a generation. For example, a major investment in primary education may not bear fruit in terms of a better work force, lower crime rates, higher college entrance tests, and so on for ten years or more. Second, there is the real question as to whether the money spent will have the desired results. Certainly there is no way of knowing for sure whether a better primary education will lead to a better work force; we believe this is true, but there are no guarantees. Third, there is the quesiton of direct causality and measurement. Does a good education lower the crime rate? If college entrance scores go up, how much of the rise is attributable to primary education rather than accumulated student skills at test taking? Finally, what if all of the indicators mentioned show an undesirable trend? Does this mean that the investment in primary education was unwarranted, or simply poorly executed? Such are the dilemmas of public policy analysts.*

SUMMARY

We have attempted in this chapter to summarize some rather weighty material which the typical business student spends a semester on in a business policy course. We hope we have conveyed two notions to you: One, that evaluation/strategy is exciting and significant; and two, that conceptually at least, it is not all that hard to comprehend. In practice, most firms carry out these processes though they may call them something else, and most probably believe that they could be doing them better. Certainly, some of the firms in the industry described below must feel that there is room for improvement in strategic planning.

"NAME THAT INDUSTRY!"†

One company . . . can boast of a 60 percent after-tax return on its invested capital, while others are going broke. No formula for success seems to exist; certainly there is no correlation between profits and the amount of product a company generated. While some . . . companies introduced over 100 new products,

---

* For the reader who is interested in finding out more about this fascinating and important subject, we recommend Yehezkel Dror, *Public Policymaking Reexamined* (San Francisco: Chandler Publishing Company, 1968).

† The answer is given in Discussion Question 3.

the one with the highest profit margin put out only ten. In search of the elusive formula, industry executives are resorting to more scientific kinds of market analysis, even though they know that a product's success still hinges on its acceptance by a relatively few early users. And the most powerful form of advertising remains free.[11]

GUIDES TO ACTION

1. A well-run organization *always* engages in some form of periodic evaluation and strategic planning. Keep this in mind in your own evaluation of a prospective employer.

2. If you are interested in a career in evaluation and planning (i.e., on a corporate planning staff), bear down in your finance and marketing classes. New products and money to make them is the basis of corporate strategy.

3. Few companies can do everything well. Therefore, be cautious of companies that are into everything. There is a fine line between reasoned diversification and random acquisition.

4. In evaluating your own career, a good starting point is to ask the three questions: (1) Where am I now? (2) Where do I want to be? and (3) How do I get there? And, does my distinctive competence match my primary task?

NOTES

1 Robert B. Buchele, "How to Evaluate a Firm," Reading No. 98 in H. Koontz and C. O'Donnell, eds., *Management: A Book of Readings,* 3d ed. (New York: McGraw-Hill Book Company, 1972), p. 808.

2 Ibid., p. 812.

3 S. Schoeffler, R. Buzzell, and D. Heany, "Impact of Strategic Planning on Profit Performance," *Harvard Business Review,* Vol. 54, no. 2 (March–April, 1976), p. 144.

4 Russell L. Ackoff, "The Meaning of Strategic Planning," in Ernest Dale ed., *Readings in Management: Landmarks and Frontiers,* 3d ed. (New York: McGraw-Hill Book Company, 1975), p. 230.

5 R. G. Murdick et al., *Business Policy: A Framework for Analysis,* 2d ed. (Columbus, Ohio: Grid Publishing, 1976), p. 101.

6 "The Fast-Food Stars: Three Strategies for Fast Growth," *Business Week,* July 11, 1977, p. 58.

7 "Texas Instruments Shows U.S. Business How to Survive the 1980's," *Business Week,* September 18, 1978, pp. 66–92.

8 Murdick et al., *Business Policy,* p. 122.

9 A. Thompson, Jr. and A. Strickland III, *Strategy and Policy, Concepts and Cases* (Dallas, Tex.: Business Publications, Inc., 1978), p. 108.

10 Ibid.

11 Peter W. Bernstein, "The Record Business: Rocking to the Big Money Beat," *Fortune,* April 23, 1979, pp. 58–68.

DISCUSSION QUESTIONS

1. Comment on the following statements:

   a. We don't have time to evaluate our organization—we're growing too fast." (Dean of a private business college.)

   b. "Sure, our costs are rising, but we must provide the skills to handle heart transplants. After all, the patient comes first." (Administrator of a middle-sized general hospital.)

c. "Product life cycle curves are good in theory, but they have no relevance to the tennis club business." (Owner of a chain of tennis clubs.)

2. Summarize the major findings of the PIMS study relative to a firm in the average category in company sales and degree of diversity.

3. An April 23, 1979 *Fortune* article entitled, "The Record Business: Rocking to the Big Money Beat," described the plight of the record industry in the following way. "The volume is way up, but so are the costs of hype and superstars. Small companies are getting squeezed and even the giants have been jolted" (p. 59). Under these circumstances, what do you see as critical elements in a strategic plan for a small record company for the 1980s?

4. How does the learning (or experience) curve relate to strategic planning? How would you employ it in bidding on a contract for, say, 500 hand-lettered T-shirts?

5. What type of "counter" counterattack strategy might Gillette have followed in light of the follower strategy employed by Schick?

6. Using Exhibit 15–7, identify the types of strategies (or combination strategies) which seem to have been employed by the following organizations:
   a. MacDavid Hamburger Restaurants (in Israel).
   b. OPEC countries in the Middle East.
   c. Fotomat stores.
   d. Three-dimensional movies in the 1950s.
   e. The Goodrich Blimp.
   f. *Penthouse Magazine.*
   g. The old World Football League.

CASE 1:   BEHIND THE HIGH COST OF TEXTBOOKS*
The average student pays $150 a year for
college texts. Reasonable or rip-off?

It's a $640-million-a-year industry, selling no one knows how many books to approximately 11 million students in over 3,300 colleges across the nation. Reasonable or rip-off? The average student, who pays $150 per year for his texts, may be inclined to think he's getting taken. But consider these financial facts:

Textbooks, particularly the fat, introductory variety, are very expensive to produce. Always long and frequently stuffed with graphs, charts, photos,

---

* Reprinted with publisher's permission from *Nutshell* © 1979/80 13–30 Corporation, 505 Market Street, Knoxville, TN 37902.

and four-color layouts, they necessarily incur production costs considerably above the average hardback novel—yet the price is not much higher. (Actually, the *average* price is about $8.50. Industry officials, however, are quick to concede that this is almost meaningless when so many highly visible texts cost $15 or more. The average price is deflated by a lot of $4 and $5 paperbounds.)

Says David Ammerman, president of the college division at Prentice-Hall: "The value in texts today is far superior to what it's ever been. We put a lot more into the writing, the illustrations, the supplementary materials—everything you can imagine. And the life cycle of textbooks is very short. To get a return, you have to get it very quickly. And from a very small universe. When there may be only 25,000 or 30,000 students taking a course in the whole country, and 15 or 20 books competing for their business, it becomes very competitive."

With some obvious and dramatic exceptions, no one involved with the production of textbooks makes a great deal of money on any single title. Large publishers doing $20 million or more a year in sales may make as much as 13 cents on the dollar (net profit) from their texts; but the more realistic figure is 10 cents. For smaller publishers doing $5 million or less in sales, the return is more like 2 cents after taxes.

Nor do college bookstores clean up. In fact, they may actually lose money on texts. Whereas publishers allow booksellers to purchase many trade books for about 60 percent of list price, most demand nearly 80 percent for texts. The reason: "The marketing is done by the publisher," says Ammerman. "Its salesmen call on the professors and provide the samples. With trade books, the bookseller does most of the promoting."

Out of that 20 percent margin, college bookstores must pay all their overhead, including the costs of warehousing the books, completing all the paper work related to ordering, and paying for the transportation of returned texts. Some college bookstores calculate that a typical store spends 23 percent of its gross textbook sales volume on overhead—meaning that it runs 3 percent in the red. "The only way college stores keep their heads above water is by selling all those sweat shirts, beer mugs and other merchandise," explains one store manager. "If we sell shirts, we can buy them from any of several different manufacturers. We can bargain on the price. But we can't do that with textbooks."

So who makes money? The author? According to Ammerman, royalties today run close to 15 percent—which sounds great only until you remember that the average text sells fewer than 5,000 copies. The shining exceptions, of course, are occasional blockbusters like James McConnell's *Understanding*

Human Behavior; these help keep costs down on the limited editions of more esoteric texts and also help underwrite every publisher's inevitable losers.

"None of us plan to publish losers," says Ammerman, "but unavoidably we're going to make some mistakes. Somebody has to pay the bill; if the publisher turns a profit, the winners take care of the losers." He is borne out by the numbers. In 1976, according to industry figures, 29 percent of all the money spent by consumers on books went for texts. Yet textbooks earned 46 percent of the industry's pretax profits.

Pricing of texts is based in part on their sales potential. The Association of American Publishers (AAP) explains that, in general, "short books with pages mostly of straight type cost less, and therefore are priced lower than longer books with many tables, formulas, equations and illustrations, which cost more to produce. But a short book with a very limited potential for use in upper level and graduate courses may carry a higher price to compensate for having to spread the initial investment over fewer copies sold."

Why are paperbound texts almost as expensive as hardbound ones? A spokesman for the AAP replies that, first, trade paperbounds are produced for the mass market; economies of scale keep their prices down.

"By contrast," he continues, "our college-textbook paperback books are intended for a far smaller audience. Sometimes they are the basic text for a course, but more often they are supplementary reading. Teachers and students expect them to be better made so that they can be resold. Since publishers are obliged to maintain quality, where can they save on costs to keep prices as low as possible?"

On the buying end, professors call the shots. They write the books. They select them. They read manuscripts (frequently receiving fees of $50 to $200 or more) and make suggestions for new books. Publishers, ever on the lookout for new ideas and authors, keep files on who's the expert in a field and what he or she might someday write. They talk to professors and survey college courses to see what's being covered, they try to tailor their books to current demand. "A few years ago they didn't want to do engineering texts because no one was taking the courses and there weren't any jobs in the field," says Parker Ladd of the AAP. "Now engineering has come back and nursing is big. We're seeing a lot of books on nursing."

Some publishers specialize. So Southwestern, in Cincinnati, and Irwin, in Homewood, Illinois, do only business texts. Addison-Wesley, in Massachusetts, started out in engineering and math and eventually took on social sciences as well. Most of the big firms—Harper & Row, Prentice-Hall, Holt, Rinehart and Winston, McGraw-Hill, and others—publish a wide range of titles and produce revisions of big introductory texts every three or four years.

To many students, this common publishers' practice seems like nothing but a profit-making ploy to keep students from reselling used texts. Ammerman admits that this is certainly one motive for the practice—and that it increases profits because revising a book is cheaper and less risky than starting again from scratch. But he adds that much of the pressure for revisions comes from the professors themselves. "The academic market is very conscious of copyright dates," he explains. "Nobody wants a book that's three or four years old."

Questions

1. What strategies do the book companies use in getting teachers to use their books?
2. Ask your instructor what his/her criteria are.
3. What criteria would *you* suggest?

CASE 2: AMERICAN SECURITY BANK*

On July 1, 1976 the saving depositors of American Security Bank of Washington, D.C., received the letter shown in Exhibit 1 regarding their savings accounts.

Mr. Carleton M. Stewart, chairman of the board of American Security and Trust Company (AS&T), provided statistics compiled by the Federal Reserve Board showing that for an average U.S. bank, the cost of simply maintaining a savings account with no active deposits and withdrawals, and posting interest was $5.74 in 1969, $9.87 in 1972, and $11.14 in 1975.

The cost to a bank for each withdrawal—manpower and technology—was 58 cents in 1972, and 70 cents by 1975.

With this sort of inflation, AS&T had no choice but to begin adding service fees, Stewart said. American Security has had 84,000 savings accounts, 44,000 of which had deposits of less than $500. Accounts with less than $500 accounted for 65.49 percent of all AS&T savings accounts in 1975 but only 3.62 percent of the dollar volume, Stewart revealed.[1]

---

* This case was prepared by Thomas L. Wheelen, McIntire School of Commerce, University of Virginia, and Moustafa H. Abdelsamad, Virginia Commonwealth University, as basis for class discussion.

Copyright © 1977 by Thomas L. Wheelen and Moustafa H. Abdelsamad. Distributed by Intercollegiate Case Clearing House, Soldiers Field, Boston, Mass., 02163. All rights reserved to the contributors. Printed in the U.S.A.

[1] William H. Jones, "AS&T Service Charge Viewed as Trend-Setter," *Washington Post,* July 25, 1976, p. k2. The three paragraphs are directly quoted from the *Washington Post* story.

Exhibit 1

July 1, 1976

Dear Customer:

We believe that most people who bank at American Security do so because they are good money managers. That is why we work hard to give you the full spectrum of financial services and to make your banking relationship more than a matter of simple convenience. We're sure that you value the security of knowing that *your* bank is one of the strongest in the nation and, therefore, responsive to all your needs.

Because of this relationship, we know you will understand it is essential for American Security Bank to observe the principles of sound money management in all of our operations. And so, because of increased costs, we have found it necessary to apply the following regulations, effective immediately, to American Security Bank savings accounts:

1. Savings accounts which have no deposit or withdrawal activity for two years will be classified as inactive. A service charge of $1.00 per month will be assessed against all inactive accounts. No statements will be mailed to these accounts.

2. Accounts with average balances during the quarter of less than $1,000 will be allowed four free withdrawals per quarter. There will be a $1.00 charge for each withdrawal in excess of four.

3. Any savings account with an average quarterly balance of less than $500 will be assessed a $1.00 service charge at the end of each month.

4. Quarterly statements will only be mailed to accounts which had deposit or withdrawal activity during the preceding quarter. Year-end statements will be mailed to all active accounts in order to show the taxable interest paid during the year. In this connection, interest will be credited as of the last business day of the quarter.

It is this kind of prudent money-management that makes it possible for us to expand and maintain our most meaningful services. For example, in recent months our Consumer Loan Division has been able to offer *new lower rates on loans for any sound purpose.*

Only a strong, well-managed bank could do this. We urge you to check these rates because you will find them more than competitive.

We value your savings account and encourage you to utilize it in such a manner that you never incur a service charge. If you wish any further advice, please contact any American Security branch office.

Sincerely,
AMERICAN SECURITY BANK

Questions

1. What are the strategic planning implications of the letter?
2. What are the social responsibility implications of the letter?
3. What do you expect will be the impact on the first-line supervisors and workers from the new policy?

SELECTION OF THE PRODUCT OR SERVICE	DESIGN OF THE SYSTEM	STAFFING THE ORGANIZATION	STARTUP OF THE ORGANIZATION	OPERATING THE ORGANIZATION IN THE STEADY STATE	IMPROVING THE ORGANIZATION	REVISION OF THE ORGANIZATION	TERMINATION OF THE ORGANIZATION
Decision-making processes; social value; goals; forecasts; policies; plans	Authority and responsibility; power; organizational structure; communications systems; job design	Work force planning; personnel management functions	Startup planning and scheduling; monitoring; alternative startup approaches	Motivation; leadership; production and operations management; control	Individual improvement programs and techniques; group conflict management; MBO	Evaluation of organizational policies; strategic choices; organizational change; organizational development	Partial terminations; cutback management; complete terminations; mergers; born-again strategies

Level of Organizational Outputs

O

t_0

Time

Chapter 16
Managing organizational change

Plus ça change, plus c'est la même chose.

Alphonse Karr (1808–1890)
Les Guêpes, January 1849, p. vi

In his popular book, *Future Shock*, Alvin Toffler asks us to think about the last 50,000 or so years in terms of 800 lifetimes of 62 years each.[1] At least 650 of these lifetimes, over 40,000 years, were taken up by cave dwellers. "Writing" has been with us for only 70 lifetimes, with the printed word (à la Gutenberg) appearing in only the last 6. Electric motors have been around for only two lifetimes. Actually, most of the things we use in our daily lives were developed in the 800th lifetime, the current one.

Toffler's point is that we are living in a world that is undergoing profound and rapid changes; changes that in their magnitude and rapidity are unmatched in the history of the family Hominidae. It has almost become trite to say that the only constant thing about today's world (and therefore our organizations) is that things are constantly changing. In reality, management does not have the option of "not changing." Thus, we must be cognizant of ways to promote and respond to change to ensure the survival of our organizations.

There are two major ways of dealing with change in organizations. The first is a *reactive* process; management adapts in a piecemeal, one-step-at-a-time manner to deal with problems or issues as they arise. The second is that management can be *proactive* and embark on a program of *planned change*.

The reactive process simply tries to keep the organization on a steady course as problems come up. For example, if complaints about salesclerks suddenly increase, we might institute a short training program to hopefully correct the problem. If a major supplier goes bankrupt, we quickly search out another source of supply. If new government regulations require more fire extinguishers, we acquire them. This approach involves little planning and is usually not viewed as being "threatening" since it is aimed at solving a visible problem. However, over time a series of small, incremental changes can accumulate to cause a significant alteration in the affairs of an organization. And sometimes the resultant alteration is not a desired state of events. Phrases like, "Before we knew it . . . ," "Suddenly we found . . . ," and "Over a period of time . . ." are usually associated with problems that occur after (and because of) a sequence of reactive changes.

Planned change on the other hand involves deliberate actions to alter the status quo. It is proactive in that it sets out to change things; to set a new course rather than to maintain the current one. Also, planned change seeks to anticipate changes in the environment and deals with ways of coping with these predicted new conditions. Because of the complexity and rapidity of change in our modern world, we feel that managers must be capable of understanding and utilizing planned change approaches.

In this chapter, we will analyze some of the causes of change, some of the ways organizations cope with change, and various sources of resistance to change that may occur within organizations. Lastly, we will discuss organizational development—an approach to change that concentrates on changing the behavior and attitudes of organizational members.

ENVIRONMENTAL AND INTERNAL FORCES FOR CHANGE

In Chapter 1 we discussed the concept of an organization as an open system. Because it is an open system an organization is influenced by environmental forces which may be outside of its control or area of influence. Just as sunspots are uncontrollable influences on radio communications on Earth, actions by a union in one of your suppliers' plants over a grievance between a worker and supervisor may well cause severe repercussions in your own organization.

George Odiorne has said (tongue in cheek), "Things that do not change remain the same."[2] Unfortunately, that is not quite true. Since the environment in which an organization exists is changing, so must the relationships that the organization has with the elements of its environment. The organization *must*, to survive, adapt to the changed environment. Rather than Odiorne's phrase, we feel that "Those organizations that fail to change, fail," is more appropriate.

Shirley Terreberry has claimed that change in organizations is increasingly externally induced and that an organization's adaptability and survival depends on its ability to learn of and perform according to these environmental changes.[3] Exhibit 16–1 illustrates how organizations affect and are affected by other organizations. Rectangles represent other formal organizations and circles represent *non*formal social units (e.g., consumer groups, lobbyists, community residents in the area of a factory, and so on). Any organization must deal with other organizations and with other social units in the environment to acquire personnel, raw materials, and other inputs. Further, the organization must deal with others in the environment to "sell" or otherwise dispose of its goods/services outputs. In our turbulent, interdependent world, everything seems to be capable of influencing everything else.* For example, children's clothing manufacturers had to find new sources of fireproofing pajamas after the chemical Tris was banned (when *private* researchers claimed it was carcinogenic), while the fireproofing requirement was retained by the federal government. Prices of petroleum products in America can be influenced by curtailed production of crude oil caused by social unrest promoted by dissident groups

---

* This may have led Mark Twain to observe that "Life is just one damned thing after another." Or, as often expressed by the character Roseanne Roseannedanna on the television program "Saturday Night Live," "Well, Jane, it just goes to show 'ya—it's always something."

Exhibit 16–1
Illustration of organization X in its environment

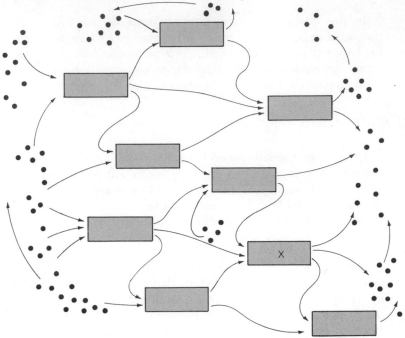

Source: Shirley Terreberry, "The Evolution of Organizational Environments," *Administrative Science Quarterly,* vol. 12, no. 4 (March 1968), p. 607.

in Middle Eastern countries. This can, in turn, cause many changes in our nation's organizations and in individual lifestyles as energy conservation practices are initiated. Indeed, many new organizations can be created (e.g., solar energy companies and electric automobile manufacturers) and others terminated (e.g., many "independent" gasoline stations and drive-in theaters) due to an externally induced change in petroleum availability.

Some forces for change are also internally generated. A new production method invented by a company engineer could abolish a number of jobs and cause those workers to be released or reassigned. Changes over time in the social values held by workers could lead to increased turnover and absenteeism which in turn could lead to new management policies. Or, a change in management's goals and policies could lead to a major reorganization. Chandler's well-known book, *Strategy and Structure,* shows how General Motors, Du Pont, Standard Oil of New Jersey, and Sears, Roebuck underwent significant structural reorganizations in response to strategy decisions made by top management.[4]

It is often difficult to differentiate between and isolate internal and environmental change forces. Certainly changes in the American family lifestyle after

World War II led Sears to build stores in suburban areas in order to cater to upwardly mobile, young families. This strategy shift, induced by an environmental change in demographics, led to a major corporate reorganization involving extensive decentralization. Then, too, the resultant proliferation of regional shopping areas by Sears and others may have further led to increased suburbanization. Ultimately, causes and effects become unclear indeed.

In order to cope with a turbulent, changing environment, organizations must develop the capacity to acquire information about the environment and stimulate adaptive responses. Responsible managers will strive to determine the areas of the environment that are most critical and will monitor them closely. Just as biological systems mutate in response to changed environments, organizations must adapt.* The alternative is extinction.

MECHANISMS OF ORGANIZATIONAL CHANGE

Change in an organization has two basic facets: *what* is to be changed, and *how* the change is to be accomplished.

What changes?

A commonly used conception of what changes in organizations is proposed by Leavitt.[5] He identifies three things that can be changed: structure, technology, and people. *Structural* change involves revisions of such things as policies, procedures, budgeting methods, the organization chart, and the like. *Technological* changes are concerned with layout, work methods, equipment used, job descriptions, and similar factors. *People* approaches concern changes in work attitudes and behavior, skills, and motivation as brought about by training programs, personnel selection procedures, or employee performance evaluation methods. Leavitt contends that a change in any one of these three areas will, in turn, lead to changes in the other areas. For example, a change in work layout (technological) may lead to a revision of the reporting relationships (structural) since the employees can now be better supervised by another foreman. The increased supervisory responsibility may necessitate additional training (people) for the affected foreman.

The manager must be cognizant of these three areas of change and their interaction. The costs and ultimate consequences of any change will normally go beyond the borders of the initial target of change.

---

* Very few creatures that ply the Earth have survived without changing. Sharks and cockroaches are, however, two examples of those that have remained the same over long periods of time. Thankfully, sharks and cockroaches rarely make it to the executive suite.

How does it change?

The power to effect a change has been analyzed by Larry E. Greiner.[6] Three main power "alternatives" are set out as shown in Exhibit 16–2. At the extreme unilateral end, management alone decides on the need to change and how the change will take place. Unilateral power can be (1) *by decree* as, for example, in a simple announcement that henceforth all purchases over $100 must be approved by the plant manager, (2) by *replacement* of certain personnel in the hope (assumption) that a change in personnel will lead to a change in some aspects of performance, and (3) by a *structural* change in jobs or relationships (e.g., relieve the loan officer of the authority to approve new car loans over $6,000 and require that the bank's branch manager concur before such a loan is issued). Note that the use of unilateral power is simply an exercise of that authority traditionally held by management.

Shared power involves permitting the affected group of persons to either select from a set of alternatives or to actually develop a recommended course of action. *Group decisions* (selection from a set of alternatives) and *group problem solving* (develop a recommended course of action) are thus the two approaches which can be used here.

There are two forms of delegated power. The *fact-finding group* involves the manager and workers collegially discussing and generating a solution to a problem (i.e., a course of action to change something). *Sensitivity training* (which will be discussed later in this chapter) places an emphasis on change via an improvement in individuals' self-awareness, which leads to improved interpersonal relationships, which leads to improved performance.

Greiner's studies led him to state that the shared approach is usually more successful than either the unilateral or delegated approaches. The reason for this finding may be that the unilateral approach tends to ignore potentially valuable inputs from workers, and the delegated approach restricts or negates the manager's own inputs. Hence, the shared approach strikes a balance and provides some independence for workers, while also permitting some policy and authority enforcement by the manager.

Exhibit 16–2
Three-power approaches to change

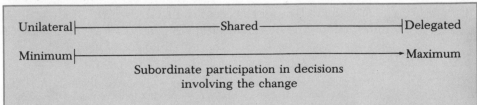

Unilateral |——————————Shared————————| Delegated

Minimum |———————————————————→ Maximum

Subordinate participation in decisions
involving the change

Exhibit 16–3
Dynamics of successful organizational change

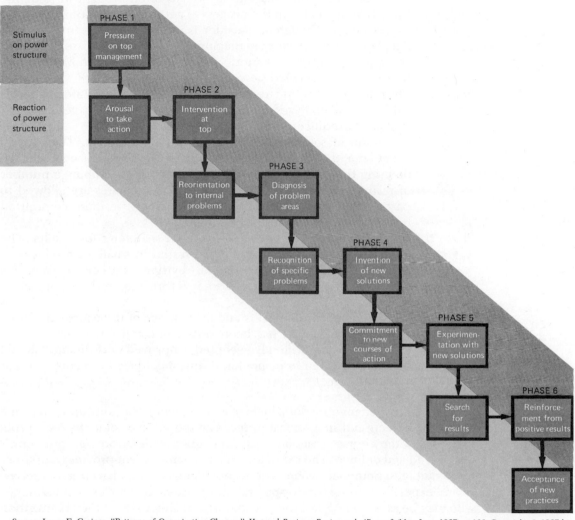

Based on his study of successful changes in organizations, Greiner has proposed the model presented in Exhibit 16–3. The model has six phases:

Phase 1:   Pressure on and arousal of top management to take action. Top management needs to feel a need or pressure for a change. This usually is caused by some significant problem(s); e.g., a sharp decline in profits, serious labor unrest, and so on.*

* Bert Lance, Jimmy Carter's first director of the Office of Management and Budget, was fond of saying, "If it ain't broke, don't fix it."

Phase 2:   Intervention by a respected person (change agent) and reorientation to the internal problems. An outsider is often brought in to define the problem and begin the process of getting organization members to focus on it. Though an outsider is most often used, internal staff people are also capable of managing the process if they are perceived as "expert" and are "trusted." In either case the problem is "attacked" by a respected person.

Phase 3:   Diagnosis of data and recognition of the problem. Information is gathered and analyzed by the change agent and management. *The* problems are uncovered.

Phase 4:   Invention of solutions and a commitment to action. The change agent should stimulate thought and try to avoid an overreliance on using the "same old methods." Creatively developing a number of plausible alternatives is desired. As subordinates are allowed to participate in this process, they will probably be more committed to the course of action finally chosen.

Phase 5:   Experimenting with new solutions and searching for results. The solutions developed in Phase 4 are tested in small-scale pilot tests and results analyzed. Perhaps one division or a certain part of a sales force tries out an idea before it is thrust upon the organization as a whole.

Phase 6:   Reinforcement from results and acceptance of the course of action. If a course of action has been tested out and found desirable, it should be (more) willingly accepted. Improved performance should be a source of reinforcement and thus should lead to a commitment to the change.

The planned change model provides a convenient checklist approach in a complete fashion and in a logical order. Far too often, "solutions seek problems"—i.e., the course of action is decided upon well before the problem is discovered and defined. The use of an outside change agent provides a number of advantages. Someone whom we do not know well and who is perceived as an "expert" is often more respected and trusted than a close acquaintance who may be as skilled.* Since the outsider is expected to leave the organization upon completion of the change, there is also the tendency to feel that the outsider will act more "professionally" and not be subject to behaving so as to achieve personal gains based upon the change. Thus, the outsider is often able to elicit information that might not be presented to an insider who may later turn it to personal gain. And, this information may be needed to better define the problem and/or analyze alternatives. What you don't know *can* hurt you.

---

* A popular definition of an expert is: "Someone who lives at least 50 miles away and carries a briefcase." Further, "A prophet is only despised in his own country and in his own house." (Matthew, 13:57)

BEHAVIORAL ISSUES IN MANAGING CHANGE

As noted earlier by Leavitt, a change in either the organizational, structural, or people areas will lead to subsequent changes in other areas. Since organizations are made up of people, the human factor will ultimately come into play in any change program.

Most views toward change involving individuals in organizations are based upon the work of Kurt Lewin who believed that for attitudinal and behavioral changes to occur, a sequence of stages must be passed through.[7] The stages are:

1. *Unfreezing.*   There is a desire for change. This is based on a felt need; some level of dissatisfaction with the status quo. Support is withdrawn for present values and behavior. The old way is no longer desirable or acceptable.
2. *Moving.*   The desired new set of behaviors and attitudes are introduced. The individual should see the new behavioral attitudes at work for other people and should begin to exhibit the new behavior themselves.
3. *Refreezing.*   Without reinforcement the newly acquired behaviors and attitudes will not endure for long. A regression back to the "old ways" needs to be countered. Sufficient reinforcement for the newly acquired behaviors and attitudes must be provided at least until the change becomes a part of the individual's "normal" repertoire.

Examples of the use of this three-stage sequence abound. Military training traditionally takes a new recruit and immediately induces a high amount of stress to develop a "felt need" to change. Recruits have their hair cut, are yelled at, are given new clothes, and so on. This all facilitates the unfreezing process. The recruit is cut off from old values and behaviors. The military indoctrination and training is the moving phase as a new set of skills, values, and behaviors are taught. By the end of basic training, the new behaviors are typically "normal" as refreezing occurs due to constant reinforcement/ punishment of desired/undesired actions.

Religious cults also seem to use this process. The convert is usually someone who is "lost" or having personal problems (i.e., the felt need to change is there). The converts are typically isolated from old friends, family, and familiar places and are subjected to a great deal of pressure aimed at getting them to reject their former beliefs (i.e., unfreezing). Next, a high degree of indoctrination is given (the movement stage). As the new, desired behaviors are exhibited, the converts are rewarded (refreezing). Ultimately, the conversion becomes complete.

One aspect of the refreezing process seems especially critical and is based upon the simple admonition "if you make a change, then *make* it." Too often when a change is introduced, for example, a new computerized billing system, the old way of doing things is not totally withdrawn. Hence, there can be a tendency to revert back to the old way whenever a problem occurs because it is easy/familiar. If this is allowed, the new computer system will likely never get all the bugs worked out and it will ultimately fail. To properly refreeze, the old system should be taken away. Certainly backup records should be kept on the old system until the new computerized system is debugged. But, these records should be kept elsewhere; inaccessible except under only the most extreme emergency to the people involved with the new system. Praise and rewards should be given to those people working the new system as they struggle and cope with problems. Allowing vestiges of the "old way" in the guise of the old forms, office titles on the door, and so on will only encourage a remission back to where unfreezing began.

It is interesting to note how often college and professional coaches practice this admonition. Almost always a new coach will dismiss those assistants and most other personnel left behind when the old coach departed. The new coach typically discards the furniture in the office and redecorates. Changing the color scheme is a virtual certainty. New uniforms and even a new logo are also common. The message in all this? "This is how it is now. I'm in charge. We'll now do it my way. Don't bother me with stories about how you used to do it. You get rewarded for what you do now, not for what you did." The unfreezing-moving-refreezing process takes place swiftly. The team can "get back to business" without all of the worrying and behind the scenes politics associated with wondering just what will happen. It happened. Now we can move forward.

Resistance to change

A major obstacle to many change attempts is simply resistance by organizational members.

1. Pragmatic considerations. Perhaps an individual perceives that the change will do him or her some harm; e.g., his or her job may be eliminated or substantially changed, old benefits may be lost, one's potential for promotion may be hampered, and so on. Just because a change may be beneficial to the organization as a whole does not mean that all concerned individuals stand to gain. Also, even in the absence of perceived harm, if the individual does not stand to benefit (i.e., has no felt need), there tends to be little incentive to alter the status quo. Also, an individual could see serious errors in the change proposal and thus generate resistance. It is not uncommon for major programs to survive experts' scrutiny only to have some lower level old-timer take one look, say "It ain't right. It won't work" and be correct.

2. Social considerations. Even in the absence of financial and related losses being caused by a potential change, individuals could resist due to social factors.

The change could result in the loss of a status symbol, cause the disruption of an informal organization, or could simply result in making a job "less fun" or "more boring."

3. Uncertainty. Fear of the unknown is typical of most people. Dark alleys (real and figurative) often create trepidation. Even if a worker has no outright complaints about a change, the change may still be resisted because of some unknown or unpredictable aspect. After all, if things are fine now, why risk a change?* When the promoters of change attempt to profess all of the benefits, they are usually greeted with skepticism. Dick Gregory once said that you shouldn't have to "sell" a change to people—if it's any good, they'll steal it. There seems to be a moral there.

John McCarthy contends that employees will be motivated to follow directions or to change if an appeal is made to at least one of the following five points:[8]

1. Am I going to make money, maybe even get rich—or is this going to cost me money?
2. Are you going to make me famous or look good—or will I look bad if I do what you want?
3. Will I be more secure or safe—or will I be taking a chance by doing what you are asking?
4. Is this going to make life easier for me—or will I have to do harder or rougher work?
5. Will my sphere of influence increase (i.e., more power, authority)—or will it be reduced if I go along with your advice or instructions?

Reducing versus overcoming resistance

Exhibit 16–4 presents what is known as a force field model. The horizontal line represents the status quo. The arrows pushing up from below are forces for change. The relative size of each arrow indicates the "weight" of each force. The arrows pushing down from above are forces resisting the change. Again weights are indicated by the arrows' size.

The line (status quo) is currently "in balance." The forces have pushed against each other and the line has moved up or down until a balance was achieved. To change the system we need to move the line (up, in this case). There are two ways to create enough imbalance to move the line. First, we could simply add more forces (arrows) and/or add to the weight of existing arrows. As in a tug-of-war, when our side adds more members and gets stronger, it can begin to overcome the other side by sheer force. Note that the other

---

* Remember Bert Lance's admonition: "If it ain't broke, don't fix it."

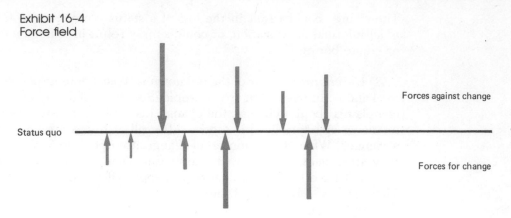

Exhibit 16–4
Force field

The second approach involves *reducing* the resistance. Here we attempt to reduce the size of the arrows acting against us while maintaining our own forces (e.g., we get a few of the opponents in the tug-of-war to drop out).

In both cases, overcoming and reducing, the horizontal line moves to a new balance point. Obviously, the "social cost" (and perhaps real costs as well) would seem to be greater in the overcoming strategy. Certainly, more ergs of energy are expended in winning a tug-of-war by this strategy. Further, by reducing resistance, there would probably be greater harmony in the organization.

The force field approach provides an easily constructed method for analyzing the impact of a change on the people in an organization. The simple exercise of creating it by listing the various forces often leads to the discovery of heretofore overlooked elements of the situation.

ORGANIZATION DEVELOPMENT

The planned change model put forth by Greiner seems well suited for those immediate and visible problems in an organization. On the other hand, organization development (OD) as a change approach does not normally seek to solve the immediate and visible problem. Instead it is a longer range change approach that seeks to affect organizational performance by focusing on changing the attitudes and behaviors of organizational members.

Warren Bennis points out that OD rests upon three basic propositions:[9]

1. Each age creates and adopts those organizational forms that are most appropriate to current conditions. As these conditions change, so must the form of the organization.
2. The only real way to change any organization is to change its "culture"; that is, the system of beliefs, attitudes, norms, patterns of interaction, and so on.
3. Since a social awareness is necessary in our current, dynamic world, a similar social awareness must be assumed by people in organizations.

The essence of OD is the use of behavioral science knowledge to aid organizations to adapt to changes that occur in the world. A widely accepted definition of OD is offered by Beckhard:

> Organization development is an effort (1) *planned,* (2) *organizationwide,* and (3) *managed* from the *top,* to (4) increase *organization effectiveness* and *health* through (5) *planned interventions* in the organization's "processes," using *behavioral science* knowledge.[10]

Each aspect of Beckhard's definition warrants examination. First, OD is *planned.* It is a systematic, deliberate effort. Second, it involves the entire *organizational system.* The system need not necessarily be an entire organization, but must be a discrete, autonomous unit (e.g., not the government as a whole, but, say, the U.S. Forest Service; or Pontiac Division of General Motors). Third, it must be *managed from the top.* Without a top-management commitment, OD can rarely accomplish much. Fourth, OD is intended to improve *organizational health* and *effectiveness* as indicated by such factors as: sound organizational design, undistorted communication, viable reward systems, a lack of win/lose confrontations, and the like. Lastly, OD uses *planned interventions* based on behavioral science knowledge. This involves the use of a number of specific techniques which are based upon research evidence.

Types of OD interventions

There is a large number of intervention techniques available for use. French and Bell have developed a classification scheme that separates interventions into 12 "families."[11]

1. *Diagnostic activities.* These are intended to determine the status of an organization; its needs, its problems, operating procedures, and so on. Methods include questionnaires, surveys, interviews, meetings, and a variety of other mechanisms limited only by one's data gathering ingenuity.
2. *Team-building activities.* These are designed to improve the performance of people in groups, or work teams. Areas of involvement include member skills, resources, and interpersonal relations. Teams may be formal work groups, committees, task forces, and any other permanent or transient aggregation of personnel.

3. *Intergroup activities.* These are designed to promote more effective inter-action *between* teams or groups. They focus on joint interaction and the inputs/outputs associated with the various groups.

4. *Survey-feedback activities.* These are related to the diagnostic activities discussed above. Included are efforts that collect data via surveys, ascertain actual or potential problems based on the data, and develop plans and activities based on the survey data. Survey results are normally fed back to organization members as an aid to developing problem solutions.

5. *Education and training activities.* The focus here is upon skills, knowl-edge, and abilities of people. These can be both technical and interpersonal in nature and may be conducted in groups or individually.

6. *Technostructure activities.* These activities involve new organizational designs or different resource allocations. The focus is upon analyzing and experimenting with organizational, technical, and/or resource constraints upon performance.

7. *Process consultation activities.* These involve a "consultant" helping the "client" understand process or procedural problems and develop solutions. The consultant asks the right questions, provides special knowledge, and guides the client in solving interpersonal problems in such "process" areas as communications, decision making, leadership, and group norms.

8. *Grid Organization Development® activities.* Grid OD was developed by Blake and Mouton and is an extension of the leadership theory discussed in Chapter 11. It is a six-phase process which can take from three to five years. Phase 1 develops managers' problem solving and leadership skills. Phase 2 is involved with team building and goal setting. Phase 3 deals with improving intergroup relations. In phase 4 top managers begin design-ing an organizational model (structure) which will aid in achieving organi-zational and individual goals. Phase 5 involves implementing the model just developed. Finally, phase 6 emphasizes a continuing evaluation of the impact of the Grid program; i.e., what was accomplished, and what needs to be done next?

9. *Third-party peacemaking activities.* These activities involve the use of a third-party consultant to help resolve a conflict between two others (indi-viduals or groups). The consultant uses a variety of mediator and conflict resolution skills and strategies.

10. *Coaching and counseling activities.* The key here is nonevaluative feed-back given to individuals. The aim is to help people (1) define learning goals, (2) learn how others see their behavior, and (3) learn new behaviors to aid in goal attainment.

11. *Life-and-career-planning activities.* These activities help individuals to articulate their personal goals and then analyze how they can go about achieving these in the organization. Specific programs here involve life/career inventories, assessment of capabilities and skills, and determination of training needs. Note how this blends into work force planning as dis-cussed in Chapter 8.

12. *Planning and goal-setting activities.* These activities involve training in organizational planning and problem solving. The intent is to help inte-

Exhibit 16–5
A typology of OD interventions based on target groups

Target group	Types of interventions
Interventions designed to improve the effectiveness of *individuals*	Life- and career-planning activities Role analysis technique Coaching and counseling T-group (sensitivity training) Education and training to increase skills, knowledge in the areas of technical task needs, relationship skills, process skills, decision making, problem solving, planning, goal-setting skills Grid OD phase 1
Interventions designed to improve the effectiveness of *dyads/triads*	Process consultation Third-party peacemaking Grid OD phases 1, 2
Interventions designed to improve the effectiveness of *teams and groups*	Team building—Task directed —Process directed Family T-group Survey feedback Process consultation Role analysis technique "Startup" team-building activities Education in decision making, problem solving, planning, goal-setting in group settings
Interventions designed to improve the effectiveness of *intergroup relations*	Intergroup activities—Process directed —Task directed Organizational mirroring (three or more groups) Technostructural interventions Process consultation Third-party peacemaking at group level Grid OD phase 3 Survey feedback
Interventions designed to improve the effectiveness of the *total organization*	Technostructural activities Confrontation meetings Strategic planning activities Grid OD phases 4, 5, 6 Survey feedback

Source: Wendell L. French and Cecil H. Bell, Jr., *Organization Development: Behavioral Science Interventions for Organization Improvement* © 1973 (Englewood Cliffs, N.J.: Prentice-Hall, Inc., 1973), p. 107. Reprinted by permission.

grate individuals and groups into the total organization by showing how each contributes to the planning and decision-making process.

Target groups of OD interventions. A convenient way to view OD interventions is by seeing what "level" of the organization is involved. In Exhibit 16–5 we show five target groups and the types of OD interventions that are often used to promote effectiveness in each area. It is readily apparent that certain interventions are applicable to several targets.

It is beyond the scope of this book to thoroughly discuss each of the interventions shown in Exhibit 16–5. There are, however, several which are widely used and ought to be understood by today's managers. Reference to any one of several books on OD can be made to gain insight into the many other interventions.*

T-groups

T-groups (or sensitivity training groups) are worthy of special mention since until fairly recently, they were viewed as the major tool of the OD field, and were thought by some to be synonymous with it. In essence, T-groups are leaderless groups which meet with a psychologist (or similar professional) over an extended period of time, with the general objective of developing an open environment so that its members may interact with one another in complete honesty. T-groups may consist of people who work together and/ or know each other ("family groups") or may be composed of total strangers. The ultimate end objective is for individuals to see themselves as others see them and to be able to use this insight to change their own attitudes and/or behavior in order to function more effectively in the work setting. This process calls for gaining "social sensitivity"—understanding how one comes across to others; and "behavioral flexibility"—being able to change attitudes and behavior in light of one's new awareness of their impact on others. What makes T-groups different from, say, a department meeting or social discussion is the emphasis on getting at people's true feelings. In the "classic" T-group, there is no agenda, no appointed "leader" and only slight input (if any) from the professional who is monitoring the members' activities. Members generally do attempt in early meetings to establish structure, exert their authority, form cliques, or in other ways establish leadership positions. As the group evolves, it develops its own norms of behavior, and individuals tend to fulfill leadership,

---

* For example, see Wendell L. French and Cecil H. Bell, Jr., *Organization Development: Behavioral Science Interventions for Organization Improvement* (Englewood Cliffs, N.J.: Prentice-Hall, Inc., 1973); Edgar F. Huse, *Organization Development and Change* (St. Paul: West Publishing Co., 1975); or the excellent 1969 Addison-Wesley Series on Organization Development, of which the following are a part: Richard Beckhard, *Organization Development: Strategies and Models;* Warren G. Bennis, *Organization Development: Its Nature, Origins, and Prospects;* Robert R. Blake and Jane S. Mouton, *Building a Dynamic Corporation through Grid Organization Development;* Paul R. Lawrence and Jay W. Lorsch, *Developing Organizations;* Edgar H. Schein, *Process Consultation;* and Richard E. Walton, *Interpersonal Peacemaking: Confrontation and Third Party Consultation* (Reading, Mass: Addison-Wesley Publishing Co., Inc., 1969). More recent volumes in the series include: Richard Beckhard and Reuben T. Harris, *Organizational Transitions: Managing Complex Change* (1977); William G. Dyer, *Team Building: Issues and Alternatives* (1977); Jay R. Galbraith, *Designing Complex Organizations* (1973); David A. Nadler, *Feedback and Organization Development* (1977); Richard J. C. Roeber, *The Organization in a Changing Environment* (1973); Fred I. Steele, *Physical Settings and Organization Development* (1973); and Stanley M. Dairs and Paul R. Lawrence, *Matrix* (1977).

group maintenance, and other such roles that the group itself creates. By experiencing this developmental process and by "seeing" one's own behavior in it, people are believed to be better able to perceive and understand their own and others' behavior in their work-a-day organizations.

An important aspect of T-groups is the development of a better understanding of oneself and of others. Such an understanding is believed to be facilitated by open communications and free expression of feelings. Just as teamwork on a sports team is aided when members can predict each others' "moves," teamwork in our organizations can be aided when we can better understand and thus better predict how co-workers will behave.

The Johari window, developed by Joe Luft and Harry Ingham, provides an interesting analytical device to measure the openness of our communications about ourselves with others. The window is illustrated in Exhibit 16–6. The four window panes are represented by columns and rows. The columns

Exhibit 16–6
The Johari window

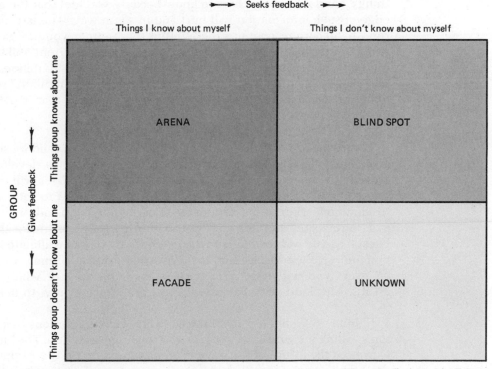

Source: Based on Philip C. Hanson, "The Johari Window: A Model for Soliciting and Giving Feedback," in John E. Jones and J. William Pfeiffer, eds., *The 1973 Annual Handbook for Group Facilitators* (La Jolla, Cal.: University Associates, 1973), p. 115. Used with permission.

represent the *self* and the rows the *group*. In the left column are the "things I know about myself" and the other column contains the "things I don't know about myself." The top row represents those "things the group knows about me" and the bottom row the "things the group doesn't know about me." The information in each area need not be static because as trust occurs so usually will more open communication and feedback. Thus the size/shape of each window pane can change in response to information sharing.

The upper left corner pane is the *Arena;* things I know and things the group knows. This area is characterized by free, open communications. The Arena will increase in size with increased trust and communication. The upper right corner is the *Blind Spot;* things the group knows but I don't. Such information can be picked up by group members from verbal cues, body language, and so on. This pane will increase in size to the extent that we are insensitive to the consequences of our own behavior. Discovering information from this pane can be quite disconcerting. It could range from finding out you have bad breath or body odor (remember those TV commercials?) to being told that you always cough just before giving someone a difficult order. A large Blind Spot would be a poker player's downfall.

The lower left-hand corner is the *Facade*. This pane represents your secrets; things you don't want others to know because you feel that the group's knowledge of such information will hurt you in some way. The last pane, the lower right-hand corner, contains those things that neither you nor the group knows about yourself. This is the *Unknown*. Such things as latent abilities, childhood memories, or even unrecognized physical or mental disabilities are included here. This pane increases/decreases in size as we "remember," solicit information, and try out new behaviors. It is very unlikely that a person will ever totally eliminate this pane.

The reduction of the Blind Spot would seem to be a valid sensitivity training goal. This will only come about when one is willing to develop a receptive attitude to encourage others to communicate freely. This will cause the right side column to shrink in size. Another goal would be to reduce the Facade; to allow co-workers to be better able to understand you and facilitate teamwork (e.g., anticipate your move to the basket so they can make that pass). The Facade can be reduced only to the extent that you are willing to share information and give feedback to others. Thus the group will know where you stand on issues and will not have to guess that much about what your behavior means. This kind of behavior will cause the bottom row to decrease in size.

Exhibit 16–7 shows several Johari window configurations based upon a person's willingness and ability to give and solicit information. The "Ideal Window" expresses the intent of sensitivity training; to increase the Arena and decrease the other panes. The "Interviewer" represents people who solicit feedback from others (to reduce the Blind Spot) but in turn give out little information

Exhibit 16–7
Representative types of Johari windows

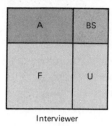

Ideal window

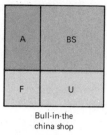

Interviewer

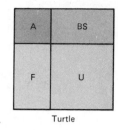

Bull-in-the
china shop

Turtle

Source: Based on Philip C. Hanson, "The Johari Window: A Model for Soliciting and Giving Feedback," in John E. Jones and J. William Pfeiffer, eds., *The 1973 Annual Handbook for Group Facilitators* (La Jolla, Cal.: University Associates, 1973), p. 118. Used with permission.

about themselves (thus keeping a large Facade). The "Bull-in-the-China Shop" has a large Blind Spot and rarely has the ability or inclination to assess the consequences of his or her own behavior. The Bull gives out information rather freely, but rarely seeks out or accepts the feedback of others. The "Turtle" hides in a shell. This could be a silent observer or someone in a group who is the "mystery person." Such people often praise themselves for being "good listeners." Because they neither solicit nor give much information, they tend to be left out of the mainstream of a group's functioning and are often viewed with distrust or hostility by more active group members.

Team building

As one might surmise, T-groups are an imprecise instrument and it seems safe to say that their use has diminished since their halcyon days of the mid-1960s. What has replaced their function in many OD activities is what is termed "team building" which as the name implies is an approach that is designed to get people to function more effectively as part of a team or work group. Team building activities are generally directed toward four major organizational improvement areas:

1. Diagnostic meetings; involving a general critique of the performance of the team; i.e., its strengths and weaknesses, and identification of promising areas for improvement.
2. Task accomplishment; usually focusing on how to proceed in making the improvements identified in the diagnostic meeting.
3. Team relationships; focusing on resolving interpersonal or interunit conflict if members are from special groups; or focusing on improving boss/subordinate relationships and peer relationships if members are from family groups.
4. Team and organization processes; centering on communications, decision making, and task allocations.

In carrying out the team building activities, it is recommended that diagnostic meetings be held separately from problem-solving meetings since their purpose is identifying problems, not solving them (an activity that may necessitate considerably more time and resources).

As in T-groups, team building uses a professional consultant, but unlike the T-group trainer, the professional's role is one of gathering information from the group prior to a meeting and presenting issues to the group based upon this information. Getting problems/opportunities out on the floor and developing action plans is a major objective of postdiagnostic team building meetings.

The role analysis technique (RAT) is a team building intervention that is designed to help clarify or develop job or role expectations and obligations of team members. In many cases team members' jobs may not be carefully spelled out or known; i.e., the "job description" is nonexistent or out of date. This can lead to conflicts over work domain, decisions not being made because no one accepts responsibility, and so on. Such problems can occur in new teams (e.g., startup teams as discussed in Chapter 9) as well as with older work groups where changes have occurred over time to the point that the old job descriptions are no longer valid.

The RAT consists of a series of steps for each person or position under consideration. To begin the RAT, one person volunteers or is chosen to start. The person (and their job) now under consideration is called the *focal role*. The following steps then take place:

1. The focal role individual analyses/describes his or her role (job). The job's duties, its place in the organization, what is done, what isn't done, what should be done, and so on are all discussed by the focal role incumbent. A blackboard may be used to list the duties, responsibilities, and so on of the focal role. The focal role incumbent makes the initial statement, but all team members may discuss additions/deletions from the list. The discussion continues until ultimately a consensus is reached about the list.
2. Step 2 involves the focal role incumbent listing his or her expectations of every other team member based upon the agreed-to-list. The team can discuss these expectations and add/delete or modify, again until a consensus is reached.
3. After each other team member's obligations are decided upon (step 2), each other team member (in turn) describes what is wanted or needed from the focal role imcumbent in order for them to live up to the step 2 agreement.

After step 3 is completed, another team member is chosen for the focal role. This continues until all team members have gone through the three steps.

4. Finally, after all team members have been through the process, each focal role incumbent must write up a summary of the job as it has been defined

and agreed-to; they create a new "job description." This document is reviewed and perhaps modified at a subsequent team meeting. It then becomes "accepted."

The result of the RAT is normally a far better understanding of other people's jobs. It is advisable to undergo a RAT periodically, especially for higher level management jobs that are dynamic and subject to periodic change. In a hospital organization where the RAT was used for the administrator and seven associate administrators, the initial RAT took place over a weekend retreat. Subsequently, one focal role per month is reviewed in regularly scheduled staff meetings. Thus, each job comes up for review every eight months.

Intergroup team building.   This OD technique attempts to do much the same as team building for a departmental unit—improve communication, reduce the amount of dysfunctional competition, enhance interactions among members—and in addition, to provide an awareness of how groups must interrelate in achieving general organizational goals. The methodology involved varies, but the guiding philosophy in the approach is solving problems through *confrontation*. That is, meeting sources of disagreements head on by bringing them out in the open and then sticking with the facts until a solution is hammered out. There are several specific approaches which can be used.

One approach is described by Beckhard:

1. The leaders (or all members) of two groups are brought together to discuss whether relations can and should be improved. If so, the subsequent steps are undertaken.
2. *Separately,* each group develops a list of the attitudes and ideas it holds about the other group; that is, what is liked and what is disliked about the other group. Also, each group develops a list of their speculations about what the other groups is listing about them.
3. The groups are then brought together and the lists are shared. Clarifications are permitted, but no discussion is allowed. Each group simply reads its lists.
4. Again separately, each group reacts to the shared information. What are the areas of agreement and disagreement about each other? How did the disagreements occur? Why? Finally, each group develops a list of "priority" issues that need to be resolved. This list is usually quite small compared to the step 2 list.
5. The groups meet and compare priority issues lists. Together a single list is developed and a commitment obtained toward attacking these problems.
6. Leaders or certain members of each group meet periodically to discuss progress.[12]

This type of intergroup intervention is often useful for headquarters-field problems. It may also be useful for certain union-management situations. Overall, its utility is greatest where the two groups have misunderstandings which are based upon poor communications or faulty perceptions.

Another popular intergroup intervention is organizational "mirroring." This approach is useful when a particular unit is having difficulties with a number of other organizational units. The focal unit (often through a consultant) invites the other units to a meeting. Prior to the meeting, the consultant interviews relevant people to begin getting a "feel" for the problem(s). At the meeting, a "fishbowl" is created: The focal group sits inside a circle of the other groups and, in an uninterrupted manner, the other groups talk among themselves about the focal group. Following this, the focal group discusses (again in an uninterrupted manner) what it just heard. Clarifications may be asked for. After this a general discussion may ensue but *no one* begins to solve any problems that are uncovered. The consultant must often ask questions and keep the discussion on track. Also, the consultant should maintain the feeling of an open, nonhostile climate. The consultant's job is not an easy one!

Subgroups are then created that are jointly composed of both focal unit members and members of other groups. These subgroups identify changes that would help improve the effectiveness of the focal group. The subgroups then report back to the whole assembly. In a general discussion, action plans are developed and tasks assigned. A follow-up meeting is usually scheduled prior to adjournment.

This intervention technique is very useful when a particular work unit seems to experience difficulties with other work-related groups. Information feedback is quick, and agreed-upon plans to resolve problems usually lead to real actions and better understandings.

Evaluation of OD

Given the great numbers of books and practitioners in the field of OD, it is apparent that someone must feel that the benefits are worth the costs. Certainly, we find it difficult to argue with the goals of OD; that is, promoting organizational effectiveness by improving the way people work together. Unfortunately, despite its popularity, there is some question as to how good OD really is.

Two recent articles on the subject argue that research in the area is generally insufficient to determine if OD does in fact work. Pfeiffer and Jones state that "No OD effort we know of can be claimed to be a success on the bottom line. It is impossible to attribute organizational achievement to OD because of the time lag involved between the 'treatment' and the 'result.' "[13] Peggy Morrison is even more critical based upon her analysis of 26 OD studies: "It is clear from the data presented . . . that the studies of OD evaluation published to date do not conform to established criteria for internal and external validity for effective social science research and evaluation."[14]

In light of these somewhat negative evaluations, the reader may be wondering why we brought the subject up! The answer is, first, that the tools of

OD do appear to be appropriate for certain organizations for dealing with certain problems. (Team building, for example, is eminently logical when workers will have to be working as a team, even though research studies can't guarantee success.) And second, modern managers should be aware of what OD is since they may very well have to participate in OD activities or even be asked to make a decision on its use in their own organizations.

SUMMARY

The rapidity of change in our modern world mandates that organizations as open systems be adaptive and undergo change themselves. Reactive changes, over time, result in significant and often unexpected alterations of an organization. Planned change takes a proactive approach and strives to create a revised, much more predictable and effective organization.

Behavioral responses to change attempts must be considered by managers. The felt need to change and the expected benefits may not be similarly perceived by both managers and workers. Strategies for reducing as well as overcoming resistance to change need to be considered in virtually all cases of change implementation. (Some basic rules of thumb are suggested in Exhibit 16–8.)

Organization development as a change approach focuses on improving organizational effectiveness by improving behavioral processes within the organization. There are many OD intervention techniques aimed at individuals, groups, intergroup relationships, and organizationwide systems. Unfortunately, despite the popularity of OD, there is great difficulty in assessing the bottom line benefits of this change approach. Still, there is face validity for OD and there is virtual certainty that most managers in the near future will be exposed to OD interventions. Hence, knowledge of this change approach should be encouraged.

Exhibit 16–8
Some rules of thumb for introducing change

1. There is a clear-cut felt need.
2. A credible source helps introduce it.
3. The implications of the change for people are spelled out.
4. The people affected should have some inputs into the what and how of the change.
5. Benefits should be shared by all those who incurred "costs" in making the change.
6. Expect some resistance. Try to reduce it first; overcome it only if reducing fails, as prescribed by the force field approach.

GUIDES TO ACTION

1. Change is inevitable. Don't fight it. Monitor your environment and adapt. When beneficial, plan your change and be proactive. You can influence the world as well as have it influence you.

2. Use of an outside change agent poses many benefits. Don't rely on internal change agents unless there are overwhelming arguments to the contrary.

3. Recognize the importance of a felt need or tension state for both organizational and human change. If the felt need isn't perceived as you desire (e.g., people may resist because they like things fine the way they are), you may have to "shake things up" to generate a certain level of tension before proceeding with the change process.

4. Once a change is made, make sure it stays made. If, for example, you changed the purchase authorization form (e.g., it is now blue rather than green and has a special line for someone else's signature), then burn or otherwise dispose of the old ones. Letting the old ones lay around will encourage people to use them. And once they do, the regression begins.

5. Once the system is unfrozen, it is advisable to go ahead with a number of intended changes rather than allowing it to refreeze for a while and then unfreeze for another small change, refreeze, and so on.

6. Despite the lack of significant validation, well-chosen OD interventions should be encouraged. Use of an outside OD consultant is a "must" in all but a few rare exceptions. Pick your consultant carefully and don't hesitate to check references and see how the consultant fared in previous work. Once chosen, trust the consultant and don't try to pull strings behind the curtain.

NOTES

[1] Alvin Toffler, *Future Shock* (New York: Bantam Books, Inc., 1971), p. 13.

[2] George Odiorne, *Management and the Activity Trap* (New York: Harper & Row Publishers, Inc., 1974), p. 154.

[3] Shirley Terreberry, "The Evolution of Organizational Environments," *Administrative Science Quarterly*, vol. 12, no. 4 (March 1968), pp. 590–613.

[4] Alfred Chandler, *Strategy and Structure: Chapters in the History of the American Industrial Enterprise* (Cambridge, Mass.: MIT Press, 1962).

[5] Harold J. Leavitt, "Applied Organizational Change in Industry: Structural, Technical, and Human Approaches," in W. W. Cooper, H. J. Leavitt, and M. W. Shelly, eds., *New Perspectives in Organization Research* (New York: John Wiley & Sons, Inc., 1964), pp. 55–71.

[6] Larry E. Greiner, "Patterns of Organization Change," *Harvard Business Review*, vol. 45, no. 3 (May–June 1967), pp. 119–30.

[7] Kurt Lewin, "Frontiers in Group Dynamics: Concept, Method, and Reality in Social Science," *Human Relations*, vol. 1, no. 1 (1947), pp. 5–41.

[8] John J. McCarthy, *Why Managers Fail . . . and What to Do about It* (New York: McGraw-Hill Book Company, 1978), p. 43.

[9] Warren G. Bennis, *Organization Development: Its Nature, Origins, and Prospects* (Reading, Mass.: Addison-Wesley Publishing Co., Inc., 1969), p. v.

[10] Richard Beckhard, *Organization Development: Strategies and Models* (Reading,

Mass.: Addison-Wesley Publishing Co., Inc., 1969), p. 9. Italics in original.

[11] Wendell L. French, and Cecil H. Bell, Jr., *Organization Development: Behavioral Science Interventions for Organization Improvement* (Englewood Cliffs, N.J.: Prentice-Hall, Inc., 1973), pp. 102–4.

[12] Beckhard, *Organization Development*, pp. 33–35.

[13] J. W. Pfeiffer, and J. E. Jones, "A Current Assessment of OD: What It Is and Why It Often Fails," *The 1976 Handbook for Group Facilitators* (La Jolla, Cal.: University Associates, 1976), p. 228.

[14] Peggy Morrison, "Evaluation in OD: A Review and Assessment," *Group and Organization Studies*, vol. 3, no. 1 (March 1978), p. 65.

DISCUSSION QUESTIONS

1. What are the ways in which management deals with change in organizations?

2. Why must managers monitor the organizational environment?

3. Identify the three things noted by Leavitt that change in an organization.

4. What are the phases in Greiner's change model?

5. Use Lewin's three-stage model (unfreeze, move, refreeze) to discuss a change in an organization with which you were involved.

6. Why do some people resist change?

7. From a force field perspective, why is overcoming resistance not the most desirable strategy?

8. What does OD do?

9. Select one of the many OD interventions discussed in the chapter and discuss how it could be applied to an organizational problem with which you are familiar.

10. Why do you suppose that OD efforts are hard to evaluate?

CASE: TEANOCO CORPORATION*

Teanoco Corporation, a Cleveland-based firm that manufactures a variety of automobile replacement parts, is planning to build a new manufacturing plant in North Platte, Nebraska. At the present time, Teanoco has three manufacturing facilities in operation. The blue-collar workers in these plants are all hourly employees with jobs ranging from machine operators to assembly-line workers where various automotive parts are assembled, inspected, tested, and packaged. This planned facility will manufacture primarily brake system parts including brake linings, wheel cylinders, brake drums and discs, master cylinders, and various other miscellaneous parts. North Platte has a population of about 20,000, and Teanoco's management believes that, with only two other

* From Theodore T. Herbert, *Organizational Behavior: Readings and Cases,* (New York: The Macmillan Co., 1976), pp. 369–71.

industries in the immediate area, they will be able to attract the type of individuals who will be willing to work. The North Platte plant will employ approximately 300 production workers and about 35 office workers.

A group of top managers responsible for the planning of this new production facility decided the time was right to do some corporate soulsearching into the reasons for every personnel policy. Every policy and procedure—from the employee's first interview, disciplinary rules, absenteeism control procedures, time clocks, buzzers, eligibility rules, to reserved parking places—was carefully examined and evaluated. The managers came to the conclusion that Teanoco's factory employee-relations policies and practices were fundamentally predicated on mistrust.

These managers decided that the North Platte plant would be designed to implement some changes in management philosophy and employee relations. They believed that an employee could be trusted and desired a certain amount of responsibility. They also believed that creating a humanistic environment within the factory would result in increased job satisfaction, higher productivity, reduced turnover and absenteeism, and a higher return on investment.

Keith Tarbett, manager of personnel, has been with Teanoco for about 12 years. He has an undergraduate degree in sociology and a master's degree in management. Keith has been selected by the group of managers to draw up a list of proposed changes that should be implemented in the North Platte plant, in order to create an environment that will be conducive to employee motivation.

Keith remembered seeing articles in several journals a few years back on the topic of job enrichment and decided that it might be a good idea to learn all he could about this topic; it might be just what Teanoco needs at a time like this. Over the next few weeks, Keith "did his homework," learning just what job enrichment was all about. He read everything he could find on the subject, including articles written by M. Scott Myers, Frederick Herzberg, Robert N. Ford, and Douglas McGregor. While doing this background preparation, Keith was surprised to read of the number of successful attempts at humanizing the work environment by various companies such as Texas Instruments, PPG Industries' Glass Division, Questor Corporation's Spalding Division, and Pitney-Bowes' Mailing Equipment Division. Although Keith was not too sure that job enrichment is everything the books say it is, not to mention what they say it can do, he was willing to talk it over with the other managers to see what their reaction would be to implementing some of the enrichment concepts into the operation of the North Platte plant.

At the next managers' planning meeting, Keith presented the job enrichment concepts to the others and suggested a number of ideas that could possibly be implemented at the North Platte plant. Keith emphasized that other industries have actually put some of these concepts into practice, resulting in increased productivity and profits, reduction in turnover and absenteeism, and a general improvement in employee motivation and job satisfaction. Among the ideas Keith presented were the following:

1. Put all employees on salary.
2. Train all supervisors to let each employee perform his own job as he sees fit.
3. Eliminate the company's 90-day probationary period for new employees.
4. Conduct an attitude survey of the employees at the other three Teanoco plants to determine what the employees really want to increase job satisfaction.
5. Eliminate company policies and rules on absenteeism and tardiness.
6. Design the work flow so that individuals have a complete module of work and use autonomous work groups to eliminate assembly-line operations.
7. Use job rotation to provide a variety of tasks for employees.
8. Hold semiannual "jobholders" meetings in which the employees can ask questions concerning their jobs and the company directly to top management.
9. Post or distribute pertinent production reports to *all* employees so they are given firsthand knowledge of how they are performing.
10. Establish a management by objectives program for setting individual goals and employee evaluation.

As soon as Keith had finished his presentation, a great deal of discussion began among the managers; comments such as these were heard:

"Keith has definitely gone overboard on this one."

"He must be joking to think this enrichment concept is really worthwhile."

"I'm not so sure Keith hasn't hit the nail right on the head. I think we ought to investigate this a bit further."

Dave Wilson, the man selected to be the plant manager of the North Platte plant, suggested that a complete investigation of the pros and cons of job enrichment be undertaken. He asked each of the managers to submit a written evaluation of each of the points presented by Mr. Tarbett to him on the Friday before the next managers' planning meeting.

Questions

1. Assume you are one of the Teanoco managers who have just heard Mr. Tarbett's job enrichment presentation. Evaluate each of the points Mr. Tarbett has presented.
2. Based on this evaluation and the information presented in the case, how would you recommend that the jobs at the North Platte plant be enriched?
3. What would you expect will be the results if these ideas are implemented in the North Platte plant?

Section eight
Termination of
the organization

A reality in life is that most organizations do, in part or in totality, close down. All too often managers ignore this reality and fail to develop skills in handling this managerial function. In this section we analyze a variety of partial and complete termination strategies with a view toward helping managers perform this function in both a humane and an economic manner.

SELECTION OF THE PRODUCT OR SERVICE	DESIGN OF THE SYSTEM	STAFFING THE ORGANIZATION	STARTUP OF THE ORGANIZATION	OPERATING THE ORGANIZATION IN THE STEADY STATE	IMPROVING THE ORGANIZATION	REVISION OF THE ORGANIZATION	TERMINATION OF THE ORGANIZATION
Decision-making processes; social value; forecasts; policies; plans	Authority and responsibility; power; organizational structure; communications systems; job design	Work force planning: personnel management functions	Startup planning and scheduling; monitoring; alternative startup approaches	Motivation; leadership; production and operations management; control	Individual improvement programs and techniques; group conflict management; MBO	Evaluation of organizational policies; strategic choices; organizational change; organizational development	Partial terminations; cutback management; complete terminations; mergers; born-again strategies

Level of Organizational Outputs

0

t₀

Time

Chapter 17
Termination processes

If you have too many problems, maybe you should go out of business. There is no law that says a company must last forever.

Peter Drucker[1]

The significance of Drucker's remark is that going out of business is an all too often overlooked potential course of action. Roy Walters has put this same idea another way: "If you're already in a hole, there's no use to continue digging."[2] Lest the reader feel that we are advocating organizational suicide, we hasten to add that we are simply urging that realistic appraisals of an organization's current status and its potential be made to ascertain whether continued operations are justified. If the justification is not there, then a planned, orderly, well-managed termination is preferable to spontaneously leaping off bridges.

Termination is an art that is often ignored in the management literature, too. Shutting down or terminating a unit or an entire organization is, however, too common an event to overlook. The U.S. Department of Commerce and the Small Business Administration periodically publish data pertaining to the mortality rate of business organizations. Small businesses are especially prone to termination. Half fail to survive a year of operations; only one third survive past year four. However, lest we assume that only small organizations are candidates for termination, we need only remember the Penn Central Railroad, W.T. Grant, Studebaker, the World Football League, the Office of Economic Opportunity, and the Atomic Energy Commission, among others. In fact, of the 100 largest business firms in the United States in 1900, only two (American Sugar and Exxon) were still in existence as late as 1968.[3] Who remembers such early 20th-century giants as Pacific Mail, Auburn Motors, Central Leather, U.S. Cordage Company, American Cotton Oil Company, Hudson Motors, and Baldwin Locomotive?

As noted, size alone does not guarantee survival. However, it no doubt helps. Large organizations may make errors which would wipe out the resources of smaller organizations, but are taken in stride due to the "slack" existent in most large organizations. Also, large organizations tend to have a wider variety of knowledgeable people in them and thus may be capable of dealing with a broader range of problems than smaller organizations. Finally, when they get into trouble, large organizations tend to be able to call upon greater amounts of outside aid and support. Note Lockheed's and Chrysler's government-backed loans and the degree of federal backing of loans to New York City. Would such aid have been as easily forthcoming to Cessna, de Lorean Motors, or Lebanon, Illinois?

500

A hallmark of organizations is that they *can* transcend the lifetimes of their human founders and members. Properly designed and managed, an organization can endure a dramatic turnover of its human component. Witness the Roman Catholic Church, the government of England, and the Hudson's Bay Company (originally chartered by Charles II in 1670 as "The Governor and Company of Adventurers of England trading into Hudson's Bay" and now Canada's oldest company). The point to remember, however, is that such immortality tends to be the exception rather than the rule.

There are many causes of organizational termination. Revolutions topple governments. As noted previously, "Sunset laws" enacted by many states force a periodic review of government agencies with the assumption that they are "terminated" and must be rejustified and created anew in order to continue to exist. Competition, poor management, or a depressed economy can terminate a business. Surprisingly, it sometimes can simply be more profitable to terminate. UV Industries (number 357 on the 1978 *Fortune* 500 list) found itself in such a position in early 1979 and did indeed begin to liquidate itself.[4] UV's situation came about due to a combination of circumstances whereby the company had a great deal of cash, and tax laws (Section 337 of the Internal Revenue Code) made it advantageous to simply liquidate and distribute the money to stockholders. Hence, the end of UV per se, and the movement of its assets and personnel to other endeavors.

As seen in the UV case, though the word termination implies failure, it may not be so. It was noted in the two preceding chapters that as the world changes so must our organizations. Some of these changes may well involve the obsolescence of a socially desirable good or service output or of the technological system that produces it. In a capitalistic society, we must accept the fact that resources will be allocated only to those organizations that produce desired outputs in the most efficient manner. Thus, we (our society) should not buy goods/services we do not desire nor should we buy goods/services that are overpriced in comparison to others. Those organizations that cannot produce desired outputs at competitive prices must, to attain a proper allocation of resources in a capitalistic economy, be terminated. Otherwise resources will not be used to their best advantage. Thus, termination of organizations, or parts of organizations, should be viewed not as "failure" per se, but as a part of a continual effort by society to attain a proper allocation of its resources.

In the sections that follow, we will look at several aspects of termination. First, we will discuss terminating a part of the organization (e.g., a single production line, one of several stores, or one of a number of plants). We will also look at cutback management, a situation where organizationwide reductions are made. Next we will consider termination of an entire organization. Fourth, we will analyze mergers as a form of termination. And, finally, we will consider "born again" organizations; those that cease one form of operations and emerge in a new role (e.g., the March of Dimes).

PARTIAL TERMINATION

Examples of partial terminations abound. A large oil company shuts down a small refinery in the Midwest. A retail chain closes a downtown store in the face of increased competition from suburban shopping malls. The ore in a copper mine begins to play out and the parent firm ceases operations until the price of copper rises enough to make the mine profitable again. An insurance company decides to get out of the life insurance business and write only fire and auto policies. Virtually all readers can remember examples of these types of closures that touched their own lives. While often traumatic, partial terminations need not be so. William Wong describes the well-managed closing of an American Oil Company refinery.[5] This well-planned termination allowed for an orderly reduction of personnel and assets in a way that minimized adverse effects on the remainder of the organization, its employees, and the community at large.

In this case, the termination was implemented via a planned phaseout of operations. Personnel were given options of moving to other jobs within the company. Suppliers had time to adjust to decreased sales. Assets were sold or donated to local government units in such a way as to neither depress values nor fuel speculation. And the local government units were given sufficient time to adjust for a decreased tax base and lowered employment.

Personnel

There are several ways of dealing with employees in a partial termination. First, employees can be permitted to transfer to other parts of the organization that are not being terminated. Second, if the terminated unit is being "sold off" perhaps the purchasing party will retain the employees. Third, employees can simply be let go. And last, some combination of the above may be used.

Retention of employees by allowing them to transfer to other organizational units is an appealing, humanistic approach. It does, however, have drawbacks as well as benefits.

On the benefits side, retention allows the organization to keep those skills for which it hired or perhaps trained the employees. If these skills are valuable or scarce, and if they are needed now or in the reasonably near future in another organizational unit, retention should be considered. Further, there may well be an increase in loyalty (and possible related improvements in morale and performance) when employees feel that the organization "takes care of its people." For example, IBM prides itself on retaining employees.[6] Thus, in the event of the termination of a unit of IBM, workers are offered jobs elsewhere in the organization.

Retention will involve a significant amount of personnel management work. As noted in Chapter 8, a personnel needs assessment is necessary for effective staffing. Thus, employees in the terminated unit need to be analyzed to ascertain how they can best fit into areas where their skills are needed by the organization. In addition, there may well be physical moves involved. It is one thing to transfer employees to another part of a plant or even to a facility in another part of town. It is another thing to transfer employees to another city. In the latter case, the organization may well pay for moving costs and provide help in selling and purchasing homes. Important decisions must be made concerning who is eligible to have various expenses paid (e.g., everyone? only those with, say, two years' seniority? and so on), the extent of these expenses (a percentage of the cost? all of the cost? only for a certain number of rooms of furniture? and so on), whether travel expenses will be paid for house-hunting visits to the new city (for the employee only? employee and spouse? employee and all dependents?), and to what extent the organization will help sell and purchase housing. Some organizations actually guarantee an employee an appraised value of a home so that in selling, perhaps quickly, a loss is not incurred.* Likewise, aid in obtaining financing or construction advice for a new home can be furnished at the new city.†

In some cases employees of a terminated unit are not only offered another job with the organization, they are given seniority rights that allow them to actually displace other workers. Thus, high seniority employees can "bump" someone elsewhere in the organization from jobs. The bumped employee may then bump someone with even less seniority, and so on. While an obvious benefit to high seniority workers, the cost to the organization of a series of bumps can be great. The general havoc created when someone is replaced on the job usually results in short-term decreased productivity as the new worker learns the job and co-workers learn to work with the new person. Further, even though they have seniority, the replacing worker may not be as skilled as the bumped worker. Can all supervisors run a drill press as well as the "average" drill press operator? Can the former manager of a typing pool type as well as a young typist? Obviously, the answer is "sometimes," but certainly not always as seniority privileges might imply.

Retention costs can be substantial. In a rational manner, the organization must weigh the benefits of retaining employees against these costs. Of course, the analysis should also include the more subjective assessment of morale and loyalty associated with retention. That the costs are often worth it is apparent in the many cases where such employee retentions are undertaken.

Not all partial terminations involve actual shutdowns. Sometimes the "termination" involves selling off a portion of the organization to another organization. For example, one store in a chain of discount stores could be sold to another chain and the employees retained (if they desire to stay) by the purchas-

---

* If the organizational termination is a large one, many houses could suddenly come on the market and temporarily depress values.

† When many people from the organization suddenly arrive in a new city looking for housing near the place of employment, local values can temporarily go up appreciably.

ing organization. Indeed this was the case when Walgreens sold several of its western states Globe stores to Zody's, a California-based chain. The stores' signs, advertising, and displays changed, but many of the same employees remained, albeit in different uniforms.

Terminations or layoffs are perhaps the most abrupt methods of dealing with displaced workers, if the organization has neither the desire nor the ability to absorb the workers in other areas.

Not all workers will be "pink slipped."* The use of early retirement programs is one way of aiding displaced workers. Here, employees of a certain age and/or seniority are allowed to elect to retire earlier than normal and begin receiving a pension, albeit at a rate less than that they would receive at the normal retirement age. During a period from 1971 to 1975 IBM offered a bonus equal to two years' salary to some 15,000 workers in an attempt to get them to retire early.[7]

"Outplacement" has also been practiced by many organizations. This involves resources being used by the organization to aid displaced employees in finding other employment. Some organizations actually provide offices and secretarial help for job hunting purposes. Outplacement has progressed to the point that special companies (e.g., THinc and Executive Progress, Inc.) exist that, for a fee, provide outplacement consulting services for companies that are cutting back on employees.

Another strategy discussed earlier in Chapter 10 is to "lend" displaced workers to another organization. Thus, the organization plays the same role as Manpower or Kelly Services. The employees remain on the original organization's payroll. In turn, the "new" organization pays the original organization a specified rate for the use of the employee. Obviously, this approach would be most useful where the displacement appears to be temporary and jobs will again be available in the original organization. This approach was recently used by Information Terminals Corp.[8] In this case, however, all the employees chose to stay with the new organization! Nevertheless the company called the approach a "success."

Physical assets

The disposal of physical assets is in some ways easier than dealing with displaced employees. Not only is there less emotionalism, physical assets yield cash whereas humans aren't (usually) subject to sale.†

---

* Told, sometimes in a pink memo, that their services are no longer required/desired.

† Except, as noted in Chapter 8, that some professional athletes' contracts (and thus their services) can be bought and sold.

Various physical assets may go with the rest of the business if a store, refinery, and so on is being sold off. Or, specific assets can themselves be sold by the organization. Some "going out of business" sales include the fixtures as well as the merchandise!

Alternatively, the assets can be distributed to other organizational units on an "as needed" basis. Rather than some other unit purchasing brand new desks, fixtures, a computer, and so on, perhaps the existing assets would be as useful and cheaper. Of course, shipment and remodeling costs need to be considered. The U.S. government routinely makes available to various other government units equipment that is no longer needed by some agency. If no federal government unit "buys" the equipment, it will eventually be made available to state and local government units at low prices prior to being auctioned or sold to the general public.

Not to be overlooked is the donation of property. In the American Oil Company refinery case mentioned earlier, several hundred acres of land were donated to the county government for a future industrial park. Thus, the company was able to take an immediate tax credit for the donation rather than waiting (perhaps for several years) to sell the property and then having to pay a capital gains tax. An "immediate bird" in the hand was worth several "future eagles." In a similar manner, office equipment was donated to local churches, and a fire truck given to a neighboring community by American Oil.

CUTBACK MANAGEMENT

Thus far we have viewed partial terminations from the perspective of closing a particular unit (e.g., a store, plant, production line, refinery). Implicit in our discussion has been the notion that such terminations result from particular problems deriving from that unit. Thus, the store closes because its sales drop or costs rise, not necessarily because of decreased sales or increased costs for other parts of the organization. Cutback management, on the other hand, involves organizationwide issues. For example, a school district may experience a long-term decline in enrollments and react by closing some schools and cutting back on the number of teachers and support staff. Or Congress could cut the Department of Defense budget in such a way as to require the number of civilian employees to be decreased by, say, 10 percent. Beginning with California's Proposition 13 in 1978, governmental budget cuts have become increasingly popular and many cutback management strategies have had to be implemented. Cutback management, while highly visible in government, is also practiced in business organizations. "Economy drives" (e.g., "let's cut everyone's budget by 5 percent") are quite popular in business and government and are sometimes effective in reducing unauthorized organizational slack (i.e., spare resources) that is often hidden away by organizational units for rainy days or other emergencies.

Following are a number of common cutback management strategies which can be used alone or in various combinations.

Budget cuts

An across-the-board budget cut is a popular action. On the surface, it implies equality in that all organizational units supposedly suffer equally. However, within particular units, some may suffer more than others. A state legislature may require all of its state agencies, including the universities, to enfore a 12 percent budget reduction. What if in a certain university this is accomplished by reducing a given college's budget by enough dollars to accomplish the necessary "universitywide" 12 percent decrease? Even if all units (including all of the various subunits) suffer the same percentage cutback, how does this affect the unit that has already "cut the fat" while others have done no such thing? If, for example, due to an oil crisis, gasoline sales to a family were restricted to 80 percent of last year's purchases, the family that had last year already reduced consumption would be penalized in comparison to their neighbors who practiced no restraints.

Budget cuts must then be used with discretion. Zero-base budgeting, discussed in Chapter 13, offers an attractive vehicle to affect these cuts. Here organizational units prioritize their programs or activities. Costs (and benefits) are determined for each program or activity. Then, the organization starts from a "zero budget" and puts in its top priority item. Then the next (in priority) item is added in. And then the next, and so on. Those items not yet included when the allowable upper limit of the budget is reached are the ones that are cut.

Hiring freeze/attrition

As a method of reducing the number of personnel, a hiring freeze is often imposed. Then, as employees quit, are fired, get transfers, and so on, they are not replaced. The number of employees, and hence costs, decrease by simple attrition.

This method also has the outward appearance of equity. However, we cannot be sure that our "more important" organizational units will not suffer disproportionate attrition. We may well find support units fully staffed (due to no turnover) and line units understaffed; an undesirable situation in most all organizations.

Attrition cutbacks can further penalize the manager who has done a good job of developing employees. Such well-qualified employees may well be attractive candidates for jobs in other organizations; especially since this organization is no longer hiring. To move up, they have to move out. Thus, attrition cutbacks can actually encourage managers to acquire and maintain a mediocre work force—one that is not likely to be offered better jobs elsewhere.

An alternative attrition strategy is to require that job openings due to quits, firings, and so on revert to a central pool. Organizational units that need additional staff make requests and these are prioritized. New employees can then be hired for top priority positions, but overall fewer people will be hired than are terminated. Attrition takes place, but supposedly only in the lower priority areas.

Consolidation

At times organizations with far-flung operations consolidate into fewer, more central locations. Such an approach is most often intended to reduce overhead and duplication. Of course, the reason operations were dispersed in the first place will suffer. No longer, for example, will the organization be as close to customers and raw materials, or will the fire department be able to reach any point in the city within 3.5 minutes.

Vacated assets may be disposed of or mothballed. Disposal of property and disposition of employees will require the use of various partial termination strategies discussed above. In essence, the closing of various facilities is a partial termination.

Mothballing may be appropriate if the organization believes that the facility will be needed again. Of course, the cost of mothballing, maintenance, and un-mothballing must be taken into consideration. Perhaps it would be economical to dispose of the property now and rebuild later.

TERMINATION OF THE WHOLE ORGANIZATION

We are all familiar with bankruptcy referees liquidating a business. Further, some businesses simply close down one day without bankruptcy; e.g., hospitals have been known to close their doors; political campaigns complete with physical assets and a paid staff, do end. While more extreme, this type of termination has much in common with partial terminations.

Personnel

The primary difference between complete and partial terminations is that with complete terminations intraorganizational transfers and "bumping" will not be an option because (by definition) the *whole* organization is being terminated. Thus, early retirement, outplacement, or simply "pink slipping" are the normal choices unless mergers are involved. Obviously, mergers permit (but do not require) the purchasing organization to retain existing employees.

Physical assets

Outside of precluding intraorganizational transfers, disposal of physical assets here tends to be similar to the case of partial termination.

Receiving book value or better for assets is often dubious. Willing or eager buyers are not always waiting in the wings. The question is often asked, "If these are such great assets and if this is such a great business, why don't you just keep things going?" Further, while small amounts of physical assets can usually be placed on the market without depressing prices, suddenly flooding the market with the assets of an entire organization may well upset the existing supply-demand balance.

THE URGE TO MERGE

Mergers are a special case of terminating an organization. Here, although the organization itself "terminates," it may well live on as a part of another organization without many, if any, changes other than ownership. Perhaps the best example of this is U.S. Industries, a large conglomerate, which purchased many companies and in virtually all cases retained the existing management and other personnel. Many of those 100 largest businesses in the United States in 1900, as well as the AEC and the OEO, in essence live on as a part of another organization with which they merged.*

There are a variety of reasons for the abundance in the last several decades of mergers. Several of these are:[9]

1. *Antitrust.*   Horizontal and/or vertical expansion is often viewed skeptically by government antitrust lawyers. Hence, acquisitions of businesses in other industries is perhaps the only feasible way for a business to "grow."
2. *Taxes.*   Especially with hard to market stock in closely held firms, tax laws often encourage mergers. Thus, rather than placing hard-to-sell stock on the market to obtain cash to pay estate taxes, mergers often provide compelling benefits by the setting of a fixed price per share for the transaction. Another tax inducement is a tax-loss carryforward. A firm with past losses and hence a carryforward that is without the future earning power to use it is often a tempting target for another firm which can thus shelter income.

---

* Sort of like a heart or kidney transplant?

3. *Excess cash.* While ostensibly an enviable problem, having excess cash (for whatever reason) is often a difficulty. Held too long, it can be an appealing target for some other firm to engineer a takeover. Also it simply represents an unused asset (i.e., opportunity cost). In mid-1978 Kennecott Copper Company had substantial cash due to an antitrust forced sale of Peabody Coal Company. Needing to invest this cash, Kennecott eventually purchased Carborundum at a price of $66 per share. Note that at the time Carborundum stock was selling for only $37 and Eaton Corporation had recently offered $47 per share for Carborundum! Money can indeed burn a hole in one's pockets—even those of a corporation.

4. *Improved management.* Often companies are poorly managed or without certain needed skills. Via mergers better talent can be made available. Thus, several small firms, none of which could afford its own computer facility and staff, could be merged into a parent whereby these services could be cost-effectively provided from a central staff unit.

Not all mergers are willing marriages. One need only read *The Wall Street Journal, Fortune,* or *Business Week* for a period of time to discover cases where the mergee is not desirous of being acquired. Marshall Field's rejection of Carter, Hawley, Hall, and McGraw-Hill's opposition to American Express are several well-publicized examples that occurred in recent years.

BORN AGAIN

If, in Rip Van Winklean fashion, one were to emerge from a long sleep and compare a number of business organizations today with what they were some years ago, significant differences would be apparent. For example, Corn Products Company is now CPC International (number 90 on the 1979 *Fortune* 500) and doesn't use all that much corn anymore. IBM has become a dominant producer of computers; quite a change for a firm that once concentrated on clocks and other such office equipment. Mary Carter Paint Company has become Resorts International, with a large role in the gambling industry, especially in Atlantic City. Most changes such as these are due to an evolution over time as the organization reacted time and again to various environmental changes and therefore continuously adapted. Such behavior is consistent with one prescribed approach to organizational change presented in the preceding chapter. With such an evolution, there is typically no clearly identifiable point where the organization terminated one mode of operation and originated a new one. There are, however, cases where the termination and new origination take place over a short time and where this point is therefore observable: a revolutionary change versus an evolutionary one. We make the analogy here with "born-again" religious "converts."

A well-known example of the revolutionary approach is the change undergone by the National Foundation for Infantile Paralysis (March of Dimes) after polio was "conquered" by the Salk vaccine.[10] Rather than terminate, the organization was "reborn" as it switched its goal very quickly to the prevention and healing of birth defects while leaving virtually intact its administrative structure and widespread volunteer organization.

Many college students have perhaps witnessed instances where a hotel or similar structure is bought and converted to student housing. Some years ago at Northwestern University a hotel for the elderly was so purchased and the staff retained as Northwestern employees. The hotel manager overnight became the director of graduate housing.* Obviously, such a shift in organizational goals and of organization members' jobs requires attention. Indoctrination pertaining to the new "industry" and training for new or changed jobs is quite often required.

Checker Auto, long known for taxicab manufacturing, declared in late 1978 that it would cease being an automobile manufacturer and henceforth concentrate on being a parts supplier to the Big Three (GM, Ford, Chrysler). At first glance, this may not seem to be a massive shift in operations. However, consider the difference in sales (to several large firms versus through a nationwide sales organization) and manufacturing (parts versus finished autos). Will there be differences in advertising? In arrangements with financial institutions? In required employee skills? In machinery utilized? And so on. The answer is obviously "yes" in all cases.

It would seem that organizations with low technological investments (i.e., plant, equipment and skills) would experience fewer born-again birth pains. There would be less of a financial cost involved in disposing of old assets and acquiring a new plant and equipment base. Also, there would be less of a shift in personnel resources. Organizations in service industries (low technology base) would thus seem to be more prone to advantageously being born again than would those in manufacturing. The hotel example above required fewer changes in technology than did Checker Auto. Thus, there would be far more personnel and plant and equipment issues for management at Checker than at Northwestern.

Our modern world may well require organizations to undergo born-again strategies. Legal as well as market requirements can often make current outputs obsolete or less desirable (e.g., lead in gasoline as produced by the Ethyl Corporation). An advisable strategy is, then, to consider alternative outputs that require as few technological changes as possible. Checker Auto stayed in the automotive industry. Heublein, during Prohibition, switched from Smirnoff Vodka to A-1 Steak Sauce. During the same period a number of other

---

* Not exactly the same kind of rebirth but certainly more bizarre is the conversion of the "whites only" restaurant (formerly owned by the former governor of Georgia, Lester Maddox) to the Georgia Institute of Technology personnel office, a change which might be called "from displacement to placement!"

distillers concentrated on using their expertise in fermentation technology to produce products that could be used by the ethical drug industry.

Thus, the lower the technological investment the easier it is to be born again. Barring a low investment, the born-again organization ought to seek a new output that utilizes, insofar as possible, the existing technology and personnel.

LOOKING FOR THE SILVER LINING

What will you do? What *will* you do?

Karl Malden*

This plaintive cry might accurately capture the feelings of the individual manager caught in a termination or merger. If your company is to be liquidated, the prudent course of action is to begin a new job search as soon as possible. If your company is to be merged, look closely at your accomplishments and abilities and dispassionately analyze how you look to the new managers. Are you really indispensible? Are they likely to find someone better? Tough questions, but they must be faced. Mergers commonly lead to compression of top-management jobs in an effort to consolidate administration. Put more simply, it means that there will be competition for such jobs with only one survivor. Less risk befalls an individual at the lower management ranks, but remember that mergers are often accompanied by reductions in force (RIF's) and in fact present one way of introducing an entire new management group.

Stories abound about the trauma of being out of work. Some executives, unable to even tell their families about losing their job, have been known to commute each day, well dressed and with briefcase, to a park bench. Others write résumés and knock on doors, looking for another job like the one they lost. Still others take the opportunity to reassess their lives and lifestyle and may even decide to change careers.

We urge an optimistic outlook for the person who has been, or will soon be, terminated. This is the time to take a close look at one's career. Was the termination due to problems within the whole industry, or within a given organization? If it is an industrywide problem, moving to another organization within that industry may well be only a temporary solution as problems may well soon catch up with the new employer, and it too could terminate. Also, to what extent was the termination due in some part to a deficiency in the worker? Perhaps abilities were not a good match with ambitions and some training or other skills improvement is needed. On the other hand, many people never really test the market for their services. More than once a fired

---

* These questions are asked by Karl Malden in the TV commercial for American Express traveler's checks.

executive finds that some other organization is willing to offer an even better job at higher pay than the job that was just lost. By approaching a job loss in a calm, objective manner, that silver lining may well be found.[11]

SUMMARY

Organizational termination need not be catastrophic nor need it be an evidence of failure. Termination should be viewed as a natural occurrence, especially in a capitalistic system, and should be as carefully managed as any other aspect of an organization's activities.

Practical strategies exist to ensure that personnel and physical assets are terminated with the least possible amount of disruption. Innovative ways of disposing of physical assets and of helping personnel find other employment should continually be developed.

Terminated organizations often continue to live on in other forms through mergers and born-again strategies. Such opportunities should constantly be considered as alternatives to continued current operations.

While organizations can transcend their human founders, few do last forever. Even those very old organizations such as the Roman Catholic Church experience some partial terminations; the Church has closed down various of its operations including a given church here and there, as well as many of its schools. Therefore, to ignore the need to know how to terminate is to ignore reality itself.

GUIDES TO ACTION

1. Always include termination as a decision-making option. There is little justification in continuing an operation that is a net loser. Managers as well as poker players can profit from Kenny Rogers' advice: "You got to know when to hold 'em; know when to fold 'em; know when to walk away; and know when to run."[12]

2. Sometimes losing a job is a blessing in disguise, Look for that silver lining.

3. Though firing someone is one of the more difficult things many managers go through, don't avoid it if it is justified.

NOTES

[1] Attributed to Peter Drucker, from Paul Dickson, *The Official Rules* (New York: Delacorte Press, 1978), p. 40.

[2] Attributed to Roy Walters, from Dickson, ibid., p. 183.

[3] Robert G. Murdick, Richard H. Eckhouse, R. Carl Moor, and Thomas W. Zimmerer, *Business Policy: A Framework for Analysis,* 2d ed. (Columbus, Ohio: Grid Publishing Company, 1976), pp. 4–6.

[4] Peter W. Bernstein, "A Company That's Worth More Dead than Alive," *Fortune,* February 26, 1979, pp. 42–44.

[5] William Wong, "Out of Business—A Plant Shutdown Is Always Painful but It Need Not Be Merciless," *The Wall Street Journal,* February 28, 1972, p. 1.

[6] See Allan J. Mayer, and Michael Ruby, "One Firm's Family," *Newsweek,* November 11, 1977, pp. 82–84.

[7] Ibid., p. 84.

[8] *The Wall Street Journal,* "Farming out Work," July 11, 1978, p. 1.

[9] Based on Joel Dean, "Causes and Consequences of Growth by Conglomerate Merger: An Introduction," in *Conglomerate Mergers and Acquisitions: Opinion and Analysis,* vol. 44, *St. John's Law Review* (special ed., 1970), pp. 15–66.

[10] David C. Sills, *The Volunteers* (New York: The Macmillan Company, 1956).

[11] Daniel D. Cook, "Are You a Prisoner of Your Industry," *Industry Week,* February 19, 1979, pp. 41–47; Irving Janis, and Dan Wheeler, "Thinking Clearly about Career Choices," *Psychology Today,* May 1978, pp. 67–76, and 121–22.

[12] Kenny Rogers, "The Gambler" (D. Schlitz), Writers Night Music, United Artists, 1978.

DISCUSSION QUESTIONS

1. Why is termination not necessarily the result of failure?

2. What are several strategies involving personnel in partial terminations? In total organization termination?

3. What are the dangers of across-the-board budget cuts? Of hiring freezes?

4. Why are mergers considered to be a subset of the termination process?

5. Discuss the "born-again" phenomena. Can you think of an organization with which you have had dealings that was "born again"?

6. How can an individual cope with being caught in a termination?

CASE: CHICKENS*

John Hartman has sold his business. It was not a matter of his inability or lack of knowledge. He had started the business himself 15 years ago and, for a while, it was fairly successful and profitable. For the past few years, however, everything seemed to be going to the birds.

John owned and operated a poultry vaccinating service. Fifteen years ago, when he started the business, the southern New Jersey area was heavily populated with small poultry farms. Each of these small farms raised two or three flocks of 1,000 to 5,000 chickens per year so as to maintain egg production at a relatively steady pace. In order to sell their eggs commercially, state law required that the hens be inoculated against most of the common poultry diseases. (Yes, chickens do get chicken pox!) In order to meet the state requirements economically, local farmers contracted this task to local vaccinating crews.

These crews were usually owned and operated by individuals who, at one time or another, owned or worked on a chicken farm but decided to forsake the monotony, dependence, and risk of the farm for the relative freedom and mobility (not to mention the profitability) of the vaccinating crews. The owner/operator's source of mobility was his truck in which he carried his crew and all his equipment from farm to farm performing his services at the rate of 2½ cents to 10 cents per bird, depending on the operation involved. His crew during the winter was usually made up of farm laborers who were unemployed during the off season. During the summer, local high school boys composed the majority of the crews.

A crew usually consisted of eight to ten people with only three or four possessing the skill or experience necessary to allow them to actually inoculate the birds. The remainder of the crew was assigned the task of rounding up, catching, and holding the birds. A good crew could average 1,100 to 1,300 birds per hour for the most common operations.

Usually the flock would be located in a coop divided into six or seven small rooms, with 250 to 500 birds in a room. The crew set up their catching frames so as to divide the room in half. Each frame was 14 to 16 feet long made up of seven to eight sections, which were approximately 4 feet high and 2 feet long. They were connected in such a fashion that they could be folded and would stand without support. This folding also created "pockets," which facilitated catching. The chickens would be herded into half of the room and six or seven catchers would go into the portion of the room with the birds, catch

---

* From Theodore T. Herbert, *Organizational Behavior: Readings and Cases* (New York: Macmillan Publishing Company, Inc., 1976), pp. 76–79.

a handful (three or four), and pass them over the frame to where the actual vaccinating was being done. As the birds were vaccinated, they were once again allowed to run free in the other half of the room. This same process would be repeated from room to room until the entire flock was completed.

Hartman's crew was one of the best. His reputation with the small farmers was earned as much by his personality as by the skill of his crew. Since farm labor rates were low and his only major capital investments were in his truck and catching frames, Hartman enjoyed a successful and profitable business.

During the mid-1960s, the poultry industry in the south Jersey area suffered what many farmers considered a major depression. Egg prices dropped sharply while the cost of operations steadily rose. To make matters worse, large poultry farms (100,000 to 500,000 pullets) in the South and Southwest were able to compete profitably under these conditions. Rather quickly, the numerous small farms in south Jersey gave way to the large mechanized poultry farms.

The modern farms were drastically different from the small farms. Rooms in the coop were much larger and could easily handle 3,000 to 5,000 birds. Most of the newer coops had raised wire floors instead of the old straw or sawdust floors. This keeps the coops and the birds cleaner. The small numerous feeding hoppers that had to be filled manually twice a day gave way to a conveyor-like feeding system that automatically circulated the feed twice a day. A similar watering system also kept a fresh supply of water available at all times. Laying roosts were constructed down the center of the rooms instead of the conventional method of hanging them on the walls. Each compartment was slanted toward the back so the egg would roll onto a conveyor belt which ran automatically twice a day. This replaced the slow, tedious method of collecting by hand. Finally, many of the new coops had no windows. Air was circulated by the use of a system of large exhaust fans. Lighting was completely artificial and was automatically turned on and off so as to provide the chickens with the proper amount of "day" and "night." In effect, the role of the farmer was reduced to that of maintaining and checking the timers to be sure that they were working on schedule.

Although John was unhappy to see the small farmers, many of whom were his friends, lose their farms, he felt that the larger farms would make his business more profitable. He felt he would be able to vaccinate more birds per day because he would be reducing his travel time from farm to farm. He recognized that the modern farm with its automated operations, cages, and wire floors would present some inconveniences. However, he felt that his method of operations was adequate to meet these obstacles without modification.

Soon he began noticing that it was difficult for his crew to average 1,000 birds per hour. This resulted in extra time spent on the job. This usually upset the farm manager because his supervisor (who was responsible for two or three farms) was anxious for the operations to return to normal. As a result Hartman began to lose business. Coupled with the increased cost of vaccine and the rising labor rates, this had the effect of turning a successful and profitable business into the red.

In looking at his competition, Hartman saw that many of the other crews were faced with a similar problem. However, some of the older crews as well as some newly formed crews were benefiting from the modernized farms. The successful crews increased their manpower, changed the ratio of vaccinators to laborers, developed new operating procedures for working in the modern coops, and adopted the latest vaccinating technique developed by the State Department of Agriculture. In fact, many of the old-time crew owners indicated, to Hartman's dismay, that business had never been any better.

The end result was Hartman selling his business and taking a job with one of the local glass manufacturers.

Questions

1. How did the change in technology of poultry farming affect the vaccination industry?
2. What could Hartman have done to avoid selling his business?

Section nine
A practical side
of organizations

Throughout this book we have attempted to help you develop important managerial skills. In this last section we pause to point out a few more "realities" of managerial life which, though important, do not normally get communicated to the novice manager.

SELECTION OF THE PRODUCT OR SERVICE	DESIGN OF THE SYSTEM	STAFFING THE ORGANIZATION	STARTUP OF THE ORGANIZATION	OPERATING THE ORGANIZATION IN THE STEADY STATE	IMPROVING THE ORGANIZATION	REVISION OF THE ORGANIZATION	TERMINATION OF THE ORGANIZATION

Level of Organizational Outputs

0

| Decision-making processes; social value; goals; forecasts; policies; plans | Authority and responsibility; power; organizational structure; communications systems; job design | Work force planning; personnel management functions | Startup planning and scheduling; monitoring; alternative startup approaches | Motivation; leadership; production and operations management; control | Individual improvement programs and techniques; group conflict management; MBO | Evaluation of organizational policies; strategic choices; organizational change; organizational development | Partial terminations; cutback management; complete terminations; mergers; born-again strategies |

t_0 Time ⟶

Chapter 18
The rest of the story

There are a million stories in the naked city. . . .

Introduction to a series of radio
programs in the 1950s

The colorful newscaster, Paul Harvey, has a syndicated radio program called "The Rest of the Story." In each broadcast, Mr. Harvey relates one or more little-known anecdotes about a famous person or event. After the obligatory commercial, the suspense is broken when the identity of the subject is divulged. Quite often, these stories add a dimension about people or things which is counter to the listener's originally held views, and thereby enriches his or her understanding about the subject.

Like Paul Harvey's program, there is a rest of the story in the study and practice of management which relates to you as you embark upon a managerial career. The purpose of this chapter is to share such information with you. Specifically, our rest of the story will highlight the routes one can take in moving through the organization; some factors to think about in obtaining your first job and subsequent jobs; sample career management strategies; some of the types of people you will meet along the way; coping with your boss (and yourself); and suggestions for further reading in management.

CAREER PATHS THROUGH THE ORGANIZATION

Throughout the book, we have used one-dimensional organization charts as referents in discussing various aspects of management. For purposes of career planning, however, the model of the organization developed by Edgar Schein much better demonstrates the alternative career paths one might take. As depicted in Exhibit 18–1, the organization can be viewed as an inverted cone, with career movements depicted as proceeding along three dimensions:

1. Vertically.   Increasing or decreasing one's rank in the organization.
2. Radially.   Increasing or decreasing one's centrality in the organization.
3. Circumferentially.   Changing one's function or area in the organization.[1]

If your career objective is to become, say, a vice president, you might enter a firm in a functional area (e.g., marketing) and strive toward moving to an important (or central) position at the apex of the bottom triangle. As you prove yourself in this position, you might then move to the next highest triangle in marketing. Of course, it is likely that such vertical movement will be along the outside of the cone; once at the next level you will have to prove yourself again in order to progress toward the center.

Other career patterns might involve simply horizontal moves to other functional fields, and may be limited in the degree of inclusion (influence) achieved

Exhibit 18–1
A three-dimensional model of an organization

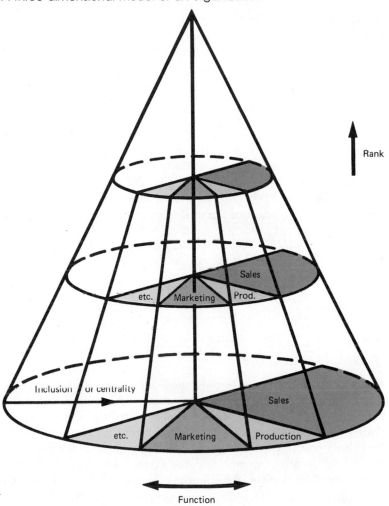

Function

Source: Edgar Schein, "The Individual, The Organization, and the Career: A Conceptual Scheme," in D. Kolb, I. Rubin, & J. McIntyre, *Organizational Psychology, A Book of Readings,* 3d ed., © 1979, p. 500. Reprinted by permission of Prentice-Hall, Inc., Englewood Cliffs, New Jersey.

within each function. From this conceptualization, it can be seen that the speed of progression can be affected by a variety of factors—number of levels in the organization, policies, need for specific skills within each area, and personnel development programs available within the organization. Further, some organizations have relatively easy access to a particular functional area, but may have barriers to various kinds of advancement within them; conversely, some may tightly control the number of people they hire, but those individuals that remain have a strong chance of moving to the center in terms of authority and formal and informal status.

What all of this means to career planning is simply that one should try to crystallize what his or her career goals are, and then seek organizations whose size, structure, and development programs are most favorable to their achievement.

GETTING STARTED AND MOVING UP

Rules for landing the first job

1. Be persistent. All books on job hunting agree on one point: sending out résumés and letters and then just sitting back and waiting for an interview invitation is a sure way to lose. Letters must be followed up by phone calls, and phone calls by more phone calls. Telegrams and registered letters may also be effective. Your objective is to make your name stick in the minds of hiring managers (without becoming a pest).

2. Know something about the company you are interviewing. Study a recent annual report and bone up on their product line and organization structure.

3. Custom design your résumé. The résumé should highlight those areas of your background which, on the basis of your study of a given organization, would appeal to that organization. In this regard, you might follow the rule:

If you can't fix it, feature it!

For example, if you have only mediocre grades in college, then emphasize the benefits to your prospective employer of the activities you engaged in rather than studying; e.g., fraternity activities developed your leadership skills; your part-time job as a bartender gave you a deep understanding of people and their problems; your travels to Tiajuana broadened your perspective on the world. In other words, find the redeeming feature(s) of the things which you *have* done rather than finding excuses for what you haven't done. (If nothing else, this will indicate moxie on your part, which is just the thing if you are going into, say, a sales-oriented firm.)

4. Dress for success. Unless you are certified as being brilliant, getting a favorable recommendation from a recruiter is a subtle mixture of what you say and how you look during the screening interview. Thus, beyond responding thoughtfully to questions posed to you, putting your best foot forward requires appropriate dress. Surprisingly, there is a lot more to dressing appropriately than most people realize. In fact, we can only touch the surface of this theoretically trivial, but practically important subject. In a book (!) on how to dress, John T. Malloy states that men "dress for failure" for three basic reasons:

1. . . . They allow their wives to select fashionable clothing for them. [Unfortunately, as evidenced by the following Malloy quote, the American corporate establishment does not in general favor high fashion.]

In one survey I conducted, 92 percent of the executives who were questioned said they would not hire a man who presented himself for a job interview wearing high fashion clothing.[2]

2. They let sales clerks sell them clothing, rather than coming into a clothing store with a firm idea in mind about what they want and how it should fit.

3. They purchase fashion designer clothes that have continental styling which though appropriate for Rome is out of place in most U.S. offices.[3]

Malloy advocates that men should choose their clothing to match the culture of where they are working. However, he also points out that we have expectations about the type of dress which is appropriate for particular jobs. Thus, an accountant in Beverly Hills should wear conservative dress even though he (or she) is in "leisure suit country."*

Liz Houston, in giving pointers to businesswomen in *MBA* Magazine, argues that women, like men, must dress for the part (job) to which they aspire. If you want to be president, dress like a president.[4] *Very* good shoes and handbags are essentials. You do not need many clothes ". . . but what you have ought to be very, very good and look like it."[5] Ultrasuedes, silk shirts and a Brooks Brothers blazer or raincoat are highly recommended. Jewelry should not be elaborate, but it should be authentic. One item from Tiffany's is better than a thousand from the "five and dime."

The well-known designer Diane von Furstenburg echoes Houston's basic advice.[6] She advises that a simple silk shirtdress should be an early purchase along with at least one good suit in a "quiet" pattern.

Six ways of not quite getting to the top

The following article from the *Financial Times* of London contains some factors to consider when interviewing for an upper level management position.

At lunch after the evidently successful final interview, the chairman of the employing company remarked to the candidate how pleasant it was to relax and be sociable.

"Oh yes," replied the would-be managing editor director engagingly. "But it's very hard to get totally away from executive work, isn't it? I think the only time when I relax properly is at the end of the month when my wife and I go to the local Rugby club and get drunk."

He received the letter of rejection the next morning.

---

* We are at a loss to explain to our students the "Tucson school" of business dress—cowboy boots, a vested suit, and baseball cap with a "Cat" patch. Professorial dress style is easier to explain—our generally impecunious condition makes it cost-effective to continue to wear serviceable 20-year-old slacks with a belt in the back.

I owe that story to head-hunter Michael Silverman, head of Merton Associates (Consultants). The demand for chief executives has risen some 20 percent over the past three years, by his count, and he estimates that each of the top opportunities attracts about 25 candidates with impressive career records.

Of these, of course, only one can get the job. But not long ago, Mr. Silverman decided to do some "action research" into why other candidates fail even though their experience and qualification fit, if not surpass, the employer's needs.

The explanation commonly given by recruitment consultants is "poor chemistry," he says. But the aim of his informal study was to investigate the cause of the adverse reaction a bit more deeply.

His findings reinforce a widespread view among recruiters that physical appearance accounts for a fair number of failures, with highly qualified people being rejected ultimately because they are short in stature, overweight and/or bald. Even so, it seems that a greater number of candidates are rejected for flaws which are far more easily avoidable.

"Most often an executive fails because of some unintended but fatal slip in his behaviour during the final interviews with the employing company's chairman or its main Board management committee," Michael Silverman told me.

"The variety of individual reasons for failure is extensive. But my recent study of 30 candidates for nine chief-executive openings, indicated that most of the mistakes made are one of six basic kinds."

The first, he added, is an inability on the candidate's part to put over his or her special competence with the polished crispness which the final interviewers not surprisingly expect in a budding chief executive.

Many managers have climbed internal promotion ladders by dint of just developing their skills without ever really thinking of how these could best be communicated verbally to other people. Hence, when faced with a need to express their abilities to relative strangers, they are liable to emit a jumble of cliches and impenetrable jargon. And the more skilful the interviewers are at making candidates feel at home, the greater is the peril of lapsing into broken Double Dutch.

Having once asked a sales director, two and a half gins and tonic into an informal party, how he got his representatives to turn in such good results, I know that Mr. Silverman's observation here is true. The sales chief's reply (which I shall never forget) was:

"Clearly, er, the balanced application of both positive and negative KITA is indispensable, but it would be no go unless the hygiene factors were interfaced with some active motivation, which should be individualised because, when all's said and done, it takes all kinds to make a world."

The second main kind of mistake is to rationalise one's own past failures, typically by explaining at length how the few blemishes in the record, although nominally one's own responsibility, really arose from the coincidence of malign circumstances and criminal lunacy among the supporting staff.

In general, interviewers would prefer to know that the candidate has made mistakes, and has learned from them. Besides, it is quite possible that the interviewers will include someone with knowledge of the failure in question, who will then take the shilly-shallying candidate to pieces, and with relish.

The third kind of mistake is to be overly critical of one's current employer. "This kind of behaviour demonstrates a lack of the discretion that is considered crucial at the highest levels of a large company," Michael Silverman added.

Fourthly, he said, the aspiring chief is all too prone to display his powers of leadership by being overpowering or even arrogant during the interview. True, the average chairman will not want a lamb as a managing director, but he may be equally chary about lying down with a lion. Moreover:

"There is another side to arrogance that puts off a selection committee just as much. Sometimes a candidate will adopt a very casual style during his interviews, offering superficial knowledge about the company and clever answers to key questions. This informality suggests he has more important things to worry about than getting the job."

The fifth type of flaw—a tendency to over explain—Mr. Silverman illustrated with the sad case of the would-be head of a big shipping concern owned by a City holding company.

The candidate knew that the shipping group had been having financial problems, primarily because of poor controls over its many divisions. He also knew that he was on the shortlist because his career record indicated that he possessed just the sort of competence that was lacking in the company.

So when he came up before the interviewers in the City, he assumed they would want to know precisely what he would do when appointed to the job. But before he could finish his detailing of the necessary technical and financial steps to be taken, a glassiness in the eyes of the selectors across the table showed that he had lost them, and the job, beyond recall.

Last but not least among the flaws is a failure to appreciate that top-level selectors may be fastidious about points of dress or grooming. Just recently a potentially first-rate insurance chief went through three successive days of interviews, only to be undone by his clothes. It wasn't that he was badly dressed. His suit was beautifully tailored. But he ought not to have worn it on all three occasions.

As a safeguard against these common errors, Mr. Silverman offered four tips for aspiring chief executives approaching their last judgments. They are:

1. Brief yourself comprehensively about the company and the executives who are likely to conduct the interview. Three years worth of annual accounts and reports in directories and the *Financial Times* [or *The Wall Street Journal* in the U.S.] should suffice in the case of the company. A person ready to say openly why he or she wants the information on the executives, could probably obtain it from other managers in the same industry or, where there is one, from the recruitment consultant.

2. While talking to the interviewers keep constantly alert for, and smoothly respond to, any signs either verbal or in their behaviour that you are not being clearly understood or are taxing their patience.

3. Respond to questions as though you were talking to an acquaintance who is about to catch a train, albeit on a line where the service is frequent.

4. If you have nothing positive really to say about any particular issue, it is best to say so.[7]

CAREER MANAGEMENT STRATEGIES

A variety of career management strategies have been followed successfully by upwardly mobile managers. For example, a study of British managers lists 11 alternatives, with "improving one's qualifications" being most frequently mentioned (see Exhibit 18–2).

Some other frequently followed strategies are:

1. "Hitch your wagon to a star" (work for a fast-rising executive).
2. "Don't make waves" (have a congenial personality, avoid controversy, play it safe).
3. "Pygmalion" (find a sponsor who finds you worthy of grooming for more important jobs).
4. "Problem solver" (crises create heroes, so be an expert in solving problems under pressure).

Which of these is best can't be answered unequivocally. The choice is dependent upon the individual's alternatives and values, and those of the organization where he or she is working. As a statement of our values, improving your qualifications is always advocated. However, if your qualifications are expanded to include socialization skills within an organization, then this may well entail recognition of power relationships and politics, thereby leading you to politically appropriate strategies.

Exhibit 18–2
A ranking of the importance of various career strategies
by 81 respondents

Improve one's qualifications	35
Choose jobs that are stepping-stones	27
Improve interpersonal relations	25
Do job well	22
Ask for move or explanation	18
Get out of dead-end job	17
Wait	15
Leave for another company	14
Make it easy to leave	5
Improve one's knowledge of the firm	5
Change content of job	5
Other	6

Source: C. Sofer, *Men in Mid-Career: A Study of British Managers and Technical Specialities* (London: Cambridge University Press, 1970), p. 245.

PEOPLE YOU WILL MEET ALONG THE WAY

The modern corporation makes special demands on its members and breeds certain types of managerial personalities. In what has been called a "troubling" book, a practicing psychologist, Michael Maccoby describes four types of managers he encountered in a seven-year study of 250 managers in high technology industries:

THE CRAFTSMAN, as the name implies, holds traditional values, including the work ethic, respect for people, concern for quality, and thrift. When he talks about his work, he shows an interest in the *process* of making something; he enjoys building. He sees others, co-workers as well as superiors, in terms of whether they help or hinder him in doing a craftsmanlike job.

THE JUNGLE FIGHTER lusts for power. He experiences life and work as a jungle where it is eat or be eaten, and the winners destroy the losers. A major part of his psychic resources are budgeted for his internal department of defense. Jungle fighters tend to see their peers as either accomplices or enemies, and their subordinates as objects to be used.

There are two types of jungle fighters, lions and foxes. The lions are the conquerors who, when successful, may build an empire. In large industry, the day of the lions—the Carnegies and Fords—seems virtually ended. The foxes make their nests in the corporate hierarchy and move ahead by stealth and politicking. The most gifted foxes we encountered rose rapidly, by making use of their entrepreneurial skills. But in each case they were eventually destroyed by those they had used or betrayed.

THE COMPANY MAN bases his sense of identity on being part of the protective organization. At his weakest, he is fearful and submissive, seeking security even more than success. At his strongest, he is concerned with the human side of the company, interested in the feelings of the people around him, and committed to maintaining corporate integrity. The most creative company men sustain an atmosphere of cooperation and stimulation, but they tend to lack the daring to lead highly competitive and innovative organizations.

THE GAMESMAN sees business life in general, and his career in particular, in terms of options and possibilities, as if he were playing a game. He likes to take calculated risks and is fascinated by techniques and new methods. The contest hypes him up and he communicates his enthusiasm, energizing his peers and subordinates like the quarterback on a football team. Unlike the jungle fighter, the gamesman competes not to build an empire or to pile up riches, but to gain fame, glory, the exhilaration of victory. His main goal is to be known as a winner, his deepest fear to be labeled a loser.[8]

Of these four, the Gamesman is best adapted to the demands of organizational life and in Maccoby's study was most likely to rise to the top. The gamesman's ability to succeed lies in his paradoxical character traits:

The gamesman is cooperative but competitive, detached and playful but compulsively drawn to succeed, a team player but a would-be superstar, a team leader but often a rebel against bureaucratic hierarchy, fair and unprejudiced but contemptuous of weakness, tough and dominating but not destructive. Competition and innovation in modern business require these gamelike attitudes, and of all the character types, only the gamesman is emotionally attuned to the environment.[9]

What makes Maccoby's findings troubling is his observation that adaption so well achieved by the Gamesman leads to the development of "the head rather than the heart." That is, to be successful, managers felt that they had to be detached emotionally from their decisions; they couldn't let their feelings interfere with their objectivity relative to doing what is best for the organization.

Maccoby doesn't argue in favor of being softhearted but rather seems to advocate a mixture of courage to do what is right and empathy with the individuals who will be affected by the manager's decision. This requires a subtle blend of traits—humility, pride, love of humanity and openness—if a manager is to be a complete human being, not just a calculating "decision maker." Unfortunately, our society is not generally geared to selecting leaders for their strength of character. Indeed, intellectual problem solving is far easier to measure than is Maccoby's strength of heart.

If you plan a career in public administration, Anthony Downs has identified some common character types that you will encounter in government bureaucracies:

1. *Climbers* who consider power, income, and prestige as nearly all important in their value structures.
2. *Conservers* who consider convenience and security as nearly all important.
3. *Zealots* who are loyal to particular policies or concepts such as the development of ballistic missiles.
4. *Advocates* who are loyal to a broader set of functions such as a strong military capability.
5. *Statesmen* who are loyal to society as a whole and seek power for the "general good" of all.[10]

COPING

. . . With an abrasive boss

There is no guarantee that the person you will work for will be the perfect supervisor. In fact, your study of the many traits which go into making a good manager presented in this book should suggest to you that you will be fortunate to work for one who is very good or superb.

One of the common sources of frustration for the neophyte manager is the boss, who though intelligent and fair-minded, has quite simply, an abrasive personality. He or she just rubs people the wrong way. Writing in the *Harvard*

Business Review, Levinson addresses this particular problem and points out some options that are available for a subordinate to cope with such an individual:

> Let us assume that you are relatively new or inexperienced in a particular area and need a certain amount of time to achieve your own competence. Chances are that because of his knowledge and competence, your abrasive boss will have much to teach. Since his high standards will ensure that the model he provides will be a good one, there will be sufficient reason for you to tolerate his abrasiveness.
>
> But after two years, or whenever you establish your own competence, you will begin to chafe under the rigid control. As you push for your own freedom, your boss is likely to become threatened with loss of control and feel that you are becoming rivalrous. He is then likely to turn on you, now no longer a disciple, and, in sometimes devious ways, get back at you. Your memos will lie on his desk, unanswered. Information being sent through channels will be delayed. Complaints, suggestions, requests will either be rejected outright or merely tabled. Sometimes he will reorganize the unit around you, which will fence you in and force you to deal with decoys—nominal bosses who have no real power.
>
> If you are in a safe position, you might tell the boss how he appears to you, and his effect on subordinates. If he is at a high level, it will usually do little good to go above his head. Certainly, you should check out how much concern his superiors have about him, how much they are willing to tolerate, and how able they are to face him in a confrontation. Few at higher management levels are willing to take on a bright, combative, seemingly self-confident opponent— especially if he has a record of achievement, and there is little concrete evidence of the negative effects of his behavior.
>
> In short, after you have learned what you can from such a person, it is probably time to get out from under him.[11]

. . . With an abrasive self

Do you have an abrasive personality? If you answer affirmatively to three or more of the questions in Exhibit 18–3 the chances are that you do, and you might be wise to try and change. (There are some management consulting firms that specialize in helping individuals to lose their abrasiveness.)

. . . With stress

A study of 130 jobs by the National Institute of Occupational Safety and Health (NIOSH) yielded the following list* of most stressful and least stressful jobs:[12]

Most stressful
1. Unskilled laborer
2. Secretary
3. Assembly line inspector

---

* Students were not included in the study.

Exhibit 18–3
Do you have an abrasive personality?

You might ask yourself these questions. Then ask them of your spouse, your peers, your friends—and even your subordinates:

1. Are you condescendingly critical? When you talk of others in the organization, do you speak of "straightening them out" or "whipping them into shape"?

2. Do you need to be in full control? Does almost everything need to be cleared with you?

3. In meetings, do your comments take a disproportionate amount of time?

4. Are you quick to rise to the attack, to challenge?

5. Do you have a need to debate? Do discussions quickly become arguments?

6. Are people reluctant to discuss things with you? Does no one speak up? When someone does, are his or her statements inane?

7. Are you preoccupied with acquiring symbols of status and power?

8. Do you weasel out of responsibilities?

9. Are you reluctant to let others have the same privileges or perquisites as yourself?

10. When you talk about your activities, do you use the word "I" disproportionately?

11. Do your subordinates admire you because *you* are so strong and capable or because, in your organization, *they* feel so strong and capable—and supported?

12. To your amazement do people speak of you as cold and distant when you really want them to like you?

13. Do you regard yourself as more competent than your peers? Than your boss? Does your behavior let them know that?

Source Harry Levinson, "The Abrasive Personality," *Harvard Business Review*, May–June 1978, p. 94. Copyright © 1978 by the President and Fellows of Harvard College; all rights reserved. Reprinted by permission.

4. Clinical lab technician
5. Office manager
6. Foreman
7. Manager/administrator
8. Waitress/waiter
9. Factory machine operator
10. Farm owner
11. Miner
12. House painter

Least stressful

1. Clothing sewer
2. Garment checker
3. Stock clerk
4. Skilled craftsman
5. Maid
6. Farm laborer

  7. Heavy equipment operator
  8. Freight handler
  9. Child care worker
 10. Factory package wrapper
 11. College professor
 12. Personnel worker

As we can see, "manager/administrator" ranks number seven in the most stressful category, indicating that the managerial career can take its toll. In light of this hazard, we asked Dr. Jerry Day, a specialist in stress, to contribute the following section on the nature of stress and how to cope with it.

After eight years on the East Coast, Jim learns that he will be transferred to the Midwest. Is Jim under stress? Bob learns that the firm has hired a young and upcoming executive to work with him to learn his job. Is this stress? Anne got a nice promotion and raise. Is that stress? Peter is getting a divorce. Al must travel 15 miles through heavy traffic to get to work. Are any or all of these people experiencing stress? Maybe these examples may not represent true stress; stress can be both positive and negative experiences, but we cannot determine if these examples represent stress unless more information is given.

Stress may be defined as physical, mental or emotional arousal without the offsetting and balancing effect of rest. In view of this definition, we should not consider Jim, Bob, Anne, Peter, or Al to be under stress if they have learned to rest and recuperate from mental, emotional, or physical arousal. Man is easily aroused when a demand is made upon his or her ability to adjust and adapt. This is called the fight or flight defense survival mechanism. However, there is yet another built-in ability to survive called the relaxation response. Thus, it is not stress (by the above definition) if we know how to deprogram arousal by exercising the relaxation response. Another way to understand stress is from the view that stress is a nonspecific response from our body to any demand made upon it. Again, stress does not become *dis*tress unless we fail to quiet our arousal.

What are the long-term effects of stress?   Every individual has a bank account of stress resistence. We can withdraw from our bank account but we cannot deposit back into it. However, we can decide how fast we will withdraw from our reserves. Every day, our work and home environments cause our system to be aroused 50 to 100 times. If we do not attend to our ability to deprogram the effects of arousal, we deplete our bank account of stress reserves too rapidly. When our reserves are low, then stress symptoms begin to appear. It should be emphasized that stress is basically silent until symptoms appear. Some of the more prominent stress symptoms are headaches, high blood pressure, chronic fatigue, heart disease, low back pain, shoulder and neck tenderness, insomnia, anxiety, depression, loss of memory and concentration, and stomach disorders.

Hard work alone does not produce these symptoms. We are built for hard work and stress arousal just helps us sharpen our work and social skills. Symptoms only appear when we do not avail ourselves of the opportunity to reduce arousal through the consistent application of what can be called "stress management techniques."

How to manage stress.   There are four basic methods to control life stress:

1. The awareness method.   As mentioned earlier, there is no way to avoid stress (unless one is dead). For some people, stress can come from a telephone call, for others it may come from a committee meeting, and for someone else, it could be from an exciting movie. The problem arises when we do not perceive our stress arousal. The best way to raise your level of awareness is to engage in a self-administered stress arousal analysis. For a week, observe and write down the many stress arousals you experience in a day. Go over your own body in your analysis. Start with your toes and work up to the top of your head, observing tightness, tender spots, joint aches, and burning spots. Write them down and observe how daily stress affects them. Physical, mental, and emotional awareness will lead to substantial stress reduction.

2. The deep relaxation method.   Given the chance the body will quickly reduce stress arousal and absorb the stress biochemical by-products generated throughout the day. Deep relaxation should be engaged in for 20 minutes once a day. Deep relaxation is easily learned. Basically, what you need to do is sit quietly, without distractions and start at your feet and tell each part in turn how to relax. The relaxation response will naturally take over, and arousal will be reduced. One can expect to experience increased pep and energy, clearness of thought, and healthy biophysical changes.

3. The inner dialogue method.   Extensive research has demonstrated that our emotional feelings are directly affected and controlled by our inner self-talk. Emotions do not occur independently from our inner dialogue. A negative life event such as failure to get a raise can give rise to negative dialogue. Yet the negative life event cannot independently cause negative feelings. The emotion of depression can occur only if there is present depressive self-talk. We are totally responsible for our own emotional life. Change negative self-talk to positive self-talk and your feelings will change correspondently.

4. The exercise method.   Very vigorous exercise is an excellent stress control method. The exercise must be vigorous enough to stimulate the heart to beat between 115–150 beats per minute for 20 minutes or more. The cardiovascular area is strengthened and the efficiency of the basic metabolism is increased, which means that every tissue will be better nourished. After a few months, a deep sense of psychological well-being is experienced, resulting in increased confidence.

In summary: Stress is arousal, and stress causes dangerous symptoms, but stress *can* be managed through the four basic techniques just described.

A SHORT LIST OF CLASSICS

The General Electric Management Development Institute has compiled a list of the 50 most significant books on business management written in the last three decades.[13] Out of their list we have chosen a representative few classics.*

Entrepreneurship and Venture Management   1975
        —Clifford M. Baumback and Joseph R. Mancuso
The successive managerial problems and decisions that occur during the life cycle of a new venture. The personal attributes—personality, upbringing, motivations—which characterize successful entrepreneurs.

My Years with General Motors   1963
        —Alfred P. Sloan, Jr.
The history of GM, showing its transformation from an ailing Ford competitor to a keystone of the U.S. economy. Describes not only events but also the company's management policies and strategic concepts as they evolved.

Administrative Behavior   1945, Revised 1976
        —Herbert A. Simon
An organization affects the decision making of the individuals in it by imposing constraints—roles, policies, loyalties, communications, unwritten laws—which bias the human choice made in any decision. Organization design, then, should consider the decision processes of the organization to ensure that this bias is functional.

The Practice of Management   1954
        —Peter Drucker
An early Drucker description of business management; what is a business; the role and structure of management; managing managers, workers, and work.

The Human Side of Enterprise   1960
        —Douglas McGregor
McGregor's classic work on the Theory X-Theory Y approach to human behavior in organizations.

Managerial Psychology   1958, Revised 1972
        —Harold J. Leavitt
Some concepts of human behavior relevant to managerial problems; how people behave as individuals, in small groups, and in large organizations.

---

* The list was trimmed in accordance with Chase's law of reading lists, to wit: For any positive number of books on a bibliography, the greater the number listed, the fewer that will be read.

Motivation and Personality   1954, Revised 1970
          —Abraham H. Maslow
     Maslow's classic, influential work on motivation theory.

The Organization Man
          —William H. Whyte, Jr.   1956
     The classic study of organizational loyalty in American society. Traces the
     gradual imprint of the bureaucratic ethic on the individual during college
     and early employment training, and its effects on his business, social, and
     personal life.

In addition to these books, we also recommend that you keep current by
subscribing to the following three periodicals:

1. *The Wall Street Journal*
2. *Harvard Business Review*
3. *Time, U.S. News and World Report,* or *Newsweek*

SUMMARY

This chapter has touched a number of bases as has the rest of the book.
This broad range in subject matter mirrors the real world of management.
Organizations (like the people in them) vary in their personalities and each
one has its own "rest of the story" to be experienced and interpreted by
the person who works for it. Our intent in this book has been to prepare
you for such experience and interpretation as you start your life cycle of management work. Naturally we hope that we have been successful in our efforts.

In closing, we have one more piece of practical advice for you in your
quest for a new job: The one visible tool which the nascent manager possesses
is a briefcase. In light of this, it stands to reason that in applying for a job,
you will want to have a briefcase which indicates that you are managerial
timber. The proper choice, according to *MBA* Magazine, is one of fine leather
which may cost up to $200 or $250. Your briefcase should not be large (important people like you let others carry the heavy stuff). It should be simplistic
and should impart a feeling of seriousness, strength of character, and good
taste. Color is very important. Deep, dark browns are good. But, the best is
a very dark burgundy with your initials simply embossed in gold lettering—
much like the covering of this book, which was designed to give you this
one last piece of advice.[14]

And now you know the rest of the story. . . .

GUIDES TO ACTION

1. Make the boss look good. This is desirable for both a boss you want to keep and for a boss you want to get rid of. If the boss is good, his or her stature will rise and your contribution will be recognized; if the boss is bad, then your efforts may lead to his or her being promoted, or better yet transferred to another position. You really can't lose.

2. Beware of the "friendship trap" with the boss. For example, if you are working for a "jungle fighter" (who sees co-workers as either allies or enemies), "you automatically acquire your boss's enemies, and your future becomes totally linked with his."[15]

3. Do not go drinking with the boss if either one of you can't hold your liquor. After a few drinks one of you is certain to say something that you will wish the other hadn't heard.

4. Accumulate a "Go to Hell" savings account (i.e., enough money to tide you over for two or three months while you look for another job). This provides you a certain amount of security and flexibility in the event that you must take a risky stand on some aspect of your job. It always feels good to be financially secure enough to be able to tell them to "Go to Hell!"

5. Keep your sense of humor. Even the most serious and pretentious organizations have their moments of absurdity. Relax and enjoy them.

NOTES

[1] Edgar Schein, "The Individual, the Organization and the Career: A Conceptual Scheme," in D. Kolb et al., *Organizational Psychology: A Book of Readings*, 3d ed. (Englewood Cliffs, N.J.: Prentice-Hall, Inc., 1979), p. 499.

[2] John T. Malloy, *Dress for Success* (New York: Warner Books, 1975), p. 13.

[3] Ibid., p. 13.

[4] Liz Houston, "Businesswomanly Wiles," *MBA*, September 1977, pp. 30–31.

[5] Ibid., p. 30.

[6] Judy Moore, "Avoid Dark Shirts, and Ties That Come to Your Navel," Chicago *Sun-Times*, Syndicated, 1979.

[7] Michael Dixon, "Six Ways of Not Quite Getting to the Top," *Financial Times*, London, June 28, 1978, p. 8.

[8] Michael Maccoby, *The Gamesman: The New Corporate Leaders* (New York: Simon & Schuster, Inc., 1976).

[9] Quotations taken from Michael Maccoby, "The Corporate Climber Has to Find a Heart," *Fortune*, December 1976, pp. 98–108.

[10] Anthony Downs, *Inside Bureaucracy* (Boston: Little, Brown & Co., 1967), pp. 87–88.

[11] Harry Levinson, "The Abrasive Personality," *Harvard Business Review*, Vol. 56, no. 3 (May–June 1978), p. 93. Copyright © by the President and Fellows of Harvard College; all rights reserved. Reprinted by permission.

[12] Pam Proctor, "How to Survive Today's Stressful Jobs," *Parade* Magazine, June 17, 1979, pp. 4–5.

[13] General Electric Company, "The Fifty Books on Business Management," G.E. Management Development Institute, Croton-on-Hudson, New York, 11 pages.

[14] "Fashion Moving up," *MBA* Magazine, February, 1977, pp. 36–37.

[15] Mort LaBrecque, "The Friendship Trap," *MBA* Magazine, November 1977, p. 67.

DISCUSSION QUESTIONS

1. In what way(s) is Schein's model different from the standard organization chart?

2. Summarize the six ways of not quite getting to the top.

3. Can you identify some career management strategies in addition to those listed in the chapter?

4. Of the types of managers and bureaucrats listed by Maccoby and Downs respectively, which type(s) do you believe are closest to your personality. (Be honest.)

5. Are you an abrasive personality? (Answer honestly and please don't become hostile.)

6. How do you handle stress now? Do you use any of Dr. Day's techniques?

Name index

Subject index